Colorado Flora: Western Slope

COLORADO FLORA: WESTERN SLOPE

by William A. Weber
Fellow of the Linnean Society of London
University of Colorado Museum
Boulder, Colorado

COLORADO ASSOCIATED UNIVERSITY PRESS

QK
150
.W39
1987

Copyright © 1987 by William A. Weber
Published by Colorado Associated University Press
Boulder, Colorado 80309
ISBN 0-87081-167-3
Library of Congress Catalog Card Number 87-70012

cba 1166

This book is dedicated

to

Constantine Rafinesque, Edward Lee Greene,
Per Axel Rydberg, Wendell Holmes Camp,
Lloyd Shinners and Áskell Löve

Funds for the art work and to some extent the publication of this book were advanced through donations from the following people and organizations:

Russell W. Allen
Amoco Foundation, Inc.
Lee Amoroso
Audrey D. and James Bell Benedict, Jr.
David A. Boyce
F. Martin Brown
Jack and Martha Carter
George R. Clark
Cities Service Foundation
Cloud Ridge Naturalists
Colorado Chapter GNSI
Colorado Native Plant Society
James C. and Carol Crain
Tommy G. Cruff
Dale L. and Miriam L. Denham
Ann Ophelia Dowden
Mary E. Edwards
William S. Eisenlohr
John C. Emerick
The Evergreen Naturalists
Catherine B. Fessenden
Jess L. Fults
Paul F. and Margaret Gilbert
Tom and Mary Hall
Frederick J. Hermann
David W. Jamieson
Lucian M. Long
Sue S. Martin
Cuvier D. and Margaret Ann McClure
Mobil Oil Corporation
Elinor R. Oakes
Steffen and Kirsten Robertson
Mrs. Mary C. Rockefeller
Rocky Mountain Biological Laboratory
John & Dorothy Rohner
William H. Romme
Katherine N. Schwarzenbach
Mr. & Mrs. Ira H. Washburn
Westcliffe Publishers, Inc.
Western Resource Development
Frederick H. and Janet L. Wingate
Robert G. and Joan W. Young
Ann H. Zwinger

CONTENTS

Foreword ix

Acknowledgments xi

Preface xv

Introduction 1

Key to the Families 23

Glossary of Terms 499

Index to Common Names 515

Index to Genera 522

FOREWORD

It is a great pleasure to provide a Foreword to Professor Weber's *Colorado Flora: Western Slope*. He is an honored member of our faculty, having spent his entire professional career with the university, first in the Department of Biology and later in the Museum, where he has built over the years the most comprehensive collection of plants of Colorado in the world. His book, Rocky Mountain Flora, has informed hosts of amateur and professional botanists, not to mention laymen who have moved to Colorado to enjoy our outdoors, in the wonders of our plant life. In 1986 the University gave him one of its highest accolades, the Robert L. Stearns award, and the Wright-Ingraham Institute honored him "for his distinguished work as a scientist in the public interest". In 1985 he was made a Fellow of the Linnean Society of London. He is known abroad as "Mr. Botany" of Colorado. The books that he has written are in the best educational tradition of the University. While intended for use in the field as well as in the laboratory, and for the general public of all ages as well as the university student body, his work represents in a concrete way the true outreach of the University. This educational outreach, especially to our western slope, is a major theme of my administration.

For too many years, the various geographical regions of Colorado have been treated as separate entities. This was especially true of the relationship of the Western Slope to the Front Range. The Continental Divide seemed to effect a separation that was sociological and political as well as geographical.

The need for consolidated approaches to common problems has finally begun to unify the State. The University of Colorado, for example, has initiated such programs as the Small Business Assistance Center, the Center for Rural Recreation and Development and the Meeker Summer Session in an effort to extend its educational and research activities to all the people of Colorado. As a public institution, the University has an obligation to serve communities and citizens throughout the State; in this sense, we are truly public servants.

Professor Weber's *Colorado Flora: Western Slope* represents a major contribution to understanding the rich and varied wonders of Colorado. Anyone wishing to become familiar with the natural profile of the Western Slope will find this book an indispensable resource. In its content and style, this is clearly a book for all of Colorado's citizens. As such, it presents a unique and valuable service to Professor Weber's profession and to the general public. This is a lasting contribution, because this book will continue to inform and educate our public for generations.

E. Gordon Gee
President
University of Colorado

ACKNOWLEDGMENTS

This project was made possible in large measure by the bequest of Mrs. Katherine Crisp, once a student at the University of Colorado under T. D. A. Cockerell and Francis Ramaley. She had a love for the herbarium and for the academic disciplines. With her bequest the University of Colorado herbarium was able to purchase a Philips MICOM word processor on which the manuscript originally was prepared. Funding for the art work came from from members of the Colorado Native Plant Society, other friends, and personal funds. If there are errors in the text, they are all my own, since I have been responsible personally for the field work, the research, final taxonomic and nomenclatural decisions and every bit of the typing and organization of this manuscript. The Little Red Hen of the nursery story is alive and well.

In order for this book to be distributed to a wide readership, a major subsidy was needed to permit a reasonable selling price. A pair of matching grants has assured publication of this volume. These came from the Pauline A. and George R. Morrison Charitable Trust, of Denver, and the University of Colorado Committee on University Scholarly Publications, to whom I am greatly indebted.

Claudia and Walter Rector, of Clifton, Colorado, accompanied me in the field and alerted me to special localities, provided housing and transportation for me and my colleagues, Vlad Siplivinsky and Hans Beck, and, most important, forced me always to keep the lay reader in mind. Joan W. Young, of Grand Junction, by her assiduous collecting, added many new records to the West Slope flora, which she knows very well. Bruce and Marion MacLeod let me use their summer home on Blue Mountain for my frequent trips to Moffat County, and alerted me to new habitats and species of the Dinosaur National Monument country.

The various directors, naturalists and staffs of the national parks and monuments encouraged me to collect in their domains, and I reciprocated by establishing herbaria for them and producing catalogs of their floras. Colleagues who contributed important collections while working on environmental impact and endangered species programs include John Anderson, David Buckner, David Johnson, Warren Keammerer, Betsy Neely, Steve O'Kane, and Jim Ratzloff.

Drs. Áskell and Doris Löve gave me invaluable help from their encyclopedic knowledge of the boreal floras of the world and the cytology of the species. Our discussions of generic limits and the biological species concept have enriched my perspective continually. Ron Wittmann has been by my side in the field, tested the keys and challenged my concepts. Ron also has been my volunteer computer programmer and helped immeasurably in transferring the manuscript to our IBM AT computer and trouble-shooting along the way. The final manuscript has been made camera-ready and the master copy printed on a Hewlett-Packard LaserJet printer. Miriam Colson Fritts (*Carex*), Alva Day (*Gilia*), David Dunn (*Lupinus*), Barry Johnston (*Potentilla*), Robert Price (*Draba*), James Reveal (*Eriogonum*), Dieter Wilken (*Ipomopsis*), and Janet Wingate (Poaceae), contributed parts or entire keys for some groups. Tom Schwab copy-edited an early version of the text. Several amateurs to whom I loaned the manuscript found typographic and substantive errors in the keys. My herbarium assistants, Tim Hogan, Jo Ann Flock, and my 'Privat Docent' Harold Dahnke tested the keys, checked the leads backwards and forwards, and suggested improvements. Copies of the manuscript in various stages of completion were made available to collectors for field-testing. I am grateful for all this help.

A large number of the illustrations are new, the work of a Boulder artist, Carolyn Ensle, now of San Francisco. Carolyn accomplished some of this work while a temporary resident of France, which meant that our communication had to be by correspondence and shipment of specimens and photographs back and forth. Her success is a tribute to her sensitivity to the essential and often intangible features of the plants. The remainder of the plates are illustrations from *Rocky Mountain Flora*, by Ann Pappageorge. The color plates are from my own photographs.

I am grateful for the encouragement of the many friends and colleagues, and devotees of the Colorado flora who first became acquainted with plants through using my *Rocky Mountain Flora*, and I hope that this new book will widen their horizons and provide them an ever greater educational experience. This is the greatest reward a teacher can expect.

Most of all, I am thankful for many things which in one way or another made this book possible: the opportunity to serve on the faculty of the University of Colorado for over forty years, first in the Biology Department and later the University Museum, and to be free to develop wide interests in floristic botany, not only in vascular plants but in lichens and bryophytes (knowledge of each group gave me increased perspective in another); the opportunities for foreign travel afforded by these added specialties; and the excellent preparation given me in high school which enabled me to master the languages I needed to read the literature of my field.

I should also mention some of the people who, in my early years, took time to give me their attention and instruction: F. Martin Brown, my lepidopterist cousin, who, when I was a five-year old shut-in, put a small microscope in my hand and taught me how to make slides; Mrs. Elizabeth Gertrude Britton, wife of the director of the New York Botanical Garden, with whom I had my first 'brush' with botany at age nine, when she drove me out of the garden with her umbrella after I, illegally, had picked a leaf of skunk cabbage to show to a young friend; José Antonio Jove, son of a Venezuelan refugee in New York, who helped me with my first botany, the identification of trees in winter in the city parks; Helene Lunt, director of adult education at New York Botanical Garden, who took me in the field and taught me plant families; Alma Ericson Moldenke, my high school biology teacher and friend for over fifty years; Mr. Mortenson, another biology teacher who gave me my first botany text, his unused copy of Gray's Manual that was required in his college class; Fräulein Stamm, who, as my German teacher in high school, found me a pen pal in Holstein from whom I learned to read and write German Script. This talent ultimately earned me my first graduate fellowship at Pullman, where I had to unravel the field notes of Wilhelm N. Suksdorf, a plant collector in Washington State; J. Otis Swift, columnist for the New York World-Telegram, who on Saturday morning field trips taught me volumes of plant-name lore and gave me my first opportunity to teach others; George Gill, of the law firm of Stockbridge & Borst, where I worked as office-boy, who asked me to try to type briefs letter-perfect without erasures, thus creating the two-fingered typist who produced this text; George Goodman, my botanical guru at Iowa State; Henry Conard, who identified my mosses of the Columbia River Gorge and gave me money to join the Sullivant Moss Society; Marion Ownbey, who, as my major professor at Pullman, taught me not only botany but everything I have learned about the discipline of writing. Most of these gave of themselves, probably never anticipating that they would contribute to a *Colorado Flora: Western Slope*. But they have; they were all educators in their fashion. I owe them more than I can ever repay.

I have learned from my students, many of whose names are memorialized on the doors of our herbarium cases. They forced me to write keys that can be used effectively. I learned much by taking into the field many of my American colleages but especially those from abroad who, visiting Colorado, enlightened me on Eurasian species occurring here: Eilif Dahl, Erling Porsild, Eric Hultén, Misao Tatewaki, to list a few. Over a hundred institutions around the world, by establishing exchanges of specimens with us, enriched our collections and permitted first-hand comparisons of specimens from our respective areas.

Last but not least, I am indebted to persons whom I tried to help abroad and to institutions which made it possible for me to do field work with them: Donald McVean and the Australian National University; the National Science Foundation; the USA-USSR botanical exchange program; INSTAAR's Man in the Biosphere program in Chile; the Galapagos International Scientific Project; the International Botanical Congress Arctic Excursion, the International Phytogeographic Excursions and the National Geographic Society. These field experiences were vital in providing perspective on the Rocky Mountain flora.

PREFACE

Plants are mankind's most precious resource. Their activities supply directly or indirectly, all of our needs. Our housing, clothing, grains, fruits, vegetables, medicines, all animal products, our watersheds, the oxygen we breathe—all depend on plants. Yet we often act, in spite of massive evidence to the contrary, as if plants are the very last things that count in our lives. Knowledge of plants is vital to the citizen's responsibility.

To know the plants by name is to distinguish more than various shades of green in the landscape. It means the difference between our unwitting support of landscape destruction or modification (and its subsequent 'revegetation') and our sober questioning of development. Intelligent citizenship in these times requires that all citizens try to understand the structure of the botanical landscape more than they have. Botany is no longer to be considered just a 'nice' subject for 'ladies' as it was in the past, made more attractive by the coinage of sweet-sounding common names such as 'Fairy Bells', 'Johnny Jump-up', and 'Love-lies-bleeding'. Even the term 'wild-flower' is in some sense demeaning of a solid science. Botany is the science that is ultimately responsible for our survival, and it needs to be recognized as such. Granted the enormous esthetic value of plants, we can no longer afford not to know the differences between the species of plants, their biological behavior, their potential as foods and medicines, and their potentials for good and ill in agriculture and landscape management.

In the tropics thousands of unknown and little-known species of potentially valuable plant species are disappearing by the thousands through the inroads of 'development' for short-term economic gain by foreign or domestic interests. Our own backyard is no less vulnerable although most of us cannot evaluate the impact because we don't know what we are losing. In western Colorado the land is under siege and will continue to be for the near future; I say the near future because the pressure on the land is so great that a far future is inconceivable at the rate we are raping the landscape.

Western Colorado for a long time was ignored, a stepchild of the state, especially botanically, for there has never been a specific guide to its flora. Now its few accessible valleys are being filled with trailer parks, 'Fun Cities', gravel pits, and condominium towns for the ski areas. Ranching, which was in some ways very sound land husbandry, is disappearing. Dams are impounding water for the use of our burgeoning population and those of other western states. Whole mountains are being leveled in the harvesting of coal and uranium. Off-road recreational vehicles are ruining the ephemeral spring flower displays of the Gunnison and Colorado River valleys. Ever wider highways are cutting swathes through our most scenic canyons. To many this is progress, but in allowing it to continue unchecked we are casting negative votes for unborn generations who, while they may not realize what was once here, should have been allowed the opportunity of their own choice.

This is the first comprehensive handbook of the flora of western Colorado. It belongs to the long tradition in Europe of what are called 'Excursion-floras'. Such a flora has no formal descriptions of plants, but provides more detailed keys and helpful information than is to be found in larger volumes which, unfortunately, cannot be carried in the field. *Rocky Mountain Flora* has been in print continuously in five editions since 1952. I am flattered that its format has been copied by at least one Eurasiatic flora: *Keys to the vascular flora of the Southern Krasnoyarsk Region*, by Vezlyanova and others (Novosibirsk, USSR, 1979).

I hope that in some measure this book may be responsible for influencing intelligent decisions in future land use, as well as being a means of educating the adults and children of the Western Slope in their botanical heritage, as well as in the English language and its roots in Latin and Greek. I find that my first volume, *Rocky Mountain Flora*, has created, in the past thirty-five years, a large group of people who through its use have learned to know the plants of the Colorado Front Range region, and have put their knowledge to good use in environmental causes. If as much progress can be achieved by this volume, I will be content.

In 1952, when the University of Colorado Press first published *Rocky Mountain Flora*, I felt that my readers might need elementary training in its use, and a brief introduction to the basics was included. The present book is something of a sequel, and the reader should consult the earlier volume for this material. Besides, now there are primers of many styles and qualities available, so I have dropped this chapter in order to save space for other discussions. Instead, in order to bring the scientific names closer to our own language experience, I have given the derivations of all of the generic names and most of the more obscure specific epithets, and I have included an enlarged glossary of scientific terms.

While I have the floor, I would like to express my deep concern about the steadily worsening state of floristic knowledge in the United States. Lloyd Shinners, in his *Spring Flora of the Dallas-Fort Worth area*, wrote: "Blessed are they that write state and local floras. They discharge the taxonomist's elementary duty to the general public." If this be so, why is there no financial support for the writers of such books? Recently two state floras, of Wyoming and New Mexico, have been published without local or national support. The first was published by a vanity press, possibly at the author's expense, and the second was published in Germany! Commercial presses hardly ever publish floras; a university scholarly press may, but its scope is understandably parochial, and such presses are sometimes seriously under-funded. A local flora may be a best-seller, but because its audience is not necessarily affluent, it has to be sold near or below cost. And, furthermore, local floras lie outside the purview of national granting foundations.

The problem goes much deeper, however. Attention to plant taxonomy is declining in the schools and universities at an alarming rate. Departments expand in the disciplines where grants are available.

Botany departments are absorbed into Biology departments, which then become laboratory-oriented and molecular in emphasis. Field identification courses lose status, and departmental herbaria are neglected. They become 'service' units and their curators, upon retirement, are replaced by 'collection managers'. Eventually the herbaria in local and regional universities are either abandoned or are given to the few large national herbaria, which are in turn reluctant to accept them.

The result of all this is that students no longer are trained in floristics. Professors are not encouraged to spend their lives learning whole floras. A few very large institutions continue to train graduate students in the most sophisticated grant-cadging parts of taxonomy, specializing more and more on small genera rather than floras. In the end these young people will find few jobs in the colleges. The whole body of science will prosper only as its parts remain healthy. Still, for economic reasons some organs are fed while others are starved. We need wise deans and department chairs who insist on maintaining balance within the discipline of biology just as we need wise chancellors to maintain balance between the arts, humanities and sciences. None can survive long without the other.

The health of the discipline of plant taxonomy depends on our scientific community educating the citizens at the grass-roots. This will not be accomplished by standing aloof and writing expensive texts that are only available to libraries. Local floras reach the general public, and should be supported. By these I mean good, complete local floras which have a mission to teach amateurs and professionals. Wild flower books are burgeoning in the bookstores, true enough. Anyone with a color camera can put together a book, but no one claims that these are complete or that they seriously try to raise the level of literacy or observation in their readers. But the floristic world is collapsing world-wide under the weight of exploitation and development. Where is the body of voting people who can see, evaluate, and finally act to stop this destruction? I therefore plead for support of local floras at the highest levels of the counsels of private and public granting agencies!

INTRODUCTION

Scope of the Book

Why only the Western Slope? I thought very hard about treating the entire state of Colorado but decided against it for two reasons: I wanted to have a book that was not too massive to carry in the field, and I felt that a book on the Western Slope would make for simpler keys by eliminating those closely related species restricted to the Eastern Slope.

This book has as its subject the vascular plants—ferns, gymnosperms and flowering plants—native and naturalized on the entire hydrologic Western Slope of Colorado—from the Continental Divide to the Utah, Wyoming, and New Mexico borders. It is a rich and varied territory, lacking only the level plains of the Eastern Slope, but possessing a rich variety of rock types: granites, limestones, sandstones and volcanics exposed at high and low altitudes. There are deep canyons, river valleys, natural lakes, high plateaus, and a substantial core of alpine tundra. The forests are equally varied, with ponderosa pine, spruce and fir, piñon pine and juniper, and white fir. Sagebrush, serviceberry and oak clothe the high plateaus and desert shrubs the lower steppe. An ephemeral spring flora blooms in the arid 'adobes' of the Colorado River valley in April and May.

Physical Geography

The elevation of the Western Slope ranges from over 14,000 ft. (ca. 4,250 meters) in the Saguache Range down to 4,500 ft. (ca. 1,400 meters) near Grand Junction. The area is drained by five river systems: the Yampa, White, Colorado (including Dolores), Gunnison, and San Juan. The high country includes the main Rocky Mountain chains near the Continental Divide, the Elk and West Elk Mountains, the San Juan Volcanic region, and several great plateaus: White River, Blue Mountain, Grand Mesa, Blue Mesa, Cochetopa and Uncompahgre. The Gunnison basin is a major intermountain basin or 'park'.

Floristic Zones

Floristic zones are rough estimates of the altitudinal coverage of the easily recognizable plant communities. They are not always consistent in mountain regions because of a phenomenon called environmental compensation. On a south-facing slope species of low altitudes may climb very high, and on north-facing slopes high altitude species may reach very low altitudes because of various factors which define their ecological requirements. Statements of the floristic zone occupied by a species should always be allowed some latitude. An especially protected cool north-facing canyonside may actually harbor typically alpine species, while an alpine tundra site with easily warmed sedimentary rock substrate and soil churned up by gophers may support typical subalpine vegetation.

In this book I use a loosely construed group of floristic zones: **desert-steppe** is the treeless semi-arid canyon-side, river bench, or talus of the lower river basins. **Riparian woodlands** or **meadows** are wetlands along the major streams. **Piñon-juniper** refers to the plant community dominated by these species (there seems to be nothing gained by changing the name to piñon-red cedar although technically these are not *Juniperus*). **Sagebrush** refers to sites dominated by various species of *Seriphidium* (formerly part of *Artemisia*). **Montane** refers to the middle-altitude, relatively dry forested zone, **subalpine** to the spruce-fir zone below the limit of trees, and **alpine** to the area above the limit of trees. **Ruderal** is a term used for sites much disturbed by the activities of man.

I prefer not to assign altitudinal limits because the Western Slope, with its great and abrupt topographic gradients, is full of compensating environments. One should always expect to find plants growing above or below the limits given by the book. Furthermore, seeds of plants growing at high altitudes are prone to wash down to lower altitudes, sprout and produce growth for a season or two until they meet an unfriendly season.

Plant Geography

The Colorado Rocky Mountain region is like a huge flattened wheel with a hub—the Rocky Mountain chain—running north to south and presenting a potential highway for plant species to move along it. Thus, it is not surprising that the majority of our high mountain species are also found to the north and to the south at least as far as the terminus of the range near Santa Fé, New Mexico. I call this the Rocky Mountain element. Because the Rocky Mountains are less continuous to the south and because of events in geoclimatic history, we have relatively few species, if any, of a Mexican mountain element, although at one time many of our species did extend into the Mexican cordillera and are still present in small patches there.

Returning to the concept of the Rockies as a hub of a wheel with radiating spokes, we see elements of other floristic regions extending into Colorado along the river valleys (the spokes), from the Great Basin, Uintah Basin, Colorado Plateau, Rio Grande Valley, the Chihuahua desert, the Northern Rockies, and the northern and southern Great Plains. At least one genus, *Psychrophila*, seems to be an Andean-Australasian group of which few other vestiges remain. Lupines and paintbrushes also occur commonly in the South American Andes.

The northern Rocky Mountain element is especially interesting because it is restricted to the Park Range north of Steamboat Springs. Here a number of species common in the Northern Rocky Mountains and Pacific Northwest survive in this very mesic mountain area and must have once extended north across what is now the Wyoming Desert. Exemplifying this distribution pattern are *Trillium ovatum*, *Mimulus lewisii*, *Azaleastrum albiflorum*, *Erocallis triphylla*,

Perideridia gairdneri and *Mimulus moschatus*.

The southern, or Colorado, Rocky Mountains have virtually no so-called Amphi-Atlantic connections characteristic of the floras of northern Europe and northeastern North America. Nevertheless, there are some curious plant distributions involving Greenland and the Rockies, such as *Sisyrinchium montanum*. This is not surprising, since Greenland was yet another great high-mountain mass before the Pleistocene, probably harbouring a large reservoir of species common to Asia and western America. But some Rocky Mountain species occur in isolated pockets around the Great Lakes, a situation that is still not clearly understood.

The San Juan Mountains belong to a volcanic system generally considered not to belong to the Rocky Mountains, and, while much of its flora is that of the main Southern Rocky Mountains, there are a number of endemics which mark the area as somewhat special: *Besseya ritteriana* and *Trifolium attenuatum* are examples. The San Juans are the most scenic, rugged, and probably least botanically explored mountains of western Colorado.

Because the Colorado Rockies are a massive, highly buffered system of mountain ranges, whose ranges are isolated from each other by intermountain basins, it is to be expected that some species evolved in this isolation and are restricted to a particular mountain mass. These are endemics. Endemics occur not only on mountain masses but also in isolated areas of the lowlands, particularly in connection with areas of high aridity and specialized rock strata.

The richest treasures of our flora are found wherever pure rock strata are exposed, undiluted by the debris and mixing from strata above. In the canyon country, therefore, look for rock strata that are highly tilted. Different communities are encountered as one walks across one formation to another. Alkaline flats are often especially interesting; they harbor rare mosses as well as locally isolated pockets of vascular plants especially tolerant of alkali. Alcove cliffs of the massive Wingate sandstone will have seepage areas with groups of rare species. The limestones of the high Elk Mountains are rich in species either endemic (restricted to the area) or disjunct (isolated) from the Canadian Rockies or more remote areas in Asia. Wetlands of all kinds, artificial as well as natural, have their special plants. Inaccessible cliffs should tempt the rock-climbing botanist. Sagebrush, aspen groves, ponderosa pine forest, mountain meadow, all have their special floras. The successful plant-hunter must learn to develop a sense of the habitat, especially the microhabitat. It is not a book-learning skill, but one that is developed by learning to discriminate.

Certain alpine areas are more rewarding than others. In my experience the major north-south-trending ranges tend to endure severe environmental stress, especially because of the drying winter Föhn winds, while the high connecting ridges such as the Elk Mountains, Hoosier Ridge and the Rabbit-ears are protected from them; this, and the different exposure of the side-ridges and canyons to the daily march of the sun, tends to permit these areas to remain more moist through the season as a result of slower snow-melt. In such areas the south slopes are quite as mesic as the north slopes. The greatest concentrations of rare alpine species occur in these areas.

The Altai Connection

In the summer of 1877, Asa Gray and Sir Joseph Dalton Hooker visited Colorado for five days as guests of the Hayden Survey team and climbed Gray's and Blanca peaks. Hooker returned to the Royal Botanic Gardens at Kew, profoundly impressed by our flora, and he began writing to Darwin and to Gray, pointing out the close floristic relationship that he saw between the Colorado Rockies and the Altai Mountains of Middle Asia. Altai is a complicated mountainous area in southern Siberia, extending south over the Mongolian and Chinese borders. Hooker even claimed to have sent Gray a manuscript on this matter, but so far we have not found it.

In 1882 Gray and Hooker published a joint paper on the floristic relationships between the Rocky Mountains and the rest of the world, but, strangely, there is no mention in it of this Asiatic connection. It is as if Gray had written the paper without using any of Hooker's contribution. Why should Hooker have been so impressed with the Altai connection and Gray not at all? Probably because he was extremely well-informed about the floras of Middle Asia including the Himalaya, and Gray was limited in his experience to North America. Nevertheless, earlier on, Gray had established a similar remarkable connection between the humid low-altitude Southern Appalachians and Japan and adjacent China. The establishment of this connection, now known to date from Tertiary times, became Gray's great contribution to plant geography.

What Hooker saw was a complementary semi-arid high-altitude floristic similarity between the Rocky Mountain region and the Altai. If there were low altitude Tertiary connections why should there not have been similar high-altitude ones? It appears that Gray evidently did not appreciate what this discovery meant to his own earlier one. I recently obtained a facsimile of Hooker's plant list from the Colorado trip. Knowing exactly what he saw and collected, we can understand his excitement; he had made a discovery fully as important as that of Gray, extending the idea of Tertiary connections to the areas of Continental climates in America and Asia.

The magnitude of the Asiatic connection is even more remarkable than Hooker realized, because he saw only relatively common species; few of the rare disjuncts (*e.g.*, *Ptilagrostis porteri*), had been discovered at that time. Later on, the Danish plant geographer Theodore Holm published a more detailed analysis which reinforced Hooker's impressions. And in the 1930s C. W. T. Penland, of Colorado College, began to make his momentous discoveries of *Eutrema*, *Saussurea*, and *Armeria* on Hoosier Ridge. The mountains continue to yield these Asiatic disjuncts to the present moment. From our enlarged perspective, the Asiatic element in the Rocky Mountain flora now appears to be the single most significant feature of Rocky Mountain phytogeography. We have species disjunct between Colorado and Altai: *Stellaria irrigua*, *Chondrophylla nutans*, *Ptilagrostis porteri*, and *Armeria scabra*. Some genera are similarly disjunct: *Clementsia*, *Claytonia*, *Saussurea*, *Avenochloa*, and *Helictotrichon*, while others, such as *Eritrichum*, have species in the intervening areas of Alaska and Kamtchatka. Thus we establish that, as in the Appalachian-eastern Asia connection, there is a similarly ancient highland Tertiary connection between the continental-climate western America and the interior of Asia. This connection is not wholly alpine, but involves the desert-steppe as well. *Artemisia frigida*, *A. laciniata*, and *Chamaerhodos erecta* are as abundant in Altai as here in Colorado.

The Rocky Mountains also have a rich relictual Tertiary flora which is endemic or otherwise disjunct here. Some examples: *Jamesia americana*, alive today and fossil in the Creede Oligocene formation; *Mahonia*, now known from the Rocky Mountains, the Redwood forest, and the Himalaya; *Paxistima*, known otherwise in a species of the Appalachians, *Asplenium andrewsii*, endemic in Colorado, Arizona and Mexico, and *Asplenium septentrionale* disjunct in isolated mountain ranges across the Northern Hemisphere.

One thing that we feel we have learned from a study of our respective floras is that it is highly unlikely that the alpine flora of the Rocky Mountains was brought to us from the Arctic along the fronts of continental glaciers, moving up to high altitudes as the Pleistocene climate retreated northward. On the contrary, it more likely was the ancient Tertiary floras of high mountain areas near the present Arctic which moved downslope with a depression of timberline, to invade freshly scoured new habitats on the Arctic plains. In other words, the Rocky Mountain flora in Colorado is long-standing, having remained essentially in place since the Tertiary. The precise manner of the Altai connection, whether across a wider Bering land bridge with a continental-type highland climate or whatever, is a problem for future geobotanical research. I prefer to use the term 'oro-boreal' rather than 'circumpolar' for this element.

The Families Treated In This Book

The following alphabetical list of plant families is grouped in four categories: ferns, gymnosperms, monocots and dicots. In three columns are the scientific names, common names, and international three-letter acronyms. Because the International Rules of Botanical Nomenclature recommends that all family names end in -*aceae*, several of the large old families have unfamiliar new names. The old name is placed in square brackets, and a reference is made to the new name by citing both of the pertinent acronyms. I do not applaud this recommendation because, while it makes things neat, we still will need to know the old names in order to use the literature. Who was it that said, "Consistency is the bugaboo of small minds"?

One hundred thirty-nine families are recognized here. A number of those usually recognized in American floras have been broken up into two or more. To aid readers in finding these segregates, the acronyms (published by the author in Taxon 31:74-88. 1982) of the families concerned are given in a second line, *e.g.* "was UMB" or "see also ASN".

Common names of families vary from place to place and often embody the name of a genus common to the area. Pea Family is not more correct than Legume Family. In this sense common names of families, genera, and species are variable, and no useful purpose is served by trying to standardize them, since they differ among different language groups as well as between local areas.

Fern Families

ADIANTACEAE	MAIDENHAIR	(was PLP)	ADI
ASPIDIACEAE	SHIELD-FERN	(was PLP)	ASD
ASPLENIACEAE	SPLEENWORT	(was PLP)	ASL
ATHYRIACEAE	ATHYRIUM	(was PLP)	ATY
CRYPTOGRAMMACEAE	ROCK BRAKE	(was PLP)	CRG
EQUISETACEAE	HORSETAIL		EQU
HYPOLEPIDACEAE	BRACKEN	(was PLP)	HPL
ISOETACEAE	QUILLWORT		ISO
LYCOPODIACEAE	CLUB-MOSS		LYC
MARSILEACEAE	PEPPERWORT		MSL
OPHIOGLOSSACEAE	ADDER'S TONGUE		OPH
POLYPODIACEAE	POLYPODY		PLP
(See also ADI, ASD, ASL, ATY, CRG, HPL, SIN, WDS)			
SELAGINELLACEAE	LITTLE CLUB-MOSS		SEL
SINOPTERIDACEAE	LIP FERN	(was PLP)	SIN
WOODSIACEAE	WOODSIA	(was PLP)	WDS

Gymnosperm Families

CUPRESSACEAE	CYPRESS FAMILY	CUP
EPHEDRACEAE	EPHEDRA	EPH
PINACEAE	PINE	PIN

Monocot Families

AGAVACEAE	AGAVE	(was LIL)	AGA
ALISMATACEAE	WATER-PLANTAIN		ALI
ALLIACEAE	ONION	(was LIL)	ALL
ASPARAGACEAE	ASPARAGUS	(was LIL)	ASG
CALOCHORTACEAE	MARIPOSA	(was LIL)	CCT
COMMELINACEAE	SPIDERWORT		CMM
CONVALLARIACEAE	MAYFLOWER	(was LIL)	CVL
CYPERACEAE	SEDGE		CYP
CYPRIPEDIACEAE	LADY'S SLIPPER		CPD
[GRAMINEAE]	GRASS		GRM/POA
HYDROCHARITACEAE	FROGBIT		HDC
IRIDACEAE	IRIS		IRI
JUNCACEAE	RUSH		JUN
JUNCAGINACEAE	ARROW-GRASS		JCG
LEMNACEAE	DUCKWEED		LMN
LILIACEAE	LILY		LIL
(see also AGA, ALL, ASG, CCT, CVL, MLN, TRI, UVU)			
MELANTHIACEAE	FALSE HELLEBORE	(was LIL)	MLN
NAJADACEAE	WATER-NYMPH		NAJ
ORCHIDACEAE	ORCHID		ORC
POACEAE	GRASS		POA/GRM
POTAMOGETONACEAE	PONDWEED		POT
RUPPIACEAE	DITCHGRASS		RUP
SPARGANIACEAE	BUR-REED		SPG
TRILLIACEAE	TRILLIUM	(was LIL)	TRL
TYPHACEAE	CAT-TAIL		TYP
UVULARIACEAE	BELLWORT	(was LIL)	UVU
ZANNICHELLIACEAE	HORNED PONDWEED		ZAN

Dicot Families

ACERACEAE	MAPLE	ACE
ADOXACEAE	ADOXA	ADX
ALSINACEAE	CHICKWEED (was CRY)	ASN
AMARANTHACEAE	AMARANTH	AMA
ANACARDIACEAE	SUMAC	ANA
APIACEAE	PARSLEY	UMB/API
APOCYNACEAE	DOGBANE	APO
ARALIACEAE	GINSENG	ARL
ASCLEPIADACEAE	MILKWEED	ASC
ASTERACEAE	SUNFLOWER	CMP/AST
BERBERIDACEAE	BARBERRY	BER
BETULACEAE	BIRCH	BET
BIGNONIACEAE	CATALPA	BIG
BORAGINACEAE (see also EHR)	BORAGE	BOR
BRASSICACEAE	MUSTARD	CRU/BRA
CACTACEAE	CACTUS	CAC
CALLITRICHACEAE	WATER-STARWORT	CLL
CAMPANULACEAE	BELLFLOWER	CAM
CANNABACEAE	HOPS	CAN
CAPPARIDACEAE	CAPER	CPP
CAPRIFOLIACEAE	HONEYSUCKLE	CPR
CARYOPHYLLACEAE (See also ASN)	PINK	CRY
CELASTRACEAE	STAFF TREE	CEL
CERATOPHYLLACEAE	HORNWORT	CTP
CHENOPODIACEAE	GOOSEFOOT	CHN
[COMPOSITAE]	SUNFLOWER	CMP/AST
CONVOLVULACEAE	MORNING-GLORY	CNV
CORNACEAE	DOGWOOD	COR
CRASSULACEAE	STONECROP	CRS
CROSSOSOMATACEAE	CROSSOSOMA	CRO
[CRUCIFERAE]	MUSTARD	CRU/BRA
CUCURBITACEAE	GOURD	CUC
CUSCUTACEAE	DODDER	CUS
DIPSACACEAE	TEASEL	DPS
DROSERACEAE	SUNDEW	DRS
EHRETIACEAE	EHRETIA (was BOR)	EHR
ELAEAGNACEAE	OLEASTER	ELE
ELATINACEAE	WATERWORT	ELT
ERICACEAE (see also MNT, PYR)	HEATH	ERI
EUPHORBIACEAE	SPURGE	EUP
FABACEAE	PEA	LEG/FAB
FAGACEAE	OAK	FAG
FRANKENIACEAE	FRANKENIA	FNK
FUMARIACEAE	FUMITORY	FUM
GENTIANACEAE	GENTIAN	GEN
GERANIACEAE	GERANIUM	GER
GROSSULARIACEAE	GOOSEBERRY (was SAX)	GRS
HALORAGACEAE	WATER-MILFOIL	HAL
HELLEBORACEAE	HELLEBORE (was RAN)	HEL

HIPPURIDACEAE	MARE'S TAIL	HPU
HYDRANGEACEAE	HYDRANGEA (was SAX)	HDR
HYDROPHYLLACEAE	WATERLEAF	HYD
HYPERICACEAE	ST. JOHNSWORT	HYP
[LABIATAE]	MINT	LAB/LAM
LAMIACEAE	MINT	LAM
[LEGUMINOSAE]	PEA	LEG/FAB
LENTIBULARIACEAE	BLADDERWORT	LNT
LIMNANTHACEAE	MEADOW-FOAM	LIM
LIMONIACEAE	THRIFT (was Plumbaginaceae)	LMO
LINACEAE	FLAX	LIN
LOASACEAE	LOASA	LOA
LYTHRACEAE	LOOSESTRIFE	LYT
MALVACEAE	MALLOW	MLV
MENYANTHACEAE	BUCKBEAN	MNY
MONOTROPACEAE	PINESAP (was ERI)	MNT
MORACEAE	MULBERRY	MOR
NYCTAGINACEAE	FOUR-O'CLOCK	NYC
NYMPHAEACEAE	WATER-LILY	NYM
OLEACEAE	OLIVE	OLE
ONAGRACEAE	EVENING-PRIMROSE	ONA
OROBANCHACEAE	BROOM-RAPE	ORO
OXALIDACEAE	WOOD-SORREL	OXL
PAPAVERACEAE	POPPY	PAP
PARNASSIACEAE	GRASS-OF-PARNASSUS	PAR
PLANTAGINACEAE	PLANTAIN	PTG
POLEMONIACEAE	PHLOX	PLM
POLYGALACEAE	MILKWORT	PGL
POLYGONACEAE	KNOTWEED	PLG
PORTULACACEAE	PURSLANE	POR
PRIMULACEAE	PRIMROSE	PRM
PYROLACEAE	WINTERGREEN (was ERI)	PYR
RANUNCULACEAE (see also HEL)	BUTTERCUP	RAN
RHAMNACEAE	BUCKTHORN	RHM
ROSACEAE	ROSE	ROS
RUBIACEAE	MADDER	RUB
SALICACEAE	WILLOW	SAL
SANTALACEAE	SANDALWOOD	SAN
SAXIFRAGACEAE (See also PAR, HDG, GRS)	SAXIFRAGE	SAX
SCROPHULARIACEAE	FIGWORT	SCR
SIMAROUBACEAE	QUASSIA	SMR
SOLANACEAE	NIGHTSHADE	SOL
TAMARICACEAE	TAMARISK	TAM
ULMACEAE	ELM	ULM
[UMBELLIFERAE]	PARSLEY	UMB/API
URTICACEAE	NETTLE	URT
VALERIANACEAE	VALERIAN	VAL
VERBENACEAE	VERVAIN	VRB
VIOLACEAE	VIOLET	VIO
VISCACEAE	MISTLETOE	VIS
VITACEAE	GRAPE	VIT
ZYGOPHYLLACEAE	CALTROP	ZYG

Some Floristic Statistics

The total number of species recognized here is roughly 2,150. The larger families and their numbers are AST (354), POA (208), FAB (138), CYP (123), BRA (119), SCR (99), PLG (63), ROS (64), CHN (55), API (51), RAN (44), PLM (45), ONA (40), SAL (27), ASN (31), JUN (29), LAM (25), SAX (25), HYD (22). The rest of the families have fewer than 20 taxa. Twenty-five families have only one taxon. Seventeen have only two. Twenty-one families have only three. This means that, while we have 139 families to reckon with, 1,585, or about 75 per cent of the taxa fall into the 'big 19' families! If you can learn to recognize these families, you can avoid using the family key that much of the time. Success in using a field guide comes when one knows the large families without using the key.

On the other hand, the large families are also the most diverse. An understanding of them comes from learning first some species, then seeing that they are related as a genus, and gradually getting a feeling for the family by association rather than by memorization of a group of characters common to the family. A family or a genus cannot be narrowly defined. Just as a species is a group of closely related individuals, a genus is a group of closely related species, and a family is a group of closely related genera. Of course, we like to measure relationship roughly by morphological similarity, but other more important things are involved. Davis and Gilmartin point out (Systematic Botany 10:417. 1985), "Species concepts have evolved to the point that morphology is now considered one of the weaker criteria of 'true' speciation. In adhering to a biological species concept the significance of morphological change in the speciation process can be trivialized on definitional grounds." The same may be said of generic concepts.

Generic Concept

Scientific names are the most concise method we have of expressing points of view. It is a human trait to use names for things just as we do for people, and a scientific name consists of a generic name (surname) and a specific epithet (Christian name). Scientists take narrower or broader views of genera and species, depending on their view of the evidence. Names that for one reason or other are not accepted by a scientist are called synonyms. Synonyms are not dead wood, but are held in the system for use when and if someone accepts them in preference to those accepted by others. Many people consider it unfortunate that names must change from time to time. Scientists do not force others to use the names they accept; they merely express their opinions by using the names they prefer. It is no more desirable to 'freeze' the names of plants than it is to force scientists to agree to 'accepted facts'. There would be no progress if the results of study and observation ('research') could not be applied to problems in science. With this in mind I should explain my generic concepts in some detail.

The most conspicuous difference between this book and the older *Rocky Mountain Flora* is in my choice of generic names. An older generation will recognize the fact that many of the names in this book were also used by Rydberg in his *Flora of the Rocky Mountains and adjacent Plains (1922)*. I believe I can say that I arrived at many of the same conclusions without realizing that I was returning to Rydberg's classification. In the Ranunculaceae, for example, he recognized *Pulsatilla*, *Viorna* (my *Coriflora*), *Atragene*, *Batrachium*, *Halerpestes*, and *Cyrtorhyncha*.

One wonders why Rydberg was so denigrated by the dominating 'eastern establishment' at Harvard. He was Swedish and might have suffered from an antagonism to foreigners. Unfortunately, we know very little about him outside of his publications, since practically all of his records at the New York Botanical Garden have disappeared. His species concepts at times were extremely narrow, but I feel that as time goes by many of his generic concepts will be vindicated by the results of new research.

The same is true of E. L. Greene, who in the first half of this century was considered nothing more than a hopeless generic 'splitter'. I suspect that there was an element of professional jealousy involved here, because Greene was a classical scholar and could and did read the classical botanical works, Greek and Latin, in the original languages. He was an acute observer in the field and was responsible for many of the genera that I have adopted but that have been ignored up to now. There was intense personal feuding between Greene and his colleagues as they strove to describe the botanical riches of the western frontier.

A proliferation of generic names began after Linnaeus' death, especially as botanists began to realize that the Linnaean system was artificial and did not reflect biological relationships. Some of the enormous waste-basket genera that are still maintained in our modern floras date from Linnaean concepts. *Potentilla* (=*Pentaphylloides*) *fruticosa*, *Potentilla* (=*Argentina*) *anserina*, and the genus *Drymocallis*, which are as 'good' genera as any in the Rosaceae, have remained undisturbed, until now, in *Potentilla*. *Polygonum*, *Saxifraga* and *Gentiana* also contain clear-cut extraneous elements. Rafinesque inveighed against the maintenance of these unnatural genera as long ago as 1837, in his attempt to bring American botanists toward a more natural generic classification. But for many reasons, including inertia and contentedness with the *status quo*, few of his, Rydberg's or Greene's proposals have been adopted.

There are almost 200 genera treated here which were not recognized by Harrington in his *Colorado Flora*. Of these, I am personally responsible for no more than four. The great bulk of 'new' names are those proposed by European botanists between the publication of Linnaeus' *Species Plantarum* (1753) and 1850. These were rejected by botanists who preferred the Linnaean classification, and they were thus lost in the literature until the present need for them arose. Most of the remainder were added by Rydberg and Greene.

Why are segregate, often small genera, still disliked *per se*? Some of the reasons are scientific, but many are emotional, practical, or psychological. A very famous British botanist told me that he dislikes the breaking up of genera, because "we simply could not keep track of so many." An American told me, "I shall never adopt your names; they are a throwback to Rydberg and Greene, who are discredited." Another, "Why should we pay attention to the Europeans; they know nothing about our plants." Or, "Asa Gray and Sereno Watson [supply other names if you wish] were fully competent botanists. Are you more so?" Or the motivation is simply a desire to keep the *status quo*. After all, if names are changed, not only must people learn them, but they must also remember the displaced ones in order to intelligently read the older literature. And if changes need to be made in an herbarium, it means annotation labels, and shifts of material from one case to another. This is messy and some would avoid it at any cost.

The genus is a concept of relationship, and our science allows us to recognize different degrees of relationship by permitting division of genera into smaller subdivisions. Many of the genera I recognize are to others subgenera, sections or series. Maintenance of these cubbyholes rests sometimes on evidence but more often for the sake of tradition, inertia, and the reputation of some person or school who is 'followed'.

In Europe, Linnaeus dominated with his 'sexual system' of classification until slowly a new group arose, favoring the 'natural system' which we continue to improve upon today. In America, the genus concept was dominated by what Greene and others called the 'eastern establishment', meaning Harvard University, with Gray, Watson and Robinson maintaining that all truth emanated from Cambridge. Western botanists resented this attitude, and Greene and Rydberg, especially, were put down and labelled 'splitters'.

It is curious that 'splitters' and 'lumpers' became synonymous with the 'bad guys' and the 'good guys'. Part of the explanation is that a *status quo* in taxonomy is desired or demanded by workers in other fields such as physiology, agriculture, and forestry, because they need to use scientific names and are annoyed when they prove to be unstable. However, we must remember that a scientific name is a concise expression of a point of view, and that taxonomists are as entitled to differing opinions as any other scientists. The 'splitter' often had a better eye than the 'lumper' and saw subtle differences in morphology, ecology, and life history. He was often a man who knew his species in the field as well as in the herbarium. Greene and Rydberg were, after Rafinesque, the ultimate generic splitters.

I recall that in the 1930s taxonomists had a very bad name because of their evident inability to stabilize nomenclature (an impossible dream at best) and because of the splitters. Everyone took pride in being a lumper (conservative). Taxonomy even changed its name several times, to 'systematics', 'biosystematics', 'plant science'. Even the great Swedish herbarium at Uppsala, where Linnaeus was professor, has now changed its name to 'Fytotek' [Gr., *phyton*, plant, + *theca*, container], capitalizing perhaps on the similarity of 'tek' to 'tech'! Perhaps all this was necessary as a short-term reaction, but soon the enormous developments in biological research made taxonomy again a respectable branch of science. The terms 'splitting' and 'lumping' are now moot.

Scientific plant breeding, crossing techniques, rapidity of shipment of live material, the electron-microscope (particularly the surface scanning electron-microscope), biochemical analytics, interdisciplinary research, have all come to the aid of taxonomy, and have made it possible for us to re-evaluate generic concepts. These developments have moved generic as well as specific concepts from an '*alpha*' kind which is essentially based on morphological features, to a '*biological genus concept*' which utilizes as many aspects of plant biology and behavior as possible. The facts are not all in, but a revolution is in progress, and I believe that the results will demonstrate that the reputations of E. L. Greene and P. A. Rydberg were unjustifiably degraded.

In 1946, when I began work in the Rocky Mountains, I was a confirmed 'lumper'. I reorganized the herbarium at the University of Colorado according to my training and eliminated all of the Rydberg-isms. I had been taught that Rafinesque was crazy (he was said to have run around his room flailing at a bat with his Stradivarius violin), and that Greene was beyond the pale. When Professor Edna Johnson discovered that I had placed *Pulsatilla* within *Anemone*, she cried, "My, you are a lumper, aren't you!" With this book I am able to finally recant my puerile preconceived notions.

It is unfortunate that in this book there is not space to discuss the justifications for each generic concept utilized here. It is not necessary, in fact, to produce detailed justification for adopting a particular taxonomic point of view (a name). Some huge genera have been maintained by inertia, despite the obvious morphological differences which fully justify their division into smaller groups: *Geum*, *Potentilla*, *Gentiana*, *Polygonum*, *Saxifraga*, *Senecio*, and *Haplopappus*. Some small genera were proposed as genera with proper justification but were simply ignored: *Teloxys*, *Seriphidium*, *Oreobatus*, *Rubacer*, *Tonestus*, *Stenotus*, *Rydbergia*, and *Tetraneuris*. Certain small genera I recognize because recent monographic studies demonstrate them in my opinion to be justified: *Gentianella*, *Gentianopsis*, *Dugaldia*. Justification for the few genera that I have proposed will be found in recent volumes of the journal, *Phytologia*.

It has taken forty years for me to gain enough experience with the flora of the world to see that lumping is not a virtue. I feel that I have gained perspective not only through my field work with floras on other continents, but through my developing specializations in the lichens and bryophytes. In the lichens, particularly, it has been demonstrated that reliance on gross morphology study had resulted in an extremely superficial taxonomy. Study of the development and microanatomy of the fruiting structures, as well as lichen biochemistry, has now ushered in a revolution in taxonomy that is upsetting the old family, generic and specific arrangements thought to be stable only thirty years ago

In preparing the manuscript for this book, I determined to cast aside my preconceptions about the genera as I had been taught, and take a fresh look at the flora, taking into account the work which has been done in other countries. Particularly, the rich Asiatic element in the Rocky Mountains forced me to utilize the *Flora USSR* and to do field work in the Altai. The result is a completely fresh treatment of the flora.

Reed Rollins, Professor Emeritus and Asa Gray Professor at Harvard, stated the case for the modern genus concept in his paper on the genus *Halimolobos* (Contrib. Dudley Herb. 3:242. 1943). "The decision as to whether *Halimolobos* should be maintained as a distinct genus in the Cruciferae or united with *Sisymbrium* is a difficult one.

The tangle of generic lines in the Sisymbrieae is well known to botanists who have dealt with the family. Clearly there was considerable unwarranted splitting of this tribe by O. E. Schulz in *Das Pflanzenreich*, but the other extreme of indiscriminately placing unrelated species into a single genus is equally objectionable. The aim should be to determine the immediate affinities of the species involved and adjust generic lines so as to make them correspond to the hiati between natural groupings of species. However difficult such a task may be, obviously it cannot be accomplished by the arbitrary selection of a single character difference which is then used as the definitive mark of the genus. Rather, the members of a genus must display a pattern of characters distinctive in itself and different from the pattern characteristic of any other genus. This pattern may be resolvable into recognizable points of a distinctive nature or the pattern as a whole may be unique. It may be based not only on morphological data but anatomical, cytological, genetic, and physiological data as well."

A common criticism of variant taxonomies produced by people working in 'the boondocks' of the Great American West is that, not being cognizant of the larger world flora (that is, not working in one of the great herbaria of the East), they tend to be provincial and do not see the forest for the trees. I am willing to run the risk of this criticism, but I do not believe that it is justified, judging from my field experience of over fifty years in the United States, Europe, the American Arctic, Central Asia, Ecuador, Chile, Australia and New Guinea.

I present this flora in the hope that it will encourage unbiased students to explore alternative classifications which from my point of view are more natural and reasonable than those which have dominated western American taxonomy up to this time. I regret that some of the applied scientists using the book will be irritated by being asked to adopt new names, but I have included the relevant synonyms if they choose not to. In my opinion we live in times of great leaps in knowledge. Freezing nomenclature is precisely what we do not need. We do need to keep open minds.

Common Names

Common or vernacular names are of relatively little consequence in our region. Such names arise along with a culture that lives on the land and utilizes plants for food, clothing and medicine. In New England common names were coined for this reason; in fact, many common names can be traced back to England, where many of the same plants occurred. In the American West, a civilization descended fullblown upon the region and common names were often transferred incorrectly to plants that were unknown in the East. This has made for continued confusion, especially now that we have visitors to Colorado who are accustomed to the traditional common names and find them misapplied here, or visitors from Eurasia who know many of our species by their botanical names, and to whom our common names mean nothing.

Another problem with common names is that sometimes a genus can be given one common name while some of its individual species may have quite different ones. Furthermore, the forest, soil conservation and range agencies seem to dislike botanical names or find they cannot expect their field men to learn them, so they may feel that a parallel system of common names has to be invented. Some of these are really ludicrous, like 'Rock Fendlerbush' for *Fendlera* and 'Threadleaf Rubber Rabbitbrush' for *Chrysothamnus greenei*. Common names that are simply translations of the scientific name, or reversal of the generic name and the specific epithet, are superfluous. In trying to make an index to common names for this book I was so frustrated by these problems that I almost decided to drop the project because I felt that this book is for people who are interested in a higher level of learning. They may or may not find, on using the book, that a species has a common name—good and well. But the purpose of this book is not to provide common names for those who are unwilling to learn the correct ones. My translations of generic names and specific epithets are intended to help the reader to relate these words and their stems to his or her own language, and thus to make scientific names mean more.

Lloyd Shinners made the most stinging remarks on common names after a lifetime of work, in his *Spring Flora of the Dallas-Fort Worth Area*: "One of the most tiresome and irritating remarks I have to listen to over and over, runs: 'Oh, don't give me those terrible Latin names; give me something I can say and understand.' People who mouth such jawbreakers as *chrysanthemum* or *asparagus* without batting an eye are simply being childish when they say they cannot manage Latin names. That is what those two words are, without a single letter changed. . . . For the 'Standardized Plant Names,' manufactured according to arbitrary rules by bureaucrats, largely by translating the Latin binomials with varying degrees of accuracy and inaccuracy, I have no use whatever. They are an insult to intelligence and a crime against good taste. There is absolutely no necessity for concocting fraudulent 'common names' for plants which the 'common man' often cannot tell apart in the first place. Anyone with serious enough interest to want to distinguish species and varieties to the same degree that a botanist does certainly ought to be serious enough to use botanical names. Those who refuse to accept the disciplines of Science are not entitled to its benefits. The botanist has enough hard work to do without being asked to put up with a lot of artificial gobbledy-gook in the form of bogus vernacular names. I have no patience with the you-do-all-the-work, give-me-something for nothing attitude which lies behind demands for 'common' names. Genuine popular names are often vivid and interesting. A study of them would be fascinating, but it belongs in the realm of folk-lore, not of science."

My experience has been that children have no trouble at all with scientific names, especially if they are told the meaning, nor with technical keys. In fact, their understanding of the English language is enhanced by seeing the similarities and derivations of scientific and vernacular words and their powers of observation are challenged by key choices. There are lots of so-called wild-flower guides that require no linguistic or scientific aptitude on the part of the reader; perhaps reluctant adults should be satisfied with those.

Pronunciation

In the pronunciation argument, I take the position that the most important question is whether one is being understood. Particularly, the English and American pronunciations of scientific names, whether 'purist' Latin or not, seem to be utterly unintelligible to people from other parts of the world. Since the Rocky Mountain flora attracts so many Eurasians because of the similarity of their floras to ours, I feel we should make an attempt to meet them halfway with pronunciation, because otherwise when we pronounce words like '*nuttallii*' with four syllables ending with a long '*i*' they simply close their ears. I find that Americans and Britons are much more likely to try to understand a European's pronunciation than *vice versa*. Since this is the case, I think we should try to reach them with something like their language, which in many ways is really more intelligible than ours. Here are my basic rules:

The letter '*a*' should always be pronounced '*ah*'.

The letter '*e*' should always be pronounced '*eh*'.

The letter '*i*' should always be pronounced '*ee*'. This goes for the double '*ii*' which may be given as either one or two syllables.

The letter '*c*' can always be given the hard sound although circumstances may dictate a soft sound; Germans often give it a '*ts*' sound.

In pronouncing a name based on a person's surname, try not to change its sound. *Núttallii* should be accented on the first, not the second syllable.

In words based on two stems, such as *Oxytropis*, try to keep the sound of the stems intact: *Oxy-trópis*, rather than accentuating an unimportant vowel—*Ox-ý-tro-pis*; *Cardio-phýlla* rather than *car-di-ó-phylla*.

In short, purist Latin as spoken by Americans and British is not necessarily pure Latin anyway, and it is not easily understood by others, even our own people. Try pronouncing a list of names and have a group of intelligent people copy them from your oral presentation and you will see what I mean. Pronouncing according to the simple rules given above will at least make our words intelligible to foreigners, and quite possibly more so to our students who were not brought up on Latin.

Miscellaneous notes

Abbreviations: in order to save space in the keys, common words are abbreviated, as lvs, fls, frt, infl, pap, spklt. These are usually self-explanatory. If not, they may be explained at the beginning of the pertinent key or in the glossary. The abbreviations, ADV and END stand for adventive and endemic, respectively.

Generic names: I have presented generic names together with their authors and dates of publication. I have also tried to present an accurate derivation of each name for its educational value.

Specific names: a specific name consists of a generic name and a specific epithet, followed by the name of the author of the name. Botanical nomenclature differs from zoölogical in the way authors of the names are cited. The name of an author in parentheses means that that author first published the species. The second author is the person responsible for the name in its present form, usually under another genus.

Author citations: in order to save space, I have deliberately omitted the initials of authors, as A. Gray and A. Nelson. I have also omitted the second author when his name follows *ex*. The citation, Nuttall *ex* Torrey & Gray means that Torrey and Gray described the plant but gave credit to Nuttall for recognizing it, informally naming it and perhaps furnishing the description. The name of Carl Linné (Linnaeus) is always abbreviated 'L'. Full citations of all names for Colorado plants are given in Weber, Johnston & Wittmann *Natural History Inventory of Colorado, 1. Vascular Plants, Lichens and Bryophytes* (1987).

Counties: Abbreviations for the Colorado counties are taken, with slight modifications*, after the Smithsonian Institution River Basin Surveys, as follows:

ARCHULETA (AA)	HINSDALE (HN)	PITKIN (PT)
DELTA (DT)	LA PLATA (LP)	RIO BLANCO (RB)
DOLORES (DL)	MESA (ME)	ROUTT (RT)
EAGLE (EA)	MOFFAT (MF)	SAGUACHE (SH)
GARFIELD (GF)	MONTEZUMA (MZ)*	SAN JUAN (SA)
GRAND (GA)	MONTROSE (MN)	SAN MIGUEL(SM)
GUNNISON (GN)	OURAY (OR)	SUMMIT (ST)

Family acronyms: Collectors should indicate on their labels the family to which a species belongs. This makes for ease in filing and retrieval from collections. Because family names are usually very long, I have developed a standard 3-letter acronym for each family, which should serve a useful purpose as a shorthand reference.

Family arrangement: Except for the Gymnosperms and Ferns, the families are listed alphabetically irrespective of whether they are Monocots or Dicots. A list of the families, with their alternative names and acronyms, under each group, is provided.

Endangered Habitats: Concern with the extremely rapid deforestation of the tropics and the concomitant urban development in western United States (made possible in part by this very deforestation) has produced a nationwide movement for the preservation of rare, threatened and endangered species. The concept of rarity is discussed below. However, in Colorado I feel that our concern really should be with special or unique habitats which in turn support populations of rare plants. If we are able to prevent destruction of their habitats, we probably need not worry about the plants.

Unfortunately, many important habitats for rare plants are going by the board. For example, while environmentalists were protesting the planned impoundment and filling of the spectacular canyon of the South Platte River for Two Forks Dam, no one seemed to be concerned about the fact that an eastern slope city had acquired water rights in South Park and within a year or two, had destroyed by ditching and draining most of the wetlands of northern South Park, where a number of very rare species occur. Probably the most threatened habitat on the Western Slope is the area of adobe hills in the lower Gunnison, Colorado and San Juan river valleys. These not

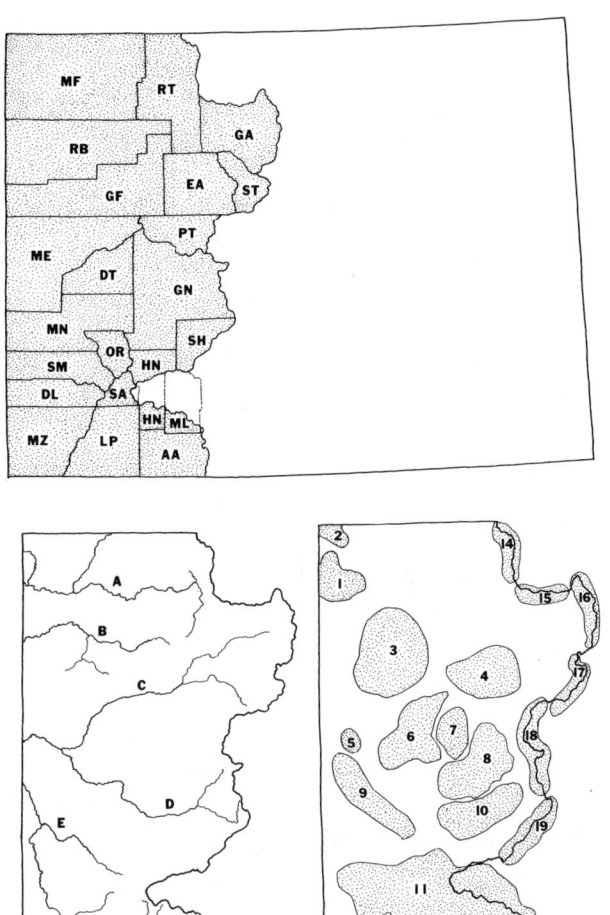

Top: Area covered by this book (shaded area); refer to text for county abbreviations.
Lower left: River systems: **A**, Yampa, Little Snake and Green; **B**, White; **C**, Colorado; **D**, Gunnison; **E**, Dolores; **F**, San Juan.
Lower right: Major topographic features: **1**, Dinosaur National Monument; **2**, Cold Spring/O-wy-u-kuts Plateau; **3**, Roan Cliffs-Piceance Basin; **4**, Flat-tops; **5**, Colorado National Monument; **6**, Grand Mesa; **7**, West Elk Mts.; **8**, Elk Mts.; **9**, Uncompahgre Plateau; **10**, Gunnison Basin; **11**, San Juan/La Plata Mts.; **12**, Mesa Verde National Park; **13**,

only provide magnificent displays of ephemeral spring flowers during good years, but they harbor a number of narrowly endemic species which may disappear unless the pressure of off-road vehicles, particularly motorbikes, can be alleviated. An effort should be made to set aside areas for motorbike recreation and allow the rest to remain undisturbed. It is claimed, however, that fencing off such areas will simply lead to vandalism! But why not give education a try?

Rarity: I have tended to omit statements about relative abundance because the term 'rare' has many connotations, and because even rare plants are often abundant where they occur, and if I say something is infrequent, someone will soon find it to be abundant. I have been unable to walk over every inch of Colorado. There are many places that I have not seen. If a species is restricted to Colorado (endemic here) I generally say so. If it is really threatened by collecting I make a note of this. Generally, our rare plants (except for cacti) are threatened less by collectors than by bulldozers and drainage ditches which destroy the habitats. Rather than using the word 'rare' I prefer to use more precise words such as 'infrequent', 'locally abundant', or 'local'.

Rarity actually is the end result of many interacting factors. These may be characteristics of the species itself: its genetic diversity or homogeneity which may make it resistant or vulnerable to changes in the habitat or environment, its mode and recentness of origin, and its 'reproductive strategy'. Others may have to do with externals: alteration of the habitat, either natural (fire, flood, climatic change) or induced by grazing or the hand of man (introduction of exotic animals, pollinators, introduced plants); and exploitation of wild plants for food, drugs, or firewood. Detailed studies of the autecology and population biology of rare plant species of Colorado have only begun. But changes in the habitat occur daily.

An important and thoughtful review of the concept of rarity was recently published in the journal Taxon, vol. 35: 502-518. 1986, by Peggy Lee Fielder, entitled: "*Concepts of rarity in vascular plant species, with special reference to the genus Calochortus Pursh (Liliaceae)*." She discusses in detail the concepts mentioned here. Among other things, she shows that the rarity of *Calochortus* not only involves unique habitats, but probably resulted in large part from the commercial bulb collection by a single dealer and his crew who claimed to have dug an average of 8,000 bulbs in ten hours. Everyone working in plant conservation should study this paper. We must refine our definition of rarity and seek to learn its basis. Each species is a unique case; generalizations are impossible.

On Colorado's Western Slope, there are several apparent reasons for rarity. In the high mountains, small populations have survived intact since Tertiary times because their microhabitats have remained in place, or have moved only slightly over millions of years. Our Asiatic rarities belong to this group. Their habitats include limestone outcrops, alpine wetlands, and virgin forests in areas untouched by glaciation. Since neither the hand of man, even in the mining days, nor sheep grazing, has destroyed these species up to now, few alpine plants are threatened or endangered. In the desert-steppe, rare and endemic species may be restricted to certain types of rock, or localized seleniferous or gypsum soils in particularly critical moisture regimes. We do not understand the specific combinations of factors that cause species to be so restricted, but can often provide educated guesses. Because these sites are localized and subject to massive injury because of quarrying and recreational vehicle use, many of these plants may prove to be truly endangered. Again, each species is a unique case, and much study of the biology of the plant is required, not only fencing off of a few acres.

But only a few species are rare here because of past human use. The Male Fern was almost exterminated by pharmaceutical collectors. At one time the Colorado Columbine was thought to be in great danger from people who gathered enormous bouquets on Sunday drives. Thus we have the only state law protecting a wild plant in Colorado. The habit of wholesale wild-flower gathering is a thing of the past. More recently, however, some rare bog plants have been endangered by digging of peat bogs for Denver gardens. Topsoil has been stripped from foothill canyon slopes, and Barrel Cacti and Banana Yucca have been exploited for landscaping of shopping malls and residences.

The preservation of crucial habitats alone is not sufficient. These sites must be sufficiently buffered so that the effect of change on adjacent sites will not wash over and affect a protected habitat. In western Colorado hindsight tells us that the Colorado National Monument should have included a larger buffering area, for we now see development right up to the fence, that the uncontrolled campsite resulted in destruction of a prime area for rare plants; that the Black Canyon National Monument was too small and should have included the north bench; that the old Mesa Verde campground on Chapin Mesa was endangering the ruins, and, of course, the plant life. These lessons we have learned at relatively small cost, but they should be constant reminders to us. In conclusion, I reiterate that it is the critical habitats that need to be preserved. Then we may have time to study over the long period the various features of the biology of plant species that makes them rare, and be better able to make intelligent rather than emotional decisions for their preservation.

Revegetation: Despite claims to the contrary, it is virtually impossible to revegetate an area in such a way as to reconstruct the original ecosystem. Therefore, the wisest action is to avoid disturbance in the first place. Attempts are commonly made nowadays to reclaim land denuded by development or exploitation by seeding to 'native' plants. From a scientific botanical standpoint this is often regrettable, since it alters the racial mixes even of species native to this area. Because of the fact that records are seldom kept, history of vegetational change of this kind is hard to reconstruct. Depending on the source of seed, weeds known to be potentially harmful may be introduced. Native species from other regions, if successful, may become undesirable weeds. My personal preference would be to allow the land to reclaim itself, providing the development has not produced an erosion crisis. In Australia enormous amounts of money have been spent in order to reverse the effects of one or two introductions (*Opuntia* cacti, Himalayan blackberry and rabbits). This could easily happen here as a result of the completely uncontrolled introduction, by well-meaning but botanically ignorant environmentalists, of plants for revegetation purposes.

Eponymy—Botanists honored in Colorado Plant Names

To identify all of the people who have been honored in the names of Rocky Mountain plants would fill this book. Most of them are mentioned briefly in the text. The ones listed here are those who, again and again, appear in the specific epithets or in generic names. Most of these were collectors in Colorado or worked intensively on Rocky Mountain plants. For additional names and details, see Joseph and Nesta Dunn Ewan. 1981. *Biographical Dictionary of Rocky Mountain Naturalists, a guide to the writings and collections of botanists, zoölogists, geologists, artists and photographers, 1682-1932.*

Baker, Charles F., 1872-1927, collected extensively in Montrose and Gunnison counties. His collections were described by Greene in a series of papers called *Plantae Bakerianae*.

Brandegee, Townshend Stith, 1843-1925, botanist with the Hayden Surveys, also surveyor of Fremont County, made important collections in the Mesa Verde area.

Clements, Frederick E., 1874-1945, ecologist, originator of plant succession concept, had experimental gardens on Pikes Peak.

Coulter, John Merle, 1851-1928, botanist with the Hayden Surveys and author of Manual of Botany of the Rocky Mountain Region, (1885).

Crandall, Charles Spencer, 1852-1929, horticulturist, professor at Colorado Agric. College, collected extensively in Colorado.

Douglas, David, 1799-1834, Scottish botanist and explorer of the West, never visited Colorado but described and collected many plants native to the State.

Eastwood, Alice, 1859-1953, high school teacher in Denver, collected around Grand Junction in 1890, later became curator at Calif. Acad. of Sciences where she gained lasting fame by segregating the type specimens and eventually saving them during the great earthquake.

Engelmann, George, 1809-1884, St. Louis physician-botanist and a founder of the Missouri Botanical Garden. Collected with Hall & Harbour in South Park, and had a cabin under Gray's Peak. Major contributions were made in the cacti and conifers.

Fendler, Augustus, 1813-1883, collector for Engelmann and Gray, mostly in New Mexico.

Frémont, John Charles, 1813-1890, explored widely in the West and collected plants and animals. Unfortunately, many of his plant specimens were lost in accidents along the way.

Gray, Asa, 1810-1888, student of Torrey and developer of the Harvard Herbarium, the dominant taxonomist of his era. Visited Colorado twice, in 1872 for the dedication of Gray's and Torrey's Peak, and for a few days in 1877, with Sir Joseph Dalton Hooker.

Greene, Edward Lee, 1843-1915, field botanist and clergyman in Colorado and New Mexico, later botanist at Univ. of California, Berkeley, one of the most knowledgeable persons of his time as to the Colorado flora.

Hall, Elihu, 1820 (or 22?)-1882, Illinois botanist, collected in South Park with J. P. Harbour in 1862.

Harbour, J. P., 1862-?, thought to be an acquaintance of Parry, and collected in South Park in 1862 with Elihu Hall.

Harrington, Harold D., 1903-1981, professor at Colorado State University, Fort Collins, author of *Manual of the Plants of Colorado* (1954), still the only complete flora of the state with keys and descriptions, indispensable to present and future floristic work.

Hayden, Ferdinand Vandiveer, 1829-1887, leader of the U. S. Geol. and Geog. Survey of the Territories 1867-1879, in which many botanists participated.

Holm, Herman Theodor, 1854-1932, Danish botanist, collected in Colorado in 1896 and 1899, published a classic paper on the plant geography of the Rocky Mountains.

Hooker, Sir William Jackson, 1785-1865, British botanist, described many western North American plants from the historic voyages of exploration and from Geyer's trip across Wyoming, director of the Royal Botanic Gardens, Kew (most species commemorating Hooker in our flora refer to W. J., rather than to his son, Sir Joseph Dalton Hooker).

Hooker, Sir Joseph Dalton, 1817-1911, director of the Royal Botanic Gardens, Kew, an early leader in plant geography, visited Colorado with Asa Gray in 1877 and was the first to note the strong Asiatic element in our flora.

James, Edwin, 1797-1861, surgeon-naturalist with the Long expedition, collected plants in 1820 from Pikes Peak to the Platte River.

Jones, Marcus Eugene, 1852-1934, exceptional field botanist, probably the greatest collector the West has known, mining engineer, contemporary and great competitor of Greene.

Letterman, George Washington, 1841-1913, a reclusive Missouri schoolteacher, collected on Long's Peak.

Nelson, Aven, 1859-1952, Wyoming botanist and founder of the Rocky Mountain Herbarium at Laramie, first life-long resident botanist of this region. Great teacher and developer of botanists, such as L. N. Goodding, Elias Nelson, J. F. Macbride, Marion Ownbey, and George J. Goodman.

Nuttall, Thomas, 1786-1859, English botanist, explorer of the West with the Second Wyeth Expedition, Harvard professor, and a perceptive taxonomist, especially in Asteraceae.

Osterhout, George E., 1858-1937, amateur naturalist and resident collector in Colorado and southern Wyoming.

Parry, Charles Christopher, 1823-1890, physician-botanist of Davenport, Iowa, collected extensively on the east slope.

Patterson, Harry Norton, 1853-1919, botanist-printer of Oquawka, Ill., collected in the Gray's Peak area.

Payson, Edwin Blake, 1893-1927, promising student of Cockerell and Nelson, collected extensively from his father's cattle ranch at Naturita. A brilliant botanist, specialized in Brassicaceae and Boraginaceae.

Penland, C. William T., 1899-1982, professor at Colorado College, avid alpine botanist, discovered many rare alpine species on Hoosier Pass, specialized in *Penstemon*.

Pennell, Francis W., 1886-1952, Pennsylvania botanist, specialized in the Scrophulariaceae of the Rocky Mt. region.

Porter, Thomas C., 1822-1901, professor at Lafayette College, Pa., collected with the Hayden Survey and published the first Colorado Flora in 1874.

Rydberg, Per Axel, 1860-1931, Swedish immigrant, curator at New York Botanical Garden, with Greene and Nelson, one of the most important figures in Rocky Mt. botany, published *Flora of the Rocky Mountains and Adjacent Plains*, 1917, ed. 2, 1923, and collected extensively in Colorado.

Schmoll, Hazel M., 1891-, Univ. of Chicago student, wrote thesis on Chimney Rock area, Pagosa-Piedra region, was curator of botany at Colorado State Museum, 1919-1923, collected at Mesa Verde Nat. Park, has been mayor and 'majordomo' of the town of Ward for many years, after giving up botany completely.

Vasey, George, 1822-1893, curator in the U. S. National Herbarium, collected extensively in eastern Colorado.

Watson, Sereno, 1826-1892, botanist on the U. S. Exploring expeditions, later assistant to Asa Gray at Harvard and then curator.

KEY TO THE FAMILIES

Note: in the longer keys, reference is made, in square brackets, to the number of the couplet from which you last came; page references are not given, since the families are in alphabetic order. Starting pages for major groups are as follows:

    Ferns and Fern allies . . . . page 43
    Gymnosperms. . . . . page 61
    Angiosperms, flowering plants . . . . page 67

1a. Plants not producing seeds or true fls, but reproducing by spores; fern-like, moss-like, rush-like plants. **Pteridophyta,** FERNS AND FERN ALLIES
1b. Plants producing seeds, either by means of fls or cones; plants of various aspects (seed plants) . . . . (2)

2a. Lvs needle-like or scale-like; evergreen trees and shrubs, never with fls; ovules and seeds on the open face of a scale or bract (rarely the cone becomes a fleshy 'berry' in *Juniperus* and *Sabina*). **Gymnosperms**
2b. Lvs various, seldom needle-like or scale-like (if so, fls are present), rarely evergreen; ovules and seeds borne in a closed cavity (carpel; ovary). **Angiosperms,** FLOWERING PLANTS. . . . . (3)

3a. Parasitic or saprophytic, often highly colored but not green (mistletoe, in this category, usually has some chlorophyll but is yellowish and epiphytic). **Key A**
3b. Not parasitic, or at least having green lvs. . . . . (4)

4a. Stems thick and succulent, spiny; true lvs absent or greatly reduced and early deciduous. **Cactaceae,** CACTUS FAMILY
4b. Not as above . . . . (5)

5a. Lvs all basal, with circular blades covered with stalked glistening red glands; fls in a raceme. **Droseraceae,** SUNDEW FAMILY
5b. Not as above, not insectivorous plants . . . . (6)

6a. Submerged plants, with or without floating lvs. **Key B**
6b. Terrestrial or semiaquatic, not wholly submerged nor with floating lvs. . . . . (7)

7a. Vines, climbing or twining among other plants, often possessing suckers or tendrils, not merely creeping on the ground. **Key C**
7b. Herbaceous or woody plants, not vines. . . . . (8)

24 Key to the Families

8a. Lvs usually parallel-veined; fl parts in threes; stem hollow or with scattered vascular bundles; herbaceous (except *Yucca*); seeds with one cotyledon. **Key D, Monocots** (but see also Limnanthaceae which has floral parts in threes, otherwise a typical dicot)
8b. Lvs usually netted-veined; fl parts in fives, fours, or twos; stems with vascular bundles arranged in a ring around the pith; herbaceous or woody; seeds usually with two cotyledons (**Dicots**). . . . (9)

9a. Trees or shrubs. **Key E**
9b. Herbaceous, sometimes woody at the very base. **Key F**

KEY A. PARASITES

1a. Attached to the bark of trees, or by suckers to the aerial stems of herbs . . . . (2)
1b. Without obvious attachments to the aerial parts of their hosts . . . . (3)

2a. Attached to the trunks of branches of evergreen trees. **Viscaceae**, Dwarf Mistletoe Family
2b. Thread-like orange or yellow plants attached by suckers to aerial parts of herbs. **Cuscutaceae**, Dodder Family

3a. Fls actinomorphic, in a spike-like erect or nodding raceme. **Monotropaceae**, Pinesap Family
3b. Fls zygomorphic . . . . (4)

4a. Fls tubular, the petals united; ovary superior. **Orobanchaceae**, Broom-rape Family
4b. Fls with separate petals; ovary inferior, often spirally twisted. **Orchidaceae**, Orchid Family

KEY B. AQUATICS

1a. Plants disk-like or thallus-like, without true stems and lvs, free floating or submerged. **Lemnaceae**, Duckweed Family
1b. Plants with stems and lvs, not thallus-like nor free-floating (2)

2a. Stems short and lacking, the lvs attached to the bottom, elongate-linear, the tips floating on the surface. **Sparganiaceae**, Bur-reed Family
2b. Plants with definite stems . . . . (3)

3a. Lvs simple, entire or slightly toothed . . . . (4)
3b. Lvs distinctly lobed, compound, or finely dissected . . . . . . (15)

4a. Lvs linear or oblong, arranged in whorls . . . . (5)
4b. Lvs variously shaped, not whorled. . . . . (6)

5a. Lvs translucent, lax, 2 cell layers thick; fls, if present, sessile (carpellate) or long-pedicelled (staminate). **Hydrocharitaceae**, Frog-bit Family
5b. Lvs opaque, rather rigid unless submerged, more than 2 cell layers thick; fls sessile in the lf axils. **Hippuridaceae**, Mare's Tail Family

6a. Lvs almost orbicular, deeply cordate, very thick and leathery; fls large, yellow, solitary. **Nymphaeaceae**, Water-lily Family
6b. Lvs narrower, not cordate; fls not as above. . . . . (7)

7a. Lvs linear or filiform . . . . (8)
7b. Lvs with distinctly broadened blades. . . . . (12)

8a. Fls in terminal or axillary spikes. **Potamogetonaceae**, Pondweed Family
8b. Fls sessile in the lf axils or on slender, often coiled, peduncles . . . . (9)

9a. Frt minute, blackish, on an elongate, often coiled peduncle; lvs filiform, over 3 cm long. **Ruppiaceae**, Ditch-grass Family
9b. Fls and frts sessile in the lf axils; lvs shorter . . . . (10)

10a. Frt rounded or emarginate, oblong or wider, not beaked. **Callitrichaceae**, Water Starwort Family
10b. Frt narrowly cylindric, tapered to a beak. . . . . (11)

11a. Frt flattened, slightly curved, with a stout beak; lvs filiform. **Zannichelliaceae**, Horned Pondweed Family
11b. Frt terete, straight, the beak whitish, not rigid; lvs linear, flat, the margins very finely toothed (under high magnification). **Najadaceae**, Water-nymph Family

12a. Lvs alternate, at least 1 cm long; fls not sessile in the lf-axils. . . . . (13)
12b. Lvs opposite, less than 1 cm long; fls inconspicuous, sessile in the lf axils . . . . (14)

13a. Floating lvs pinnately veined; fls pink, with showy pink perianth parts. *Persicaria*, in **Polygonaceae**, Buckwheat Family
13b. Floating lvs with parallel veins, or floating lvs absent; fls greenish, not showy. **Potamogetonaceae**, Pondweed Family

14a. Stipules lacking; calyx and corolla absent; ovary 4-locular; floating and submerged lvs often strikingly different. **Callitrichaceae**, Water-starwort Family
14b. Stipules present; calyx and corolla often present; ovary 3- or 5-locular; lvs not dimorphic. **Elatinaceae**, Waterwort Family

15a. Lvs 3-foliolate; fls white, petals fringed. **Menyanthaceae**, Buckbean Family

15b. Lvs not 3-foliolate . . . . (16)

16a. Lvs bearing small balloon-like traps; fls showy, yellow, spurred, on racemes projecting above water level. **Lentibulariaceae**, BLADDERWORT FAMILY
16b. Lvs not bearing bladders; fls not spurred . . . . (17)

17a. Lvs alternate; fls with white or yellow petals. **Ranunculaceae**, BUTTERCUP FAMILY
17b. Lvs whorled; fls greenish, inconspicuous . . . . (18)

18a. Lf divs dichotomous, finely serrate; fls sessile in the axils of normal lvs. **Ceratophyllaceae**, HORNWORT FAMILY
18b. Lf divs pinnate, entire; fls in an interrupted spike resembling a knotted cord. **Haloragaceae**, WATER MILFOIL FAMILY

KEY C. VINES

1a. Lvs simple . . . . (2)
1b. Lvs compound (Caution! Poison Ivy in this category). . . . . . (6)

2a. Lvs palmately lobed, sometimes only slightly so . . . . (3)
2b. Lvs not lobed . . . . (5)

3a. Plants with tendrils . . . . (4)
3b. Tendrils absent. *Humulus*, in **Cannabaceae**, HOPS FAMILY

4a. Herbaceous; frt a papery, spiny balloon or a gourd. **Cucurbitaceae**, CUCUMBER FAMILY
4b. Woody; fruit a fleshy 'grape'. **Vitaceae**, GRAPE FAMILY

5a. Fls 1 cm long or more; petals united, pleated. **Convolvulaceae**, MORNING-GLORY FAMILY
5b. Fls smaller; perianth parts (tepals) separate. **Polygonaceae**, BUCKWHEAT FAMILY

6a. Lvs pinnately compound . . . . (7)
6b. Lvs trifoliolate, palmately 5-7-foliolate, or ternately compound; fls not as above . . . . (8)

7a. Lfls entire; fls with banner, wings, and keel (sweet-pea type). **Fabaceae**, PEA FAMILY
7b. Lfls serrate; fls tubular. **Bignoniaceae**, CATALPA FAMILY

8a. Lvs palmately 5-7-foliolate. **Vitaceae**, GRAPE FAMILY
8b. Lvs not as above . . . . (9)

9a. Lvs with 3 shiny lfls; fls greenish; plant short (scarcely viny in this area), commonly bearing clusters of greenish-white berries. *Toxicodendron*, Poison Ivy, in **Anacardiaceae**, SUMAC FAMILY
9b. Lvs twice ternately compound, or if 3-foliolate, the fls blue or yellow, with long feathery styles in frt. **Ranunculaceae**, BUTTERCUP FAMILY

KEY D. MONOCOTS

1a. Woody plants with stiff evergreen dagger-like lvs and racemes or panicles of large white fls, later large 3-locular pods. **Agavaceae**, AGAVE FAMILY
1b. Herbs . . . . (2)

2a. Tall fern-like plants, the true lvs minute, triangular, papery, subtending clusters of filiform green cladodes; fls small, yellowish; fruit a red berry. **Asparagaceae**, ASPARAGUS FAMILY
2b. Not as above . . . . (3)

3a. Fls minute, enclosed in chaffy bracts; 3- or 6-parted perianth lacking; fls arranged in spikes or spikelets (grasses and sedges). . . . . (4)
3b. Flowers not enclosed in chaffy bracts or scales; perianth usually present, with 3 or 6 parts which may themselves appear papery or chaffy. . . . . (5)

4a. Lvs 2-ranked (in 2 rows on the stem), the sheaths usually open, the margins not fused (few exceptions); stems cylindric or flattened and almost always hollow; anthers attached to filaments at their middles. **Poaceae**, GRASS FAMILY
4b. Lvs 3-ranked, sometimes absent; sheaths usually closed, the margins fused; stems almost always triangular and solid (a few cylindric and hollow); anthers attached at one end. **Cyperaceae**, SEDGE FAMILY

5a. Fls with a rudimentary perianth consisting of bristles or scales, or none . . . . (6)
5b. Fls with sepals and petals (sometimes the two are similar in shape and texture: tepals). . . . . (7)

6a. Fls in elongate terminal spikes, the looser staminate fls in a separate group above the dense brown carpellate ones. **Typhaceae**, CAT-TAIL FAMILY
6b. Fls in spherical clusters, staminate ones above the carpellate ones. **Sparganiaceae**, BUR-REED FAMILY

7a. Carpels numerous (over 6), separate and distinct, in a whorl or ball. **Alismataceae**, WATER-PLANTAIN FAMILY
7b. Carpels 3 or 6 . . . . (8)

8a. Ovary wholly inferior, the floral parts attached to the top of the ovary. . . . . (9)
8b. Ovary superior or only partly inferior . . . . (11)

9a. Fls radially symmetrical; lvs gladiate. **Iridaceae**, IRIS FAMILY
9b. Fls bilaterally symmetrical; leaves not gladiate. . . . . . . (10)

10a. Fls large, slipper-shaped with a rounded toe; lvs more than 1; functional stamens 2. **Cypripediaceae**, LADY'S SLIPPER FAMILY

10b. Fls small (if slipper-shaped, the toe pointed and lf solitary); functional stamens 1. **Orchidaceae**, ORCHID FAMILY

11a. Perianth of 6 chaffy or scale-like similar segs, hardly petal-like, but arranged in 2 alternating groups of 3; grass-like plants. **Juncaceae**, RUSH FAMILY
11b. Perianth segs petal- or sepal-like, not chaffy or scale-like . . . (12)

12a. Tepals minute, greenish; stamens sessile; carpels separating as units at maturity; annual, or perennial from a rhizome; grass-like plants of alkaline flats and mountain bogs. **Juncaginaceae**, ARROW-GRASS FAMILY
12b. Not as above . . . . (13)

13a. Outer and inner perianth segs strongly differentiated in color or size . . . . (14)
13b. Outer and inner perianth segs similar (tepals) . . . . (16)

14a. Petals less than 2 cm long, all purple or two blue, one white. **Commelinaceae**, DAY-FLOWER FAMILY
14b. Petals over 2 cm long, white or rose-colored . . . . (15)

15a. Lvs broadly ovate, in a whorl of three; fl white, with green sepals. **Trilliaceae**, TRILLIUM FAMILY
15b. Lvs linear, alternate; fl white or rose, with a prominent gland of colored hairs. **Calochortaceae**, MARIPOSA FAMILY

16a. Fls in umbels subtended by a group of papery bracts; stem arising from a bulb. **Alliaceae**, ONION FAMILY
16b. Fls not in umbels; stems from fibrous roots, rhizomes or bulbs . . . . (17)

17a. Inner tepals with a prominent gland at the base; ovary with prominent styles; carpels separate part way down. **Melanthiaceae**, FALSE HELLEBORE FAMILY
17b. Tepals without glands; ovary usually without styles (don't confuse these with separate stigmas); carpels united. . . . . (18)

18b. Lvs basal, if not then the fls large and showy. **Liliaceae**, LILY FAMILY
18a. Lvs alternate, cauline; fls small, 2 cm or less . . . . (19)

19a. Infl a terminal raceme or panicle; tepals white, wide spreading; frt a small red or greenish berry. **Convallariaceae**, MAYFLOWER FAMILY
19b. Infl axillary or terminal, fls solitary or a few; fl bell-shaped, tepals yellowish. **Uvulariaceae**, BELLWORT FAMILY

KEY E. WOODY DICOTS

1a. Lvs minute (less than 5 mm long), scale-like, overlapping and appressed to the stem. **Tamaricaceae**, TAMARISK FAMILY
1b. Lvs larger and otherwise not as above . . . . (2)

Key to the Families—Woody Dicots 29

2a. [1] Lvs covered by silvery or brownish peltate scales. **Elaeagnaceae**, OLEASTER FAMILY
2b. Lvs not covered by peltate scales . . . . (3)

3a. [2] Lvs opposite. . . . . (4)
3b. Lvs alternate or scattered. . . . . (19)

4a. [3] Frt a samara. . . . . (5)
4b. Frt not a samara (or frts not present) . . . . (6)

5a. [4] Lvs pinnately-veined, mostly simple, or a few with one or two lfls; lvs leathery. *Fraxinus*, in **Oleaceae**, OLIVE FAMILY
5b. Lvs palmately veined, simple or compound (*Negundo* sometimes has 5 lfls, thus pinnately compound); lvs not leathery. **Aceraceae**, MAPLE FAMILY

6a. [4] Lvs palmately lobed or compound (*Negundo* sometimes has 5 lfls, thus pinnately compound) . . . . (7)
6b. Lvs neither palmately lobed nor palmately compound . . . . . . (9)

7a. [6] Terminal bud long-pointed, not protected by overlapping scales; frt a berry. *Viburnum*, in **Caprifoliaceae**, HONEYSUCKLE FAMILY
7b. Terminal bud blunt or merely acute, protected by overlapping scales; frt a samara . . . . (8)

8a. [7] Most lvs simple; lvs leathery, oval; samara simple, one-winged. *Fraxinus*, in **Oleaceae**, OLIVE FAMILY
8b. Lvs never simple nor leathery; samara double, with 2 wings. **Aceraceae**, MAPLE FAMILY

9a. [6] Lvs evergreen . . . . (10)
9b. Lvs deciduous . . . . (12)

10a. [9] Lvs entire, paler beneath; plants of subalpine bogs. *Kalmia*, in **Ericaceae**, HEATH FAMILY
10b. Lvs serrulate or crenate, not pale beneath . . . . (11)

11a. [10] Lvs elliptic; low spreading shrubs, lvs spreading in one plane; fls small, axillary, reddish. **Celastraceae**, STAFF-TREE FAMILY
11b. Lvs broadly oval; creeping plant with only slightly woody stems; fls in pairs, pendent from an erect stalk. *Linnaea*, in **Caprifoliaceae**, HONEYSUCKLE FAMILY

12a. [9] Lvs linear, with smaller lvs fascicled in the axils . . . . . . (13)
12b. Lvs broader, not in axillary fascicles. . . . . (14)

13a. [12] Lvs glabrous, appearing terete, the margins tightly revolute; fls white; restricted to gypsum soils. **Frankeniaceae**
13b. Lvs densely appressed-pubescent, margins not tightly revolute; fls lacking corolla; not gypsiferous. *Coleogyne*, in **Rosaceae**, ROSE FAMILY

Key to the Families—Woody Dicots

14a. [12] Lvs pinnately compound. **Caprifoliaceae**, HONEYSUCKLE FAMILY
14b. Leaves simple. . . . . (15)

15a. [14] Twigs red; buds not covered by scales; lvs oval, ± parallel-veined; fls in compound cymes. **Cornaceae**, DOGWOOD FAMILY
15b. Twigs not red; buds scaly; lvs and fls not as above. . . . . . . (16)

16a. [15] Bark exfoliating; lvs oblong or oval, commonly distinctly hairy; fls white, waxy-textured; frt a dry capsule. **Hydrangeaceae**, HYDRANGEA FAMILY
16b. Bark not exfoliating; lvs ovate, if oblong then glabrous or very minutely hairy, sometimes slightly lobed; venation pinnate, netted, or lvs with numerous ± parallel veins . . . . (17)

17a. [16] Tall shrubs of streambottoms and mountain streamsides. . . (18)
17b. Low, much-branched shrubs of plateaus and gulches; lvs narrowly to broadly oval, up to twice as long as wide, often with some lateral lobes; fls pink or white, short-or long-tubular; frt a white juicy berry. *Symphoricarpos*, in **Caprifoliaceae**, HONEYSUCKLE FAMILY

18a. [17] Much-branched shrub with small, thick, dark green oval lvs, resembling privet; fls minute, greenish, not in pairs; frt a black berry. *Forestiera*, in **Oleaceae**, OLIVE FAMILY
18b. Little-branched shrub with large thin ovate-oblong light green lvs; fls yellow or white, in pairs; berry red or purple-black. *Distegia*, in **Caprifoliaceae**, HONEYSUCKLE FAMILY

19a. [3] Lvs compound. . . . . (20)
19b. Lvs simple . . . . (25)

20a. [19] Lvs spine-margined, evergreen (resembling holly); inner bark yellow. **Berberidaceae**, BARBERRY FAMILY
20b. Lvs not as above . . . . (21)

21a. [20] Lvs with 3 lfls (Caution! Poison Ivy is in this category). **Anacardiaceae**, SUMAC FAMILY
21b. Lvs not trifoliolate, usually pinnately compound. . . . . (22)

22a. [21] Frt a legume; lfls more than 9, entire. **Fabaceae**, PEA FAMILY
22b. Frt not a legume; lfls various, but if numerous, then serrate or with shallow lobes or auricles at the base of the lfl . . . . . . (23)

23a. [22] Lfls more than 11; branches stout, the pith occupying a major portion of the cross-section. . . . . (24)
23b. Lfls 11 or fewer; if more, then the pith not as above. **Rosaceae**, ROSE FAMILY

24a. [23] Lfls serrate; frts red, round, with a velvety surface. **Anacardiaceae**, SUMAC FAMILY
24b. Lfls entire except for basal auricles; frt an elongate samara with a central seed. **Simaroubaceae**, QUASSIA FAMILY

25a. [19] Stems with thorns or spines. . . . . (26)
25b. Stems spineless . . . . (33)

26a. [25] Thorns often more than 1 cm long, formed by modification of whole branchlets . . . . (27)
26b. Thorns shorter, formed at the nodes (modified lvs or stipules . . . . (31)

27a. [26] Lvs linear, often somewhat thick and succulent . . . . . . (28)
27b. Lvs not succulent, broader . . . . (29)

28a. [27] Rigid, short-branched dense low shrub less than 1 m tall, with narrowly oblong pale green lvs, the older branches rigid, thorn-like; fls small, greenish, with petals and sepals. **Crossosomataceae**
28b. Shrubs either over a m tall, or not rigidly branched, with succulent or gray-farinose lvs; fls lacking petals, subtended by characteristic bracts. **Chenopodiaceae**, GOOSEFOOT FAMILY

29a. [27] Lvs crenate, serrate or lobed; thorn a modified branchlet. *Crataegus*, in **Rosaceae**, ROSE FAMILY
29b. Lvs entire . . . . (30)

30a. [29] Lvs with 3 prominent veins; thorn a modified branchlet; low shrub. *Ceanothus*, in **Rhamnaceae**, BUCKTHORN FAMILY
30b. Lvs with pinnate venation; thorn replacing a stipule; introduced tree. *Maclura*, in **Moraceae**, MULBERRY FAMILY

31a. [26] Lvs linear; young twigs woolly-tomentose. *Tetradymia*, in **Asteraceae**, SUNFLOWER FAMILY
31b. Lvs broader; young twigs not tomentose . . . . (32)

32a. [31] Lvs elliptic, entire, toothed, or spine-toothed; frt elliptical. **Berberidaceae**, BARBERRY FAMILY
32b. Lvs ovate, lobed and toothed; frt globose. **Grossulariaceae**, GOOSEBERRY FAMILY

33a. [25] Lvs pinnately lobed or spine-toothed, leathery; frt an acorn. **Fagaceae**, OAK FAMILY
33b. Lvs not as above; frt not an acorn. . . . . (34)

34a. [33] Lf-blades unequal at the base (one side attached lower than the other). **Ulmaceae**, ELM FAMILY
34b. Lf-blades not unequal at the base . . . . (35)

35a. [33] Lvs broadly ovate-cordate or deeply 5-7-lobed, crenate; frts juicy, blackberry-like (a fleshy catkin); introd. **Moraceae**, MULBERRY FAMILY
35b. Not as above . . . . (36)

36a. [35] Lvs palmately lobed (sometimes shallowly) . . . . (37)
36b. Lvs not palmately lobed . . . . (38)

Key to the Families—Woody Dicots

37a. [35] Stamens numerous; carpels few to numerous, separate; frt dry; fls never tubular. **Rosaceae**, ROSE FAMILY

37b. Stamens 5 or fewer; carpels 2, united, forming a fleshy berry; fls often tubular. **Grossulariaceae**, GOOSEBERRY FAMILY

38a. [35] Lf buds (in the lf-axils) with a single covering scale; lvs from narrowly linear to broadly lanceolate or elliptic. *Salix*, in **Salicaceae**, WILLOW FAMILY

38b. Not as above . . . . (39)

39a. [38] Petiole flattened perpendicular to the lf face; lvs deltoid-serrate, evenly serrate or crenulate. *Populus*, in **Salicaceae**, WILLOW FAMILY

39b. Petiole not flattened . . . . (40)

40a. [39] Either staminate or carpellate catkins present at most times (in *Alnus* the carpellate catkin is persistent and woody); lvs irregularly serrate; horizontal lenticels present on the trunk. **Betulaceae**, BIRCH FAMILY

40b. Catkins not present . . . . (41)

41a. [40] Fls in heads, each fl cluster surrounded by an invol; mostly low desert shrubs. **Asteraceae**, SUNFLOWER FAMILY

41b. Fls not as above. . . . . (42)

42a. [41] Desert shrubs with farinose pubescence. **Chenopodiaceae**, GOOSEFOOT FAMILY

42b. Not as above . . . . (43)

43a. [42] Lvs never with 3 prominent veins; fls usually vase-shaped (except in *Azaleastrum*); petals united, waxy. **Ericaceae**, HEATH FAMILY

43b. Not as above . . . . (44)

44a. [43] Lvs entire, elliptic or ovate, with 3 prominent veins (or, in *Rhamnus*, with many parallel lateral veins); stamens opposite the petals. **Rhamnaceae**, BUCKTHORN FAMILY

44b. Lvs toothed or lobed (rarely entire in *Peraphyllum*, which has inconspicuous lateral veins); stamens numerous or not opposite the petals. **Rosaceae**, ROSE FAMILY

KEY F (HERBACEOUS DICOTS)

1a. Fls several to many, sessile in heads, each fl-cluster surrounded or subtended by an invol. . . . . (2)

1b. Fls not as above. . . . . (6)

(Flowers in heads with invol)

2a. [1] Lvs linear, all basal; head single, scapose; fls pink, the head papery-textured; ovary superior. **Limoniaceae**, THRIFT FAMILY

2b. Not as above; ovary inferior . . . . (3)

3a. [2] Invol papery or umbrella-like, consisting of a single, undivided cup; fls obviously separate and not tightly confined by the invol. **Nyctaginaceae**, FOUR-O'CLOCK FAMILY
3b. Invol not papery or umbrella-like, the fl cluster confined in a dense head . . . . (4)

4a. [3] Lvs in a single whorl on a short stem; invol white; berries red. *Chamaepericlymenum*, in **Cornaceae**, DOGWOOD FAMILY
4b. Not as above . . . . (5)

5a. [4] Corolla 4-lobed; stamens separate. **Dipsacaceae**, TEASEL FAMILY
5b. Corolla 5-lobed or strap-shaped or of both types; stamens with united anthers. **Asteraceae**, SUNFLOWER FAMILY

(Fls not in heads)

6a. [1] Perianth none or of a single set of parts (tepals), these all much alike in color and texture . . . . (7)
6b. Perianth present, evidently double, the outer segments (sepals) and inner segments (petals) usually conspicuously different in texture, color, or both . . . . (29)

(Perianth absent or of tepals)

7a. [6] Plants dioecious; staminate fls in racemes, carpellate in clusters; frt nutlike; lvs digitately compound with narrow serrate lfls. *Cannabis*, in **Cannabaceae**, HOPS FAMILY
7b. Plants not dioecious, otherwise not as above . . . . (8)

8a. [7] Ovary inferior . . . . (9)
8b. Ovary superior . . . . (13)

9a. [8] Ovary with 2 locules, one ovule in each; frt 2-seeded . . . . (10)
9b. Ovary with one locule, this with 1-2 ovules (or ovary with 1-3 locules but only one locule containing an ovule); frt 1-seeded
. . . . (11)

10a. [9] Petals united at the base; lvs opposite or whorled; fls in cymes, never umbels. **Rubiaceae**, MADDER FAMILY
10b Petals separate; lvs alternate or basal; fls in umbels. **Apiaceae/ Umbelliferae**, CARROT FAMILY

11a. [9] Lvs alternate, glaucous; fls greenish-white. **Santalaceae**, SANDALWOOD FAMILY
11a. Lvs opposite; fls white or pink . . . . (12)

12a. [11] Lvs simple, entire; fls pinkish or flesh-colored; frts hard and bony or with papery wings. **Nyctaginaceae**, FOUR-O'CLOCK FAMILY
12b. Lvs pinnately lobed or divided; fls white; frts provided with a delicate parachute of feathery bristles. **Valerianaceae**, VALERIAN FAMILY

Key to the Families—Herbaceous Dicots

(Perianth of tepals; ovary superior)

13a. [8] Carpels separate, several to many in each fl; stamens usually numerous . . . . (14)
13b. Carpels solitary or several united; stamens one to many (usually not over 10 in most families . . . . (15)

14a. [13] Carpels consisting of dehiscent, several-seeded follicles. **Helleboraceae**, HELLEBORE FAMILY
14b. Carpels consisting of 1-seeded indehiscent akenes. **Ranunculaceae**, BUTTERCUP FAMILY

15a. [13] Ovary with 2 or more locules . . . . (16)
15b. Ovary with one locule . . . . (20)

16a. [15] Plants with milky juice. **Euphorbiaceae**, SPURGE FAMILY
16b. Plants without milky juice . . . . (17)

17a. [16] Fls unisexual; ovary on a stalk (in this group the fls are reduced to single stamens on single gynoecia, but the stamens and gynoecium are surrounded by a cup-like invol which resembles a perianth). **Euphorbiaceae**, SPURGE FAMILY
17b. Fls perfect . . . . (18)

18a. [17] Lvs opposite or whorled, entire; stamens one to many (rarely 2); fls axillary, solitary of in small clusters. **Alsinaceae**, CHICKWEED FAMILY
18b. Lvs alternate or crowded at the base of the stem, usually toothed; stamens 2; fls in terminal spikes or racemes . . . . . (19)

19a. [18] Perennials; fls in spikes; frt several-seeded. *Besseya*, in **Scrophulariaceae**, FIGWORT FAMILY
19b. Annuals; fls in racemes; frt 2-seeded (one seed in each locule. *Lepidium*, in **Brassicaceae/Cruciferae**, MUSTARD FAMILY

20a. [15] Ovary with several to many ovules; frt a capsule, several- to many-seeded . . . . (21)
20b. Ovary with one ovule; frt a one-seeded ak or utricle . . . . . (22)

21a. [20] Perianth of united tepals, pink; lvs oblong, glaucous. *Glaux*, in **Primulaceae**, PRIMROSE FAMILY
21b. Perianth of separate tepals; leaves otherwise. **Alsinaceae**, CHICKWEED FAMILY

22a. [20] Lvs with stipules either papery or sheathing the stem . . . (23)
22b. Lvs without stipules, or these, when present, neither papery nor sheathing the stem . . . . (24)

23a. [22] Lvs opposite; stipules papery. *Paronychia*, in **Alsinaceae**, CHICKWEED FAMILY
23b. Lvs alternate; stipules united around the stem in a sheath just above the nodes. **Polygonaceae**, BUCKWHEAT FAMILY

Key to the Families—Herbaceous Dicots 35

24a. [22] Conspicuous, persistent stipules present; lvs opposite. . . . . (25)
24b. Stipules lacking; lvs usually alternate. . . . . (26)

25a. [24] Stipules papery; plants small, with spreading, prostrate, or densely caespitose stems rarely over 30 cm tall; stinging hairs not present. **Alsinaceae**, CHICKWEED FAMILY
25b. Stipules not papery; plants with erect stems usually over 30 cm tall; stinging hairs present. **Urticaceae**, NETTLE FAMILY

26a. [24] Fls perfect, the fl clusters subtended by a cup-like invol; stamens 6 to 9; frt an ak. **Polygonaceae**, BUCKWHEAT FAMILY
26b. Fls perfect or unisexual but not subtended by a cup-like invol; stamens 1 to 5; frt an ak or utricle. . . . . (27)

27a. [26] Bracts and perianth ± papery or membranaceous. **Amaranthaceae**, AMARANTH FAMILY
27b. Bracts and perianth herbaceous to fleshy, not papery or membranaceous. . . . . (28)

28a. [27] Style and stigma one; lvs alternate and entire; frt an ak; annuals. *Parietaria*, in **Urticaceae**, NETTLE FAMILY
28b. Styles and stigmas 1 to 3 (but if one the lvs toothed); frt a utricle; annuals or perennials; weedy sp, often coarse and scurfy-pubescent. **Chenopodiaceae**, GOOSEFOOT FAMILY

(Perianth with sepals and petals)

29a. [6] Petals separate. . . . . (30)
29b. Petals united (at least at the base). . . . . (77)

30a. [29] Sepals and petals 3, petals shorter than sepals; ovary superior, frt a schizocarp of 3 nutlets; delicate wetland plants with pinnatifid lvs. **Limnanthaceae**, MEADOW-FOAM FAMILY
30b. Floral parts not in 3's; otherwise not as above. . . . . (31)

31a. [30] Ovary inferior, at least the lower half fused to the hypanthium or calyx-tube . . . . (32)
31b. Ovary superior (if hypanthium is present the ovary may seem to be inferior but upon dissection it is seen not to be imbedded in the hypanthium tissues, *cf.* rose hips) . . . . (40)

(Ovary inferior, petals separate)

32a. [31] Stamens as many as the petals and opposite them. **Portulacaceae**, PURSLANE FAMILY
32b. Stamens fewer or more numerous than the petals, or, if the same number, then alternate with them. . . . . (33)

33a. [32] Ovules and seeds more than one in each locule; ovary with 1 to 4 locules. . . . . (34)
33b. Ovules and seeds only one in each locule; ovary with 2 to 6 locules. . . . . (37)

Key to the Families—Herbaceous Dicots

34a. [33] Two or more styles present. . . . . (35)
34b. Only one style present (stigmas may be lobed). . . . . (36)

35a. [34] Branched staminodia alternating with the stamens; petals white; lvs basal or with one on the flower stalk. **Parnassiaceae,** GRASS-OF-PARNASSUS FAMILY
35b. Branched staminodia absent; petals white, pink or yellow. **Saxifragaceae,** SAXIFRAGE FAMILY

36a. [34] Stamens 10 or more; plants sand-papery, with minutely barbed hairs. **Loasaceae,** LOASA FAMILY
36b. Stamens 4 or 8; plants lacking barbed hairs. **Onagraceae,** EVENING-PRIMROSE FAMILY

37a. [33] Lvs whorled, entire; ovary usually with 2 locules and only one style; frt a cluster of red berries. *Chamaepericlymenum*, in **Cornaceae,** DOGWOOD FAMILY
37b. Lvs alternate, opposite, or basal, toothed or entire (never whorled); ovary with 4 locules, or, if with 2, then 2 styles present. . . . . (38)

38a. [37] Stamens 2, 4 or 8; petals 2 or 4; style one, locules usually 4 (2 in *Circaea*). **Onagraceae,** EVENING-PRIMROSE FAMILY
38b. Stamens 5, rarely 4; petals usually 5; styles 2 or more; locules 2 to 6. . . . . (39)

39a. [38] Locules 4 to 6; frt a several-seeded berry; lvs basal, ternately compound. **Araliaceae,** GINSENG FAMILY
39b. Locules 2; frt dry, separating into 2 one-seeded schizocarps. **Apiaceae/Umbelliferae,** CARROT FAMILY

40a. [31] Corolla bilaterally symmetrical . . . . (41)
40b. Corolla radially symmetrical . . . . (47)

(Ovary superior, corolla bilaterally symmetrical)

41a. [40] Lvs pinnately or palmately compound . . . . (42)
41b. Lvs simple, entire, to deeply lobed or pinnatifid, but never truly compound . . . . (44)

42a. [41] Sepals 2, very minute and scale-like; corolla spurred; lvs greatly dissected. **Fumariaceae,** FUMITORY FAMILY
42b. Sepals 4 or 5; corolla not or very inconspicuously spurred; lvs once or twice compound . . . . (43)

43a. [42] Ovary with one placenta; petals 5 (a banner, two wings, and a keel consisting of two partly united petals that enclose the stamens and style); fls usually shaped like those of sweet-pea. **Fabaceae/Leguminosae,** PEA FAMILY
43b. Ovary with 2 placentae on opposite sides of the ovary; petals 4; stamens exserted. **Capparaceae,** CAPER FAMILY

44a. [41] Stamens many; carpels usually more than one; if one, then a few-seeded red berry. **Helleboraceae**, HELLEBORE FAMILY
44b. Stamens 10 or fewer; ovary of a single or several united carpels; frt a dehiscent capsule or legume . . . . (45)

45a. [44] Fls spurred (violets). **Violaceae**, VIOLET FAMILY
45b. Fls not spurred, but with a larger upper petal (the banner) . . . (46)

46a. [45] Plant strictly herbaceous; lvs orbicular, glaucous; frt a legume; fls like sweet-pea. *Astragalus asclepiadoides*, in **Fabaceae/Leguminosae**, PEA FAMILY
46b. Plant with a stout woody base; lvs linear or oblong; frt a flat 2-loculed capsule; fls zygomorphic but not like sweet-pea. **Polygalaceae**, MILKWORT FAMILY

(Ovary superior, corolla radially symmetrical)

47a. [40] Stamens of the same number as the petals and opposite them . . . . (48)
47b. Stamens fewer or more numerous than the petals, or, if the same number, then alternate with them . . . . (50)

48a. [47] Sepals, petals and stamens each 6 in number, 3 of the sepals petal-like; lf margins spiny. **Berberidaceae**, BARBERRY FAMILY
48b. Sepals, petals and stamens 2 to 5 (sepals rarely 6); branches and lvs spineless . . . . (49)

49a. [48] Styles and stigmas 1; sepals usually 5. **Primulaceae**, PRIMROSE FAMILY
49b. Styles and stigmas 2 or more; sepals usually 2. **Portulacaceae**, PURSLANE FAMILY

50a. [47] Ovary one (a single unit) with one locule. . . . . (51)
50b. Ovaries more than one (several separate units), or, if one, then with 2 or more locules. . . . . (63)

(Corolla radial, ovary one, with one locule)

51a. [50] Stamens 13 or more . . . . (52)
51b. Stamens 12 or fewer. . . . . (57)

52a. [51] Ovary simple (of a single carpel having one placenta, one style, one stigma; many such ovaries may be present in a single flower) . . . . (53)
52b. Ovary compound (two or more placentae, styles, or stigmas) . . (54)

53a. [52] Frt a one-seeded ak. **Ranunculaceae**, BUTTERCUP FAMILY
53b. Frt a several-seeded dehiscent follicle or a fleshy berry. **Helleboraceae**, HELLEBORE FAMILY

54a. [52] Placenta free-central or basal. **Portulacaceae**, PURSLANE FAMILY

Key to the Families—Herbaceous Dicots

54b. Placentae parietal . . . . (55)

55a. [54] Ovary with 2 parietal placentae; plants usually viscid and ill-smelling. **Capparaceae**, CAPER FAMILY
55b. Ovary with 3 or more placentae; plant not viscid nor ill-smelling . . . . (56)

56a. [55] Lvs opposite, entire, with minute translucent dots (hold up to the light); juice not milky; lvs and petals often with black marginal dots. **Hypericaceae**, ST. JOHNSWORT FAMILY
56b. Lvs alternate, toothed or lobed, without translucent dots; juice milky; calyx forced off intact as a cone by the swelling petals; fls white or cream-colored, rarely yellow or orange. **Papaveraceae**, POPPY FAMILY

57a. [51] Gynoecium composed of a single carpel (one placenta, style, and stigma). . . . . (58)
57b. Gynoecium compound (more than one placenta, style, or stigma). . . . . (59)

58a. [57] Stamens and petals attached to the rim of the calyx-tube (hypanthium). **Rosaceae**, ROSE FAMILY
58b. Stamens and petals not attached to the calyx tube. **Fabaceae/Leguminosae**, PEA FAMILY

59a. [57] Petals inserted on the throat of a bell-shaped or tubular calyx. **Lythraceae**, LOOSESTRIFE FAMILY
59b. Petals inserted on the receptacle; calyx of separate or united sepals . . . . (60)

60a. [59] Ovules attached to base of ovary or to a free-central placenta (never parietal) . . . . (61)
60b. Ovules attached to two or more parietal placentae . . . . (62)

61a. [60] Calyx of united sepals; petals with claws. **Caryophyllaceae**, PINK FAMILY
61b. Calyx of separate sepals; petals not stalked. **Alsinaceae**, CHICKWEED FAMILY

62a. [60] Ovary with 2 parietal placentae; sepals and petals 4 each. **Capparaceae**, CAPER FAMILY
62b. Ovary with 3 to 5 parietal placentae; sepals and petals 5. **Hypericaceae**, ST. JOHNSWORT FAMILY

(Corolla radial, ovary superior, more than one, or compound)

63a. [50] Plants with milky juice or stinging hairs; ovary stipitate, exserted from the 'calyx cup'. **Euphorbiaceae**, SPURGE FAMILY
63b. Plants without milky juice or stinging hairs. . . . . (64)

64a. [63] Fl parts in 2's or 4's. **Brassicaceae/Cruciferae**, MUSTARD FAMILY
64b. Fl parts in 5's or numerous. . . . . (65)

65a. [64] Lvs trifoliolate, acrid tasting. **Oxalidaceae**, WOOD-SORREL FAMILY
65b. Lvs not trifoliate nor acrid-tasting. . . . . (66)

66a. [65] Stamens united in a column around the styles. **Malvaceae**, MALLOW FAMILY
66b. Stamens not united in a column around the styles . . . . (67)

67a. [66] Lvs linear or oblong, succulent. **Crassulaceae**, STONECROP FAMILY
67b. Lvs not as above . . . . (68)

68a. [67] Stamens numerous. (69)
68b. Stamens not more than 10 . . . . (71)

69a. [68] Lvs elliptic, with translucent dots and often minute black marginal dots on lvs and petals; stamens tending to be in 5 groups; frt a capsule. **Hypericaceae**, ST. JOHNSWORT FAMILY
69b. Lvs and stamens not as above; frt an ak . . . . (70)

70a. [69] Stipules lacking; hypanthium not developed. **Ranunculaceae**, BUTTERCUP FAMILY
70b. Stipules present; hypanthium always developed. **Rosaceae**, ROSE FAMILY

71a. [68] Petals waxy; anthers opening by terminal pores; lvs often leathery. **Pyrolaceae**, WINTERGREEN FAMILY
71b. Petals not waxy; anthers opening by slits . . . . (72)

72a. [71] Frt 5-carpellate, separating at maturity into 5 one-seeded segments (mericarps). (73)
72b. Frt not 5-carpellate, not separating into mericarps. . . . . . . (74)

73a. [72] Fls pink or white; mericarps not spiny. **Geraniaceae**, GERANIUM FAMILY
73b. Fls yellow; pericarps stoutly spiny. **Zygophyllaceae**, CALTROP FAMILY

74a. [72] Stamens alternating with branched staminodia. **Parnassiaceae**, GRASS-OF-PARNASSUS FAMILY
74b. Branched staminodia lacking . . . . (75)

75a. [74] Petals yellow, copper or blue, falling within a few hours; capsule 10-locular (5 locules each with an additional septum). **Linaceae**, FLAX FAMILY
75b. Petals white, yellow or pink-purple, not fugacious; capsule not as above . . . . (76)

76a. [75] Calyx completely free from the ovary but tightly surrounding it; petals mounted on the calyx tube. **Lythraceae**, LOOSESTRIFE FAMILY

Key to the Families—Herbaceous Dicots

76b. Calyx fused to the lower part of the ovary only; petals on the margin of a hypanthium. **Saxifragaceae**, SAXIFRAGE FAMILY

(Petals united, at least at the base)

77a. [29] Corolla radially symmetrical . . . . (78)
77b. Corolla bilaterally symmetrical. . . . . (93)

78a. [77] Plants with milky juice. . . . . (79)
78b. Plants without milky juice . . . . (80)

79a. [78] Corolla bell-shaped or trumpet-shaped, without special horn-like structures. **Apocynaceae**, DOGBANE FAMILY
79b. Corolla rotate, with a central body consisting of the fused stigmas and stamens; corona present, enclosing horn-like structures. **Asclepiadaceae**, MILKWEED FAMILY

80a. [78] Ovary superior . . . . (81)
80b. Ovary inferior or half-inferior . . . . (96)

81a. [80] Stamens more numerous than the corolla lobes, 6 to many. . (82)
81b. Stamens as many as the corolla lobes or fewer. . . . . (83)

82a. [81] Stamens many, united into a tube around the style. **Malvaceae**, MALLOW FAMILY
82b. Stamens 6 to 10, separate and distinct; anthers opening by pores at the basal end; petals waxy. **Pyrolaceae**, WINTERGREEN FAMILY

83a. [81] Stamens 5, opposite the petals; ovary with 1 locule; placenta basal or free-central. **Primulaceae**, PRIMROSE FAMILY
83b. Stamens alternate to the petals or fewer; ovary more than 1-loculed or if 1-loculed then the placenta rarely basal or free-central. . . . . (84)

84a. [83] Ovary 4-lobed, developing into 4 (or by abortion fewer) one-seeded nutlets. . . . . (85)
84b. Ovary not four-lobed; frt a capsule or berry, usually several-seeded. . . . . (86)

85a. [84] Style deeply 2-cleft; plant prostrate, dichotomously branched; fls minute; lvs small, with veiny ovate blades. **Ehretiaceae**
85b. Style undivided; otherwise not as above. **Boraginaceae**, BORAGE FAMILY

86a. [84] Ovary with 1 locule . . . . (87)
86b. Ovary with 2 or more locules . . . . (89)

87a. [86] Lvs basal; fls solitary, scapose; stoloniferous plants rooted in mud. *Limosella*, in **Scrophulariaceae**, FIGWORT FAMILY
87b. Not as above . . . . (88)

88a. [87] Lvs opposite or whorled, entire; style 1 or none; plants mostly glabrous; infl not curled in the bud. **Gentianaceae,** GENTIAN FAMILY
88b. Lvs usually alternate (if opposite, then not entire); styles 2, or single and 2-cleft above; plants mostly hairy; infl commonly curled in the bud. **Hydrophyllaceae,** WATERLEAF FAMILY

89a. [86] Stigma 3-lobed or style 3-branched; ovary with 3 locules. **Polemoniaceae,** PHLOX FAMILY
89b. Stigma entire or 2-lobed, or style 2-cleft; ovary usually with 2 locules. . . . . (90)

90a. [89] Fls yellow, in dense terminal spikes or racemes over 20 cm long; filaments hairy. *Verbascum*, in **Scrophulariaceae,** FIGWORT FAMILY
90b. Fls variously colored, never in spikes or elongate racemes . . . (91)

91a. [90] Styles 2, distinct, each one again 2-cleft; ovules 2 in each locule; fls axillary, the corolla lavender, with darker pleats; foliage silky-hairy. **Convolvulaceae,** MORNING-GLORY FAMILY
91b. Style 1, or if 2, rarely separate to the base, never again 2-cleft; ovules usually more than 2 per locule; infl various . . . . (92)

92a. [91] Style 1, the stigma entire or 2-lobed; frt a capsule or berry. **Solanaceae,** POTATO FAMILY
92b. Styles 2 or definitely 2-branched below the stigmas; frt a capsule. **Hydrophyllaceae,** WATERLEAF FAMILY

(Petals united, bilateral; ovary superior)

93a. [77] Stem 4-angled; lvs opposite. . . . . (94)
93b. Stem not 4-angled; lvs opposite, alternate or basal. . . . . . . (95)

94a. [93] Corolla usually strongly 2-lipped; style arising from the base of the gynoecium between the nutlets; foliage usually with a minty odor. **Lamiaceae,** MINT FAMILY
94b. Corolla open, flat, from a narrow tube; style terminal; foliage never with a minty odor. **Verbenaceae,** VERVAIN FAMILY

95a. [93] Corolla papery; lvs basal; infl a spike; frt a circumscissile capsule (dehiscent as one would open a soft-boiled egg). **Plantaginaceae,** PLANTAIN FAMILY
95b. Corolla not papery; otherwise not as above. **Scrophulariaceae,** FIGWORT FAMILY

(Petals united; ovary inferior)

96a. [80] Lvs ternately compound, basal; fls in a few-fld tight umbel-like cyme; delicate herbs. **Adoxaceae,** ADOXA FAMILY
96b. Not as above . . . . (97)

97a. [96] Lvs opposite or whorled . . . . (98)
97b. Lvs alternate or basal. **Campanulaceae,** BELLFLOWER FAMILY

98a. [97] Stem creeping, slightly woody; lvs opposite, crenate; fls 2, pink, pendent from an erect stalk. *Linnaea*, in **Caprifoliaceae**, HONEYSUCKLE FAMILY
98b. Stem erect or sprawling, herbaceous; lvs opposite or whorled, entire; fls white, minute, in cymes. **Rubiaceae**, MADDER FAMILY

DIVISION PTERIDOPHYTA
FERNS AND FERN ALLIES

1a. Stems jointed, hollow, green (except the fertile stems of *Equisetum arvense*, which are yellowish-brown), the nodes circled by sheaths. **Equisetaceae**, HORSETAIL FAMILY
1b. Stems not jointed, seldom green; sheaths absent . . . . (2)

2a. Plants aquatic, inhabiting lake shores or actually submerged in ponds and lakes. . . . . (3)
2b. Plants terrestrial, growing on soil or rocks . . . . (4)

3a. Lvs grass-like, their bases swollen, each bearing a pair of sporangia, the whole forming an onion-like bulb; plants submerged in shallow water of mountain lakes and ponds for the greater part of the growing season. **Isoetaceae**, QUILLWORT FAMILY
3b. Lvs with distinct petioles and blades, the blades 4-parted, resembling a four-leaf clover; spores borne at the base of the plant in round nut-like 'sporocarps'; borders of ponds and sandy streamsides at lower altitudes. **Marsileaceae**, PEPPERWORT FAMILY

4a. Lvs very numerous, lanceolate or linear, often bract-like, sessile, spirally or oppositely arranged in 4 to many ranks upon branched perennial stems. . . . . (5)
4b. Leaves relatively few, broad or ± dissected (except in *Asplenium septentrionale*, the GRASS FERN, which has linear leaves), arising from an underground stem . . . . (6)

5a. Leaves minute (less than 3 mm long). **Selaginellaceae**, LITTLE CLUB-MOSS FAMILY
5b. Leaves larger (5 mm to 1 cm or more long). **Lycopodiaceae**, CLUB-MOSS FAMILY

6a. Fronds (the 'leaves' of ferns) linear, undivided except for a few narrow forks at the tip. *Asplenium septentrionale*, in **Aspleniaceae**, SPLEENWORT FAMILY
6b. Fronds broader, ± dissected (fern-like). . . . . (7)

7a. One entire branch of each frond completely altered in appearance, modified for spore production, the remainder of the frond green and not producing spores. **Ophioglossaceae**, ADDER'S TONGUE FAMILY

7b. Fronds without conspicuously altered branches; entire fronds modified for spore production (there being two forms of fronds) or spores borne on the undersides of relatively unmodified fronds. . . . . (8)

8a. Fronds of two kinds, the sterile ones short, yellow-green, with much-divided pinnae, their ultimate divisions blunt-tipped; fertile fronds taller, with pod-shaped pinnules. **Cryptogrammaceae, Rock Brake Family**
8b. Fronds all similar, whether fertile or sterile. . . . . (9)

9a. Fronds with the lower pair of branches ± equalling the central branch or facing forward, creating the illusion of a 3-branched frond . . . . (10)
9b. Fronds distinctly pinnate, with one main axis from which the pinnae arise along the sides. . . . . (11)

10a. Fronds tall and coarse, forming thicket-like stands; sporangia, when present, borne on the infolded edges of the pinnules. **Hypolepidaceae, Bracken Family**
10b. Fronds small, delicate; sporangia, when present, borne on the flat undersides of the pinnules. *Gymnocarpium*, in **Athyriaceae, Lady Fern Family**

11a. Fronds with submarginal sori, the indusium formed by the rolled or folded edge of the pinnule. . . . . (12)
11b. Fronds with the sori on the face of the pinnule . . . . (13)

12a. Pinnules large, thin, smooth, green, fan-shaped or reniform. **Adiantaceae, Maidenhair Family**
12b. Pinnules small, often thickish, hairy or scaly or waxy-coated below. **Sinopteridaceae, Lip Fern Family**

13a. Frond merely deeply pinnatifid, the pinnae not separated from the stipe. **Polypodiaceae, Polypody Family**
13b. Frond distinctly pinnate . . . . (14)

14a. Sori linear-elliptic, indusium curved, crescentic. **Athyriaceae, Lady Fern Family**
14b. Sori round; indusia not crescent-shaped . . . . (15)

15a. Plants large, stout; indusium forming a somewhat circular shield, attached at the sinus. **Aspidiaceae, Shield-fern Family**
15b. Plants small, delicate; indusia not as above . . . . (16)

16a. Indusium cup-like, attached at the center below the sporangia, deeply cleft at maturity; pinnae thickish, widest above the middle. **Woodsiaceae, Woodsia Family**
16b. Indusium hood-like, attached by one side at the base, not cleft at maturity; pinnae thin, broadest below the middle or at the base. *Cystopteris*, in **Athyriaceae, Lady Fern Family**

ADIANTACEAE—MAIDENHAIR FAMILY (ADI)

ADIANTUM L. 1753 [ancient word meaning unwetted, shedding raindrops]
1a. Frond dichotomously branched with two main axes, the pinnae reniform. **A. pedatum** L. [arranged like toes], MAIDENHAIR FERN, **2A**. Infrequent, rich spruce forests, San Juan Range.
1b. Frond pinnate, with a single main axis, the pinnae fan-shaped. **A. capillus-veneris** L., VENUS' HAIR FERN, **2B**. Rare, on seeping cliffs of canyonlands.

ASPIDIACEAE—SHIELD-FERN FAMILY (ASD)

1a. Frond simply pinnate, the pinnae spine-toothed, with an auricle at the upper base. **Polystichum**, CHRISTMAS FERN
1b. Frond more than once-pinnate. **Dryopteris**, SHIELD FERN

DRYOPTERIS Adanson 1763 [Gr., *drys*, oak, + *pteris*, fern]. SHIELD FERN
1a. Frond bipinnatifid, the ultimate divs blunt; indusium very prominent. **D. filix-mas** (L.) Schott, MALE FERN, **1A**. Infrequent, shaded canyons. Formerly gathered for the oil in the rhizomes, from which a worm medicine was prepared; no longer gathered commercially, but could easily be exterminated and should be protected.
1b. Frond bipinnate, the ultimate divs sharp-pointed; indusium not so prominent. **D. expansa** (C. Presl) Fraser-Jenkins & Jermy (*D. assimilis*), **2G**. Rare, in rich subalpine forests, known only from Rocky Mt. Nat. Park.

POLYSTICHUM Roth 1799 [Gr., *polys*, many, + *stichos*, row, referring to the sori]. CHRISTMAS FERN
One sp, **P. lonchitis** (L.) Roth [a name used by Pliny for some plant with a tongue-shaped lf], HOLLY FERN, **1B**. Infrequent among rocks, alpine and subalpine.

ASPLENIACEAE—SPLEENWORT FAMILY (ASL)

ASPLENIUM L. 1753 [Gr., *Asplenon*, a name used by Dioscorides for some fern supposed to cure spleen diseases]. SPLEENWORT
1a. Fronds linear, simple or only forked at the tips, in dense clumps in rock crevices, resembling dark green grass. **A. septentrionale** (L.) Hoffmann [northern], GRASS FERN, **7A**. Collected once, long ago, in Box Canyon, Ouray. A species widely scattered in the mountains of the Northern Hemisphere, incl Altai, The Alps, Pyrenees, Caucasus and Scandinavia.
1b. Fronds with oblong-orbicular pinnae . . . . (2)

2a. Pinnae not twice as long as wide, thin, not evergreen; stipe green. **A. trichomanes-ramosum** L. [green], GREEN SPLEENWORT, **3F**. Rare, limestone cliffs near timberline (*A. viride*).
2b. Pinnae oblong, thick, evergreen. **A. trichomanes** L., MAIDENHAIR SPLEENWORT, **1C**. Infrequent, San Juans.

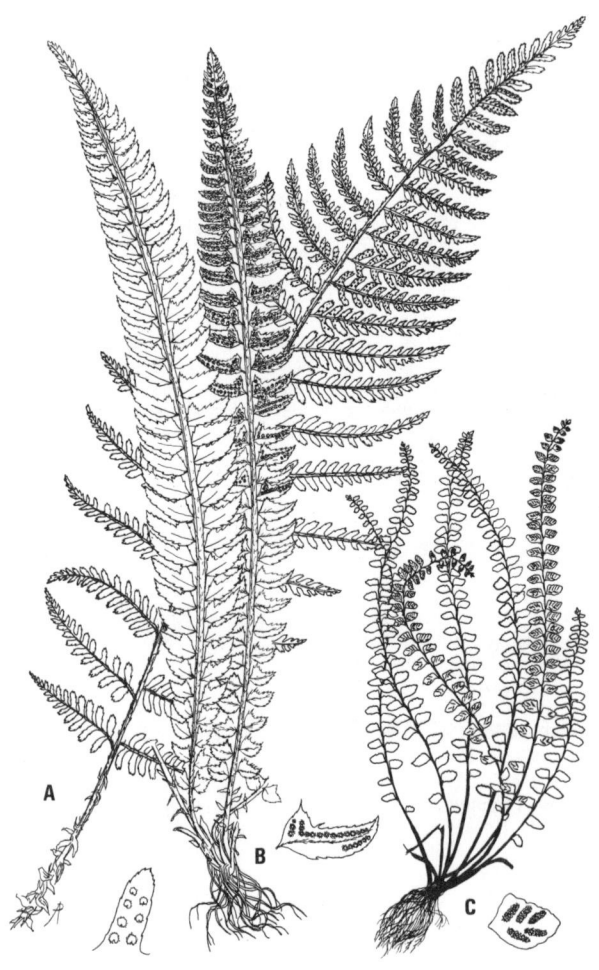

Figure 1. A, *Dryopteris filix-mas*; B, *Polystichum lonchitis*; C, *Asplenium trichomanes*

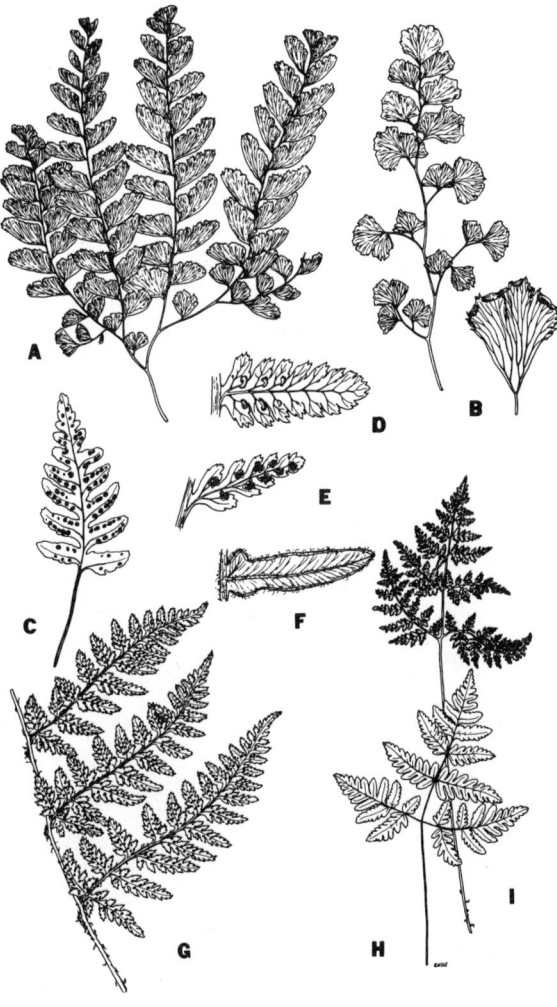

Figure 2. A, *Adiantum pedatum*; B, *A. capillus-veneris*; C, *Polypodium hesperium*; D, *Athyrium filix-femina*; E, *Cystopteris fragilis*, pinna; F, *Pteridium aquilinum*, pinnule; G, *Dryopteris expansa*; H, *Gymnocarpium dryopteris*; I, *Cystopteris montana*

ATHYRIACEAE—LADY FERN FAMILY (ATY)

1a. Fronds large, over 3 dm. long, up to 15 cm or more wide. **Athyrium**, LADY FERN
1b. Fronds less than 3 dm long, up to about 10 cm wide. . . . . . . (2)

2a. Frond broadly triangular, with three main branches . . . . (3)
2b. Frond pinnate. **Cystopteris**, BRITTLE FERN

3a. Pinnules oblong, not deeply toothed, broadly rounded. **Gymnocarpium**, OAK FERN
3b. Pinnules tapered, deeply toothed or lobed. **Cystopteris**, BRITTLE FERN

ATHYRIUM Roth 1799 [Gr., *athyros*, doorless, the sporangia only tardily forcing back the margin of the indusium]. LADY FERN
1a. Indusium crescentic, usually plainly visible; frond well-expanded, the pinnae not appearing crowded or directed sharply toward the apex of the frond; fronds few to a clump. **A. filix-femina** (L.) Roth, **2D**. Forests of the lower altitudes, never at or above timberline.
1b. Indusium rarely seen, minute, withering early; frond narrow, the pinnae rather crowded or directed sharply toward the frond apex. **A. distentifolium** Tausch. Subalpine screes (*A. alpestre* ssp *americanum*).

CYSTOPTERIS Bernhardi 1805 [Gr., *cystis*, a bladder, + *pteris*, fern]. BRITTLE FERN
(key adapted from Lellinger, *Field Manual of Ferns*, 1985)
1a. Frond broadly triangular, with three main branches. **C. montana** (Lamarck) Bernhardi, **2I**. Local in moist, rich spruce forests.
1b. Frond pinnate. . . . . (2)

2a. Frond compact, narrow, mostly (2.5)3-4 times longer than wide; basal pinnules sessile, truncate to obtuse at the base; indusia lanceolate . . . . (3)
2b. Frond lax, broad, mostly 2-2.5(3) times longer than wide; basal pinnules short-stalked to sessile, obtuse to cuneate at the base; indusia round to ovate. (4)

3a. Spores echinate, appearing slightly spiny at 60x magnification. **C. fragilis** (L.) Bernhardi, **2E**. Our most common fern, from low to high altitudes. The stipes are produced in clusters and are very brittle.
3b. Spores rugose-verrucose, appearing smooth at 60x magnification. **C. dickieana** Sim [for George Dickie, Scottish algologist, 1812-1882].

4a. Pinnules with a broad, uncut center; segments mostly rounded at the apex; frond pinnate-pinnatifid to 2(3)-pinnate-pinnatifid; basal pinnules cuneate in less divided forms, obtuse in more divided ones; usually on rock. **C. tenuis** (Michaux) Desvaux.

4b. Pinnules lacking a broad, uncut center; segments mostly acute at the apex; fronds 2-3-pinnate-pinnatifid; basal pinnules mostly cuneate at the base; plants usually on soil. **C. reevesiana** Lellinger.

GYMNOCARPIUM Newman 1851 [Gr., *gymno*, naked, + *carpium*, fruit. OAK FERN
One sp, **G. dryopteris** (L.) Newman ssp **disjunctum** (Ruprecht) Sarvela, 2H. Shaded woods and thickets, montane, subalpine.

CRYPTOGRAMMACEAE
ROCK BRAKE FAMILY (CRG)

CRYPTOGRAMMA R. Brown 1823 [Gr., *cryptos*, hidden, + *gramme*, a line, alluding to the lines of sporangia]. ROCK BRAKE
1a. Fronds robust, crowded on a short rhizome; lower parts of the stipes persistent. **C. acrostichoides** R. Brown [like the genus *Acrostichum*], **3D**. Rocky places, montane to alpine [*C. crispa* ssp].
1b. Fronds delicate, one or two together. **C. stelleri** (Gmelin) Prantl [for the Russian explorer], STELLER'S CLIFF BRAKE, **3B**. Extremely rare, crevices of limestone cliffs.

EQUISETACEAE—HORSETAIL FAMILY (EQU)

1a. Green stems bearing numerous branches in whorls at the nodes (fertile simple brown stems also belong here). **Equisetum**, HORSETAIL
1b. Green stems stout, simple or occasionally with a few short branches scattered irregularly on the main stem. **Hippochaete**, SCOURING-RUSH

EQUISETUM L. 1753 [Gr., *equus*, horse, + *seta*, bristle]. HORSETAIL

1a. Sterile stems with ascending branches, 4-angled; central cavity a fourth the diam of the stem; rhizome with scattered blackish tubers; fertile stems brown, abruptly wilting; stem smoothly tuberculate, the teeth in whorls of 3-5(6). **E. arvense** L., FIELD HORSETAIL, **4C**. Wet ditches and floodplains. The stems are of two kinds, branched and sterile, or brown, unbranched and bearing a sporangiate cone at the apex. The latter are produced in early spring and soon wither.
1b. Stems with horizontal or gently down-curving branches, 3-angled; central cavity about half the stem diam; rhizome without tubers; cone produced at the apex of the green branched stem; stem sharply papillate with whorls of 8-15 teeth. **E. pratense** Ehrhardt, MEADOW HORSETAIL. Wet spruce-fir forests, less common than the last.

HIPPOCHAETE Milde 1865 [Gr., *hippos*, horse, + *chaite*, mane]. SCOURING-RUSH [formerly incl in *Equisetum*]
1a. Stems slender, 5-12-angled and -grooved; sheaths loose, with fine-pointed persistent teeth; central cavity of stem usually half

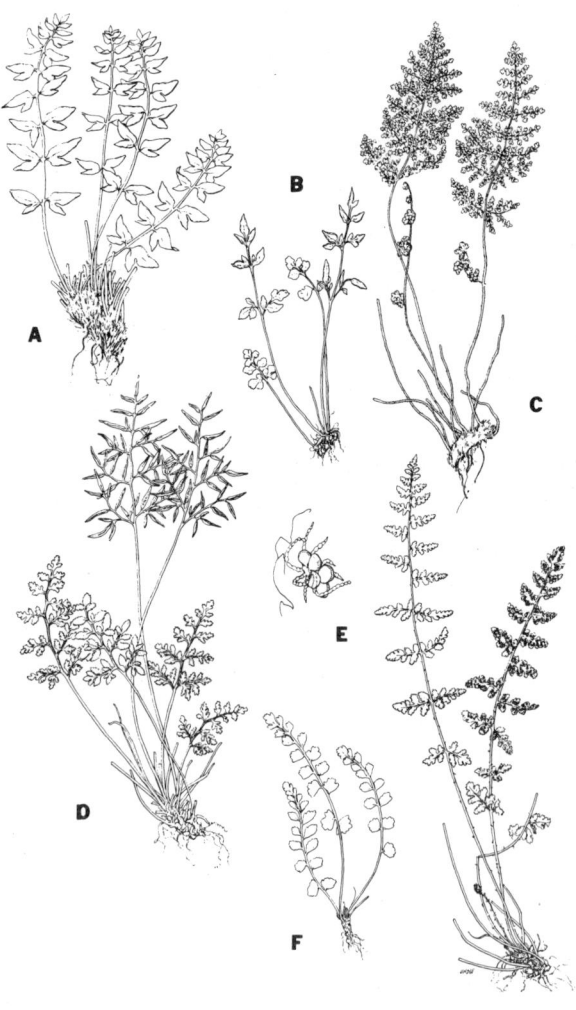

Figure 3. A, *Pellaea breweri*; B, *Cryptogramma stelleri*; C, *Cheilanthes feei*; D, *Cryptogramma acrostichoides*; E, *Woodsia scopulina*, plant and sorus; F, *Asplenium trichomanes-ramosum*

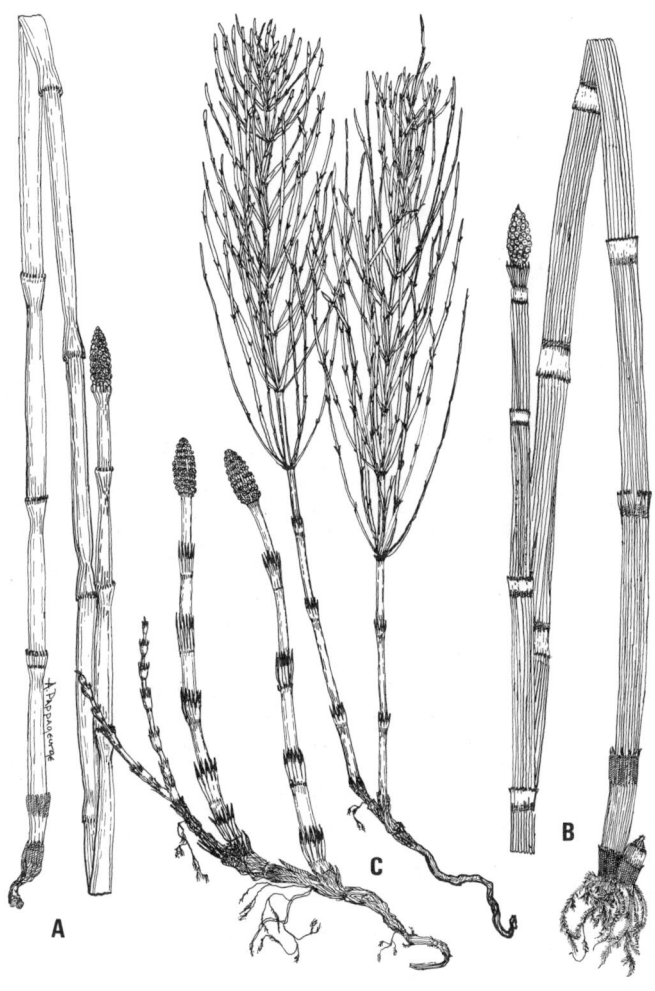

Figure 4. A, *Hippochaete laevigata*; B, *H. hyemalis*; C, *Equisetum arvense*

its diam. **H. variegata** (Schleicher) Bruhin. Sandy bars of streams.
1b. Stems stout, 16-48-angled and -grooved; sheaths loose or tight, the teeth persistent or deciduous; central cavity of the stem more than half its diam . . . . (2)

2a. Stem dying after one season; sheaths lacking a dark band at base; cone rounded at apex. **H. laevigata** (A. Braun) Farwell. [smooth], **4A**. Wet ground of ditches and streamsides; called scouring-rushes because of the deposits of silica on the stems; they are effective for scouring pots and pans.
2b. Stem enduring several years; sheaths commonly with a dark band at the base; cone pointed at the apex. **H. hyemalis** (L.) Bruhin ssp **affinis** (A. Braun) Weber [of winter; related], **4B**. Similar habitats.

HYPOLEPIDACEAE—BRACKEN FAMILY (HPL)

PTERIDIUM Gleditsch 1760 [dim. of *Pteris*, another genus]. BRACKEN
One sp, **P. aquilinum** (L.) Kuhn ssp. **lanuginosum** (Bongard) Hultén [of an eagle, from the wing-shaped fronds; woolly], **2F**. Dry open woodlands. Our largest native fern.

ISOËTACEAE—QUILLWORT FAMILY (ISO)

Identification of the quillworts is a technical task requiring examination of the megaspores with a high-powered dissecting microscope and comparison material of correctly named specimens. Mature plants are needed, which means collecting in late summer or fall, when the spores in the leaf-bases are ripe, and the plants then tend to fall apart.

ISOËTES L. 1753 [name used by Pliny for a sp of *Sedum*]. QUILLWORT
1a. Megaspores with scattered low tubercles becoming joined to form low ridges. **I. bolanderi** Engelmann [for H. N. Bolander, California botanist], **6D**. Small lakes and ponds, upper montane and subalpine. Abundant on Grand Mesa.
1b. Megaspores with high, sharp spines and jagged ridges. **I. lacustris** L. Deep water of larger lakes. The plants are often washed ashore by wave action.

LYCOPODIACEAE—CLUB-MOSS FAMILY (LYC)

The spores of *Lycopodium* were once used as a fine baby powder and an inflammable powder for flash photography. In Scandinavia, where they are abundant ground cover in forests, lycopods are gathered in enormous quantities for ornamental Christmas greens. In Colorado they are so infrequent as to be considered in need of protection.

1a. Stem not creeping, the erect branches tightly bunched; sporangia in the axils of unmodified lvs, not in discrete cones. **Huperzia**, FIR CLUB-MOSS

1b. Stem creeping extensively, the erect branches not tightly bunched; spores produced in an elongate cone. **Lycopodium**, CLUB-MOSS

HUPERZIA Bernhardi 1801 [for Johann Peter Huperz, died 1816]. FIR CLUB-MOSS

One sp, **H. selago** (L.) Bernhardi [the ancient generic name], **6B**. Local in rocky cirque-basins and cliffs near or above timberline (*Lycopodium*). A separate family, Huperziaceae, may be used for this sp and its relatives.

LYCOPODIUM L. [Gr., *lycos*, a wolf, + *pous*, paw]. CLUB-MOSS

1a. Lvs widely spreading or somewhat reflexed, rich green, 5-10 mm long, acute, regularly toothed; branches 10-15 mm wide. **L. annotinum** L. [a year old, from the marked separation of annual branches], STIFF CLUB-MOSS, **6A**. Subalpine spruce forests and under willow thickets.
1b. Lvs ascending. yellowish-green, 3-7 mm long, sparingly toothed or entire; branches 3-7 mm wide. **L. dubium** Zoëga. Infrequent, upper subalpine and alpine.

MARSILEACEAE—PEPPERWORT FAMILY (MSL)

Plants of *Marsilea* are very un-fernlike and might be passed off as four-leaf clovers, but in late summer the sporocarps, hard nutlike organs at the base of the plants, are conspicuous. The sporocarps of Nardoo, *M. drummondii*, of Australia, are edible and gathered by the aborigines, who taught the early explorers to use this wild food as a last resort against starvation in the outback.

MARSILEA L. 1753 [for Luigi Marsigli, 1658-1730, Italian naturalist]. PEPPERWORT

One sp, **M. mucronata** A. Braun, HAIRY PEPPERWORT, **6C**. Edges of muddy streams and ponds at low altitudes. Not yet found on the W slope, but occurring in E Utah. The plants become conspicuous in August and September when ponds dry up.

OPHIOGLOSSACEAE
ADDER'S TONGUE FAMILY (OPH)

All of the members of this family are rare subalpine and alpine species and should not be collected with their roots. Fortunately for them, they are exceedingly difficult to see in the field; one either stumbles on them or finds them only after much diligent searching. Populations are usually very small. Although few of these are reported for the Western Slope, all Colorado species are included in the key since they may be expected.

1a. Several dm. tall, the green, sterile portion ± less triangular in gross outline, very delicately and finely dissected; fertile branch narrow, consisting of a spike of brown, spore-bearing branches. **Botrypus**, RATTLESNAKE FERN

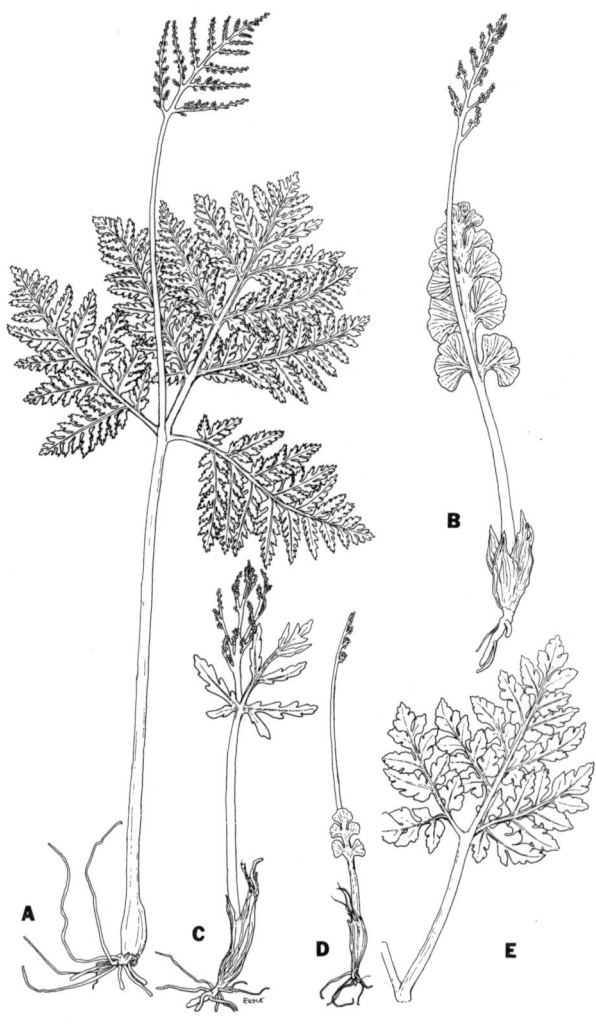

Figure 5. **A**, *Botrypus virginianus;* **B**, *Botrychium lunaria;* **C**, *B. lanceolatum;* **D**, *B. simplex;* **E**, *B. multifidum*

1b. Small (15 cm or less tall), the green sterile portion unbranched or only pinnatifid; fertile branch short, yellowish-brown, sporangia in a grape-like cluster like the rattles of a snake. **Botrychium**, GRAPE FERN

BOTRYCHIUM Swartz 1801 [Gr., *botrys*, a cluster of grapes]. GRAPE FERN
(Key adapted from Wagner & Wagner, Am. Fern J. 76:33-47. 1986)

1a. Usually over 5 cm high, with leathery, much-divided fronds. **B. multifidum** (Gmelin) Ruprecht ssp **coulteri** (Underwood) Clausen [for J. M. Coulter, collector on the Hayden Surveys, 1872-3], **5E**. Mt meadows, RT.
1b. Plants less than 5 cm tall; fronds merely pinnate or with the lower lobes ternate . . . . (2)

2a. Lower pinnae linear, lanceolate, or ovate, with a central or at least a basal midrib . . . . (2)
2b. Lower pinnae or pinnules lunulate, fan-shaped, wedge-shaped or square, with flabellate venation, a central midrib lacking . . . . . (6)

3a. Trophophore (sterile segment) broadly deltate, usually subsessile; pinnae linear; sporophore (fertile segment) divided near base into two or more major axes. **B. lanceolatum** (Gmelin) Ångström, **5C**.
3b. Trophophore mostly oblong to ovate, subsessile to long-stalked; segments linear to oblong to spatulate; sporophores with only one major axis or, if more, the laterals arising well above the base . . . . (4)

4a. Pinnae usually well-separated, linear to oblanceolate with pointed tips; basal pinnae mostly cleft into a smaller lower segment and larger upper segment; frond shiny green in life. **B. echo** W. Wagner [for Echo Lake].
4b. Pinnae usually approximate, oblong to ovate with rounded or blunt tips; basal pinnae not cleft in two; luster various . . . . . . (5)

5a. Pinnae with few lobes, these mainly on the basal side; lowest pinnae mostly exaggerated, ascending and commonly subclasping; pinnae broadly adnate, strongly asymmetrical; frond dull gray in life. **B. hesperium** (Maxon & Clausen) Wagner & Lellinger [western].
5b. Pinnae with numerous lobes, these roughly equal in number on upper and basal sides; lowest pinnae symmetrical, mostly equal in length to those above; frond bright shiny green in life. **B. pinnatum** St. John.

6a. Apex of trophophore usually not deeply divided, commonly concave (in life); upper pinnae or lobes tending to be somewhat irregularly fused; sporophore arising at various positions, from ground level to near the apex; trophophore sessile to long-stalked. **B. simplex** E. Hitchcock, **5D**.
6b. Apex of trophophore usually deeply divided, mostly flat (in life); upper lateral pinnae and lobes regularly separated; sporophore

Figure 6. A, *Lycopodium annotinum*; **B**, *Huperzia selago*, habit, sporophylls; **C**, *Marsilea mucronata*; **D**, *Isoëtes bolanderi*, habit, megaspore above, microsporangium below

attachment high on the common stalk; trophophore sessile to short-stalked . . . . (7)

7a. Pinnae lunate to broadly cuneate, the sides of the lower pinnae at a 90°-180° angle, remote to overlapping. **B. lunaria** (L.) Swartz, MOONWORT, **5B**.
7b. Pinnae cuneate to oblong, the sides of the pinnae at a 0°-90° angle, usually remote. **B. minganense** Victorin [of the Mingan Islands, Quebec].

BOTRYPUS Michaux 1803 [name derived from *Botrychium*]. RATTLESNAKE FERN
   One sp, **B. virginianus** (L.) Holub, **5A**. Infrequent and local, in cool moist ravines (*Botrychium*).

POLYPODIACEAE—POLYPODY FAMILY (PLP)

POLYPODIUM L. 1753 [Gr., *polys*, many, + *pous*, foot]. POLYPODY

1a. Rhizome scales with a dark median stripe; fronds narrowly oblong, rarely over 2 cm wide, pinnae usually about 12 pairs, the lowermost often smaller. **P. amorphum** Suksdorf [formless]. Rocks in dry woods, Gunnison Basin.
1b. Rhizome scales concolorous; fronds more triangular-oblong, usually over 2 cm wide, pinnae usually fewer pairs, the lowermost commonly largest. **P. hesperium** Maxon [western], **2C**. San Juan Mts.

SELAGINELLACEAE
LITTLE CLUB-MOSS FAMILY (SEL)

This family contains the strange 'resurrection-plants' of Texas and Mexico, that roll into balls when dry and revive spectacularly under humid conditions. As in the Isoetaceae, the spores are of two sizes (micro- and megaspores). This difference is evident even with the hand-lens or naked eye. The orange-yellow sporangia are in the upper leaf-axils, the megasporangia containing no more than four spores and bulging irregularly by their contours. Microsporangia contain hundreds of very minute spores. The different spores produce male and female gametophytes, respectively.

SELAGINELLA P. Beauvois 1805 [dim. of *Selago*, ancient name for a club-moss]. LITTLE CLUB-MOSS
1a. Lvs thin and soft, without a dorsal groove; cone not four-sided; sporophylls lax. **S. selaginoides** (L.) Link [like *Selaginella*; Linnaeus included this sp in *Lycopodium*], **7C**. Boggy places by beaver ponds and wet spruce forests. E side Park Range, probably W also.
1b. Lvs thick and firm, with a dorsal groove; cone 4-sided; sporophylls appressed . . . . (2)

2a. Lvs blunt, ciliate-margined but lacking a white hair-point. **S. mutica** Eaton [blunt], **7E**. Rocky canyonsides.

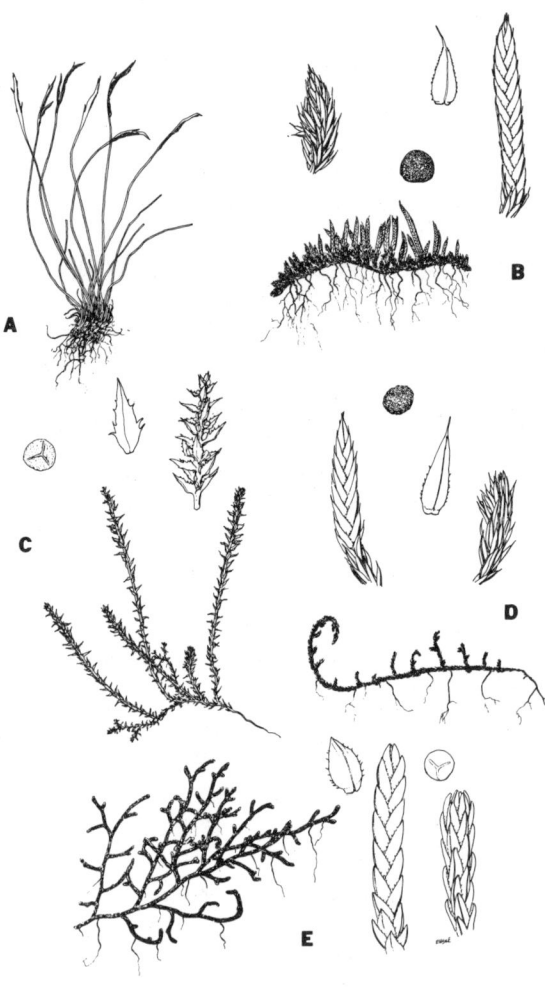

Figure 7. A, *Asplenium septentrionale*; B, *Selaginella densa*; C, *S. selaginoides*; D, *S. underwoodii*; E, *S. mutica*

2b. Lvs narrowed to a slender white hair-point. . . . . (3)

3a. Creeping stems very short, the lvs curved upward, gray-green; fruiting branches erect, elongate, four-angled. **S. densa** Rydberg [clumpy], **7B**. Common on rocks and soil, summits of the plateaus up to the tundra. By the inexperienced, this plant will be mistaken for the common hair-cap moss, *Polytrichum piliferum*, which has similar lvs, but lacks the creeping branches.
3b. Stems elongate, the lvs not strongly upcurved, bright green; fruiting branches inconspicuous. **S. underwoodii** Hieronymus [for L. M. Underwood, American fern specialist], **7D**. Cliffs of moist protected canyonsides.

SINOPTERIDACEAE—LIP FERN FAMILY (SIN)

1a. Fronds green and glabrous. **Pellaea**, CLIFF BRAKE
1b. Fronds either hairy, scaly, or with a white wax on the underside. **Cheilanthes**, LIP FERN

PELLAEA Link 1841 [Gr., *pellos*, dusky, from the dark stipes]. CLIFF BRAKE
1a. Most middle and lower pinnae deeply two-lobed; stipe bases persistent; plant green. **P. breweri** Eaton [for Prof. W. H. Brewer, collector in California from 1860-1864], **3A**. Rocky summits, Dinosaur Nat. Mon.
1b. Most pinnae simple, or a very few of the lower ones ternate or pinnate; plant blue-green. **P. suksdorfiana** Butters [for Wilhelm N. Suksdorf, botanist of Washington, 1850-1932]. Rimrock and cliffs, ME, MF.

CHEILANTHES Swartz 1806 [Gr., *cheilos*, margin, + *anthos*, flower]. LIP FERN
1a. Fronds pinnate, densely brown-hairy or with brown scales beneath . . . . (2)
1b. Fronds 2-3-pinnate with zig-zag branches and ternate pinnae, white waxy beneath. **C. cancellata** Mickel [latticed] (*Notholaena fendleri*). Talus of arid canyonsides.

2a. Fronds reddish-hairy beneath, lacking scales. **C. feei** Moore [for Antoine L. A. Fée, French pteridologist, 1789-1874], **3C**. Sandstone cliffs and overhangs.
2b. Fronds scaly beneath, lacking hairs. **C. fendleri** Hooker. Infrequent, San Juans, on granitic rocks.

WOODSIACEAE—WOODSIA FAMILY (WDS)

WOODSIA R. Brown 1810 [for Joseph Woods, 1776-1864, English botanist]
1a. Stems and fronds with stiffly spreading hairs. **W. scopulina** Eaton [of rocks], **3E**. Rock crevices in cool canyons.
1b. Stems and fronds not hairy. . . . . (2)

2a. Lower half of stipe usually reddish-black; cilia of the indusium either obscured by the sorus or just visible beyond it; epidermal cells regular in shape. **W. oregana** Eaton. Similar habitats, more common than the last.

2b. Lower half of stipe usually brown; cilia of the indusium usually surrounding the sorus and quite evident; cells of the epidermis with jagged walls. **Woodsia mexicana** Fée. Canyons of the San Juan range.

GYMNOSPERMS

The gymnosperms are woody vascular plants that do not produce true flowers, but instead bear mega- and microsporangia on the open faces of sporophylls that are often grouped together in cones. In Colorado these fall into three families, separated by the following key.

1a. Shrubs with jointed green stems, the lvs represented by small black triangular scales in whorls at the joints; microsporangiate cones yellow, the scales stamen-like; megasporangiate (ovulate) cones green, of a few loose thin scales. **Ephedraceae**, EPHEDRA FAMILY
1b. Trees or shrubs with either needle-like or scale-like overlapping lvs, producing berry-like gray cones or cones with woody scales . . . . (2)

2a. Frt a gray berry-like cone, the scales fused together and only detectable by their protruding tips; shrubs or small trees with decussately arranged scale-like lvs or flat sharp needles. **Cupressaceae**, CYPRESS FAMILY
2b. Frt a woody cone with spirally arranged scales; small or large trees with needle lvs. **Pinaceae**, PINE FAMILY

CUPRESSACEAE—CYPRESS FAMILY (CUP)

1a. Low sprawling shrub with strongly bicolored needle-lvs, white above, green below; cones almost sessile (on extremely short shoots with a few scale-lvs), in the axils of the large vegetative needles; needles three at a node. **Juniperus**, JUNIPER
1b. Erect small tree with decussate triangular scale-lvs appressed to the branches (a few injured or juvenile branches may revert to the *Juniperus* type); cones terminating short shoots not differentiated in any way from the vegetative branches; lvs two at a node. **Sabina**, RED CEDAR, SAVIN, JUNIPER

JUNIPERUS L. [old Lat. name used by Virgil and Pliny]. JUNIPER
One sp, **J. communis** L. ssp **alpina** (Neilreich) Celakovsky, **8A**. Common undershrub throughout the coniferous forest area (*J. sibirica*).

SABINA Miller 1754 [the ancient Latin name]. RED CEDAR, SAVIN

1a. All branchlets stout, not tapering; berries more than 5 mm diam. **S. osteosperma** (Torrey) Antoine, UTAH JUNIPER (*S. utahensis*), **8C**. Piñon-juniper from EA westward. Reports of *S. monosperma* on the W slope are incorrect. While the habit of immature plants

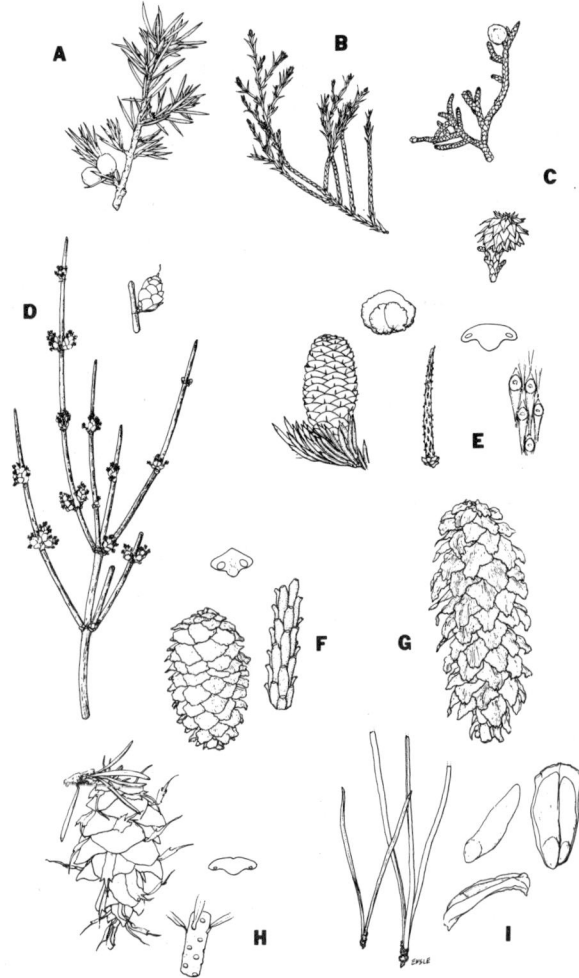

Figure 8. A, *Juniperis communis*; B, *Sabina scopulorum*, showing some juvenile lvs; C, *S. osteosperma* (below: gall); D, *Ephedra*, branches, male cone; E, *Abies lasiocarpa*, cone, cone axis, needle section, lf scars; F, *Picea engelmannii*, cone, lf section, twig; G, *P. pungens*, cone; H, *Pseudotsuga*, cone, twig, lf-section; I, *Pinus* sp., needles, seed, face and side view of cone scale

may be confusing, the spp are easily distinguished by their cones: in *S. osteosperma* the cones are dry and mealy when crushed while in *S. monosperma* they are full of liquid resin.

1b. Ultimate branchlets slender and elongate; berries less than 7 mm diam. **S. scopulorum** (Sargent) Rydberg, ROCKY MT JUNIPER, **8B**. Abundant at higher altitudes, requiring more moisture.

EPHEDRACEAE—EPHEDRA FAMILY (EPH)

EPHEDRA L. 1753 [Gr. name used by Pliny for *Hippuris*]. MORMON TEA

1a. Branches gray, widely spreading; lvs and cone-scales 3 at a node; bracts of ovulate cones stalked, scarious. **E. torreyana** Watson, **PL 33-34**. Desert sites, less common than the next and restricted to drier and lower areas. The branches make a palatable tea.

1b. Branches rich green, usually erect or ascending parallel; lvs and cone-scales 2 at a node; bracts of cones sessile, only the margins scarious. **E. viridis** Coville, **8D**. More abundant than the last and ascending to higher altitudes (cliffs of Glenwood Canyon). A variety **viscida** (Cutler) Benson, comprises plants with sticky branches and longer-stalked ovulate cones.

PINACEAE—PINE FAMILY (PIN)

1a. Lvs sheathed at the base, at least when young, usually in clusters of 2 or more; cone-scales thick and woody, with swollen tips; bracts minute, much shorter than the scales; frt maturing the second year. **Pinus**, PINE

1b. Lvs not sheathed at the base, nor in clusters; cone scales not thick and woody nor swollen at the tip; bracts relatively large; frt maturing in one season . . . . (2)

2a. Older twigs studded with the persistent stumps of fallen needles. **Picea**, SPRUCE

2b. Older twigs smooth . . . . (3)

3a. Lf-scars elliptical; needles stalked; cones hanging down, the scales persistent at maturity and the cone falling in one piece; bracts of the cone-scales longer than the scales, 3-cleft. **Pseudotsuga**, DOUGLAS-FIR

3b. Lf-scars round; needles sessile; cones erect, the scales falling away from the axis at maturity; cone-scales not much exceeded by the bracts. **Abies**, FIR

ABIES Miller 1754 [Lat. name of an Old World species]. FIR

1a. Cones grayish-green; bracts of the cone-scales with a short triangular tip; cones 7-12 cm long; resin-ducts of the lvs (in X-section) near the lower epidermis. **A. concolor** (Grenier & Godron) Lindley, WHITE FIR. Montane canyonsides, S counties. A handsome fir, usually easily recognized by its long needles, but needle-length alone can be misleading.

64   Pinaceae (PIN)

1b. Cones dark brown-purple; bracts of the cone-scales with long subulate tips; cones 5-10 cm long; resin ducts of the needles equidistant from each epidermis. . . . . (2)

2a. Bark strongly checkered with large lenticels, very thick and spongy under hand pressure. **A. arizonica** Merriam. Common on Wolf Creek Pass at medium altitudes.

2b. Bark not strongly checkered, relatively thin and not spongy under hand pressure. **A. lasiocarpa** (Hooker) Nuttall, SUBALPINE FIR, **8E**. Characteristic associate of Engelmann spruce at high altitudes. It has been suggested, on biochemical grounds, that our plant should be called *A. bifolia* Murray and the name *A. lasiocarpa* must be applied to a NW coast sp, but the evidence is still somewhat inconclusive.

PICEA A. Dietrich 1824 [Lat. name of some pine, from *pix*, pitch]. SPRUCE

1a. Young branches and lf-bases minutely pubescent; needles acute or acutish at apex, not rigid; cones about 5 cm long, the scales ± rounded and distinctly thinner at apex. **P. engelmannii** (Parry) Engelmann, ENGELMANN SPRUCE, **8F**. Dominant forest tree of the subalpine, not necessarily near streamsides.

1b. Young branches glabrous; needles rigid, almost spine-tipped; cones commonly 8 cm long, the scales truncate and not distinctly thinner at the apex. **P. pungens** Engelmann, COLORADO BLUE SPRUCE, **8G**. Always very close to streamsides in the canyons.

PINUS L. [the classical Lat. name]. PINE, **8I**

1a. Fascicles (leaf clusters) containing 5 needles . . . . (2)
1b. Fascicles containing 2 or 3 needles . . . . (4)

2a. Needles commonly less than 5 cm long, usually strongly curved, with a few resin drops on the surface; cone-scales bristle-tipped. **P. aristata** Engelmann, BRISTLECONE PINE. Upper montane and subalpine.

2b. Needles usually longer than 5 cm, straight or only slightly curved, not sticky; cone lacking bristles . . . . (3)

3a. Small tree with irregular trunk and branching pattern; needles not toothed near the apex. **P. flexilis** James, LIMBER PINE. Common on rocky tors and gravelly knolls, upper montane and subalpine, usually in open sites.

3b. Tall tree with straight trunk; needles with a few very minute teeth near the apex. **P. strobiformis** Engelmann, MEXICAN WHITE PINE. A forest tree of the SW counties.

4a. Needles 10-18 mm long, in 3's or 2's; cones 7-12 cm long; fascicles crowded at ends of branches, at least in older trees. **P. ponderosa** Douglas ssp **scopulorum** (Watson) Weber, PONDEROSA PINE. On the W slope this forms a more majestic tree than to the east, especially near Pagosa Springs, characteristically on the Uncompahgre and Blue Mountain plateaus, where the under-

story is manzanita.
4b. Needles 3-7 cm long, usually in pairs; cones 5 cm long or less; fascicles scattered along the branches . . . . (5)

5a. Tall, slender tree, cone-scales bristle-tipped; cones persistent for several years after maturity; needle in x-section with two vascular bundles. **P. contorta** Douglas ssp **latifolia** (Engelmann) Critchfield, LODGEPOLE PINE. Forming uniform forests with little underbrush, following fires, montane and subalpine.
5b. Low, bushy tree; cone-scales not bristle-tipped; cones falling soon after maturity; needle in x-section with one vascular bundle. **P. edulis** Engelmann, PIÑON PINE. Abundant at lower elevations of the plateaus and mesas.

PSEUDOTSUGA Carriere 1867 [false (differing from) *Tsuga*]. DOUGLAS-FIR

One sp, **P. menziesii** (Mirbel) Franco, **8H**. Moist canyon walls and slopes, montane. The 3-pronged bracts are diagnostic.

ANGIOSPERMS (MONOCOTS AND DICOTS)
ACERACEAE—MAPLE FAMILY (ACE)

Maples of our area can always be recognized by the combination of three characters: palmately-lobed (rarely pinnately compound) leaves; opposite arrangement; and two-winged fruits (*samaras*). Several genera of the Rosaceae as well as the genus *Ribes* have 'maple leaves' but lack the other features. In Japan there are maples with elm-like leaves, so really the only reliable features if flowers are lacking are the opposite leaf-arrangement and the samara.

1a. Lvs simple and 3- to 5-lobed, or sometimes palmately 3-parted; twigs slender, reddish, with a narrow pith. **Acer**, MAPLE
1b. Lvs pinnately compound, with 3 to 5 lfls; twigs stout, green or gray, with a thick pith. **Negundo**, BOX-ELDER

ACER L. 1753 [the ancient Lat. name]. MAPLE

1a. Lf-lobes biunt, with few incisions; fall coloration salmon-pink. **A. grandidentatum** Nuttall, BIG-TOOTH MAPLE, **9C**. Rare, N face of Mesa Verde cliffs. Abundant in Utah.
1b. Lf-lobes acute, with many incisions; lvs sometimes 3-parted; fall color brilliant red. **A. glabrum** Torrey, MOUNTAIN MAPLE, **9A**. 3-parted lvs (forma **trisectum** Sargent) are more common in the S counties. In midsummer the lvs develop large bright red blotches. These are galls containing Eriophyid mites.

NEGUNDO Boehmer 1760 [a Malayan name for *Vitex negundo*, according to E. L. Little]. BOX-ELDER

One sp, **N. aceroides** (L.) Moench ssp **interius** (Britton & Shafer) Löve & Löve, **9B**. gulches and streamsides at low elevations. This, the native W race, has the branchlets covered with short hairs, while ssp **violaceum**, introd as a shade tree, has smooth, pale, glaucous twigs (*Acer negundo*).

ADOXACEAE—ADOXA FAMILY (ADX)

A monotypic family, that is, one consisting of a single genus and species. *Adoxa* occurs in mountains throughout the Northern Hemisphere. The inflorescence is unique. The terminal flower has a two-lobed calyx (bracts?) and a 4-lobed greenish corolla, and four stamens alternating with the lobes. The filaments are deeply divided, giving the impression of eight stamens. The lateral flowers (close to the terminal one) have a three-lobed calyx and a 5-lobed greenish corolla and 5 (looking like 10) stamens. The ovary is half-inferior, of 3-4 united carpels.

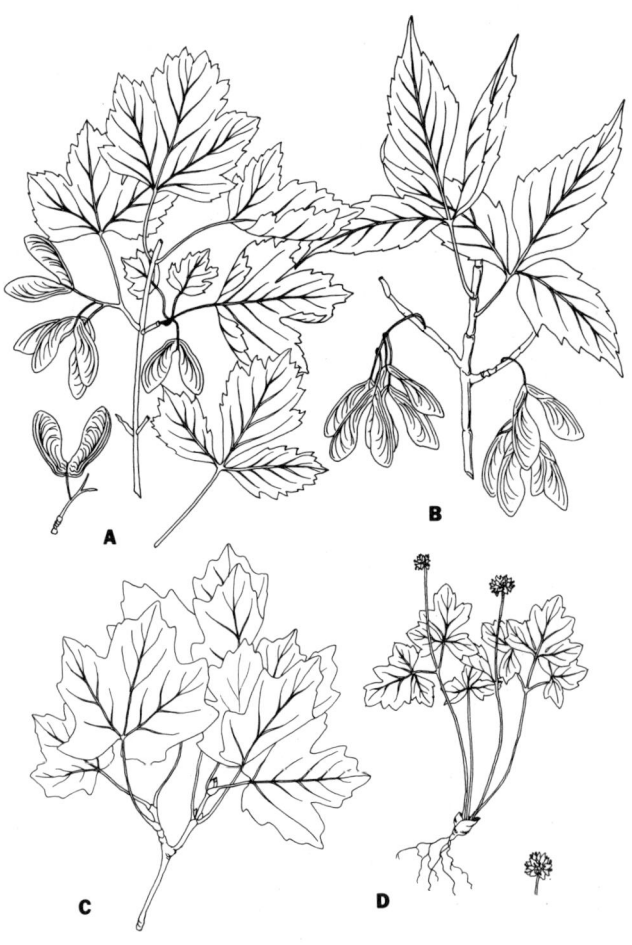

Figure 9. A, *Acer glabrum*, with lf of f. *trisectum*; B, *Negundo aceroides*; C, *Acer grandidentatum*; D, *Adoxa moschatellina*

Adoxaceae (ADX) 69

However, Robert F. Thorne, Rancho Santa Ana Bot. Garden, has evidence to indicate that the Adoxaceae is not monotypic after all, and places *Sambucus* (CPR) in this family!

ADOXA L. 1753 [from Gr., *adoxos*, without glory], MOSCHATEL

One sp, **A. moschatellina** L., **9D**. Moist, often shaded sites, upper montane, subalpine and alpine. Inconspicuous and growing in such diverse sites as forested streambanks and alpine rockslides. The pale green fls have a musky odor. With its ternate lvs and umbel-like fl cluster, the plant suggests a small umbellifer.

AGAVACEAE—AGAVE FAMILY (AGA)

Plants of the Agave family, along with the cacti, create much of the exotic living landscapes of the American Southwest. These plants also have been some of the most useful plants for native Americans, giving fibre for sandals, baskets, food from the seeds, and fermented drinks from the sap, such as pulque and tequila. Our only genus, *Yucca*, is of consuming biological interest because it illustrates the phenomenon of symbiosis. *Yucca* is visited by a night-flying 'pronuba' moth, *Tegeticula yuccasella*. Alighting on the flower, the moth first stabs the ovary and lays an egg inside. Then it mounts a stamen and collects a mass of pollen from the anther. It is not possible to pollinate *Yucca* by merely brushing the stigma with pollen accidentally, for the stigmatic surface is deeply seated in the bottom of the funnel-shaped style. As if understanding the problem, the moth proceeds to stuff the wad of pollen deep in the funnel, thus assuring pollination, and consequently ample food for the developing larva inside. Pollination results in the production of hundreds of seeds, so that neither actor in the drama loses anything and each achieves posterity. The hole bored in the ovary is easily visible on mature fruits.

YUCCA L. [from *yuca*, the Carib name for the manihot, erroneously used]. SPANISH BAYONET
1a. Plants with thick, rigid, broad curved lvs; frt indehiscent, fleshy; fls pendent in dense panicles. **Y. baccata** Torrey, BANANA YUCCA. Rocky piñon-juniper stands from the Colorado R valley southward.
1b. Plants with slender, flexible, narrow straight lvs; frt dehiscent, dry; fls erect or spreading, only drooping in age, in narrow panicles. **Y. harrimaniae** Trelease [for Mrs. Edward H. Harriman, sponsor of the Harriman Alaska Expedition in which Trelease participated; the returning party discovered this sp when their train was stopped at Helper, Utah]. Canyonsides and rocky piñon-juniper, very variable in lf length and thickness (*Y. angustissima* and *Y. neomexicana* of Colorado reports).

ALISMATACEAE—WATER-PLANTAIN FAMILY (ALI)

The English family name alludes to the resemblance of the leaves of *Alisma*, with its numerous parallel veins, to those of *Plantago major*. These plants always grow with their "feet in the water." Their petioles and stems are spongy, filled with air spaces, permitting oxygena-

Alismataceae (ALI)

tion of the tissues. The rhizomes of arrowheads were the '*wappata*' eaten by native Americans, and some species are cultivated by the Chinese for food. The numerous akenes produced by each flower are eaten by waterfowl.

1a. Lvs sagittate; fls in whorls of three along a central axis; aks in a tight ball. **Sagittaria,** ARROWHEAD
1b. Lvs oval or almost linear; fls in a diffusely-branched panicle; fls in umbels; aks in a ring. **Alisma,** WATER-PLANTAIN

ALISMA L. 1753 [anc. name for a water plant]. WATER-PLANTAIN

1a. Lvs usually elliptic to ovate-elliptic, 2-20 cm wide, rarely narrower; pedicels ascending to erect; petals 3.5-6.0 mm long; infls surpassing the lvs; aks centrally grooved at the tip, the style straight. **A. triviale** Pursh, **10D**. Muddy ditches and ponds (*A. plantago-aquatica* of manuals).
1b. Lvs linear to narrowly elliptic, less than 3 cm wide; pedicels widely spreading and curved; petals 2-4 mm long; infl usually not much longer than the lvs; aks centrally ridged, with two grooves near the tip, the style curled. **A. gramineum** Lejeune [grasslike], **10A**. Rare or infrequent, drying ponds, MF.

SAGITTARIA L. 1753 (Lat., *sagitta*, arrow]. ARROWHEAD

1a. Beak of ak horizontal or nearly so (at right angles to the long axis). **S. latifolia** Willdenow, **1C**. Muddy ditches and pond shores.
1b. Beak of ak erect or nearly so (parallel to the long axis). **S. cuneata** Sheldon, **10B**. Similar habitats.

ALLIACEAE—ONION FAMILY (ALL)

Usually included in the Lily family, the onions, for reasons other than their distinctive odors, stand alone because of their umbellate flower clusters and papery spathe-like bract, as well as numerous other technical features. In the family we find the culinary leek: *Allium porrum,* Garlic: *Allium sativum,* commercial onion: strains of *Allium cepa,* and Chives: *Allium schoenoprasum. Allium* is a particularly diversified genus in the arid West and in southwest Asia and contributes many showy species to rock garden culture.

1a. Tepals free to the base; stamens separate; fls numerous in the umbel, white or pink; lvs and bulb onion-scented. **Allium,** ONION

1b. Tepals united half-way; stamens united by the filaments into a tube; fls few, dull blue with olive-green midribs, sometimes white; lvs and bulb not onion-scented. **Androstephium,** WILD HYACINTH

ALLIUM L. 1753 [ancient Lat. name of garlic]. ONION

1a. Lvs hollow, terete. **A. schoenoprasum** L. [rush-leek], WILD CHIVES, **11C**. Wet meadows in the mt parks.

Figure 10. A, *Alisma gramineum*; B, *Sagittaria cuneata*, plant, carpel; C, *S. latifola*, carpel; D, *Alisma triviale*

1b. Lvs not hollow (but may be flat or terete) . . . . (2)

2a. Most fls replaced by fleshy reddish bulblets. **A. rubrum** Osterhout, **11D**. Springs and marshy places. Considered by some to be a race of *A. geyeri* (var *tenerum* Jones).
2b. Bulblets absent . . . . (3)

3a. Umbel nodding. **A. cernuum** Roth, **11B,G**. Grassy slopes and dry meadows. Fls pink, the petals rounded, concave, the tips not spreading.
3b. Umbel erect . . . . (4)

4a. Bulb coats persisting as a network of coarsely woven fibers. . . . (5)
4b. Bulb coats either non-fibrous or with parallel, not woven, fibers. . . . . (7)

5a. Invol bracts mostly 3-5-nerved; ovary usually strongly crested; lvs mostly 2 per scape. **A. macropetalum** Rydberg, **11I**. Adobe clay hills, Colorado R southward.
5b. Invol bracts mostly 1-nerved . . . . (6)

6a. Lvs 3 or more per scape; tepals pink. **A. geyeri** Watson [for Carl A. Geyer, collector on the Oregon Trail], **11E**. Moist meadows, montane and subalpine.
6b. Lvs usually only 2 per scape; tepals white or slightly pinkish. **A. textile** Nelson & Macbride. [ref. to the 'woven' bulb-coat]. Adobes and piñon-juniper, more common than *A. macropetalum*.

7a. Bulb elongate, terminating a stout short *Iris*-like rhizome; outer bulb coats with elongate cells in vertical rows. **A. brevistylum** Watson. Meadows and dry wooded slopes, N counties.
7b. Bulb ovoid to globose; outer bulb coats patterned but not with vertical rows of elongate cells. . . . . (8)

8a. Fls red-purple, tepals acuminate with flaring tips. **A. acuminatum** Hooker, **11F,J**. Sagebrush zone.
8b. Fls pale pink or white . . . . (9)

9a. Lf solitary, terete or subterete. **A. nevadense** Watson, **11H**. Infrequent, piñon-juniper zone, MF-ME.
9b. Lvs 2 or more per scape, flat and falcate. **A. brandegei** Watson. Mt sagebrush and oak, forming large colonies.

ANDROSTEPHIUM Torrey 1859 [Gr., *andros*, man, + *stephanos*, crown, alluding to the staminal corona]. WILD HYACINTH

One sp, **A. breviflorum** Watson, **11A, PL 38**. Adobe clay hills in the lower valleys, inconspicuous in fl but very striking in frt because of the few very large green flat-topped spheroidal capsules.

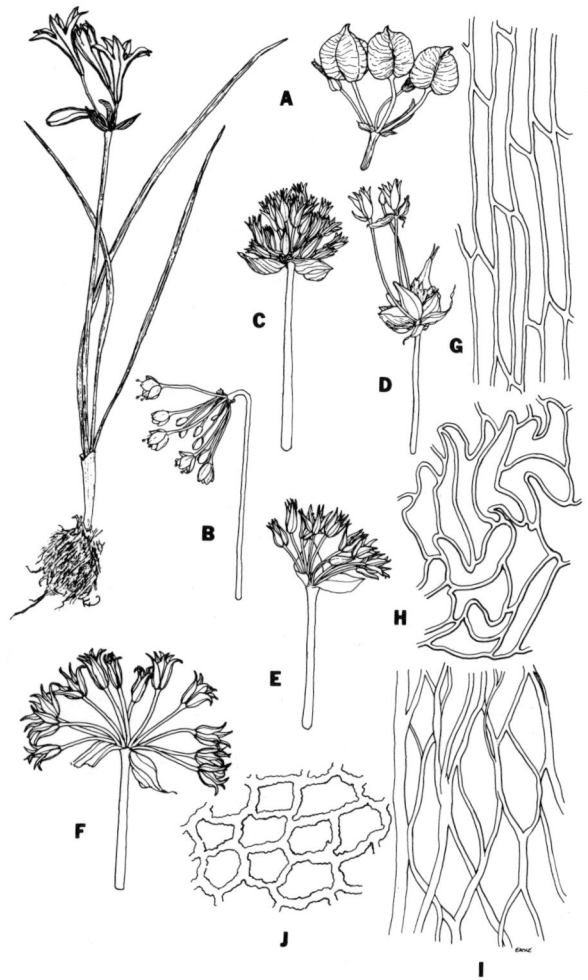

Figure 11. A, *Androstephium breviflorum*, habit & frt; B, *Allium cernuum*; C, *A. schoenoprasum*; D, *A. rubrum*; E, *A. geyeri*; F, *A. acuminatum*, G, bulbcoat detail of *A. cernuum*; H, *A. nevadense*; I, *A. macropetalum*; J, *A. acuminatum*

ALSINACEAE—CHICKWEED FAMILY (ASN)

This family is usually placed as a subfamily of Caryophyllaceae, but differs obviously in having its flowers constructed differently, with separate instead of united sepals and petals without narrow basal claws. The family is founded upon *Alsine media*, the common garden weed. To beginners, the chickweeds and sandworts seem to be an exasperating group, so many of them looking alike, but careful study shows a number of discrete genera with clear-cut characters.

Alert observers will note that the petals of *Lidia obtusiloba*, *Alsinanthe* and several other alsinoids will vary a great deal in length and showiness from plant to plant in the same population. Closer examination will reveal differences in the size and development of the stamens and carpels. Plants with small petals, often hardly longer than the sepals, will tend to have abortive and nonfunctional anthers but well developed ovaries, while plants with showy petals often have well-developed anthers and poorly developed ovaries. In other words, different plants will show different degrees of 'maleness' and 'femaleness' and in fact may be quite dioecious. The phenomenon, floral or sexual dimorphism, is very common in certain families and is especially well developed in the Alsinaceae and Apiaceae, where the variation in floral structure may occur on the same plant and within the same umbel!

1a. Lvs with colorless, papery stipules. . . . . (2)
1b. Lvs lacking stipules . . . . (3)

2a. Annual; glandular-pubescent herb with pink petals. **Spergularia**, SAND SPURRY
2b. Perennial, somewhat woody at the base; variously pubescent or glabrous, but seldom glandular. **Paronychia**, NAILWORT

3a. Minute (2 cm or less high) from a slender taproot; lvs mostly basal, linear; stems one-fld; muddy or moist sites, upper montane to subalpine. **Sagina**, PEARLWORT
3b. Larger, rarely less than 5 cm high, or if low, then perennial or lvs otherwise . . . . (4)

4a. Styles 5; caps cylindric, often curved, dehiscent by 10 apical teeth. **Cerastium**, MOUSE-EAR
4b. Styles 3; caps short, ovoid or oblong, splitting into 3 or 6 segs . . . . (5)

5a. Petals deeply 2-lobed . . . . (6)
5b. Petals entire or only shallowly notched. . . . . (8)

6a. Lvs ovate, or at least the lower ones petiolate; number of fl parts variable; stem with 2 lines of hairs. **Alsine**, CHICKWEED
6b. Lvs never distinctly petiolate, the blades elliptic or lanceolate to linear . . . . (7)

7a. Plant arising from fleshy tubers (easily detached in collecting),

glandular-pubescent; petals 6-8 mm long, cleft not more than half-way to the base; lvs lanceolate. **Pseudostellaria**, TUBER STARWORT
7b. Plant not glandular-pubescent; petals not over 5 mm long; lvs various. **Stellaria**, CHICKWEED

8a. Delicate early spring annual weed; stem simple or branched only at the very base, with a single terminal simple umbel of flowers; stem lvs about 2 pairs, glaucous. **Holosteum**
8b. Not as above . . . . (9)

9a. Lvs elliptic, 5 pairs or more on slender, relatively unbranched stems . . . . (10)
9b. Lvs linear, mostly basal; fls solitary or in many-fld cymes or clusters . . . . (11)

10a. Stems usually elongate, branched and sprawling, stems and lvs densely and minutely short-pubescent; nodes and lf-pairs numerous; the lvs acute. **Spergulastrum**
10b. Stems simple or branched only from the base, erect, the stems and lvs sparsely and inconspicuously pubescent; nodes about 5; the lvs obtuse or rounded at the apex. **Moehringia**

11a. Lvs narrowly linear or filiform, grasslike, over 1 cm long; ovary splitting at maturity into 3 valves which are again partly split to form 6 teeth. **Eremogone**, DESERT SANDWORT
11b. Lvs linear but very short and thickish, less than 1 cm long; ovary splitting at maturity into 3 valves . . . . (12)

12a. Sepals cucullate at the tip; stems short, one-fld and plants usually tightly matted at ground level. **Lidia**, ALPINE SANDWORT
12b. Sepals acute or acuminate; stems with simple or compound cymes; plants loosely caespitose . . . . (13)

13a. Plants delicate, from a slender taproot, with numerous unbranched stems bearing simple cymes at the apex; calyx and pedicels glandular-pubescent. **Tryphane**
13b. Plants well-developed, with a strong taproot supporting numerous leafy, branched stems with more developed cymes. . . . . . . (14)

14a. Totally glabrous; lvs and calyx soft, not rigidly pointed, the lvs appressed or somewhat secund; capsule conical, 4 mm long; on alpine tundra. **Alsinanthe**
14b. Covered with very slender multicellular gland-tipped hairs; lvs rigidly spreading; lvs and calyx with sharp yellowish subulate tips; capsule subglobose, 2 mm long; sagebrush lands. **Minuopsis**

ALSINANTHE Reichenbach 1841 [from resemblance to *Alsine*]
    One sp, **A. macrantha** (Rydberg) Weber [large-fld].Common on tundra (*Arenaria*). Two markedly different petal sizes occur (see notes on floral dimorphism).

ALSINE L. 1753 [ancient name for chickweeds, possibly *Alysson* of Dioscorides]. CHICKWEED

One sp, **A. media** L., **13B**. ADV weed of poorly drained shaded lawns (*Stellaria*). Flower parts are variable in number. The ovate lvs, abruptly narrowed to the petiole, are diagnostic.

CERASTIUM L. 1753 [Gr., *cerastes*, horned, alluding to the curved capsule]. MOUSE-EAR

1a. Petals at least half again as long as the sepals; capsule not much longer than the sepals; native perennials . . . . (2)
1b. Petals about as long as the sepals or slightly exceeding them; capsule about twice as long as sepals; annual or weedy biennial or perennial. **C. fontanum** Baumgartner. ADV ruderal weed (*C. vulgatum*).

2a. Bracts of the infl not at all scarious; fl stems usually without lfy tufts in their axils; calyx glandular with long multicellular hairs; low, loosely matted plants. **C. beeringianum** Chamisso & Schlechtendal ssp **earlei** (Rydberg) Hultén [for Graf von Beering; for F. S. Earle, collector with C. F. Baker], **13E**. Tundra and alpine rockslides. In areas of compensating environment the next (lowland) species may come into contact with and presumably hybridize with *C. beeringianum* in which case there is no sure way to distinguish them.
2b. Bracts of the infl scarious-margined; fl stems with tufts of sterile shoots in the lf axils; plants with tall erect fl stems. **Cerastium strictum** L. *emend.* Haenke [straight], **13D**. Abundant in meadows and openings of pine forests, from medium to high altitudes (*C. arvense* of manuals). *C. arvense* is a northern European tetraploid occurring in America at low altitudes only as a weed. Our plants are diploid and are related to if not identical, to the diploid *C. strictum* of the high mountains of Eurasia.

EREMOGONE Fenzl 1833 [Gr., *erem-*, desert]. DESERT SANDWORT (formerly incl in *Arenaria*)
1a. Fls crowded into dense clusters or heads . . . . (2)
1b. Fls in open cymes. . . . . (3)

2a. Sepals about 3 mm long; fls in a tight head; fl stems usually over 15 cm tall. **E. congesta** (Nuttall) Ikonnikov, **12C**. Gravelly soil, upper montane and subalpine.
2b. Sepals about 6 mm long; fls in a condensed cyme but not a tight head; fl stems rarely over 10 cm tall. **E. hookeri** (Nuttall) Weber [for Sir Joseph Hooker], **12B**. Desert-steppe.

3a. Infl glandular. **E. fendleri** (Gray) Ikonnikov, **12A**. Common in forested and high mountain areas.
3b. Infl not glandular. **E. kingii** (Watson) Ikonnikov ssp **uintahensis** (Nelson) Weber [for Clarence King, leader U. S. Exploring Exped. 1867-68]. Desert-steppe (*Arenaria eastwoodiae*).

Figure 12. A, *Eremogene fendleri*; B, *E. hookeri*; C, *E. congesta*

HOLOSTEUM L. 1753 [unexplained, from Gr., *holo*, all + *osteon*, bone, possibly alluding to the very early-blooming plant which dries quickly to a simple straw]

One sp, **H. umbellatum** L. ADV. Recently discovered along roadsides in western ME. The umbellate infl is very distinctive.

LIDIA Löve & Löve 1976 [for Johannes Lid, Norwegian botanist].
ALPINE SANDWORT

One sp, **L. obtusiloba** (Rydberg) Löve & Löve, **14D**. Abundant mat-former on dry tundra (*Minuartia*). Very closely related to the Eurasian *L. biflora* but forming very dense mats in contrast. Two distinct petal sizes occur (see notes on floral dimorphism). We used to think that small-petaled, juvenile, loosely matted plants occurring on pioneer, open unstable sites were distinct (*biflora*) from the tightly-matted, large-fld plants on stable sites (*obtusiloba*), but they are not clearly separated.

Alsinaceae (ASN)

MINUOPSIS Weber 1985 [resembling *Minuartia*]

One sp, **M. nuttallii** (Pax) Weber. Sagebrush-saltbush stands on gravelly slopes, MF, RB (*Arenaria*).

MOEHRINGIA L. 1753 [for Paul H. G. Moehring, German botanist, 1710-1792]

1a. Sepals rounded at the apex; lvs about as long as the internodes, narrowly oval, rounded at the apex. **M. lateriflora** (L.) Fenzl. Moist or swampy forest, montane and subalpine. Stems delicate and slender, finely pubescent with recurved hairs.
1b. Sepals acute or acuminate; lvs often longer than the internodes, broader, ovate-oblong, with distinct points. **M. macrophylla** (Hooker) Torrey. More common than the last, spruce-fir and aspen.

PARONYCHIA Miller 1754 [Gr. name for whitlow, a disease of the nails, and for plants with whitish or scaly parts, thought to cure it]. NAILWORT

1a. Densely matted alpine; lvs elliptic, obtuse; fls sessile; aerial branches absent. **P. pulvinata** Gray, **14A**. Gravelly tundra, the most extreme of dwarf mat plants.
1b. Plants freely branching or with foreshortened aerial branches, not alpine; lvs linear, sharp-pointed . . . . (2)

2a. Fls solitary or in pairs; lvs and bracts of equal length; lvs and stipules 4-6 mm long. **P. sessiliflora** Nuttall. Sagebrush in the intermountain basins.
2b. Fls numerous, in branched cymes; lvs 6-20 mm long, longer than the bracts and stipules. **P. jamesii** Torrey & Gray, **14B**. Infrequent, eastern Gunnison Basin.

PSEUDOSTELLARIA Pax 1934 [false *Stellaria*]. TUBER STARWORT

One sp, **P. jamesiana** (Torrey) Weber & Hartman, **13A**. Forest openings, middle altitudes (*Stellaria*). Most of the showy (functionally staminate) white fls do not produce seeds. The few fertile ones point to the ground, and their capsule valves roll outward, forming a flat shiny disk. The genus is Eurasian, this being the only American sp. Rhizomes are rarely collected because the stem is so brittle.

SAGINA L. 1753 [Lat., *sagina*, fattening, applied earlier to *Spergula*, a European forage plant]. PEARLWORT

One sp, **S. saginoides** (L.) Karstens. Subalpine, alpine, common but overlooked because of its small size; among rocks or in muddy depressions.

SPERGULARIA Presl & Presl 1819 [derived from *Spergula*]. SAND SPURRY

One sp, **S. rubra** (L.) Presl. ADV. A prostrate pink-fld weed coming in especially along logging trails.

SPERGULASTRUM Michaux 1803 [*Spergula*, + Lat., *-astrum*, related]

One sp, **S. lanuginosum** Michaux ssp **saxosum** (Gray) Weber. Rocky open sites of forested zones, S counties (*Arenaria*). Variable in size and branching.

Plate 1. **Wyethia amplexicaulis** Weber
Mule's Ears

Plate 2. **Trillium ovatum** Roberts

Plate 3. *Fritillaria pudica* Roberts
YELLOWBELLS

Plate 4. *Epipactis gigantea* Roberts

Plate 5. *Amsonia jonesii* — Weber

Plate 6. *Polygala subspinosa* — Weber
SPINY MILKWORT

Plate 7. ***Lewisia rediviva*** Roberts
BITTERROOT

Plate 8. ***Chamaepericlymenum canadense*** Roberts
BUNCHBERRY

Plate 9. *Gentianodes algida* — Roberts

Plate 10. *Castilleja scabrida* — Weber

Plate 11. ***Chrysothamnus nauseosus*** Roberts
RABBITBRUSH

Plate 12. ***Abronia elliptica*** Weber

Plate 13. ***Pediomelum megalanthum*** Weber

Plate 14. ***Ligularia soldanella*** Weber

Plate 15. *Besseya ritteriana* — Roberts

Plate 16. *Shepherdia canadensis* — Weber
BUFFALO-BERRY

Figure 13. A, *Pseudostellaria jamesiana*; B, *Alsine media*; C, *Stellaria umbellata*; D, *Cerastium strictum*; E, *C. beeringianum*

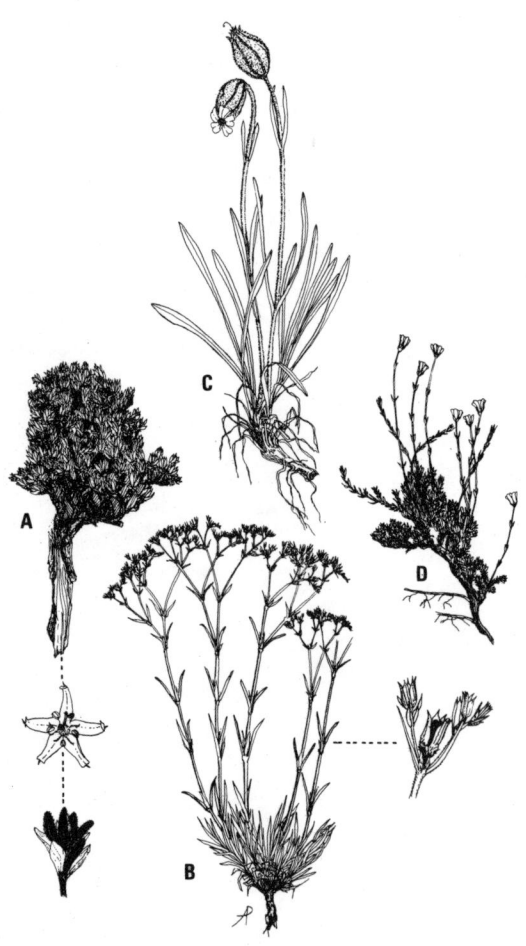

Figure 14. **A**, *Paronychia pulvinata*; **B**, *P. jamesii*; **C**, *Gastrolychnis apetala*; **D**, *Lidia obtusiloba*

Alsinaceae (ASN) 81

STELLARIA L. 1753 [Lat., stella, star]. CHICKWEED

1a. Fls subtended by scarious bracts (in *S. irrigua* and *S. umbellata*, the infl is condensed and the bracts may be somewhat hidden) . . (2)
1b. Flowers subtended by green lvs. . . . . (5)

2a. Lvs elliptic-oblong; infl sub-umbellate and condensed or cymose and open, pedicels tending to be reflexed. . . . . (3)
2b. Lvs lanceolate or lance-linear; infl cymose, pedicels ascending or divaricate, rarely actually reflexed. . . . . (4)

3a. Petals absent; plants green, extremely variable (in shaded places with long internodes and very open cymes; in sunny alpine sites dwarfed, fleshy, with short internodes and condensed cymes). **S. umbellata** Turczaninow, 13C. Subalpine, lower alpine (*S. weberi*).
3b. Petals present, filiform, 2-divided to the base; plants strongly purplish-tinged in all parts; pedicels short, infl always congested and somewhat hidden in the upper lvs; internodes about as long as the lvs, the lower ones longer; lvs fleshy, rather blunt, shriveling when pressed. **S. irrigua** Bunge, ALTAI CHICKWEED. Locally common on screes at high altitudes. First discovered in the Altai Mts. of Siberia, where it evidently is rare.

4a. Calyx 2-3 mm long, broadly acute or obtuse, sepals almost nerveless; cymes commonly axillary as well as terminal; lvs very minutely tuberculate on the margins, dull. **S. longifolia** Mühlenberg, STITCHWORT. Common in moist meadows in the mts.
4b. Calyx 4-8 mm long, sharply acute or acuminate, strongly 3-nerved; cymes terminal; lvs with smooth margins, shiny, sometimes slightly ciliate at the base. **S. longipes** Goldie ssp **stricta** (Rydberg) Weber, STITCHWORT. Wet ground, montane and subalpine.

5a. Low, decumbent and creeping; lvs less than 1 cm long, almost round, pointed, subpetiolate; fls solitary, axillary or terminal, on short pedicels less than 1 cm long. **S. obtusa** Engelmann. Gravelly streamsides, RT.
5b. Erect; lvs usually over 1 cm long, elliptic-lanceolate, lanceolate, or lance-linear; fls solitary or cymose, on longer pedicels. . . . . (6)

6a. Stem copiously pilose with multicellular hairs; lvs strongly ciliate, elliptic-oblong, acute; petals vestigial (1 mm long), with narrowly oblong divisions. **S. calycantha** (Ledebour) Bongard [cupped flower]. A sporadic variant that has been recognized by some as *S. simcoei* (Howell) C.L. Hitchcock. Subalpine meadows and willow bogs.
6b. Stem glabrous or very nearly so; lvs smooth or somewhat ciliate at the base, lanceolate to lance-linear; petals well-developed (about as long as or longer than the sepals). . . . . (7)

7a. Lvs lustrous, firm, thick and keeled, green or glaucous; plant usually with a single terminal fl, sometimes irregularly cymose; sepals smooth, rarely ciliate; petals about twice as long as the

82 Alsinaceae (ASN)

sepals. **S. longipes** Goldie ssp **monantha** (Hultén) Weber. Subalpine, alpine (incl. *S. laeta*?).
7b. Lvs not lustrous, flat, not keeled; fls solitary or in cymes; petals equalling or shorter than the sepals. . . . . (8)

8a. Lf margins completely smooth and the surfaces glabrous. **S. crassifolia** Ehrhart. Wet mountain meadows.
8b. Lf margins ciliate, at least lower half. **S. calycantha** (Ledebour) Bongard. Wet forests, meadows and willow bogs.

TRYPHANE Reichenbach 1841 [Gr., *trypheros*, delicate]
One sp, **T. rubella** (Wahlenberg) Reichenbach [reddish]. Moraines, gravel bars, and unstable tundra slopes, subalpine and lower alpine (*Arenaria, Minuartia*).

AMARANTHACEAE—AMARANTH FAMILY (AMA)

The family name comes from a Greek word meaning unfading, alluding to the 'everlasting' quality of the papery perianth parts. Many amaranths are cultivated for this quality: the Prince's Feather, *Amaranthus hypochondriacus*, with red, nodding, 'melancholy' spikes, and the Cockscomb, *Celosia argentea*. Our local amaranths are weeds of late summer, growing in waste or fallow ground, but in tropical America and Asia 'grain amaranths' are important food crops at high elevations. The seeds are popped and made into balls with a syrup binder, or ground to meal and baked into cakes or drunk in a slurry.

1a. Lvs covered by a dense mat of minute white stellate hairs; prostrate, dichotomously branched, the fls clustered in rosettes of lvs at the branch-tips. **Cladothrix**, ESPANTA VAQUERO
1b. Lvs green, glabrous. **Amaranthus**, AMARANTH

AMARANTHUS L. 1753 [Gr., *amarantos*, unfading]. AMARANTH

1a. Fls in bracteate clusters in the lf-axils; lvs seldom more than 5 cm long, oblong or obovate, with whitish margins and veins . . . (2)
1b. Fls in dense spikelike panicles at the ends of the branches . . . . (3)

2a. Prostrate, branching in all directions; seeds over 1 mm broad. **A. blitoides** Watson [like the genus *Blitum*], **15B**. Ruderal weed, but evidently native in America (*A. graecizans* of some manuals).
2b. Erect with widely open or ascending branches; seeds less than 1 mm broad. **A. albus** L. Less common, ADV.

3a. Tepals of carpellate fls obtuse or truncate (do not confuse these with the bracts!). **A. retroflexus** L. ADV ruderal weed of late summer.
3b. Tepals of carpellate fls acuminate or acute. **A. powellii** Watson [for John Wesley Powell, explorer of the West]. One record, MZ.

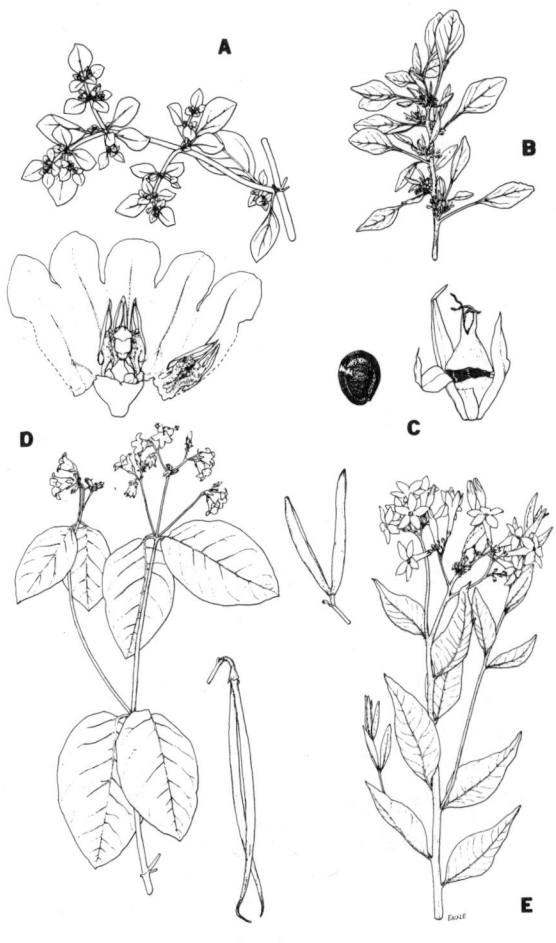

Figure 15. A, *Cladothrix lanuginosa*; B, *Amaranthus blitoides*; C, *Apocynum androsaemifolium*; D, *Amsonia jonesii*

84   Amaranthaceae (AMA)

CLADOTHRIX Watson 1880 [Gr., *klados*, twig, + *trichos*, hair]. ESPANTA VAQUERO

One sp, **C. lanuginosa** Nuttall, **15A**. Sandy and gravelly benches, MZ (*Tidestromia*).

ANACARDIACEAE—SUMAC FAMILY (ANA)

While a bout with poison ivy will instill certain knowledge of this family, it is nice to know that the anacards contain some of our most delicious fruits and nuts. *Anacardium occidentale* is the Cashew, *Pistacia vera* the Pistachio, and *Mangifera indica* the Mango, which has to be picked dead ripe from the tree to be appreciated. Under cultivation as an ornamental in city parks is *Cotinus coggygria*, the Smoke Tree, so named for the exceedingly slender plumose sterile branches of the inflorescence that create an illusion of mist. The ubiquitous cultivated Pepper Tree, *Schinus molle* of Southern California, also belongs to this family.

1a. Lfls 3, shiny; terminal lfl petiolate; frts white, smooth. **Toxicodendron**, POISON IVY
1b. Lfls 3 or more, dull and pubescent (if lfls 3, terminal lfl sessile); frt red, hairy. **Rhus**, SUMAC

RHUS L. 1753 [the ancient name]. SUMAC

1a. Lfls 9 or more, regularly serrate; tall shrub with thick twigs and much pith; frts in pyramidal clusters. **R. glabra** L., SMOOTH SUMAC, **16A**. Infrequent on canyonsides. The Staghorn Sumac, *R. typhina* L., is occasionally found as an escape from cult. It differs by having velvety-hairy twigs. *Ailanthus*, in the Simaroubaceae, looks like a sumac but has entire lvs with a few shallow lobes at the bases of the lfl, and produces papery samaras.
1b. Lfl 3 or sometimes 1, coarsely crenate; frts in dense small clusters. **R. aromatica** Aiton ssp **trilobata** (Nuttall) Weber, SKUNKBRUSH (*R. trilobata*), **16B**. Canyonsides and rimrock. In Mesa County many plants tend to have simple lvs (var *simplicifolia*), but all gradations occur.

TOXICODENDRON Miller 1754. POISON IVY, POISON OAK

One sp, **T. rydbergii** (Small) Greene, **16C**. Common at the bases of cliffs and increasing with trampling of the ground. Never climbs high into trees like its eastern counterpart.

APIACEAE/UMBELLIFERAE
PARSLEY FAMILY (API/UMB)

The so-called 'umbels' are recognized by the usually ternately (sometimes pinnately) compound leaves with a sheathing petiole (the edible part of celery), the umbellate flower clusters, the fruits that separate at maturity into two one-seeded nutlets (think of caraway seeds), and a generally pungent specific odor or taste. Many important culinary herbs belong here: Dill (*Anethum graveolens*), Carrot (*Daucus carota*),

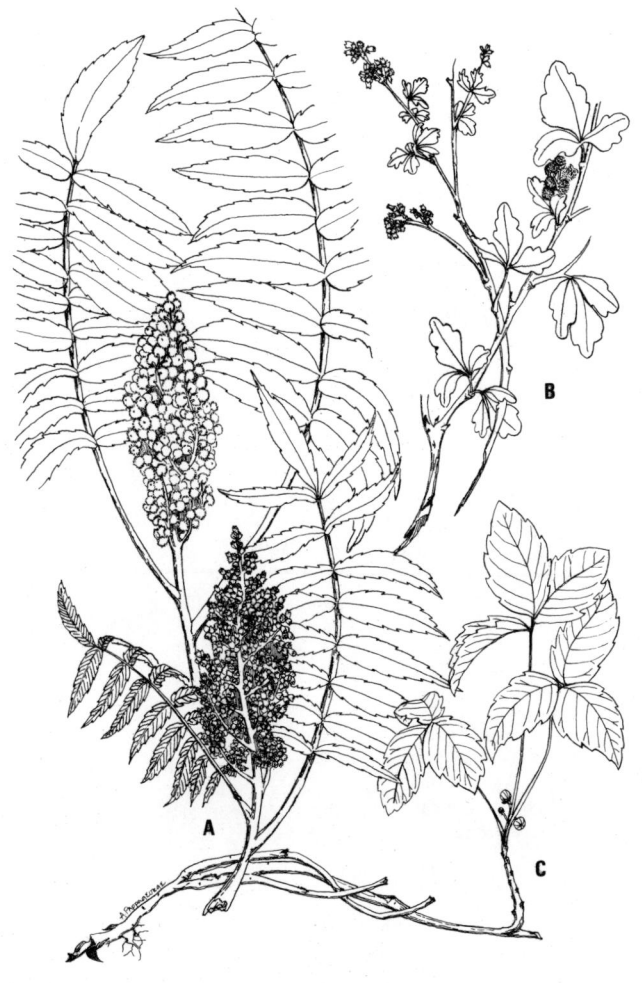

Figure 16. **A**, *Rhus glabra*; **B**, *Rhus aromatica*; **C**, *Toxicodendron rydbergii*

Coriander or cilantro (*Coriandrum sativum*), Cumin (*Cuminum cyminum*), Fennel (*Foeniculum vulgare*), Celery (*Apium graveolens*), Parsley (*Petroselinum hortense*), Anise (*Pimpinella anisum*), Parsnip (*Pastinaca sativa*), Caraway (*Carum carvi*), and Myrrh (*Myrrhis odorata*). But beware of chewing the leaves, stalks, roots or seeds of any umbel whose identity is the slightest bit doubtful! Two of the most poisonous plants in our region are *Conium*, Poison Hemlock, and *Cicuta*, Water Hemlock. Cases of fatal or near-fatal poisoning are reported every season. Learn to recognize these species before using wild umbels for food.

In order to use the key successfully, knowledge of the type of root system, presence or absence of caudices, and leaves on the flowering stem, flower color, characteristics of the mature fruit, and type of odor of the foliage, may all be helpful. Also, the flowers are not always alike in the same umbel, often showing a division of labor, some being functionally male, female, or neuter.

Thorne would place this family under the smaller, mostly tropical family Araliaceae.

1a. Lvs palmately cleft into 5 to 9 simple, toothed segs; fls yellow; frt covered with hooked bristles. **Sanicula**, BLACK SNAKEROOT
1b. Lvs various; frts not covered by bristles, or if so, fls white . (2)

2a. [1] Lvs simple, undivided; umbels few, condensed, subtended by a ring of broad bractlets fused at the base; dwarf alpine plants. **Bupleurum**
2b. Lvs never simple . . . . (3)

3a. [2] Lvs basically pinnately compound, only the lowermost pair of lfls occasionally incised or lobed . . . . (4)
3b. Lvs basically ternate, or if pinnate, the lfls commonly further subdivided . . . . (8)

4a. [3] Fls yellow; lfls large and coarsely toothed; weed of cult ground. **Pastinaca**, PARSNIP
4b. Fls white; native sp . . . . (5)

5a. [4] Lfls linear, entire; plant very slender, arising from a globose or fusiform corm. Yampa drainage only. **Perideridia**, YAMPA
5b. Lfls broader, toothed or lobed; plant not arising from a corm; widely distributed. . . . . (6)

6a. [5] Lfls elongate, broadly linear, finely toothed; tall marsh plant. **Sium**, WATER PARSNIP
6b. Lfls broader, coarsely toothed or incised . . . . (7)

7a. [6] Lfls broadly elliptic-ovate, crenate. Plants of mt streamsides. **Oxypolis**, COWBANE
7b. Lfls narrowly elliptic-oblong, deeply-toothed, the lowest pair usually with a large lobe; plants of irrigation ditches. **Berula**, WATER PARSNIP

8a. [3] Low plants of tundra, sagebrush or arid clay areas . . . . . . (9)

8b. Tall or coarsely weedy plants of mt forests or roadsides . . . . (17)

9a. [8] Very slender and weak, arising singly from a globose or fusiform corm; lvs ternate with usually linear (only rarely wider) lfls. **Orogenia**, TURKEY-PEAS
9b. Stout, the stems never arising singly from a corm; lvs various . . . . (10)

10a. [9] Plants of subalpine meadows and alpine tundra. . . . . . . (11)
10b. Plants of desert-steppe or sagebrush . . . . (13)

11a. [10] Lvs ternately pinnate, the lfl long and narrow. **Pseudocymopterus** (dwarfed forms of high altitudes)
11b. Lvs pinnately-divided or if somewhat ternate the lfls very short and crowded . . . . (12)

12a. [11] Lfls digitately incised, the group distinctly fan-shaped; fl stems erect, the umbel very conspicuous, fls bright yellow; subalpine meadows. **Podistera**
12b. Lfls incised but not distinctly fan-shaped; fl stems spreading, fls pale yellow, rarely purplish, inconspicuous; tundra plants. **Oreoxis**, ALPINE PARSLEY

13a. [10] Stemless; lvs all basal, none on the fl stem . . . . (14)
13b. Stem present; lvs either on the fl stem or on a pseudoscape . . . (15)

14a. [13] Over 10 cm tall, with numerous stout caudices; arid, rocky ledges or clay-shale slopes. **Aletes**
14b. Less than 10 cm tall, with few caudices; sagebrush communities in the intermountain basins. **Oreoxis**, ALPINE PARSLEY

15a. [13] Frts strongly dorsiventrally flattened, laterally thin-margined and winged. **Lomatium**
15b. Frts not strongly flattened dorsiventrally, the dorsal ribs conspicuous and often winged . . . . (16)

16a. [15] Frts strongly corky-winged; arid steppe-desert, piñon-juniper, and sagebrush; fls white, yellow, or dull red. **Cymopterus**
16b. Frts with conspicuous dorsal ribs but with poorly-developed wings; pine, aspen forests and subalpine meadows. **Pseudocymopterus**, MOUNTAIN PARSLEY

17a. [8] Fls yellow . . . . (18)
17b. Fls white . . . . (19)

18a. [17] Frts strongly dorsiventrally flattened, laterally thin-margined and winged. **Lomatium dissectum**
18b. Frts with conspicuous dorsal ribs but with poorly-developed wings; pine, aspen forests and subalpine meadows. **Pseudocymopterus**

19a. [17] Frts 4-5 times longer than wide; frts and roots with an anise odor when crushed. **Osmorhiza**, SWEET CICELY

19b. Frts short, about as wide as long; frt and roots lacking anise odor. . . . . (20)

20a. [19] Tall, coarse plants, the ultimate lf-segs 1 cm or more broad; lvs generally not more than twice pinnately compound. . (21)
20b. Slender plants, or, if tall and coarse, the ultimate lf-segs less than 0.5 cm wide; lvs generally very finely dissected, fernlike . . . . (23)

21a. [20] Principal lvs divided into 3 or 5 huge, maple-shaped lfls, the lf sheath over 2 cm wide; stems up to 3-4 cm thick. **Heracleum**, COW PARSNIP
21b. Principal lvs not as above . . . . (22)

22a. [21] Lf-segs lanceolate; ribs of frt prominent but not forming wings; roots tuberous, clustered; sloughs and ditches in the valleys. **Cicuta**, WATER HEMLOCK
22b. Leaf-segs ovate; ribs of frt forming wings; plant with a taproot; mt streamsides and screes. **Angelica**

23a. [20] Frts covered with hooked bristles; umbels subtended by a conspicuous ring of lflike bracts, sometimes equalling the umbel rays. **Daucus**, WILD CARROT
23b. Frts not bristly; umbels subtended by very inconspicuous small bracts or none . . . . (24)

24a. [23] Introd weeds of irrigation ditches, roadsides, or cult ground. . . . . (25)
24b. Natives of forests and subalpine streamsides . . . . (26)

25a. [24] Stem spotted with purple; tall plants with hollow stems over 1 m tall and huge fern-like basal lvs; fruit (do not chew!) with a soapy or celery odor. **Conium**, POISON HEMLOCK
25b. Stem not spotted; plants not over 1 m tall, smaller in all details; frt with caraway odor. **Carum**, CARAWAY

26a. [24] Lfl linear, 1-3 mm wide. **Ligusticum**, LOVAGE
26b. Lfl ovate, oblong, or lanceolate, 5-40 mm broad . . . . (27)

27a. [26] Less than 1 m tall, unbranched, with one to two stem lvs; ultimate lf-lobes with one principal vein, the lateral veins, if present, inconspicuous; frts oval, flattened dorsally. **Conioselinum**, HEMLOCK PARSLEY
27b. Over 1 m tall, branched, with numerous large lvs; ultimate lf-lobes with many lateral veins as conspicuous as the mid-vein; frts oblong, not flattened dorsally. **Ligusticum**, LOVAGE

ALETES Coulter & Rose 1888 [Gr., *Aletes*, a wanderer, from the fact that *A. acaulis* was known under at least six generic names prior to *Aletes*, including *Lomatium*]

1a. Lfls over 5 mm wide.; forming broad mats. **A. latiloba** (Rydberg) Weber. Sandstone ledges, canyonlands of W ME.
1b. Lfls less than 4 mm wide. . . . . (2)

2a. Crushed lvs with a strong anise or citronella odor; lfls not differentiated well from the rachises, sharp-pointed. **A. anisata** (Gray) Theobald & Tseng. A variable sp, occurring on many substrates: shales in the Piceance Basin, and volcanics at Black Canyon.
2b. Crushed lvs with a celery or soapy odor; lfls either distinct from the rachis by a constriction, or not . . . . (3)

3a. Lfls oblong, crowded, often appearing fan-shaped, on very short pinnae, the general outline narrowly pinnate. **A. eastwoodiae** (Coulter & Rose) Weber, **18A**. Piñon-juniper, N base of Uncompahgre Plateau, ME. Blossoming extremely early (March, April) and rarely seen in fl.
3b. Lfls not as above . . . . (4)

4a. Umbels not over 2 cm broad in fl or frt; lfls well-separated from the rachis, broadest in the middle. **A. macdougalii** Coulter & Rose ssp **breviradiata** Theobald & Tseng. Sandstone ledges, Mesa Verde.
4b. Umbels at least 3-4 cm diam; lfls not at all separate, scarcely wider than the rachis . . . . (5)

5a. Umbels with the lower rays not reflexed. **A. petraea** (Jones) Weber. Rocky terraces, Gates of Lodore. This is similar to the next but habitat is different.
5b. Umbels with the lower rays strongly reflexed. . . . . (6)

6a. Lateral lf lobes linear, entire. **A. lithophila** (Mathias) Weber [rock-loving]. END. Eocene clays in southern LP; common on volcanic outcrops in southern counties of E slope.
6b. Lateral lf lobes with a few short, flaring teeth. **A. nuttallii** (Gray) Weber. Locally abundant on soft black shale slopes, sagebrush of Middle Park near Kremmling. The type collection was collected by Nuttall in southern Wyoming or Nebraska but its name has been misapplied to another sp of Utah. Nelson gave the name *Lomatium* [=*Aletes*] *megarrhiza* to our plant. The Utah plant that has gone under the name *Lomatium nuttallii* should be called *Aletes kingii* but the combination has not yet been made.

ANGELICA L. 1753 [named *angelic* from cordial and medicinal properties of some spp].
1a. Coarse, stout herbs of streambanks, middle altitudes; over 2 m tall with very large umbels. **A. ampla** Nelson.
1b. Lower herbs less than 2 m tall; aspen zone to alpine screes . . . . (2)

2a. Involucel (bract of the smallest umbel) lacking. **A. pinnata** Watson. Aspen groves and streamsides, uncommon but widely distributed.

2b. Involucel present . . . . (3)

3a. Frt glabrous; involucel of lanceolate bracts often longer than the fls; alpine screes. **A. grayi** (Coulter & Rose) Coulter & Rose.
3b. Frt scabrous; involucel of filiform or linear bracts; habitat unknown. **A. roseana** Henderson [for J. N. Rose]. One collection known, from "Cassell's Canyon", possibly near Mt. Harvard.

BERULA Besser 1826 [Lat. name of some aquatic plant]. WATER PARSNIP
One sp, **B. erecta** (Hudson) Coville. Weak herb of sloughs and irrigation ditches in the lower valleys.

BUPLEURUM L. 1753 [Gr., *bous*, an ox + *pleuron*, a rib].
One sp, **B. triradiatum** Adams ssp **arcticum** (Regel) Hultén. Rare, tundra of Needle Mts., San Juans. The genus is unique in its simple lvs. Our specimen is only 2 cm tall.

CARUM L. 1753 [mod of old Lat. name, *Careum*]. CARAWAY
One sp, **C. carvi** L. ADV. A locally common weed, in mt town sites. The caraway flavor of the crushed mericarp is distinctive.

CICUTA L. 1753 [Ancient Lat. name of Poison Hemlock]. WATER HEMLOCK
One sp, **C. douglasii** (de Candolle) Coulter & Rose, **17B**. Swamps and roadside ditches in the lower valleys. Extremely poisonous. Certain identification can be made by making a longit. section of the thick root; it has cross-partitions separating air-spaces.

CONIOSELINUM G. Hoffm. 1814 [merger of two generic names of umbels, *Conium* and *Selinum*]. HEMLOCK-PARSLEY
One sp, **C. scopulorum** (Gray) Coulter & Rose. Wet meadows and roadside ditches in the mts. A low herb with usually one or two stem lvs, little-branched, never tall and rank like its close relative, *Ligusticum porteri*.

CONIUM L. 1753 [Gr., *coneion*, the Hemlock, by which Socrates and various criminals were put to death]. POISON HEMLOCK
One sp, **C. maculatum** L. [spotted], **17A**. An abundant tall, rank ADV weed in towns, especially near irrigation ditches and wet ground. The plant produces a rosette of fern-like lvs the first year and can be hoed out easily at that stage. Children have been poisoned by using the hollow stems for whistles. Every effort should be made to eliminate this from our area because of the potential danger of poisoning.

CYMOPTERUS Rafinesque 1819 [Gr., *cyma*, a wave + *pteron*, a wing, alluding to frt wings].
1a. Fls yellow or dull red . . . . (2)
1b. Fls white or pink . . . . (6)

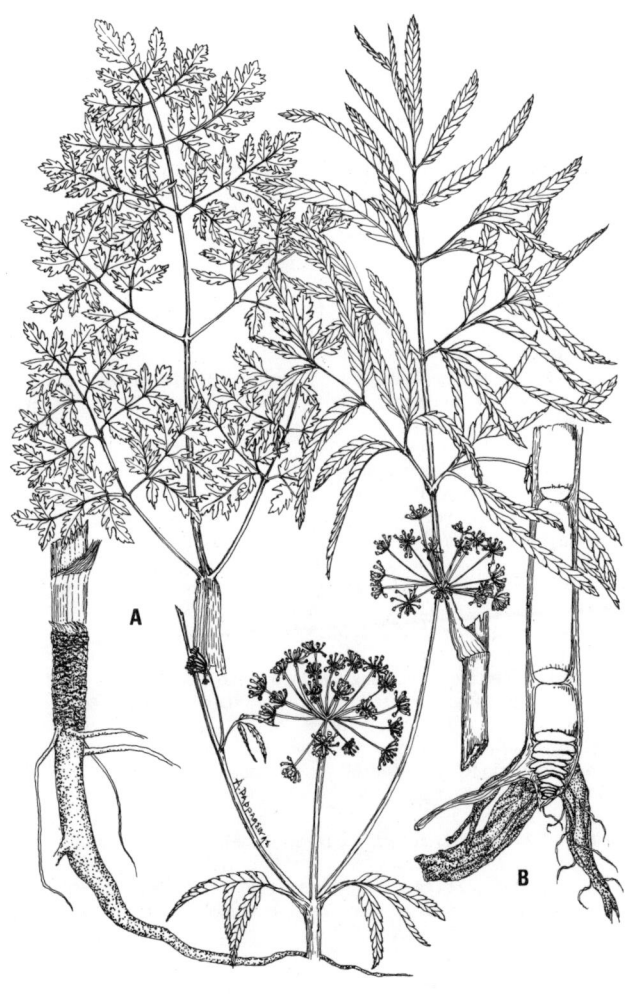

FIGURE 17. A, *Conium maculatum*; B, *Cicuta douglasii*

2a. Lvs gray or glaucous. . . . . (3)
2b. Lvs green, shiny. . . . . (5)

3a. Plant with a long, slender, deeply buried pseudoscape, the lvs spreading out at ground level. **C. planosus** (Osterhout) Mathias [flat, prostrate]. Sagebrush meadows, upper mountain valleys, blooming in early spring. Red-fld and yellow-fld plants occur in the same population.
3b. Pseudoscape short, stout, not buried, the lvs ascending . . . . . . (4)

4a. Lvs with very broad segs. **C. duchesnensis** Jones [from Duchesne, Utah], **18F**. Clay buttes, White R and Yampa basins.
4b. Lvs with linear segs. **C. terebinthinus** (Hooker) Torrey & Gray var **calcareus** (Jones) Cronquist [with turpentine odor; of limestone] Steppe-desert, White and Yampa R basins.

5a. Pseudoscape conspicuous, up to 15 cm long; umbels usually sessile; involucel of broad green bracts. **C. fendleri** Gray. Clay soils, lower valleys.
5b. Pseudoscape short, stout; umbels with well-developed rays; involucel of a few inconspicuous narrow bracts. **C. purpureus** Watson. Similar habitats.

6a. Involucel of slender, inconspicuous bracts; lvs with narrow segs, spreading out across the ground; fls dull red. See 3a, above.
6b. Involucel of broad white papery bracts; lvs with broad segs, ascending; fls pink . . . . (7)

7a. Bracts many-nerved. **C. multinervatus** (Coulter & Rose) Tidestrom. Desert-steppe, not as common as the next.
7b. Bracts 1-3-nerved. . . . . (8)

8a. Umbels somewhat spreading, the rays 10-50 mm long; frt ovoid-oblong, the wings generally narrower than the body. **C. bulbosus** Nelson. Adobe soils, lower valleys.
8b. Umbels densely globose, the rays 4-10 mm long; frt ovoid, the wings 2-3 times the width of the body. **C. purpurascens** (Gray) Jones. Four Corners area.

DAUCUS L. 1753 [the ancient Greek name]. CARROT; QUEEN ANNE'S LACE

One sp, **D. carota** L. ADV weed or garden escape, estab along roadsides in the mt valleys. The first blooming fl (center of umbel) is often deep purple.

HERACLEUM L. 1753 [dedicated to Hercules, Pliny having thought our sp to be of great medicinal value]. COW PARSNIP

One sp, **H. sphondylium** L. ssp **montanum** (Schleicher) Briquet [*Sphondylium*, a pre-Linnaean genus name for this]. A plant of giant proportions, in swampy thickets and stream-sides in the middle mts. The outer petals of the outer fls of the umbel are usually enlarged and 2-cleft, creating the impression of a single large fl, not an umbel of small ones.

Apiaceae/Umbelliferae (API/UMB) 93

LIGUSTICUM L. 1753 [Lat., *ligusticus*, of the country Liguria, where the garden lovage abounded]. LOVAGE

1a. Lfl linear, 1-3 mm broad; low, slender plant less than 0.5 m tall. **L. filicinum** Watson var **tenuifolium** (Watson) Mathias & Constance. Wet mountain meadows, grassy slopes, subalpine.
1b. Lfl ovate, oblong, or lanceolate, 5-40 mm wide; tall, rank plants over 1 m tall. **L. porteri** Coulter & Rose [for T. C. Porter]. OSHA. Forested ravines and aspen groves.

LOMATIUM Rafinesque 1819 [Gr., *lomation*, a little border, alluding to the winged frt].

1a. Fls white or pale yellow . . . . (2)
1b. Fls bright yellow . . . . (4)

2a. Bractlets ± tomentose or villous; frts at least 1 cm long; stout plants with pseudoscapes. **L. macrocarpum** (Hooker & Arnott) Coulter & Rose. Sagebrush, Yampa Valley, Rt to MF.
2b. Bractlets glabrous; frts smaller; slender plants . . . . (3)

3a. Fls clearly white, with red anthers. **L. orientale** Coulter & Rose. Blooming in very early spring, mostly a plant of the E plains, but recurring in MF and RB.
3b. Fls distinctly pale yellow, anthers concolorous. **L. juniperinum** (Jones) Coulter & Rose. Piñon-juniper, MF, much more common than the last.

4a. Well over 2 dm tall, with large ternate lvs, usually more than one elongate internode, and large umbels (more resembling *Ligusticum* than *Lomatium*). **L. dissectum** (Nuttall) Mathias & Constance. Frequent in the oak zone. Easily confused with *Ligusticum porteri* but not so tall, and the ultimate lf-lobes have only a single midvein, while in *Ligusticum* the venation is pinnate.
4b. Low or slender, less than 2 dm tall, the internodes few and short; umbels small . . . . (5)

5a. Lvs densely pubescent with very short stiff hairs. **L. foeniculaceum** (Nuttall) Coulter & Rose ssp **macdougalii** (Coulter & Rose) Theobald [resembling the genus *Foeniculum*; for D. T. MacDougal, USDA plant collector]. Local, on clay-shale slopes, W RB.
5b. Lvs glabrous . . . . (6)

6a. Ultimate lf-segs narrowly linear, less than 5 mm long. **L. grayi** Coulter & Rose, **18B**. Very common on barren clay hillsides.
6b. Ultimate lf-segs broader, more remote, more than 5 mm long. . . (7)

7a. Lfl few, long and narrow, lvs not more than twice ternate; plants with usually one erect fl stem. **L. triternatum** (Pursh) Coulter & Rose ssp **platycarpum** (Torrey) Cronquist [broadfruited]. Sagebrush meadows.
7b. Lfl numerous, more than twice ternate; plants with several spreading fl stems. (8)

8a. Lvs with broader-than-linear ultimate lobes; frts broadly oval. **L. concinnum** (Osterhout) Mathias [neat, elegant]. END. Very rare, adobe hills near Montrose.
8b. Lvs with linear lobes; frts narrowly oblong, stiffly erect in a sessile umbel. **L. leptocarpum** (Nuttall) Jones [narrow-fruited]. Sagebrush meadows, Yampa R drainage.

OREOXIS Rafinesque 1830 [Gr., *oros*, mountains]. ALPINE PARSLEY

1a. Bractlets linear, entire, green . . . . (2)
1b. Bractlets broad, toothed at the apex, often purplish. **O. bakeri** Coulter & Rose [for C. F. Baker]. Tundra, San Juan Mts.

2a. Glabrous and glossy. **O. alpina** (Gray) Coulter & Rose. Common dwarf alpine on granitic central mts.
2b. Distinctly puberulent. **O. alpina** ssp **puberulenta** Weber. Sagebrush, high interior basins.

OROGENIA Watson 1871 [Gr., *oros*, mountain, + *genia*, alluding to resemblance to the genus *Erigenia*]. TURKEY-PEAS
One sp, **O. linearifolia** Watson. Sagebrush meadows. Very inconspicuous and easily overlooked, blooming in May. This and *Perideridia* are our only umbels arising from a globose or fusiform corm; lfls are usually narrowly oblong to linear, but some plants may have very broad lfls (var **lata** Payson).

OSMORHIZA Rafinesque 1819 [Gr., *osmo*, scent + *rhiza*, root]. SWEET CICELY [corruption of a genus name, *Seseli*]
1a. Lvs distinctly pinnate-ternate with several pairs of lateral ternate lfls, the lobes shallow and also finely-toothed; frt glabrous or sparsely bristly at base, obtuse at apex, not caudate; frts and umbel rays stiffly ascending. **O. occidentalis** (Nuttall) Torrey. Oak-aspen and mt meadows.
1b. Lvs clearly ternate, with one pair of lateral ternate lfls, the lobes deep and simple; frts bristly-hispid, caudate at the base with conspicuous tails; frts and umbel rays spreading-ascending or divaricate . . . . (2)

2a. Rays and pedicels spreading-ascending; frt linear-oblong, cylindric. **O. chilensis** Hooker & Arnott. Not as common as the next, shaded forests along streams.
2b. Rays and pedicels divaricate; frt clavate, widest near the apex. **O. depauperata** Philippi. Very common, montane.

OXYPOLIS Rafinesque 1825 [Gr., *oxys*, sharp + *polios*, white, from the slender involucels and white petals]. COWBANE
One sp, **O. fendleri** (Gray) Heller, 18E. Along rivulets in subalpine forests.

PASTINACA L. 1753 [Lat., *pastino*, to prepare the ground for planting of the vine]. PARSNIP
One sp, **P. sativa** L. Commonly escaped from cult and ADV, becoming estab in neglected agricultural land.

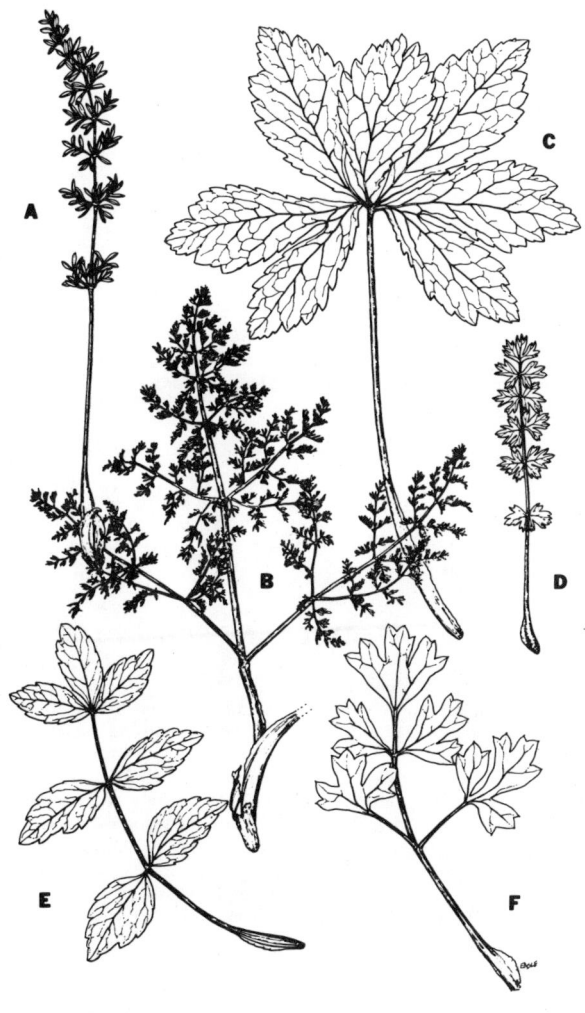

FIGURE 18. A, *Aletes eastwoodiae*; B, *Lomatium grayi*; C, *Sanicula marilandica*; D, *Podistera eastwoodiae*; E, *Oxypolis fendleri*; F, *Cymopterus duchesnensis*

PERIDERIDIA Reichenbach 1837 [Gr., *peri*, around + *derris*, a leather coat]. YAMPA

One sp, **P. gairdneri** (Hooker & Arnott) Mathias ssp **borealis** Chuang & Constance. Wet meadows, Yampa Valley. Corms of this plant were gathered for food by the Indians.

PODISTERA Watson 1887 [alluding to the entanglement of the pedicels and involucels in the original sp].

One sp, **P. eastwoodiae** (Coulter & Rose) Mathias & Constance, **18D**. END, subalpine meadows from the Elk Mts southward.

PSEUDOCYMOPTERUS Coulter & Rose 1888 [Gr. *pseudo*, false + *Cymopterus*]. MOUNTAIN PARSLEY

One sp, **P. montanus** (Gray) Coulter & Rose. Probably the most abundant yellow umbel in the mts, from the pine-oak to subalpine, extremely variable in height and leaf-cutting.

SANICULA L. 1753 [Lat., *sanara*, to heal]. SNAKEROOT

One sp, **S. marilandica** L., **18C**. An E foothills sp uncommon on the W slope, in cool shaded woods along streams, known from near Steamboat Springs and Piedra.

SIUM L. 1753 [Gr., *sion*, the name of a water plant]. WATER PARSNIP

One sp, **S. suave** Walter. Swales of the larger valleys. Lvs typically simply pinnate with serrulate margins, but in 'drowned' situations some may develop more dissection. The stem base is partitioned internally as in *Cicuta*.

APOCYNACEAE—DOGBANE FAMILY (APO)

The dogbane family is diversified in the tropics, where members are used as fiber plants, sources of india rubber, and arrow poisons. In recent years, *Rauwolfia*, a tropical tree, was found to yield a wonder drug for high blood pressure. Most of the well-known genera are ornamentals. In our gardens, *Vinca minor*, Periwinkle, is a standard ground cover in shaded corners, and the extremely poisonous Oleander, *Nerium oleander*, separates lanes of divided highways in California and Arizona. *Plumeria* provides the lovely Frangipani flowers of the Hawaiian lei.

1a. Fls elongate, tubular, chalky-blue; lvs alternate. **Amsonia**
1b. Fls short, bowl-shaped, white, greenish-white, or pink; lvs opposite. **Apocynum**, DOGBANE

AMSONIA Walter 1788 [for Dr. Charles Amson, 18th century traveller in America]

One sp, **A. jonesii** Woodson [for Marcus Jones], **15D**, **PL 5**. Rare in runoff-fed draws on sandstone, steppe-desert, blooming in May. The masses of powder-blue fls make a most unexpected show in springtime. The corolla is completely closed by stiff, inpointing hairs.

APOCYNUM L. 1753 [Gr., *apo*, away, + *cyno*, dog]. DOGBANE

1a. Corolla pink, 3 times the length of the calyx; branching mostly dichotomous; lvs usually drooping. **A. androsaemifolium** L., SPREADING DOGBANE, **15C**. This and the next sp hybridize freely in the wild. Intermediates are called *Apocynum x medium*. Gravelly soil, open pine woods.
1b. Corolla greenish-white, 1.5-2.0 times the length of the calyx; branching opposite; lvs erect or spreading, not drooping. **A. cannabinum** L., INDIAN HEMP. Roadside ditches. Plants with sessile, clasping lower lvs (*A. sibiricum*), while possibly once distinct, merge with *A. cannabinum*. The lower leaves soon fall away.

ARALIACEAE—GINSENG FAMILY (ARL)

Rice paper is not made from rice at all but from an aralia, *Tetrapanax papyrifera*. The English Ivy, symbolic of the 'ivory tower', is an aralia, *Hedera helix*. The spiny Devil's Club of the rain forests of the Pacific Northwest is an aralia, *Oplopanax horrida*. And Ginseng, one of the most ancient of medicines, is an aralia, *Panax ginseng*. Aralias are very close relatives of the Apiaceae, differing in their flowers which have five carpels instead of two.

ARALIA L. 1753 [origin of name unknown]

1a. Umbels numerous in a large compound panicle or raceme; cauline lvs present. **A. racemosa** L., SPIKENARD. Shaded streamsides. Recently collected for the first time on the W slope, north of Durango, LP. An eastern relictual sp first noted, but not collected, near the mouth of the Platte R by Edwin James.
1b. Umbels few in a corymb; leaf solitary, basal, long-petioled. **A. nudicaulis** L(naked-stemmed), WILD SARSAPARILLA. Infrequent in cool ravines, foothills and montane. Our only collections from the W slope come from North Inlet in Rocky Mt Nat Park. A plant of the NE American forests disjunct in our E foothills. Formerly used as a substitute for sarsaparilla.

ASCLEPIADACEAE—MILKWEED FAMILY (ASC)

To understand the milkweed flower some explanation is needed. The milkweed flower contains 5 sepals, 5 petals (which are usually reflexed), 5 stamens which, as such, cannot easily be recognized, and a gynoecium composed of two carpels which are free for most of their length, but united at the apex. Each carpel (follicle) splits down one side at maturity, liberating the seeds, which are equipped with a tuft of silky hairs (coma) at one end, serving as a parachute.

Milkweed flowers are unique in their possession of what would appear to be a whorl of floral organs between the petals and the stamens. This whorl of 5 petal-like parts is called a corona, and each segment is a hood. On its inner surface, the hood may or may not have a protruding horn-like structure. The base of the hood may be expanded into flap-like structures called auricles.

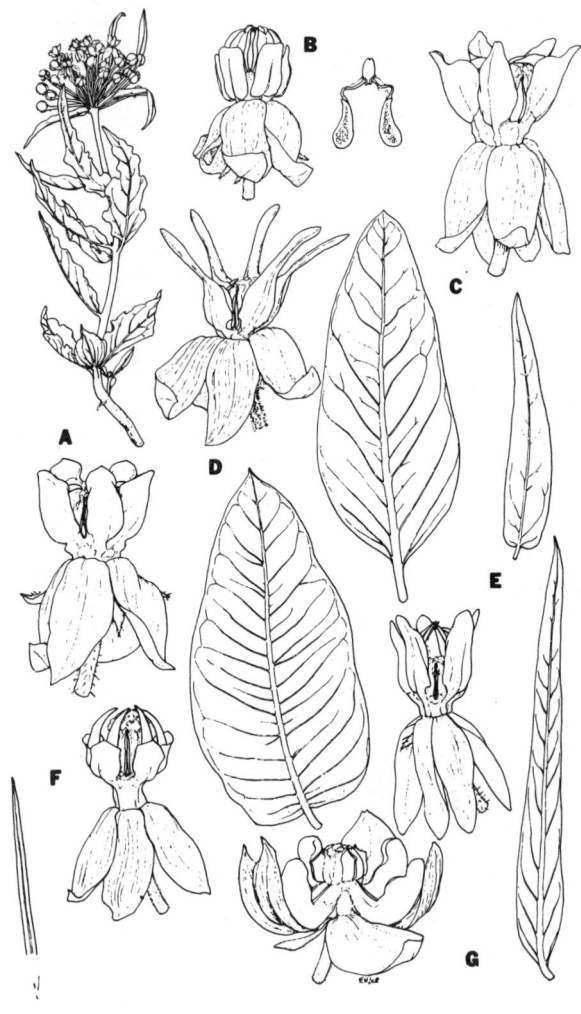

FIGURE 19. A, *Asclepias macrosperma*, plant (fl below); B, *A. engelmanniana*, fl, pollinia; C, *A. hallii*, fl, (lf below left); D, *A. speciosa*, fl (lf below); E, *A. tuberosa* (fl below left, lf above right); F, *A. subverticillata*, fl, lf; G, *A. asperula*, fl left, lf right

The stamens themselves are united to the style, the two structures together forming a unit in the central part of the flower. The pollen grains formed within the anther sacs are sticky and hang together in masses called pollinia. The pollinia of adjacent anthers are united by a thread-like structure called a translator. The pollinia and connecting translator are hidden in the style column except for a black center piece protruding from a vertical slit. Insects, during visits to the flowers, accidentally catch the spines of their feet on the translators, yanking the pollinia free (or sometimes losing a leg) and carry the pollen to other flowers, where it must be deposited on the stigmatic surface. This is no easy chance, which explains why this overspecialization of pollination mechanism results in very few fertilizations. However, one fertilization can compensate for this, because the enormous number of pollen grains in a pollinium can fertilize an enormous number of ovules in a single follicle!

ASCLEPIAS L. 1753 [Gr., *Aesculapius*, god of Medicine]. MILKWEED

1a. Corolla lobes erect or only spreading at anthesis. **A. asperula** Woodson, **19G**. [rough], CREEPING MILKWEED. Piñon-juniper. The long purple hoods curve out and up, contrasting with the large spreading greenish petals.
1b. Corolla lobes reflexed . . . . (2)

2a. Fls orange, petals usually darker than the hoods. **A. tuberosa** L. ssp **terminalis** Woodson, ORANGE MILKWEED; BUTTERFLY-WEED, **19E**. Local, near springs, ME-MN.
2b. Flowers not orange . . . . (3)

3a. Lvs linear; fls white or greenish-white . . . . (4)
3b. Lvs lanceolate, ovate or round; fls not white . . . . (5)

4a. Hoods and anther head distinctly stalked and elevated above the corolla; lvs tending to be whorled. **A. subverticillata** (Gray) Vail, WHORLED MILKWEED, **19F**. Roadsides, lower valleys.
4b. Hoods and anther head sessile; lvs not whorled. **A. engelmanniana** Woodson, **19B**. Dry shale slopes and canyonsides.

5a. Low sprawling plants of early spring. . . . . (6)
5b. Tall erect plants of midsummer . . . . (7)

6a. Lvs orbicular, glaucous; fls bicolored, with cream-colored petals and purple hoods. **A. cryptoceras** Watson [hidden horn], ADOBE MILKWEED, **PL 17**. On clay or shale knolls in the valleys, blooming in early spring, one of the crown jewels of our flora. This species bears an uncanny resemblance to *Astragalus asclepiadoides*, which has glaucous lvs reduced to a single orbicular lfl; sometimes the two spp grow side by side.
6b. Lvs ovate-lanceolate, wavy-margined; fls pale greenish tinged with purple. **A. macrosperma** Eastwood, **19A**. Peripheral, on clay soils, desert, MZ. The seeds of this small plant are indeed big, 1-1.3 cm long!

100   Asclepiadaceae (ASC)

7a. Almost glabrous; hoods 2-3 times as long as the anther head, abruptly acute or acuminate, erect or only slightly spreading. **A. hallii** Gray, **19C**. Sagebrush, central (*e.g.* Gunnison) basins.
7b. Densely tomentose, especially the infl; hoods 3-4 times as long as the anther head, long acuminate, widely spreading. **A. speciosa** Torrey, SHOWY MILKWEED, **19D**. Abundant along fencerows and irrigation ditches in the valleys.

ASPARAGACEAE—ASPARAGUS FAMILY (ASG)

This family consists of one genus, most species of which occur around the Mediterranean region and most of Africa and Asia. A few, like our vegetable, and some ornamental greenhouse species, are rather delicate plants, but many of the others are horribly spiny shrubs that make impenetrable thickets. The potted 'Asparagus Fern' is *Asparagus sprengeri*, a broad-'leaved' type, and the one used by florists in bouquets is *A. plumosus*.

ASPARAGUS L. 1753 [the name given it by Theophrastus]
   One sp, **A. officinalis** L., **20A**. Escaped and ADV along irrigation ditches in the Colorado River valley. The young shoots, which we eat, are extraordinarily different in appearance from the older, mature ones. The succulent shoots possess triangular scale lvs which are lost when the shoot elongates, shrinks in diameter, and branches to form an intricate fern-like growth. The filiform green 'lvs' are modified shoots and not true lvs at all. The plants bear bright red berries.

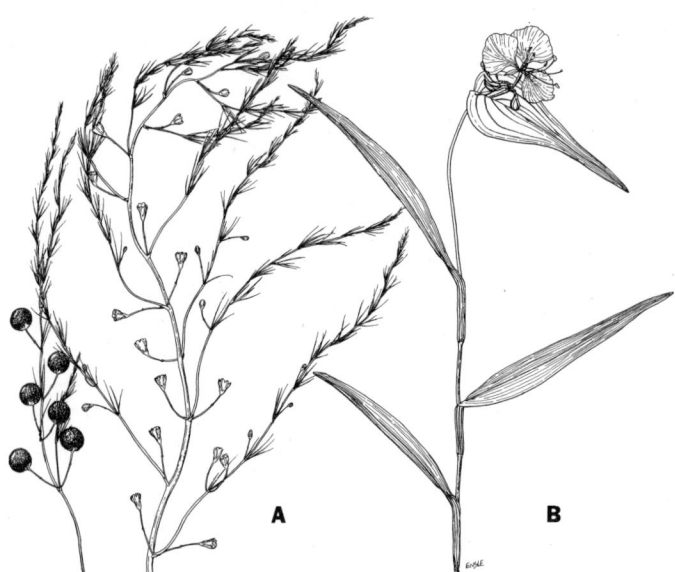

Figure 20. **A**, *Asparagus officinalis*; **B**, *Commelina dianthifolia*

ASTERACEAE/COMPOSITAE
SUNFLOWER FAMILY (AST/CMP)

Except for the cockleburs and ragweeds, which may be regarded better as a separate family, this family is easily recognized if one can think of a dandelion and a sunflower as being representative of the group. The family illustrates a very interesting evolutionary tendency: when the number of flowers in an inflorescence is enormously increased at the same time as the flower size is decreased, the visibility of the flowers to pollinating insects probably is decreased as well. This disadvantage is often compensated for in some plant families by massing the flowers into tight clusters, and setting up a division of labor among the flowers. This is usually accomplished by enlarging and changing the shape of the marginal flowers of the cluster in such a way as to cause the entire flower cluster to resemble a single flower and thus restore the visibility of the inflorescence. The composites achieve this in a variety of ways, making them a very complex and diverse family.

Note abbreviations: **pap**=pappus; **phyls**=phyllaries

1a. Fls all strap-shaped (ligulate) and perfect; juice milky. **Key A**
1b. Fls not all ligulate; ray-(ligulate) fls, when present, marginal, either with stigmas only or with neither stigmas nor stamens; juice usually watery . . . . (2)

2a. Heads with flattened and opened ray-fls . . . . (3)
2b. Heads with only disk-fls (sometimes as large as ray-fls but then distinctly radially symmetrical) . . . . (5)

3a. Rays yellow or orange (sometimes marked with purple or reddish-brown at the base) . . . . (4)
3b. Rays white, pink, purple, red, or blue. **Key B**

4a. Pap chaffy or of firm awns, or absent; receptacle chaffy, bristly, or naked. **Key C**
4b. Pap partly or wholly of numerous capillary, sometimes plumose, bristles. **Key D**

5a. Invol either a spiny bur or with phyllaries that are either fringed or spiny or in one genus very broadly rounded with a broad papery margin. **Key E**
5b. Invol not as above. . . . . (6)

6a. Pap partly or wholly of numerous capillary, sometimes plumose, bristles. **Key F**
6b. Pap absent or of scales or awns or very short, chaffy bristles or of a few low teeth, never plumose. **Key G**

KEY A

1a. Fls blue, pink, purple, or white . . . . (2)
1b. Fls yellow or orange (sometimes drying pinkish) . . . . (9)

2a. Fls sky-blue (rare mutants white), sessile on nearly lfless, stiffly branched stems; pap a crown of blunt scales. **Cichorium**, CHICORY
2b. Fls a shade of pink, lavender or purple, rarely white; pap of capillary bristles. . . . . (3)

3a. Pap bristles plumose. . . . . (4)
3b. Pap bristles simple. . . . . (5)

4a. Lvs elongate, grasslike; tall, relatively unbranched; heads large, with swollen peduncle. **Tragopogon**, SALSIFY
4b. Lvs short, inconspicuous; richly branched, wiry; heads small; peduncles not swollen. **Stephanomeria**, WIRE-LETTUCE

5a. Stems low, branched; lvs linear, bractlike, or small and runcinate . . . . (6)
5b. Stems tall, simple; lvs well-developed, often large . . . . (7)

6a. Lvs linear; invol over 1 cm long; peduncles ascending. **Lygodesmia**, SKELETON-WEED
6b. Lvs coarsely runcinate-toothed; invol less than 1 cm long; peduncles widely divergent. **Prenanthella**

7a. Lvs lanceolate, tapered to a point, entire or variously toothed or lobed; frts flattened. **Lactuca**, LETTUCE
7b. Lvs oblanceolate, rounded, very shallowly if at all toothed . . . . (8)

8a. Lvs glabrous and glaucous; heads nodding, in a raceme. **Prenanthes**
8b. Lvs hirsute; heads few, erect in an open panicle. **Chlorocrepis**, HAWKWEED

9a. Pap bristles ± united at the base and falling readily as a unit from the frt. **Malacothrix**, DESERT DANDELION
9b. Pap bristles not united, falling separately. . . . . (10)

10a. Lvs primarily basal, the stem lvs near the base of the plant and greatly reduced upwards . . . . (11)
10b. Lvs not primarily basal; stem-lvs well-developed . . . . (16)

11a. Pap of plumose bristles. **Microseris**
11b. Pap of simple bristles . . . . (12)

12a. Heads solitary on a lfless scape . . . . (13)
12b. Heads (or buds) few to numerous, rarely solitary; stem usually with one or more well-developed lvs. . . . . (14)

13a. Frt 10-ribbed or 10-nerved, without minute spines on the surface; outer phyls erect. **Agoseris**, FALSE DANDELION
13b. Frts 4-to 5-ribbed, with minute spines at least near the apex; phyls reflexed (except in a few tundra spp). **Taraxacum**, DANDELION

14a. Pap white; frts tapering upwards; phyls ± thickened at base and on the midrib. . . . . (15)
14b. Pappus brownish or reddish; frts not tapering upwards; phyls not thickened. **Chlorocrepis**, HAWKWEED

15a. Dwarf alpine rosette-plants with succulent, simple, glabrous, entire lvs and infl no longer than the lvs. **Askellia**, ALPINE HAWKSBEARD
15b. Tall plants with basal, usually hairy, often deeply pinnatifid lvs and elongate fl stem; never alpine. **Psilochenia**

16a. Lvs simple, grasslike, not toothed or divided. **Tragopogon**, SALSIFY
16b. Lvs toothed, lobed, or pinnatifid . . . . (17)

17a. Frts beaked; invol cylindric or ovoid-cylindric. **Lactuca**, LETTUCE
17b. Frts not beaked; invol turbinate or hemispheric. **Sonchus**, SOWTHISTLE

KEY B

1a. Plants stemless, the extremely short-rayed heads almost hidden in clusters of oblanceolate basal lvs crowning several stout caudices; gypsophile. **Bolophyta**
1b. Plants with distinct stems, or otherwise not as above. . . . . . . (2)

2a. [1] Lvs opposite, pinnatisect; annual; pap of 2-4 retrorsely hispid awns; rays pink. **Cosmos**
2b. Lvs alternate; annual or perennial; pap not as above . . . . (3)

3a. [2] Receptacle chaffy, at least in the middle; rays white, rarely pinkish . . . . (4)
3b. Receptacle not chaffy . . . . (6)

4a. [3] Rays few, commonly 3 to 5, short and broad, less than 5 mm long; perennial. **Achillea**, YARROW
4b. Rays numerous, mostly 5-10 mm long or more . . . . (5)

5a. [4] Native perennial with prominent rosettes and tall, few-lvd fl stems. **Hymenopappus**
5b. Introd annual weeds with leafy stems. **Anthemis**

6a. [3] Pap lacking . . . . (7)
6b. Pap present, of capillary or stouter bristles . . . . (8)

7a. [6] Lvs simple, toothed or the basal somewhat pinnatifid; perennial. **Leucanthemum**, OX-EYE DAISY
7b. Lvs finely pinnatisect; annual. **Matricaria**

8a. [6] Lvs cordate-triangular, sagittate, white beneath; stem leaves reduced to bracts. **Petasites**, SWEET COLTSFOOT
8b. Leaves not as above . . . . (9)

9a. [8] Pap (at least in the disk fls) of several to many rigid bristles; aks pubescent with 2-forked or glochidiate hairs; usually low, often stemless plants. **Townsendia**, EASTER DAISY
9b. Pap of many long capillary bristles; aks glabrous or pubescent with simple hairs . . . . (10)

10a. [9] Rays very numerous, filiform and short, scarcely surpassing the disk; annuals . . . . (11)
10b. Rays linear or broader, obviously flattened, longer than the disk fls (absent in one sp of *Machaeranthera*); usually perennials. . . (13)

11a. [10] Lvs oblanceolate, usually obtuse at the apex; pap often reddish-brown. **Erigeron** (*lonchophyllus* group)
11b. Lvs linear, acute; pap always white . . . . (12)

12a. [11] Invol 5-10 mm high; pap longer than the fls, very conspicuous in frt (powderpuff). **Brachyactis**
12b. Invol less than 5 mm high; pap not longer than the fls. **Conyza**, HORSEWEED

13a. [10] Phyls subequal or ± imbricate, often green in part but neither definitely lflike nor with chartaceous base and herbaceous green tip; style branches lanceolate or broader, acute to obtuse, 0.5 mm long or less. **Erigeron**, FLEABANE
13b. Phyllaries either subequal and the outer lflike, or more commonly imbricate, with chartaceous base and evident green tip, sometimes chartaceous throughout; style branches lanceolate or narrower, acute or acuminate, usually over 5 mm long . . . . . (14)

14a. [13] Lvs linear, less than 1 cm long; ray-fls white, rarely pink; plants much branched, forming low rounded clumps. **Leucelene**
14b. Lvs broader; rays white or colored; plants not as above. . . . . (15)

15a. [14] Lvs toothed or divided; rays either lavender or yellow. **Machaeranthera**, TANSY ASTER
15b. Lvs entire; rays never yellow . . . . (16)

16a. [15] Plants with numerous strongly woody caudices; heads large, with white rays, solitary on long stems; on seleniferous soils in the valleys. **Xylorhiza**, POISON ASTER
16b. Plants not as above . . . . (17)

17a. [16] Inner phyls dry and chartaceous, strongly keeled, in 4-5 very distinct imbricate rows; pap often brownish. **Eucephalus**
17b. Inner phyls at least with green tips, commonly chartaceous on the sides and base; pap white . . . . (18)

18a. [17] Phyls glandular-puberulent. **Virgulus campestris**
18b. Phyls not glandular . . . . (19)

19a. [18] Invol 3-4 mm high; lvs linear or oblong, short; lvs and stems generally stiff-hairy; heads very numerous. **Virgulus**

19b. Invol 5-15 mm high; lvs broader, elongate; lvs usually glabrate except above; heads relatively few. . . . . (20)

20a. [19] Stems from a woody thickened corm-like base, with 3-nerved basal lvs; aks fusiform, strigose; phyls glandular or stipitate-glandular. **Virgulus**
20b. Plants not as above. **Aster**

KEY C

1a. Deep-seated perennials with massive tap-roots and caudices, very large basal lvs and large heads . . . . (2)
1b. Annuals or perennials, but not as above . . . . (3)

2a. [1] Lvs lanceolate or lance-oblong, glutinous or hirsute. **Wyethia**, MULE'S-EARS
2b. Lvs cordate or pinnatifid, appressed hairy or hirsute-scabrous. **Balsamorhiza**, BALSAM-ROOT

3a. [1] Phyls covered with a sticky-gummy exudate . . . . (4)
3b. Phyls not sticky-gummy, but sometimes with glandular hairs . . . (6)

4a. [3] Lvs opposite; exudate confined to very narrow lines. **Flaveria**
4b. Lvs alternate; exudate generally covering the phyls . . . . (5)

5a. [4] Lvs lanceolate or oblong, commonly toothed; heads large, over 10 mm diam. **Grindelia**, GUMWEED
5b. Lvs narrowly linear, entire; heads small, less than 5 mm diam. **Gutierrezia**, SNAKEWEED

6a. [3] Receptacle chaffy or bristly . . . . (7)
6b. Receptacle naked (rarely with a few chaffy scales between the ray and disk fls) . . . . (17)

7a. [6] Receptacle bristly; rays usually bicolored, yellow and orange-red. **Gaillardia**, BLANKET-FLOWER
7b. Receptacle chaffy . . . . (8)

8a. [7] Phyls in two distinct dissimilar series; aks strongly flattened at right angles to the radius of the head . . . . (9)
8b. Phyls in one or more series, all ± similar; aks either not flattened, or flattened parallel to the radius of the head . . . . . . (11)

9a. [8] Pap of 2 to 4 firm, retrorsely barbed awns; lvs entire, pinnatifid or pinnately compound. **Bidens**, BEGGAR'S TICK
9b. Pap of two minute teeth, or lacking; lvs pinnately divided, mostly basal . . . . (10)

10a [9] Lobes of disk-fls equal, triangular, about twice as long as wide, shorter than the broad upper part of the tube. **Coreopsis**
10b. Lobes of disk-fls unequal, oblong or linear-lanceolate, more than twice as long as wide, equalling or longer than the widened upper part of the tube. **Thelesperma**

11a. [8] Phyls in a single series, the margins curved around and enclosing the disk-aks; rays very short, inconspicuous; weedy glandular annual. **Madia**, TARWEED
11b. Phyls not as above. . . . . (12)

12a. [11] Receptacle distinctly conical or elongate . . . . (13)
12b. Receptacle flat or only slightly convex. . . . . (14)

13a. [12] Receptacle elongate-cylindric; rays often partly maroon; lvs strigose, with narrow divs. **Ratibida**, PRAIRIE CONEFLOWER
13b. Receptacle merely conic; rays always pure yellow; lvs either simple or with relatively broad divs. **Rudbeckia**, BLACK-EYED SUSAN

14a. [12] Rays with well-developed styles, producing seeds; lvs mostly alternate, silvery-white pubescent beneath, coarsely toothed; annual weed. **Ximenesia**. CROWNBEARD; COW-PEN DAISY
14b. Rays lacking functional styles, not producing aks . . . . (15)

15a. [14] Pap lacking; rays up to 1.5 cm long. **Heliomeris**
15b. Pap present, although sometimes falling away when the ak is ripe; rays longer. . . . . (16)

16a. [15] Pap persistent; disk-aks strongly flattened, thin-edged. **Helianthella**, LITTLE SUNFLOWER
16b. Pap deciduous; frts only slightly compressed, plump. **Helianthus**, SUNFLOWER

17a. [6] Some lvs pinnatifid or ternately divided. . . . . (18)
17b. Lvs simple and undivided . . . . (20)

18a. [17] Basal rosette lvs with many divs; ultimate lobes with rounded tips. **Bahia**
18b. Basal rosette lvs with relatively few divs; ultimate lobes linear with pointed tips . . . . (19)

19a. [18] Phyls in two distinct series, the outer ones shorter, united at their bases to form a shallow cup; heads less than 2 cm diam; middle altitudes. **Picradenia**
19b. Phyls not in two distinct series, the outer ones not at all united; heads solitary, over 3 cm diam; tundra. **Rydbergia**, OLD-MAN-OF-THE-MOUNTAIN

20a. [17] Plants woolly-pubescent; rays broad and short, persistent and becoming papery. **Psilostrophe**, PAPER-FLOWER
20b. Rays not persistent . . . . (21)

21a. [20] Annual; lvs opposite; invol cylindric. **Flaveria**
21b. Perennial with alternate or basal lvs . . . . (22)

22a. [21] Lvs linear, basal. **Tetraneuris**
22b. Lvs not linear nor all basal. . . . . (23)

23a. [22] Desert plants with several slender woody caudices and petiolate oval-oblong, often mostly basal lvs. **Platyschkuhria**, Desert Bahia
23b. Mountain plants with a few stout caudices and sessile oblanceolate lvs . . . . (24)

24a. [23] Lvs decurrent on the stem; top of peduncle not lanate. **Helenium**, Sneezeweed
24b. Lvs not decurrent on the stem; top of peduncle lanate. **Dugaldia**, Orange Sneezeweed

KEY D

1a. True shrubs with woody stems; lvs linear. **Stenotopsis**
1b. Herbaceous, sometimes woody at the very base . . . . (2)

2a. Lvs mostly opposite. **Arnica**
2b. Lvs alternate or basal . . . . (3)

3a. Phyls narrow, in a single series except for one or two shorter ones from the base of the head . . . . (4)
3b. Phyls in two or more series, subequal or imbricate. . . . . (8)

4a. Heads turbinate, usually nodding in bud, succulent; lvs succulent, coarsely dentate, often with purplish and clasping petiole bases; roots little-branched, ropy; plants with a strong lemon scent when crushed or after drying. **Ligularia**
4b. Heads not turbinate or nodding, rarely succulent; lvs not as above; roots fibrous-branched; plants lacking lemon scent . . . . (5)

5a. Lvs progressively reduced in size upward. . . . . (6)
5b. Lvs about equally distributed along the stem or concentrated upward . . . . (7)

6a. Plants rhizomatous or with an erect caudex, with branching fibrous roots; basal lvs entire to pinnatisect but only rarely with callous denticles along the margin; relatively low, less than a half m tall. **Packera**
6b. Plants either with a short, coarse lateral or suberect rhizome or with a very short, button-like caudex, and with long unbranched fleshy fibrous roots; lvs entire to repand-dentate, often with small callous teeth on the margins. **'Senecio'**: *Lugentes* and *Integerrimi*

7a. Plants with numerous stems from the base, forming bushy clumps; lvs linear or with few linear lobes; plants of open steppe or desert. **'Senecio'**: *Suffruticosi*
7b. Plants with relatively few stems; lvs broader, entire, dentate or pinnatifid. **'Senecio'**: *Triangulares*

8a. Heads usually very small and numerous, in panicles; phyls rarely distinctly herbaceous at apex . . . . (9)

8b. Heads usually few and relatively large; phyls usually distinctly herbaceous at apex . . . . (11)

9a. Lvs linear throughout the stem . . . . (10)
9b. Lvs broader, or only uppermost linear. **Solidago**, GOLDENROD

10a. Plants low, matted, with many basal lvs. **Petradoria**, ROCK GOLDENROD
10b. Plants very tall, without basal lvs. **Euthamia**

11a. Lvs pinnatifid; phyls graduated. **Machaeranthera**, TANSY ASTER
11b. Lvs entire or merely toothed . . . . (12)

12a. Lvs not chiefly basal, the lvs always entire . . . . (13)
12b. Lvs chiefly basal; stems with reduced lvs, sometimes toothed . . . (14)

13a. Pap double, the inner of capillary bristles, the outer of paleae or short bristles; invol with narrow imbricate phyls. **Heterotheca**, GOLDEN ASTER
13b. Pap single, of capillary bristles; invol with broad herbaceous-tipped phyls. **Oreochrysum**

14a. Plants low, caespitose, with a woody caudex, stiff shiny evergreen linear-lanceolate lvs and solitary scapose heads. **Stenotus**
14b. Plants with wholly herbaceous stem, woody only in the short caudex; lvs not evergreen, neither stiff nor shiny . . . . (15)

15a. Plants with a taproot and basal lvs larger than the cauline; heads solitary or racemose on elongate peduncles; disk-fls widened upwards. **Pyrrocoma**
15b. Plants with short caudices or rhizomes; heads on short peduncles little exceeding the basal lvs; disk-fls tubular. **Tonestus**

KEY E

1a. Lvs spiny-margined, thistle-like; invol with spine-tipped or fringed phyls . . . . (2)
1b. Lvs not spiny-margined . . . . (4)

2a. Pap plumose; receptacle densely bristly. **Cirsium**, THISTLE
2b. Pap bristles simple, merely barbellate . . . . (3)

3a. Receptacle densely bristly, neither honeycombed nor obviously fleshy. **Carduus**, THISTLE
3b. Receptacle fleshy, conspicuously honeycombed on the surface, not bristly or only sparsely and shortly so. **Onopordum**, SCOTCH THISTLE

4a. Heads spherical, phyls slender, with hooked tips; lvs huge, cordate-ovate. **Arctium**, BURDOCK
4b. Heads not as above . . . . (5)

5a. Heads with the phyls fused into a single spine-studded bur. . . . (6)
5b. Heads with separate phyls, the spines, if present, along the margins . . . . (7)

6a. Burs very small, less than 1 cm, the spines not hooked. **Ambrosia**, RAGWEED
6b. Burs large, over 1 cm long, the spines hooked. **Xanthium**, COCKLEBUR

7a. Phyls very broad and rounded, with a broad papery entire margin; rhizomatous perennial with usually simply lvs. **Acroptilon**, RUSSIAN KNAPWEED
7b. Phyls either with margin spinose or fringed, or lacerate; annuals or perennials, not rhizomatous . . . . (8)

8a. Phyls brown, broad, with papery-lacerate margins. **Jacea**, BROWN KNAPWEED
8b. Phyls white, with fringed or spiny margins. . . . . (9)

9a. Phyls with a soft white fringe; lvs simple or weakly divided; fls large, blue, pink, or white. **Leucacantha**, CORNFLOWER
9b. Phyls with stiff marginal spines; lvs strongly pinnatifid. **Acosta**, KNAPWEED

KEY F

1a. True shrubs . . . . (2)
1b. Herbs or only woody at the base . . . . (5)

2a. Plants dioecious; staminate and carpellate heads on different plants. **Baccharis**, GROUNDSEL TREE
2b. Plants with perfect fls in the heads . . . . (3)

3a. Fls white or greenish; lvs scabrous. **Brickellia**
3b. Fls yellow; lvs not scabrous. . . . . (4)

4a. Phyls of the same length, in a single series (a few short ones sometimes at the base). **Tetradymia**, HORSEBRUSH
4b. Phyls imbricated, in vertical rows. **Chrysothamnus**, RABBITBRUSH

5a. Plants tending to be woody, at least at the base . . . . (6)
5b. Plants herbaceous . . . . (9)

6a. Fls yellow . . . . (7)
6b. Fls white or cream-colored. . . . . (8)

7a. Phyls in well-marked vertical files; corolla gradually expanded from the base, the tube and limb not strongly differentiated. **Chrysothamnus**, RABBITBRUSH

7b. Phyls not in well-marked vertical files; corolla limb abruptly expanded from a slender basal tube. **Isocoma**

8a. Twigs covered with a white felt; plants woody at the base, forming hemispherical compact clumps. **Macronema**
8b. Twigs naked; lvs scabrous; plants irregularly formed. **Brickellia**

9a Lvs opposite or whorled . . . . (10)
9b. Lvs alternate . . . . (12)

10a. Fls yellow. **Arnica**
10b. Fls white or purplish . . . . (11)

11a. Lvs opposite; fls white or cream-colored; invol 2-4 mm long; phyls almost nerveless. **Ageratina**
11b. Lvs whorled; fls purplish; invol about 1 cm long, phyls strongly several-nerved. **Eupatorium**, JOE PYE WEED

12a. Fls all alike, perfect and fertile . . . . (13)
12b. Outer fls of the head carpellate or, in some heads, all carpellate, or plants dioecious, with staminate and carpellate heads on different plants . . . . (19)

13a. Fls yellow . . . . (14)
13b. Fls lavender, purple, white, or cream-colored . . . . (17)

14a. Phyls in one series, elongate, equal, with a few outer ones (not in a whorl) near the base of the head . . . . (15)
14b. Phyls imbricate in two or more series (rayless forms of *Aster* and *Erigeron*), **Key B**

15a. Annual; lvs pinnatifid; phyls black-tipped; garden weed. **Senecio** (True *Senecio*)
15b. Perennial; lvs simple; phyls not black-tipped; native plants of the high mts . . . . (16)

16a. Heads turbinate, nodding, succulent; lvs not tomentose. **Ligularia**
16b. Heads erect, not succulent; lvs densely tomentose. **Packera cana**

17a. Fls white or cream-colored to pale pinkish; heads in loose panicles. **Brickellia**
17b. Fls purple . . . . (18)

18a. Heads in an elongate raceme, rarely solitary. **Liatris**, GAY- FEATHER
18b. Heads in a dense, flat-topped cluster, sometimes exceeded by the lvs. **Saussurea**

19a. Basal lvs over 10 cm long, triangular-cordate, white beneath. **Petasites**, SWEET COLTSFOOT
19b. Basal lvs not as above . . . . (20)

20a. Lvs and stems ± white-woolly; phyls with dry, scarious tips. . . (21)

20b. Lvs and stems not white-woolly; phyllaries not scarious (rayless forms of *Erigeron* and *Aster*), **Key B**

21a. Plants with tap-root, annual or perennial; heads all with outer carpellate and inner perfect fls . . . . (22)
21b. Plants fibrous-rooted, perennial, often with rhizomes or stolons, without tap-root; dioecious or nearly so, the heads on some plants all staminate or carpellate. . . . . (23)

22a. Heads very small, imbedded in wool, the clusters lfy-bracted; low annuals, seldom more than 20 cm high. **Filaginella**, CUDWEED
22b. Heads medium-sized (5 mm or more wide), not lfy-bracted; plant usually 30 cm or more high (resembling Pearly Everlasting). **Gnaphalium**, CUDWEED

23a. Basal lvs forming a conspicuous, persistent tuft; stem seldom very lfy, often with stolons or rhizomes; strictly dioecious, the staminate and carpellate plants often very different in appearance. **Antennaria**, PUSSYTOES
23b. Basal lvs soon withering, not larger than the numerous stem lvs; plants with rhizomes but never stolons; heads of carpellate plants usually with a few centrally located staminate fls. **Anaphalis**, PEARLY EVERLASTING

KEY G

1a. Phyls extremely sticky-gummy, the tips usually recurved. **Grindelia**, GUMWEED
1b. Phyls not sticky-gummy nor with recurved tips . . . . (2)

2a. Heads of two kinds, staminate and carpellate . . . . (3)
2b. Heads all alike . . . . (6)

3a. Invol of the carpellate heads burlike or nutlike, with hooked prickles, spines or tubercles; staminate invol unarmed; corollas small and inconspicuous, green . . . . (4)
3b. Invol not as above; staminate fls with disk-corollas; carpellate fls lacking corollas. . . . . (5)

4a. Carpellate invol with hooked spines. **Xanthium**, COCKLEBUR
4b. Carpellate invol with tubercles or straight spines. **Ambrosia**, RAGWEED

5a. Perennial with tall rushlike stems; lvs pinnately parted into filiform divs. **Oxytenia**
5b. Annual; lvs simple, oblong-fusiform, petioled. **Dicoria**

6a. Lvs opposite . . . . (7)
6b. Lvs alternate or basal . . . . (8)

7a. Phyls with prominent glandular spots; low weedy aromatic plants with finely pinnatifid lvs. **Dyssodia**, FETID MARIGOLD

7b. Phyls without glands; tall weeds with large cordate lvs resembling those of sunflower. **Cyclachaena**, MARSH-ELDER

8a. Lvs basal; heads solitary, scapose . . . . (9)
8b. Lvs alternate, with or without a basal rosette . . . . (10)

9a. Lvs about 1 cm diam; head erect, on a short peduncle; caespitose, with several short caudices from a long taproot. **Chamaechaenactis**
9b. Lvs much larger; head nodding, on a long peduncle; not caespitose. **Enceliopsis**

10a. Receptacle chaffy or bristly. . . . . (11)
10b. Receptacle not as above, sometimes with weak hairs . . . . . . (13)

11a. Heads large (over 1 cm), cylindric, purple-black. **Rudbeckia**, BLACK-EYED SUSAN
11b. Heads small, flat or rounded, not dark . . . . (12)

12a. Lvs oblong; heads single in the lf axils, nodding; low plants. **Iva**, POVERTY WEED
12b. Lvs triangular-ovate; heads in a panicle; tall rank weeds. **Cyclachaena**, MARSH-ELDER

13a. Pap of scales . . . . (14)
13b. Pap absent, or a minute crown of teeth. . . . . (15)

14a. Phyls with broad papery tips. **Hymenopappus**
14b. Phyls with narrow green tips. **Chaenactis**, PINCUSHION

15a. Phyls in one equal series, each enclosing an ak; linear-lvd annuals with glandular heads. **Madia**, TARWEED
15b. Phyls in several series, not individually enclosing the aks; annuals, perennials, or shrubs. . . . . (16)

16a. Heads yellow, in flat-topped clusters or solitary. . . . . (17)
16b. Heads greenish-yellow, in spikes, panicles or racemes . . . . . (19)

17a. Lvs 3-lobed, tomentose, on short shoots near the ground; heads 2-5, on long peduncles. **Sphaeromeria**
17b. Lvs pinnatisect, not chiefly basal nor tomentose. . . . . (18)

18a. Low herb less than a 0.5 m high, with pineapple odor. **Lepidotheca**, PINEAPPLE-WEED
18b. Tall herb over 1 m high, with a 'tansy' odor. **Tanacetum**, TANSY

19a. Ray-fls absent; disk fls present and fertile (with functional styles, stigmas, and ovary); shrubs. **Seriphidium**, SAGEBRUSH [note: *Artemisia bigelovii* resembles this but has heads with only 2-4 fls, one or two of these with short rays and lacking stamens].
19b. Ray-fls (small) present. (20)

20a. Disk-fls present and fertile; herbaceous or slightly woody at the base. **Artemisia**, SAGEWORT; WORMWOOD
20b. Disk-fls present but sterile, their aks aborting; herbs or shrubs
. . . . (21)

21a. Dwarf subshrub with branchlets ending in spines; fls and aks arachnoid-tomentose. **Picrothamnus**, SPINY SAGEBRUSH
21b. Herbaceous or shrubby, the branchlets not ending in spines. **Oligosporus**, TARRAGON; SAGEWORT

ACHILLEA L. 1753 [so called because its healing powers were thought to have been discovered by Achilles]. YARROW
   One sp, **A. lanulosa** Nuttall. Meadows and roadsides from sagebrush to alpine. In the tundra, a local race occurs with the phyllaries strongly margined with dark brown-black (var *alpicola* Rydberg). Very closely related but effectively isolated from the Eurasian and introd *A. millefolium*, a hexaploid (*A. lanulosa* is tetraploid).

ACOSTA Adanson 1763 [presumably for Jose d'Acosta, botanist-missionary in Peru from 1569-1588]. **Knapweed** (formerly in *Centaurea*)
1a. Phyls with a black spot; heads 1 cm high or more; stems relatively little-branched. **A. maculosa** (L.) Holub, SPOTTED KNAPWEED. To be expected with the next, and hybridizing with it. Fls usually purple.
1b. Phyls pale, not spotted; heads smaller; stems much-and widely-branched. **A. diffusa** (Lamarck) Sojak, TUMBLE KNAPWEED. Abundant ADV along highway rights-of-way on the E slope and expected to invade the W slope at any time. Fls white or lavender.

ACROPTILON Cassini 1827 [Gr., *akron*, summit, + *ptilon*, feather, alluding to the hairy tip of the inner phyls]. RUSSIAN KNAPWEED
   One sp, **A. repens** (L.) de Candolle. Abundant ADV weed. Miles of roadside are dominated by this plant in the Colorado-Gunnison R valleys (*Centaurea*).

AGERATINA Spach 1841 [dim. of *Ageratum*]
   One sp, **A. herbacea** (Gray) King & Robinson. Pine forests, S counties (ME-MT) (*Eupatorium*). The fls are white, the lvs triangular ovate and deeply crenate-dentate.

AGOSERIS Rafinesque 1819 [Gr., *aix*, goat, + *seris*, chicory]. FALSE DANDELION
1a. Annual. **A. heterophylla** (Nuttall) Greene. Sagebrush, MF.
1b. Perennial, from a heavy taproot. . . . . (2)

2a. Fls yellow, often drying pinkish or bluish; frt beak usually comparatively stout, nerved throughout, much shorter than the body (but see var. *laciniata*!). **A. glauca** (Pursh) Rafinesque. Extremely variable in leaf outline and plant size, it forms apomictic populations, each differing slightly from another. Among the better marked ones are var **laciniata** (Eaton) Smiley, with a scape less than 2 dm tall, pinnatifid lvs, and a narrow head with usually long-beaked aks, and var **dasycephala** (Torrey & Gray) Jepson, a tall, coarse plant with large woolly heads.

2b. Fls burnt-orange, often drying purplish; frt beak slender, not nerved throughout, elongate. **A. aurantiaca** (Hooker) Greene. Meadows, montane, subalpine.

AMBROSIA L. 1753 [food of the gods, a misnomer!]. RAGWEED

1a. Lvs entire to palmately 3-to 5-lobed; invol of staminate heads with black ribs. **A. trifida** L., GIANT RAGWEED. ADV ruderal weed. An important hay-fever plant.
1b. Lvs once to thrice pinnatifid; invol of staminate heads not ribbed . . . . (2)

2a. Frting invol naked or with a few very short knobs or spines. **A. psilostachya** de Candolle var **coronopifolia** (Torrey & Gray) Farwell. Indigenous ruderal weed, uncommon on the W slope.
2b. Frting invol bur-like, with long, sharp spines. . . . . (3)

3a. Lvs ovate or deltoid in outline, 1-to 3-pinnatifid, green or only slightly paler beneath; frt 1-beaked, armed with 6 to 30 flattened, straight, spreading spines 2-5 mm long; annual. **A. acanthicarpa** Hooker, SAND-BUR, **23C**. Indigenous ruderal weed.
3b. Lvs oblong in outline, interruptedly pinnatifid, with a strongly toothed or lobed rachis, green above, densely white-canescent beneath; frt 2-or 3-beaked, bearing about 4-9 thick-subulate spines 1-2 mm long, flattened only at the base; perennial from rhizomes. **A. tomentosa** Nuttall. Infrequent, sandy places, MF.

ANAPHALIS de Candolle 1838 [anagram of *Gnaphalium*]. PEARLY EVERLASTING

One sp, **A. margaritacea** (L.) Bentham & Hooker. Meadows and forest openings, montane and subalpine.

ANTENNARIA Gaertner 1791 [from the resemblance of the pap of staminate fls to the antennae of some insects]. PUSSY-TOES

Note: a very difficult group because the spp hybridize and subsequent generations often are apomictic; also, some populations may be equally divided between male plants and female plants, while in others only one sex may occur; it is useful to note this in the field. This key gives only a rough guide to the taxonomy.

1a. Heads solitary; low mat-plants; fl stems hardly higher than the lvs . . . . (2)
1b. Heads more than one to a fl stem (or if occasionally solitary, flowering stems developed). . . . . (3)

2a. Phyls strongly brown-tinged; staminate invol 5-7 mm high, carpellate 10-15 mm high with narrow, taper-pointed phyls; plants with well-developed caudices; fibrous roots not particularly conspicuous. **A. dimorpha** (Nuttall) Torrey & Gray. Sagebrush zone. Very unlike any other sp, possibly deserving generic recognition.

2b. Phyls white-tomentose; carpellate invol smaller; plants with numerous wiry fibrous roots. **A. rosulata** Rydberg. Sagebrush flats, S counties.

3a. Not mat-forming, never with stolons. . . . . (4)
3b. Mat-forming, usually with leafy stolons . . . . (5)

4a. Invol scarious to the base, glabrous or nearly so; basal lvs linear-oblanceolate, middle cauline lvs linear. **A. luzuloides** Torrey & Gray. Meadows, RT.
4b. Invol with a densely pubescent lower portion, not at all scarious below; lvs with prominent parallel venation. **A. pulcherrima** (Hooker) Greene ssp **anaphaloides** (Rydberg) Weber. Dry meadows, sagebrush and open forests.

5a. Lvs green above. **A. marginata** Greene. Southern counties, AA-MZ, in ponderosa pine and piñon pine woods. Greene called this *marginata* because the lvs curl slightly at the margins, creating a narrow white rim around the green lf surface.
5b. Lvs white-tomentose on both sides . . . . (6)

6a. Terminal scarious part of phyls discolored or brownish to dirty blackish-green; high altitudes. . . . . (7)
6b. Terminal part of phyls white, yellowish or pink. . . . . (9)

7a. Plant glandular (easily seen on the phyls), with citronella odor when fresh; lvs very short and broad. **A. aromatica** Evert. Limestone tundra, Saguache Range.
7b. Not glandular, odorless; lvs usually oblanceolate . . . . (8)

8a. Outer phyls pointed, distinctly brown but not blackish, paler at the tip; underground caudices well-developed, elongate and branched; stems often 1 dm tall or more, typically with loose elongate underground stems. **A. umbrinella** Rydberg. Dry subalpine meadows, rarely alpine.
8b. Outer phyls blunt, blackish-green to the apex; underground branching relatively slight; plants usually less than 1 dm tall, often dwarfed, usually lacking extensive underground parts. **A. media** Greene (incorrectly referred to the European *A. alpina*).

9a. Phyls with a conspicuous dark spot at the base of the scarious portion; basal lvs narrowly oblanceolate. **A. corymbosa** Nelson. Common, moist meadows and glades.
9b. Phyls not as above; lvs rounded obovate or fusiform. . . . . . (10)

10a. Phyls distinctly yellow-greenish; infl and upper stem lvs glandular; basal lvs small, fusiform. **A. microphylla** Rydberg. Sagebrush, forest openings.
10b. Phyls pink or white; infl and upper stem lvs not glandular; basal lvs usually oblanceolate, rounded at apex. . . . . (11)

11a. Heads large, invol 7-11 mm high, the dry carpellate corollas 5-8 mm long; staminate plants very rare. **A. parvifolia** Nuttall. Common in open montane forests.
11b. Heads smaller, invol 4-6 mm high, the dry carpellate corollas less than 5 mm long; sexes about equally represented. **A. rosea** Greene. Abundant everywhere.

ANTHEMIS L. 1753 [the ancient name]. CHAMOMILE

1a. Receptacular chaff stiff and awnlike, restricted to the center (upper part) of the conic invol; usually branched above the base. **A. cotula** L. ADV ruderal weed.
1b. Receptacular chaff flat, lanceolate, subtending most of the disk florets; branched from the base and spreading on the ground. **A. arvensis** L. ADV ruderal weed, GN.

ARCTIUM L. 1753 [Gr., *arctos*, a bear, alluding to the shaggy invol]. BURDOCK
1a. Heads racemosely arranged, 1.5-2.5 cm wide, short-pedunculate or sessile. **A. minus** (Hill) Bernhardi, **23I**. ADV ruderal weed, low and middle altitudes.
1b. Heads in flat-topped corymbs, 2.5-4 cm wide, long-pedunculate. **A. lappa** L. ADV ruderal weed, ME, OR.

ARNICA L. 1753 [origin of name unknown]

1a. Heads rayless, nodding in bud. **A. parryi** Gray. Meadows and open forests, middle altitudes.
1b. Heads with rays. . . . . (2)

2a. Stems relatively lfy, the cauline lvs mostly 5-12 pairs, no basal rosettes . . . . (3)
2b. Stems less lfy, the cauline lvs mostly 2-4 pairs exclusive of the basal rosette (if present), often more or less reduced in size upwards . . . . (4)

3a. Phyls obtuse or merely acutish, bearing a tuft of hairs at the tip or just within it; tube of disk-fls 3-4.5 mm long. **A. chamissonis** Lessing ssp **foliosa** (Nuttall) Maguire. Common in montane meadows.
3b. Phyls sharply acute, the tip not more hairy than the body; tube of disk-fls 2-3 mm long. **A. longifolia** Eaton. Subalpine talus slopes.

4a. Pap subplumose, brownish. **A. mollis** Hooker. Subalpine spruce-fir forests.
4b. Pap only barbellate, white . . . . (5)

5a. Lvs ovate, at least those of the sterile rosettes with petioles equalling the blades; rhizomes naked or clothed with overlapping scales and lf-bases only near the tip, typically 3-branched near the apex . . . . (6)
5b. Lvs lanceolate, sessile or with petioles shorter than the blades;

rhizomes clothed with overlapping scales and lf-bases, unbranched near the apex . . . . (7)

6a. Stem lvs sessile; lvs of basal rosettes narrowly ovate; sparingly hairy, often quite green and glabrous; basal lvs not cordate but ovate-truncate; aks brown. **A. latifolia** Bongard. Moist subalpine forests. A sexual species.
6b. Stem lvs petiolate; lvs of basal rosettes cordate or broadly ovate; hairy, the invol usually rather densely so; aks dark gray. **A. cordifolia** Hooker. Dry forests, widely distributed from foothills to subalpine. A completely apomictic species with no known sexual populations. Its great variability is due to many slightly different apomictic clones.

7a. Old lf-bases at base of stem with tufts of tawny hairs in their axils; lower stem-lvs petioled; plants of montane meadows. **A. fulgens** Pursh. Infrequent on W slope.
7b. Old lf-bases at base of stem lacking tufts of tawny hairs; lower stem-lvs sessile; subalpine or alpine sp. . . . . (8)

8a. Phyllaries densely pilose from base to apex; lvs narrowly lanceolate, gray-pubescent; heads usually solitary. **A. alpina** (L.) Olin ssp **tomentosa** (Macoun) Maguire. Rare, known from a single alpine locality, PT.
8b. Phyllaries sparsely pilose, mostly at the base; lvs elliptic-lanceolate, green; heads usually 3. **A. rydbergii** Greene. Common on rocky slopes near timberline.

ARTEMISIA L. 1753 [ancient name in memory of *Artemisia*, wife of *Mausolus*, who was buried in 353 B.C. in the first 'mausoleum']. SAGEWORT, WORMWOOD

1a. Plant with finely-dissected silvery-hairy lvs, densely massed along long offshoots which may be slightly woody near the base; fl spikes slender, erect. **A. frigida** Willdenow [cold], SILVER SAGE. Abundant in dry meadows and hillsides.
1b. Not as above . . . . (2)

2a. True shrubs, woody not only at the very base, the annual growth not dying back to the ground each year; lvs 3-notched, resembling woody sagebrushes (*Seriphidium*) but with 1-2 short ray-fls. **A. bigelovii** Gray
2b. Herbaceous plants . . . . (3)

3a. Dwarf alpines, hardly more than 10 cm high, the lvs pinnatisect, mostly basal; phyls conspicuously dark-bordered; receptacle long-hairy between the fls . . . . (4)
3b. Taller plants, if alpine, the receptacle not hairy between the fls
. . . . (5)

4a. Heads 5 to 25; phyls with very broad dark margin, appearing uniformly dark; lvs mostly twice pinnatifid (pinnatifid with the primary divisions divided again). **A. scopulorum** Gray. Common, alpine and subalpine.

4b. Heads 1 to 4; phyls with a narrow distinct dark margin, appearing bicolored; lvs once pinnatifid or cleft. **A. pattersonii** Gray. Tundra, Rocky Mt. Nat. Park.

5a. With taproots or short woody caudices . . . . (6)
5b. With well-developed rhizomes. . . . . (12)

6a. Stem lvs not reduced in size upwards; basal rosettes withering by fl time . . . . (7)
6b. Stem lvs reduced in size upwards; basal rosettes usually still evident at fl time . . . . (8)

7a. Biennial; lvs green, pinnatisect, the segs with sharp points; rachis with short segs between the principal ones. **A. biennis** Willdenow. ADV in disturbed forest sites such as logging roads, check dams, campgrounds.
7b. Perennial; lvs silvery-hairy, pinnatisect with rounded lobes. **A. absinthium** L., ABSINTHE. ADV., Gunnison Basin.

8a. Heads in a raceme, large, nodding; phyls prominently dark-margined; lvs green and glabrate or gray-hairy. **A. arctica** Lessing ssp **saxicola** (Rydberg) Hultén. Rocky alpine slopes and meadows.
8b. Heads in spikes or panicles, small, erect; phyls not prominently dark-margined; lvs usually very hairy . . . . (9)

9a. Lf-lobes rounded at the apex; infl secund. **A. franserioides** Greene. Talus slopes, cliffs, and openings in spruce-fir forests. Pleasantly fragrant with a sweet heavy odor.
9b. Lf-lobes, or lvs (if undivided) acute; infl not secund. . . . . . (10)

10a. Lvs silky-pubescent to glabrous, never woolly or tomentose; plants with distinct basal lvs. **A. laciniata** Willdenow ssp **parryi** (Gray) Weber. Cobbly creek margins in the Creede area and possibly crossing the divide, resembling a very tall *A. arctica* with distinctly pinnately compound lvs with acute lfls and nodding heads (*A. parryi*). *A. franserioides* has rounded leaflets and lvs tomentose beneath.
10b. Lvs tomentose or woolly, especially beneath; plants lacking differentiated basal lvs . . . . (11)

11a. Lvs green, glandular; main lvs divided into slender elongated or linear-filiform lobes 0.5-1.0 mm wide. **A. ludoviciana** Nuttall ssp **incompta** (Nuttall) Keck. Rocky slopes and cliffs, middle altitudes. One of the more well marked races.
11b. Lvs white, at least underneath; main lvs entire, toothed or divided into broader segs. (12)

12a. Invol small (1-2 mm wide and high), densely tomentose, as the lvs; phyls not strongly hyaline-margined; corollas yellow; lvs ranging from simple, entire, to toothed and lobed or very deeply dissected. **A. ludoviciana** Nuttall. Abundant except in alpine and desert-steppe; the races are legion, and impossible to place into pigeonholes, and their geography becomes clouded by mass movement of soil and seeds by man.

12b. Invol larger (2-3 X 3-4 mm), almost glabrous, with very wide hyaline, often purplish-margined phyls; corollas also purplish; lvs always deeply incised, with narrow, serrate lobes, strongly bicolored, rarely almost green on both surfaces. **A. michauxiana** Besser. Scree and talus slopes, montane and subalpine.

ASKELLIA Weber 1984 [for Áskell Löve, Icelandic botanist]. ALPINE HAWKSBEARD

One sp, **Askellia nana** (Richardson) Weber, PL 56. A dwarf, fleshy, glabrous alpine with slender roots, growing on unstable scree slopes; lvs oval, often lacking lobes. Infrequent, high peaks (*Crepis*).

ASTER L. 1753 [Gr., *aster*, a star]

The nomenclature of 'asters' is now in a state of flux. If one accepts the divisions that are being made of *Aster*, then there are no members of the genus in America, the type species of *Aster* belonging to an exclusively Eurasian group. Our species may all become *Symphyotrichum*.

1a. Dwarf tundra plant not over 20 cm tall, with the habit of a low *Erigeron*; lvs mostly basal, the stem-lvs progressively reduced; ray-fls characteristically rolling back after flowering. **A. alpinus** L. var **vierhapperi** (Onno) Cronquist. Very rare, collected only once, a century ago, on Berthoud Pass.
1b. Lvs not mostly basal, or not dwarf tundra plants . . . . (2)

2a. Invol and ultimate branchlets glandular-pubescent; lvs elongate-linear, glaucous, succulent, 1-nerved. **A. pauciflorus** Nuttall, anomalous even among American asters and recently segregated as the genus *Almutaster pauciflora* (Nuttall) Löve. Alkaline swales, interior basins.
2b. Invol and branches not glandular-pubescent . . . . (3)

3a. Very slender; lvs linear, 2-5 mm wide; rhizomes seldom elongate, over 2 mm thick. **A. junciformis** Rydberg. Cold bogs, mt parks, PA.
3b. Plants not as above . . . . (4)

4a. Pubescence of stem and branchlets occurring in distinct lines decurrent from the lf-bases. **A. hesperius** Gray. A late-summer aster of wet meadows and ditches.
4b. Pubescence of stem and branchlets not in lines . . . . (5)

5a. Invol strongly graduated, at least the outer ones obtuse, markedly shorter than the inner and never foliaceous, instead, with strongly thickened pale cartilaginous margins and base. **A. ascendens** Lindley. Abundant weedy sp of roadsides and gravelly flats in the mts. Another very tall, rhizomatous clump-forming sp of alkaline river-flats keys to this but evidently is *A. orthophyllus* Greene, which is possibly an amphidiploid sp derived from the cross, *A. ascendens* x *A. hesperius*.

5b. Invol not strongly graduated, or if so then the phyls acute (if obtuse, they are enlarged and foliaceous). . . . . (6)

6a. Glabrous except for short lines of hairs in the infl; lvs glaucous, entire or toothed. **A. laevis** L. var **geyeri** Gray. Common montane sp of late summer.
6b. Variously pubescent, not glaucous. . . . . (7)

7a. Lvs and bracts relatively small and narrow, the middle cauline lvs mostly less than 1 cm wide and less than 7 times as long as wide; phyls oblong, the outer ones never enlarged and foliaceous. **A. occidentalis** (Nuttall) Torrey & Gray. Open, often alkaline meadows.
7b. Lvs and bracts relatively large; middle cauline lvs mostly over 1 cm wide and less than 7 times as long as wide; some of the outer bracts enlarged and lflike. **A. foliaceus** Lindley. Extremely variable, ranging from dwarf plants with very showy heads, to tall plants with medium-sized ones, abundant, montane and subalpine.

BACCHARIS L. 1753 [ancient name of a shrub dedicated to Bacchus]. GROUNDSEL-TREE

One sp, **B. salicina** Torrey & Gray. Tall shrub of floodplains, SW counties. Lvs oblong or elliptic; invol pale, up to 1 cm high and wide.

BAHIA Lagasca 1816 [for Concepción Bay, Chile, where the first sp was collected]

One sp, **B. dissecta** (Gray) Britton. Common in bare gravelly soil, mostly along roadsides in the canyons.

BALSAMORHIZA Nuttall 1840. BALSAM-ROOT
1a. Lvs cordate, entire, appressed silvery-pubescent; root massive beneath several ascending woody caudices; scapes numerous. **B. sagittata** (Pursh) Nuttall, **PL 25**. Abundant in deep soils, sagebrush. Very long-lived, not flowering before the fourth or fifth year and continuing for over 50 years. Hybridization occurs where this comes in contact with the next. Evidence is seen in intermediate lf shapes, teeth and irregular lobing.
1b. Lvs deeply pinnatifid, green and hirsute-scabrous; root and caudices comparatively slender. **B. hispidula** Sharp. Thin rocky soils of desert hills, MF, RB.

BIDENS L. 1753 [Lat. *bidens*, two-toothed, alluding to the pappus]. BEGGAR'S TICK
1a. Lvs with many narrow divs. **B. tenuisecta** Gray. Indigenous weedy roadside plant, S counties.
1b. Lvs with a few broad, toothed divs. **B. frondosa** L., 23E. Infrequent ADV weed in the valley wetlands, ME.

BOLOPHYTA Nuttall 1840 [Gr., *bolus*, lump, clod, + *phyton*, plant]

One sp, **B. ligulata** (Jones) Weber. END on gypsum ridges, MF (*Parthenium*). An inconspicuous plant forming cushions of oblanceolate rosettes from thick woody caudices, the heads hidden among the lf-bases and the rays extremely short (1-2 mm). It commonly occurs along with a similar dwarf, *Eriogonum tumulosum*.

BRACHYACTIS Ledebour 1845 [Gr., *brachy*, short, + *aktis*, ray]
1a. Rays about 2 mm long, purplish, surpassing the short styles; phyls obtuse or acutish. **B. frondosa** (Nuttall) Gray. Alkaline swales in the valleys, MF (*Aster*).
1b. Ray-fls tubular, shorter than the styles, virtually absent; phyls distinctly acute. **B. ciliata** Ledebour ssp **angusta** (Lindley.) A. Jones. Similar sites (*Aster*).

BRICKELLIA Elliott 1823 [for Dr. John Brickell, American colonial naturalist]
1a. Lvs triangular-ovate, regularly crenate or serrate dentate, the largest over 2 cm long. . . . . (2)
1b. Lvs linear, elliptic, oblong or, if ovate, smaller, entire or irregularly toothed . . . . (3)

2a. Lvs crenate; heads small (not over 1 cm high), erect. **B. californica** (Torrey & Gray) Gray. Dry rocky canyonsides.
2b. Lvs coarsely and deeply serrate-dentate; heads over 1 cm high, nodding. **B. grandiflora** (Hooker) Nuttall. Common on canyonsides, but going higher in the mts than the last.

3a. Pap plumose; strictly herbaceous. **B. rosmarinifolia** (Ventenat) Weber ssp **chlorolepis** (Wooton & Standley) Weber (*Kuhnia chlorolepis*). Dry meadows in the lowlands.
3b. Pap simple; plants shrubby or semi-woody . . . . (4)

4a. Lvs elongate-linear; tall, bushy-branched shrubs with very white stems. **B. longifolia** Watson. Dry canyonsides, piñon-juniper, ME-MN.
4b. Lvs ovate to elliptic or oblong; low semi-woody herbs . . . . . . (5)

5a. Lvs ovate, entire or few-toothed, ranging from only a few mm to about 2 cm long, very scabrous. **B. microphylla** (Nuttall) Gray ssp **scabra** (Gray) Weber (*B. scabra*). Piñon-juniper and rimrock.
5b. Lvs elliptic or oblong, almost or quite entire . . . . (6)

6a. Heads about 9-fld, solitary or few, terminal or from the upper axils. **B. brachyphylla** Gray. Piñon-juniper, SW counties, MZ-AA.
6b. Heads 40-50-fld, more numerous, on diverging peduncles from the upper lf-axils. **B. oblongifolia** Nuttall. Piñon-juniper, Colorado R Valley southward.

CARDUUS L. 1753 [the ancient Lat. name]. THISTLE
1a. Stem slender; invol 1-1.5 cm high and wide, arachnoid; phyls slender, the outer not conspicuously spreading or reflexed. **C. acanthoides** L. ADV. Frequent roadside weed in some of the mt valleys, PT, EA.
1b. Stem stout; invol over 2 cm wide and high, glabrous; phyls broad and stout, the outer conspicuously spreading-reflexed. **C. nutans** L. ssp **macrolepis** (Peterman) Kazmi, MUSK THISTLE. ADV.

Abundant weed in overgrazed or neglected fields and roadsides. In *Carduus* and *Onopordum*, the entire length of the stem is covered by the decurrent lf-bases.

CHAENACTIS de Candolle 1836 [from Gr., *chaino*, gaping, + *aktis*, ray]. PINCUSHION
1a. Ephemeral annual. **C. stevioides** Hooker & Arnott. Desert soils in the warm river valleys, early spring.
1b. Biennial or perennial . . . . (2)

2a. Biennial with lfy stem terminating in a flat-topped infl of several heads; pap scales 8 to 14; plants usually 2 dm high or more. **C. douglasii** (Hooker) Hooker & Arnott. Common in dry open piñon-juniper and oak woods.
2b. Perennial with numerous slender caudices; stem with one, rarely up to three heads; lvs mostly basal; pap scales 4 to 6. **C. alpina** (Gray) Jones. Alpine screes.

CHAMAECHAENACTIS Rydberg 1906 [Gr., *chamae*, dwarf, + *Chaenactis*]
One sp, **C. scaposa** (Eastwood) Rydberg, **PL 54**. Infrequent or rare in piñon-juniper and desert-steppe, W counties.

CHLOROCREPIS Grisebach 1853 [Gr., *chloros*, green, + *Crepis*, a genus]. HAWKWEED (formerly incl in *Hieracium*)
1a. Lvs glabrous (with many minute stalked glands) and glaucous; infl a loose raceme; invol glandular-pubescent with black hairs. **C. tristis** (Willdenow) Löve & Löve ssp **gracilis** (Hooker) Weber. Subalpine spruce-fir forests (*H. gracile*).
1b. Lvs with long stiffish hairs; infl a cyme or panicle of heads; invol not glandular-pubescent. . . . . (2)

2a. Fls white; heads numerous (over 20); invol 8-10 mm high; ak 3 mm long excluding pap; phyls with a prominent dark median line. **C. albiflora** (Hooker) Weber. Common in dry forested montane canyons.
2b. Fls yellow; heads few (less than 10); invol 12-15 mm high; ak 6 mm long; phyls green, without a dark median line. **C. fendleri** (Schultz-Bipontinus) Weber. Infrequent, montane and subalpine.

CHRYSOTHAMNUS Nuttall 1840 [Gr., *chrysos*, gold, + *thamnos*, bush]. RABBITBRUSH
1a. Twigs covered with a felt-like tomentum (scratch with fingernail will remove it) . . . . (2)
1b. Twigs glabrous or puberulent, not tomentose . . . . (3)

2a. Heads in lfy spike-like or racemose clusters, these sometimes branching to form panicles; outer phyls often prolonged into slender herbaceous tips or appendages. **C. parryi** (Gray) Greene. Upper montane, subalpine, with sagebrush, and open forests.
2b. Heads cymose at the ends of the branches; infl sometimes compound and elongated; phyls obtuse to acute, outer ones shortened and without herbaceous tip. **C. nauseosus** (Pallas) Britton,

PL 11. The most abundant and showy species in the area, represented by several races, the most common of which is ssp **graveolens**, a tall gray-leaved shrub especially common in deep soils or arroyos, along with big sagebrush. ssp **leiospermus** is a dwarf plant less than 3 dm tall, MF, MZ.

3a. Heads 9-13 mm high; phyls strongly keeled, in very conspicuous vertical ranks; lvs oblanceolate to spatulate; rarely over 30 cm tall. **C. depressus** Nuttall. Low shrub, open slopes, replacing sagebrush. Abundant in the Gunnison Basin.

3b. Heads 5-8 mm high; phyls not strongly keeled, the vertical rows not pronounced; lvs and plants various . . . . (4)

4a. Ak glabrous or nearly so, longitudinally 10-striate, 5 mm long. **C. vaseyi** (Gray) Greene. S counties.

4b. Ak usually densely hairy, or at least never striate, 3-4 mm long . . . . (5)

5a. Phyls attenuate or abruptly narrowed to a subulate tip; corollas 4.0-4.5 mm long; lvs very narrow (1.2 mm). **C. greenei** (Gray) Greene. Known in our area only from MZ.

5b. Phyls obtuse or acute; corollas 4.5-7.0 mm long; lvs broader. . . . (6)

6a. Very tall (over 1 m high), relatively unbranched plants of riparian sites; lvs 5 mm wide or more, elongate and hardly twisted. **C. linifolius** Greene [flax-leaved]. Common on floodplains in canyon country.

6b. Lower, bushy-branched plants of dry desert-steppe and sagebrush-piñon-juniper; lvs narrower, typically twisted. **C. viscidiflorus** (Hooker) Nuttall [sticky-flowered] Abundant throughout, with several races.

CICHORIUM L. 1753 [altered from the Arabian name for the plant]. CHICORY

One sp, **C. intybus** L. ADV locally estab as a ruderal weed. The roasted roots are a coffee substitute.

CIRSIUM Miller 1754 [Gr., *cirsos*, a swollen vein, for which the thistle was considered a remedy]. THISTLE

1a. Perennial reproducing by underground rhizomes (growing in patches often many meters across); heads usually less than 3 cm high; plants dioecious . . . . (2)

1b. Biennials with taproots (stems single or few together); heads usually more than 3 cm high; flowers perfect . . . . (3)

2a. Lvs and heads glabrous. **C. arvense** (L.) Scopoli [of cult fields], CANADA THISTLE. ADV, abundant noxious weed of cult ground.

2b. Lvs strongly tomentose beneath; heads somewhat larger than in the last. **C. incanum** (Gmelin) Fischer [hoary]. ADV, probably widespread on the W slope but known thus far from GN. Introd from SW Asia and SE Europe.

3a. Lvs beset on the upper surface with small sharp spines; decurrent lf-bases extending as narrow wings from node to node; heads conspicuously cobwebby-pubescent. **C. vulgare** (Savi) Tenore, BULL THISTLE. ADV pasture weed.
3b. Lvs not spiny above, never decurrent all the way from node to node. . . . . (4)

4a. Phyls and/or their spines reflexed or spreading . . . . (5)
4b. Phyls and spines straight, not reflexed nor widely spreading . . (11)

5a. Cauline lvs not at all decurrent . . . . (6)
5b. Cauline lvs decurrent . . . . (8)

6a. Spines of phyls about 2 mm long, often with an erose fringe at the sides, or the tips erose and without spines. **C. perplexans** (Rydberg) Petrak. END, adobe hills, Colorado and Gunnison R valleys (*C. vernale*).
6b. Spines of phyls over 2 mm long, never with an erose fringe at the tip or sides . . . . (7)

7a. Longest phyl spines about 5 mm; heads with purple fls. **C. undulatum** (Pursh) Sprengel. Common on roadsides.
7b. Longest phyl spines 3 mm long; heads white or very pale purplish. **C. tracyi** (Rydberg) Petrak. Common, mostly S of the Colorado R.

8a. Heads with purple fls . . . . (9)
8b. Heads with white or very pale purplish fls . . . . (10)

9a. Plant completely white-tomentose; lvs with the lobes directed forward and twisted, not pressing flat; heads small, 2 cm or less high; longest phyl spines about 3 mm. **C. barnebyi** Welsh & Neese. Dry shale slopes of Piceance Basin, GF, RB.
9b. Lvs less tomentose above than below, the lobes not twisted; heads larger with longer spines. **C. ochrocentrum** Gray. An E slope sp occurring in Middle Park.

10a. Invol conspicuously floccose with long cobwebby hairs; lower phyls strongly reflexed, spines over 5 mm long. **C. neomexicanum** Gray. Canyonsides, W counties.
10b. Invol not conspicuously floccose; lower phyls not strongly reflexed, spines less than 5 mm long. **C. canescens** Nuttall. An E plains sp found in Middle Park.

11a. Fls with lobes as long as or longer than the corolla throat; invol cylindric (in life, not so obvious after pressing) . . . . . (12)
11b. Fls with lobes shorter than the corolla throat; heads spherical, or so densely crowded that the shape is not apparent. . . . . . (13)

12a. Lvs glabrous, pinnatifid with narrow divisions, strongly decurrent, the uppermost reduced mostly to spines; heads ± hidden in the mass of spines. **C. ownbeyi** Welsh. Canyonsides, W MF.

12b. Lvs tomentose at least beneath, rarely almost glabrous, with relatively broad lobes; heads exserted from the upper lvs; heads more than 2 cm high; longest phyl spines 7-8 mm long. **C. calcareum** (Jones) Wooton & Standley. Rimrock areas, piñon-juniper, ME-MZ.

13a. Inner phyls with dilated, fringed tips, lacking terminal spine. **C. centaureae** (Rydberg) Schumann. Common in forests in the mountains near the Continental Divide.

13b. Inner phyllaries tipped with a spine, sometimes ciliate-fringed along the sides . . . . (14)

14a. Heads in loose clusters, not strongly arachnoid-pubescent, rarely much exceeded by the lvs; infl usually branched. **C. eatonii** (Gray) Robinson. Montane forests and meadows. Fls usually ochroleucous.

14b. Heads mostly congested in terminal clusters or spicate along the stem (if in loose branched infl the heads exceeded by the lvs and strongly arachnoid-pubescent with long multicellular hairs) . . . . (15)

15a. Heads not conspicuously arachnoid-pubescent with long multicellular hairs, only the phyl margins cottony at best, the inner ones with flattened spines; plants either acaulescent or tall. **C. coloradense** (Rydberg) Cockerell. Abundant, montane meadows.

15b. Heads conspicuously arachnoid-pubescent with long multicellular hairs; inner phyllaries with terete spines . . . . (16)

16a. Outer phyls with spinulose-ciliate margins as well as stout terminal spines; fls yellow. **C. parryi** (Gray) Petrak. Common in moist montane meadows.

16b. Outer phyls without spinulose-ciliate margins; fls yellow or purplish to purple . . . . (17)

17a. Heads congested in massive, heavy, commonly nodding terminal clusters or spikes; fls either yellow (N populations) or pale purplish (S pops); upper subalpine and lower alpine. **C. scopulorum** (Greene) Cockerell. Common along the Continental Divide.

17b. Heads in narrow, erect spikes; fls deep purple; subalpine and upper montane. **C. hesperium** (Eastwood) Petrak [for Mount Hesperus], PL 61. Common, the San Juan Mts.

CONYZA Lessing 1832 [Gr., *konops*, a flea, hence fleabane]. HORSE-WEED

1a. Lvs linear, entire, neither arachnoid-tomentose nor minutely glandular; invol about 3 mm high; heads very numerous, in diffuse panicles. **C. canadensis** (L.) Cronquist. ADV abundant roadside and field weed.

1b. Lvs oblanceolate, coarsely toothed, with minute golden glandular hairs in addition to the tomentum; upper stems arachnoid-tomentose; heads 3.5-5.0 mm high, on short axillary shoots or in somewhat pyramidal branched panicles. . . . . (2)

2a. Very narrow ray-fls present, about as long as the pap; pap off-white or tawny; heads 4-5 mm high. **C. schiedeana** (Lessing) Cronquist. Infrequent in pine forests, LP.
2b. Ray-fls absent; plants tending to be dioecious; pap white; heads 3.0-3.5 mm high. **C. coulteri** Gray. Infrequent in the foothills on the E slope, not yet seen but expected on the W slope in pine forests.

COREOPSIS L. 1753 [Gr., *coris*, a bug, + *opsis*, appearance, from the form of the ak]

One sp, **C. tinctoria** Nuttall. ADV, waste places in the Colorado R Valley, ME.

COSMOS Cavanilles 1791 [Gr., *cosmos*, a decoration]

One sp, **C. parviflorus** (Jacquin) Humboldt, Bonpland & Kunth. A somewhat weedy plant known from AA, with pink-purple rays, smaller-headed than the common cult garden sp, *C. bipinnatus* Cavanilles.

CYCLACHAENA Fresenius 1838 [Gr., *kyklos*, circle, + *achaenia*, akene, alluding to the rounded obovate ak]. MARSH-ELDER

One sp, **C. xanthifolia** (Nuttall) Fresenius [with lvs like *Xanthium*]. Tall weed with triangular-ovate lvs and greenish heads in a terminal panicle. Phyls 10, the five outer green, the five inner more membranous, partly enfolding the aks (*Iva*).

DICORIA Torrey & Gray 1859 [Gr., *di*, two, + *coreo*, a bug, from the form of the akenes]

One sp, **D. brandegei** Gray, said to be found along the San Juan River between McElmo Canyon and Recapture Creek. It is questionable whether this was in Colorado or Utah.

DUGALDIA Cassini 1828 [for Dugald Stewart, Scottish philosopher, 1753-1828]. ORANGE SNEEZEWEED

One sp, **D. hoopesii** (Gray) Rydberg. Tall, coarse lfy plant with orange-yellow ray-fls, common in the aspen zone. Very poisonous to livestock, particularly sheep, causing what is called the 'spewing sickness' (*Helenium*).

DYSSODIA Cavanilles 1803 [Gr., *dysodia*, stench]. FETID MARIGOLD

One sp, **D. papposa** (Ventenat) Hitchcock. Native roadside weed, S counties. The glandular spots on the phyllaries are distinctive.

ENCELIOPSIS Nelson 1909 [for a resemblance to the genus *Encelia*]

One sp, **E. nutans** Eastwood, locally abundant on adobe soils. Easily recognized by the single large rayless head on a tall scape, and the broad orbicular basal lvs. Just across the state line in Utah a second sp, *E. nudicaulis*, occurs. This sp has silvery-silky pubescence and the heads have conspicuous rays. One might mistake it for *Balsamorhiza sagittata* but the lvs are not at all cordate.

ERIGERON L. 1753 [Gr., *eri*, early, + *geron*, old man, ancient name for an early-blooming hairy plant]. FLEABANE; DAISY
Note: The type species of *Erigeron* is *E. acre*. Our *E. elongatus* and *E. lonchophyllus* are true erigerons. Most other American spp do not belong to *Erigeron* but a name has not been proposed for them.

1a. At least some of the lvs 3-toothed, ternately lobed or pinnatifid . . . . (2)
1b. Lvs entire . . . . (6)

2a. [1] Lvs oblanceolate, narrowed to the base without a distinct petiole, at least some of them 3-toothed at the apex; invol woolly-villous at the base. **E. lanatus** Hooker [woolly]. Very local on alpine scree slopes, Elk Mts.
2b. Lvs distinctly petiolate and lobed; invol not woolly-villous . . . . (3)

3a. [2] Caudices numerous, slender and elongate; lvs flabellate, the blade with three broad rounded lobes. **E. vagus** Payson [wandering, allusion to rock slides]. Alpine scree slopes. The long, elastic caudices are especially adapted to shifting talus.
3b. Caudices few, stout, erect; lvs with slender divs. . . . . (4)

4a. [3] Lvs 3-lobed or repeatedly ternately-lobed, hirsute. **E. compositus** Pursh. Gravelly soil, middle elevations; rays may be white or violet; rayless forms are common.
4b. Lvs pinnately lobed, glabrous except for cilia along the petioles . . . . (5)

5a. [4] Rays conspicuous, violet; lvs with many pinnatifid divs. **E. pinnatisectus** (Gray) Nelson. Rocky tundra.
5b. Rays absent; lvs with few divs. **E. mancus** Rydberg [crippled]. La Sal Mts of Utah, very close to the Colorado line.

6a. [1] Annuals or short-lived perennials with very shallow root systems, if appearing perennial, the basal lvs coarsely toothed . . . . (7)
6b. Perennials . . . . (12)

7a. [6] Carpellate (ray-) fls very numerous, with very narrow, short, erect ligules, these sometimes not exceeding the disk, or the inner carpellate corollas tubular, without an expanded ligule (two subalpine spp). . . . . (8)
7b. Carpellate fls few to numerous (rarely absent), the ligules, when present, well-developed and spreading, not short, narrow or erect. . . . . (9)

8a. [7] Inner phyls usually long-attenuate; infl ± flat-topped; pap reddish brown. **E. elongatus** Ledebour. Subalpine meadows (*E. acre* var *debilis*). This and the next are only distantly related to our W American so-called *Erigeron*.
8b. Inner phyls merely acute or acuminate; infl racemose, not flat-topped; pap usually white. **E. lonchophyllus** Hooker [lance-lvd].

Wet meadows and seepage areas of screes and rocky slopes near timberline.

9a. [7] Plants broad-lvd, hardly branched, with large, coarsely toothed basal lvs and numerous very slender rays. **E. philadelphicus** L. Moist meadows, intermountain basins.

9b. Plants with narrow, entire (very rarely a few toothed basal) lvs, much branched; rays narrow but not unusually numerous. . . . . (10)

10a. [9] Stem hairs spreading perpendicularly . . . . (11)

10b. Hairs of the stem appressed; plant slender, with stolons arising from the base of the plant and rooting at the tips. **E. flagellaris** Gray. Dry montane meadows.

11a. [10] Heads solitary on elongate, mostly lfless stems from the basal lf clusters; plants developing long non-rooting stolon-like spreading shoots. **E. colo-mexicanus** Nelson. Dry gravelly floodplains and meadows, mimicking *E. flagellaris* but with spreading stem hairs.

11b. Heads numerous in lfy branches usually terminating stout erect stems. **E. divergens** Torrey & Gray [spreading]. A weedy sp of ruderal sites and gravelly floodplains.

12a. [6] Tall and erect; woodland and meadow plants with well-developed, lanceolate or broader, stem lvs. . . . . (13)

12b. Low; lvs linear or spatulate; plants of various, not usually forested, sites . . . . (21)

13a. [12] Invol woolly-villous with multicellular hairs. **E. elatior** (Gray) Greene [taller]. Aspen and spruce-fir forests.

13b. Invol not woolly-villous but often hirsute. . . . . (14)

14a. [13] Rays white; invol. hairs with black cross-walls. **E. coulteri** Porter [for John M. Coulter]. Aspen and spruce-fir forests.

14b. Rays lavender, only white in mutant plants; invol hairs without black cross-walls . . . . (15)

15a. [14] Rays mostly 2-3 mm wide; pap simple. **E. peregrinus** (Banks) Greene ssp **callianthemus** (Greene) Cronquist [wandering; beautiful-fld] Open rocky slopes and subalpine meadows. Commonly mistaken for *Aster*, since the rays are so much wider than they should be in *Erigeron*. The pap bristles are also stouter. The pubescence of the phyls and uppermost stem is very distinctive. The stem just below the phyls is covered by a close white pubescence of multicellular, partly glandular hairs; the phyls contrast by being quite dark and covered by short club-shaped red-tipped glandular hairs. The basal lvs are largest.

15b. Rays narrower; pap usually double (with long and short bristles) . . . . (16)

16a. [15] Cauline lvs glabrous or slightly glandular, not even ciliate on the margins, comparatively few in number and little if at all longer than the internodes. **E. eximius** Greene [extraordinary].

Aspen and spruce-fir forests (*E. superbus*).
16b. Stem lvs either obviously pubescent or at least ciliate on the margins, sometimes also glandular, relatively numerous and longer than the internodes . . . . (17)

17a. [16] Lvs glandular or glandular-scabrous and sparsely pubescent with long hairs. **E. uintahensis** Cronquist. High forested plateaus, NW MF.
17b. Lvs hairy or ciliate, or the uppermost ones only slightly glandular. . . . . (18)

18a. [17] Plants uniformly lfy, middle lvs commonly as large as the lower ones . . . . (19)
18b. Plants with upper lvs abruptly reduced, the middle ones commonly smaller than the lowermost ones. . . . . (20)

19a. [18] Upper and middle stem lvs glabrous except for the ciliate margins. **E. speciosus** (Lindley) de Candolle [showy]. Abundant, aspen and spruce-fir.
19b. Upper and middle stem lvs hairy. **E. subtrinervis** Rydberg. In similar areas but in drier, more open sites. This simply may be a race of the above.

20a. [18] Stem and invol glandular or viscid, sometimes also hairy; stem curved at the base. **E. formosissimus** Greene [very handsome]. Forest openings and mountain meadows.
20b. Stem and invol ± hairy, scarcely glandular or viscid; stem usually erect. **E. glabellus** Nuttall [dim. of smooth]. Similar sites. Hybridization evidently occurs among most of these leafy spp, and identifications are often inconclusive, probably for this reason.

21a. [12] Plants of desert-steppe sites at lower altitudes and intermountain basins (except *E. caespitosus*, which ranges higher in Utah and Wyoming). . . . . (22)
21b. Plants of higher elevations, from montane to tundra . . . . . . (32)

22a. [21] Lvs spatulate, rounded at the apex; plants spreading with slender caudices, forming stolons late in the season. **E. kachinensis** Welsh & Moore, [for Kachina Natural Bridge, Utah]. Extremely rare, on seepy bases of sandstone alcoves, MN.
22b. Lvs linear, or if broader, acute or acuminate; otherwise not as above . . . . (23)

23a. [22] Lvs in a prominent spreading rosette from a tap-root, broadly linear, broadest in the middle, triple-nerved, the basal ones half as long as the fl stems, spreading in a rosette, the fl stems spreading before ascending (base S-shaped) . . . . (24)
23b. Lvs and infl not as above. . . . . (25)

24a. [23] Biennial with one or only a few caudices; lf-segs broad (2-3 mm wide), many lvs usually simple; heads larger. **E. caespitosus** Nuttall. Rare, gravelly streambeds, MF.

24b. Stem hairs appressed or ascending; lvs acute, tapering above and below. **E. eatoni** Gray [for the collector, Daniel C. Eaton]. Common in sagebrush.

25a. [23] Pubescence of stem and lvs stiffly spreading, or if not, at least the petioles strongly stiff-ciliate . . . . (26)
25b. Pubescence of stem and lvs closely appressed, often giving the plant a grayish cast . . . . (28)

26a. [25] Stem pubescence appressed, but petioles stiffly ciliate. **E. engelmannii** Nelson. Closely related to the next, but a smaller plant in every way, never with many caudices.
26b. Stem and lf pubescence spreading; coarse plant with many caudices, forming a dense clump . . . . (27)

27a. [26] Rays well-developed, white or lavender. **E. pumilus** Nuttall ssp **concinnoides** Cronquist [little; like *E. concinnus*]. Abundant, desert-steppe and piñon-juniper zone.
27b. Rays lacking. **E. aphanactis** (Gray) Greene [rayless]. Transitions with short rays occur, strongly suggestive that this is only a minor variant of the last. Similar habitats.

28a. [25] Lvs ranging from almost glabrous to sparsely strigose; heads small (invol less than 1 cm diam). **E. nematophyllus** Rydberg [thread-lvd]. NW counties, RT-MF, in a variety of sites: shale outcrops, sandstone rubble of canyons, gravelly tops of plateaus.
28b. Lvs and stems densely strigose (appearing gray); heads over 1 cm diam . . . . (29)

29a. [28] Stems low (under 15 cm), fl stems with a few reduced lvs below. **E. consimilis** Cronquist [like in all respects (to *E. compactus*, a similar sp]. Gypsum hills, MF.
29b. Stems tall (over 20 cm), fl stems with several well-developed lvs; invol clearly and regularly imbricate . . . . (30)

30a. [29] Basal lvs withering and disappearing before fls open. **E. utahensis** Gray. Canyonsides, ME-MN.
30b. Basal lvs forming strong tufts at flowering time . . . . (31)

31a. [30] Aks glabrous; old lf-bases persisting and becoming strongly fibrous. **E. canus** Gray [hoary]. Infrequent, S half of the range. The rays of this and the next are wider than in most spp.
31b. Aks ± hairy; old lf-bases, if persistent, becoming somewhat chaffy, not strongly fibrous. **E. pulcherrimus** Heller [very beautiful]. Adobe hills.

32a. [21] Rays very narrow and short, 3-6 mm long, 0.3-1.0 mm wide; phyls purple-black, narrow and attenuate. **E. humilis** Graham [low]. Extremely rare on mossy tundra on high peaks, GN. Plants are minute, less than 3 cm tall; heads on very short stems no longer than the basal lvs.
32b. Rays well-developed, 7-15 mm long, 1.0-2.5 mm wide. . . . . (33)

33a. [32] Stems and usually lvs glandular; basal lvs linear-lanceolate; caudex branches very stout. **E. vetensis** Rydberg, [for La Veta Pass]. Common dwarf sp of gravelly slopes or dry meadows, montane and subalpine.

33b. Stems and lvs not glandular; lvs not linear-lanceolate, often rounded at the apex . . . . (34)

34a. [33] Invol woolly-villous with multicellular hairs . . . . (35)

34b. Invol variously pubescent or sometimes glabrous but not woolly-villous . . . . (37)

35a. [34] Invol hairs with black or very dark purple cross-walls; rays white. **E. melanocephalus** Nelson, [black-headed]. One of the most common dwarf daisies on subalpine slopes and meadows, usually replaced by *E. simplex* on tundra; where they occur together, the soil is more moist under plants of *E. melanocephalus*.

35b. Invol hairs with clear cross-walls, or the lowermost cross-walls sometimes bright reddish-purple; rays lavender . . . . (36)

36a. [35] Pap bristles mostly about a dozen, sometimes as many as 15; outer pap conspicuous, setose-squamellate; invol and upper stem with moderate long hairs, never appearing shaggy or obscuring the phylls. **E. simplex** Greene. Common dwarf alpine sp.

36b. Pap bristles mostly 15 to 20; outer pap obscure; invol and upper stem with very long shaggy (3-4 mm) hairs, obscuring the phylls. **E. grandiflorus** Hooker. Uncommon or rare, on tundra. This seems to have many more ray-fls than the last, and deeper-colored.

37a. [34] Plant with slender rhizomes, these freely rooting along their length; most lvs elongate and acute at the apex. **E. ursinus** Eaton [of Bear R Canyon, Utah]. Dry meadows at and above timberline. Commonly confused with *E. simplex* although in the field the rhizomatous character is very evident.

37b. Plant with slender or stoutish elongate caudices, these not rooting freely along their length; most lvs oblanceolate and rounded at the apex. **E. leiomerus** Gray [with smooth parts]. Alpine and subalpine screes and rockslides.

EUCEPHALUS Nuttall 1840 [Gr., *eu*, well-developed, + *kephalos*, head] (formerly incl in *Aster*)

1a. Outer phylls obtuse at apex, ivory-white with a green tip; plants glaucous, up to 5 dm tall, strongly rhizomatous and forming extensive clumps. **E. glaucus** Nuttall. Abundant, base of talus and rimrock, piñon-juniper and oak (*A. glaucodes*).

1b. Outer phylls acute at apex, green with reddish border; plants not strongly glaucous, over 5 dm tall, not forming extensive clumps. . . . . (2)

2a. Lvs large, mostly 15-35 mm wide; rays white, turning pinkish in age; 6-15 dm tall; phylls elongate, some with narrow flexuous tips; invol about 1 cm high. **E. engelmannii** (Eaton) Greene. Spruce-fir and aspen forests.

2b. Lvs smaller, 3-15 mm wide; rays deep violet; plants 3-6 dm tall; invol about 5 mm high. **E. perelegans** (Nelson & Macbride) Weber. Open slopes and summits, MF.

EUPATORIUM L. 1753 [from *Mithridates Eupator*, King of Pontus, who found one species to be an antidote against poison]. JOE PYE WEED (after an Indian of that name)

One sp, **E. maculatum** L. Rare on the W slope, known from a spring bank, ME.

EUTHAMIA Nuttall 1818 [Gr., *thameios*, crowded, alluding to the fls]

One sp, **E. occidentalis** Nuttall. Common along irrigation ditches in the valleys (*Solidago*).

FILAGINELLA Opiz 1854 [dim. of the genus *Filago*]. CUDWEED (formerly in *Gnaphalium*)
1a. Subtending lvs linear or narrowly oblanceolate, much exceeding the clusters of heads; phyls usually dark. **F. uliginosa** (L.) Opiz. Common in drying pools and muddy ditches in the mts (*G. exilifolium*).
1b. Subtending lvs oblong or oblanceolate, little exceeding the clusters of heads; phyls pale. **F. palustris** (Nuttall) Holub. Similar situations).

FLAVERIA Jussieu 1789 [Lat., *flavus*, yellow, the original sp used as a dye plant]

One sp, **F. campestris** Johnston. Infrequent in wetlands of lower Colorado R Valley, ME. The heads are narrow, broadest at the base, few-fld (with usually only one very pale yellow or white ray); the clusters mimic a single head!

GAILLARDIA Fougeroux 1786 [for Gaillard de Charentonneau, French amateur botanist]. BLANKET-FLOWER
1a. Lvs deeply and narrowly pinnatifid. **G. pinnatifida** Torrey. Common on adobe hills, early spring.
1b. Lvs entire, or some toothed or broadly pinnatifid . . . . (2)

2a. Disk-fls and often the bases of the rays red-purple; lvs large, over 5 cm long, more than 1 cm broad, stiff-hairy. **G. aristata** Pursh [awned, referring to the pap], **23F**. Common, sagebrush and lower montane, midsummer.
2b. Disk-fls yellow; rays short; lvs up to 3 cm long, to 1 cm wide, smooth. **G. spathulata** Gray [spatula-shaped]. Desert-steppe, rimrock, Dolores R Valley.

GNAPHALIUM L. 1753 [Gr., *gnaphallon*, a lock of wool]. CUDWEED

1a. Leaves bicolored, glandular above, tomentose below; phyllaries white. **G. viscosum** Humboldt, Bonpland & Kunth. ADV, common in disturbed soil, montane forest clearings (*G. macounii*).
1b. Leaves tomentose on both sides, not at all glandular; phyllaries yellowish. **G. stramineum** Humboldt, Bonpland & Kunth. ADV at a hot spring in the Gunnison Basin (*G. chilense*).

GRINDELIA Willdenow 1807 [for D. H. Grindel, 1776-1836, Russian botanist]. GUMWEED
1a. Phyls not squarrose-recurved. **G. arizonica** Gray. Clay soils, SW counties.
1b. Phyls strongly squarrose-recurved . . . . (2)

2a. Basal lvs withered by fl time; annual or short-lived perennial. **G. squarrosa** (Pursh) Dunal. Abundant weed in the lower valleys. Two varieties occur; var **serrulata** is the common one; var **quasiperennis** (slightly perennial) is found in and around RT.
2b. Basal lvs much larger than stem lvs, in basal rosettes at fl time; fl stems naked at the base (two seasons required to produce one, the basal lvs disappearing by fl time); strongly perennial
. . . . (3)

3a. Rays present. **G. fastigiata** Greene. Common on adobe soils, W counties, mostly N of the Colorado R.
3b. Rays lacking. **G. aphanactis** Greene. Local, Mesa Verde.

GUTIERREZIA Lagasca 1816 [for Pedro Gutierrez, 1816, correspondent of the Bot. Garden of Madrid]. SNAKEWEED
1a. Rays 1-2, disk-fls 1-2; phyls fewer than 10; heads usually in small clusters. **G. microcephala** (de Candolle) Gray. Desert and adobe hills, DL-MZ.
1b. Rays 3-5, disk-fls usually more than 2; phyls usually more than 10; heads single or in clusters. **G. sarothrae** (Pursh) Britton & Rusby. Fl. in late summer in desert and sagebrush, roadsides.

HELENIUM L. 1753 [Gr. name of some plant, said by Linnaeus to commemorate Helen of Troy, wife of King Menelaus of Sparta]. SNEEZEWEED
One sp, **H. autumnale** L. var **montanum** (Nuttall) Fernald. Montane meadows and roadsides.

HELIANTHELLA Torrey & Gray 1842 [dim. of *Helianthus*]. LITTLE SUNFLOWER
1a. Phyls ovate, strongly graduated; heads numerous, the rays very short; disk-fls purple-brown. **H. microcephala** (Gray) Gray. Rocky canyons, SW counties.
1b. Phyls lanceolate, subequal; heads solitary or few, the rays ample; disk-fls yellow . . . . (2)

2a. Phyls uniformly pubescent, not distinctly ciliate; lvs acute or obtuse, tapering to short petioles; enlarged basal lvs absent; heads erect. **H. uniflora** (Nuttall) Torrey & Gray. Sagebrush and lower montane (pine), N counties.
2b. Phyls conspicuously ciliate, slightly pubescent on the face; lvs acute or acuminate, tapering to long petioles; enlarged basal lvs present; heads turned at right angles to the stem. . . . . (3)

3a. Tall and stout; heads 4-5 cm broad excluding the rays; lvs up to 50 cm long, attenuate at both ends, prominently 5-veined. **H. quinquenervis** (Hooker) Gray, **PL 31**. Abundant, aspen zone.

3b. Low and slender; heads 1.5-2.0 cm broad excluding the rays; lvs less than 10 cm long, acute. **H. parryi** Gray, **23B**. Montane (ponderosa pine) zone, S counties.

HELIANTHUS L. 1753 [Gr., *helios*, the sun, + *anthos*, flower]. SUNFLOWER
1a. Lvs linear-lanceolate, elongate; tall rank plants often over 2 m tall. **H. nuttallii** Torrey & Gray. Abundant in the lower valleys along wet ditches and in swales.
1b. Lvs broader, rhomboidal to triangular . . . . (2)

2a. Lvs mostly opposite, narrowly rhomboidal; perennial from rhizomes. **H. rigidus** (Cassini) Desfontaines var **subrhomboideus** (Rydberg) Heiser. Infrequent, open pine forests, AA.
2b. Lvs mostly alternate, broadly ovate . . . . (3)

3a. Perennial with tuberous roots, escaped from cultivation. **H. tuberosus** L., JERUSALEM-ARTICHOKE. ADV, estab along fencerows in the Colorado R. Valley.
3b. Annual with a taproot . . . . (4)

4a. Phyls hispid-ciliate, ovate or obovate, with acuminate tips. **H. annuus** L., COMMON SUNFLOWER. Very abundant and variable native roadside weed.
4b. Phyls not ciliate, appressed-short-hairy, lanceolate. **H. petiolaris** Nuttall, PRAIRIE SUNFLOWER. Similar to the preceding and commonly hybridizing with it.

HELIOMERIS Nuttall 1848 [Gr., *helios*, the sun, + *meris*, a part]
One sp, **H. multiflora** Nuttall. Common small-headed sunflower of montane roadsides and desert hills (*Viguiera*). Lvs opposite, usually narrowly elliptic. Var **nevadensis** is a desert form with very narrow lvs. Heads numerous, cymosely arranged. Flowering in mid- and late summer.

HETEROTHECA Cassini 1817 [Gr., *hetero*, different, + *theca*, case, alluding to the unlike achenes]. GOLDEN ASTER
Note: The spp are notoriously variable, with distinct local races, and many specimens cannot be definitely placed. Treatments vary enormously as well; unfortunately the monographer never published a definitive study of them.
1a. Upper stems, lvs and invol densely hirsute, nonglandular or only with small inconspicuous sessile glandular dots; upper lvs not markedly coarse or rigid; outer pap inconspicuous, of narrow setaceous scales. **H. villosa** (Pursh) Shinners. Abundant weedy perennial throughout the lower mts and canyons.
1b. Herbage less densely pubescent, distinctly greenish, copiously covered with conspicuous large sessile and stipitate glands, or, if more densely pubescent and less conspicuously glandular, then the upper lvs markedly coarse and stiff, and peduncular lvs broad and closely subtending the heads; outer pap conspicuous, of lanceolate fringed scales . . . . (2)

2a. Heads ± sessile, closely subtended by peduncular lvs not grading into the phyls. **H. fulcrata** (Greene) Shinners. Upper montane, subalpine.
2b. Heads appearing pedunculate; peduncular lvs distant from the heads or (if closer) reduced and grading into the phyls. **H. horrida** (Rydberg) Harms. Middle altitudes.

HYMENOPAPPUS L'Heritier 1788 [Gr., *hymen*, membrane, + pappus]

1a. Plants with showy white ray-fls. **H. newberryi** (Gray) Johnston. Open hillsides, SE counties (*Leucampyx*).
1b. Ray-fls lacking. **H. filifolius** Hooker, **23G**. Common, piñon-juniper. Several fairly well-marked races occur. . . . . (2)

2a. Basal lf-axils without a dense tomentum. Var **parvulus** (Greene) Turner. Infrequent, Gunnison Basin to Four Corners.
2b. Basal lf-axils densely tomentose. . . . . (3)

3a. Corollas 2-3 mm long; fls averaging 20 per head. Var **luteus** (Nuttall) Turner. A Uintah Basin race in MF.
3b. Corollas 3-7 mm long; fls 20-70 per head . . . . (4)

4a. Anthers 3-4 mm long; corolla 4-7 mm long. Var **megacephalus** Turner. Lower Colorado and Gunnison valleys.
4b. Anthers 2-3 mm long; corolla 2.5-4.5 mm long. Var **cinereus** (Rydberg) Johnston. The most abundant race throughout the area.

ISOCOMA Nuttall 1840 [Gr., *isos*, equal, + *coma*, mane, alluding to the pap)

One sp, **I. drummondii** (Torrey & Gray) Greene. Peripheral, deserts, MZ. Somewhat resembling a low sp of *Chrysothamnus*. but having deep goblet-shaped corollas; lvs elliptic-lanceolate, flat (*Haplopappus*).

IVA L. 1753 [anc. name of some medicinal plant]. POVERTY WEED

One sp, **I. axillaris** Pursh. Abundant weedy rhizomatous perennial, alkaline soil in cult river valleys.

JACEA Miller 1754 [a pre-Linnaean name for this group]. BROWN KNAPWEED

One sp, **J. pratensis** Lamarck. ADV locally escaped around Glenwood Springs (*Centaurea jacea*).

LACTUCA L. 1753 [Gr., *lac*, milk, alluding to the juice]. LETTUCE

1a. Lvs spiny-margined and often with spines along the midrib and veins. **L. serriola** L., PRICKLY LETTUCE. ADV common weed in fields and gardens. Fls yellow. Hybridizes in nature with the cultivated lettuce.
1b. Lvs not spiny-margined . . . . (2)

2a. Fls yellow . . . . (3)

2b. Fls blue or purplish . . . . (4)

3a. Invol 1-1.4 cm long; aks and heads 5-6 mm long; pap 5-7 mm long; lvs mostly strongly pinnatifid. **L. canadensis** L., CANADIAN WILD LETTUCE. Infrequent, montane gulches.
3b. Invol 1.5-2.2 cm long; mature aks including beak 7-10 mm long; pap 9-12 mm long; lvs mostly undivided. **L. graminifolia** Michaux. Local, near Ouray.

4a. Strongly rhizomatous perennial; lvs simple or narrowly pinnatifid; pap white. **L. tatarica** (L.) Meyer ssp **pulchella** (Pursh) Stebbins. Abundant along roadsides in the valleys. An American race of a Siberian sp.
4b. Biennial with a basal rosette and taproot; lvs with broad triangular pinnatifid divs; pap brownish. **L. biennis** (Moench) Fernald. One old record, RT.

LEPIDOTHECA Nuttall 1841 [Gr., *lepido*, scaly, + *theca*, container, akene]. PINEAPPLE WEED

One sp, **L. suaveolens** Nuttall. Common low herb of disturbed areas, notably unpaved parking areas in the mts. The crushed foliage has a pineapple odor (*Matricaria matricarioides*).

LEUCACANTHA Nieuwland & Lunell 1917 [Gr., *leucos*, white, + *acantha*, thorn]. CORNFLOWER

One sp, **L. cyanus** (L.) Nieuwland & Lunell. ADV, commonly escaped from cultivation and spreading to fields.

LEUCANTHEMUM Miller 1754 [Gr., *leuco*, white, + *anthos*, flower]. OX-EYE DAISY

One sp, **L. vulgare** Lamarck. ADV, escaped from gardens and estab in meadows, around mines and ghost towns in the mts. Common in the E U. S. (*Chrysanthemum leucanthemum*).

LEUCELENE Greene 1896 [Gr., *leucos*, + lenis, soft]. SAND-ASTER

One sp, **L. ericoides** (Torrey) Greene [like heather, from the leaf shape]. Common on arid gravels or clays, desert-steppe (*Aster arenosus*). Forming small hemispherical clumps, each branch with a single head.

LIATRIS Gaertner 1791 [derivation unknown]. GAY-FEATHER

1a. Heads numerous, small, cylindric; individual fls few; lvs linear. **L. punctata** Hooker [with translucent dots]. Roadsides, Gunnison Basin. Mostly an E slope sp.
1b. Heads few, as broad as or broader than long; individual fls numerous; lvs spatulate or oblanceolate. **L. ligulistylis** (Nelson) Schumann. Wet hay-meadows, Gunnison Basin.

LIGULARIA Cassini 1816 [Lat., *ligula*, strap, alluding to the rays] (formerly incl in *Senecio*)
1a. Dwarf alpines, or, if taller and subalpine, heads with rays . . . . (2)

Asteraceae/Compositae (AST/CMP)   137

Figure 21. **A**, *Ligularia holmii*; **B**, *L. soldanella*

1b. Tall plants of montane forests and roadsides; rays absent; cauline lvs several . . . . (6)

2a. Plants small, with long slender elastic caudices; lvs cordate-reniform, crenate, usually less than 2 cm diam. **L. porteri** (Greene) Weber. END. Rare on alpine screes, Elk, Saguache and San Juan Mts.

2b. Plants larger in all respects; caudices stout, short . . . . (3)

3a. Cobwebby-pubescent. **L. taraxacoides** (Gray) Weber, **22B**. END. High rocky alpine slopes. Lvs usually runcinate-pinnatifid.

3b. Glabrous . . . . (4)

4a. Basal lvs withering by fl time; cauline lvs elongate, usually sessile and clasping the stem (rarely tapered to a narrow base). **L. amplectens** (Gray) Weber, **22A**. END, subalpine meadows and forest clearings.

4b. Lvs chiefly basal, present at fl time, all rounded or cordate, with distinct petioles; alpine . . . . (5)

5a. Lvs broadly rounded at apex, abruptly narrowed to the petiole, the teeth remote or almost lacking; rays short and not twice as long as the invol; plant succulent, strongly reddish-tinged. **L. soldanella** (Gray) Weber, **21B, PL 14**. END, boulderfields and screes of the higher peaks.

138   Asteraceae/Compositae (AST/CMP)

Figure 22. A, *Ligularia amplectens*; B, *L. taraxacoides*; C, *L. pudica*; D, *L. bigelovii*

5b. Lvs more tapered to base and apex, usually strongly dentate; rays twice as long as invol, showy; plants not strongly succulent, green or only reddish-tinged on the petioles. **L. holmii** (Greene) Weber, **21A**. END, frequent on tundra.

6a. Heads large, turbinate, thick and fleshy, on stout peduncles, mostly racemosely arranged. **L. bigelovii** (Gray) Weber, **22D**. Aspen groves, roadsides, montane.
6b. Heads small, cylindric, not fleshy, on slender peduncles, mostly arranged in panicles. **L. pudica** (Greene) Weber, **22C**. Canyons in the foothills and montane.

LYGODESMIA Don 1829 [Gr., *lygos*, a pliant twig, + *desme*, a bundle]. SKELETON-WEED

1a. Rays 10-12 mm long, ca. 4 mm wide; pap 6-9 mm long. **L. juncea** (Pursh) Don. Infrequent in the W valleys.
1b. Rays 1.5-2.5 cm long, 6-10 mm wide; pap 12-17 mm long . . . . (2)

2a. Invol of 8 or 9 principal phyls; rays 8-22 to a head. **L. grandiflora** (Nuttall) Torrey & Gray, **PL 43**. Abundant on adobe flats and alluvial fans of the valleys.

2b. Invol of 5 or 6 principal phyls; rays usually 5 per head. . . . . . (3)

3a. Much branched from the base, all lvs very narrow and filiform (ca. 3 mm wide). **L. doloresensis** Tomb. END on benches of Dolores R Valley.
3b. Sparsely branched from the base, not all lvs narrow and filiform, some at least wider than 3 mm. **L. arizonica** Tomb. Peripheral, Four Corners.

MACHAERANTHERA Nees 1832 [Gr., *machaira*, sword, + *anthera*, anther, alluding to lanceolate processes of the anthers]. TANSY ASTER

1a. Rays lacking. **M. grindelioides** (Nuttall) Shinners. Common on dry roadsides and hills, canyon country (*Haplopappus australis*). This and *M. gracilis* have bristle-tipped leaf teeth.
1b. Rays present . . . . (2)

2a. Rays yellow . . . . (3)
2b. Rays lavender to purple . . . . (4)

3a. Annuals with toothed lvs, each tooth with a very slender bristle on the tip; branched from above the base. **M. gracilis** (Nuttall) Shinners. Common, ponderosa pine and piñon-juniper woods, from ME southward (*Haplopappus*).
3b. Perennials with pinnatifid lvs; branched from the base. **M. pinnatifida** (Hooker) Shinners. Common weedy plant with many races, steppe-desert and piñon-juniper (*Haplopappus spinulosus*).

4a. Lvs pinnatifid; annual . . . . (5)
4b. Lvs merely toothed; biennial or perennial. . . . . (6)

5a. Heads very small, invol about 5 mm high; phyllaries appressed; rays less than 7 mm long. **M. parviflora** Gray. Alkaline flats, MN (*Aster parvulus*).

5b. Heads large, invol about 1 cm high; phyllaries spreading-recurved; rays 8-12 mm long. **M. tanacetifolia** (Humboldt, Bonpland & Kunth) Nees. Common weedy plant in ruderal and overgrazed sites in the lowlands (*Aster*).

6a. Low or prostrate mat-plant with woody caudices; heads solitary on short peduncles. **M. coloradoensis** (Gray) Osterhout. Gravelly places in the higher mountain parks and on dry tundra (*Aster*).

6b. Erect branching weedy plant, lower and middle altitudes. . . . . (7)

7a. Lvs broad; heads relatively few, very large; phyls foliose, very glandular. **M. pattersonii** (Gray) Greene. Frequent on Grand Mesa.

7b. Lvs narrow; heads very numerous, small; phyls hardly foliose, canescent or somewhat glandular. **M. canescens** (Pursh) Gray (including *M. linearis*, *M. rubrotinctus*). Abundant roadside weed with many poorly defined races, subject to being moved around through road construction, possibly hybridizing freely.

MACRONEMA Nuttall 1840 [Gr., *macro*, long, + *nema*, thread, alluding to the styles]

One sp, **M. discoideum** Nuttall. Frequent on montane slopes. The branches are closely felted as in *Chrysothamnus* but the heads are rayless and cream-colored (*Haplopappus macronema*).

MADIA Molina 1781 [from *madi*, the Chilean name]. TARWEED

One sp, **M. glomerata** Hooker. ADV frequent roadside weed. The foliage and heads are so viscid that they catch dust easily and become very dirty.

MALACOTHRIX DC. 1838 [Gr., *malacos*, soft, + *trichos*, hair, alluding to the pap]. DESERT DANDELION

1a. Inner phyls up to 8 mm long, the sides parallel to near the apex; ribs of the aks all similar. **M. sonchoides** (Nuttall) Torrey & Gray. Common on adobe hills, early spring.

1b. Inner phyls up to 11 mm long, the sides tapering from the base, very narrowly acuminate; five of the ak ribs much stouter than the others. **M. torreyi** Gray. Similar sites and probably almost as abundant.

MATRICARIA L. 1753 [Gr., *matrix*, womb, for reputed medicinal value]. WILD CHAMOMILE

One sp, **M. perforata** Merat. ADV, abundant in disturbed ground of montane roadsides, pastures and townsites esp. along the Blue River (*M. inodora*).

MICROSERIS Don 1832 [Gr., *micro*, small, + *seris*, a kind of endive]

One sp, **M. nutans** (Geyer) Schultz-Bipontinus. Dry wooded slopes and meadows, montane and subalpine. Resembles *Agoseris*, but has several heads per stalk, nodding at least in bud.

OLIGOSPORUS Cassini 1817 [Gr., *oligo*, few, + *spora*, seed] [formerly incl in *Artemisia*]. TARRAGON, SAGEWORT
1a. Dwarf plants of desert-steppe, with finely divided pedatifid lvs and fl spikes very short and hidden among the lvs. **A. pedatifidus** (Nuttall) Poljakov. Clay soils, MF, peripheral.
1b. Not as above . . . . (2)

2a. Perennial from rhizomes; basal lvs absent by fl time; lvs glabrate and simple at maturity; heads almost sessile, with pedicels 1-2 mm long; lvs commonly 2 mm or more wide. **O. dracunculus** (L.) Poljakov ssp **glauca** (Pallas) Löve & Löve, WILD TARRAGON. Frequent throughout the area, often weedy.
2b. Biennial, monocarpic, or perennial, with a rosette of basal lvs
. . . . (3)

3a. Heads in an open panicle, the bracts inconspicuous; invol 2-3 mm high, 2-3.5 mm broad; biennial or monocarpic from a taproot. **O. campestris** (L.) Cassini ssp **pacificus** (Nuttall) Weber. Common in dry open meadows, montane basins.
3b. Heads in a condensed spikelike panicle, the bracts conspicuous in the infl; invol 3-4 mm high, 3.5-5.0 mm broad; perennial, developing several caudices. **O. groenlandicus** (Hornemann) Löve & Löve. Upper subalpine and alpine (*A. borealis* of manuals).

ONOPORDUM L. 1753 [Gr., *onos*, donkey, + *porde*, flatulence; Pliny stated that it caused this in donkeys]. SCOTCH THISTLE
One sp, **O. acanthium** L. ADV. A huge, heavily armored weedy thistle with tomentose foliage and spiny decurrent lf bases, lower river valleys. *O. tauricum* Willdenow, with glabrous lvs, may also be expected.

OREOCHRYSUM Rydberg 1906 [Gr., *oros*, mountain, + *chrysos*, gold]
One sp, **O. parryi** (Gray) Rydberg. Common in spruce-fir and aspen forests (*Haplopappus*).

OXYTENIA Nuttall 1848 [Gr., *oxys*, sharp, alluding to the rigid lf-tips]
One sp. **O. acerosa** Nuttall. A tall gray shrub, blooming in late summer, abundant on floodplains of lower valleys, ME-MZ.

PACKERA Löve & Löve 1976 [for John Packer, contemporary Canadian botanist]. GROUNDSEL (previously incl in *Senecio*)
1a. Stem scapose (the stem lvs reduced to linear or bractlike vestiges), less than 2 dm high. **P. werneriifolia** (Gray) Weber & Löve. Rocky alpine and subalpine ridges. Variable in lf width and tomentum.
1b. Stems with at least a few well-developed lvs . . . . (2)

2a. Basal lvs entire, ± permanently white-tomentose. **P. cana** (Hooker) Weber & Löve. Gravelly moraines and alpine ridges.
2b. Basal lvs, at least some of them, toothed or pinnatifid, glabrous or becoming so in age . . . . (3)

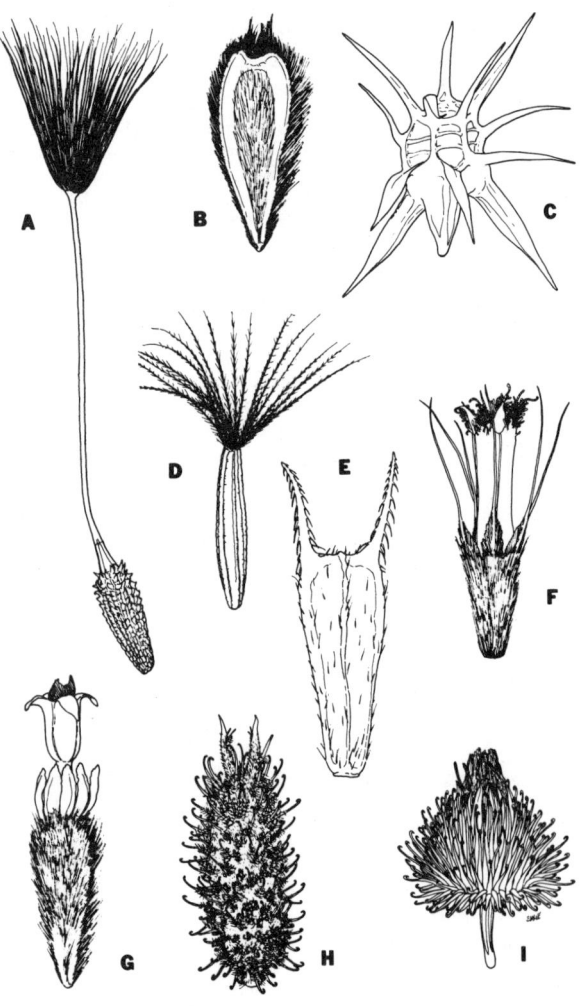

Figure 23. **A**, *Taraxacum officinale*; **B**, *Helianthella parryi*; **C**, *Ambrosia acanthicarpa*; **D**, *Stephanomeria pauciflora*; **E**, *Bidens frondosa*; **F**, *Gaillardia aristata*; **G**, *Hymenopappus filifolius*; **H**, *Xanthium strumarium*; **I**, *Arctium minus*

3a. Basal lvs and most stem lvs deeply pinnatifid or runcinate-pinnatifid. . . . . (4)
3b. Basal lvs oval, rarely pinnatifid except sometimes at the very base. . . . . (5)

4a. Not rhizomatous; lf-lobes irregular, deep; lvs glabrous or at least not white-tomentose. **P. multilobata** (Torrey & Gray) Weber & Löve. Piñon-juniper and adobe hills.
4b. Producing rosettes from long slender rhizomes; lf-lobes uniform, shallow; lvs white-tomentose. **P. fendleri** (Gray) Weber & Löve. Gravelly soil, open forests.

5a. Basal lvs oval or cordate, on long slender petioles, regularly crenate. . . . . (6)
5b. Basal lvs narrower, on winged petioles, irregularly toothed or lobed or entire . . . . (8)

6a. Basal lvs thick and leathery, oval, cuneate at the base; strongly rhizomatous plants forming broad mats. . . . . (7)
6b. Basal lvs relatively thin, cordate-ovate; stems produced singly or a few together. **P. pseudaurea** (Rydberg) Weber & Löve. Wet montane streamsides.

7a. Glabrous; cauline lvs sharply serrate, stem lvs usually pinnatisect. **P. streptanthifolia** (Greene) Weber & Löve. Infrequent, open forests, GA-RT.
7b. Floccose-pubescent; lvs crenate, basal ones never pinnatisect. **P. oödes** (Rydberg) Weber. Common, EA and southwestward, in dry forests.

8a. Stems clustered, from a taproot with short caudices; upper stem lvs without auriculate or enlarged bases . . . . (9)
8b. Stems solitary or a few together, from a short rhizome; upper stem lvs with enlarged, auriculate-clasping bases . . . . (10)

9a. Lvs narrowly oblanceolate, commonly three-toothed at the apex but sometimes generally toothed or pinnatifid, usually glabrous. **P. tridenticulata** (Rydberg) Weber & Löve. Open gravelly flats. Distinct in its characteristic glabrous, 3-toothed form, but completely merging, through hybridization, with the next.
9b. Lvs oval or broadly oblanceolate, variably toothed or lobed, usually distinctly pubescent. **P. neomexicana** (Gray) Weber & Löve. Abundant in relatively dry meadows and open montane forests. Extremely variable, probably due to a tendency to hybridize with other *Packera* spp.

10a. Ray-fls deep orange. **P. crocata** (Rydberg) Weber & Löve. Moist meadows, usually at lower altitudes than the next.
10b. Ray-fls yellow. **P. dimorphophylla** (Greene) Weber & Löve. Dry gravelly montane and subalpine meadows.

144 Asteraceae/Compositae (AST/CMP)

PETASITES Miller 1754 [Gr. name for coltsfoot, from *petasos*, a broad-brimmed hat]. SWEET COLTSFOOT

One sp, **P. sagittata** (Banks) Gray. Marshy meadows in the intermountain parks and valleys, especially abundant in the Gunnison Basin. Lvs triangular-cordate, green above, white-woolly beneath; flowering very early, the fruiting heads very conspicuous because of the copious white pap.

PETRADORIA Greene 1895 [Gr., *petra*, rock, + *Doria*, an old name for a goldenrod]. ROCK GOLDENROD

One sp, **P. pumila** (Nuttall) Greene. Rocky flats in the sagebrush-piñon-juniper, W counties (*Solidago*).

PICRADENIA Hooker 1833 [Gr., *picros*, bitter, + *aden*, gland, alluding to the very bitter floral glands]

1a. Strong perennial with numerous caudices; lf-segs narrow; heads few or numerous, small (less than 1.5 cm diam excluding rays). **P. richardsonii** Hooker. Abundant on gravelly flats, intermountain parks (*Hymenoxys*). Several races occur, differing in the size and number of heads.

1b. Biennial with one or only a few caudices; lf-segs broad (2-3 mm wide), many lvs usually simple; heads larger (about 2 cm diam). **P. helenioides** Rydberg. Known in Colorado from only two localities, one on the W slope, HN (*Hymenoxys*).

PICROTHAMNUS Nuttall 1841 [Gr., *picros*, bitter, + *thamnos*, shrub]. SPINY SAGEBRUSH

One sp, **P. desertorum** Nuttall. A dwarf spiny shrublet with finely pedatifid lvs, on desert hills, lower valleys (*Artemisia spinescens*).

PLATYSCHKUHRIA Rydberg 1906 [Gr., *platy*, broad, alluding to the lvs, which are broader than in *Schkuhria*]. DESERT BAHIA

One sp, **P. integrifolia** (Gray) Rydberg var **oblongifolia** (Gray) Ellison. Arid gulches, lower valleys (*Bahia*).

PRENANTHELLA Rydberg 1906 [dim. of *Prenanthes*]

One sp, **P. exigua** (Gray) Rydberg. Infrequent, desert flats, MZ.

PRENANTHES L. 1753 [Gr., *prenes*, drooping, + *anthe*, flower]. WHITE-LETTUCE

One sp, **P. racemosa** Michaux. Rare or infrequent in forested areas along streamsides and in willow bogs, AA.

PSILOCHENIA Nuttall 1841 [Gr., *psilo*, bare, + *achaenia*, akene] (formerly incl in *Crepis*; see also *Askellia*). AMERICAN HAWKSBEARD

1a. Invol turbinate-campanulate; stem lvs generally all reduced, narrow, inconspicuous or rarely the lowest one similar to the basal lvs. **P. runcinata** (James) Löve & Löve. A very common and variable species of wet montane and subalpine meadows. Easily distinguished from the other spp by the broad invol.

1b. Invol narrowly or broadly cylindrical, 1 to 3 stem lvs well-developed; plants of dry situations. . . . . (2)

2a. Invol, or lower part of stem, or both, conspicuously setose but not at all glandular. **P. modocensis** (Greene) Weber. Infrequent, MF.
2b. Invol and/or stem not conspicuously setose, but if setose, then the setae gland-tipped . . . . (3)

3a. Inner phyls glabrous. **P. acuminata** (Nuttall) Weber. Common on dry montane slopes.
3b. Inner phyls ± tomentose, often glandular or setose as well
. . . . (4)

4a. Invols thick-cylindric, 5-10 mm wide at the middle, ± glandular-pubescent or glandular setose; plants rarely over 3.5 dm high. **P. occidentalis** Nuttall. Common in dry sagebrush areas. Foliage usually very tomentose.
4b. Invols narrow-cylindric, 3-5 mm wide at the middle, never glandular; plants commonly taller . . . . (5)

5a. Aks dark to light green; lf-lobes lanceolate to linear, usually entire. **P. atribarba** (Heller) Weber. Canyonsides and chaparral.
5b. Aks yellowish, buff or brown; lf-lobes lanceolate, usually toothed. **P. intermedia** (Gray) Weber. Similar sites.

PSILOSTROPHE de Candolle 1838 [Gr., *psilos*, bare, + *tropheus*, bearer, alluding to the receptacle]. PAPER-FLOWER
One sp, **P. bakeri** Greene. Common in the Colorado and Gunnison R valleys. The rays are very broad and short, and dry without shrinking, as do those of *Zinnia*. The lvs and heads are loosely woolly.

PYRROCOMA Hooker 1833 [Gr., *pyrrhos*, tawny, + *coma*, mane, alluding to the pappus] (formerly incl in *Haplopappus*)
1a. Invol 11-22 mm high; pap light brown. . . . . (2)
1b. Invol 6-10 mm high; pappus white . . . . (3)

2a. Phyls very broad and rounded-obtuse; invol over 15 mm high; aks glabrous. **P. crocea** (Gray) Greene [saffron yellow]. Forest openings and aspen groves. Variable in height, sometimes up to 1 m tall, with huge glaucous basal leaves.
2b. Phyls acute; invol less than 15 mm high;, aks villous. **P. clementis** Rydberg [for F. E. Clements]. Gravelly flats, intermountain parks, and dry alpine limestone tundra.

3a. Head solitary on each stem. **P. uniflora** (Hooker) Greene. Infrequent, open summits, GN, ME.
3b. Heads racemosely arranged along the stem. **P. lanceolata** (Hooker) Greene. Alkaline flats, GN, RT.

RATIBIDA Rafinesque 1817 [derivation?]. PRAIRIE CONEFLOWER

One sp, **R. columnifera** (Nuttall) Wooton & Standley. Dry meadows, S counties at relatively low altitudes. In the pure sp the rays are yellow and the receptacle long-cylindric. Plants with shorter-cylindric heads and rays with some red color are introgressants with the SE species, *R. tagetes*.

RUDBECKIA L. 1753 [for Professors Olaf Rudbeck, father and son, predecessors of Linnaeus at Uppsala]. BLACK-EYED SUSAN
1a. Lvs entire; stem less than 1 m tall; rays present. **R. hirta** L. Frequent in mountain meadows.
1b. Lvs lobed or divided; stems usually over 1 m tall; rays present or absent. . . . . (2)

2a. Rays absent; disk becoming cylindrical in frt, 3-5 cm long, purplish-black from the first. **R. occidentalis** Nuttall var **montana** (Gray) Perdue, **PL 63**. Moist mt meadows.
2b. Rays present; disk ovoid in fruit, less than 2.5 cm long, dull yellowish at least when young. **R. ampla** Nelson (*R. laciniata* var *ampla*), GOLDEN-GLOW. Common along montane streamsides.

RYDBERGIA Greene 1898 [for Per Axel Rydberg, dean of Rocky Mountain botanists]. OLD-MAN-OF-THE-MOUNTAIN

One sp, **R. grandiflora** (Torrey & Gray) Greene. A stunning large-headed dwarf yellow tundra plant (*Hymenoxys*).

SAUSSUREA de Candolle 1810 [for Swiss philosopher H. B. de Saussure, 1740-1799].

One sp, **S. weberi** Hultén, **PL 23**. Locally common on alpine solifluction lobes, ST. The deep purple stamens and style protruding well out of the corolla, and the beautifully plumose pap, are distinctive features. *Saussurea* is an Asiatic genus with a few spp in W North America. *S. weberi* also occurs in N Wyoming and W Montana.

SENECIO L. 1753 [Lat., *senes*, old man, alluding to the white pap. GROUNDSEL; BUTTERWEED

Note: *Senecio* is an enormous, very unnatural genus. *Senecio* proper, represented in Colorado by *S. vulgaris*, only occurs as a garden weed. Except for *Packera*, which has a different chromosome base number from the rest of our spp, and *Ligularia*, genera have not been proposed for the other Colorado groups of spp.

SENECIO: True *Senecio*

One sp, **S. vulgaris** L. ADV ruderal weed. The rayless fls, pinnatifid lvs, and black-tipped phyls are diagnostic.

'SENECIO': *Lugentes* and *Integerrimi*

1a. Plants with a thick rhizome. . . . . (2)
1b. Plants with an abruptly shortened button-like caudex . . . . . . (3)

2a. Tall, up to 1 m high, produced in great masses, tomentose to glabrate; lvs elongate, oblanceolate, margins with dark cartila-

ginous denticles. **S. atratus** Greene. Abundant on scree slopes and road embankments, montane.
2b. Low, less than 0.5 m high, growing singly or a few together, glabrous and glaucous; basal lvs broadly oblanceolate; lf denticles few or lacking. **S. wootonii** Greene. Open dry montane forests.

3a. Pubescent, losing much of the pubescence in age. **S. integerrimus** Nuttall. Very common in moist meadows.
3b. Glabrous. . . . . (4)

4a. Very tall glaucous plants, usually over 1 m tall, of swamplands, with numerous very small heads. **S. hydrophilus** Nuttall. Wet meadows and oxbows, N counties.
4b. Low glabrous green plants of dry mountainsides and meadows; heads few and large. **S. crassulus** Gray. Common, upper montane and subalpine.

'SENECIO': *Suffruticosi*

1a. Lower outermost phyls prominent, some of them up to half as long as the principal ones, or if smaller, than the plant distinctly woolly-tomentose. **S. douglasii** de Candolle ssp **longilobus** (Bentham) Weber. Desert-steppe sites, Four Corners (*S. longilobus*).
1b. Lower outermost phyls very short, less than 4 mm long; plants mostly glabrous, never woolly-tomentose . . . . (2)

2a. Lvs mostly pinnately divided into narrow, linear segs, seldom more than 1 mm wide. **S. multicapitatus** Greenman. Desert-steppe and piñon-juniper, NW counties, ME-MF, flowering throughout the summer.
2b. Lvs mostly simple and linear, at least some 2 mm wide or wider. **S. spartioides** Torrey & Gray. Gravelly mesa slopes and open parklands, flowering in late summer and fall, GN.

'SENECIO': *Triangulares*

1a. Low succulent many-stemmed plants with 1-3 heads per stem; lvs oblong-ovate, sharply dentate. **S. fremontii** Torrey & Gray var **blitoides** (Greene) Cronquist. Common on scree slopes near timberline.
1b. Tall plants with relatively few stems and thin lvs . . . . (2)

2a. Lvs pinnately lobed or irregularly incised. **S. eremophilus** Rydberg ssp **kingii** (Rydberg) Douglas & Ruyle-Douglas. Common along roadsides and trails, montane and lower subalpine.
2b. Lvs finely or coarsely dentate but not lobed or incised . . . . . . (3)

3a. Lvs triangular, truncate at the base; coarsely dentate. **S. triangularis** Hooker. Subalpine forest streamsides.
3b. Lvs lanceolate, finely serrate-dentate. **S. serra** Hooker var **admirabilis** (Greene) Nelson. Similar sites.

SERIPHIDIUM Poljakov 1961 [Gr., *seriphos*, wormwood] (formerly incl in *Artemisia*). SAGEBRUSH

1a. Lvs simply pinnatifid with 3-4 short stiff linear lobes, green, glandular; dwarf shrub with very heavy root system. **S. pygmaeum** (Gray) Weber, PYGMY SAGEBRUSH. A Great Basin sp reaching Colorado only in extreme W RB.
1b. Lvs 3-notched at apex. . . . . (2)

2a. Lvs many times longer than wide, usually simple and entire but occasionally 3-lobed (in hybrids with *S. tridentatum*); heads usually large (4-5 mm high). **S. canum** (Pursh) Weber, HOARY SAGEBRUSH. Moist mountain meadows, only mixing with *S. tridentatum* on drier ground, N counties.
2b. Lvs relatively short and broad, three-lobed; heads smaller. . . . . (3)

3a. Invol glabrous or nearly so, yellowish or brownish; shrub low, dark-colored in mass effect (less tomentose than other spp). **S. novum** Nelson, BLACK SAGEBRUSH. At lower elevations and on poorer, stonier soils than *S. vaseyanum*, but higher than *S. tridentatum*.
3b. Invol tomentose or canescent, not yellowish. . . . . (4)

4a. Heads very numerous in open panicles; tall shrubs of deep soils, especially along arroyos. **S. tridentatum** (Nuttall) Weber, BIG SAGEBRUSH. Abundant in the lower plateaus and river valleys.
4b. Heads in narrower panicles; lower shrubs of more rocky and shallow soils. **S. vaseyanum** (Rydberg) Weber, MOUNTAIN SAGEBRUSH. Characteristic of highland sagebrush zones, mostly above the *S. novum* zone. On the arid steppe-desert along the Wyoming border a little-understood race called ssp *wyomingensis* (Beetle & Young) Weber. Its only reliable separation from the two above is on chemical grounds.

SOLIDAGO L. 1753 [Lat., *solidus*, whole, for curative powers]. GOLDENROD

1a. Heads in a terminal simple or branched thyrse (oblong spikelike panicle), the branches not at all one-sided or scarcely so . . . . (2)
1b. Heads in a terminal, usually large, spreading panicle, its branches arching or recurved and distinctly one-sided (with the heads arranged along the upper side). . . . . (4)

2a. Lvs ± uniformly short-pubescent. **S. nana** Nuttall. Infrequent in open grasslands at low altitudes, MF.
2b. Lvs essentially glabrous . . . . (3)

3a. Lowermost lvs with ciliate-margined petioles; rays mostly about 13 (or more numerous on the terminal head); phyls not strongly imbricate. **S. multiradiata** Aiton ssp **scopulorum** (Gray) Weber. Common in open sunny and rocky places, subalpine.
3b. None of the lvs with ciliate-margined petioles; rays mostly about 8; phyls clearly imbricate. **S. spathulata** DC. Montane and sub-

alpine. Alpine plants belong to var **nana**, while taller plants of lower altitudes belong to var **neomexicana**.

4a. Lvs, at least the lower ones, oblanceolate, spatulate, or obovate, the upper usually smaller, never regularly sharply serrate. . . . . (5)
4b. Stem rather equably leafy, basal lvs not larger than the middle stem lvs, all lanceolate, sharply serrate. . . . . (7)

5a. Glabrous or nearly so; lvs somewhat leathery in texture; upper lvs often very narrow. **S. missouriensis** Nuttall. Sagebrush, intermountain basins.
5b. Short-pubescent; lvs thin, or at least not leathery in texture . . . . (6)

6a. Basal lf rosette not present at flowering time; lvs characteristically with three prominent veins. **S. velutina** de Candolle [velvety]. Piñon-juniper and oak zones (*S. sparsiflora*).
6b. Basal lf rosette present at flowering time; lvs with one prominent vein. **S. nemoralis** Aiton [of woodlands].

7a. Stem glabrous up to the infl. **S. serotinoides** Löve & Löve. A very tall goldenrod of wet places in the valleys (*S. gigantea* ssp *serotina*).
7b. Stem ± pubescent. . . . . (8)

8a. Invol 2-3 mm high. **S. canadensis** L., CANADA GOLDENROD. Wet meadows and streamsides in the valleys.
8b. Invol 3.5-5.0 mm high. **S. altissima** L., TALL GOLDENROD. Similar habitats.

SONCHUS L. 1753 [the ancient Gr. name]. SOW-THISTLE

1a. Annual; invol glabrous. . . . . (2)
1b. Perennial from deep-seated rhizomes; invol glandular-pubescent or with glandular dots. . . . . (3)

2a. Aks strongly 3- to 5-ribbed on each face, thin-margined, not transversely wrinkled; lf-base auricles rounded. **S. asper** (L.) Hill [harsh], SPINY SOW-THISTLE. ADV ruderal weed in cult ground.
2b. Ak striate and also strongly wrinkled transversely, not thin-margined; lf-base auricles acute. **S. oleraceus** L. [of kitchen gardens], ANNUAL SOW-THISTLE. ADV. Similar sites.

3a. Invol glandular-pubescent with spreading yellowish hairs. **S. arvensis** L., PERENNIAL SOW-THISTLE. ADV tall weed over 1 m tall, in wet meadows and cult ground.
3b. Invol glabrous and usually with large glandular spots. **S. uliginosus** Bieberstein, SWAMP SOW-THISTLE. ADV in similar sites. The species of *Sonchus* resemble Prickly Lettuce (*Lactuca serriola*) but the invols are broad at the base instead of narrowly cylindric.

Asteraceae/Compositae (AST/CMP)

SPHAEROMERIA Nuttall 1841 [Gr., *sphaero*, spherical, + *meris*, part, alluding to the shape of the head]

1a. Heads several, distinct; lf lobes short, relatively wide. **S. argentea** Nuttall. Local, desert flats. MF.
1b. Head solitary (rarely with an abortive one just below); lvs with narrowly linear lobes. **S. capitata** Nuttall. Similar habitats, MF.

STENOTOPSIS Rydberg 1900 [resembling *Stenotus*]

One sp, **S. linearifolius** (de Candolle) Rydberg. ssp **interior** Coville) Macbride. A low desert shrub with linear lvs and fairly large heads with long rays. Collected only once, a hundred years ago, on Surface Creek at the N base of Grand Mesa (*Haplopappus*).

STENOTUS Nuttall 1841 [Gr., *stenos*, narrow, alluding to the lvs] (formerly incl in *Haplopappus*).

1a. Phyls ovate to ovate-lanceolate, 7-9 mm long, the apex acute or acuminate, not distinctly graduated; lvs 3 cm long or less. **S. acaulis** Nuttall. Common on rimrock and dry hillsides, MF-RB.
1b. Phyls broadly oblong or oval, 10-11 mm long, the apex rounded-obtuse, distinctly graduated; lvs 3-8 cm long. **S. armerioides** Nuttall. Piñon-juniper rimrock, W counties.

STEPHANOMERIA Nuttall 1841 [Gr., *stephanos*, crown, + *meris*, part, alluding to the pap]. WIRE-LETTUCE

1a. Annual, biennial, or short-lived perennial with tap root and conspicuously white-glaucous stem; pap plumose in upper half only; heads tending to be racemosely arranged along slender unbranched axes, the peduncles short, not usually more than once or twice the length of the head. **S. exigua** Nuttall. Adobe soils, lower valleys.
1b. Perennial, otherwise not as above . . . . (2)

2a. Aks pitted and tuberculate; plants low, mostly 1-2 dm tall, with the principal lvs runcinate-pinnatifid. **S. runcinata** Nuttall. Infrequent, dry slopes, MF-RB.
2b. Aks smooth or nearly so, only longitudinally ribbed; plants low or tall; lower lvs usually disappearing by flowering time . . . . . (3)

3a. Pap pure white, plumose to the base; low and stout-stemmed, ± divaricately-branched, forming hemispherical bushy growths. **S. wrightii** Gray [for Charles Wright, plant collector of the Southwest]. Dry open places in the valleys, often behaving as a weed (*S. tenuifolia*).
3b. Pap (at least the main axis of the plumose bristles) sordid or tawny white, not plumose all the way to the base; tall and slender-stemmed, the branches appressed-ascending, forming tall broom-like growths. **S. pauciflora** (Torrey) Nelson, **23D**. Common along canyon walls.

TANACETUM L. 1753 [Gr., *athanatos*, immortal]. TANSY

One sp, **T. vulgare** L. ADV. Common along fencerows in the valleys. Tall rank-smelling herb with finely pinnatisect lvs and flat-topped infl of yellow button-like heads.

TARAXACUM G. H. Weber [from Arabic *Tharakhchakon*]. DANDELION
The genus has been revised for us by Dr. R. Doll, Univ. of Greifswald, East Germany.

1a. Outer phyls recurved-spreading. **T. officinale** Weber, COMMON DANDELION, **23A**. ADV. Abundant and ever-present weed in lawns, overgrazed meadows and pastures, responsible, nevertheless, for magnificent early spring floral displays in the mountains. Experimental evidence indicates that *T. laevigatum*, the RED-SEEDED DANDELION, is not distinct.
1b. Outer phyls appressed, erect; tundra plants . . . . (2)

2a. Brownish hairs present in the axils of the basal lvs; scapes often cobwebby-pubescent. **T. eriophorum** Rydberg. Infrequent and widely scattered, on tundra.
2b. Basal lvs and scapes without hairs . . . . (3)

3a. Outer phyls green, with horn-shaped swellings at the tips; plants large (over 5 cm tall); heads large; lvs broad, entire or shallowly sinuate-dentate. **T. ovinum** Rydberg. Common on tundra (*T. ceratophorum* of Colo. lit.).
3b. Outer phyls dark blackish-green, lacking horns; plants minute (1-5 cm tall); heads very small (about 1 cm); lvs regularly sinuate-lobed. **T. scopulorum** (Gray) Rydberg. Among boulders of fellfields on the higher peaks (*T. lyratum* of Colo. lit.).

TETRADYMIA de Candolle 1838 [Gr., *tetradymos*, four-sided, alluding to the invol]. HORSEBRUSH

1a. Branches not thorny. **T. canescens** de Candolle. Common in mountain sagebrush.
1b. Branches thorny . . . . (2)

2a. Branchlets densely white-tomentose even in age; heads solitary in the upper lf axils, not corymbose; fls 5-9 to a head; phyls 5-6. **T. spinosa** Hooker & Arnott, COTTONTHORN, **PL 24**. Clay soil, desert-steppe and lower sagebrush. Young shoots are white and covered with curved spines.
2b. Branchlets glabrate in age; heads clustered-corymbose at ends of branches; fls 5 to a head; phyls usually 4. **T. nuttallii** Torrey & Gray. Stony ground, river benches, valleys.

TETRANEURIS Greene 1898 [Gr., *tetra*, four, + *neuron*, nerve] (formerly incl in *Hymenoxys*).

1a. Stems 2-3 dm high, usually with 2-6 stem lvs. **T. ivesiana** Greene [for the Ives western exploring expedition]. Common, piñon-juniper, W counties. Some plants may lack any stem lvs.
1b. Stems low, lvs all basal . . . . (2)

2a. Lvs almost glabrous and conspicuously gland-dotted; lf-bases set in a conspicuous tuft of long white hairs. **T. torreyana** (Nuttall) Greene. Rock pavements wet in springtime, ponderosa pine, MF.
2b. Lvs strongly pubescent, not conspicuously gland-dotted; lf bases not set in a tuft of long white hairs . . . . (3)

3a. Lvs appressed-silky. **T. acaulis** (Pursh) Greene. Sagebrush, intermountain basins, GN.
3b. Lvs loosely villous. **T. brevifolia** Greene. Dwarf caespitose alpine tundra plant.

THELESPERMA Lessing 1831 [Gr., *thele*, nipple, + *sperma*, seed]
 One sp, **T. subnudum** Gray. Infrequent on adobe soils in the river valleys, ME.

TONESTUS Nelson 1904 [anagram of *Stenotus*] (formerly incl in *Haplopappus*)
1a. Phyls lanceolate to linear-lanceolate, tapering to an acute apex; stems and lvs glandular; lvs 5-12 mm wide; plants not strongly caespitose. **T. lyallii** (Gray) Nelson. Infrequent on tundra.
1b. Phyls broadly oblong, rounded-obtuse or cuspidate at the apex; stems and lvs not glandular; lvs less than 5 mm wide; plants caespitose. **T. pygmaeus** (Torrey & Gray) Nelson. Common on rocky tundra.

TOWNSENDIA Hooker 1834 [for J. K. Townsend, 1809-1851, companion of Nuttall on his western travels]. EASTER DAISY
1a. Phyls linear to narrowly lanceolate, in 5-7 series; apices acuminate or acute . . . . (2)
1b. Phyllaries broadly lanceolate to ovate or elliptic, in 2-5 series; apices obtuse or acute . . . . (4)

2a. Phyls linear, acuminate, with a tuft of tangled cilia at the apex. **T. hookeri** Beaman [for Sir Joseph Hooker]. Blooming in early spring in open, rocky sagebrush.
2b. Phyls narrowly lanceolate, acute, without a tuft of tangled cilia at the apex. . . . . (3)

3a. Disk pap more than 6.5 mm long; lf mid-vein usually conspicuous; lvs ± densely strigose. **T. exscapa** (Richardson) Porter [stemless]. Similar sites; the distinction is difficult until one gains experience with each.
3b. Disk-pap less than 6.5 mm long (if longer, then the ray-pap less than half the length of the disk-pap); lf blades glabrous or lightly pubescent. **T. leptotes** (Gray) Osterhout. Local, generally at very high altitudes on plateaus and alpine peaks, but abundant on arid seleniferous hills in Middle Park.

4a. Lvs and aks glabrous or slightly pubescent . . . . (5)
4b. Lvs and aks conspicuously pubescent . . . . (6)

5a. Lvs succulent-thickened; phyls obovate, ovate, or broadly lanceolate, mostly obtuse. **T. rothrockii** Gray [for J. T. Rothrock], **PL 58**. Late-snow areas above timberline, or (on the Uncompahgre Plateau) on level rocky ridgetops in openings in ponderosa pine forest.
5b. Lvs not succulent-thickened; phyls lanceolate, acute. **T. glabella** Gray. On steeply sloping shale slopes, lower altitudes in the S counties.

6a. Disk pap of stout bristles, shorter than the disk-corolla; annual. **T. annua** Beaman. On clay (usually gypsum) soils, from DT southwestward.
6b. Disk pap of slender bristles, as long as or longer than the disk-corolla; biennial or perennial . . . . (7)

7a. Perennial, usually with well-developed caudices, lacking a rosette of withered basal lvs; stems white with dense appressed pubescence. **T. incana** Nuttall [hoary]. Very common in piñon-juniper.
7b. Winter annual or biennial from a taproot; withered basal lvs present; lvs and stems merely strigose, the stems green. **T. strigosa** Nuttall [with short, stiff hairs]. Rare, clay hills, MF.

TRAGOPOGON L. 1753 [Gr., *tragos*, a goat, + *pogon*, beard]. SALSIFY; OYSTER-PLANT

1a. Fls violet-purple. **T. porrifolius** L. [with lvs like *Allium porrum*]. ADV common dandelionlike weed with grasslike leaves on a tall stem. Hybridizes with *T. dubius*, producing paler fls.
1b. Fls yellow . . . . (2)

2a. Fls pale lemon-yellow, all shorter than the phyls; phyls about 13 (sometimes as many as 17 on the first head or as few as 8 on the latest heads), long and narrow, not margined with purple, longer than the outer fls; peduncles strongly inflated in frt. **T. dubius** Scopoli ssp **major** (Jacquin) Vollmann. ADV ruderal weed in dry hot valleys.
2b. Fls chrome yellow, the outer ones about equalling the phyl length; phyls about 8 or 9 on the first head, rarely as many as 13, broad and short, margined with purple, about equalling the outer fls in length. **T. pratensis** L. [of meadows]. ADV, replacing *T. dubius* at higher altitudes in more mesic meadow sites.

VIRGULUS Rafinesque 1837 [dim. of Gr., *virga*, twig, rod] [formerly incl in *Aster*]
1a. Phyls glandular-pubescent; plants with simple erect stems and lavender rays. **V. campestris** (Nuttall) Reveal & Keener. Mountain meadows.
1b. Phyls stiffly short-hairy but not glandular; plants with spreading branched stems and white rays (hybrids, *V. x amethystinus*, have pink-lavender rays) . . . . (2)

2a. Stem hairs spreading. **V. falcatus** (Lindley) Reveal & Keener. Abundant weedy aster along roadsides and fence rows, blooming in late summer at low altitudes.
2b. Stem hairs appressed or ascending. **V. ericoides** (L.) Reveal & Keener. Not as common as the last, in similar habitats. There is ample justification biologically for separating *Virgulus* from *Aster*, but the morphological distinctions are not easily explained.

WYETHIA Nuttall 1834 [for Nathaniel J. Wyeth, early western American explorer]. MULE'S EARS

1a. Lvs linear to linear-lanceolate; basal lvs absent, reduced, or similar in size to the stem lvs. **W. scabra** Hooker. We have two well-marked races: ssp **scabra**, with the outer phyls coarsely hirsute (MF), and ssp **canescens** Weber, with the phyls closely imbricated with recurved tips, and covered with fine appressed hairs (MZ).
1b. Lvs lanceolate to ovate-lanceolate; basal lvs present and usually much larger than the cauline lvs. . . . . (2)

2a. Upper stem lvs clasping; huge plants with several large heads and basal lvs . . . . (3)
2b. Upper stem lvs petioled; plants with usually only one well-developed head per stem; lvs and stems strongly hirsute. **W. arizonica** Gray. SW counties, MZ-LP. Pure stands occur on the Mesa Verde, but almost all others (*W. x magna* Nelson) show evidence of hybridization with the next. *W. arizonica* is not frost-hardy, and the heads easily freeze in unseasonal frosts. Intermediates with *amplexicaulis* traits are frost-hardy in the same places.

3a. Completely glabrous. **W. amplexicaulis** (Nuttall) Nuttall, **PL 1**. Abundant and forming large stands in mt meadows throughout the area except in the extreme SW. Pure stands of this sp occur in the N counties, but in the middle of W Colorado populations with the essential habit of *W. amplexicaulis* have pubescent lvs and stems. This is a stable hybrid population stemming from a time when the Pleistocene climate compressed the range, bringing this sp into close contact with *W. arizonica*. Probably the greatest floral display of this sp is to be found on the S slopes of McClure Pass.
3b. Plant densely hirsute to almost glabrous. **W. x magna** Nelson. Hybrid, *W. amplexicaulis x W. arizonica*.

XANTHIUM L. 1753 [Gr., *xanthos*), yellow]. COCKLEBUR.
Nuttall, starting out on a journey to Arkansas in 1818, mentions fighting through masses of 'Cuckoldburs' in Ohio. In this instance, the modern word 'cocklebur' may be a later bowdlerism, since 'cuckoldbur' more aptly alludes to the two horns on the fruit!
One sp, **X. strumarium** L., **23H**. ADV common weed, especially around drying ponds in the valleys.

XIMENESIA Cavanilles 1794 [for Jose Ximenes, Castilian pharmacist and botanical illustrator]. CROWNBEARD; COW-PEN DAISY
One sp, **X. encelioides** Cavanilles. ADV common weed in disturbed, dry ground in the valleys (*Verbesina*).

XYLORHIZA Nuttall 1841 [Gr., *xylon*, wood, + *rhiza*, root]. POISON ASTER (formerly incl in *Aster*)
1a. Fl stems slender, lfy to within 2-3 cm of the head; phyls up to 10 mm long; lvs narrowly oblanceolate. **X. glabriuscula** Nuttall.

Clay hills, MF. *Xylorhiza* spp are indicators of soils containing selenium. They absorb toxic amounts of the element and are poisonous to livestock.
1b. Fl stems stout, essentially naked for 10 cm (except for a small bractlike lf); phyls up to 15 mm long; lvs usually broadly oblanceolate. **X. venusta** (Jones) Heller. Abundant on clay hills in the lower valleys.

BERBERIDACEAE—BARBERRY FAMILY (BER)

The barberries are 'living fossils' which were common on hillsides of the Florissant region in Tertiary times. They include the true barberries, which have spiny stems and simple leaves, very abundantly represented in Central Asia and South America, and the Holly-grapes, represented by a number of species in western North America, the Himalaya, and east Asia. The flowers are especially interesting because of the anthers, which open by side-flaps instead of splitting down the sides.

1a. Lvs simple, deciduous, with marginal teeth or weak spines; stems with branched spines at the base of the lf clusters; sparingly-branched, wand-like shrub. **Berberis**, BARBERRY
1b. Lvs compound, evergreen, with stout marginal spines; stems not spiny. **Mahonia**, HOLLY-GRAPE

BERBERIS L. 1753 [from *Berberys*, the Arabic name for the fruit]. BARBERRY
One sp, **B. fendleri** Gray, Barberry, **24D**. Common in the river valleys, S counties.

MAHONIA Nuttall 1818 [for Bernard MacMahon, a friend of Nuttall who introduced ornamental plants to the U. S.]. HOLLY-GRAPE; OREGON-GRAPE
1a. Above-ground stem short or almost lacking; lvs with numerous small, slender teeth; plants of uplands and open coniferous forests, widespread. **M. repens** (Lindley) Don, **24E**. The glaucous-blue berries make a good jelly.
1b. Stems shrubby, well-developed; lvs with few coarse and strong teeth. **M. fremontii** (Torrey) Fedde, YELLOW-WOOD, **24F**. Rare but locally abundant where found, in piñon-juniper, lower Gunnison and Colorado drainages. An attractive tall rounded densely-branched shrub with light yellow or pinkish berries. The wood yields a yellow dye. Here at the northern edge of its range, it is subject to severe winter-kill.

BETULACEAE—BIRCH FAMILY (BET)

From Goethe's *Erl-king* to Robert Frost, birches have always evoked romanticism; they figure in poetry and prose in many languages, especially in the northern world. Birch-bark canoes play a part in our conception of the American Indian. The bract of the carpellate catkin of birch is distinctive, recalling for some the *fleur-de-lys*, for others the Tenderfoot pin of the Boy Scouts. These catkins fall apart at

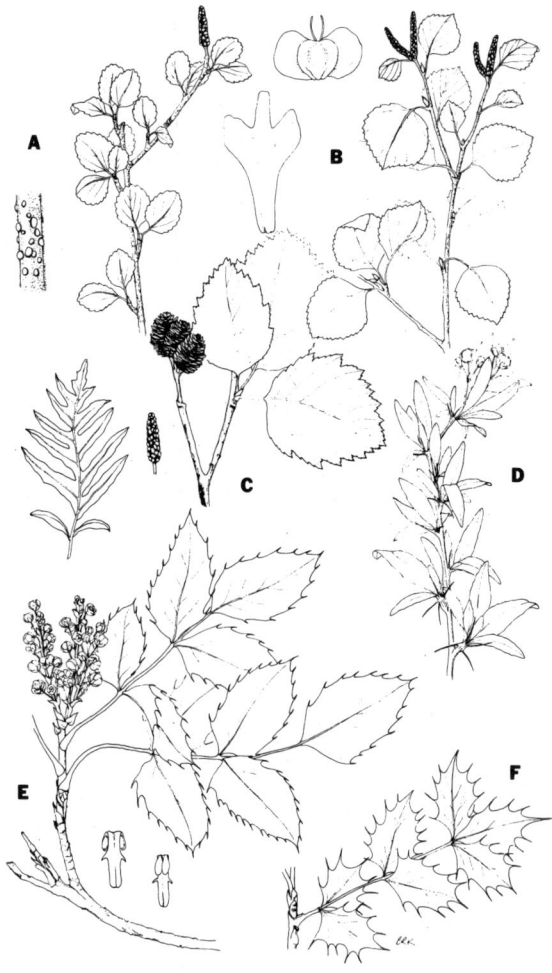

Figure 24. **A**, *Betula glandulosa*, twig, branch; **B**, *B. fontinalis*, branch, bract, frt; **C**, *Alnus incana*, branch, staminate ament, lf of forma *incisa*; **D**, *Berberis fendleri*; **E**, *Mahonia repens*; **F**, *M. fremontii*

maturity, freeing the tiny winged seeds. Birches in spring time yield a sweet sap that, while not collected for sugar-making, has been used to make vinegar. The bark of *B. lenta*, the black birch, has a wintergreen odor.

1a. Scales of the carpellate catkins thin, falling separately from the axis at maturity; lvs flat; pith round in cross-section. **Betula,** BIRCH
1b. Scales of the carpellate catkin thick, woody, and persistent, resembling a small pine cone; lvs wrinkled; pith triangular in cross-section. **Alnus,** ALDER

ALNUS Miller 1754 [the classical Lat. name]. ALDER

One sp, **A. incana** (L.) Moench ssp **tenuifolia** (Nuttall) Breitung, **24C**. Montane streambanks and pond borders (*A. tenuifolia*). A mutant (*forma* **incisa** Weber) with deeply pinnatifid lvs occurs along the Blue River.

BETULA L. 1753 [the classical Lat. name]. BIRCH

1a. Low shrub of subalpine bogs; lvs almost round, thick, crenate-serrate; young twigs dotted thickly with warty resinous glands. **B. glandulosa** Michaux, BOG BIRCH, **24A**. Common around slow streams and beaver ponds, subalpine. Autumn foliage deep red.
1b. Tall shrubs or small trees; lvs ovate or obovate, sharply serrate; young twigs naked or with relatively few glands. **B. fontinalis** Sargent, RIVER BIRCH, **24B**. Canyon bottoms, always close to water, montane. Relatively uncommon on the W slope.

BIGNONIACEAE—CATALPA FAMILY (BIG)

Most Bignoniaceae are tropical lianas, but some are trees, including the best known American one, *Catalpa*, that is widely cultivated on our city streets. The family includes some of the best ornamental climbers and trees in gardens of the warmer parts of the world, and some real oddities, such as *Kigelia*, the Sausage Tree so much in evidence in Hawaii. The flowers resemble those of scrophs: tubular, showy; sometimes a few stamens are lost or replaced by staminodes. The fruit is often an elongate pod filled with flat winged seeds.

CAMPSIS Loureiro 1790 [Gr., *kampe*, a bending, for the curved stamens]. TRUMPET CREEPER

One sp, **Campsis radicans** (L.) Seeman. ADV, commonly cult in Grand Junction and commonly escaped and estab along fence rows. The lvs are pinnately compound, coarsely toothed, the flowers are tubular, red-orange, and the pod is linear (*Tecoma*).

BORAGINACEAE—BORAGE FAMILY (BOR)

The borages share with the mints and verbenas the unique feature of a gynoecium lobed or divided into four discrete nutlets. When in doubt as to which family you have, remember that the borages alone have a radially symmetrical corolla and alternate leaves. Most bor-

Boraginaceae (BOR)

have a radially symmetrical corolla and alternate leaves. Most borages, with a few exceptions (some *Mertensia* species), characteristically have very stiff and harsh hairs on stems and leaves. The name, borage, comes from a Middle Latin source, *burra*, meaning rough hair or short wool, just as the modern word, *bur*; in fact the pronunciation of borage used to rhyme with courage.

1a. Fls yellow or greenish-yellow. **Lithospermum**, Puccoon
1b. Fls white, blue, or red-purple . . . . (2)

2a. Fls blue, pink, red or purple (white mutants occur in normal stands . . . . (3)
2b. Fls white (yellow 'eyes' may be present) . . . . (10)

3a. Dwarf alpines, often forming cushions . . . . (4)
3b. Tall plants of lower altitudes . . . . (5)

4a. Plants forming cushions of small, white silky-hairy lvs, and very short to ± elongate peduncles. **Eritrichum**, Alpine Forget-me-not
4b. Plants not cushion-forming, with several oblong basal lvs; lvs green, not silky-hairy; peduncles 5-10 cm tall. **Myosotis**, Forget-me-not

5a. Fls deep blue, with a well-developed cylindric tube and limb, and short corolla lobes . . . . (6)
5b. Fls otherwise . . . . (7)

6a. Weedy escape from gardens; nutlets with a thickened basal rim that surrounds the basal attachment stipe. **Symphytum**, Comfrey
6b. Native plants of the mountains; nutlets not as above. **Mertensia**, Chiming Bells; Bluebells

7a. Fls dull red; nutlets large, flat-topped, covered by short, hooked bristles. **Cynoglossum**, Hound's Tongue
7b. Fls blue or purple; nutlets otherwise . . . . (8)

8a. Fls in the axils of the stem lvs; fruiting calyx much larger than the fls; weak-stemmed annual with retrorsely prickly-hispid lvs. **Asperugo**, Madwort
8b. Fls in terminal racemes (actually helicoid cymes); in other respects not as above . . . . (9)

9a. Tall perennials over 0.5 m tall; fls and frts large, with pedicels recurved or deflexed in fruit; styles shorter than the nutlets. **Hackelia**, Stickseed
9b. Low annuals rarely 0.5 m tall; fls and frts minute; pedicels erect in fruit; styles surpassing the nutlets. **Lappula**, Stickseed

10a. Corolla limb 15-20 mm diam, pentangular in outline, obscurely or very broadly if at all lobed. **Euploca**, Bindweed Heliotrope
10b. Corolla limb less than 10 mm diam, distinctly lobed . . . . . . (11)

11a. Completely glabrous, succulent, with long narrow helicoid cymes of small white fls. **Heliotropium**, HELIOTROPE
11b. Sparsely or densely hirsute, the cymes relatively dense and only elongating somewhat in age. . . . . (12)

12a. Annuals without rosettes of basal lvs; fls minute, less than 5 mm diam, short-tubed with inconspicuous eye . . . . (13)
12b. Biennial or perennial from rosettes of basal lvs; fls more than 5 mm diam, often distinctly long-tubular with prominent yellow eye. **Oreocarya**

13a. Delicate weak, sparingly pubescent green annuals of muddy places. **Plagiobothrys**
13b. Strongly hirsute, stiffer annuals of arid steppe-desert and piñon-juniper stands. **Cryptantha**

ASPERUGO L. 1753 [Gr., *asper*, rough]. MADWORT
One sp, **A. procumbens** L., **25F**. ADV in MF. The enlarged and flat-open calyx becomes conspicuous after the fls wither, and it is provided with hooked bristles. An unmistakeable plant.

CRYPTANTHA Lehmann 1837 [Gr., *krypto*, hidden, + *anthos*, flower]

1a. Calyx circumscissile a little below the middle, the persistent basal portion scarious and of a different texture than the upper herbaceous part; fls solitary in the upper lf axils, not forming elongate spikes. **C. circumscissa** (Hooker & Arnott) Johnston. Desert-steppe, MF.
1b. Calyx not as above . . . . (2)

2a. Nutlets (all but one) with prominent winged margins. **C. pterocarya** (Torrey) Greene, **26B**. Common under piñon-juniper. The cymes do not elongate, and the sp is recognized by its ball-like fl clusters.
2b. Nutlets not winged . . . . (3)

3a. Calyx slender, distinctly outcurved. **C. recurvata** Coville. A delicate plant with pretty elongate cymes, common under piñon-juniper.
3b. Calyx not as above . . . . (4)

4a. Fruiting calyx only 2-3 mm long, the cymes tardily elongating, only one nutlet usually developed. **C. gracilis** Osterhout, **26D**. This sp, with *C. recurvata* and *C. pterocarya*, are constant companions in the shade of piñons and junipers. All are delicate plants.
4b. Fruiting calyx longer. . . . . (5)

5a. Nutlets all smooth. . . . . (6)
5b. Nutlets, or some of them, rough with tubercles or papillae on the dorsal surface . . . . (7)

6a. Nutlet margins prominent, sharply angled, especially above. **C. watsonii** (Gray) Greene. Infrequent, piñon-juniper, MF.

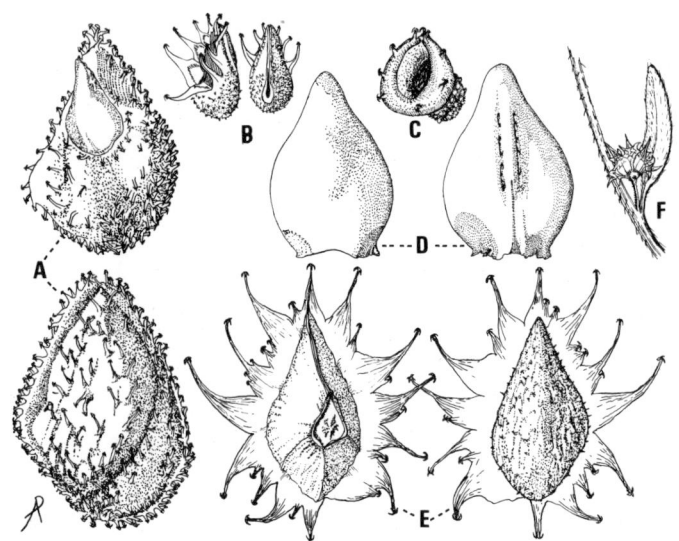

Figure 25. **A**, *Cynoglossum officinale*; **B**, *Lappula redowskii*; **C**, *L. marginata*; **D**, *Lithospermum incisum*; **E**, *Hackelia floribunda*; **F**, *Asperugo procumbens*

6b. Nutlet margins rounded or obtuse, not prominent. **C. fendleri** (Gray) Greene. Common weedy sp in arid sites.

7a. Nutlets heteromorphic—one nearly smooth and somewhat larger and more firmly attached than the other three tuberculate ones; cymes generally lacking bracts . . . . (8)
7b. Nutlets all alike in size and texture when normally developed
. . . . (9)

8a. Odd nutlet (the largest of the four) minutely papillate on the back; flowers (except for a few of the lowest ones) without any bracts. **C. crassisepala** (Torrey & Gray) Greene var **elachantha** Johnston. Abundant weedy desert annual, particularly on Mancos shale.
8b. Odd nutlet completely smooth; flowers mostly with bracts. **C. minima** Rydberg, 26C. Similar sites, often growing together with the last.

9a. Nutlets lanceolate, 0.5-0.7 mm wide. **C. scoparia** Nelson. [broomy]. Rare, piñon-juniper, MF.
9b. Nutlets ovate, 0.9-1.5 mm wide. **C. ambigua** (Gray) Greene. Infrequent, piñon-juniper, MF.

Boraginaceae (BOR) 161

CYNOGLOSSUM L. 1753 [Gr., *kyno*, dog, + *glossa*, tongue]. HOUND'S TONGUE
One sp, **C. officinale** L., **25A**. ADV Eurasian weed in forest clearings in the mts and along fence-rows.

ERITRICHUM Schrader 1828 [Gr., *erion*, wool, + *trichos*, hair]. ALPINE FORGET-ME-NOT
One sp, **E. aretioides** (Chamisso) de Candolle, on dry stony alpine and upper subalpine mountainsides. White-fld mutants are not uncommon. Plants show fls of strikingly different sizes: 'thrum' plants with large fls and conspicuous stamens, are most common, and 'pin' plants with minute flowers and conspicuous stigmas are less. The original spelling is *Eritrichum*, not *Eritrichium*, and must be used. The genus belongs to a distinct Asiatic element in our flora.

EUPLOCA Nuttall 1836 [Gr., *plocamos*, a braid, alluding to the infl]. BINDWEED HELIOTROPE
One sp, **E. convolvulacea** Nuttall ssp **californica**(Greene) Abrams. Rare on the W slope, in sandy ground, ME. The morning-glory fls are unique in the family (*Heliotropium*).

HACKELIA Opiz 1838 [for P. Hackel, 1850-1926, author of *Flora of Bohemia*]. STICKSEED
1a. Stems hispid, the hairs with pustulose bases; stems with lvs mostly near the base. **H. gracilenta** (Eastwood) Johnston. END, oak brush, canyons, Mesa Verde.
1b. Stems hirsute, pilose or otherwise pubescent, but hairs not pustulose; stems lfy throughout. **H. floribunda** (Lehmann) Johnston, **25E**. Common in mt clearings and along roadsides. This sp is said to be biennial or barely perennial, often single-stemmed from a tap-root, and the nutlets have a very few or no small prickles between the principal marginal ones. A close relative, **H. micrantha**, differing by being strongly perennial from underground caudices, with numerous intra-marginal prickles on the nutlets, is alleged to occur on the W slope, but better collections in fruit, and observations of their behavior in the field, are needed.

HELIOTROPIUM L. 1753 [Gr., *helios*, the sun, + *trope*, turning]. HELIOTROPE
One sp, **H. curassavicum** L. ssp **oculatum** (Heller) Thorne [from Curaçao, + with an eye]. ADV, alkaline flats, MF.

LAPPULA Moench 1794 [Gr., *lappa*, a bur]. STICKSEED; BEGGAR'S TICK
1a. Nutlets with marginal prickles in two rows. **L. squarrosa** (Retzius) Dumortier. ADV, the most robust of the lappulas, common in the N counties (*L. echinata*, *L. myosotis*).
1b. Nutlets with marginal prickles in a single row. . . . . (2)

2a. Branched from the base; nutlets with inflated margin (resembling horse-collars); blooming in early spring, common on adobe soils. **L. marginata** (Bieberstein) Guerke, **25C** (incorrectly given earlier

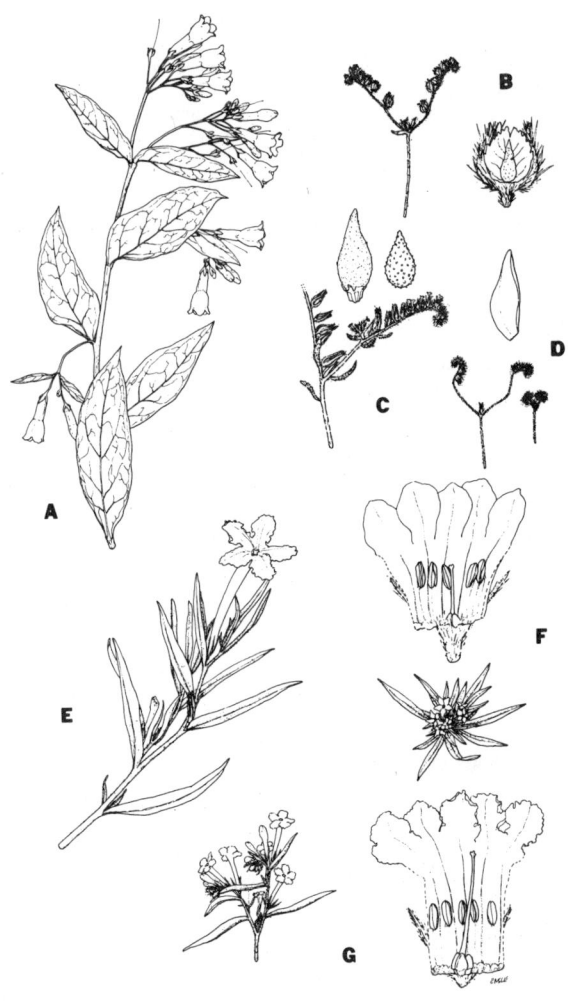

Figure 26. A, *Mertensia ciliata*; B, *Cryptantha pterocarya*; C, *C. minima*; D, *C. gracilis*; E, *Lithospermum incisum*; F, *L. ruderale*; G, *L. multiflorum*

as *L. diploloma*). Probably late-blooming plants hybridize with early-blooming *L. redowskii*, but there are two distinct entities here.
2b. Branched from well above the base, the lateral branchlets typically being almost at the apex of the stem; nutlets rarely with inflated margins; abundant in forested and sagebrush areas; blooming in summer. **L. redowskii** (Hornemann) Greene, **25B**.

LITHOSPERMUM L. 1753 [from Gr., *lithos*, stone, + *sperma*, seed]. PUCCOON

The puccoons are biologically interesting. *L. incisum*, late in the season, produces a strange sprawling, much-branched plant with very narrow lvs and cleistogamous fls that produce seed without opening. *L. multiflorum* exhibits floral dimorphism, some plants having fls with long styles ('pin' flowers) and others with short styles and stamens attached high in the corolla tube ('thrum' fls). This is a device that helps to insure cross-pollination. Read Charles Darwin, *The different forms of flowers on plants of the same species*.

1a. Corolla very pale yellow, almost greenish-white. **L. ruderale** Douglas, **26F**. Common in the oak belt on the plateaus. A robust species, with many stout lfy stems from a single base. Fls commonly of two distinct sizes on different plants.
1b. Corolla bright yellow. . . . . (2)

2a. Corolla-tube 3-4 times as long as the calyx, the lobes fringed, prominent crests in the throat. **L. incisum** Lehmann, **25D, 26E**. Common, piñon-juniper and sagebrush.
2b. Corolla-tube about twice as long as the calyx, the lobes rounded; crests of the corolla-throat inconspicuous. **L. multiflorum** Torrey, **26G**. Later-flowering than the preceding (June-July), mesic sites at higher altitudes.

MERTENSIA Roth 1797 [for F. K. Mertens, German botanist, 1764-1831]. CHIMING BELLS, BLUEBELLS

1a. Plants with several pairs of prominent veins in the stem lvs; stems usually 4 dm or more tall; plants of moist sites, flowering in late spring and summer . . . . (2)
1b. Plants without lateral veins in the stem lvs or with only one or two pairs; stems mostly less than 4 dm high; plants of fairly dry, open habitats, flowering in early spring, or later at much higher altitudes . . . . (4)

2a. Lvs with pustulate-based hairs on the upper surface. **M. franciscana** Heller [for the San Francisco Peaks]. Montane and subalpine streamsides.
2b Lvs glabrous or showing papillae above, but not hairy . . . . . . (3)

3a. Calyx-lobes 1.5-3.0 mm long, obtuse at the apex; corolla tube 6-8 mm long, the limb about the same length. **M. ciliata** (James) G. Don, **26A**. Mountain streamsides, subalpine and lower alpine.
3b. Calyx-lobes 3-4 mm long, triangular-acute; corolla tube 4-6 mm long, the limb somewhat longer. **M. arizonica** Greene var **gra-**

hamii Williams [for Edward H. Graham, botanist of the Uinta Basin]. Infrequent, GF.

4a. Hairs of the upper side of the lf appressed, and pointing away from the mid-vein . . . . (5)
4b. Hairs of the upper side of the lf not distinctly oriented as above . . . . (6)

5a. Style short, 1-2.5 mm long; anthers virtually sessile, usually included in the tube, their tips about reaching the level of the fornices. **M. brevistyla** Watson. Common in aspen, lodgepole pine and sagebrush, N counties.
5b. Style at least 4 mm long; filaments well-developed, nearly as long as the anthers, the anther-bases elevated above the level of the fornices. **M. fusiformis** Greene. Abundant, aspen and oak brush. The plants arise from a distinctive fusiform tuberous root.

6a. Corolla limb definitely shorter than the tube. **M. oblongifolia** (Nuttall) Don. High sagebrush plateaus, MF.
6b. Corolla limb longer than or about equal to the tube. **M. lanceolata** (Pursh) de Candolle. A variable and complex sp, separable into alpine and lowland, pubescent and glabrous, broad- and narrow-lvd races, all evidently merging and recombining in puzzling ways. In this sense, we include here *M. bakeri* and *M. viridis*. The alpine *M. viridis*, in the Front Range at least, seems to have received genes from *M. alpina*.

MYOSOTIS L. 1753 [Gr., *myos*, mouse, + *otos*, ear]. FORGET-ME-NOT

1a. Slenderly rhizomatous, with broadly oblong lvs, basal lvs not developed; delicate plant of streamsides in the mountains. **M. scorpioides** L. ADV. Estab as an escape, but growing in wild places where it appears at home.
1b. Tufted plant with basal lvs longer than those of the stem; tundra plant. **M. asiatica** (Vestergren) Schischkin & Sergievskaja. Local, tundra of the White River Plateau (*M. alpestris*).

OREOCARYA Greene 1887 [Gr., *oreos*, mountain, + *karyon*, nut] (formerly incl in *Cryptantha*)

1a. Corolla tube elongate, distinctly surpassing the calyx; fls usually heterostyled ('pin' and 'thrum' fls) . . . . (2)
1b. Corolla tube short, scarcely if at all surpassing the calyx; fls not dimorphic. . . . . (7)

2a. [1] Fls bright yellow; nutlets all smooth and shiny. **O. flava** Nelson. Abundant on plateaus of the W counties, piñon-juniper and adobe hills.
2b. Fls white, usually with a yellow eye . . . . (3)

3a. [2] Nutlets uniformly muricate or papillose. **O. nitida** Greene. Rocky sandstone or limestone ridges, piñon-juniper. The habit is distinctive: densely caespitose, relatively unbranched with a stiffly erect narrow spike, and the calyces are uniformly slender and not expanded at the base (*O. fulvocanescens* of Colo lit).

3b. Nutlets ± tuberculate or rugose, or sometimes with a few inconspicuous murications . . . . (4)

4a. [3] Lvs conspicuously pustulate on the upper side; corolla tube 12-16 mm long, the calyx segs 3.0-5.7 mm long in anthesis. **O. longiflora** Nelson, PL 37. Locally abundant on adobe, Colorado and Gunnison R valleys.
4b. Lvs sparsely if at all pustulate on the upper side; corolla tube 5.5-12.0 mm long; calyx segs 3.0-5.7 mm long in anthesis . . . . (5)

5a. [4] Infl 0.1-0.4 dm long; corolla tube 10-12 mm long; margin of nutlets not in contact; less than 1.2 dm tall. **O. paradoxa** Nelson. END on gypsum, DT-MN.
5b. Infl 0.5-3.0 dm long; corolla tube 5-10 mm long; margin of nutlets in contact of nearly so; usually over 1.2 dm tall . . . . (6)

6a. [5] Scar of nutlets (adaxial face) surrounded by an elevated margin but tightly closed; style 1-2 mm long; calyx 3.5-4.0 mm long in anthesis. **O. bakeri** Greene. Common in the SW counties.
6b. Scar of nutlets conspicuously open; style 3-8 mm long; calyx 4.5-7.0 mm long in anthesis. **O. flavoculata** Nelson. Probably the most common and variable sp, from Gunnison basin W, in sagebrush and piñon-juniper.

7a. [1] Nutlets smooth on the dorsal surface, not rugose, muricate, or tuberculate; elongate caudices commonly developed . . . . . . (8)
7b. Nutlets ± roughened, rugose, muricate or tuberculate at least on the dorsal surface . . . . (9)

8a. [7] Foliage gray-pubescent; lvs pubescent above. **O. suffruticosa** (Torrey) Greene. The most slender and the least harshly pubescent member of this prickly group (*Cryptantha jamesii*; *C. cinerea*).
8b. Foliage green, not densely pubescent; lvs glabrous above. **O. pustulosa** Rydberg. Not yet found on the W slope but known adjacent Utah and the Great Sand Dunes.

9a. [7] Ventral surface of the nutlets smooth or nearly so . . . . . (10)
9b. Ventral surface of the nutlets rugose . . . . (12)

10a. [9] Corolla tube 7-9 mm long; calyx 6-9 mm long in anthesis. **O. rollinsii** (Johnston) Weber. Peripheral, shale ridges, RB.
10b. Corolla tube 2-6 mm long; calyx 2.5-6.0 mm long in anthesis . . (11)

11a. [10] Less than 2 dm tall; nutlets 2.0-2.3 mm long, the scar cuneate or narrowly triangular. **O. weberi** (Johnston) Weber. END on volcanic ash, Cochetopa Pass area.
11b. More than 3 dm tall; nutlets 2.6-3.7 mm long, the scar closed or narrowly linear and open only at the forked base. **O. stricta** Osterhout. Common in sagebrush plateaus, MF, RB. END in Uintah Basin.

12a. [9] Densely caespitose, low in stature, with many rosettes of basal lvs and fl stems occurring together . . . . (13)

Boraginaceae (BOR)

12b. Not at all caespitose, tall, with a few stems occurring together . . . . (15)

13a. [12] Infl short, broad, with ± elongated lower branches, the hairs white, more appressed; plants with relatively few stems. **O. osterhoutii** Payson. END in rim-rock crevices, Colorado Nat Mon.

13b. Infl narrow, oblong, with spreading distinctly yellowish stiff hairs; caespitose, with many stems covered for several seasons with marcescent leaves. . . . . (14)

14a. [13] Lvs linear, hardly widened at the apex; corolla tube 3-4 mm long; nutlets 3.0-3.5 mm long. **O. caespitosa** Nelson. Adobe-gypsum soils, N MF.

14b. Lvs distinctly broader at the apex; corolla tube 2.0-2.6 mm long; nutlets 2.3-3.0 mm long. **O. humilis** Greene ssp **nana** (Eastwood) Weber. Adobe, Colorado R Valley.

15a. [12] Nutlets conspicuously muricate and with a few irregular ridges. **O. breviflora** Osterhout. Peripheral and infrequent, desert soils, MF. END in the Uintah Basin.

15b. Nutlets not exclusively muricate but tuberculate or rugose, with a few murications between the ridges . . . . (16)

16a. [15] Upper lf surface uniformly appressed strigose, lacking pustulate hairs. **O. sericea** (Gray) Greene. Sagebrush areas, middle elevations, Colorado R Valley, GA-GF.

16b. Upper lf surface with both strigose and pustulate hairs. . . . . (17)

17a. [16] Tall and unbranched except for the infl branches; mature calyx exceeding the nutlets by 2-4 mm. **O. elata** Eastwood. END, local on steep slopes of draws in the adobe hills, ME.

17b. Low and branched from the base; mature calyx exceeding the nutlets by 4-8 mm. . . . . (18)

18a. [17] Nutlet margins obtuse, not in contact; nutlet scar open some distance from the base, with an elevated margin; crests at base of corolla tube lacking. **O. mensana** Jones. Piñon-juniper north of the Colorado R in W GF.

18b. Nutlet margins acute, in contact; scar closed or nearly so, the margin not elevated; crests of corolla tube conspicuous. **O. aperta** Eastwood. END, "Grand Junction." Not collected since the type, in 1890.

PLAGIOBOTHRYS Fischer & Meyer 1836 [Gr., *plagio*, oblique, + *bothros*, pit, alluding to the nutlet scar]

One sp, **P. scouleri** (Hooker & Arnott) Johnston ssp **penicillata** (Greene) Löve. Muddy places in meadows, stock pond margins, etc., in the mts. A very small and inconspicuous weedy plant with small white fls (*P. scopulorum*).

SYMPHYTUM L. 1753 [Gr., *symphyton*, grown together, alluding to the decurrent lvs]. COMFREY

One sp, **S. officinale** L. ADV roadside weed, MF.

BRASSICACEAE (CRUCIFERAE)
MUSTARD FAMILY (BRA/CRU)

Crucifers are distinctive because of their cross-shaped flowers but they can be confused with the Onagraceae, which also have four petals in that arrangement, but an inferior ovary. Crucifers typically have the flowers in racemes, and usually there are no subtending bracts. Many crucifers are used in gardens (Sweet Alyssum, Rocket, Silver-dollar plant) and many are standard table vegetables: *Brassica oleracea* in its many varieties gives us Kale, Brussels Sprouts, Cabbage, Broccoli, Cauliflower and Kohlrabi. Other brassicas include Rutabaga, Turnip, Rape, White and Black Mustard, and many Chinese vegetables. Water-cress is *Nasturtium officinale*, no relative of the garden *Nasturtium* which belongs to the Tropaeolaceae. The foliage or seeds of most crucifers have distinctive tart flavors.

1a. Frt short (called a silicle), hardly more than twice as long as broad. **Key A (silicles)**
1b. Frt long (called a silique), at least 3 times as long as broad. **Key B (siliques)**

Key A (silicles)

1a. Sil sessile, pubescent, very short, indehiscent, almost spherical, with a recurved beak. **Euclidium**, SYRIAN MUSTARD
1b. Sil not as above. . . . . (2)

2a. Sil flattened . . . . (3)
2b. Sil not flattened but spherical and sometimes strongly inflated and papery in texture . . . . (11)

3a. Sil flattened parallel to the papery internal partition (replum), i.e. the shape of the replum is also the shape of the sil in face view (the valves are flat). (4)
3b. Sil flattened perpendicular to the replum; the replum bisects the sil in face view (the valves are folded). . . . . (6)

4a. Sil round in face view. **Alyssum**
4b. Sil oblong, ovate, or elliptical, never round. . . . . (5)

5a. Sil oval, not more than twice as long as wide; styles 2-3 mm long; petals white, deeply bilobed. **Berteroa**, HOARY ALYSSUM
5b. Sil longer and narrower, or styles shorter; petals white or yellow, not deeply bilobed. **Draba**, WHITLOW-WORT

6a. Sil double (resembling a pair of spectacles). **Dimorphocarpa**, SPECTACLE-POD
6b. Sil single. . . . . (7)

7a. Sil elliptic or oval. . . . . (8)
7b. Sil triangular-obovate or obcordate . . . . (9)

8a. Very delicate glabrous annuals; sil football-shaped, not notched at apex; lvs mostly narrowly oblong, but a few basal ones commonly lyrate-pinnatifid; frt not tartly-flavored. **Hymenolobus**
8b. Wiry or stout annuals or perennials; sil almost circular, with a notch at the apex; lvs commonly pinnatifid; frt with a tart taste when chewed. **Lepidium**, PEPPERGRASS

9a. Basal lvs pinnatifid; sil triangular-obovate. **Capsella**, SHEPHERD'S PURSE
9b. Basal lvs entire or merely toothed; sil not triangular . . . . . . (10)

10a. Annual weed; sil large, flat, orbicular, over 1 cm long. **Thlaspi**, PENNYCRESS
10b. Native perennial; sil obovate or oblong-cuneate, shovel-shaped, less than 1 cm long. **Noccaea**, WILD CANDYTUFT

11a. Silicle inflated and papery-textured, sometimes double . . . . . (12)
11b. Silicle neither strongly inflated nor papery, never appearing double. . . . . (13)

12a. Fls white; sil not constricted down the middle to form twin pods; green, lfy-stemmed. **Cardaria**, WHITETOP
12b. Fls yellow; sil of twin papery sacks, ovary constricted down the middle; plants low, with rosettes of basal lvs, silvery-pubescent with flat stellate hairs. **Physaria**, DOUBLE BLADDERPOD

13a. Plants of marshy places and moist ditches; lvs often deeply pinnatifid. **Rorippa sphaerocarpa**
13b. Plants of dry sites; lvs never pinnatifid. . . . . (14)

14a. Annual introd weed; stems simple or branched above; sil pear-shaped; lvs green. **Camelina**, FALSE FLAX
14b. Perennial native; fl stems arising from a cluster of stellate-pubescent silvery basal lvs. **Lesquerella**, BLADDERPOD

Key B (fruit a silique)

1a. Sil with a long stalk between the point of attachment of the petals and the seed-bearing portion of the ovary; tall, showy plants of adobe hills, selenium indicators. **Stanleya**, PRINCE'S PLUME
1b. Sil sessile on the pedicel or nearly so. . . . . (2)

2a. [1] Petals narrow, attenuate, involute, dull red-purple . . . . . . (3)
2b. Petals broad, flat, not as above . . . . (4)

3a. [2] Stem inflated, hollow; calyx pilose; lvs pinnatifid; sil not flattened. **Caulanthus**
3b. Stem not inflated; calyx glabrous; lvs entire or the basal toothed; sil flattened. **Streptanthus**

4a. [2] Sil flattened parallel to the replum (if sils are very slender, try to roll them between the thumb and forefinger, to be sure). . . . . (5)

4b. Sil terete or 4-angled or 4-ribbed . . . . (10)

5a. [4] Valves (sil walls) veinless . . . . (6)
5b. Valves veined. . . . . (8)

6a. [5] Sil hanging, broadly oblong, blunt at the tip, winged. **Isatis,** DYER'S WOAD
6b. Sil erect or spreading, not winged . . . . (7)

7a. [6] Lvs either pinnately compound or triangular-cordate; sil always elongate, elastically dehiscent. **Cardamine,** BITTERCRESS
7b. Lvs always simple, usually lanceolate; sil never more than 5-6 times as long as wide, not elastically dehiscent. **Draba,** WHITLOW-WORT

8a. [5] Perennial, from several short woody caudices, basal lvs green at flowering time; sil distinctly flattened, if long and slender, not erect. **Boechera,** FALSE ARABIS
8b. Annual, biennial, or monocarpic; basal lvs withering at flowering time; sil very long and slender, not very distinctly flattened, erect. . . . . (9)

9a. [8] Cauline lvs glabrous and glaucous, clasping the stem; basal lvs and stem with simple and forked hairs. **Turritis,** TOWER MUSTARD
9b. Cauline lvs green, not glaucous, usually somewhat hairy, along with the stem. **Arabis,** ROCK CRESS

10a. [4] Lvs round-oval, glaucous, entire, rounded at apex; sil slightly flattened but distinctly 4-angled and -ribbed; fls pale yellow; annual weed. **Conringia,** HARE'S EAR
10b. Plants not as above . . . . (11)

11a. [10] Without basal lvs, or these very early deciduous; lvs entire or remotely denticulate. . . . . (12)
11b. Usually with well-developed basal lvs or lvs mostly pinnatifid
. . . . (15)

12a. [11] Perennial with elongate rhizomes, fl stems slender and reedy; basal lvs lacking, most lvs simple and narrowly lanceolate; fls yellow. **Schoenocrambe,** SKELETON MUSTARD
12b. Plants with a slender taproot; basal lvs early-deciduous
. . . . (13)

13a. [12] Sil spreading but not reflexed, very slender and torulose (constricted between the seeds). **Thelypodium**
13b. Sil sharply reflexed, not torulose . . . . (14)

14a. [13] Beak of sil about 4 mm long; plant totally glabrous; common plant of piñon-juniper. **Streptanthella**
14b. Beak of sil about 1 mm long; stem stiff-hairy below; rare plant of rocky canyonsides. **Pennellia**

15a. [11] Lvs all entire, neither pinnatifid, toothed nor lobed; dwarf alpine perennials, not over 15 cm tall . . . . (16)
15b. Lvs (at least some) dentate, pinnatifid, or lobed. . . . . (17)

16a. [15] Totally glabrous; basal lvs long-petioled; sil with 4 strong ribs, plump, not torulose; replum incomplete. **Eutrema**
16b. Pubescent with forked hairs; lvs not petiolate; sil not 4-ribbed, somewhat constricted (torulose) between the seeds; replum complete. **Braya**

17a. [15] Sil with a stout beak extending much beyond the ovule-bearing portion, indehiscent . . . . (18)
17b. Sil without a beak or with a beak not more than 3 mm long, dehiscent. . . . . (20)

18a. [17] Fls white or yellow; sil without transverse partitions between the seeds; lower lvs often pinnatifid . . . . (19)
18b. Flowers pink or purplish; sil with transverse partitions and usually constricted between the seeds; basal lvs merely dentate. **Chorispora**, PURPLE MUSTARD

19a. [18] Sil valves one-nerved. **Brassica**, MUSTARD
19b. Sil valves with 3 to 7 veins. **Sinapis**, CHARLOCK

20a. [17] Pubescence of forked or stellate hairs (included in this category are the unique hairs of the wallflower, *Erysimum*, which are straight but pointed at each end and attached in the middle) . . . . (21)
20b. Pubescence of simple hairs, or none . . . . (25)

21a. [20] Lvs entire or moderately pinnatifid; glandular hairs absent. . . . . (22)
21b. Lvs pinnately or bipinnately divided or very deeply pinnatifid; pubescence often partly glandular . . . . (24)

22a. [21] Hairs straight, pointed at each end and appressed to the stem and lvs; fls. yellow, rarely clear violet. **Erysimum**, WALLFLOWER
22b. Hairs obviously stellate-branched; fls never yellow. . . . . . . (23)

23a. [22] Annual, widely spreading and low; fls rose-purple; weed of alkaline flats. **Malcolmia**, PURPLE MUSTARD
23b. Short-lived perennial, tall and slender, unbranched; fls white or pale pink; native plants of sandy places in wet mountain parks. **Halimolobos**

24a. [21] Weedy annuals with small yellow fls. **Descurainia**, TANSY MUSTARD
24b. Native alpine perennials with white or pinkish fls. **Smelowskia**

25a. [20] Sil somewhat 4-angled, elongate. **Barbarea**, WINTERCRESS
25b. Sil terete, elongate or club-shaped. . . . . (26)

26a. [25] Sil 3 cm or more long, about 1 mm wide . . . . (27)
26b. Sil not more than 2 cm long, often more than 1 mm wide; aquatic or marsh plants . . . . (29)

27a. [26] Cauline lvs entire, glaucous, auriculate-clasping. **Thelypodiopsis**
27b. Cauline lvs not auriculate-clasping. . . . . (28)

28a. [27] Stem lvs deeply and regularly pinnatifid; sil not torulose, stiff, four-angled; fls yellow. **Sisymbrium**, JIM HILL MUSTARD
28b. Stem lvs not deeply and regularly pinnatifid, often simple or lyrately lobed; sil torulose; fls white or purple. **Thelypodium**

29a. [26] Fls white; lvs succulent, with rounded lfls. **Nasturtium**, WATERCRESS
29b. Fls yellow; lvs not especially succulent, with acute lobes or lfls. **Rorippa**, YELLOWCRESS

ALYSSUM L. 1753 [Gr. *a*, without + *lyssa*, madness, the plants having been recommended as a cure for rabies]
1a. Sepals persistent and clasping the base of the sil; stellate hairs present on the sil but extremely small and not clearly visible with a lens; petals persistent and turning whitish; plants, when well-developed, profusely branching and spreading from the base. **A. alyssoides** (L.) L. ADV, preferring more natural areas than the next, often on wooded slopes.
1b. Sepals deciduous immediately after flowering; mature sil with no trace of the sepals. . . . . (2)

2a. Sil completely glabrous. **A. desertorum** Stapf, **29F**. ADV, locally abundant Asiatic weed in dry sagebrush areas.
2b. Sil with large stellate hairs, easily visible with a lens. **A. minus** (L.) Rothmaler, **29E**. ADV, extremely abundant European weed, producing its growth and flowering and dying in very early spring before other plants appear to give it competition. Its dense stands color large areas pale yellow.

ARABIS L. 1753 [from the country, Arabia, according to Linnaeus]. ROCK CRESS
One sp, **A. hirsuta** (L.) Scopoli. ADV, infrequent in disturbed areas and meadows in the forested zone. All other species previously listed under *Arabis* will be found under *Boechera* except *Arabis glabra*, which becomes *Turritis*.

BARBAREA R. Brown 1812 [anciently called the Herb of St. Barbara, the seed of *B. verna* being sown near St. Barbara's day, in mid-December]. WINTERCRESS
1a. Beak of mature sil 2-3 mm long, the sil appearing slender-pointed; petals usually 6-8 mm long; upper lvs shallowly lobed to merely toothed, sessile and clasping. **B. vulgaris** R. Brown. ADV on wet irrigated valley floors; difficult to distinguish from the next without mature frts.

1b. Beak of mature sil to 1 mm long, the sil appearing blunt; petals usually 3-5 mm long; upper lvs pinnatifid or if not, then narrowed to a winged petiole. **B. orthoceras** Ledebour. [straight-beak]. Probably the more abundant of the two; similar habitats.

BERTEROA de Candolle 1821 [for Carlo Giuseppe Bertero, Italian botanist, 1789-1831). HOARY ALYSSUM

One sp, **B. incana** (L.) de Candolle [hoary]. ADV. Originally in the lower mt valleys of the E slope, but now abundant in the Blue River Valley and expected to spread throughout the middle altitudes of the W slope. It forms dense stands of tall white-fld plants in meadows, roadsides.

BOECHERA Löve & Löve 1976 [for Tyge Böcher, contemporary Danish botanist] (formerly incl in *Arabis*). FALSE ARABIS

1a. Mature sil strictly erect, mostly appressed to the rachis; plants glabrous, or pubescent only at the base; seeds biseriate; stem lvs conspicuously auricled. **B. drummondii** (Gray) Löve & Löve [for Thomas Drummond, 1780-1835, botanist with the Franklin Expedition]. The most common *Boechera* in the mt forests. Most of the others are in sagebrush, piñon-juniper, or alpine.

1b. Mature sil slightly spreading to wide-spreading or reflexed; seeds uniseriate. . . . . (2)

2a. Mature sil only very slightly spreading; lvs and stems very finely pannose-pubescent, the individual hairs difficult to make out without a lens. **B. crandallii** (Robinson) Weber [for C. S. Crandall]. Rocky sagebrush, Gunnison Basin.

2b. Mature sil ascending-spreading, widely spreading, to reflexed; lvs and stems with various kinds of hairs . . . . (3)

3a. Mature sil pedicels ascending, never diverging at right angles to the stem, or sil ascending similarly. . . . . (4)

3b. Mature sil pedicels diverging at nearly right angles to the stem, or reflexed. . . . . (6)

4a. Basal lvs sparsely and loosely pubescent, or glabrous, not grayish; stems single or few. **B. divaricarpa** (Nelson) Löve & Löve. Open woods, middle altitudes.

4b. Basal lvs densely gray-canescent. . . . . (5)

5a. Stems few, from a tap root crowned by a few rosettes of basal lvs; plants not forming an extensive mat; sil usually gracefully curved; petals 6-8 mm long. **B. selbyi** (Rydberg) Weber [for the collector, A. D. Selby, 1859-1924]. Common, piñon-juniper and sagebrush.

5b. Stems many from slender branching caudices, forming an extensive mat; petals 9-14 mm long. **B. fernaldiana** (Rollins) Weber [for M. L. Fernald, Harvard botanist]. Sandy soil, bases of cliffs, Dinosaur Nat Mon.

6a. Basal lvs ranging from glabrous to hirsute, often with the marginal hairs longer . . . . (7)

6b. Basal lvs pubescent, never hirsute nor glabrous . . . . (8)

7a. Seeds uniseriate; sil pedicels 3-7 mm long; stems caespitose, several to many, 10-30 cm. tall. **B. oxylobula** (Greene) Weber [sharp-fruited]. A very characteristic dainty low sp, with gracefully downward-curving pedicels and fruits, on rocky ledges in the piñon-juniper and oak (*B. demissa*).
7b. Seeds biseriate; sil pedicels 10-20 mm long; stems not caespitose, 1 to few, 25-60 cm tall. **B. fendleri** (Watson) Weber [for August Fendler]. Common, piñon-juniper-sagebrush.

8a. Petals 12-20 mm long, limb spreading at right angles; seeds biseriate; sil densely pubescent. **B. pulchra** (Jones) Weber [lovely]. Common and very handsome early spring-blooming sp in the piñon-juniper.
8b. Petals 4-12 mm long, the limb not spreading; seeds uniseriate or imperfectly biseriate. (9)

9a. Basal lvs not over 2 cm long; cauline lvs not over 1 cm long; petals 4-6 mm long; stems 6-20 cm tall . . . . (10)
9b. Basal lvs 2-10 cm long; cauline lvs 1-8 cm long; petals 5-14 cm long; stems usually over 20 cm tall. . . . . (11)

10a. Sil pedicels 2-5 mm long; sil 2-3.5 mm wide; basal lvs spatulate, cauline lvs usually ovate. **B. lemmonii** (Watson) Weber [for J. G. Lemmon, 1832-1908, SW botanist]. Strictly alpine, near melting snowbanks.
10b. Sil pedicels 5-8 mm long; sil 1.0-1.5 mm wide; basal lvs linear-oblanceolate, cauline lvs oblong. **B. gunnisoniana** (Rollins) Weber. END, Gunnison Basin, sagebrush. Similar to *B. oxylobula* but with very different pubescence of stellate hairs.

11a. Sil pedicels and sil strictly reflexed and appressed to the rachis. **B. retrofracta** (Graham) Löve & Löve [reflexed]. Very common in subalpine meadows and forests (*Arabis holboellii* var *retrofracta*).
11b. Sil pedicels spreading or descending but not appressed to the rachis . . . . (12)

12a. Basal lvs generally not toothed, finely pubescent, the trichomes minute, no long simple or forked hairs along the petioles. **B. lignifera** (Nelson) Weber [woody]. Widespread in sagebrush zone. Intermediates connecting this with *A. retrofracta* may reflect hybridization.
12b. Basal lvs coarsely toothed, with some simple or forked hairs especially along the petioles. **B. perennans** (Watson) Weber [becoming perennial]. Piñon-juniper-sagebrush, from Colorado R drainage SW.

BRASSICA L. 1753 [Lat. name of the cabbage]. MUSTARD
One sp, **B. napus** L. [ancient name for *Bunias*, or Nape]. Rape. ADV field weed, GN. Other spp of *Brassica* are to be expected as weeds in cult fields. This one is glaucous and essentially glabrous, the

upper cauline lvs with clasping auriculate bases (*B. rapa* ssp *silvestris* of manuals).

BRAYA Sternberg & Hoppe 1815 [for Fritz Gabriel, Count de Bray, 1765-1832, of Rouen]

One sp, **B. humilis** (C. A. Meyer) Robinson ssp **ventosa** Rollins [small; of windy places], **PL 55**. Infrequent on alpine tundra, confined to the Leadville Limestone, GN, PT, ST.

CAMELINA Crantz 1762 [Gr., *chamae*, on the ground, + *linon*, flax, alluding to the presence of *C. sativa* in flax fields]. FALSE FLAX

1a. Petals distinctly yellow, less than 5 mm long; basal lvs usually withering by anthesis; plants little branched, the branches ascending. **C. microcarpa** Andrzejowski, **29G**. ADV weed, common in early spring along roadsides and in fallow fields. Characterized by the plump, terete, slightly ellipsoid pods topped by a rather long style.

1b. Petals white outside, very pale yellow inside, 6-9 mm long; basal lvs usually present at anthesis; plants with several spreading branches. **C. rumelica** Velenovsky [from Rumelia, in Bulgaria]. ADV, recently found near Montrose.

CAPSELLA Medikus 1792 [Lat., *capsa*, a box]. SHEPHERD'S PURSE

One sp, **C. bursa-pastoris** (L.) Medikus, **29D**. ADV, abundant weed in early spring in waste ground, gardens and roadsides.

CARDAMINE L. 1753 [Gr., *kardamon*, used by Dioscorides for some cress]. BITTERCRESS

1a. Lvs simple, rounded-cordate. **C. cordifolia** Gray, **28D**. Very common along forest streams. The plant is typically glabrous and only very shallowly sinuate-margined. In the S counties populations occur with strongly pubescent lvs, and one is known in which they are deeply lobed.

1b. Lvs pinnately compound . . . . (2)

2a. Tall; lvs over 3 cm long; petals 5-6 mm long. **C. breweri** Watson [for W. H. Brewer, 1828-1910, geologist and botanist] Infrequent in meadows, aspen, Park Range, RT.

2b. Dwarf; lvs less than 2 cm long; petals 2-4 mm long. **C. pensylvanica** Mühlenberg. Infrequent, wet mountain meadows, N counties.

CARDARIA Desvaux 1815 [for the heart-shaped frt of *C. draba*]. WHITETOP

1a. Sil densely pubescent. **C. pubescens** (Meyer) Jarmolenko, **29I**. ADV. All of the whitetops are introd noxious weeds abundant in irrigated lowlands. Millions of dollars have been expended in unsuccessful attempts to eradicate them.

1b. Sil glabrous. . . . . (2)

Plate 17. ***Asclepias cryptoceras***   Weber

Plate 18. ***Pedicularis centranthera***   Weber

Plate 19. *Mirabilis glandulosa* Weber
FOUR-O'CLOCK

Plate 20. *Corydalis caseana* Roberts

Plate 21. *Astragalus asclepiadoides* — Weber

Plate 22. *Phacelia splendens* — Weber

Plate 23. *Saussurea weberi* Weber

Plate 24. *Tetradymia spinosa* Weber

Plate 25. ***Balsamorhiza sagittata***   Weber
BALSAM ROOT

Plate 26. ***Astragalus oöcalycis***   Weber

Plate 27. ***Azaleastrum albiflorum***   Weber
WHITE RHODODENDRON

Plate 28. ***Stanleya pinnata***   Weber
PRINCE'S PLUME

Plate 29. *Gilia penstemonoides*　　　　　　　　　Weber

Plate 30. *Drosera rotundifolia*　　　　　　　　　Weber
SUNDEW

Plate 31. *Helianthella quinquenervis* Weber
LITTLE SUNFLOWER

Plate 32. *Mimulus eastwoodiae* Weber

2a. Sil triangular-cordate (broad at the base and coming to a point below the style; main axis of infl pubescent. **C. draba** (L.) Desvaux, **29J**.
2b. Sil rounded top and bottom, broadest at the middle; main axis of infl glabrous. **C. chalepensis** (L.) Handel-Mazzetti [of Aleppo, Syria], **29H**.

CAULANTHUS Watson 1871 [Gr., *caulon*, stem, + *anthos*, flower]
One sp, **C. crassicaulis** (Torrey) Watson [thick-stemmed], **PL 45**. An unmistakeable plant characterized by a massively swollen stem, broadest near the base, a cluster of pinnatifid basal lvs, and a terminal raceme of fls with spreading-pilose calyces and narrow deep red petals. Desert-steppe, MF, RB.

CHORISPORA R. Brown 1821 [Gr. *chori*, separated, + *spora*, seed, alluding to the torulose sil]. PURPLE MUSTARD
One sp, **C. tenella** (Pallas) de Candolle [slender], **28B**. ADV from SW Asia, an abundant early spring weed of fallow fields.

CONRINGIA Heister 1759 [for Hermann Conring, 1606-1661, professor at Helmstadt]. HARE'S EAR
One sp, **C. orientalis** (L.) Dumortier. ADV, locally abundant spring-flowering Eurasian weed. The large rounded entire, clasping-based lvs and pale yellow fls are diagnostic.

DESCURAINIA Webb & Berthelot 1836 [for Francois Descourain, 1658-1740, French apothecary]. TANSY MUSTARD
1a. Sil very long and narrow, 20-30 mm long; lower lvs 2-3-times pinnate. **D. sophia** (L.) Webb [*Sophia*, a generic name]. ADV abundant Eurasian weed of roadsides and cult fields. The other spp are native.
1b. Sil usually less than 20 mm long, relatively plump; lower lvs 1-2-times pinnate . . . . (2)

2a. Sil plump and blunt at the ends, style almost obsolete; pedicels wide-spreading and sil ascending. **D. pinnata** (Walter) Britton. Early spring weed of the valleys, replacing *D. richardsonii* at lower altitudes.
2b. Sil slenderly pointed, style distinct and up to 0.5 mm long
. . . . (3)

3a. Sil elongate, with parallel sides, more than 4 times as long as wide. **D. richardsonii** (Sweet) Schulz [for Sir John Richardson, botanist on the Franklin Expeditions]. The common sp of forested areas, but occurring along with *D. pinnata* in lower areas. Many minor races occur.
3b. Sil short, fusiform, less than 4 times as long as wide. **D. californica** (Gray) Schulz. Tall, branched plant, most common in the SW counties.

DIMORPHOCARPA Rollins 1979 [Gr., *di*, two + *morpho*, shape, + *carpa*, fruit]. SPECTACLE-POD

One sp, **D. wislizenii** (Engelmann) Rollins. ADV in Colorado, peripherally native in New Mexico, a roadside weed in the Four Corners area, MZ (*Dithyrea*).

DRABA L. 1753 [Gr., *drabe*, acrid, applied by Dioscorides to some cress]. WHITLOW-WORT

(Key contributed by Robert Price)

1a. Style length 0.15 mm or less; annual or perennial; seeds 1 mm long or less. **Group I**
1b. Style length more than 0.15 mm; perennial; seed length various. **Group II**

Group I

1a. Cauline lvs absent (rarely 1-2 reduced near-basal lvs); stems glabrous or sparsely pubescent near the base; lvs prominently ciliate (glabrous), or pubescent with simple or forked hairs (if hairs stellate go to 15); alpine and subalpine . . . . (2)
1b. Cauline lvs present; lf and stem pubescence various; submontane to low alpine . . . . (3)

2a. Fls white; caespitose alpine perennial; sil 3-6 x 1.5-2.0 mm, apiculate; style 0.1-0.3 mm. **D. fladnizensis** Wulfen [of Fladnitz, Austria]. Occasional among rocks on the highest mountains.
2b. Fls yellow; short-lived subalpine to alpine perennial (biennial); well-developed sil often longer than 6 mm and wider than 2 mm, rarely apiculate; style 0.0-0.15 mm. **D. crassifolia** Graham [thick-lvd]. Abundant and widely distributed on rocky slopes and meadows (*D. stenoloba* of Harrington, in part).

3a. Submontane (usually below 6,000 ft) fls white; sils often crowded in an umbel-like raceme . . . . (4)
3b. Low alpine to subalpine; fls yellow; sils spread evenly on the stem. . . . . (5)

4a. Infl axis and pedicels pubescent; sil often over 2 mm wide; cauline lvs usually dentate. **D. cuneifolia** Nuttall [with wedge-shaped lvs]. Occasional in dry open places, piñon-juniper.
4b. Infl axis and pedicels glabrous; sil rarely over 2 mm wide; cauline lvs usually entire. **D. reptans** (Lamarck) Fernald [creeping], **29L**. Occasional in dry, open habitats.

5a. Infl markedly pubescent with branched hairs. **D. rectifructa** Hitchcock (upright-fruited]. Simple or branched annual (biennial?), occasional, montane meadows and forest clearings.
5b. Infl glabrous or becoming so . . . . (6)

6a. Lowest pedicel 1.5 or more times as long as the sil; sil elliptic to elliptic-oblanceolate, often hispidulous (usually glabrous), apex (excluding the style) usually obtuse. **D. nemorosa** L. [of woods]. ADV, disturbed woodland. submontane to subalpine.

6b. Lowest pedicel less than 1.5 times as long as the mature sil; sil usually linear to linear-oblong, glabrous, apex usually acute. **D. albertina** Greene [of Alberta]. Biennial to short-lived perennial. Widespread and locally abundant, particularly in moist habitats (*D. stenoloba* and *D. crassifolia* of Harrington).

Group II

1a. Most fls bracteate; cauline lvs 0-2, reduced; basal lvs linear to linear-oblanceolate, margins ciliate and surfaces glabrous. **D. graminea** Greene [grass-like]. Yellow-fld alpine perennial, usually in late snowmelt areas. END, San Juan Mts.
1b. Few if any fls bracteate; cauline lvs 0 to many; basal leaves not as above . . . . (2)

2a. Plants scapose (may have one reduced lf in *D. incerta*), often forming extended mats; petals yellow (occasionally whitish in *D. oligosperma*), usually over 3 mm long; sil 2-6 mm wide; lvs stellate-pubescent . . . . (3)
2b. Fl stems bearing 1 to many cauline lvs, or plants small, white-fld perennials with narrower sils or shorter petals . . . . (6)

3a. Stellate hairs sessile or short-stalked, with long axis parallel to the lf surface. . . . . (4)
3b. Stellate hairs long-stalked . . . . (5)

4a. Lf surfaces with sessile, highly symmetric doubly pectinate hairs; lvs averaging less than 1.5 (0.75-1.75) mm wide; fl stems lfless. **D. oligosperma** Hooker [few-seeded]. Some populations apparently reproduce asexually by seed, others are sexual. Alpine scree slopes of central ranges but piñon-juniper in MF (incl *D. juniperina*).
4b. Lf surfaces with short-stalked stellate hairs; basal lvs averaging 2 (1.5-3.5) mm wide; fl stems sometimes with one lf. **D. incerta** Payson [puzzling]. Alpine, Elk Mts.

5a. Long-stalked stellate hairs on both lf surfaces. **D. ventosa** Gray [windy]. Alpine, Elk Mts.
5b. Long-stalked stellate hairs on lower lf surface only, upper surface with simple or forked hairs. **D. paysonii** Macbride. Alpine scree slopes, Elk Mts.

6a. White-fld alpine plants; style usually less than 0.5 mm long. . . . (7)
6b. Yellow-fld montane or alpine plants; style usually over 0.5 mm long. . . . . (11)

7a. Cauline lvs 0-2, reduced; plants small, caespitose . . . . (8)
7b. Cauline lvs 2 or more; not caespitose; stems often elongate . . . (10)

8a. Stellate hairs absent; stems glabrous; lvs markedly ciliate. **D. fladnizensis** Wulfen [of Fladnitz, Austria]. Occasional among rocks on the highest mts.

8b. Stellate hairs present on the lvs; stems pubescent or glabrous; lf margin various . . . . (9)

9a. Lvs bearing fine, multiple-branched stellae (may have simple or forked hairs as well), often cinereous; sil linear to narrowly elliptic (typically 6-12 x 1-2 mm). **D. lonchocarpa** Rydberg [with spear-shaped sils]. Found sporadically on rocky alpine slopes, sometimes locally abundant (*D. nivalis* of Harrington).

9b. Lvs with a mixture of simple, forked, cruciform and 5-8-armed stellae, usually not cinereous; sil obovate (typically 4-8 x 2-3 mm). **D. porsildii** Mulligan [for A. E. Porsild, contemporary Danish-Canadian botanist]. Alpine, ST.

10a. Lvs densely canescent with branched stellate hairs on both surfaces; usually some fls bracteate; petals ca. 4 mm long; seeds ca. 1 mm or more long or less. **D. cana** Rydberg [hoary]. Widespread but sporadic on alpine slopes (*D. lanceolata* of Harrington).

10b. Lvs less densely pubescent with 4-6-rayed stellae; fls not bracteate; petals ca 5 mm long; seeds a bit over 1 mm long. **D. borealis** de Candolle [northern]. Local alpine, ST.

11a. Basal lvs semi-succulent, oblanceolate to obovate, ciliate with surfaces glabrous; widest basal lvs often over 5 mm wide and 4 cm long; cauline lvs averaging 4- (3-8) in number. **D. crassa** Rydberg [thick]. Thick-rooted alpine rosette plant, found sporadically on talus and boulderfields on the highest mts.

11b. Basal lvs not succulent, bearing hairs on lower surface (may be few in number), dimensions various; cauline lvs 1 to many . . . (12)

12a. Cauline lvs 4 or more, entire or dentate; longest styles usually over 1 mm long (usually over 1.5 mm except in *D. aurea*, where the range is 0.5-1.5); pollen normal; montane to alpine . . . . . (13)

12b. Cauline lvs 1-3(4), entire; alpine only; style usually less than 1 mm long; pollen abortive. . . . . (16)

13a. Plants conspicuously hairy with long (often 1-2 mm), stiff, simple or forked hairs; cruciform or stellate hairs absent; lvs usually entire; sil often conspicuously twisted, glabrous except for stiff marginal cilia. **D. streptocarpa** Gray [with twisted frts]. Open ground, montane to alpine slopes near the Continental Divide.

13b. Simple hairs softer, shorter or absent; cruciform or stellate hairs predominant on lvs; lvs dentate or entire; sil plane or twisted, lacking stiff marginal cilia . . . . (14)

14a. Lower lf surface with appressed (usually sessile) cruciform hairs with greatly unequal arm lengths; pubescence usually not dense; cauline lvs dentate or denticulate. **D. spectabilis** Greene [showy]. Locally abundant, montane to alpine, SW counties.

14b. Lower lf surface with stalked, equal-armed cruciform or stellate hairs; pubescence of lvs usually dense; cauline lvs entire or dentate. . . . . (15)

15a. Longest styles usually over 1.5 mm ([1.0]1.5-3.5) long; cauline lvs usually toothed; seeds averaging 1.3 mm; petals 4-8 mm. long. **D. helleriana** Greene [for A. A. Heller, California botanist]. Montane to alpine slopes, reaching northern limit in AA.

15b. Longest styles less than 1.5 (0.5-1.5) mm long; cauline lvs usually entire; seeds about 1 mm; petals 4-6 mm long. **D. aurea** Vahl [golden]. Widespread and abundant throughout the mountains.

16a. Short-stalked cruciform or stellate hairs present on lvs and infl; sil pubescent or glabrous. **D. streptobrachia** Price [with twisted trichome arms]. Uncommon on alpine scree and fellfields from ST southwestward.

16b. Cruciform or stellate hairs absent; frt glabrous . . . . (17)

17a. Petals clawless, equalling the sepals, both very tardily deciduous; upper stem glabrous or becoming so; well-formed sil usually 3 or more times as long as wide. **D. exunguiculata** (Schulz) Hitchcock [clawless]. END in N and C Colorado from the Continental Divide eastward. Occasional in alpine fellfields, GA, ST.

17b. Petals clawed, exceeding the sepals, both early deciduous; stems with dense tangled pubescence; well-formed sil less than 3 times as long as wide. **D. grayana** (Rydberg) Hitchcock [for Gray's Peak, the type locality]. Occasional to locally abundant in alpine fellfields. END in N and NC Colorado, often mixed with the last but ranging farther W, GA-ST.

ERYSIMUM L. 1753 [Gr., *eryomai*, help or save, because of medicinal properties]. WALLFLOWER

1a. Petals 12-20 mm long, yellow, orange or lavender; biennial or perennial; native plants. . . . . (2)

1b. Petals usually under 10 mm long; annual or biennial . . . . (3)

2a. Sils and pedicels densely gray-pubescent, spreading stiffly at a wide angle from the stem. **E. asperum** (Nuttall) de Candolle [rough]. Characteristically a plant of the E plains, but infrequent in the NW counties.

2b. Sils green and almost glabrous, ascending, usually nearly parallel to the stem, although the pedicels may spread widely. **E. capitatum** (Douglas) Greene. Very common on the W slope and extremely variable, with perennial alpine races having clear yellow or lavender flowers, and montane races with clear yellow or orange petals purplish-brown on the back (incl *E. nivale*).

3a. Low, widely branching weedy annual plants with sinuate margined lvs and widely-spreading sils; pedicels nearly as thick as the sils. **E. repandum** L. [sinuate]. ADV ruderal weed, open fields in the lower valleys.

3b. Tall, slender, almost unbranched annuals or biennials; sils ascending; pedicels more slender than the sils. . . . . (4)

4a. Petals 3.5-5.0 mm long; annual; basal lvs usually gone by fruiting time; sil 1.5-3.0 cm long. **E. cheiranthoides** L. ssp **altum** Ahti

[resembling *Cheiranthus*; tall]. ADV along roadsides and in waste places.
4b. Petals 7-11 mm long; biennial; basal lvs present at fruiting time; sils 2.5-5.0 cm long. **E. inconspicuum** (Watson) MacMillan. Similar habitats, but evidently native. Except for smaller petals, this resembles *E. capitatum*.

EUCLIDIUM R. Brown 1812 [Gr., *eu*, quite, + *klio*, closed]. SYRIAN MUSTARD

One sp, **E. syriacum** (L.) R. Brown, **28A**. ADV along dirt roads on the N side of Grand Mesa. The short, hard, globose and beaked, almost indehiscent sil is unmistakeable.

EUTREMA R. Brown 1823 [Gr., *eu*, well-developed, + *trema*, hole, alluding to the replum, whose membrane does not extend from side to side, resembling an unstrung tennis racket]

One sp, **E. edwardsii** R. Brown ssp **penlandii** Rollins [for John Edwards, surgeon on the *Hecla*; for C. W. T. Penland, botanist of Colorado Springs]. Very rare, on solifluction lobes of tundra, Hoosier Pass region. Recognized by the totally glabrous lvs and frt, the long-petioled ovate basal lvs, and the quadrangular sil with four strong ribs (*E. penlandii*).

HALIMOLOBOS Tausch 1836 [Gr., *halimon*, for *Atriplex halimus*?, + *lobon*, capsule]

One sp, **H. virgata** (Nuttall) Schulz [wand-like]. Local in wet meadows of the mt parks, EA. The pedicels stand out from the stem at an angle, but the sils are stiffly erect.

HYMENOLOBUS Nuttall 1838 [Gr., *hymeno*, membranous, + *lobon*, capsule]

One sp, **H. procumbens** (L.) Nuttall. ADV. A delicate annual occurring in the Gunnison Basin and at Hot Sulphur Springs. Superficially this resembles *Draba nemorosa* but tends to be much branched from the base, and the sils are only 2-3 times as long as wide. Evidently an infrequent species native in both the Old and New World.

ISATIS L. 1753 [the ancient Gr. name]. DYER'S WOAD

One sp, **I. tinctoria** L., **28F**. ADV in Middle Park, where it probably was exterminated by county weed-controllers before it got a foothold. Abundant weed in the Salt Lake City area. In ancient times *Isatis* provided a blue dye. It is the only crucifer that produces hanging indehiscent sils resembling the winged samaras of *Fraxinus*.

LEPIDIUM L. 1753 [Gr., *lepidion*, a little scale, alluding to the silicle]. PEPPERGRASS
1a. Lvs of two strikingly different types, the lower pinnately dissected, the upper simple, orbicular, clasping the stem; fls yellow. **L. perfoliatum** L., CLASPING PEPPER-GRASS, **27C**. ADV, extremely abundant roadside weed in the warm valleys. The simple 'lvs' represent the petiole bases of lvs in which the dissected portion has been suppressed. Transitions are found on most plants.

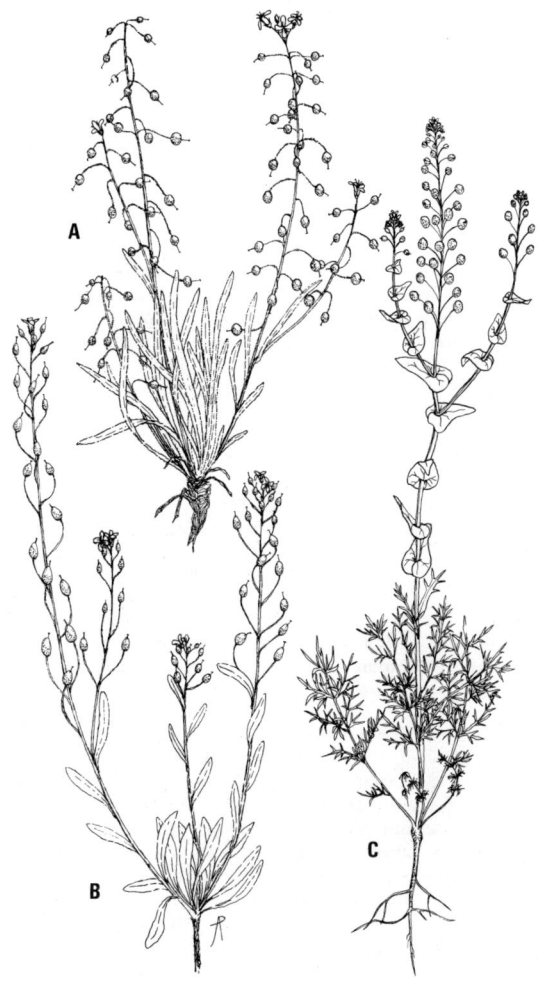

Figure 27. **A**, *Lesquerella ludoviciana*; **B**, *L. rectipes*; **C**, *Lepidium perfoliatum*

1b. Lvs uniform; fls white or greenish. . . . . (2)

2a. Lvs with auriculate bases; sil with winged margin and apex, surfaces minutely lumpy. **L. campestre** (L.) R. Brown, FIELD CRESS. ADV weed. Possibly better placed in the genus *Lepia*.
2b. Lvs without auriculate bases . . . . (3)

3a. Tall wiry perennial from deep-seated rhizomes, forming enormous colonies. **L. latifolium** L., PERENNIAL PEPPERGRASS. ADV, potentially a very bad weed that can choke out all competing vegetation, now apparently estab in MF. Fortunately the plants reproduce chiefly by rhizomes and do not seem to be able to colonize rapidly by seed.
3b. Annuals or biennials with tap-roots . . . . (4)

4a. Style up to 1.3 mm long, exceeding the depth of the sinus; strong perennial. **L. montanum** Nuttall. A characteristic plant of the piñon-juniper, flowering from late spring through midsummer. There are several distinct races; the normal form in piñon-juniper is slender, with few stems; a late summer-flowering race on greasewood flats is more succulent, with many densely lfy stems.
4b. Style short, not exceeding the depth of the sinus; annuals or perennials . . . . (5)

5a. Sil (and stems) covered with short, stiff, spreading hairs. **L. lasiocarpum** Nuttall [hairy-fruited]. Adobe soils of the lower valleys.
5b. Sil glabrous or minutely puberulent along the margin . . . . . . (6)

6a. Petals conspicuous, as long as or slightly longer than the sepals. **L. virginicum** L. ADV, infrequent ruderal weed.
6b. Petals inconspicuous, shorter than the sepals or lacking entirely(7)

7a. Sil 3.0-3.5 x 2.5-3.0 mm, round-obcordate to short oblong-obovate, rounded to abruptly curved into obtuse apical teeth. **L. densiflorum** Schrader, 29M. ADV, very common, especially in early spring, lower valleys. Usually erect and symmetrical, each main branch terminating in an erect raceme.
7b. Sil 2.5 x 1.5-2.0 mm, nearly elliptic, narrowed into acute apical teeth. **L. ramosissimum** Nelson. Flowering in midsummer at higher altitudes than the last, in the intermountain parks and oak-aspen. Often strongly asymmetrical, with the main stems widely spreading and the racemes erect along one side.

LESQUERELLA Watson 1888 [for Leo Lesquereux, 1805-1899, paleobotanist and bryologist]. BLADDER-POD
1a. Sil glabrous. . . . . (2)
1b. Sil stellate-pubescent . . . . (3)

2a. Basal lvs broadly ovate, distinctly petiolate; sil loosely racemose

	on sigmoid pedicels. **L. pruinosa** Greene. Narrowly endemic on clay-shale, AA.
2b.	Basal lvs linear, not differentiated into blade and petiole; sils crowded on stiffly erect pedicels. **L. fendleri** (Gray) Watson. Peripheral, entering Colorado at the Four Corners.

3a. Pedicels recurved, sils pendent . . . . (4)
3b. Pedicels sigmoid or curved, sometimes straight, sils erect . . . . . (5)

4a.	Perennial; inner basal lvs involute and usually entire; racemes not secund; valves often pubescent inside. **L. ludoviciana** (Nuttall) Watson, **27A**. Common on arid hills.
4b.	Annual or short-lived perennial; inner basal lvs flat and generally dentate or somewhat angular; racemes usually secund; valves glabrous on the inside. **L. parviflora** Rollins. END on shales, Piceance Basin, RB.

5a.	Lowermost lvs more than 5 mm wide, usually with a distinct blade and petiole, rosulate with a clear distinction between basal and cauline lvs. **L. rectipes** Wooton & Standley, **27B, 29K**. Piñon-juniper. In the S counties, *L. rectipes* evidently introgresses with *L. montana*, an E slope sp. In *L. rectipes* the sils are globose to obovoid; in *L. montana* they are ellipsoid, a difference difficult to define. It also is sometimes difficult to distinguish *L. rectipes* from *L. ludoviciana* for the same reasons. *L. rectipes* sometimes has a few pendent sils and narrow lvs; the sils of *L. ludoviciana* are usually much longer.
5b.	Lowermost lvs narrow, 1-5 mm wide, usually with no clear distinction between blade and petiole, tufted at stem bases but not rosulate; basal and cauline lvs somewhat similar; racemes umbelliform, hardly exceeding the basal lvs . . . . (6)

6a.	Caudices several, distinct, forming a loose crown; trichomes with the arms free almost to the center. **L. alpina** (Nuttall) Watson (*L. subumbellata*). Common on sandstone pavements of the high plateau summits in NW MF, producing elegant dwarf 'alpine gardens'. Ssp **parvula** (Greene) Rollins & Shaw has narrowly linear lvs and is abundant in Middle Park and on summits of the Ten Mile Range.
6b.	Caudices extremely short or none; plant forming a single tight and dense crown; trichomes with the arms short, more massive and distinctly fused toward the center, said to be half the size of those of the above. **L. congesta** Rollins. END, recently discovered on shale slopes of the Piceance Basin.

MALCOLMIA R. Brown 1812 [for William Malcolm, 18th cent. London nurseryman]

One sp, **M. africana** R. Brown, **28C**. ADV annual purple-fld spring-blooming ruderal weed common on adobe flats of the lower valleys. It may be confused with *Chorispora tenella*, but that is stipitate-glandular with simple hairs; in *Malcolmia* the hairs are 3-forked and non-glandular.

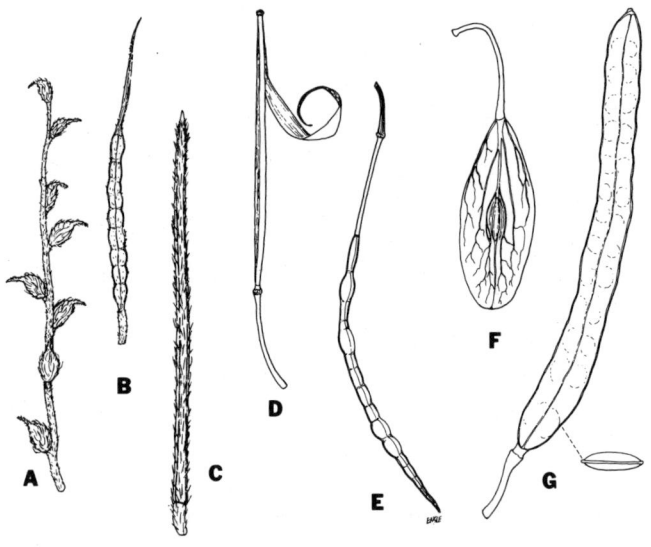

Figure 28. A, *Euclidium syriacum*; B, *Chorispora tenella*; C, *Malcolmia africana*; D, *Cardamine cordifolia*; E, *Stanleya viridiflora*; F, *Isatis tinctoria*; G, *Streptanthus cordatus*

NASTURTIUM R. Brown 1812 [so-called, according to Pliny, *a narribus torquendus*, *i.e.* a writhing of the nostrils, because of the sharp smell of the seed]. WATERCRESS

One sp, **N. officinale** R. Brown [of the shops]. ADV in slow-flowing ditches and springs in the lower valleys (*Rorippa nasturtium-aquaticum*). While this plant makes a very fine salad ingredient, contamination of the water in which wild plants are growing may be a health hazard.

NOCCAEA Moench 1802 [for Domenico Nocca, 18th cent. Italian botanist]. WILD CANDYTUFT

One sp, **N. montana** (L.) Meyer, **29A**. A ubiquitous sp, occurring through the gamut of habitats from piñon-juniper to tundra (*Thlaspi*).

PENNELLIA Nieuwland 1918 [for Francis W. Pennell, American botanist, scroph specialist]

One sp, **P. micrantha** (Gray) Nieuwland. Local on cliffs and talus slopes, montane, La Plata Mts.

PHYSARIA Gray 1848 [Gr., *physa*, bellows]. DOUBLE BLADDER-POD

1a. Plants strictly alpine, above 11,000 ft. alt; petals very large (10-12 mm long), orange-yellow. **P. alpina** Rollins, **PL 57**. END on rocky tundra, NE Gunnison Basin and Mosquito Range.
1b. Plants of sagebrush, grassland and piñon-juniper below tree-line; petals yellow, from very small to large. . . . . (2)

2a. Sil with widely spreading upper part, inversely heart-shaped. **P. obcordata** Rollins. END on white shales, Piceance Basin, RB.
2b. Sil not obviously heart-shaped . . . . (3)

3a. Coarse, with large lvs, fls and sils; sinuses of sil equal above and below. **P. acutifolia** Rydberg, **29C**. Abundant, piñon-juniper and canyon country, W counties.
3b. Relatively small and delicate in all respects; sinuses of sil unequal, the upper very deep, the lower shallow or absent . . . . . (4)

4a. Basal lvs entire or with a single broad tooth on each side, linear-oblanceolate, less than 4 cm long; replum narrowly obovate. **P. rollinsii** Mulligan [for Reed C. Rollins, crucifer specialist]. Sagebrush, Gunnison Basin NW to Grand Mesa (*P. acutifolia* of Harrington).
4b. Basal lvs divided, broadly oblanceolate, more than 4 cm long; replum linear, constricted in the middle. **P. floribunda** Rydberg. Sagebrush, mostly at lower altitudes than the last, Gunnison and Colorado R Basins. A fairly distinct form with pendent sils, localized in Middle Park, has been called *P. osterhoutii* Payson.

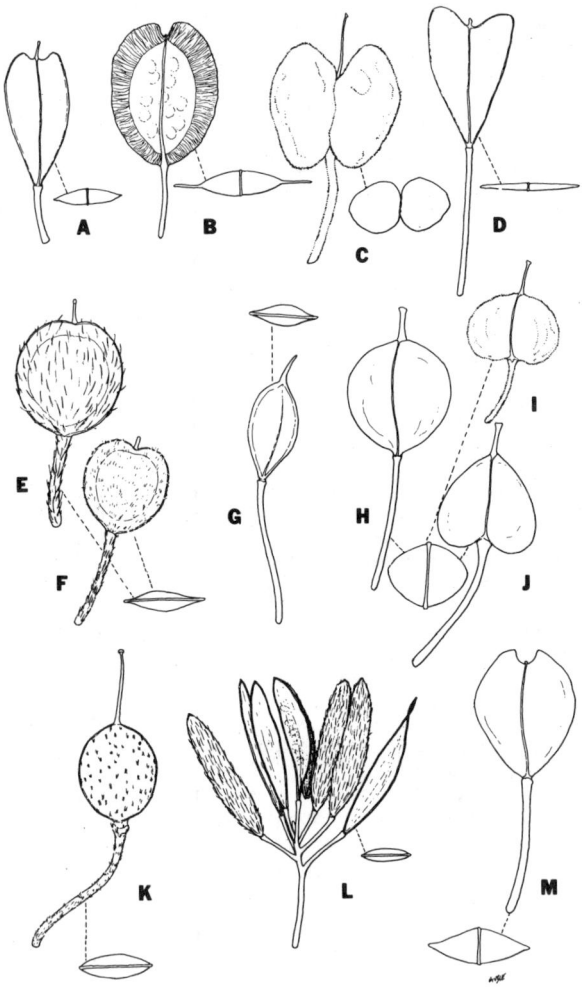

Figure 29. A, *Noccaea montana*; B, *Thlaspi arvense*; C, *Physaria acutifolia*; D, *Capsella bursa-pastoris*; E, *Alyssum minus*; F, *A. desertorum*; G, *Camelina microcarpa*; H, *Cardaria chalepensis*; I, *C. pubescens*; J, *C. draba*; K, *Lesquerella rectipes*; L, *Draba reptans*; M, *Lepidium densiflorum*

RORIPPA Scopoli 1760 [Old Saxon name for a cress, *Rorippen*]. YELLOWCRESS

1a. Rhizomatous perennial; petals well exceeding the sepals; lvs regularly pinnatifid. **R. sinuata** (Nuttall) Hitchcock. Abundant on wet roadside ditches and meadows.
1b. Annual or biennial with a taproot; petals scarcely exceeding the sepals; lvs lyrate-pinnatifid or only toothed. . . . . (2)

2a. Sil nearly spherical, the replum almost circular as well. **R. sphaerocarpa** (Gray) Britton. Rare or at least very little known, SW counties.
2b. Sil oblong . . . . (3)

3a. Stem lvs unlobed, the margin entire or serrate; low spreading plant. **R. curvipes** Greene var **alpina** (Watson) Stuckey. Common on muddy shores of drying ponds and streams, montane to subalpine.
3b. Stem lvs pinnatifid; mostly tall, erect plants. . . . . (4)

4a. Upper lf surface and stem with scattered 'vesicular trichomes' (these appear as small round blisters on the lf surface which often break, leaving holes in the lf); seeds under 0.5 mm long. **R. teres** (Michaux) Stuckey. This and the next are common in muddy places.
4b. Upper lf surface and stem lacking vesicular trichomes, but often with ordinary hairs; seeds over 0.5 mm long. **R. palustris** (L.) Besser ssp **hispida** (Desvaux) Jonsell.

SCHOENOCRAMBE Greene 1896 [Gr., *schoinos*, a rush, alluding to the lfless appearance, + *Crambe*, a genus]. SKELETON MUSTARD

One sp, **S. linifolia** (Nuttall) Greene [flax-lvd]. Common in piñon-juniper, sagebrush and oak. A nondescript tall rhizomatous yellow-fld crucifer with mostly undivided linear lvs, perennial but producing few stems (*Sisymbrium*).

SINAPIS L. 1753 [ancient name for mustard]. CHARLOCK

One sp, **S. arvensis** L. Common ADV yellow-fld mustard invading cult fields as a weed (*Brassica kaber*).

SISYMBRIUM L. 1753 [Gr. name for some mustard]. JIM HILL MUSTARD

1a. Fls pale yellow; pedicels stout, 4-10 mm long, nearly as thick as the frt; sil widely spreading, rigid, 5-10 cm long. **S. altissimum** L. [very tall]. Abundant ruderal weed at low altitudes, believed to have spread into the West along the railroads (Jim Hill was an early railroad magnate).
1b. Fls bright yellow; pedicels slender, 7-20 mm long, not as thick as the frt; sil ascending to erect, 2.0-3.5 cm long. **S. loeselii** L. [for J. A. Loiseleur des Longchamps]. Common weed N of the Colorado R drainage, mostly at higher altitudes in moister sites.

Brassicaceae (Cruciferae) (BRA/CRU)

SMELOWSKIA C. A. Meyer 1830 [for T. Smelovskii, Russian botanist]

One sp, **S. calycina** (Stephan) Meyer [with calyx]. Scree slopes and rocky tundra, Continental Divide and San Juans. A sp of our Asiatic element, ranging to Altai and Central Asia.

STANLEYA Nuttall 1818 [For Lord Stanley, British statesman, 1799-1869]. PRINCE'S PLUME

1a. Stem lvs sessile, auriculate; fls pale greenish-yellow. **S. viridiflora** Nuttall [green-fld], **28D**. Desert steppe, MF, peripheral from Wyoming.
1b. Stem lvs tapering to a petiole; fls either bright yellow or creamy white . . . . (2)

2a. Fls bright yellow; plants green. **S. pinnata** (Pursh) Britton, **PL 28**. Common on seleniferous soils in the valleys. The presence of *Stanleya* is indicative of the poisonous element, selenium, in the soil. The plants concentrate the metal in the tissues; selenium indicator plants have a strong unpleasant odor.
2b. Fls creamy white; plants glaucous. **S. albescens** Jones [whitish]. Abundant on adobe flats in the Gunnson and Colorado R valleys between Delta and Grand Junction. In certain years the plant dominates the landscape for miles, and in other years hardly any are to be seen.

STREPTANTHELLA Rydberg 1918 [dim. of *Streptanthus*]

One sp, **S. longirostris** (Watson) Rydberg [long-beaked]. Common spring-flowering mustard in piñon-juniper. Easily recognized by the slender reflexed long-beaked siliques.

STREPTANTHUS [Gr., *strept-*, alluding to the twisted petals]. TWIST-FLOWER

One sp, **S. cordatus** Nuttall, **28G**. A common odd and striking sp of the piñon-juniper, characterized by large oval clasping lvs (the basal coarsely toothed) and long raceme of fls with linear, twisted, deep maroon petals, replaced later by broad, flat, erect sils.

THELYPODIOPSIS Rydberg 1907 [resembling *Thelypodium*]

1a. Lvs linear-lanceolate, tapering to the base; fls purple. **T. linearifolia** (Gray) Al-Shehbaz. Piñon-juniper SW counties.
1b. Lvs broadly oblong, sessile and clasping at the base; fls various . . . . (2)

2a. Fls bright golden-yellow. **T. aurea** (Eastwood) Rydberg. Frequent in canyons of SW counties.
2b. Fls white, pinkish or purple . . . . (3)

3a. Fls white or pale pink; sepals spreading or reflexed in anthesis. **T. elegans** (Jones) Rydberg. Abundant on canyonsides, Gunnison, Colorado and White R drainages.
3b. Fls deep pink-purple; sepals erect at anthesis. **T. juniperorum** (Payson) Rydberg. Piñon-juniper, MN-ME. There is still some doubt as to the status of this sp.

THELYPODIUM Endlicher 1839 [Gr., *thelys*, woman, + *podium*, foot. Significance?]

1a. Sls not more than 2 cm long, lightly over 1 mm thick, curving upward from widely-spreading pedicels, crowded into a short terminal raceme. **T. integrifolium** (Nuttall) Endlicher. Stream benches in sagebrush of interior valleys.
1b. Sils 3-4 cm long, 1mm or less thick, widely spreading or downcurved, in a very lax raceme. **T. laxiflorum** Al-Shehbaz. Roadsides, cut-banks and moiost thickets, piñon-juniper to oak brush.

THLASPI L. 1753 [Gr., *thlaein*, to crush, alluding to the flat sil]. FANWEED; PENNYCRESS

One sp, **T. arvense** L., **29B**. ADV ruderal weed. So-called because the large, erect, almost orbicular flat silicles resemble fans or pennies. For other spp, see *Noccaea*.

TURRITIS L. 1753 [anc. name from Lat. *turritus*, towered]. TOWER MUSTARD

One sp, **T. glabra** L. Disturbed sitres, particularly in forested areas, along logging roads and campgrounds, very likely ADV here (*Arabis*).

CACTACEAE—CACTUS FAMILY (CAC)

Except for the prickly-pears (*Opuntia* spp), we should consider our cacti as threatened or endangered plants and refrain from collecting them in the wild. They are rapidly disappearing because of exploitation for the international rock garden trade. In Arizona the collecting of cacti is prohibited by state law, a precedent that should be followed in Colorado. Generic lines are very difficult to draw in the cacti, and each cactologist seems to have his own notion of them; they change frequently.

1a. Areoles bearing glochids (minute, sharp-pointed, barbed bristles that penetrate the flesh without at first being felt); new stem bearing a fleshy lf just below each areole. . . . . (2)
1b. Areoles not bearing glochids; stem lfless or with only slight bulges or scales representing them. . . . . (3)

2a. Joints of the stem cylindrical, elongate; glochids small and inconsequential; epidermis of the spine separating into a thin papery sheath; erect or scrambling shrubs. **Cylindropuntia**, CHOLLA
2b. Joints of the stem flat, oval or potato-like; glochids well-developed, barbed and effective; succulent, prostrate or spreading plants. **Opuntia**, PRICKLY-PEAR

3a. Fls borne clearly below the branch apex, on old growth; stems ribbed. **Echinocereus**, HEDGEHOG CACTUS
3b. Fls borne at the apex of the branch, on the current growth; stems ribbed or tuberculate. . . . . (4)

4a. Plants with vertical ribs, or with tubercles that are not grooved on the upper side . . . . (5)
4b. Plants with tubercles that are grooved along the upper side. **Coryphantha**, NIPPLE CACTUS

5a. Plants with ribs, the tubercles coalesced so as to be less noticeable than the ribs. **Sclerocactus**, BEAR-CLAW
5b. Plants with very well-defined high tubercles. **Pediocactus**, BALL CACTUS

CORYPHANTHA Lemaire 1868 [Gr., *koryphe*, summit, + *anthos*, flower, alluding to the position of the fls]. NIPPLE CACTUS
1a. Fls pink; fruit green or brown. **C. vivipara** (Nuttall) Britton & Rose var **radiosa** (Engelmann) Backeberg. Frequent in piñon-juniper and sagebrush. Our *Coryphantha* spp are currently regarded by some as belonging to the genus *Escobaria*.
1b. Flowers green or yellow; fruit red, maturing the following year. **C. missouriensis** (Sweet) Britton & Rose. Very inconspicuous and probably infrequent, sagebrush.

CYLINDROPUNTIA Knuth 1935. CHOLLA

1a. Only about a foot high, producing spreading spiny thickets; branches about 1 cm diam; fls yellow. **C. whipplei** (Engelmann & Bigelow) Knuth [for Lt. A. Whipple, head of the Pacific R. R. Survey], RAT-TAIL CACTUS. Four Corners.
1b. Plants 1 m high or more, producing erect shrubs; branches about 2 cm wide or more; fls purple. **C. imbricata** (Haworth) Knuth, CANDELABRA CACTUS. A colony alleged to be this occurs in AA. The plants answer the above description, but some believe this colony to be hybrid. *C. imbricata* is common on the E slope.

ECHINOCEREUS Engelmann 1848 [Gr., *echinos*, hedgehog, + *Cereus*, a genus]. HEDGE-HOG CACTUS
1a. Fls pink-purple; petals not rounded or cupped; stems solitary or a few together. **E. fendleri** (Engelmann) Rumpler, SITTING CACTUS. Canyon bottoms, Mesa Verde.
1b. Fls scarlet; petals rounded and cupped; stems numerous. **E. triglochidiatus** Engelmann [with three spines], CLARET CUP. A splendid species producing several short cylindrical stems from which brilliant fls arise on the sides. Several varieties are recognized, the most remarkable being the spineless forma **inermis**, **PL 51**, which may grow side by side with the typical form.

OPUNTIA Miller 1754 [name used by Theophrastus for some plant, not this]. PRICKLY-PEAR
1a. Frt with at least an apical rim of spreading, barbed spines, often spiny all over, green but becoming tan and dry as the seeds mature; seeds usually rough and irregular . . . . (2)
1b. Frt nearly always spineless but with glochids, fleshy and juicy as the seeds mature, usually red or purple; seeds usually smooth and regular in outline. **O. phaeacantha** Engelmann [brown-spined], NEW MEXICAN PRICKLY-PEAR. Usually the pads are

very large, glaucous, with wide spaces between areoles, and long brown-tipped spines. Canyons, piñon-juniper.

2a. Pads potato-like, very easily broken apart; fls yellow. **O. fragilis** (Nuttall) Haworth var **brachyarthra** (Engelmann & Bigelow) Coulter [brittle; with short joints], POTATO CACTUS. Abundant on the plateaus, especially on seasonally flooded rocky pavements. Probably a great amount of the variability of *Opuntia* is related to hybridization between this and other spp. A spineless variant occurs.
2b. Pads broad and flat, not breaking at the merest touch; fls red, yellow or coppery. . . . . (3)

3a. Spines all circular or broadly elliptic in cross-section (roll between the fingers). **O. polyacantha** Haworth. Abundant on desert flats and canyonsides.
3b. Spines flattened at least basally, and some spines elliptic or narrowly elliptic in cross-section. **O. erinacea** Engelmann & Bigelow [fig-like]. Abundant on canyonsides. To distinguish between this and the last is often impossible, since the spp undoubtedly hybridize, sometimes three and four ways.

PEDIOCACTUS Britton & Rose 1913 [from Gr., *pedion*, flatland]. BALL CACTUS
1a. Mature plants only 2.5 cm diam; spines pubescent, a central spine never present. **P. knowltonii** Benson. Peripheral and extremely rare, on the state line in AA.
1b. Mature plants well over 5 cm diam; spines smooth when mature; dark reddish-brown central spine(s) present. **P. simpsonii** (Engelmann) Britton & Rose [for J. H. Simpson, army engineer whom Engelmann assisted in the field]. Common in sagebrush areas on the plateaus, to the upper limit of piñon-juniper. On the W slope the plants are usually much larger than those on the E slope and the fls are yellowish rather than pink.

SCLEROCACTUS Britton & Rose 1922 [Gr., *sklero*, hard], also called *Ferocactus*. BEAR-CLAW
1a. Fls yellow-green; plant short and squat, the spines short, radial; central spines, when present, sometimes hooked. **S. mesaeverdae** Boissevain & Davidson, MESA VERDE CACTUS. END, rare on adobe hills, Four Corners.
1b. Fls rose-purple . . . . (2)

2a. Central spine strongly hooked; seeds 3-4 mm diam. **S. whipplei** (Engelmann & Bigelow) Britton & Rose var **intermedius** (Peebles) Benson. Adobe hills.
2b. Central spine not hooked; seeds at most 2.5 mm broad. **S. glaucus** (K. Schumann) Benson. Rare on adobe soils, Colorado R Valley. Perhaps only a variant of the last.

CALLITRICHACEAE
WATER-STARWORT FAMILY (CLL)

While the water-starworts are easily recognized as a genus by their slender stems, opposite linear or oblong leaves and sessile fruits in the leaf-axils, the species are very difficult to identify partly because of their environmental plasticity. Stem length, leaf shape and succulence vary with the degree of submergence. The species are very complex genetically, most of them being partially apomictic. Fortunately, in Colorado there seem to be only two.

CALLITRICHE L. 1753 [Gr., *callos*, beautiful, + *thrix*, hair]. WATER STARWORT
1a. Lvs uniformly linear, all submerged. **C. hermaphroditica** L. Pond margins, slow streams and ditches.
1b. Lvs both linear and oblong, the submerged ones linear, the upper and emergent or floating lvs broadly oblong. **C. verna** L. [of spring-time], **30**. Common in similar habitats. As wet places dry out, the plants, being weak, become matted on the mud (*C. palustris*).

Figure 30. *Callitriche verna*

CALOCHORTACEAE—MARIPOSA FAMILY (CCT)

A monotypic family embracing a single genus (formerly placed in Liliaceae) that is restricted to western North and Central America. Its flowers are of remarkable beauty because of their large, often highly colored petals, and especially because each bears an elaborate 'gland' near the base, consisting of a depression surrounded by colored hairs. The petals themselves may be hairy inside or marginally ciliate, wine-glass- or bowl-shaped. In California, many species are exceedingly rare and endangered, partly because of their restricted habitats and partly from historical exploitation by plant diggers for the garden trade.

CALOCHORTUS Pursh 1814 [Gr., *kalos*, beautiful, + *chortos*, grass]. MARIPOSA; SEGO LILY

1a. Petal gland not, or only slightly, depressed, not surrounded by a membrane; petals with a transverse band of yellow at the gland. **C. flexuosus** Watson. Desert flats, Four Corners. Stems usually very contorted.
1b. Petal gland depressed and surrounded by a membrane . . . . . . (2)

2a. Gland circular and surrounded by a continuous membranous margin; petal hairs simple, not branched nor enlarged. **C. nuttallii** Torrey & Gray, **PL 36**. Adobe hills in the lower valleys. Fls white to deep rose, with a reddish-brown or purple band or spot above the gland. The Utah State fl.
2b. Gland transversely oblong and elongate, discontinuously surrounded by a margin; petal hairs branched or enlarged. **C. gunnisonii** Watson. Mt meadows and aspen. Fls white, the petal hairs golden.

CAMPANULACEAE—BELLFLOWER FAMILY (CAM)

This family includes some choice rock-garden plants, many of them originally native to the meadows and tundra of Eurasia. Most species of *Campanula* are known by the deep bell-shape of the usually blue to purple corolla, and the species differ in the ways the flowers are grouped together as well as by their sizes and shapes. The family also includes the lobelias, a group of plants differing from the bellflowers in having a bilaterally symmetrical corolla, reminding one of *Penstemon* but belonging here by virtue of the three style branches and inferior ovary. None occurs on the western slope. Lobelias are commmonly cultivated as flowering border plants.

1a. Lvs all ovate, toothed, ciliate; fls small, in the lf axils; slender, unbranched, very inconspicuous. **Heterocodon**
1b. Lvs linear, entire, or only a few of the lowest ones ovate. **Campanula**, HAREBELL

CAMPANULA L. 1753 [dim. of Lat., *campana*, bell]. HAREBELL

1a. Corolla narrowly bell-shaped, with deep and narrow lobes; plants usually less than 8 cm tall; anthers 1.5-2.5 mm long. **C. uniflora** L., ALPINE HAREBELL, **31A**. Alpine tundra. The fruit is elongate, club-shaped, in contrast to the short, cup-shaped fruit of the next.
1b. Corolla broadly bell-shaped, shallowly and broadly lobed; plant usually well over 10 cm tall; anthers 4.0-6.5 mm long . . . . . . (2)

2a. Corolla lobed half-way, the lobes widely spreading and the bell shallow; capsule erect, opening by pores near the summit; bases of lower lvs ciliate. **C. parryi** Gray, **31C**. Subalpine to near timberline. Fls usually more purple than in the next.

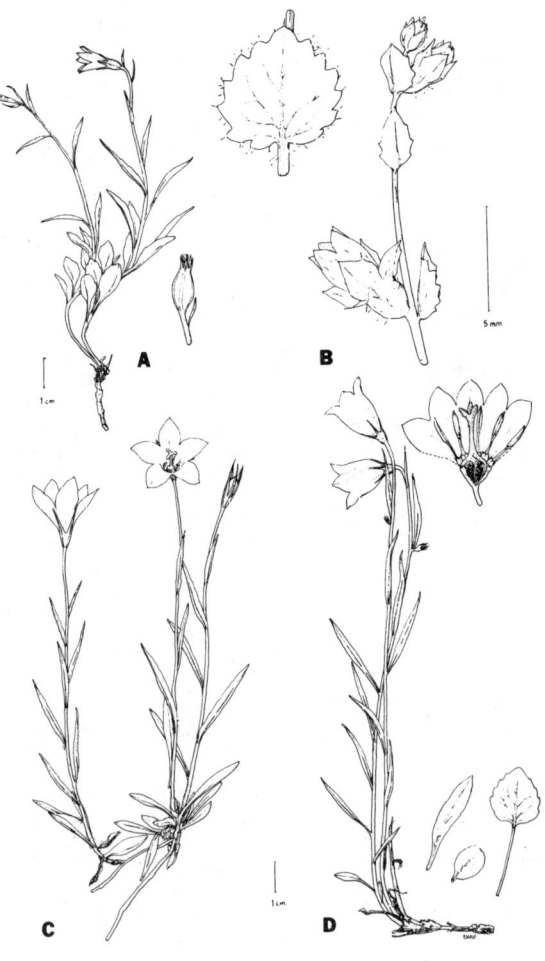

Figure 31. A, *Campanula uniflora*; B, *Heterocodon rariflorum*; C, *Campanula parryi*; D, *C. rotundifolia*

Campanulaceae (CAM) 195

2b. Corolla lobed only about one-third, the lobes not flaring and the bell deep; capsule nodding, opening by pores near the base; lf bases not ciliate. **C. rotundifolia** L., COMMON HAREBELL, **31D**. Abundant on dry mountainsides from foothills to the tundra; the alpine race is low, with very larg solitary fls; these may represent ssp *groenlandica*.

HETEROCODON Nuttall 1843 [Gr., *hetero*, various, + *kodon*, bell]

One sp, **H. rariflorum** Nuttall, **31B**. Very rare, known from a single collection near Steamboat Springs, in 1890.

CANNABACEAE—HOPS FAMILY (CAN)

This is a very small family, formerly placed in the Mulberry Family (Moraceae) but differing in the herbaceous habit and the 5- rather than 4-parted flowers. Although small, this family contains two of the most important species, where mankind is concerned—*Cannabis*, the Marijuana, Hashish, or Hemp, and *Humulus*, Hops. Each plant, in its own unique manner, is used to elevate the spirit or increase perception. The flowers are unisexual; the carpellate flowers are surrounded by large persistent bracts, large and conspicuous in *Humulus*.

1a. Erect herb up to several m tall; lvs palmately compound with narrow serrate lflts. **Cannabis**, MARIJUANA
1b. Trailing vine; lvs palmately lobed with broad rounded sinuses; lvs and stems very harsh to the touch. **Humulus**, HOPS

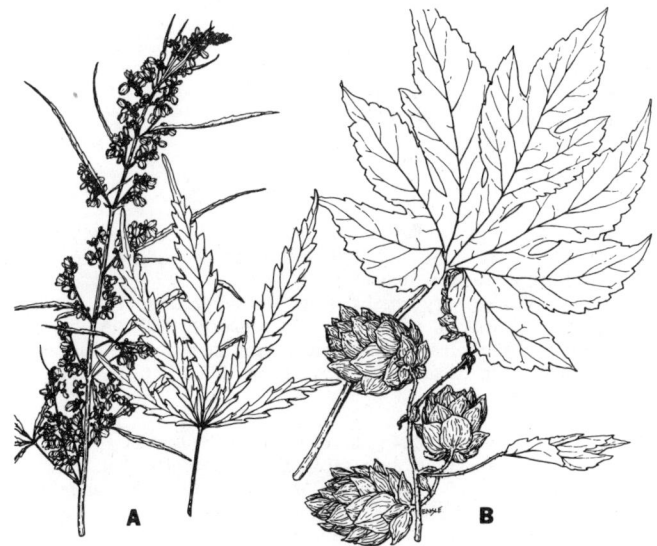

Figure 32. A, *Cannabis sativa*; B, *Humulus lupulus*

CANNABIS L. 1753 [the ancient Gr. name, possibly from the Persian, Kanab]. MARIJUANA

One sp, **C. sativa** L., **32A**. ADV, clandestinely cultivated and probably occurring as an escape along fencerows.

HUMULUS L. 1753 [Late Lat. name of Teutonic origin]. HOPS

One sp, **H. lupulus** L. ssp **americanus** (Nuttall) Löve & Löve [*Lupulus*, an early generic name], WILD HOPS, **32B**. This is a distinctly native race of the sp, having been found fossilized in the Oligocene formation at Florissant. Bases of talus slopes and along fencerows at medium altitudes.

CAPPARACEAE—CAPER FAMILY (CPP)

Capers are the pickled flower buds of *Capparis spinosa* and are essential to the preparation of the German meatball dish called 'Königsberger Klops'. The plant is a usually spiny shrub of the Mediterranean region. The giant 'Spider-flower' of gardens, so called because of its slender petals and long-exserted stamens, is *Cleome spinosa*, a giant relative of our common Rocky Mountain Bee Plant. Many capparids have sticky and unpleasant smelling foliage and pods. 'Cutting capers' has nothing to do with this name but with the Greek word *caper* meaning billy-goat.

1a. Sticky-glandular pubescent; stamens 8 or more; capsule almost sessile; fls pale pink or white, rarely deeply colored. **Polanisia**, CLAMMY-WEED
1b. Glabrous; stamens 6; capsule stipitate; fls yellow or purple . . . . (2)

2a. Pods several times longer than wide, somewhat contracted between the seeds. **Cleome**, BEE-PLANT
2b. Pods short and broad, angular, box-like. **Cleomella**, STINKWEED

CLEOME L. 1753 [of uncertain derivation, applied early to a mustard-like plant]. BEE-PLANT
1a. Fls yellow; lvs with more than three lfls. **C. lutea** Hooker, YELLOW BEE-PLANT, **33C**. A tall little-branched plant common on adobe flats, a selenium indicator.
1b. Fls pink-purple, very rarely white; lvs with three lfls. **C. serrulata** Pursh, ROCKY MOUNTAIN BEE-PLANT, **33D**. Abundant in midsummer along roadsides. Usually the stamens are longer than the petals, but occasionally a form is found, *f*. **inornata**, with short stamens.

CLEOMELLA de Candolle 1824 [dim. of *Cleome*]. STINKWEED

One sp, **C. palmerana** Jones [for Edward Palmer, botanist of the SW], **33B**. Low plant of adobe soils, usually forming large pure stands, blooming very early in the spring.

POLANISIA Rafinesque 1819 [Gr., *poly*, + *anisos*, alluding to the numerous unequal stamens]. CLAMMYWEED

One sp, **P. dodecandra** (L.) de Candolle. [with 12 stamens], **33A**.

Figure 33. **A**, *Polanisia dodecandra*; **B**, *Cleomella palmerana*; **C**, *Cleome lutea*; **D,E**, *C. serrulata*

Roadsides and gulches in the valleys. The fls are cream-white with red stamens. The pods are broad and flat.

CAPRIFOLIACEAE—HONEYSUCKLE FAMILY (CPR)

Every gardener is familiar with Elderberry, Viburnum, Honeysuckle, and Snowberry. Fewer know the most famous plant of the family—the Twinflower, *Linnaea*, which covers forest floors across the Northern Hemisphere. Linnaeus was so proud of this little plant that many of his portraits show him holding a sprig of it. With characteristic modesty he wrote that "*Linnaea* was named by the celebrated Gronovius and is a plant of Lapland, lowly, insignificant, flowering but for a brief space, after Linnaeus who resembles it."

1a. Lvs pinnately compound. **Sambucus,** ELDERBERRY
1b. Lvs simple . . . . (2)

2a. Plant with prostrate-creeping stems, only slightly woody; fls pink, in nodding pairs on an elongate, erect peduncle. **Linnaea,** TWINFLOWER
2b. Plants definitely shrubby, with erect stems . . . . (3)

3a. Lvs three-lobed, maple-like. **Viburnum,** BUSH-CRANBERRY
3b. Lvs simple or pinnately lobed, not maple-like. . . . . (4)

4a. Fls yellow, in pairs on long axillary peduncles; berry purplish-black, seated in a conspicuous lf-like cup of bracts. **Distegia,** BUSH HONEYSUCKLE
4b. Fls white or pink; berry red or white . . . . (5)

5a. Fls zygomorphic, with elongated lobes; lvs broadest at the base; berry red; introd ornamental shrubs sometimes escaped on floodplains. **Lonicera,** HONEYSUCKLE
5b. Fls with short triangular lobes; lvs broadly elliptic or oblong; berry snow-white; native shrubs. **Symphoricarpos,** SNOWBERRY

DISTEGIA Rafinesque 1838 [Gr., *di*, two, + *stegos*, roof, alluding to the bract subtending the berries]. BUSH HONEYSUCKLE

One sp, **D. involucrata** (Banks) Cockerell, **34C**. Common along mountain streams (*Lonicera*). The frt, a pair of red-juiced black berries, is extremely bitter and possibly poisonous. The fls are small, yellow, and cylindric-campanulate, not zygomorphic as in *Lonicera*.

LINNAEA L. 1753 [for derivation, see above]. TWINFLOWER

One sp, **L. borealis** L. Subalpine spruce-fir forests. Our mountain race has fls more the shape of the European type than the American ssp. **longiflora** (Torrey) Hultén.

LONICERA L. 1753 [for Adam Lonitzer, 16th century German herbalist]. HONEYSUCKLE

One sp, **L. morrowii** Gray [for its discoverer, James Morrow, 1820-1865], FLY HONEYSUCKLE, **34F**. ADV, escaped and locally established on the floodplain of the Animas River (LP). This was ori-

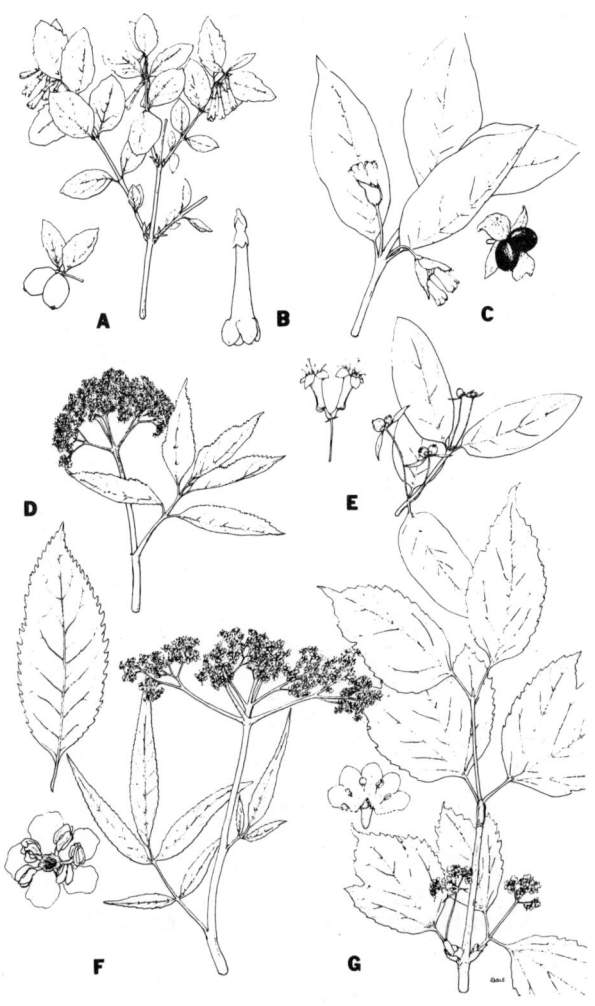

Figure 34. A, *Symphoricarpos rotundifolius*; B, *S. longiflorus*, flower; C, *Distegia involucrata*; D, *Sambucus racemosa*; E, *S. coerulea*; F, *Lonicera morrowii*; G, *Viburnum edule*

ginally reported as *L. utahensis*, a sp that might be expected in the area. The lvs of *L. morrowii* are oblong-ovate with truncate base, and minutely pubescent; those of *L. utahensis* are elliptical, somewhat glaucous, and with scattered long hairs on the underside. The fls are white, with elongate lobes; berry red.

SAMBUCUS L. 1753 [Gr., *sambuce*, an ancient musical instrument, hence a bark whistle]. ELDERBERRY
1a. Lvs green, not at all glaucous; infl broadly pyramidal, with the main axis extended beyond the lowermost floral branches. **S. racemosa** L. ssp **pubens** (Michaux) House, **34D**. The common elderberry of the region. Berries red (var **microbotrys**) or black (var **melanocarpa**).
1b. Lvs glaucous; infl flat-topped; berries glaucous blue-gray. **S. coerulea** Rafinesque, BLUE ELDERBERRY, **34E**. Common on arid mesa-slopes, W counties.

SYMPHORICARPOS Duhamel 1755 [Gr., *symphorein*, to bear together, + *carpos*, fruit]. SNOWBERRY
1a. Corolla bell-shaped, the lobes about as long as or slightly longer than the tube; fls in rather dense clusters in the uppermost lf axils. **S. occidentalis** Hooker. Forming dense colonies in rather moist open grassy swales. Only one W slope record, from MF.
1b. Corolla tubular or funnel-shaped, the tube much longer than the lobes; fls in pairs in the lf axils. . . . . (2)

2a. Fls subsalverform (tapering distinctly from top to bottom and with flaring lobes); anthers sessile; style short, pilose; nectary only one in the fl base. **S. longiflorus** Gray, **34B**. Canyonlands, MF-MN. The lvs are less than 1.5 cm long, but small-lvd specimens of the next are also common.
2b. Fls tubular-campanulate, the sides more parallel; anthers with distinct short filament; style longer, naked; nectaries five in the corolla base. **S. rotundifolius** Gray, **34A**. Abundant on steep canyonsides, gulches, oak-aspen (incl. *S. oreophilus*, *S. vaccinioides*, *S. palmeri*). Extremely variable in lf and stem pubescence.

VIBURNUM L. 1753 [the classical Latin name]. BUSH-CRANBERRY
One sp, **V. edule** (Michaux) Rafinesque [edible], **34G**. Local along streams in spruce-fir forests, N ranges near the Continental Divide (GA).

CARYOPHYLLACEAE—PINK FAMILY (CRY)

A very easily recognized family containing some handsome cultivated plants such as Carnations, Garden Pinks, and Baby's-breath. In this book I am recognizing those types with a united calyx and generally long-clawed petals as belonging to the Caryophyllaceae, while the forms usually included in the family but differing in having free calyx parts and clawless petals (among other characters) as belonging to the Alsinaceae. A good vegetative character of both families, rarely mentioned in the keys, is the distinctly swollen node at which each pair of leaves arises.

1a. Calyx closely invested at the base by two short bracts. **Dianthus**, PINK; CARNATION
1b. Calyx without two bracts at the base. . . . . (2)

2a. Styles 5; capsule opening by 5 or 10 teeth . . . . (3)
2b. Styles 2 or 3; capsule splitting into 3, 4, or 6 parts. . . . . (4)

3a. Fls unisexual, plants dioecious; petals with blades over 5 mm long; tall broad-lvd introd weeds of pastures. **Melandrium**, CAMPION
3b. Fls perfect; petals smaller; native, narrow-lvd plants of mountains and tundra. **Gastrolychnis**, ALPINE CAMPION

4a. Calyx 10-20-nerved; styles 3; capsule 3- or 6-valved. . . . . . . (5)
4b. Calyx 5-nerved or 5-angled, or terete and only obscurely nerved; styles 2; capsule 4-valved. . . . . (6)

5a. Fls in few-fld cymes subtended by unreduced lvs; plants functionally dioecious, dichotomously branched, with slender rhizomes; forest plants. **Anotites**
5b. Fls in cymes with subtended by reduced bractlike lvs; plants with perfect fls, not slenderly rhizomatous; annual weeds and native perennials, one an alpine dwarf mat plant. **Silene**, CAMPION

6a. Fls less than 4 mm long, very numerous, in much-branched cymes. **Gypsophila**, BABY'S-BREATH
6b. Fls over 5 mm long, relatively few in number. . . . . (7)

7a. Calyx 5-angled; fls deep pink; annual. **Vaccaria**, COW COCKLE
7b. Calyx terete; fls white or pink; perennial. **Saponaria**, BOUNCING BET; SOAPWORT

ANOTITES Greene 1905 [derivation unexplained, probably from *a*, not, + *notites*, marked, hence unrecognized]
One sp, **A. menziesii** (Hooker) Greene [for Alex. Menzies, explorer of the Pacific Northwest]. Low, dichotomously branched, glandular-pubescent, somewhat brittle; calyx small, less than 5 mm long. Common in forests (*Silene*).

DIANTHUS L. 1753 [Gr., *Dios*, Jupiter, + *anthos*, flower]. PINK; CARNATION
1a. Fls in clusters; bracts lance-linear, as long as the calyx tube; lvs hairy; annual. **D. armeria** L. [for the genus *Armeria*], DEPTFORD PINK, 35C. ADV weed of meadows. This and the next are not yet reported on the W slope, but judging by the rapidity of spread on the E slope both are to be expected.
1b. Fls solitary; bracts ovate, half as long as the calyx; perennial. **D. deltoides** L. [triangular, alluding to the bracts].

GASTROLYCHNIS Reichenbach 1841 [Gr., *gastridos*, pot-bellied, + *Lychnis*, a genus]. ALPINE CAMPION [formerly incl in *Melandrium* or *Silene*].

202 *Caryophyllaceae (CRY)*

1a. Dwarf alpines, usually less than 10 cm tall . . . . (2)
1b. Taller plants of various altitudes. **G. drummondii** (Hooker) Löve & Löve [for Thomas Drummond, Franklin Expedition botanist]. Dry slopes, foothills to subalpine; very similar in general appearance to *Silene scouleri*. There are more well-developed lf pairs in *G. drummondii* and they are not as abruptly reduced above.

2a. Fls nodding at anthesis; petals included or barely exserted; calyx inflated like a Japanese lantern; seeds 1.5-2.0 mm, rounded. **G. apetala** (L.) Tolmatchev & Kozhanchikov ssp **uralensis** Löve & Löve, **14C**. Unstable tundra or scree slopes.
2b. Fls erect; petals included, barely exserted, or conspicuously exserted; calyx cylindric, only slightly inflated; seeds 0.5-1.0 mm, angular. **G. kingii** (Watson) Weber [for Clarence King, western explorer]. On relatively stable tundra. Various Arctic specialists suggest that this is equivalent to *G. furcatum* or related spp, but there has been no serious revision recently and the relationships are still not clear.

GYPSOPHILA L. 1753 [Gr., *gypsos*, gypsum, + *philein*, to love]. BABY'S-BREATH

1a. Tall glaucous perennial from stout rhizomes; infl bushy-branched, with many tiny fls; calyx 1.5-2.0 mm long. **G. paniculata** L., **35A**. ADV. Estab along roadsides and fence-rows.
1b. Low (to 50 cm) green annual; infl relatively few-fld, the petals about 6 mm long; calyx 3-5 mm long. **G. elegans** Bieberstein. ADV, commonly sown in 'native plant' mixes, MF.

MELANDRIUM Roehling 1812 [Gr., *melas*, black, + *drys*, oak, used by Homer to denote the dark heartwood of oak, but later used for this plant by Clusius, 1601, in *Rariorus Plantarum Historia*. Why?]. CAMPION

One sp, **M. dioicum** (L.) Cosson & Germain [dioecious]. ADV common weed of mountain pastures (*Lychnis alba*).

SAPONARIA L. 1753 [from Gr., *sapo*, soap]. SOAPWORT; BOUNCING BET

One sp, **S. officinalis** L. [of the shops], **35D**. ADV, escaped from cult (old gardens from the mining days) and very well estab along roadsides, flowering in midsummer. The lvs make a fair lather when crushed and rubbed under water. Double-flowered sports are frequent.

SILENE L. 1753 [for *Silenus*, drunken foster-father of *Bacchus*]. CATCHFLY; CAMPION

1a. Low and densely matted, moss-like; fls scarcely higher than the short basal lvs. **S. acaulis** L. ssp **acaulescens** (Williams) Hitchcock & Maguire, MOSS PINK. Fls pink, very rarely white. Common on dry tundra. Races occur in the Arctic and most mountain areas of the N Hemisphere.
1b. Plants with tall, lfy stems, or at least not matted or moss-like; growing at various altitudes. . . . . (2)

Figure 35. A, *Gypsophila paniculata*; B, *Vaccaria pyramidata*; C, *Dianthus armeria*; D, *Saponaria officinalis*

2a. Annual weed; petals entire or shallowly cleft; stems with localized dark bands of sticky fluid on the upper internodes. **S. antirrhina** L. [with lvs like *Antirrhinum*], SLEEPY CATCHFLY.
2b. Perennial; petals deeply cleft; stems without sticky bands. . . . . . (3)

3a. Glabrous and glaucous, tall and branched; lvs ovate; calyx smooth, inflated, with 20 pale and inconspicuous veins. . . . . . (4)
3b. Pubescent; lvs narrow; calyx not inflated, strongly 10-veined . . . . (5)

4a. Calyx with very prominent reticulations, with translucent areas between veins. **S. vulgaris** (Moench) Garcke. ADV, estab in pastures and roadsides in the mts.
4b. Calyx with faint reticulations, the surface ± uniform. **S. czerei** Baumgartner. ADV, similar sites.

5a. Infl with long, somewhat dichotomous branches; fls sessile along one side of the branch. **S. dichotoma** Ehrhart. ADV, Gunnison Basin.
5b. Infl without elongate dichotomous branches; fls not secund. **S. scouleri** Hooker ssp **hallii** (Watson) Hitchcock & Maguire. Dry montane and subalpine slopes.

VACCARIA Wolf 1781 [Sanskrit, *vaca*, cow]. COW COCKLE ['Cockle' being an Anglo-Saxon word meaning tare or weed]

One sp, **V. pyramidata** Medikus, **35B**. ADV weed of cult fields (RB). The sharply five-angled calyx and glaucous lvs are distinctive features.

CELASTRACEAE--STAFF TREE FAMILY (CEL)

This small family includes Bittersweet, *Celastrus scandens*, a woody vine noted for its seed encased in a brilliant orange aril. The dry capsules dehisce, exposing but not releasing the seed. Sprays of Bittersweet are gathered in autumn for dry arrangements. *Euonymus*, the Spindle-tree, includes several species, either evergreen or deciduous, with similar arillate dull red seeds. These are desirable ornamentals, often having cork-ridged stems. The fine-grained hard wood was used in making spindles. Possibly the name 'Staff-tree' derives not from a walking-stick, but from the spinning distaff. *Forsellesia* has usually been placed in this family, but Thorne has recently shown that it really belongs with the Crossosomataceae.

PAXISTIMA Rafinesque 1838 [Gr., *pachy*, thick, + *stigma*]. MOUNTAIN-LOVER

One sp, **P. myrsinites** (Pursh) Rafinesque. A low evergreen shrub with opposite crenate lvs and inconspicuous reddish fls, common in the forests. This is one of our Tertiary relicts, with a close relative, *P. canbyi*, found in the southern Appalachians. The original spelling of the name was *Paxistima*; it was not an error and must be followed.

CERATOPHYLLACEAE—HORNWORT FAMILY (CTP)

This family consists of a single genus, and, depending on who is speaking, either one or thirty species of obligately submerged aquatic plants. Slow streams and ponds are often clogged with dense growths of these plants, which can be easily mistaken for the green alga, *Chara*. The repeatedly dichotomous linear leaf-segments are distinctive, but the strange one-seeded fruit, with a stiff, spine-like style and often a few spines spreading from the fruit base, is unique.

CERATOPHYLLUM L. 1753 [Gr., *ceras*, horn, + *phyllon*, leaf].
HORNWORT
  One sp, **C. demersum** L., **36B**. Lakes and ponds in the mts (Trapper's Lake). The whorled lvs are dichotomously branched, with narrow linear divs, very densely grouped toward the stem apex. The similar *Batrachium* (RAN) has alternate lvs, and the green alga *Chara*, sometimes confused with Hornwort, has jointed stems and a characteristic fetid odor.

CHENOPODIACEAE—GOOSEFOOT FAMILY (CHN)

Disturbed soils, particularly in urban or ruderal sites, assume a late summer and fall aspect characterized by a welter of unattractive hairy, white-mealy or spiny plants with inconspicuous greenish flowers, most belonging to the Goosefoot Family. Many ignore them because they are so nondescript and presumably difficult. But chenopods make up such an important part of the landscape, especially in desert-steppe, and mean so much, in terms of interpreting the condition of the land, that everyone should know the common species. Chenopods find their way to the dining table too. *Beta vulgaris* (Red Beets, Swiss Chard and Sugar Beets) and Spinach (*Spinacia oleracea*) belong here. The fruits of spinach have spines or prickles, hence the old name Spinage. Chenopods are among the most poorly collected of our plants, with the result that we are unsure of what we really have here. *Atriplex* and *Chenopodium*, particularly, need to be collected with ripe fruit, and small packets of additional fruit should be collected, since they fall away easily.

1a. True shrubs, not merely woody at the base . . . . (2)
1b. Herbaceous or only woody near the base . . . . (3)

2a. Plants with linear, semiterete green succulent lvs and spine-tipped branchlets. **Sarcobatus**, GREASEWOOD
2b. Plants without spine-tipped branches, or if so, then the lvs flattened. **Atriplex** (including *Grayia*), SHADSCALE

3a. Stems jointed and bearing opposite scale lvs, the fls sunken in depressions in the stem; succulent annuals. **Salicornia**, GLASSWORT
3b. Stems not as above, bearing green lvs, the fls not sunken in the stem. . . . . (4)

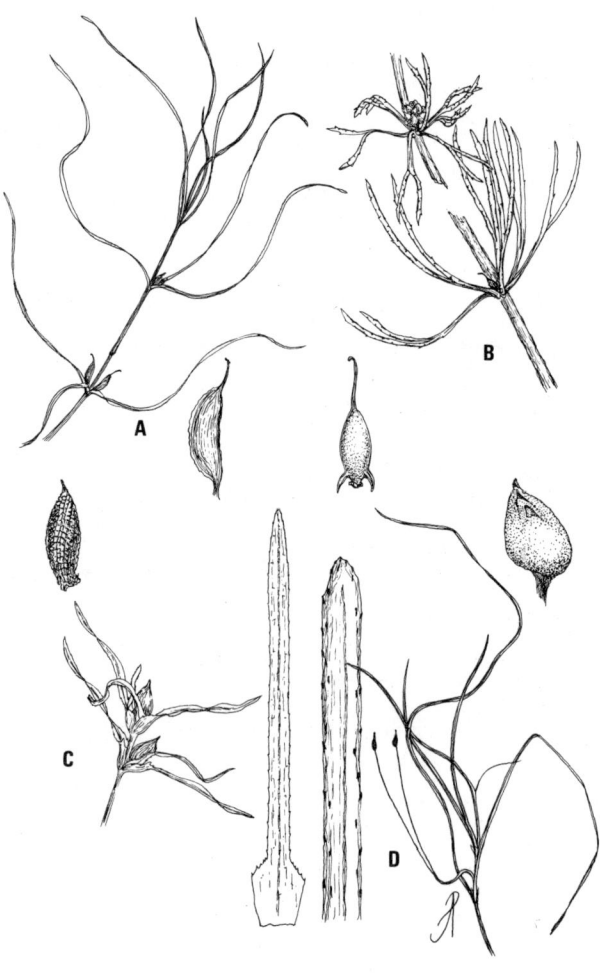

Figure 36. A, *Zannichellia palustris*; B, *Ceratophyllum demersum*; C, *Najas guadalupensis*; D, *Ruppia cirrosa*

4a. Lvs succulent, terete, sausage-shaped, each with a fine bristle at the tip. **Halogeton,** WIENERLEAF
4b. Lvs not as above . . . . (5)

5a. Lvs rigid, spine-tipped; plants stiffly branched and forming large tumbleweeds. **Salsola,** RUSSIAN-THISTLE
5b. Lvs otherwise. . . . . (6)

6a. Lvs and stem stellate-pubescent. . . . . (7)
6b. Lvs and stems not stellate-pubescent. . . . . (8)

7a. Lvs and stem densely stellate-tomentose, linear or oblong, with revolute margins; fruiting calyx with tufts of straight hairs; very white plants, becoming rusty in age. **Krascheninnikovia,** WINTERFAT
7b. Lvs green, elliptic-oblong, not revolute. **Axyris**

8a. Foliage with a strong unpleasant odor; lvs pinnatifid or at least marginally toothed or lobed, glandular. **Teloxys,** WORMSEED
8b. Foliage without a distinctive odor; lvs entire or coarsely lobed, if regularly toothed then with farinose pubescence. . . . . (9)

9a. Plants with pilose hairs on the foliage and stems. . . . . (10)
9b. Plants with farinose pubescence (small inflated hairs) or glabrous . . . . (11)

10a. Fruiting calyx with a strong hook arising from each calyx-lobe. **Bassia,** IRONWEED
10b. Fruiting calyx with a weakly to very strongly developed horizontal veiny wing arising from each calyx-lobe. **Kochia**

11a. Monoecious or dioecious, the carpellate fls enclosed by a pair of bracts of characteristic shape, either separate and forming a sandwich, or fused (like pita-bread) around the frt. **Atriplex,** SHADSCALE; SALTBUSH
11b. Plants with perfect fls, without specialized enclosing bracts
. . . . (12)

12a. Fruiting calyx with a continuous horizontal wing completely surrounding it; tumbleweed with sinuate-dentate lvs. **Cycloloma,** WINGED PIGWEED
12b. Fruiting calyx wingless or at least not as above . . . . (13)

13a. Lvs linear, not farinose . . . . (14)
13b. Lvs wider than linear, or if so, then farinose . . . . (15)

14a. Fls solitary in the axils of scarious-margined bracts; calyx consisting of a single delicate sepal on the inner side; smooth widely-branching tumbleweeds, never succulent. **Corispermum,** BUGSEED
14b. Fls in clusters in the axils of the lvs; calyx complete; succulent-lvd plants of salt flats. **Suaeda,** SEA-BLITE

15a. Calyx a solitary green bract-like fleshy sepal; lvs succulent, not mealy, hastate, passing gradually into lflike bracts; stem prostrate-spreading. **Monolepis**, POVERTYWEED

15b. Calyx 5-parted, ± enveloping the frt; lvs often white-farinose; stems ascending to erect. **Chenopodium**, GOOSEFOOT; LAMB'S QUARTERS

ATRIPLEX L. 1753 [the ancient Lat. name]. SHAD-SCALE; SALTBUSH

1a. Perennials or shrubs, erect or rarely prostrate, but definitely woody at the base. . . . . (2)
1b. Annual herbs. . . . . (8)

2a. [1] Prostrate gray mat-former; lvs sessile, succulent, oblong, under 2 cm long. **A. corrugata** Watson [wrinkled], MAT SALTBUSH, **38B**. Dominant on adobe hills, often the only plant.
2b. Not prostrate, or lvs narrowed to petioles, not succulent, longer. . . . . (3)

3a. [2] Plants with some branches modified to form spines . . . . . . (4)
3b. Plants not at all spiny . . . . (5)

4a. [3] Tall shrubs with large circular fruiting bracts becoming yellow or red at maturity; lvs narrow, green, oblanceolate, whitish at the tip. **A. grayi** Collotzi, SPINY HOP-SAGE, **38J**. Level sagebrush benches and plateaus (*Grayia spinosa*).
4b. Low subshrubs with oblong to obovate glaucous lvs, the frt bracts of the same color and texture. **A. confertifolia** (Torrey & Fremont) Watson [crowded lvs], **38H**. Common on adobe hills; aspects vary in plants of different sexes and ages.

5a. [3] Woody only at the base; fl stems herbaceous and lfy. . . . . . (6)
5b. Shrubby throughout . . . . (7)

6a. [5] Plants spreading out from the base, the ratio of fl stalks to lfy portion high; lvs green, exceedingly variable, from narrowly oblong to broadly elliptic; frt bracts not broader than long, with dorsal warty processes. **A. gardneri** (Moquin) Standley [for the collector, Alexander Gordon, his name misspelled by Moquin!]. Very common and variable in stature and lf shape. A number of spp have been proposed in this complex, but they are not clearly distinguishable.
6b. Plants rigidly erect from the base, the lfy portion about equal to the fl portion and grading into it; lvs silvery with hardly a trace of green, broadly elliptic, not more than twice as long as wide; frt bracts broader than long, distinctly stipitate, fan-shaped, rounded at the top, lacking dorsal processes. **A. obovata** Moquin. Desert flats, Four Corners area.

7a. [5] Frt bracts with the margins spreading apart, creating four wings; plant widely and stiffly branched. **A. canescens** (Pursh) Nuttall, FOUR WINGED SALTBUSH, **38A**. Common, sagebrush zone and greasewood flats. A lower shrub with poorly developed

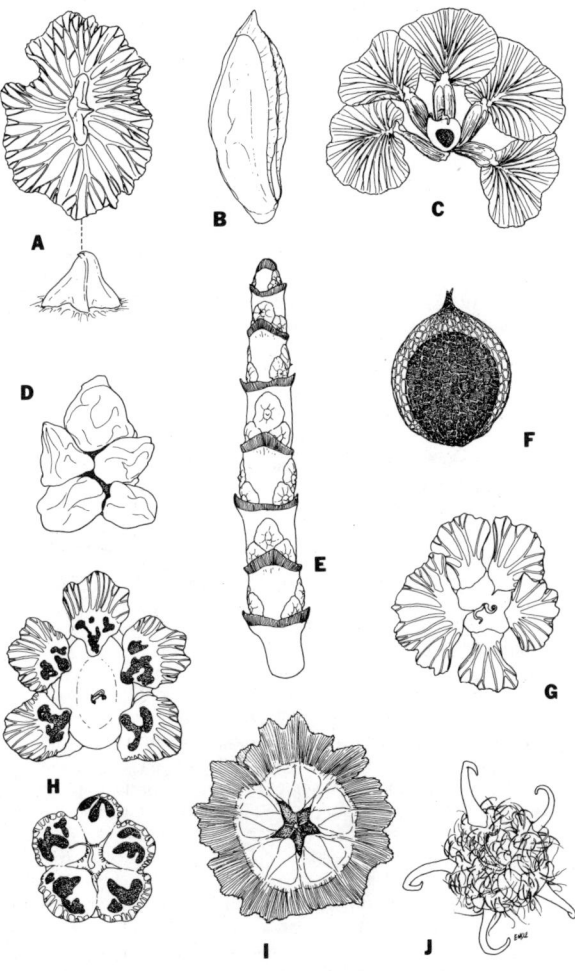

Figure 37. A, *Sarcobatus vermiculatus*; B, *Corispermum hyssopifolium*; C, *Halogeton glomeratus*; D, *Suaeda calceoliformis*; E, *Salicornia rubra*; F, *Monolepis nuttalliana*; G, *Salsola australis*; H, *Kochia sieversiana*; I, *Cycloloma atriplicifolium*; J, *Bassia hyssopifolia*

or no wings, *A. aptera* Nelson may occur here but better collections are needed of plants with fruit and data on stature.

7b. Frt bracts keeled, but not creating four wings; plant with erect branches. **A. brandegei** (Gray) Collotzi, **38K**. Rocky slopes and arroyos. Two distinct populations occur, distinguished by their lf shapes: one with linear lvs, the other with oblanceolate or obovate lvs. They appear to be genetically controlled, but it is not known if these may constitute two spp (*Grayia*).

8a. [1] Lvs green or greenish on both sides, sparsely mealy or scurfy if at all, only when young . . . . (9)
8b. Lvs gray or whitish with a permanent scurf, at least on the lower surface. . . . . (14)

9a. [8] Bracts not orbicular, less than 5 mm broad; lvs narrowly fusiform; slender erect, sparingly branched. **A. suckleyi** (Torrey) Rydberg [for George Suckley, 1830-1869, collector for the Pacific Railroad Exped.]. Infrequent on clay hills, RB (*A. dioica*).
9b. Frt bracts orbicular or rounded-ovate, often over 10 mm broad . . . . (10)

10a. [9] Coarse weedy herbs up to 1 m or more tall . . . . (11)
10b. Low native spp usually less than 3 dm tall . . . . (13)

11a. [10] Carpellate fls of two kinds, some with horizontal seeds and a 3-5-lobed perianth, the rest with vertical seeds and 2 bracts, the veins of the latter meeting above the base. **A. hortensis** L., GARDEN ORACHE, **38E**. ADV ruderal weed; plants becoming deep red-purple at maturity.
11b. Carpellate fls all of one kind, all with vertical seeds and two bracts, the veins of the latter meeting near or at the base. . . . (12)

12a. [11] Bracts less than 5 mm long, broadly rhombic, entire or denticulate, smooth or tuberculate on the back; lvs varying from almost linear to ovate with forward-pointing basal lobes. **A. patula** L. ADV ruderal weed.
12b. Bracts up to 6 mm long, elliptical or round-cordate, usually entire, smooth; lvs broadly triangular-hastate. **A. heterosperma** Bunge [with variable seeds]. ADV ruderal weed, Colorado R Valley.

13a. [10] Bracts containing several fls, each with scarious tepals. **A. pleiantha** Weber [with more fls than usual], **38G**. Local on clay knolls, known from a few small populations on the Ute Reservation, Four Corners and in adj. New Mexico.
13b. Bracts containing a single ovary, lacking tepals. **A. graciliflora** Jones. Local on adobe soils, ME, MZ. The staminate fls form an elongate, slender interrupted spike.

14a. [8] Lvs narrowly linear; slender, sparingly branched. **A. wolfii** Watson. Barren clay flats.
14b. Lvs wider, oblong-ovate or triangular-ovate . . . . (15)

15a. [14] Fruiting bracts broadest below the middle; lvs coarsely dentate; bracts becoming hard. **A. rosea** L. ADV, alkaline flats and roadsides.
15b. Fruiting bracts broadest at or above the middle . . . . (16)

16a. [15] Lvs cordate at the base or bracts cuneate at the base and truncate at the apex . . . . (7)
16b. Lvs neither cordate at the base nor bracts cuneate or truncate . . . . (19)

17a. [16] Lvs deltoid to elliptic, the base not cordate; bracts truncate at the apex. **A. truncata** (Torrey) Gray, **38I**. Alkali flats.
17b. Lf base cordate . . . . (18)

18a. [17] Bracts orbicular to oblong, with broad flat margins. **A. graciliflora** Jones (see 13b).
18b. Bracts cuneate, with narrow appendages on the faces. **A. saccaria** Watson [baggy]. Adobe clay flats.

19a. [16] Bracts becoming hard, almost bone-like. **A. rosea** L., **38F**.
19b. Bracts not becoming especially hard . . . . (20)

20a. [19] Lvs thick, triangular, pinnately veined; bracts irregularly toothed across the summit, without a horizontal wing-like lobe. **A. argentea** Nuttall [silver], **38D**. Alkaline flats and pond margins.
20b. Lvs not succulent, oval, with three prominent veins; bracts with appendages on the lower sides of the faces, but with a smooth rounded apex. **A. powellii** Watson [for Major John W. Powell, western explorer and surveyor], **38C**. Roadsides and shale slopes.

AXYRIS L. 1753 [Gr. *axyros*, unshorn]
One sp, **A. amaranthoides** L. ADV, estab in fields in the vicinity of South Park, thus very likely present on the W slope in grazing lands of the mt parks.

BASSIA Allioni 1766 [for Ferdinand Bassi, 18th century Italian botanist]. IRONWEED
One sp, **B. hyssopifolia** (Pallas) Kuntze, **37J**. ADV, common weed of alkaline flats in the valleys. Very similar to *Kochia* but distinguished when mature by the hooks on the calyx.

CHENOPODIUM L. 1753 [Gr., *chen*, a goose, + *pous*, foot, alluding to the leaf shape]. GOOSEFOOT; LAMB'S QUARTERS
1a. Fls in dense globose clusters, fleshy or red at maturity, in stout interrupted spikes; lvs green and glabrous, triangular or triangular-hastate and coarsely dentate . . . . (2)
1b. Fls in smaller clusters, not becoming markedly fleshy or red; lvs often mealy-pubescent (actually with minute inflated hairs). . . . (3)

2a. Fls becoming bright red and fleshy at maturity; clusters about 1 cm diam, not numerous. **C. capitatum** (L.) Ascherson, STRAWBERRY BLITE. ADV along trails and in shaded woods in the mts.

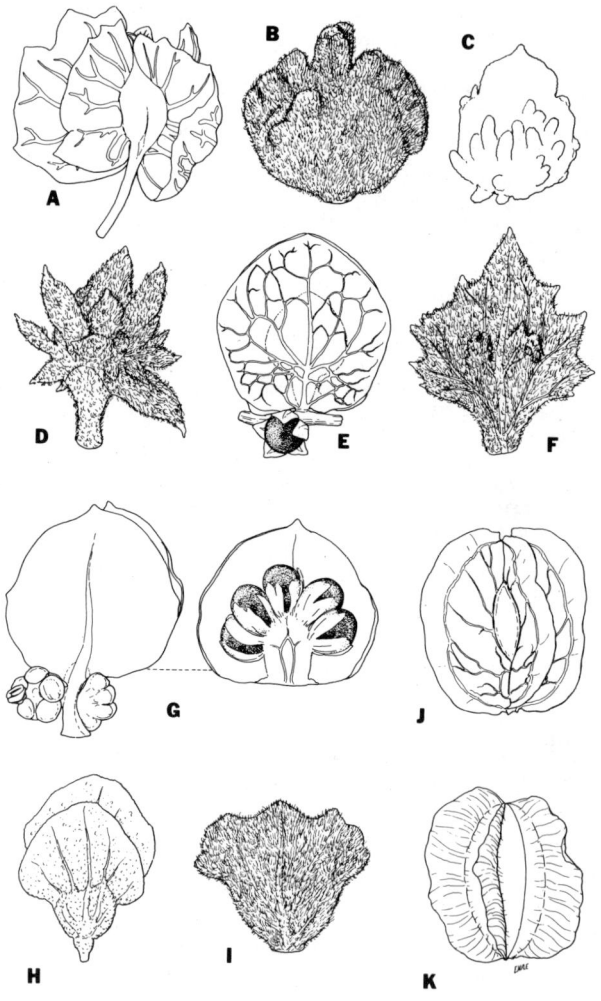

Figure 38. A, *Atriplex canescens*; B, *A. corrugata*; C, *A. powellii*; D, *A. argentea*; E, *A. hortensis*; F, *A. rosea*; G, *A. pleiantha* (with bract removed, right); H, *A. confertifolia*; I, *A. truncata*; J, *A. grayi*; K, *A. brandegei*

2b. Fls remaining green, even at maturity when the seeds are shed; clusters less than 5 mm diam, very numerous in a terminal spike interrupted by leafy bracts. **C. foliosum** (Moench) Ascherson. ADV. Similar sites, more common than the last (*C. overi*, which was thought to be native).

3a. Seed usually vertical (the frt thus laterally flattened), or some of them horizontal in the same cluster . . . . (4)
3b. Seed usually horizontal, the frt then flattened from the top. . . . (6)

4a. Lvs densely mealy beneath. **C. glaucum** L., **39C**. ADV, common in drying mud of pond shores.
4b. Lvs green, glabrous or only slightly mealy beneath . . . . (5)

5a. Fl clusters less than 4 mm thick; calyx not becoming reddish; seeds nearly always erect; terminal spike commonly branching. **C. rubrum** L. ADV, on muddy pond shores.
5b. Fl clusters often over 4 mm thick; calyx often becoming reddish; seeds occasionally horizontal in the same clusters with erect seeds; terminal spike usually simple. **C. foliosum** (Moench) Ascherson. ADV. This phase has been called *C. chenopodioides*. One very old record from Gunnison.

6a. Principal lvs entire or nearly so, usually ovate, lanceolate, oblong, linear or elliptic, rarely over 10(13) mm wide, often with 1-3 somewhat parallel veins . . . . (7)
6b. Principal lvs (often deciduous by the time frt is mature) mostly lobed or toothed or else deltoid or deltoid-ovate, often over 10 mm wide, usually pinnately veined . . . . (8)

7a. Lf blades often 2-3 times as long as wide, elliptic to ovate; tepals exposing mature frt laterally and dorsally; frts maturing unevenly in different parts of the infl. **C. atrovirens** Rydberg [dark green]. Frequent along roadsides, up into the middle altitudes.
7b. Lf blades often over 3 times as long as wide, lanceolate to oblong or linear; tepals mostly covering the mature frt; frts maturing evenly; rarely in the mts. **C. leptophyllum** (Moquin) Watson [narrow-lvd]. Sagebrush and piñon-juniper.

8a. Lvs glabrous, very large, thin-textured, slender-petioled, with a few broad, coarse, sharp-pointed lobes (duck-footed); tepals not at all dorsally keeled in frt. **C. gigantospermum** Aellen. Rather deeply shaded woods, on W slope known from a very old record from Durango.
8b. Lvs usually somewhat or quite mealy, if glabrous then small, with ± blunt basal lobes; tepals usually dorsally keeled . . . . . . (9)

9a. Lvs broadly triangular-ovate, with blunt apex and hastate basal lobes; slender and low in stature. . . . . (10)
9b. Lvs ovate or narrowly triangular-ovate, commonly dentate; tall and coarse thick-stemmed weeds of late summer . . . . (11)

Figure 39. A, *Chenopodium album*; B, *C. fremontii*; C, *C. glaucum*; D, *Teloxys botrys*

10a. Slender, not rigidly branched; lvs only slightly mealy, thin-textured. **C. fremontii** Watson [for J. C. Frémont], **39B**. Common woodland plant, especially in piñon-juniper and oak.
10b. Rigidly branched from near the base; lvs strongly mealy, thickish. **C. incanum** (Watson) Heller [hoary]. Bare clay flats.

11a. Seed distinctly pitted, the pericarp usually tight around the seed; lvs thick-textured. **C. berlandieri** Moquin [for Jean Louis Berlandier, 1805-51, Swiss botanist collector in Texas]. Abundant native ruderal weed.
11b. Seed smooth, the pericarp usually loose around the seed; lvs thin-textured. **C. album** L., **39A**. ADV, much less common than the last, but in similar sites.

CORISPERMUM L. 1753 [Gr., *coris*, bedbug, + *sperma*, seed]. BUGSEED
1a. Frt 3.5-4-5 mm long; lower bracts as broad as or broader than the frt. **C. hyssopifolium** L., **37B**. ADV, sand blowouts, MF.
1b. Frt 2.0-3.5 mm long; lower bracts narrower than the frt. **C. nitidum** Kitaibel [shining]. ADV, similar sites.

CYCLOLOMA Moquin 1840 [Gr., *cyclos*, a circle, + *loma*, a border, from the encircling calyx wing]. WINGED PIGWEED
  One sp, **C. atriplicifolium** (Sprengel) Coulter, **37I**. Native weed of sandy ground, an old record from "Elk Canyon" (RT?).

HALOGETON C. A. Meyer 1829 [Gr., *halo-*, salt, + *geiton*, neighbor]. WIENERLEAF
  One sp, **H. glomeratus** (Bieberstein) Meyer, **37C**. ADV, an Asiatic weed, common in the Colorado R Valley around Grand Junction on adobe soils. A poisonous plant once expected to be of grave economic impact on livestock, but evidently coexisting with them with no serious effects.

KOCHIA Roth 1801 [for Wilhelm D. J. Koch, 1771-1849, German botanist].
1a. Native perennial, branching from the base, not over 3 dm tall, blooming in the spring. **K. americana** Watson. Common on clay flats, lower river valleys.
1b. Introd weed, branched above the base, over 1 m tall, blooming in late summer and fall. **K. sieversiana** (Pallas) Meyer [for J. Sievers, the collector], **37H**. ADV, very abundant along roadsides and on alkaline flats in the lower river valleys [*K. iranica*, erroneously]. The wings on the tepals rarely develop on fls of early season but appear on later fls of the same plant! The annual *Kochia* species have recently been merged with *Bassia*, a reasonable realignment.

KRASCHENINNIKOVIA Guldenstaedt 1772 [for I. M. Krascheninnikov, Russian botanist]. WINTERFAT
  One sp, **K. lanata** (Pursh) Meeuse & Smit [woolly]. Forming large pure stands on gravelly benches in the lower river valleys (*Eurotia*, *Ceratoides*).

216 Chenopodiaceae (CHN)

MONOLEPIS Schrader 1831 [Gr. *monos*, single, + *lepis*, scale]. POVERTYWEED

1a. Prostrate; lvs hastately lobed at base, over 12 mm long; fls in axillary clusters. **M. nuttalliana** (Schultes) Greene, **37F**. Muddy ditches and edges of drying ponds. The translucent ovary wall has a beautifully cellular-reticulate pattern!
1b. Very slender, erect; lvs entire, not over 10 mm long; fls paniculate, on slender pedicels. **M. pusilla** Torrey. Clay soil, a single old record from Grand Junction.

SALICORNIA L. 1753 [Gr., *sal*, salt, + *cornu*, horn]. GLASSWORT

One sp, **S. europaea** L. ssp **rubra** (Nelson) Breitung, **37E**. Infrequent on borders of alkaline ponds and river oxbows. Easily spotted from a distance by its brilliant red autumn color.

SALSOLA L. 1753 [Lat., *salsus*, salty]. RUSSIAN-THISTLE

1a. Bracts broad-based, with stiffly flaring spine-tips; plant extremely prickly, difficult to handle, the branches stiffly spreading. **S. australis** R. Brown [southern], **37G, 40B**. Abundant native tumbleweed (*S. iberica, S. pestifer*).
1b. Bracts narrow-based, the tips directed forward; plant easily handled, the branches elongate, gracefully curving. **S. collina** Pallas [of hills], **40A**. ADV, thus far known only from the E slope, but to be expected here.

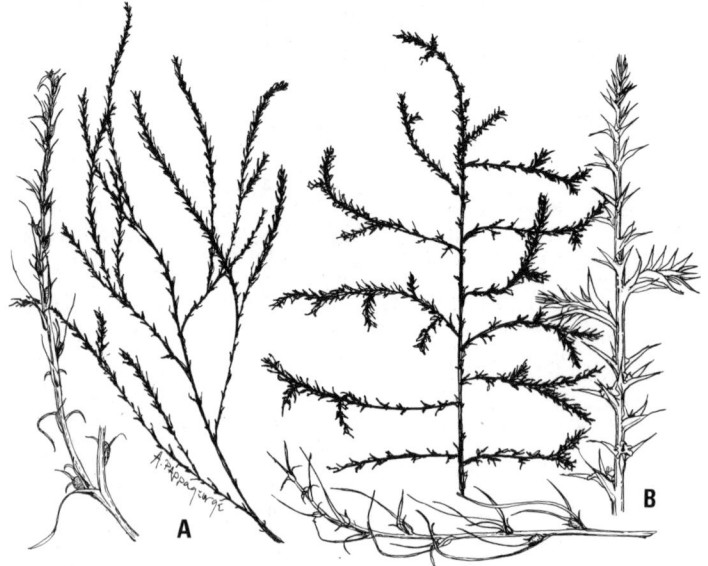

Figure 40. **A**, *Salsola collina*; **B**, *S. australis*

SARCOBATUS Nees 1841 [Gr. *sarco-*, fleshy, + *batia*, bush]. GREASEWOOD
One sp, **S. vermiculatus** (Hooker) Torrey [worm-eaten], **37A**. Abundant on alkaline flats. A poisonous plant containing calcium oxalate, nevertheless a useful forage plant if the diet is mixed and sheep do not graze in pure stands.

SUAEDA Forskål 1777 [an Arabic name]. SEA-BLITE

1a. Perennial, woody and branched at the base; stems over 3 dm tall, forming bushy growth. **S. moquinii** Torrey [for French chenopod student, C. Moquin-Tandon, 1804-1863]. Seasonally wet clay flats along the lower river valleys (*S. torreyana*).
1b. Annual, appearing in late summer and flowering late into the fall; stems less than 2 dm tall, branched but not forming bushy growth. . . . . (2)

2a. A fleshy conical outgrowth on the back of one or more tepals, this shriveling in age, giving the fl a contorted appearance. **S. calceoliformis** (Hooker) Moquin [like a little shoe], **37D**. Locally abundant on drying alkaline mud flats (*S. depressa*).
2b. Tepals thin, not developing as above. **S. nigra** (Rafinesque) Macbride [black]. Similar habitats.

TELOXYS Moquin 1834 [Gr., *telos*, tip, + *oxys*, sharp, referring to the suppressed lateral floral branchlets which become a terminal spine] (formerly incl in *Chenopodium*). WORMSEED

1a. Infl of small sessile clusters along straight, elongate spikes; lvs often 10 cm or more long. **T. ambrosioides** (L.) Weber [like *Ambrosia*]. ADV, not yet reported from the W slope, but to be expected as a weed in cult land.
1b. Infl open, cymosely branched; lvs less than 4 cm long, deeply pinnatifid . . . . (2)

2a. Cymes with central fl developed, lateral ones abortive and their pedicels becoming naked and almost spine-like; **T. graveolens** (Willdenow) Weber [heavy-odor]. ADV, reported from the upper Arkansas Valley and probably present on the W slope.
2b. Cymes with all fls equally developed. **T. botrys** (L.) Weber [bunch of grapes], **39D**. ADV along roadsides, thriving in gravelly soils. One old record, Durango.

COMMELINACEAE—SPIDERWÓRT FAMILY (CMM)

The genus from which the family takes its name contains a homely little weed in city back yards in the eastern U. S. and northern Europe called the Dayflower. The fls last only through one day, then simply melt into a slimy residue. Linnaeus explained the name he gave the plant. "*Commelina* has flowers with three petals, two of which are showy [blue] while the third [white] is not conspicuous; [named] from the two botanists called Commelin; for the third died before accomplishing anything in botany." The stamen filaments of these fls have long hairs composed of beadlike strings of enormous cells which

Figure 41. **A**, *Echinocystis lobata*; **B**, *Cucurbita foetidissima*

can be seen by the naked eye; cell division can be followed with a microscope without special treatment.

1a. Petals three, all purple; fls long-pediceled, the bracts not different from foliage lvs. **Tradescantia**, SPIDERWORT
1b. Petals three, two blue and one white; fls arising on short pedicels from a folded ovate bract with a long attenuate apex. **Commelina**, DAYFLOWER

COMMELINA L. 1753 [see above]. DAYFLOWER
  One sp, **C. dianthifolia** Delile [with lvs like *Dianthus*, CRY], **20B**. Infrequent, talus slopes in canyons, San Juan Mts., LP.

TRADESCANTIA L. 1753 [for John Tradescant, gardener to Charles I of England]. SPIDERWORT
  One sp, **T. occidentalis** (Britton) Smyth. An E slope sp to be expected here, since it reappears in Utah. Commonly found in gravelly soil along the bases of roadcuts.

CONVALLARIACEAE—MAYFLOWER FAMILY (CVL)

Recently segregated from Liliaceae as a family and characterized by having leafy stems from rhizomes. The flowers are white, with very narrow tepals, and the fruits are red or green berries. Our only genus, *Smilacina*, was recently reunited with *Maianthemum*, which includes the Canada Mayflower of the eastern and far western states. *Convallaria majalis* is Lily-of-the-Valley.

MAIANTHEMUM G. H. Weber 1780 [Gr., *Maia*, May, + *anthemum*, flower] (formerly *Smilacina*). FALSE SOLOMON'S SEAL
1a. Fls few, in a simple raceme; lvs lanceolate. **M. stellatum** (L.) Link. Throughout the lower and middle altitudes, in meadows, gulches, streamsides and forests.
1b. Fls numerous, in a panicle; lvs broadly oval. **M. amplexicaule** (Nuttall) Weber [clasping-leaved]. The common name comes from the resemblance of the circular lf-scar on the rhizome to a signet. Our sp is a diploid, while *M. racemosum*, under which it often has been treated, is tetraploid. Contrary to claims, these do not intergrade.

CONVOLVULACEAE
MORNING-GLORY FAMILY (CNV)

Morning-glories are favorite ornamental climbers for porches and patios, but several members of the family are used in other important ways. *Dichondra repens* is used as a ground cover in place of grass for lawns in southern California. *Ipomoea batatas* is the true Sweetpotato (as opposed to the Yam, *Dioscorea*, a monocot in the Dioscoreaceae). It is a staple crop in Melanesia, and its introduction, probably from America, is thought to have been effected through Polynesian migrations. *Ipomoea tuberosa* is the curious 'Wooden-rose' of dry bouquets. The parasitic Dodder, formerly included in this family, now is placed in the Cuscutaceae.

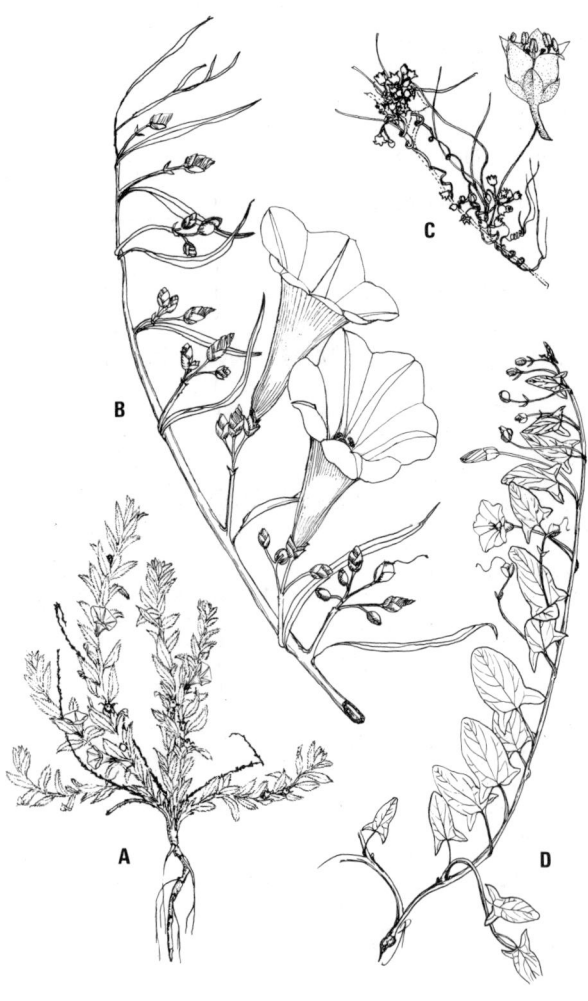

Figure 42. A, *Evolvulus nuttallianus*; B, *Calystegia sepium*; C, *Grammica sp.*; D, *Convolvulus arvensis*

Convolvulaceae (CNV) 221

1a. Erect, not at all climbing or creeping or twining; fls lavender; lvs elliptic-oblong, gray-pilose. **Evolvulus**
1b. Creeping or twining; fls white, or pink on the back; lvs triangular-hastate, smooth or nearly so. . . . . (2)

2a. Calyx enclosed by large bracts; fls over 3 cm long; lvs over 5 cm long. **Calystegia**, HEDGE BINDWEED
2b. Calyx not enclosed by large bracts; fls less than 2 cm long; lvs also small. **Convolvulus**, BINDWEED

CALYSTEGIA R. Brown 1810 [Gr., *calyx*, + *stegos*, roof, cover, alluding to the bracts]. HEDGE BINDWEED
One sp, **C. sepium** (L.) R. Brown ssp **americana** (Sims) Brummitt, **42B**. ADV but infrequent and local, on fences and hedgerows, ME.

CONVOLVULUS L. 1753 [Lat., *convolvere*, to entwine]. BINDWEED
One sp, **C. arvensis** L., **42D**, CREEPING-JENNY. ADV, common creeping weed on roadsides and in lawns, very difficult to eradicate because of its deep roots and brittle rhizomes.

EVOLVULUS L. 1753 [Lat., *evolvere*, to unroll, hence, not twining]
One sp, **E. nuttallianus** Roemer & Schultes, **42A**. Infrequent in sagebrush, our only W slope record from ME.

CORNACEAE—DOGWOOD FAMILY (COR)

The name 'dogwood' is given to a great number of unrelated trees, and the origin of the name is unknown. An old Century Dictionary mentions that the wood is so free from scratchy silica that jewelers used small splinters of it to clean out the pivot-holes in watches, and opticians for removing dust from small deep-seated lenses. Flowering Dogwoods (*Cornus*) are found in the ancient relictual Tertiary forests of Eastern and Pacific North America and Japan.

1a. Shrub with red branches; infl not subtended by petal like bracts; lvs opposite. **Swida**, RED-OSIER
1b. Herb (10-20 cm tall) from a woody rhizome; infl subtended by 4 to 5 white, petal-like bracts (a miniature 'flowering dogwood'); lvs in a whorl at the top of the stem. **Chamaepericlymenum**, BUNCHBERRY

CHAMAEPERICLYMENUM Hill 1756 [Gr., *chamae*, dwarfed, + *Periclymenium*, a honeysuckle]. BUNCHBERRY
One sp, **C. canadense** (L.) Ascherson & Graebner, **43B, PL 8**. Subalpine forests, not yet found on the W slope but to be expected in the moist spruce forests just west of the Divide, in Middle Park (*Cornus*).

SWIDA Opiz 1838 [derivation obscure]. RED-OSIER
One sp, **S. sericea** (L.) Holub, **43A**. Common in shaded montane canyons (*Cornus stolonifera*).

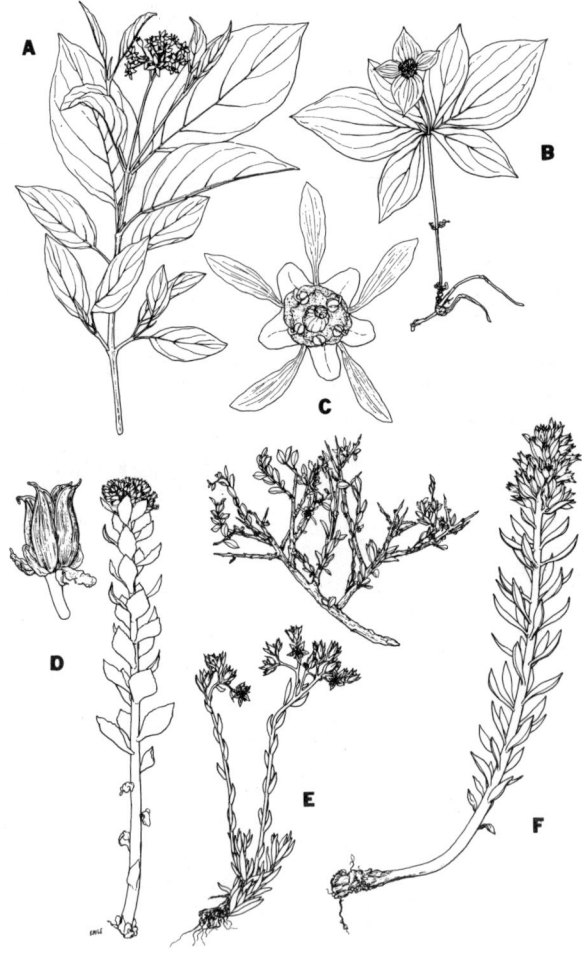

Figure 43. A, *Swida sericea*; B, *Chamaepericlymenum canadense*; C, *Forsellesia meionandra*, fl above, habit below; D, *Rhodiola integrifolia*; E, *Amerosedum lanceolatum*; F, *Clementsia rhodantha*

CRASSULACEAE—STONECROP FAMILY (CRS)

Most sedums are succulents, but not all succulents are sedums. Desert and alpine areas all over the world have evolved the succulent habit in several unrelated families. The Mesembryanthemaceae of South Africa are famous for their succulent leaves that resemble pebbles, North African euphorbias resemble our Saguaro cacti, and many chenopods of saline ground are succulents. In order to make good herbarium specimens of members of this family the stems must be briefly boiled or subjected to a heat lamp to destroy the protective function of the epidermis. Otherwise, plants will survive long periods and actually keep growing in a plant press.

1a. Fls yellow or white; lvs fleshy, plump to almost round in cross-section; fl shoots up to 1 dm high. . . . . (2)
1b. Fls purple, pink or white; lvs thin; fl shoots up to several dm tall . . . . (3)

2a. Fls yellow; lvs several times longer than wide, crowded on short basal rosettes, scattered on the fl stem; plants not strongly rhizomatous. **Amerosedum**, YELLOW STONECROP
2b. Fls white; lvs about 5 mm long, broadly ovate, not crowded in basal rosettes; plants loosely rhizomatous. **Sedum**, STONECROP

3a. Petals pink or white; fls perfect, clustered in the axils of the upper lvs; midrib prominent on lf under-side. **Clementsia**, ROSE CROWN
3b. Petals deep red-purple; fls usually unisexual (and plants dioecious), in a flat-topped terminal cluster; midrib imbedded, not easily visible. **Rhodiola**, KING'S CROWN

AMEROSEDUM Löve & Löve 1985. [American + *Sedum*], YELLOW STONECROP
One sp, **A. lanceolatum** (Torrey) Löve & Löve, **43E**. Common on stony ground from the plains up to the tundra (*Sedum*).

CLEMENTSIA Rose 1903 [for F. E. Clements]. ROSE CROWN
One sp, **C. rhodantha** (Gray) Rose, **43F**. Common along subalpine rivulets and in peat bogs (*Sedum*). END in the S Rockies, but a close relative, *C. semenovii*, almost identical to it, grows in the mts of central Asia.

RHODIOLA L. 1753 [Gr., *rhodon*, rose-colored]. KING'S CROWN
One sp, **R. integrifolia** Rafinesque, **43D**. Moist slopes and tundra, usually at higher altitudes than the preceding but often growing with it (*Sedum*). Because of its peculiar sexuality, this species has been placed in the new genus *Tolmatchevia* by Löve & Löve.

SEDUM L. 1753 [Lat., *sedere*, to sit, alluding to the habitat on rocks and walls]. STONECROP
One sp, **S. acre** L. ADV garden plant on sand bars of the Roaring Fork River, PT.

CROSSOSOMATACEAE
CROSSOSOMA FAMILY (CRO)

A very small family, until recently thought to include only the two genera, *Apacheria* and *Crossosoma*, of the desert Southwest. Recently our only genus was reassigned to this family from the Celastraceae.

FORSELLESIA Greene 1893 [for Jacob H. af Forselles, 1785-1855, Swedish mining engineer]
    One sp, **F. meionandra** (Koehne) Heller, **43C**. A low, densely branched, spiny shrub with small oblanceolate or elliptic lvs and small greenish axillary fls. Sandstone outcrops in or below the piñon-juniper zone.

CUCURBITACEAE—GOURD FAMILY (CUC)

Cultivated cucurbits are a legacy to us from aboriginal man, who used them not only for food but for all sorts of kitchen utensils, musical rattles, floats for fish nets, and drinking cups. To emphasize their importance in our culture, one only has to list a few: Squash, Pumpkin, Calabash or Gourd, Watermelon, Canteloupe, Cucumber. Besides these, there are dozens of cucurbits used throughout the tropical regions that are quite unknown to northerners. The inner spongy pulp of the genus *Luffa* is the original 'chore-boy', called Dishcloth Gourd. Flowers of cucurbits are usually unisexual. Food crops depend on pollination by honeybees and solitary bees.

1a.   Vine trailing over the ground and over low plants; lvs rough-pubescent, ovate to triangular, denticulate; fls yellow, about 10 cm long; frt a woody dry striped baseball-shaped gourd. **Cucurbita**, GOURD; CALABAZILLA
1b.   Vine climbing over fences and on tall shrubs; lvs palmately 5-lobed, glabrous; fls small, white, in racemes or panicles; frt prickly, papery balloon-like with a spongy center. **Echinocystis**, WILD BALSAM-APPLE; MOCK CUCUMBER

CUCURBITA L. 1753 [the classical name]. GOURD
    One sp, **C. foetidissima** Humboldt, Bonpland & Kunth. [stinking], Calabazilla, **41B**. ADV. Native on the E slope, but introduced in ME and MZ along roadsides.

ECHINOCYSTIS Torrey & Gray 1840 [Gr., *echinos*, hedgehog, + *kystis*, bladder]. BALSAM-APPLE; MOCK CUCUMBER
    One sp, **E. lobata** (Michaux) Torrey & Gray, **41A**. Native on E slope but evidently introd near Ouray.

CUSCUTACEAE—DODDER FAMILY (CUS)

The dodders are parasitic plants lacking green leaves and consisting only of long, slender, intertangled orange threads climbing over various kinds of plants and attaching themselves to the stems by suckers (haustoria) that penetrate the tissues of the host. The flowers are globular and white. Identification is difficult at best, and impossible without the presence of well-developed flowers and mature fruit. Until recently, most texts included this family with the Convolvulaceae. The seeds evidently have enough food supply to permit them to germinate on the ground, but they must very soon attach their stems to the proper host. Some dodders are very injurious to crops, at least in Eurasia. The name, dodder, seems to have its origin in old northwestern European languages, describing 'yellowness'. In all of our species, the capsule is circumscissile. The species are still too little known here to enable us to give much information about their distribution. They are too often collected in immature stages.

1a. Stigmas elongated. **Cuscuta**
1b. Stigmas capitate. **Grammica**

CUSCUTA L. 1753 [derivation uncertain, thought to be from Arabic]. DODDER
   One sp, **C. approximata** Babington. Known in W Colorado from one collection, MF.

GRAMMICA Loureiro 1790 [Gr., *grammicos*, linear, alluding to the stringy stems]. DODDER, **42C**
1a. Calyx with separate sepals; infl with many bracts. **G. cuspidata** (Engelmann) Hadaç & Chrtek.
1b. Calyx with united sepals; infl not very bracteate. . . . . (2)

2a. Capsules mostly globose or depressed-globose, sometimes thickened about the style-bases . . . . (3)
2b. Capsules ovoid, conic or beaked, commonly longer than wide . . . (5)

3a. Capsule globose, with a definitely thickened style base; fls ± thick and fleshy, papillate or glandular. **G. indecora** (Choisy) Weber.
3b. Capsule not especially thickened at the top . . . . (4)

4a. Internal corolla-scales lacking, not forming a low crown below the stamens. **G. occidentalis** (Millspaugh) Weber.
4b. Internal corolla-scales present, forming a crown below the stamens. **G. campestris** (Yuncker) Hadaç & Chrtek.

5a. Fls small, about 2 mm long; embryo thickened in a terminal knob; capsule 1-seeded. **G. denticulata** (Engelmann) Weber.
5b. Fls larger; capsules mostly 2-4-seeded; embryo not as above, embedded in endosperm. **G. umbrosa** (Hooker) Weber.

CYPERACEAE—SEDGE FAMILY (CYP)

The word 'sedge' is derived as far back as Middle English *segge* and Teutonic *seg*, and is related to the modern German *Säge*, meaning saw. Many sedges have sharp cutting edges on the leaves, and some of them are actually minutely saw-toothed. Relatively few sedges are of major economic importance, but *Cyperus papyrus* was famous from antiquity as a paper source, and the incas of Peru used (and still do) the giant reeds (*Scirpus totora*) of Lake Titicaca for making rafts to create land surfaces in the shallow water and for building their houses. Thor Heyerdal proved that such papyrus rafts are seaworthy. And of course, the most famous cradle of Biblical history was fashioned from papyrus.

1a. Fl cluster resembling a powderpuff or tassel, the perianth consisting of many long white silky hairs. **Eriophorum**, COTTON-SEDGE, BOG-WOOL
1b. Fl cluster not as above. (2)

2a. Fl bracts (scales) in two distinct rows, the spike flattened. . . . . (3)
2b. Fl bracts arranged in ascending spirals, the spikes not distinctly flattened . . . . (4)

3a. Rachilla of the spike articulated at base, the spikelets falling whole. **Mariscus**
3b. Rachilla of the spike not articulated, the individual scales falling from the rachis. **Cyperus**

4a. Fls unisexual, the plants and spikes either entirely staminate or entirely carpellate, or with both staminate and carpellate fls in the same spike; gynoecium enclosed in a sac-like structure (perigynium, abbr. perig). . . . . (5)
4b. Fls perfect (all alike and never grouped into different types of spikes on the same plant); gynoecium merely subtended by a scale-like bract . . . . (6)

5a. Perig split down the middle throughout its length with overlapping margins (like the open sheath of a grass). **Kobresia**
5b. Perig completely closed except at the apex where the style protrudes (like the closed sheath of a grass). **Carex**

6a. Spike solitary, terminal. . . . . (7)
6b. Spikes more than one, or if solitary, not terminal but protruding from the side of the stem . . . . (8)

7a. Ak red-brown to black, with a differentiated conical or flattened cap (stylopodium); lvs lacking blades. **Eleocharis**, SPIKE-RUSH
7b. Ak black, lacking a differentiated stylopodium (cap); lvs with short but definite blades. **Baeothryon**

8a. Spikes protruding sideways from the side of the stem, or if appearing terminal, a single erect bract appearing to continue the stem upward . . . . (9)
8b. Spikes terminal, subtended by several lflike bracts. . . . . . . (10)

9a. Spikes numerous, oval, pedunculate, and culms terete, or spikes few, sessile and lateral, and stems trigonous. **Schoenoplectus**
9b. Spikes few, cylindric, sessile at the tip of the stem; culms terete. **Amphiscirpus**

10a. Spikes large, over 1 cm long, almost sessile. **Bolboschoenus**

10b. Spikes small, less than 5 mm long, panicled, the ultimate spikes in sessile clusters. **Scirpus**

AMPHISCIRPUS Oteng-Yeboah 1974 [Gr., *amphi*, around, + *Scirpus*]
One sp, **A. nevadensis** (Watson) Yeboah. Uncommon on the W slope, alkaline shale flats, RB. The aks in this genus are distinctly cellular-reticulate under a lens (*Scirpus*).

BAEOTHRYON Dietrich 1833 [Gr., *baios*, little, scanty, + *thryon*, rush]
One sp, **B. pumilum** (Vahl) Löve & Löve. Known only from South Park, but extremely inconspicuous and inhabiting wet moss in rills in calcareous willow fens, thus to be expected on the W slope. The plants are slender-rhizomatous, with a few slender stems up to 10 cm tall, each with a small few-fld spike. As each scale falls away the tiny black shiny akene remains attached for a time. Recently rediscovered in Colorado after not being seen for over a century (*Scirpus pumilus*).

BOLBOSCHOENUS Palla 1907 [Gr., *bolbos*, a swelling, + *schoinos*, rush, alluding to the stylopodium]
One sp, **B. maritimus** (L.) Palla ssp **paludosus** (Nelson) Löve & Löve, 47A. Sloughs and ditches in the lower valleys. The large, football-shaped spikelets, lfy subtending bracts and triangular stem are diagnostic (*Scirpus paludosus*).

CAREX L. 1753 [Gr, *keirein*, to cut, alluding to the sharp lvs of many spp] (Key contributed by Miriam Colson Fritts)
1a. Spikes one to a culm (careful observation needed here; several spp may appear to have one spike but on close examination show more than one rachis). **Key A**
1b. Spikes more than one to a culm, although sometimes crowded so as to appear single (careful examination will reveal separate rachises or branches of the infl). . . . . (2)

2a. Spikes in a ball-like cluster, the individual ones not easily detected by manipulation, only by dissection; scales brown, never black. **Key B**
2b. Spikes either separate or clustered but always distinguishable without dissection. . . . . (3)

3a. Spikes sessile, never black unless perigynia wing-margined or very sharp-edged, usually with staminate and carpellate fls in the same spike, the terminal spike never markedly different from the rest. **Key C**
3b. Spikes pedunculate (at least the lowermost one), or black, or with markedly different staminate terminal spikes. **Key D**

KEY A : SOLITARY SPIKES

1a. Plants in dense clumps, not obviously rhizomatous; lf-blades always narrow and filiform. . . . . (2)
1b. Plants with obvious rhizomes, the culms solitary or a few together; lf-blades up to 3 mm wide. . . . . (6)

2a. Spike short and broad, shiny brown or black, the terminal staminate portion inconspicuous or spike broadly triangular with conspicuous staminate fls at the apex . . . . (3)
2b. Spike elongate, narrow, often pale, with a distinct elongate narrow staminate portion, only a few carpellate fls at the base, bulging when mature . . . . (5)

3a. Spike globose or triangular; stigmas 2; perig not stipitate. **C. capitata** L. ssp **arctogena** (Smith) Böcher [in a head; of the Arctic]. Rare or local in upper subalpine and alpine peat-bogs.
3b. Spike not globose; stigmas 2 or 3; perig stipitate. . . . . (4)

4a. Lvs 0.25 mm wide; perig barely stipitate, serrulate above; scales not early deciduous. **C. nardina** Fries ssp **hepburnii** (Boott) Löve et al. [resembling the grass, *Nardus*; for James Hepburn]. On the highest tundra ridges, often on very dry sites with sedimentary rock.
4b. Lvs 0.5-1.5 mm wide; perig long-stipitate, smooth above; scales early-deciduous. **C. crandallii** Gandoger [for C. S. Crandall]. Snowmelt areas, alpine, subalpine (*C. pyrenaica* of Colorado lit).

5a. Perig rounded on the angles, truncately short-beaked, puberulent above; carpellate scales with broad hyaline margins; basal sheaths usually shredded and filamentose; style exserted. **C. filifolia** Nuttall [thread-like lvs]. Dry grasslands, plains to montane.
5b. Perig more sharply triangular, slender-beaked, the body slightly puberulent or glabrous at base of beak; margin of scales not as strongly hyaline; basal sheaths not shredded, the old culms and lvs broken (or grazed off by animals) forming dense fascicles. **C. elynoides** Holm [for *Elyna*, another name for *Kobresia*]. Very abundant, subalpine and alpine, and often confused with *Kobresia*.

6a. Spikes unisexual, the plants dioecious . . . . (7)
6b. Staminate and carpellate fls in the same spike. . . . . (10)

7a. Perig faces pubescent . . . . (8)
7b. Perig faces glabrous . . . . (9)

8a. Culms aphyllopodic, strongly purplish-red-tinged at the base; scales slightly shorter than the perig. **C. scirpoidea** Michaux [resembling *Scirpus* (actually *Eleocharis*, which Michaux included in it)]. Rare, snowmelt areas, subalpine and alpine.
8b. Culms phyllopodic, brownish, reddish-brown or slightly reddish-tinged at the base; scales longer than the perig. **Carex pseudoscirpoidea** Rydberg. Occasional in mesic sites, rocky slopes, meadows, subalpine, alpine.

9a. Perig broadly obovate to suborbicular, nerveless or nearly so except for marginal nerves; stigmas 3. **C. parryana** Dewey ssp **hallii** Murray [for C. C. Parry, Elihu Hall]. Open gravelly meadows, subalpine. This sp may have 1 to 3 minute carpellate spikes (see 8a, Key D)

9b. Perig slenderly ovate, finely many-nerved dorsally, obscurely so ventrally; stigmas 2. **C. dioica** L. ssp **gynocrates** (Wormskjöld) Hultén [dioecious, female-dominant]. Infrequent in swampy meadows, subalpine. The solitary spike may be carpellate below and staminate above (see 14b).

10a. Perig few, yellowish, narrow and pointed, sharply reflexed, a well-developed hooked rachilla protruding from the beak orifice. **C. microglochin** Wahlenberg [small hooks], **44A**. Subalpine willow-bogs, often with *Sphagnum*.
10b. Perig not as above. (11)

11a. Spikes broad and densely-fld, with numerous perig; scales dark brown or black . . . . (12)
11b. Spikes few-fld, with only a few perig; scales pale or reddish-brown . . . . (13)

12a. Perig reflexed at maturity, narrow and long-stipitate; lvs 1.5-2.0 mm wide. **C. nigricans** Meyer [blackish]. Common on wet streamsides, subalpine and alpine.
12b. Perig erect to spreading at maturity, broadly obovate and barely stipitate; lvs 0.3-0.5 mm wide. **C. engelmannii** Bailey. Infrequent and local on tundra.

13a. Lvs straight, up to 1.5 mm wide. . . . . (14)
13b. Lvs drying and curling at the tip, up to 3 mm wide . . . . . . (15)

14a. Perig beak smooth, with two broad, flaring hyaline tips; lvs 1-1.5 mm wide. **C. obtusata** Liljeblad [obtuse, probably the perig beak]. Dry montane to subalpine slopes.
14b. Perig beak sparingly serrulate without the two flaring hyaline tips; lvs 0.5 mm wide. **C. dioica** L. ssp **gynocrates** (Wormskjöld) Hultén [dioecious; female-dominant]. Swampy meadows, often dioecious (see 9b above).

15a. Spikes closely-fld with 6 to 15 perig; staminate and carpellate fls close together with no exposed rachis. **C. rupestris** Allioni ssp **drummondiana** (Dewey) Holub [of rocks; for Thomas Drummond]. Dry alpine and upper subalpine slopes.
15b. Spikes loosely-fld with 1 to 3 perig; staminate and carpellate fls separated, exposing the rachis between them. **C. geyeri** Boott [for Carl Andreas Geyer, collector on the Oregon Trail], ELK SEDGE, **44E**. Dominant understory in open spruce-fir and Douglas-fir, foothills to subalpine.

KEY B : GLOBOSE SPIKES

1a. Culms exceeding the lvs; lvs about 2-4mm wide, mostly stiffly erect, not withering nor curled at the tips; perig ovate-lanceolate, not inflated. **C. vernacula** Bailey [indigenous, as opposed to a European sp from which he was distinguishing it]. Infrequent, alpine tundra.

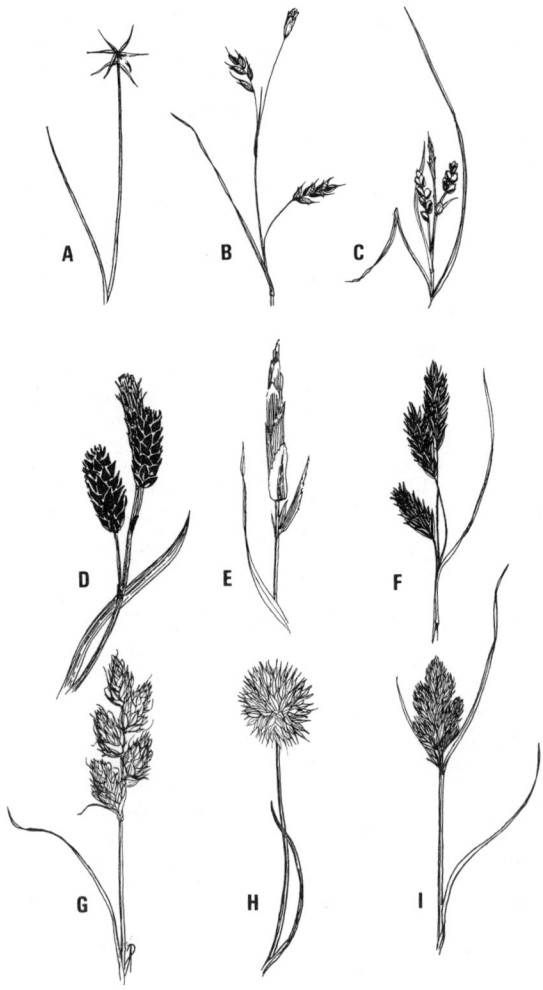

Figure 44. A, *Carex microglochin*; B, *C. capillaris*; C, *C. aurea*; D, *C. scopulorum*; E, *C. geyeri*; F, *C. misandra*; G, *C. brevior* (E slope only); H, *C. perglobosa*; I, *C. athrostachya*

Figure 45. A, *Carex ebenea*; B, *C. microptera*; C, *C. stipata*; D, *C. utriculata*; E, *C. hystericina*; F, *C. lanuginosa*; G, *C. chalciolepis*; H, *C. aquatilis*

1b. Fl culms hardly exceeding the lvs; lvs 15 mm or less wide, with a strong tendency to wither and curl at the tips . . . . (2)

2a. Spikes forming a broadly conical cluster, the basal scales preventing the infl from becoming spherical; perig oblong-lanceolate, scarcely inflated. **C. maritima** Gunnerus [of seashores]. Frost scars and wet gravels, alpine (*C. incurviformis*).
2b. Spikes forming a shaggy globose cluster, the lower spikes spreading downward; perig broad, almost orbicular, inflated. **C. perglobosa** Mackenzie [very globose], **44H**. Alpine scree slopes.

KEY C : SESSILE BISEXUAL SPIKES

1a. Spikes few-fld, green, scattered along the culm; perig conspicuous, usually spreading. (2)
1b. Spikes many-fld in definite spikes rather than short, few-fld clusters . . . . (7)

2a. [1] Culms very slender and weak, commonly nodding or reclining. . . . . (3)
2b. Fl culms ± stiffly erect. (5)

3a. [2] Perig with slender beak half as long as the body, nerveless ventrally; lvs 2-5 mm wide. **C. deweyana** Schweinitz [for Chester Dewey, *Carex* specialist]. Moist foothill-montane ravines.
3b. Perig with short beak, at least lightly nerved on both sides; lvs not more than 2 mm wide . . . . (4)

4a. [3] Terminal spike gynaecandrous; beak 1/4 to 1/3 the length of the body. **C. laeviculmis** Meinshausen. [smooth-culmed]. Uncommon on boggy streambanks or moist woods, montane.
4b. Terminal spike androgynous; beak minute. **C. disperma** Dewey [with 2 perig]. Moist forests, bogs and thickets, montane and subalpine.

5a. [2] Perig ascending, the inner faces not exposed, broadest near the middle; terminal spike with inconspicuous apical staminate portion (androgynous). **C. occidentalis** Bailey [western]. Foothills to subalpine (see 20b).
5b. Perig widely spreading, exposing their very flat inner sides, broadest just above the base; terminal spike with several staminate scales sheathing the base of the peduncle (gynaecandrous)
. . . . (6)

6a. [5] Perig 1.5-2.0 mm wide, the beak 1/4 to 1/3 the length of the body, shallowly bidentate with short, broad teeth. **C. interior** Bailey [of the midlands]. Moist meadows and forest openings, foothills to subalpine.
6b. Perig 1-1.4 mm wide, the beak from more than half to about the length of the body, deeply and sharply bidentate. **C. angustior** Mackenzie [narrower]. Similar habitats.

7a. [1] Culms arising singly or a few together from long-creeping rhizomes. . . . . (8)
7b. Culms caespitose or the rhizomes short, with short internodes, never long-creeping. . . . . (16)

8a. [7] Perig narrowly wing-margined, the beak deeply bidentate; most spikes gynaecandrous, but the lowest usually carpellate and the middle often staminate. **C. foenea** Willdenow [hay-like]. Dry gravels, foothills to subalpine.
8b. Perig not wing-margined or winged only at the junction of the beak and body, the beak obliquely-cut dorsally, becoming only slightly bidentate . . . . (9)

9a. [8] Plants dioecious or very nearly so. . . . . (10)
9b. Plants not dioecious, at least the terminal spike androgynous
. . . . (12)

10a. [9] Carpellate scales clasping the perig, usually completely concealing them; lf sheaths dark brown or black. **C. praegracilis** Boott [very slender]. Wet meadows and roadside ditches, valleys, foothills (see 14a).
10b. Carpellate scales not clasping the perig; lf-sheaths light brown
. . . . (11)

11a. [10] Perig winged at the junction of the beak and body, very small, not longer than 3 mm; beak very short; scales dark brown. **C. simulata** Mackenzie [imitative]. Wet meadows and swamps, foothills to subalpine (see 15a).
11b. Perig not at all winged, 3.5-4.0 mm long, the beak as long as the body; scales straw-colored. **C. douglasii** Boott [for David Douglas]. Roadside ditches and alkaline flats.

12a. [9] Infl broad, 1-2.5 cm wide; perig beak as long as the body. **C. douglasii** Boott].
12b. Infl linear-oblong, 5-10 mm wide. . . . . (13)

13a. [12] Upper lf sheaths green-striate ventrally except near the mouth; staminate fls unusually conspicuous, most of the middle, and often the upper, spikes entirely staminate. **S. sartwellii** Dewey [for Henry Parker Sartwell]. Infrequent, montane marshes and bogs.
13b. Upper leaf sheaths hyaline ventrally. . . . . (14)

14a. [13] Lower lf sheaths dark brown or black; carpellate scales clasping the perig at the base. **C. praegracilis** Boott [very slender] (see 10a).
14b. Lower lf sheaths light brown; carpellate scales not as above. . . (15)

15a. [14] Scales dark brown; perig winged at the junction of beak and body, abruptly narrowed to a very short beak. **C. simulata** Mackenzie (see 11a).
15b. Scales chestnut to light brown; perig not at all winged, contracted to a beak 1/4 to 1.3 the length of the body. **C. steno-**

phylla Wahlenberg ssp **eleocharis** (Bailey) Hultén [narrow-leaved, allusion to genus *Eleocharis*]. Grassy slopes, montane and subalpine.

16a. [7] Terminal spike androgynous . . . . (17)
16b. Terminal spike gynaecandrous. . . . . (22)

17a. [16] Perig tapering into a beak almost from the base; infl thick, up to 2 cm wide, the spikes stiffly spreading, like a pin-cushion. **C. stipata** Mühlenberg [crowded], **45C**. Swamps, known from one collection in the San Juans.
17b. Perig abruptly contracted into a beak; infl slender, 5-10 mm wide, the spikes ascending . . . . (18)

18a. [17] Perig tapering gradually to the beak almost from the base, widest near the base. . . . . (19)
18b. Perig abruptly contracted into the beak, widest near the middle
. . . . (20)

19a. [18] Lf sheaths transversely wrinkled ventrally; culm stout (3.5 mm thick). **C. neurophora** Mackenzie [with nerves, on the perig]. Wet meadows, montane to subalpine.
19b. Lf sheaths not cross-rugulose ventrally; culm slender (2 mm thick at base). **C. jonesii** Bailey [for Marcus E. Jones]. Meadows, montane to subalpine, N counties.

20a. [18] Perig deeply plano-convex, the marginal nerves pulled to the flat ventral face by the expanding dorsal face; lvs 1-1.5 mm wide. **C. vallicola** Dewey [of valleys]. Dry open slopes and forest clearings.
20b. Perig not as above, slightly plano-convex or flat-concave with sharp green margins; lvs 1.5-3.5 mm wide . . . . (21)

21a. [20] Perig ovate, dark glossy-brown, broadly margined, the vivid green margins conspicuously serrulate above the middle, rather abruptly long-beaked, the beak conspicuously bidentate; scales lustrous, dark chestnut-brown; infl stiff. **C. hoodii** Boott [for Sir Samuel Hood]. Montane and subalpine meadows, N counties.
21b. Perig elliptic, greenish-straw-colored to brown-centered, the green margins narrow, usually less serrulate, the beak shorter, shallowly bidentate; scales greenish-brown; infl lax. **C. occidentalis** Bailey (see 5a).

22a. [16] Perig not wing-margined but plano-convex and thin-edged
. . . . (23)
22b. Perig wing-margined to the base, thin and scale-like or plano-convex. . . . . (27)

23a. [22] Scales hyaline with green center (may be brownish-tinged at maturity. . . . . (24)
23b. Scales medium to dark brown or black. . . . . (25)

24a. [23] Perig apiculate to very short-beaked (beak usually 0.25 mm long or less), appressed-ascending; spikes many-fld (9 to 20 perig); lvs glaucous, 2-4 mm wide. **C. canescens** L. Marshes, lake shores, montane and subalpine.

24b. Perig distinctly beaked (beak 0.5 mm long or more), serrulate, loosely spreading; spikes few-fld (5-10 perig); lvs green, 1-2.5 mm wide. **C. brunnescens** (Persoon) Poiret [brownish]. Marshes and lake shores, montane, subalpine; uncommon.

25a. [23] Scales black; perig partly black; infl broadly triangular-conic, the spikes very closely aggregated. **C. illota** Bailey [dirty]. Wet subalpine and alpine meadows.
25b. Scales medium to dark brown; perig yellow-brown; infl not triangular-conic, the spikes distinct . . . . (26)

26a. [25] Spikes 2-4; perig obovate, 2.0-3.5 mm long, beak smooth, 0.5-1.0 mm long. **C. lachenalii** Schkuhr [for Werner de Lachenal]. Alpine and upper subalpine.
26b. Spikes 4-5; perig oval-ovate, 1.5-2.5 mm long, beak often slightly serrulate, 0.25-0.33 mm long. **C. praeceptorum** Mackenzie [for "the teachers", Professors Morton E. Peck and J. C. Nelson]. Tundra and grassy slopes, upper subalpine and alpine.

27a. [22] Bract of the lowest spike 1-6 cm long, often exceeding the infl (not present on all culms, however!). **C. athrostachya** Olney [swollen spike], **44I**. Wet meadows, montane and subalpine.
27b. Bract of the lowest spike shorter than the infl or the infl bractless (occasionally *C. microptera* will have a setaceous bract) . . . . (28)

28a. [27] Beak flat and serrulate to the tip . . . . (29)
28b. Beak terete (at least at the tip), not flat and serrulate . . . . . (32)

29a. [28] Scales shorter than the perig, noticeably narrower above and largely exposing them . . . . (30)
29b. Scales about the same length as the perig, nearly the same width above and nearly concealing them . . . . (31)

30a. [29] Perig 3-3.5 mm long, narrowly wing-margined to the base. **C. bebbii** Olney [for M. S. Bebb]. Moist meadows and banks of ditches, montane.
30b. Perig 6-8 mm long, broadly winged, the margins somewhat crinkled. **C. egglestonii** Mackenzie [for W. W. Eggleston, collector, 1863-1935]. Dry, open meadows, montane to subalpine.

31a. [29] Perig broadest above the middle, finely-nerved ventrally; spikes usually aggregated into a definite head; spikes subtended by several very pale, hyaline, papery staminate scales, contrasting with the darker carpellate scales above. **C. arapahoensis** Clokey [for Arapahoe Peak]. Rocky places, alpine and subalpine.
31b. Perig usually broadest below the middle, nerveless ventrally; spikes in a somewhat moniliform infl or nearly approximate; staminate scales not markedly different from the carpellate

scales above. **C. xerantica** Bailey [of dry places]. Ponderosa pine, mesas and montane.

32a. [28] Perig flat and scale-like, only distended over the ak . . . . (33)
32b. Perig plano-convex or concavo-convex, often spongy at the base and/or up the sides . . . . (36)

33a. [32] Spikes predominantly green and brown, the brown scales usually contrasting with the green perig . . . . (34)
33b. Spikes predominantly brown to blackish-brown, the perig themselves partly brown and contributing to the generally dark appearance of the spikes. . . . . (35)

34a. [33] Spikes clearly separate and distinguishable; perig appressed, the infl thus tapered to the apex and base; scales dark chestnut to blackish-brown. **C. festivella** Mackenzie [dim., compared to *C. festiva*]. Meadows and open slopes, montane and subalpine.
34b. Spikes congested and often scarcely distinguishable; perig spreading-ascending, the tips conspicuous in the heads, which are more 'bristly' as a result; scales dull brown. **C. microptera** Mackenzie [small-wing], **45B**. More common than the last, in similar habitats, but usually drier sites.

35a. [33] Perig lanceolate, 5-7 mm long; scales dark brown, appearing black. **C. ebenea** Rydberg [black], **45A**. The most abundant subalpine meadow and roadside sedge.
35b. Perig ovate, 4-6 mm long; scales dark brown. **C. haydeniana** Olney [for F. V. Hayden]. Alpine tundra.

36a. [32] Scales shorter and narrower than the perig (except sometimes in *C. pachystachya*). . . . . (37)
36b. Scales about the same width and length as the perig (beaks may protrude slightly) . . . . (40)

37a. [36] Perig 2.5-4.3 mm long, usually with 1 or 2 conspicuous transverse folds (tucks) ventrally across the center of the body, not spongy at the base or along the sides. . . . . (38)
37b. Perig 3.5-5.0 mm long, without transverse folds ventrally, spongy at the base, sometimes along the sides . . . . (39)

38a. [37] Perig ovate-lanceolate to narrowly lanceolate, 2.5-3.5 mm long, 1.0-1.3 mm wide. **C. limnophila** Hermann [pond-loving]. Wet meadows, foothills to subalpine.
38b. Perig ovate, 3.5-4.3 mm long, 1.5-1.9 mm wide; scales with conspicuous white-hyaline margins. **C. macloviana** Urville [of the Falkland Islands, Iles Malouines]. Meadows, montane and subalpine.

39a. [37] Perig oblong-lanceolate to narrowly ovate-lanceolate, 4.5-5.0 mm long, 1.0-1.5 mm wide, ascending in the spike; scales oblong-lanceolate, pale to chestnut-brown, not concealing the perig, midrib pale yellowish-brown. **C. stenoptila** Hermann [slender-wand]. Dry montane forest openings.

39b. Perig ovate, 3.5-5.0 mm long, 1.5-2.5 mm wide; scales spreading in the spike, brown or blackish, about as wide as perig and nearly as long, midrib green. **C. pachystachya** Chamisso [thick-spiked]. Meadows, open woods, montane to subalpine.

40a. [36] Spikes separated along the culm so as to barely overlap the base of one with the apex of the next, the spikes thus forming a slender nodding graceful group (moniliform, like a string of beads). **C. praticola** Rydberg [of prairies]. Montane and subalpine meadows.
40b. Spikes more densely aggregated; culm stiff . . . . (41)

41a. [40] Perig lanceolate, 5-8 mm long. **C. petasata** Dewey [with a traveling cap on, that is, ready for a journey]. Occasional, foothills, montane.
41b. Perig concavo-convex, ovate, 4-6 mm long. **C. phaeocephala** Piper [brown-headed]. Common, subalpine and alpine.

KEY D : PEDUNCLED OR BLACK OR WITH STAMINATE SPIKES

1a. Perig pubescent on the faces, not merely ciliate-margined . . . . (2)
1b. Perig faces glabrous . . . . (8)

2a. [1] Tall plants of bogs, wet meadows and ditches; staminate spikes 1 or 2, clearly different from the 2 to 4 elongate carpellate spikes distributed along the culm. **C. lanuginosa** Michaux [woolly], **45F**. Wet places from lowest altitudes to subalpine.
2b. Low, spreading, matted plants of dry forested areas or otherwise not as above . . . . (3)

3a. [2] Fertile culms with all spikes approximate, sessile or short-peduncled . . . . (4)
3b. Fertile culms with staminate and upper carpellate spikes approximate, the other carpellate spikes widely separated, nearly basal, long-peduncled, appearing as separate culms . . . . (5)

4a. [3] Perig body (excluding stipitate base and beak) oval-obovoid; scales about half the length of the mature perig bodies, ciliate and somewhat pubescent. **C. concinna** R. Brown [elegant]. Rare or overlooked in moist subalpine forests.
4b. Perig body suborbicular or suborbicular-obovoid or very short-oval, about as long as wide; scales longer than the mature perig bodies, glabrous. **C. pensylvanica** Lamarck ssp **heliophila** (Mackenzie) Weber [of Pennsylvania; sun-loving]. The earliest-flowering *Carex* in the foothills.

5a. [3] Bract of lowest non-basal carpellate spike squamiform, somewhat sheathing, usually shorter than the culm, the spike sometimes bractless. **C. geophila** Mackenzie [ground-loving]. Dry wooded slopes in the foothills.
5b. Bract of lowest non-basal carpellate spike lflike, not sheathing, normally exceeding the culm . . . . (6)

6a. [5] Upper carpellate spikes with 1 to 3 fls; perig beak obliquely cut, in age shallowly bidentate, the margins little if at all ciliate-serrulate. **C. pityophila** Mackenzie [pine-loving]. Occasional in dry pinelands and in sagebrush-grass parks, foothills and montane.

6b. Upper carpellate spikes normally with 3-20 fls; perig beak shallowly to deeply bidentate, the margins ciliate-serrulate. . . . . . (7)

7a. [6] Perig 2.5-3.25 mm long, the beak 0.25-0.75 mm long, shallowly bidentate. **C. brevipes** Boott [short-stem]. Subalpine up to timberline.

7b. Perig 3.5-4.5 mm long, the beak more than 1 mm long, deeply bidentate. **C. rossii** Boott [for Capt. J. C. Ross]. Ponderosa pine forests on the mesas and foothills up to dry subalpine forests.

8a. [1] Fertile culm with a single staminate spike and 1-3 small, one- or few-fld carpellate spikes immediately below it, often so close as to appear to be part of the same spike; some culms entirely staminate or carpellate or with a single unisexual spike (see Key A, 7a). **C. parryana** Dewey ssp **hallii** (Olney) Murray. Open gravelly subalpine meadows.

8b. Fertile culm with several staminate or carpellate spikes, the carpellate usually many-fld. . . . . (9)

9a. [8] Scales green, pale brown or pale reddish-brown, never purple-black; infl never appearing very dark. . . . . (10)

9b. Scales dark reddish-brown or purple-black, sometimes with a green or lighter midrib, the infl appearing very dark. . . . . . (21)

10a. [9] Perig beakless, very round at apex . . . . (11)
10b. Perig strongly beaked and/or tapered to the apex . . . . (12)

11a. [10] Mature perig whitish-papillose, elliptic-obovoid, not fleshy or translucent, rather obscurely ribbed; scales appressed. **C. hassei** Bailey [for H. E. Hasse, California lichenologist]. Moist canyons in the piñon-juniper belt. Doubtfully distinct from the next and distinguished mostly by the perig color and taller stature.

11b. Mature perig golden-yellow or orange when fully mature or brownish, orbicular-obovoid, fleshy, translucent, coarsely ribbed; carpellate scales widely spreading at maturity. **C. aurea** Nuttall [golden], **44C**. Wet mt meadows.

12a. [10] Carpellate spikes dangling on slender peduncles . . . . . . (13)
12b. Carpellate spikes on erect peduncles (lower spikes may droop when over-mature. . . . . (15)

13a. [12] Lowest bract long-sheathing, that is, with a portion sheathing the stem between the blade and the node of attachment; perig nerveless except for the two marginal nerves. **C. capillaris** L. [finely thread-like], **44B**. Subalpine and alpine streamsides and willow-bogs.

13b. Lowest bract not sheathing. . . . . (14)

14a. [13] Staminate spikes 4-12 mm long; carpellate scales much narrower and longer than the perig, early deciduous. **C. magellanica** Lamarck ssp **irrigua** (Wahlenberg) Hultén [from Straits of Magellan; inundated]. Lake shores and willow-bogs, subalpine.
14b. Staminate spikes 15-27 mm long; carpellate scales as broad as or broader than the perig and barely exceeding them in length, persistent. **C. limosa** L. [of bogs]. *Sphagnum* bogs and wet meadows, subalpine.

15a. [12] Lowest bract long-sheathing . . . . (16)
15b. Lowest bract not sheathing (or slightly sheathing in *C. retrorsa*) . . . . (17)

16a. [15] Carpellate spikes 3-11 mm long, oblong or globose-oblong; terminal staminate spike 1; perig with slightly bidentate beak; lf-sheaths glabrous. **C. viridula** Michaux [greenish]. Rare, borders of streams and ponds.
16b. Carpellate spikes 5-12 cm long, narrowly cylindric; terminal staminate spikes 2-6; lf-sheaths with long, soft hairs. **C. atherodes** Sprengel [swollen, referring to the perig body]. Marshy roadsides and edges of lakes and streams, montane.

17a. [15] Perig reflexed or horizontally spreading; lowest bract several times exceeding the infl; lf-sheaths loose, forming a prolonged, truncate ventral apex. . . . . (18)
17b. Perig ascending (sometimes spreading in *C. utriculata*); lowest bracts only moderately exceeding the infl; lf-sheaths tight and concave at the mouth . . . . (19)

18a. [17] Perig with numerous, close, strong raised nerves (about 7 visible on a side). **C. hystericina** Mühlenberg [like a porcupine], **45E**. In swales at low altitudes; one record from western MN.
18b. Perig with few, widely separated raised nerves (about 4-5 visible on a side). **C. retrorsa** Schweinitz [reflexed]. Infrequent in marshes, wet meadows or along river bottoms, montane.

19a. [17] Long, slender, horizontal rhizomes formed; lower lf-sheaths not shredding and becoming filamentose; culms thick and spongy at the base, bluntly triangular below the spikes. **C. utriculata** Boott [like a small skin bag], **45D**. Abundant, forming zones on shores of ponds, montane, subalpine (*C. rostrata* of manuals, incorrectly).
19b. Rhizomes short-creeping; lower lf-sheaths shredding and becoming filamentose; culms rarely spongy-based, sharply triangular below the spikes . . . . (20)

20a. [19] Perig ovoid to globose-ovoid, 3.5-8.0 mm long, 3 mm wide, abruptly narrowed into the beak. **C. vesicaria** L. [bladder-like]. Very wet habitats, montane and subalpine. Sometimes forms a sterile hybrid (aks are undeveloped) with the last.
20b. Perig lanceolate, 7-10 mm long, 2-3 mm wide, tapering from near the base into the beak. **C. exsiccata** Bailey [dried up]. Rare, wet habitats, montane and subalpine.

21a. [9] Bract at base of the lowest spike long-sheathing . . . . . . (22)
21b. Bract at base of the lowest spike not sheathing . . . . (23)

22a. [21] Perig broadly oval to oblong-oval, rounded at the apex; beak short, 0.3 mm; bract blades exceeding the infl; all spikes gynaecandrous. **C. bella** Bailey [pretty]. Aspen groves and open hillsides, subalpine.
22b. Perig narrowly lanceolate with long ill-defined beak; bract blades short or lacking; terminal spike gynaecandrous. **C. misandra** R. Brown (man-hater, because of the few staminate fls), **44F**. Tundra slopes and basins.

23a. [21] Terminal spike staminate; stigmas 2 or 3 . . . . (24)
23b. Terminal spike gynaecandrous; stigmas 3 . . . . (32)

24a. [23] Carpellate spikes nodding. . . . . (25)
24b. Carpellate spikes erect . . . . (27)

25a. [24] Perig shining, with a short slender beak 0.5 mm long; spikes usually widely-spaced; stigmas 2 or 3. **C. saxatilis** L. ssp **laxa** (Trautvetter) Kalela [of rocks, not stiff]. Pond shores and willow-bogs, subalpine.
25b. Perig dull, somewhat glaucous, not shining, beak minute; spikes approximate; stigmas 3. . . . . (26)

26a. [25] Staminate spikes 4-12 mm long; carpellate scales much narrower and longer than the perig, early deciduous. **C. magellanica** Lamarck ssp **irrigua** (Wahlenberg) Hultén [of Straits of Magellan; inundated]. Lake shores and willow-bogs, subalpine.
26b. Staminate spikes 15-27 mm long; carpellate scales as broad as or broader than the perig and barely exceeding them in length, persistent. **C. limosa** L. [of bogs]. Local, in *Sphagnum* bogs and wet meadows, subalpine.

27a. [24] Stigmas 3. **C. paysonis** Clokey [for E. B. Payson]. Infrequent, mountain meadows and alpine slopes.
27b. Stigmas 2. . . . . (28)

28a. [27] Carpellate spikes appearing very dark, the scales entirely purple-black; perig strongly purple-tinged, irregular-inflated. **C. scopulorum** Holm [of rocks], **44D**. Abundant in wet basins, subalpine and alpine.
28b. Carpellate spikes green-and-black, perig mostly green, contrasting with the darker scales . . . . (29)

29a. [28] Perig nerveless on the faces; spikes slender and elongate. **C. aquatilis** Wahlenberg [of wet places], **45H**. Lake shores, alpine and subalpine.
29b. Perig slenderly-nerved or strongly ribbed. . . . . (30)

30a. [29] Perig persistent, strongly ribbed; lvs short, broad, spreading, conspicuously glaucous; spikes plump. **C. nebrascensis** Dewey [from Nebraska]. Streamsides, springs and often alkaline mea-

dows, plains to subalpine, readily grazed by stock. Ranges from 1 to 17 dm tall. Forms glaucous stands in early spring.
30b. Perig early-deciduous, slenderly-nerved . . . . (31)

31a. [30] All culms aphyllopodic. **C. emoryi** Dewey [for Maj. Wm. H. Emory, Mexican Boundary Survey]. Swampy meadows or springy places, often along irrigation ditches in the valleys. One of the most early-flowering spp, often already dropping the perig by mid-June, before most *Carex*-hunters are abroad!
31b. Fertile culms phyllopodic. **C. lenticularis** Michaux var. **lipocarpa** (Holm) Standley [lens-shaped; early-deciduous, as to the perig]. Lake margins and marshy meadows, subalpine, N counties (*C. kelloggii*).

32a. [23] Spikes slender, not more than 5 mm wide, scattered along the culm, never forming a dense cluster . . . . (33)
32b. Spikes up to 1 cm wide or more, in a rather dense terminal cluster. . . . . (34)

33a. [32] Perig finely many-nerved, the beak minute, 0.2 mm long; fertile culms aphyllopodic. **C. buxbaumii** Wahlenberg [for J. C. Buxbaum]. Aspen groves, upper montane, subalpine.
33b. Perig not nerved, the beak short, 0.5 mm long; fertile culms phyllopodic. **C. norvegica** Retzius ssp **stevenii** (Holm) Murray [of Norway; Stevens' Mine on Gray's Peak]. Aspen forests and upper mt forest openings. **C. norvegica** ssp. **norvegica**, a stouter plant with a more compact infl, occurs on wet tundra.

34a. [32] Spikes short and plump, in a ± dense terminal cluster; all spikes sessile . . . . (35)
34b. Spikes either slightly spaced apart or conspicuously nodding or at least twice as long as broad. . . . . (37)

35a. [34] Plants usually less than 2 dm tall. the spikes pointed; perig with narrow, sloping shoulders and much purple pigmentation on the faces. **C. nelsonii** Mackenzie [for Aven Nelson]. Alpine snowmelt areas.
35b. Plants usually more than 2 dm tall, the spikes almost globose
. . . . (36)

36a. [35] Perig scabrous-margined (the cells high-papillose), the base substipitate; scales blunt, the midrib obsolete; culms erect. **C. nova** Bailey [new]. Subalpine and alpine wet spring-slopes.
36b. Perig smooth-margined, the base rounded, not stipitate; scales acuminate with ± prominent midrib; culms slender, generally flexuous. **C. pelocarpa** Hermann [dark-frted]. Frequent, subalpine and alpine slopes and meadows.

37a. [34] Spikes nodding . . . . (38)
37b. Spikes erect . . . . (39)

38a. [37] Upper carpellate scales exceeding the perig (usually conspicuously so), dark copper-brown; lowest peduncle less than half the length of the spike; apex of perig body acute. **C. chalciolepis** Holm [bronze-scaled], **45G**. Abundant, alpine and subalpine slopes.

38b. Upper carpellate scales usually exceeded by the perig, dark red- to blackish-brown, fading with age; lowest peduncle 1-2 times the length of the spike; apex of perig body obtuse. **C. atrata** L. [blackened]. Infrequent, subalpine meadows and rocky alpine slopes. There is no agreement among botanists that true *C. atrata* occurs in America; however, our plants, which Hermann called *C. heteroneura* W. Boott var. *brevisquama* Hermann, compares favorably with the European *C. atrata*.

39a. [37] Scales conspicuously white-hyaline along the sides and at the apex, nearly equalling or wider than the perig. **C. albonigra** Mackenzie [white-and-black]. Alpine tundra, fairly common.
39b. Scales not white-hyaline or only slightly so, shorter and narrower than the perig. (40)

40a. [39] Perig slightly and irregularly inflated, narrowly elliptic, the upper margins forming two sides of a triangle. **C. atrosquama** Mackenzie [black-scaled]. Infrequent, open meadows, subalpine and lower alpine.
40b. Perig flat, not inflated, broadly ovate to orbicular, the upper margins forming an arc of a circle. **C. epapillosa** Mackenzie [not papillose]. Meadows and margins of lakes, subalpine and alpine.

CYPERUS L. 1753 [*Kypeiros*, the ancient Gr. name]

1a. Diminutive annual less than 5 cm tall; floral spikes less than 1 cm long, the scales attenuate and strongly recurved at the apex. **C. aristatus** Rottboell. Not reported from the W slope, but recurrent in Utah and Arizona, undoubtedly overlooked since it develops late in the season on muddy floodplains (*C. inflexus*).
1b. Taller, relatively stout annual; floral spikes over 1 cm long, scales not attenuate nor recurved at the apex . . . . (2)

2a. Spikelet axis persistent as a unit after the aks and scales fall away. **C. erythrorhizos** Mühlenberg [red-rooted], **46D**. Muddy shores of the Colorado R near Grand Junction.
2b. Spikelet axis breaking up into units consisting of a scale, the next lowest internode and the attached wings and clasped ak; internodes becoming thickened and cartilaginous. **C. odoratus** L. Local, hot springs, GN.

ELEOCHARIS R. Brown 1810 [Gr., *helos*, marsh, + *charis*, grace]. SPIKE-RUSH
1a. Stigmas 2; aks lenticular. **E. palustris** (L.) Roemer & Schultes [of swamps], **46A**. The most common, and extremely variable, sp in wet places throughout (*E. macrostachya*). It rarely is collected in good fruiting condition, since it evidently takes more time to reach maturity than any other sp.
1b. Stigmas 3; achenes trigonous . . . . (2)

Figure 46. A, *Eleocharis palustris*; B, *E. acicularis*; C, *E. rostellata*; D, *Cyperus erythrorhizos*

2a. Tubercle confluent with the ak, not forming a distinct apical cap . . . . (3)
2b. Tubercle forming a distinct apical cap . . . . (4)

3a. Lowest scale subtending a fl; stems slender and short, not over 1 mm wide; spklts 4-8 mm long with 3-9 fls. **E. quinqueflora** (Hartman) Schwartz. Subalpine wet meadows and bogs (*E. pauciflora*).
3b. Lowest scale empty; stems tall and robust, more than 1 mm wide, the sterile ones forming stolons and rooting at the tips; spklts 8-13 mm long with 10-20 fls. **E. rostellata** (Torrey) Torrey, **46C**. Springs and seeps in the lower desert canyons.

4a. Extremely delicate and thin-stemmed; ak whitish or pale gray, longitudinally many-ribbed and horizontally cross-ribbed. **E. acicularis** (L.) Roemer & Schultes, **46B**. Mt pond margins.
4b. Not delicate or thin-stemmed; ak golden or pale yellow, not ribbed . . . . (5)

5a. Spikes few-fld, ovate, the scales purple-black; ak pale yellow; tubercle broader than high; plants in clumps, not rhizomatous; lvs green. **E. bolanderi** Gray [for H. N. Bolander, California botanist]. Springs on the plateaus.
5b. Spikes many-fld, cylindric, the scales brown, with hyaline sides and light midrib; ak golden yellow; tubercle as high as wide; plants with stout black rhizomes; lvs glaucous. **E. montevidensis** Kunth. In silt of drying pond margins, Colorado R Valley.

ERIOPHORUM L. 1753 [Gr., *erion*, wool, + *phoros*, bearing]. COTTON-SEDGE; BOG-WOOL

1a. Culms with well-developed lvs; heads several, on distinct peduncles. **E. angustifolium** Honckeny, **47E**. Subalpine pond margins and sedge meadows (*E. polystachion*).
1b. Culms lacking well-developed lf blades; head solitary at the stem apex. . . . . (2)

2a. Cottony bristles white; plant rhizomatous. **E. altaicum** Meinshausen var **neogaeum** Raymond [from Altai; New World race], **47F**. Local, in bogs in the high Elk and San Juan Mts.
2b. Cottony bristles russet brown; caespitose. **E. russeolum** Fries. Local, in bogs of the high Elk Mountains.

KOBRESIA Willdenow 1805 [for J. P. von Cobres, 1747-1823, naturalist of Augsburg] Note: in *Kobresia* the perigynium is an open sheath with margins overlapping abaxially, and never has a bidentate beak. It often encloses a staminate and a carpellate floret; these fl pairs are called spikelets. Groups of spikelets on distinct major axes are called spikes.

1a. Spklts consisting of one staminate and one carpellate floret; spikes simple . . . . (2)
1b. Spklts unisexual, 1-fld, the upper ones staminate, the lower carpellate; spikes several, the lower ones distinct. **K. simplicius-**

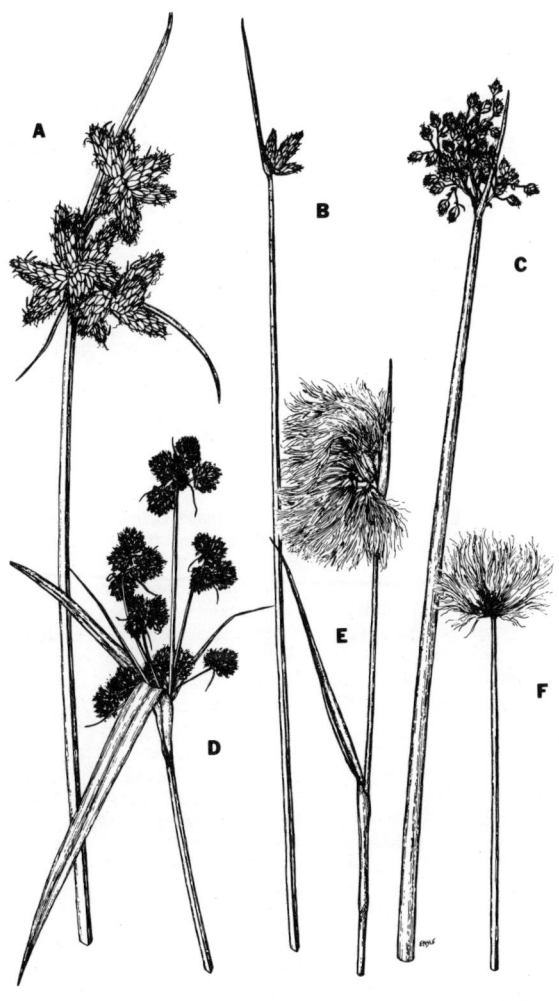

Figure 47. A, *Bolboschoenus maritimus*; B, *Scirpus microcarpus*; C, *Schoenoplectus pungens*; D, *S. lacustris*; E, *Eriophorum angustifolium*; F, *E. altaicum*

cula (Wahlenberg) Mackenzie. Moist gravelly tundra, near the Continental Divide of the Front Range. Strongly rhizomatous, not forming dense clumps.

2a. Spike 1-3 cm x 2-3 mm; scales 2-3 mm long; perig 3-3.5 x 1.25 mm; very densely caespitose, forming hummocks; fl culms very slender. **K. myosuroides** (Villars) Fiori & Paoli. The climax dominant on mature soils of relatively dry but peaty alpine tundra. In autumn the tundra slopes are colored a rich bronze-yellow by the drying foliage of this sp. Very similar to *Carex elynoides*, and distinguished certainly only by the closed perig of the latter.

2b. Spike 1-2 c x 4-5 mm; scales 4-5 mm long; perig 5.5 x 1.25 mm; fl culms stout. **K. sibirica** Turczaninow. Forming dense hummocks in moist tundra, solifluction slopes and gravelly alpine lake shores, Continental Divide in the Hoosier Pass region.

MARISCUS M. Vahl 1806 [name used by Pliny for a kind of rush]
One sp, **M. fendlerianus** (Böckeler) Koyama, a perennial with bulbous stem bases; floral axes clustered to form a condensed greenish head. Dry rocky hillsides at low altitudes, San Juan Mts (*Cyperus*).

SCHOENOPLECTUS Palla 1888 [Gr., *schoinos*, rush, + *plectos*, braided, probably alluding to use in making baskets and cradles]. TULE; BULRUSH

1a. Culms triangular; infl of a few sessile, obviously lateral, spikes. **S. pungens** (Vahl) Palla, **47C**. Abundant in very wet portions of stream valleys, occupying a zone somewhat comparable to that of the dark green *Juncus arcticus*, and like that sp, visible from a distance because of its color (*Scirpus americanus* of Colo lit).

1b. Culms terete; infl of oval pedunculate subterminal spikes. . . . . (2)

2a. Spklts appearing dull gray-brown, the individual scales with prominent red-brown striae on a paler background. **S. lacustris** (L.) Palla ssp **acutus** (Mühlenberg) Löve & Löve, **47D**. Very common on muddy shores of the lower river valleys (*Scirpus acutus*).

2b. Spikelets more reddish-brown, the scales with a darker ground cover so that the red-brown striae are less distinct. **S. lacustris** ssp **creber** (Fernald) Löve & Löve [thick]. Same habitats, evidently not as common as the last (*Scirpus validus*).

SCIRPUS L. 1753 [the classical Lat. name]. BULRUSH

1a. Lf sheaths reddish; midrib of the scales exserted as a short, stiff awn; styles 3. **S. pallidus** (Britton) Fernald. Wet pond shores and ditches at low altitudes.

1b. Lf sheaths green; midrib of the scales not exserted or very minutely so; styles 2. **S. microcarpus** Presl, **47B**. Same habitats.

CYPRIPEDIACEAE
LADY'S SLIPPER FAMILY (CPD)

Traditionally, the Lady's Slippers have been placed in the orchid family, but recent studies have shown that there is little relationship between these and the true orchids. Not only are the fundamental features of the embryo sac development different, but in the Cypripediaceae there are two functional stamens, and neither of these corresponds to the single stamen of the true orchids. Curiously enough, the family was proposed by John Lindley back in 1833! All species of *Cypripedium* are rare and potentially endangered and should not be disturbed.

CYPRIPEDIUM L. 1753 [Gr., *Kypris*, Venus, + *pes*, foot]. LADY'S SLIPPER

1a. Fls yellow. **C. calceolus** L. ssp **parviflorum** (Salisbury) Hultén. Local, and very vulnerable to extermination by collectors, LP.
1b. Fls purple or dull brown-purple. **C. fasciculatum** Kellogg. Local and vulnerable, openings in subalpine forests, usually under overhanging lower branches of *Abies*, RT.

DIPSACACEAE—TEASEL FAMILY (DPS)

The teasel head is a perfect device for raising the nap on woolen fabrics. The process, called 'fulling' has been used since ancient Roman times, and the English surname, *Fuller*, comes from this operation. Although teasels are still grown for this purpose, modern technology has found metal substitutes. To be a satisfactory teasel, the bristles on the head need to be hooked and stiff enough to stand up to tension without shattering and getting caught in the wool. *Dipsacus sativus* is the commercial teasel. Our weedy species has straight bristles and is of little use. The family name comes from the Greek *dipsa*, thirst. 'Dipsomaniac' comes from the same stem. When one speaks of 'teasing' something apart, or of 'teasing' someone in the sense of annoying, the word comes from the same source as 'teasel'. The wild teasels are commonly silvered or gilded and they make striking additions to winter bouquets.

1a. Stems 4-angled, these and the simple lvs very harshly hooked; infl an elongate-oval head, the fls commonly blossoming from the center of the head and proceeding upwards and downwards, few blooming at any one time. **Dipsacus**, TEASEL
1b. Stems not 4-angled, not armed; lvs toothed, lobed, the upper usually pinnatifid; infl capitate, like that of most Asteraceae, with purple fls, the basal bracts forming an invol. **Knautia**

DIPSACUS L. 1753 [Gr., *dipsa*, thirst, the plant figuring in ancient Dionysian rituals involving drinking]. TEASEL
One sp, **D. sylvestris** Hudson, **48**. ADV, estab along irrigation ditches.

KNAUTIA L. 1753 [for Christian Knaut, 1654-1716, Saxon botanist]. Linnaeus said: "*Knautia* has a regular flower made up of irregu-

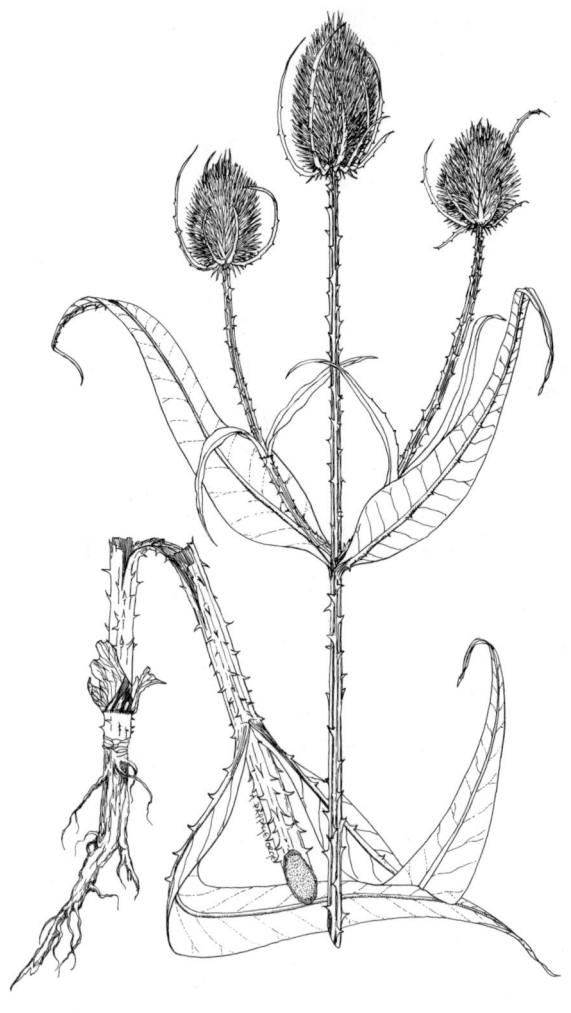

Figure 48. *Dipsacus sylvestris*

lar florets, and seeds enclosed in a hard coat, being called after a man who zealously sought to promote the welfare of Botany by his study of regularity and irregularity in flowers, and whose works were never bare and unadorned."

One sp, **K. arvensis** (L.) Duby. ADV, estab on roadsides, RT.

DROSERACEAE—SUNDEW FAMILY (DRS)

The sundews include, in North America, two genera of insectivorous plants: *Drosera*, the sundew, and *Dionaea*, the Venus' Fly-trap. Unlike *Dionaea*'s 'bear-trap' mechanism, the trapping of insects by *Drosera* is by sticky glandular hairs on the leaf-surfaces. When an insect is stuck on a hair, the other hairs move to fix themselves on all the parts, and the insect is slowly digested by proteolytic enzymes. *Dionaea* grows only in bogs on the south Atlantic coastal plain, and until very recently *Drosera* was known no closer to Colorado than Yellowstone National Park.

DROSERA L. 1753 [Gr., *droseros*, dewy]. SUNDEW

One sp, **D. rotundifolia** L, **PL 30**. Known in Colorado only from a small iron-permeated bog in Gunnison County, where it is being given special protection. The plants consist of a cluster of petiolate, reddish basal lvs with circular blades covered by long glistening glandular-tipped hairs. The delicate pink or white fls are produced in a slender raceme about 5-10 cm. tall. Under no circumstances should this sp be collected. It is abundant enough in the sphagnum bogs of northern North America, and is available from biological supply houses.

EHRETIACEAE (EHR)

A small, mostly tropical family related to the borages but differing in the fruit, which, instead of having four nutlets, is a berry or drupe. The subtropical and tropical genus, *Cordia*, is most well-known, being a tall shrub with campanulate yellow or white flowers.

TIQUILIA Persoon 1805 [from a vernacular name, Tiquilo]

One sp, **T. nuttallii** (Bentham) Richardson, found in unstable sand dunes peripheral in MF. A prostrate herb cymosely (appearing dichotomously) branched, with ovate, impressed-veined lvs less than a cm long subtending small fl clusters at the branch tips (*Coldenia*).

ELAEAGNACEAE—OLEASTER FAMILY (ELE)

This family is unique because of the peculiar peltate scales that cover the leaves and fruits, giving the foliage a satiny or a rusty tint. All are trees or shrubs and many are ornamental cultivars of which the best known is the Russian-olive, one of the hardiest introduced trees on the Great Plains and on western slope homesteads. Deserted homesteads are often recognizable by the persisting wind-rows of Russian-olive trees. In Siberia, a relative, *Hippophaë rhamnoides*, is being bred to improve the yield of its orange berries which are high in vitamin-C content, for which there is a great need in that climate.

Eleagnaceae (ELE)

1a. Lvs and branches opposite. **Shepherdia**, SILVERBERRY; BUFFA-LOBERRY
1b. Lvs and branches alternate. **Elaeagnus**, RUSSIAN-OLIVE

ELAEAGNUS L. 1753 [Gr., *elaia*, the olive, + *agnos*, Gr. name of *Vitex*]. RUSSIAN-OLIVE

One sp, **E. angustifolia** L., **49C**. ADV. A hardy dry-land sp, consisting of many cultivars. Extremely variable in shape and vesture of lvs, the young plants or shade-branches have lvs often almost green above and broadly elliptic. Such plants have been called *E. orientalis*, but I doubt that these types represent different spp.

SHEPHERDIA Nuttall 1818 [for John Shepherd, 1764?-1836, curator of Liverpool Bot. Garden]. SILVERBERRY; BUFFALOBERRY

1a. Lvs silvery on both sides, oblong-elliptic; berries silvered. **S. argentea** (Pursh) Nuttall, SILVERBERRY, **49B**. Abundant in river-bottoms and irrigation ditches.
1b. Lvs green, broadly elliptic with rusty scales; berries orange-red. **S. canadensis** (L.) Nuttall, BUFFALO-BERRY, **49A**, **PL 16**. Open lodgepole pine forests and rocky slopes and summits, montane and subalpine. Dioecious, with unisexual fls, appearing in early spring before the lvs.

ELATINACEAE—WATERWORT FAMILY (ELT)

A small family of semiaquatic plants, containing only two small genera, *Elatine* and *Bergia*, **50B**. The latter occurs only on the eastern plains. *Elatine* is infrequent, small and inconspicuous and of no economic importance whatever. The genus is so rarely collected that we do not know if we have one or more species in Colorado. Anyone collecting *Elatine* should deposit specimens with the Herbarium.

ELATINE L. 1753 [classical name of some low and creeping plant]. WATERWORT

One sp, **E. rubella** Rydberg, **50A**. It has only been collected once, near Gothic, GN, and did not have seeds. Since identification of the species is impossible without them, we must await further collections of more mature plants (= *E. triandra*?).

ERICACEAE—HEATH FAMILY (ERI)

Heaths or heathers are characteristic plants of almost every mountain region of the world, but they are not well represented in the Southern Rocky Mountains and are mostly absent from our tundra because of our arid continental climate and the lack of acidity in the tundra soils. Even the blueberries (incorrectly called huckleberries) rarely set abundant fruit here, possibly because of unseasonal frosts at flowering time. The flowers of ericads are beautiful creations, like porcelain easter-eggs into which one peers to see exotic scenes, and exotic they are, for the stamens have anthers that open by terminal pores and are often adorned with peculiar horns. The family once included

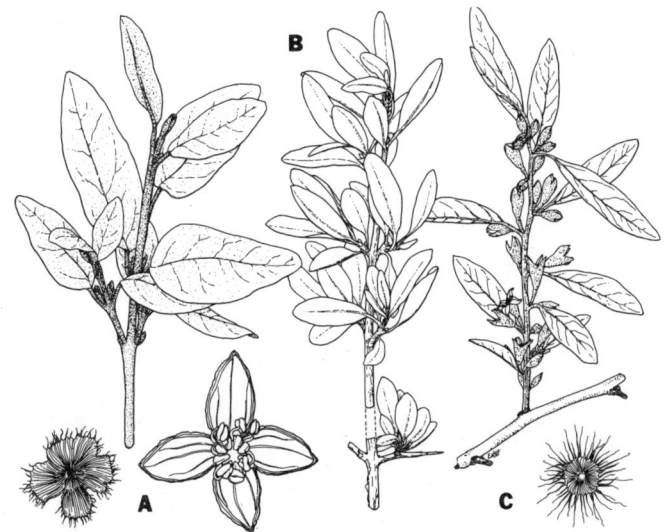

Figure 49. A, *Shepherdia canadensis*; B, *S. argentea*; C, *Elaeagnus angustifolia*

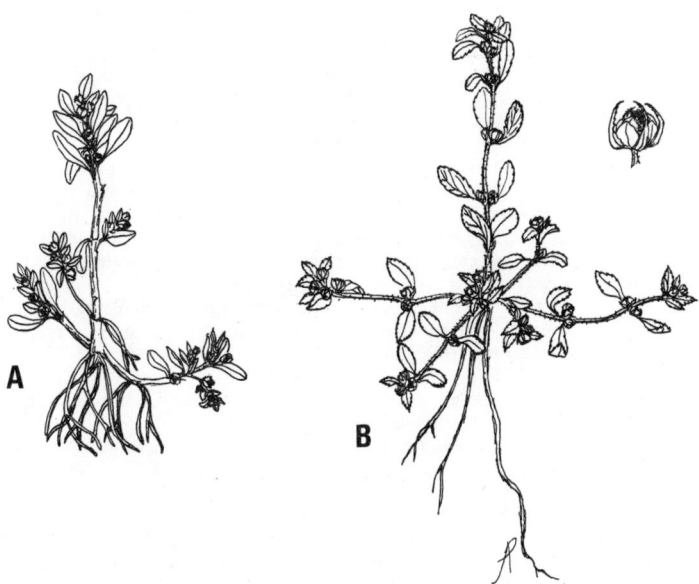

Figure 50. A, *Elatine sp.*; B, *Bergia texana*

plants that are now removed to two families, the Pyrolaceae and Monotropaceae. *Vaccinium* is probably more properly placed in its own family, the Vacciniaceae.

1a. Lvs thick and evergreen . . . . (2)
1b. Lvs thin in texture, usually deciduous . . . . (3)

2a. Lvs green on both sides, the margins not revolute; not bog plants, the fls urn-shaped. **Arctostaphylos**, BEARBERRY; MANZANITA
2b. Lvs paler beneath, with revolute margins; bog plants with pink parasol-shaped fls. **Kalmia**, SWAMP-LAUREL

3a. Creeping plants of mossy forests. **Gaultheria**, CREEPING WINTERGREEN
3b. Erect shrubs . . . . (4)

4a. Lvs entire, sparsely rusty-hairy, clustered at the ends of the branches; fls large, white, open-campanulate. **Azaleastrum**, WHITE RHODODENDRON
4b. Lvs crenulate-serrate or serrate, glabrous, not clustered at the ends of the branches; fls small, urn-shaped. **Vaccinium**, BLUEBERRY; BILBERRY; HUCKLEBERRY

ARCTOSTAPHYLOS Adanson 1763 [Gr., *arctos*, a bear, + *staphyle*, a bunch of grapes]. BEARBERRY; MANZANITA
1a. Creeping on the ground; lvs oblanceolate with rounded apex, tapering to the base. **A. adenotricha** (Fernald & Macbride) Löve & Löve, BEARBERRY, **51E**. Gravelly or stony forest openings. Diploid. This characteristically has glandular-hairy young twigs (*A. uva-ursi* ssp *adenotricha*). *A. uva-ursi* ssp *coactilis* (Fernald & Macbride) Löve & Kapoor [thickened], a tetraploid, is frequent on the E slope and lacks glandular hairs.
1b. Erect, forming bushes up to 1 m or more high; lvs broad oval, with distinct petioles. **A. patula** Greene ssp **platyphylla** (Gray) Wells, MANZANITA, **51D**, **PL 50**. Locally abundant and forming huge stands of acres of plants, reproducing vegetatively by layering. On the highest points of the Uncompahgre and Blue Mountain Plateaus, under well-developed stands of ponderosa pine. The two spp of *Arctostaphylos* hybridize, producing plants of intermediate stature and lf-shape, which reproduce vegetatively to form distinctively different stands.

AZALEASTRUM Rydberg 1900 [resembling *Azalea*, a *Rhododendron* segregate]. WHITE RHODODENDRON
One sp, **A. albiflorum** (Hooker) Rydberg, **PL 27**. Lake-shores and moist forests, Park Range (*Rhododendron*).

GAULTHERIA L. 1753 [for Jean-Francois Gaultier, 1708?-1756, Quebec naturalist and court physician]. CREEPING WINTERGREEN
One sp, **G. humifusa** (Graham) Rydberg, **51F**. Cool, mossy subalpine forests. Lvs thin, almost round, the lateral veins prominent. Fls inconspicuous, greenish-white; berries red.

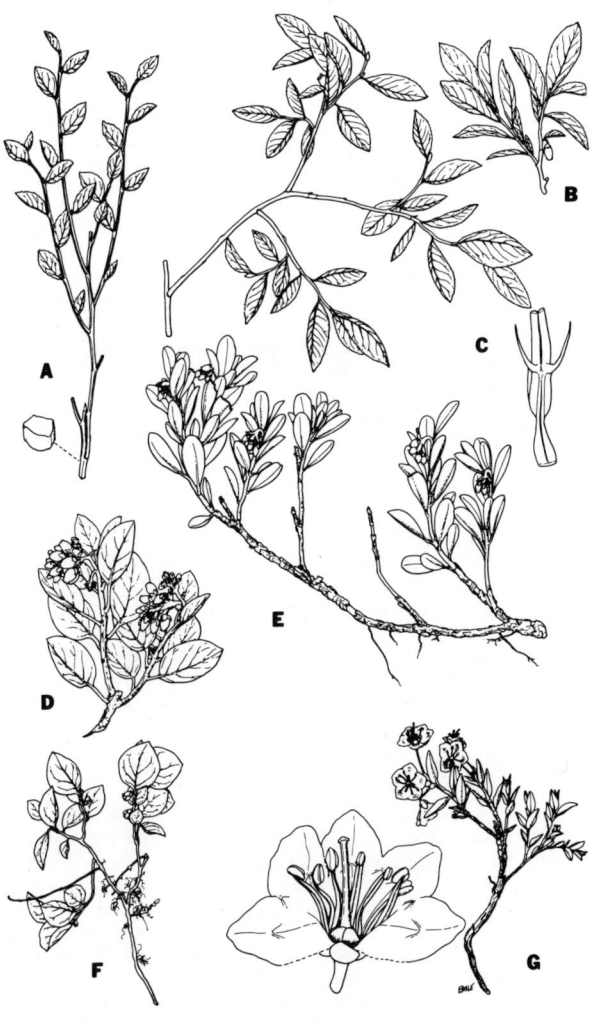

Figure 51. A, *Vaccinium scoparium*; B, *V. myrtillus*; C, *V. cespitosum*; D, *Arctostaphylos patula*; E, *A. adenotricha*; F, *Gaultheria humifusa*; G, *Kalmia microphylla*

KALMIA L. 1753 [for Pehr Kalm, who collected in America for Linnaeus]. PALE or SWAMP LAUREL

One sp, **K. microphylla** (Hooker) Heller, **51G**. Infrequent but locally abundant, borders of ponds and streams, subalpine (*K. polifolia* var *microphylla*).

VACCINIUM L. 1753 [Lat., *vaccinus*, of cows, as reflected in the germanic folk-name, *Kuhteke*]. BLUE-, BIL-, or HUCKLEBERRY

1a. Lvs broadest above the middle, crenulate-serrate above the middle; branchlets not angled and twigs usually brown rather than green. **V. cespitosum** Michaux, DWARF BILBERRY, **51C**. Mossy forest floors, shores of ponds, and moist subalpine slopes.
1b. Lvs broadest at or below the middle, serrate or serrulate from base to apex; branchlets angled, green . . . . (2)

2a. Lvs more than 10 mm long; berry blue-black; branches spreading, not crowded . . . . (3)
2b. Lvs less than 10 mm long; berry red; branches erect, often crowded as broomstraws. **V. scoparium** Leiberg, BROOM HUCKLEBERRY, **51A**. Usually found at higher altitudes than the preceding, often above timberline.

3a. Lvs over 3 cm long, usually very broadly elliptic and obtuse at the apex; plants usually 0.5 m or more tall. **V. globulare** Rydberg. What seems to be this sp occurs in the Park Range, but it has not been collected in fl or frt. It looks like a gigantic form of the next, but needs further study in the field. The fls appear during the leafing-out period and are short and squat (globular), unlike the longer ones of *V. myrtillus*.
3b. Lvs about 2 cm long, usually narrowly elliptic and acute at the apex; plants usually less than 0.5 m tall. **V. myrtillus** L. ssp **oreophilum** (Rydberg) Löve *et al*, **51B**, BLUEBERRY. Common understory, montane and subalpine forests under spruces.

EUPHORBIACEAE—SPURGE FAMILY (EUP)

In this family a curious evolutionary trend is demonstrated in fantastic variety. Whole flower clusters are reduced to one essential part (one stamen or one gynoecium). Bracts take the place of the sepals, and colored glands the place of the petals. Yet each flower cluster assumes the aspect of a single flower. Look closely at the stamen or the gynoecium and you will see that it has its own stalk, marked by a joint, so each is a separate flower and not a floral part. Next Christmas, examine the *Poinsettia* and learn that the beautiful red 'petals' are not petals at all but colored leaves surrounding a number of these strange flower clusters or 'cyathia'. In a number of families, reduction in size of flowers, which might make the flower-insect relationship difficult, is compensated for by grouping the reduced flowers together in such a way as to simulate one large flower.

1a. Lvs silvery, covered by stellate hairs. **Croton**
1b. Lvs glabrous or with simple hairs . . . . (2)

2a. Lvs bristly with irritating hairs (Sorry!), sharply serrate; a true calyx present. **Tragia**
2b. Lvs without stinging hairs, entire, dentate. or obscurely serrate; fls reduced to single stamens and gynoecia, in a cyathium; true calyx absent . . . . (3)

3a. Stem lvs opposite, with united or connected stipules, 2-ranked; main stem much shorter than the branches or absent, the plant many-stemmed (branched from the base). **Chamaesyce**
3b. Stem lvs without united or connected stipules, spirally or radially arranged, alternate, opposite or whorled; main stem well-developed, longer than the branches . . . . (4)

4a. Uppermost lvs and bracts with broad white margins. **Agaloma**, SNOW-ON-THE-MOUNTAIN
4b. Uppermost lvs and bracts not margined . . . . (5)

5a. Lvs coarsely dentate; petioles up to half the length of the blades; lvs opposite, often with a dark central spot. **Poinsettia**
5b. Lvs entire or serrulate, sessile or narrowed to the base; lvs alternate (except in the infl). **Tithymalus**

AGALOMA Rafinesque 1838 [Gr., *agalma*, a delight]. SNOW-ON-THE-MOUNTAIN

One sp, **A. marginata** (Pursh) Löve & Löve, **53D**. Common on the mesas and plains of E Colorado, but on the W slope only ADV near Montrose.

CHAMAESYCE Rafinesque 1817 [Gr., *chamae*, creeping, + *sykon*, fig]

1a. Perennial with deep-seated woody root system, with a cluster of slender contorted woody stems below ground level. **C. fendleri** (Torrey & Gray) Small, **53B**. Common in sandy places in dry valleys and piñon-juniper. The plants are often reddish-brown.
1b. Annual with a taproot . . . . (2)

2a. Seeds with distinct transverse ridges and furrows . . . . (3)
2b. Seeds smooth . . . . (4)

3a. Lvs extremely long and narrow, revolute; stems erect, slender and delicate. **C. revoluta** (Engelmann) Small. Infrequent or overlooked non-weedy sp, our only collection from near Durango.
3b. Lvs elliptic, flat; stems prostrate and wide-spreading. **C. glyptosperma** (Engelmann) Small, **52A, 53C**. Native ruderal weed.

4a. Lvs narrowly elliptic, entire. **C. parryi** (Engelmann) Rydberg. Infrequent or overlooked sp, our only record from Mancos.
4b. Lvs broadly elliptic, serrulate. **C. serpyllifolia** (Persoon) Small. ADV ruderal weed.

Figure 52. **A**, *Chamaesyce glyptosperma*; **B**, *Tithymalus montanus*; **C**, *Tragia ramosa*; **D**, *Croton texensis*

CROTON L. 1753 [Gr., *croton*, a tick, from the seed shape].
   One sp, **C. texensis** (Klotsch) Müller-Argoviensis, **52D**. Not yet seen on the W slope, but to be expected in the SW corner. The sp occurs in adjacent Arizona and New Mexico and on the E slope.

POINSETTIA Graham 1836 [for J. R. Poinsett, 1799-1851, U. S. minister to Mexico]
   One sp, **P. dentata** (Michx.) Klotsch & Garcke. ADV ruderal weed in the Colorado R Valley.

TITHYMALUS Gaertner 1790 [ancient Gr. name for a plant with milky sap] (usually placed in the wastebasket genus *Euphorbia*). SPURGE
1a. Perennials with rhizomes or woody bases; lvs entire . . . . (2)
1b. Annuals with taproots; lvs crenulate near the apex. . . . . (5)

2a. Lvs oblong or oblanceolate, succulent or thick and leathery, with numerous stems clustered on a woody base. . . . . (3)
2b. Lvs linear, thin-textured; plants rhizomatous . . . . (4)

3a. Foliage and stems, with rare exceptions, completely glabrous, at least the upper lvs broadest at the base. **T. montanus** (Engelmann) Small, **52B**. Dry sites throughout the lower elevations (incl *T. robustus*).
3b. Foliage and stems minutely pubescent, the lvs narrowed at base and apex. **T. incisus** (Engelmann) Norton var **mollis** Norton. Evidently restricted, in Colorado, to sandstone rimrock of the Mesa Verde.

4a. Stem lvs oblanceolate or narrowly oblanceolate-oblong, rounded at the apex, broadest above the middle, cuneate attenuate at the base. **T. esula** (L.) Scopoli [*Esula*, a pre-Linnaean genus name], LEAFY SPURGE. ADV weed, not as common as the next.
4b. Stem lvs narrowly linear, broadest at or below the middle or of uniform breadth, sharply acute; usually branched from the base with numerous sterile branches. **T. uralensis** (Fischer) Prokhanov, LEAFY SPURGE, **53A**. ADV weed, locally abundant especially in mt meadows.

5a. Glands of the cyathium elliptical and symmetrical, without the development of slender lateral 'horns'. **T. spathulatus** (Lamarck) Weber. Infrequent on river benches (*Euphorbia dictyosperma*).
5b. Glands of the cyathium crescentic, with slender lateral 'horns'. **T. crenulatus** (Engelmann) Heller. Local, Four Corners.

TRAGIA L. 1753 [for the early herbalist, Hieronymus Bock, 1498-1554, Latinized *Tragus*, 'Bock' and 'Tragus' meaning goat]
   One sp, **T. ramosa** Torrey, **52C**. Rocky or grassy hillsides, pinon-juniper and sagebrush. The foliage, applied to the back of the hand, can give one a nettlesome experience.

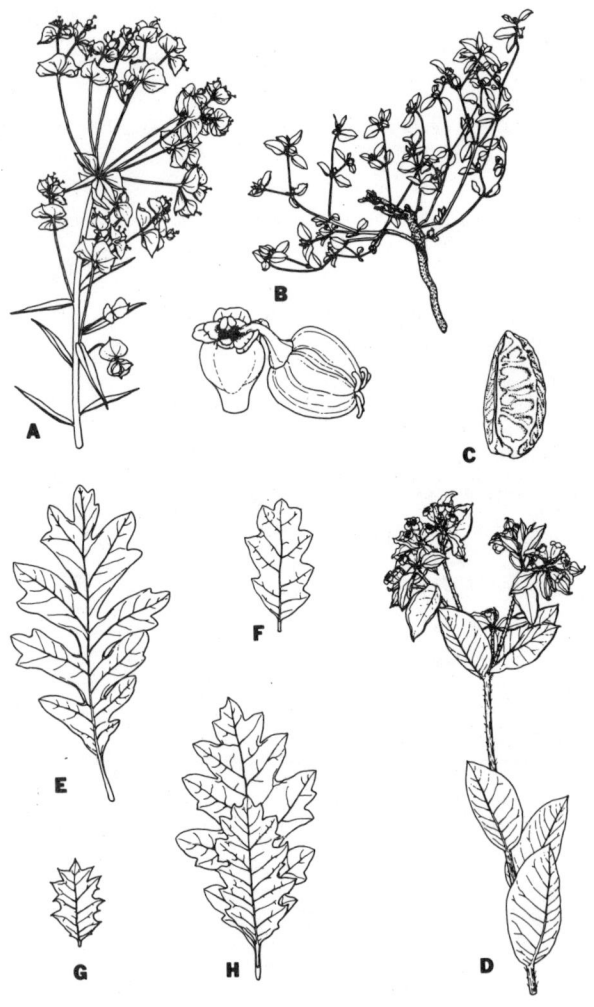

Figure 53. A, *Tithymalus uralensis*; B, *Chamaesyce fendleri*; C, *C. glyptosperma*, seed; D, *Agaloma marginata*; E, *Quercus gambelii*; F, *Q. turbinella*; G, *Q. ajoensis*; H, *Q. gambelii* X *havardii* (range of variation)

FABACEAE (LEGUMINOSAE)
PEA FAMILY (FAB/LEG)

Eric Partridge suggests that the word *legume* probably is derived from the Latin verb *legere* (stem, *leg* + suffix,-*umen*), "what one gathers or picks, thus a vegetable." In French, the word *legume* still refers to any vegetable, not only those we call legumes: peas, beans, soy beans, lima beans and pinto beans. A curious extension of the word is also French, in which "*les grosses legumes*" means "the bigwigs". Aside from their food value, many legumes are poisonous. Species of *Astragalus* absorb large amounts of poisonous selenium salts, and, when grazed, cause the ailments of cattle known as 'blind staggers' or 'alkali disease'. Another disease, 'loco', evidently is not caused by selenium although the toxic principle is not definitely known. Some *Astragalus* and most *Oxytropis* species are 'loco-weeds'. The ability of plants to absorb minerals differentially from the soil opened up a new field—geobotanical prospecting, now used to search for uranium and heavy metals, and to analyze the extent of heavy-metal pollution in the environment.

1a. Woody plants (shrubs or trees) . . . . (2)
1b. Herbs . . . . (3)

2a. Lvs and stems with thorns at the petiole base (modified stipules); lflts broadly oval; fls white or purple. **Robinia**, LOCUST
2b. Lvs and stems without thorns; low sprawling shrub with pinnately compound lvs with many filiform lfls and slender racemes of greenish-yellow fls; corolla lacking. **Parryella**

3a. Filaments all separate to the base or very nearly so; plants tall, erect, with large, yellow fls. **Thermopsis**, GOLDEN BANNER
3b. Stamens united by their filaments (10 together, or 9 united and 1 separate); fls variously colored. . . . . (4)

4a. Lvs digitately compound with more than three lfls. . . . . (5)
4b. Lvs pinnately or digitately compound, if digitate then with not more than 3 lfls. . . . . (6)

5a. Annual or perennial, never with deep tuberous roots; anthers of 2 forms, large and small; lfls commonly more than 5. **Lupinus**, BLUEBONNET
5b. Perennial with deep tuberous root; low sprawling plants of desert sites; anthers not of two forms. **Pediomelum**, INDIAN POTATO

6a. Lvs gland-dotted . . . . (7)
6b. Lvs not gland-dotted . . . . (8)

7a. Lvs pinnately compound; pod with hooked prickles (like a small cuckoldbur). **Glycyrrhiza**, WILD LIQUORICE
7b. Lvs with 3 lfls; pods unarmed, small, one-seeded. **Psoralidium**

8a. Lvs even-pinnately compound (the terminal lfl missing), terminated by a coiled tendril or a bristle. . . . . (9)
8b. Lvs odd-pinnately compound or digitately compound or simple; tendrils absent . . . . (10)

9a. Style terete, with a tuft of hairs at the apex. **Vicia**, VETCH
9b. Style flat, hairy along one side. **Lathyrus**, PEAVINE

10a. Lf margins denticulate to serrate; lvs 3-foliolate. . . . . (11)
10b. Lf margins entire; lvs various. . . . . (13)

11a. Fls in elongate loose racemes; corolla yellow or white. **Melilotus**, SWEET-CLOVER
11b. Fls in heads or short, dense spikes; corolla white, pink or purple (sometimes with green cast). . . . . (12)

12a. Lvs pinnately trifoliate (terminal lfl with a short petiole jointed to the top of the elongated rachis). **Medicago**, ALFALFA, MEDIC
12b. Lvs palmately trifoliate, terminal lfl not as above. **Trifolium**, CLOVER

13a. Fls in umbels or capitate clusters . . . . (14)
13b. Fls in racemes, spikes, or solitary . . . . (15)

14a. Fls variegated pink-purple-and white; lvs pinnately compound. **Coronilla**, CROWN VETCH
14b. Fls yellow; lvs trifoliolate. **Lotus**

15a. Fls solitary in the lf axils, yellow with brown tones; pod elongate, terete, narrow, reflexed. **Lotus**
15b. Fls not as above, if solitary in the lf axils then not yellow; pod various. . . . . (16)

16a. Keel petals with an abruptly narrowed tip or beak . . . . . . (17)
16b. Keel petals not beaked but rounded or gradually acute; plants usually, but not always, with lfy stems. . . . . (18)

17a. Lvs all cauline; plants rhizomatous; pods terete, woody, constricted between the seeds. **Vexibia**, WHITE LOCO
17b. Lvs mostly basal; plants caespitose; pods not woody nor constricted between the seeds. **Oxytropis**, LOCO-WEED

18a. Tall, lfy-stemmed, with axillary racemes of orange-red fls and inflated, stipitate papery pods; introd weed of irrigated ground. **Sphaerophysa**, BUYAN
18b. Not as above . . . . (19)

19a. Keel longer than the banner and wings, the end squared, apex blunt (**54F**); pods flat, jointed, forming reticulated, one-seeded, indehiscent segs. **Hedysarum**, CHAINPOD
19b. Keel usually not conspicuously longer than the banner and wings, or if so then canoe-shaped (curved to the apex, see **54A**); pods not jointed between the seeds. **Astragalus**, MILK VETCH

ASTRAGALUS L. 1753 [ancient Gr. name for a plant]. MILK VETCH

1a. Lvs with distinctly spine-tipped leaflets . . . . (2)
1b. Lvs with rounded, pointed or emarginate, never spine-tipped lfls . . . . (3)

2a. [1] Stems with elongate, more or less erect branches, the internodes 1-5 cm long; lfls up to 1 cm long, stiffly spreading. **A. kentrophyta** Gray ssp. **elatus** (Watson) Weber [*Kentrophyta*, an older generic name for this group; tall], **54A**. Dry steppe-desert sites, NW counties.
2b. Stems short, prostrate, matted, not rigid, the internodes very short; lfls shorter, relatively soft, not stiffly spreading. **A. kentrophyta** Gray ssp **implexus** (Canby) Weber [matted]. Sagebrush of intermountain parks, and bare ground up to near timberline. These races are so very different that they could be regarded as separate spp except for the fact that they intergrade farther W.

3a. [1] Pods papery-inflated, thin-textured. . . . . (4)
3b. Pods not papery-inflated, thick-textured . . . . (11)

4a. [3] Plants with very slender underground caudices and with slender or thick rhizomes. (5)
4b. Plants with strong taproots or caudices . . . . (7)

5a. [4] Pods glabrous, mottled. **A. ceramicus** Sheldon [like pottery]. Lfls narrowly oblong or linear; plants with very slender stems and elongate buried caudices, easily breaking away from the root-crown which is rarely collected. Sand dunes and blowouts. Two races occur: var **ceramicus**, with magenta fls and well-developed lfls, in the Four Corners area, and var **filifolius**, with ochroleucous fls and the lfls reduced or absent.
5b. Pods gray-strigose, not mottled . . . . (6)

6a. [5] Lfls few (7-11); annual or very short-lived perennial, often flowering the first season, never developing a strong root system; pod less than 2 cm long; fls magenta. **A. fucatus** Barneby [rouged]. Local, sandy ground or dunes, END, Four Corners region.
6b. Lfls numerous (15-25), closely-ranked; plants appearing stemless but with elongate slender underground caudices; pod up to 2 cm long; fls white with a lilac-tinged keel. **A. lutosus** Jones [muddy, from the gypsum when wet]. END, Gypsum knolls in the Piceance Basin and adj Utah.

7a. [4] Pods 3-6 cm long, long-pointed . . . . (8)
7b. Pods less than 2 cm long . . . . (9)

8a. [7] Pod glabrous; plants slightly caulescent; fls purple with white tips on the wings, or ochroleucous. **A. oöphorus** Watson var **caulescens** (Jones) Jones [egg-stemmed, from the stipitate pod; with stems]. Common in sagebrush, central plateaus and basins.

8b. Pod short-appressed-pubescent; plants almost stemless; fls white with a pink flush. **A. megacarpus** (Nuttall) Gray [big-fruited]. Desert gulches, Colorado to Green R drainages.

9a. [7] Pods red-mottled, almost spherical. **A. jejunus** Watson [hungry]. Known only from MF. The banner is purple, wings white, and keel lavender. The rachises of the lvs of the previous year persist as dried straws, but they are hardly rigid or spine-like.
9b. Pods not mottled, strigose . . . . (10)

10a. [9] Plants in clumps, strongly perennial, with several short lfy stems from a stout taproot; lvs narrowly oblong; pods sessile. **A. cerussatus** Sheldon [white-lead-colored]. Rare on rocky hillsides, S side Gunnison Basin.
10b. Plants solitary or a few together, either with long slender caudices or with a slender taproot; lfls broadly oval or orbicular; pod stipitate; short-lived perennials with a slender taproot. **A. wetherillii** Jones [for B. A. Wetherill]. Piñon-juniper, Colorado and Yampa R valleys.

11a. [3] Scapose or appearing so, lvs usually basal, the stems in often dense clusters from stout or slender underground caudices; if lfy-stemmed, the aerial stems foreshortened and the racemes hardly over-topping the lvs. . . . . (12)
11b. Plants lfy-stemmed, often tall, the lvs never mostly basal. . . . (35)

12a. [11] Lvs simple, or with 3 lfls. . . . . (13)
12b. Lvs pinnately compound, with more than 3 lfls (plants may have occasional lvs with 3 or fewer lfls) . . . . (14)

13a. [12] Lvs simple; dwarf mat plants with linear, silvery appressed-pubescent basal lvs; fls small, purple or ochroleucous, in short racemes. **A. spatulatus** Sheldon. Common on stony ground, plateaus of the NW counties.
13b. Lvs with three lfls. **A. aretioides** (Jones) Barneby [in habit resembling an Aretian *Androsace*]. Densely matted, only a few cm tall, from flexible caudices; lvs woolly white-hairy, the fls one or two in a short raceme almost hidden in the lvs. Gypsum soils, MF, peripheral from southern Wyoming.

14a. [12] Plants forming very low tight mats on sandstone rocks; old lf rachises persisting into the second season. . . . . (15)
14b. Plants not as above . . . . (16)

15a. [14] Old lf rachises rigid, spine-like; caudices few, short and stout. **A. humillimus** Gray [very humble]. Extremely local, known in Colorado only from the Four Corners area in Colorado and Arizona.
15b. Old lf rachises not rigid or spine-like; caudices slender, elongate. **A. sesquiflorus** Watson [1 1/2-fld]. Local, on slickrock formations in the Dolores R Valley.

Figure 54. **A**, *Astragalus kentrophyta*, lf; **B**, *Pediomelum megalanthum*; **C**, *Hedysarum boreale*; **D**, *Glycyrrhiza lepidota*; **E**, **F**, **G**, keels of *Astragalus, Hedysarum, Oxytropis*

264 Fabaceae (Leguminosae) (FAB/LEG)

16a. [14] Pods covered by a dense white woolly pubescence, in some spp completely obscuring the surface. . . . . (17)
16b. Pods not densely white-woolly pubescent but commonly appressed-strigose or hirsute . . . . (19)

17a. [16] Racemes elongate, usually overtopping the lvs; lvs and scapes often over 2 dm tall; fls 2 cm long, purple. **A. mollissimus** Torrey var **thompsoniae** (Watson) Barneby [very soft; for Mrs. E. P. Thompson, sister of Capt. Powell]. Common in piñon-juniper, W counties.
17b. Racemes short, usually shorter than the longest lvs; plants usually less than 1 dm tall; fls ochroleucous, with a purple spot on the keel . . . . (18)

18a. [17] Pubescence of lvs and pods straight; pod not entirely obscured by the pubescence. **A. argophyllus** Nuttall var **martinii** Jones [silver-lvd; for Rev. G. W. Martin]. Sagebrush, piñon-juniper, ME-MF.
18b. Pubescence of lvs flexuous and matted, obscuring the surface of lvs and pods and giving the lvs a felt-like texture. **A. purshii** Douglas [for Frederick Pursh]. Similar habitats and range.

19a. [16] Racemes producing several pods (more than 3), on usually elongate, erect peduncles, never spreading out on the ground below the basal lvs . . . . (20)
19b. Racemes producing only 1-3(4) pods, the short peduncles spreading out on the ground below the basal lvs . . . . (28)

20a. [19] Pods about 1 cm diam, inflated and tough-chartaceous, straw-colored, pendent and often persisting through the winter; stems very numerous, forming broad clumps; fls up to 2 cm long, purple. **A. eastwoodiae** Jones. Desert gulches, Colorado R Valley.
20b. Pods much narrower, not inflated, dark in color, not persisting; stems relatively few, forming small clumps; fls smaller. . . . . (21)

21a. [20] Racemes elongate, many-fld; fls yellow (or white in SW counties); pods only about twice as long as wide; lfls linear. **A. flavus** Nuttall [yellow]. Common on adobe hills in the warm river valleys.
21b. Racemes short or few-fld, if elongating then only at frt maturity; fls never yellow; pods more than twice as long as wide . . . (22)

22a. [21] Pods erect, in a close terminal cluster (not elongating much at maturity); lvs usually with 3-7 lfls . . . . (23)
22b. Pods widely spreading or pendent, like little flags (the raceme elongating at maturity); lvs pinnately compound with many lfls . . . . (24)

23a. [22] Lvs with 3-5 narrowly linear lfls; pods about 2 cm long, sparsely strigose. **A. detritalis** Barneby [of rubble]. Local, on knolls, lower White R Valley.
23b. Lvs with broadly oval lfls; pods up to 1.5 cm long, densely gray-strigose. **A. calycosus** Gray var **scaposus** Jones. Piñon-juniper and sagebrush, LP, MZ.

24a. [22] Pods hirsute with widely spreading hairs . . . . (25)
24b. Pods appressed-pubescent . . . . (26)

25a. [24] Pods with minutely bulbous-based hairs; plants almost scapose. **A. desperatus** Jones [despairing; Jones was looking for an unused name in this enormous genus]. Piñon-juniper and canyonlands, ME, S of the Colorado R.
25b. Pods with long lustrous white (not bulbous-based) hairs; usually definitely caulescent. **A. pubentissimus** Torrey & Gray [very downy]. White R valley near Rangely.

26a. [24] Calyx tube 3.5-6.5 mm long; fls pink-purple or whitish tipped with purple; pod leathery-textured . . . . (27)
26b. Calyx tube 3-3.5 mm long; fls ochroleucous; pod papery. **A. deterior** (Barneby) Barneby [meaner (than *naturitensis*)]. Mesa Verde.

27a. Infl lengthening in frt; pods less than 1.5 cm long, essentially straight except for the beak. **A. naturitensis** Payson [from Naturita]. Piñon-juniper, Local, ME, MN and MZ.
27b. Infl subumbellate in frt; pods 2 cm long or more, strongly upcurved. **A. monumentalis** Barneby. Local, on sandstone along canyon rims, MZ.

28a. [19] Lfls 3-5, rarely 7, fusiform (pointed at each end and broadest in the middle); pods densely spreading- or appressed-strigose. **A. musiniensis** Jones [of Musinia Peak, Utah]. Sagebrush hills, W ME and GF.
28b. Lfls more numerous, oval; pods various . . . . (29)

29a. [28] Pod leathery-inflated, mottled. **A. chamaeleuce** Gray [creeping; white poplar]. Common on adobe hills. Too recently described to be included in the key, a new sp, *A. piscator* Barneby & Welsh [from Fisher Towers, Utah] has been found in the Dolores River Valley. It is unique in that the epicarp of the pod exfoliates. The fls are pale lilac and the ripe pod is laterally compressed. The pods are like those of *A. chamaeleuce* but have a prominent dorsal suture and elliptic cross-section.
29b. Pod chartaceous or almost woody, not mottled. . . . . (30)

30a. [29] Fls ochroleucous with purple-tipped keel; stems and lvs spreading-pilose. **A. parryi** Gray. Open forests near the Continental Divide, GN.
30b. Fls purple; stems and lvs appressed-pubescent. . . . . (31)

31a. [30] Pubescence basifixed (hairs attached at the very base) . . . (32)
31b. Pubescence dolabriform (hairs attached at the middle and pointed at each end) . . . . (33)

32a. [31] Pods glabrous; lfls 8-15; pubescence variable but not really silky. **A. iodopetalus** (Greene) Barneby [violet petals]. Sagebrush, Gunnison Basin and AA.
32b. Pods strigose; lfls rarely more than 3-8; pubescence very silky-

glossy. **A. shortianus** Nuttall [for Charles Wilkins Short]. Sagebrush hillsides, GA, uncommon W of the Continental Divide.

33a. [31] Pod narrowly oblong to oblong-ellipsoid, straight or nearly so, laterally compressed when ripe, keeled on both sutures, persistent. **A. missouriensis** Nuttall var **missouriensis**. Adobe hills, Four Corners.
33b. Pod obliquely ovoid to narrowly ellipsoid, mostly in curved, but if straight then dorsiventrally compressed either at base or in the middle, one or both sutures more or less depressed. . . . . (34)

34a. [33] Pod readily deciduous. **A. amphioxys** Gray var **vespertinus** (Sheldon) Jones [sharp at both ends (of pod); western]. Abundant in piñon-juniper and desert-steppe. Of the two spp in this couplet, this is by far the most common.
34b. Pod persistent or very tardily deciduous. **A. missouriensis** Nuttall var **amphibolus** Barneby [ambiguous]. Generally distributed from the Colorado R Valley southward. Thought to represent *A. amphioxys x A. missouriensis*.

35a. [11] Stems tall, erect, or if decumbent or spreading, then rather stout; fls usually large (10-20 mm). . . . . (36)
35b. Stems low, delicate, wiry, slender-stemmed, spreading or prostrate; fls usually smaller . . . . (60)

36a. [35] Lvs simple (reduced to the greatly expanded lf-base), orbicular, glaucous; fls large, bright purple; pods stipitate, fleshy-inflated, woody when ripe. **A. asclepiadoides** Jones [resembling *Asclepias cryptoceras*], **PL 21**. Common on adobe hills.
36b. Lvs pinnately compound. . . . . (37)

37a. [36] Pod with two grooves (sulci) along the upper (adaxial) side; racemes elongate, finger-width; fls numerous, ochroleucous. **A. bisulcatus** (Hooker) Gray. Two races occur: ssp **haydenianus** (Gray) Weber, with long racemes of very small fls, and ssp **bisulcatus**, with shorter racemes of larger, often bicolored, fls. Common in selenium soils.
37b. Pod without a double groove . . . . (38)

38a. [37] Calyx inflated, densely spreading-hirsute; fls yellow, mostly enclosed in the calyx. **A. oöcalycis** Jones [egg-shaped calyx], **PL 26**. END, San Juan Valley, AA and LP. Poisonous plant indicator of selenium soils.
38b. Calyx not as above . . . . (39)

39a. [38] Densely spreading-hairy; fls white. **A. drummondii** Douglas [for Thomas Drummond]. Infrequent, dry grassland, Yampa and Gunnison R valleys. Abundant on the E slope.
39b. Glabrous or appressed-pubescent . . . . (40)

40a. [39] Pods rigid, thick-walled, strongly keeled along each suture; stipules connate. . . . . (41)
40b. Pods not as above. . . . . (44)

41a. [40] Fls clear white (no keel spot); lvs regularly pinnate, lfl of upper lvs not reduced in size or number. **A. nelsonianus** Barneby. Gullies and flats, N MF. Ill-smelling because of uptake of selenium.
41b. Fls pink-purple or if white, with purple spot on keel; lvs with lfl much reduced in size or number . . . . (42)

42a. [41] Pod erect or ascending; fls white, with purple spot on keel. **A. linifolius** Osterhout [flax-lvd]. END, canyonsides, E base Uncompahgre Plateau and Dolores R.
42b. Pod declined or deflexed. . . . . (43)

43a. [42] Pod elliptic or oblong-elliptic in profile, the terminal cusp 2.5-4.0 mm long; stems glabrous or nearly so, the growing tips never gray-pubescent; fls white or pale purple. **A. rafaelensis** Jones [of San Rafael Swell, Utah]. Dolores Canyon-bottom near Uravan.
43b. Pod linear-oblong or narrowly oblanceolate in profile, reticulate but not wrinkled, the terminal cusp 0.5-1.0 mm long; growing tips commonly cinereous; fls deep pink-purple. **A. saurinus** Barneby [from Dinosaur Nat. Mon.]. Not yet known from Colorado, but extremely close to the border on Raven Ridge, RB.

44a. [39] Pods compressed, either laterally, dorsally or triquetrously . . . . (45)
44b. Pods not compressed. . . . . (53)

45a. [43] Pods triquetrously compressed, slightly grooved adaxially . . . . (46)
45b. Pods laterally or dorsiventrally compressed . . . . (47)

46a. [45] Raceme dense, the fls and frts strongly ascending in a tight head; pods 3 times as long as wide; fls either purple or ochroleucous; stems in clumps. **A. adsurgens** Pallas [upstanding]. Common in mt meadows.
46b. Raceme loose, elongate; pods reflexed, plump, only twice as long as wide; fls purple; stems solitary or few. **A. eucosmus** Robinson [becoming]. Frequent along subalpine streamsides.

47a. [45] Pods laterally compressed. . . . . (48)
47b. Pods dorsiventrally compressed . . . . (52)

48a. [47] Lfls broadly elliptic; fls purple. **A. cibarius** Sheldon [suitable for fodder]. Infrequent on sagebrush hills, MF.
48b. Lfls linear or narrowly oblong; fls ochroleucous. . . . . (49)

49a. [48] Pods not stipitate, not more than 2-3 times as long as wide, erect or pendulous. **A. eucosmus** Robinson. Frequent along subalpine streamsides.
49b. Pods stipitate, elongate, pendulous. . . . . (50)

50a. [49] Fls purple; foliage cinereous. **A. coltonii** Jones var **moabensis** Jones [for W. F. Colton; of Moab, Utah]. Piñon-juniper, ME, MN.

50b. Fls white or ochroleucous; lvs green . . . . (51)

51a. [50] Lfls linear, filiform or very narrowly oblong; fls white; pod not sulcate. **A. osterhoutii** Jones. END, Middle Park, on clay soils.
51b. Lfls oblong to elliptic; fls ochroleucous; pod longitudinally sulcate. **A. scopulorum** T. C. Porter [of Rocky Mts]. Piñon-juniper S of Colorado R valley.

52a. [47] Pod glabrous; lfls 1-9, the upper ones sometimes almost without lfls; terminal lfl not jointed to the rachis. **A. lonchocarpus** Torrey [long-podded]. Common in piñon-juniper.
52b. Pod strigose; lfls 11-20, the uppermost one jointed to the rachis. **A. schmolliae** C. L. Porter [for Hazel Schmoll]. END, Mesa Verde. Possibly derived from the cross, **A. lonchocarpus** x **A. scopulorum.**

53a. [44] Pods crowded, not more than twice as long as wide; plants of mesic sites. . . . . (54)
53b. Pods loosely arranged, about 3 times as long as wide; plants of desert selenium soils. . . . . (55)

54a. [53] Pods ovoid or globose, hirsute. **A. cicer** L. [generic name of the chick-pea]. ADV, introd in reclamation projects in the forested areas.
54b. Pods plump short-cylindric, glabrous, stiffly erect (fls tend to be spreading or even somewhat reflexed). **A. canadensis** L. var **brevidens** (Gandoger) Barneby. Gravelly meadows, often along streams, middle altitudes.

55a. [53] Pod with a stout, elongated beak sharply set off from the body proper; sprawling succulent plants with broadly oval lfls. **A. lentiginosus** Douglas var **palans** (Gray) Jones [freckled; straggling]. Piñon-juniper.
55b. Pod without a differentiated beak, the body simply terminated by the persistent style . . . . (56)

56a. [55] Plants elongate, with relatively few stems from the base, often decumbent . . . . (57)
56b. Plants forming dense clumps of low, slender stems; lfls narrowly elliptic to linear; pod thin, pliable. . . . . (59)

57a. [56] Fls purple; lfls oblong to elliptic; pod rigid. **A. hallii** Gray. Frequent in the intermountain valleys.
57b. Fls ochroleucous . . . . (58)

58a. [57] Calyx and petals ochroleucous; blades of the keel half-obovate, incurved through 90-105° to the blunt rectangular apex; stems green. **A. praelongus** Sheldon. Adobe hills. This and the next are selenium indicators.
58b. Calyx and petals pure white; blades of the keel lunately half-elliptic, incurved through less than 90° to the rather sharply triangular apex; stems usually red. **A. pattersonii** Gray. Replacing the last at higher altitudes (oak zone and intermountain parks).

59a. [56] Fls purple. **A. eastwoodiae** Jones. Adobe hills, Colorado R Valley near Grand Junction.
59b. Fls white or ochroleucous. **A. debequaeus** Welsh. END, Colorado R valley near DeBeque. A recently described taxon, which I tend to regard as a mere color form of the last.

60a. [35] Pods shaggy-pilose with spreading hairs, the body short, curved. **A. pubentissimus** Torrey & Gray. White R Valley.
60b. Pods glabrous or appressed-pubescent . . . . (61)

61a. [60] Annual or short-lived perennial with a slender taproot . . . (62)
61b. Perennial with variously developed root systems. . . . . (63)

62a. [61] Annual; pods oblong, strongly curved; fls purple, in short racemes. **A. nuttallianus** de Candolle var **micranthemiformis** Barneby [small-flowered form]. Piñon-juniper and *Atriplex* zones from Colorado R Valley southward.
62b. Perennial, sometimes blooming the first year; pods obovoid; fls white, scattered along delicate flagelliform racemes. **A. brandegei** T. C. Porter. Infrequent on gravelly river benches, Gunnison Basin. Extremely inconspicuous.

63a. [61] Weak, decumbent, with very slender and delicate root systems, often stoloniferous or rhizomatous; plants of subalpine meadows, streamsides and alpine tundra . . . . (64)
63b. Plants not as above . . . . (66)

64a. [63] Pod stipitate; racemes 7-24-fld; keel surpassing the wings and almost as long as the banner; fls purple-and-white. **A. alpinus** L. Common in subalpine meadows and streamsides, the most common subalpine *Astragalus*.
64b. Pod very short-stipitate (not over 1.5 mm) or sessile; racemes 3-6-fld; keel much shorter than the wings; fls white or purple . . (65)

65a. [64] Plants very small, densely strigose; fls purple. **A. molybdenus** Barneby [from Climax molybdenum area]. Gravelly tundra, Mosquito, Elk Mts (*A. plumbeus*).
65b. Plants lax, elongate; green and sparsely strigose; fls white. **A. leptaleus** Gray [slender]. Uncommon or inconspicuous, wet meadows and aspen, Gunnison Basin and Middle Park.

66a. [63] Pods laterally compressed. . . . . (67)
66b. Pods not laterally compressed but either dorsiventrally compressed, terete, or somewhat triangular (triquetrous) in cross section. . . . . (72)

67a. [66] Pods stipitate . . . . (68)
67b. Pods sessile. . . . . (70)

68a. [67] Pod short, broadly oblong, abruptly short-pointed; stipe short, included in the calyx; pods and lvs often turning black on drying. **A. tenellus** Pursh. Pine-oak; fls usually white, purple in the upper Gunnison Basin.
68b. Pod slenderly tapering at each end; stipe more evident . . . . . (69)

69a. [68] Fls white; pod glabrous, straight along one suture and very convex along the other. **A. aboriginum** Richardson [of indian tribes who gathered the root for food]. On the W slope we have only an alpine race known from the Mosquito Range; plants are 1-2 dm tall, branched from the base, with very short racemes of white fls and spreading-pilose lvs.
69b. Fls purple; pod strigose, somewhat convex on both surfaces. **A. robbinsii** Gray var **minor** (Hooker) Barneby [for J. W. Robbins, M.D.]. Subalpine streambanks, fell-fields and dry tundra, Gunnison and San Juan basins.

70a. [67] Pods 1-2 cm long, broadly oblong, abruptly pointed, glabrous; hairs basifixed. **A. wingatanus** Watson [from Fort Wingate]. Very common, piñon-juniper.
70b. Pods 2-3 cm long, narrowly oblong, gradually pointed, strigose; hairs dolabriform . . . . (71)

71a. [70] Some or all lvs reduced to the linear main rachis, all or most lfls lacking. **A. convallarius** Greene [of valleys]. Common, piñon-juniper.
71b. Lfls well-developed, from narrowly linear to broadly oblong. **Astragalus miser** Douglas var. **oblongifolius** (Rydberg) Cronquist [wretched, *re* the original specimen]. Common in mt meadows, usually above the piñon-juniper.

72a. [66] Pod triquetrously compressed, dorsal side grooved . . . . . (73)
72b. Pod compressed dorsiventrally or terete . . . . (74)

73a. [72] Forming dense low, erect clumps; heads dense, many-fld, the fls large, over 1 cm long, erect, crowded. **A. agrestis** Douglas [of fields]. Grassy meadows, lower montane.
73b. Wiry-stemmed, spreading, few-branched, not forming erect clumps; heads loose, the fls about 8 mm long. **A. cronquistii** Barneby [for Arthur Cronquist, contemporary American botanist]. Local, Four Corners.

74a. [72] Pod dorsiventrally compressed in the proximal half, becoming more or less laterally compressed distally; fls bicolored, with white wings and reddish-purple banner and keel; like *A. convallarius* but lfls better developed. **A. duchesnensis** Jones [of Duchesne, Utah]. Local, piñon-juniper, MF.
74b. Pod essentially terete . . . . (75)

75a. [74] Pod small, up to 8 mm long, short and fat, slightly dorsiventrally compressed; raceme few-fld, a raceme in the axil of a lf usually paired with another shoot bearing a lf and a short raceme. **A. microcymbus** Barneby [little boat]. END, rare, dry hillsides, Gunnison Basin.
75b. Pod over 1 cm long, oblong; racemes not as above. . . . . . . (76)

76a. [75] Lfls 11-25; pod pubescent, very rarely glabrous; banner 7-11 mm long. **A. flexuosus** (Hooker) Douglas. Common in piñon-juniper and oak.

76b. Lfls 7-11; pod always glabrous; banner 6-7 mm long. **A. proximus** (Rydberg) Wooton & Standley [close relative (of *flexuosus*)]. END, AA-LP.

CORONILLA L. 1753 [dim. of Lat., *corona*, crown]. CROWN VETCH

One sp, **C. varia** L. ADV pasture plant used extensively for revegetation. The pinkish fls have a slender purple-tipped keel. The plants thrive in shade and quickly form a dense cover up to several feet high.

GLYCYRRHIZA L. 1753 [Gr., *glycys*, sweet, + *rhiza*, root]. WILD LIQUORICE

One sp, **G. lepidota** Pursh, **54D, PL 35**. Abundant along irrigation ditches and on floodplains. Fls greenish-white. The spiny pods are unique in the family. Extracts of the roots of two S European spp, *G. glabra* L. and *G. echinata* L. are a commercial source of liquorice.

HEDYSARUM L. 1753 [Gr. name used by Theophrastus for some legume]. CHAINPOD

1a. Upper calyx lobes broader but considerably shorter than the lower three; wing petals with a slender, basal auricular lobe nearly as long as the claw, the 2 petals weakly joined by these lobes above the ovary; pods not noticeably cross-corrugated, the reticulations almost isodiametric. **H. occidentale** Greene. Less frequent than the next. Habitat differences have not been noted.

1b. Upper calyx lobes slender, subequal to the lower ones and to the calyx tube; basal lobe of the wing-petals broad, much shorter than the claws, not joined over the ovary; pods plainly cross-corrugated, the reticulations laterally elongated. **H. boreale** Nuttall, **54C**. Common on soil embankments at low and medium altitudes. The report of *H. alpinum* from the Gunnison Basin was a misidentification of *Astragalus bisulcatus*.

LATHYRUS L. 1753 [Gr., *la*, very, + *thyros*, passionate, the original sp thought to be an aphrodisiac]. PEAVINE

1a. Fls purple, pink, or red . . . . (2)
1b. Fls white. . . . . (4)

2a. Fls bright pink, rarely white (mutants); lfls 2; stem strongly winged. **L. latifolius** L., PERENNIAL SWEET PEA. ADV garden escape commonly colonizing fencerows.

2b. Fls blue, purple, or variegated pink-and-white; lfls numerous; stem not strongly winged. . . . . (3)

3a. Keel definitely shorter than the wings; calyx glabrous or the teeth merely ciliate, the teeth usually longer than the calyx-tube. **L. pauciflorus** Fernald. Open woods, especially oak zone, SW counties.

3b. Keel and wings equal or nearly so; calyx sparsely hairy, the teeth shorter than the calyx-tube. **L. eucosmus** Butters & St. John [becoming]. Similar habitats. Lfl shape and width are extremely variable in most spp.

4a. Fls 11-14 mm long; lfls usually fewer than 6; tendrils hardly curling. **L. arizonicus** Britton. Oak zone, SW counties. Doubtfully distinct from the next.
4b. Fls 14-18 mm long; lfls usually 6 or more; tendrils strongly curling. **L. leucanthus** Rydberg [white-fld]. Oak woodlands.

LOTUS L. 1753 [ancient Gr. plant name, used in many senses]

1a. Fls bright yellow, in a terminal umbel. **L. tenuis** Waldstein & Kitaibel. ADV in E Colorado, not yet found on the W slope but to be expected in cult and pasture land.
1b. Fls yellow with brown, solitary in the lf axils. **L. wrightii** (Gray) Greene [for Charles Wright]. Dry open forests, S counties.

LUPINUS L. 1753 [Lat., *lupus*, wolf, because of an old belief that it ruins the soil].
(Key contributed by David B. Dunn)

1a. Annual or biennial; cotyledons usually present at flowering time . . . . (2)
1b. Perennials . . . . (4)

2a. [1] Racemes rather loose and usually over 3 cm long; pods 2 cm long or more, constricted somewhat between the seeds; seed faces concave, the sides perpendicular. **L. pusillus** Pursh [very small]. Sandy soil, MF. In places where this is common, the pinkish seeds are gathered by ants and used to cover their hills. Local residents call these seeds 'ant money'.
2b. Racemes short, dense, head-like, usually less than 2 cm long; pods less than 2 cm long, not much constricted between the seeds; seeds convex on both surfaces. . . . . (3)

3a. [2] Plants acaulescent or nearly so, the lfy stem scarcely a cm long; lower calyx lip more than twice as long as the upper. **L. brevicaulis** Watson. Steppe-desert, NW counties.
3b. Plant with distinct stems, branched; calyx lips about equal. **L. kingii** Watson [for Clarence King, geologist]. Common, S counties.

4a. [1] Dwarf, forming low spreading clumps, the infl shorter than the lvs. **L. caespitosus** Nuttall. Sagebrush parks.
4b. Tall, usually erect; infl exceeding the lvs. . . . . (5)

5a. [4] Banners reflexing at or near the midpoint, leaving a relatively wide gap above the wings; longest petioles near the base, the upper ones often much reduced . . . . (6)
5b. Banners reflexing above the midpoint, and the ventral groove clasping enough of the wings so the tip of the banner leaves a small opening between the wing tip and the banner tip; lvs mostly short-petioled, occasionally somewhat longer below . . . (13)

6a. [5] Banner glabrous dorsally; plants erect or decumbent-spreading. . . . . (7)
6b. Banner pubescent dorsally, at least distally along the crest;

plants erect, often in dense clumps . . . . (11)

7a. [6] Lfls densely sericeous on both surfaces, somewhat sparser above, most of the lvs long-petioled. **L. wyethii** Watson [for Nathaniel J. Wyeth, western explorer]. Not known in Colorado but to be expected in the NW, since it occurs in adjacent Wyoming and Utah.

7b. Lfls glabrous above, rarely with a few scattered hairs near the margins . . . . (8)

8a. [7] Lvs with spreading pilose hairs 2-3 mm long. . . . . (9)
8b. Lvs appressed-puberulent to glabrate. . . . . (10)

9a. [8] Rhizomatous, with slender caudices; the pilose hairs aging yellowish. **L. ammophilus** Greene [sand-loving]. Sandy soil, SW counties and Four Corners.

9b. Not rhizomatous, with stout caudices; pilose hairs more hyaline. **L. prunophilus** Jones [chokecherry-loving]. Sagebrush, W counties.

10a. [8] Fls white to pinkish, drying tan, brownish or bluish, about 12 mm diam, viewed laterally; lfls succulent; stems decumbent. **L. crassus** Payson [thick]. Piñon-juniper, MN.

10b. Fls blue, about 18 mm diam, viewed laterally; in pine-oak woodland on the high benches E La Sal Mts. **L. lasalensis** Dunn, unpublished.

11a. [6] Lfls sericeous on both sides; banner pubescent over the central half of the dorsal side. **L. sericeus** Pursh [silky]. Gunnison Basin and MF. Var **flexuosus** (Lindley) Smith has appressed pubescence, small fls and lax racemes; var **egglestonianus** Smith [for W. W. Eggleston] has spreading pubescence.

11b. Lfls strigose-pilose to glabrous above; banner pubescent in the central area along the dorsal crest; plants in dense clumps from a woody caudex; stems ± fistulose . . . . (12)

12a. [11] Lfls thinly to densely pilose above and sericeous below; stems with spreading pilose hairs of multiple lengths. **L. bakeri** Greene ssp **bakeri** [for C. F. Baker], PL 44. Sagebrush slopes.

12b. Lfls glabrate to glabrous above and thinly pilose to sericeous below. **L. bakeri** Greene ssp **amplus** (Greene) Fleak & Dunn. Sagebrush up to spruce-fir.

13a. [5] Keel generally ciliate above and below, as well as ahead of the claw (sometimes cilia below and ahead of the claw are missing); often some lower lvs with longer petioles; lfls sericeous or sparsely pilose to glabrate above; calyx spur often well-developed . . . . (14)

13b. Keel glabrous above, below, and ahead of the claw; lvs usually all short-petioled; lfls often glabrous above and conduplicate, sometimes thinly pilose to sparsely strigose above . . . . (15)

14a. [13] Some petioles longer below; spur often developed, or the calyx only gibbous at the base; lfls strongly sericeous on both sides (plants with gibbous calyx may have the ciliation near the keel claw missing). **L. caudatus** Kellogg [spurred]. Common in sagebrush stands, plateaus.

14b. Petioles all short; spurs well-developed on the calyx; ciliation near the claw usually well-developed. **L. caudatus** Kellogg ssp **argophyllus** (Gray) Phillips. Sagebrush, S counties (*L. aduncus*).

15a. [13] Tip of keel short and bent back; fls small and numerous in elongate racemes . . . . (16)
15b. Tip of keel long and slender, erect or slanting forward; fls 8-12 mm long, in short or long racemes. . . . . (19)

16a. [15] Lfls and stems pubescent, strigose above and below. **L. parviflorus** Nuttall ssp **floribundus** (Greene) Harmon. In sagebrush, central Colorado.
16b. Lfls all glabrous above, strigose below, conduplicate or plane, broadly or narrowly oblanceolate . . . . (17)

17a. [16] Lfls narrowly oblanceolate, often conduplicate on drying; banner with an eyespot. **L. parviflorus** ssp **myrianthus** (Greene) Harmon. The most prevalent ssp, on sagebrush benches and plateaus.
17b. Lfls broadly oblanceolate, mostly plane. . . . . (18)

18a. [17] Stems slender, in clusters; plants to about 5 dm tall; eyespot poorly developed or absent. **L. parviflorus** ssp **parviflorus**. Infrequent in the NW counties.
18b. Stems subfistulose in clusters of several from a caudex, often taller; eyespot brown on drying. **L. parviflorus** ssp **myrianthus** var **fulvomaculatus** (Payson) Harmon [tawny-spotted].

19a. [15] Lfls evenly strigose above; calyx gibbous at base above and sericeous. **L. x alpestris** Nelson. Hybrids of *L. caudatus* with any of the following.
19b. Lfls glabrous, thinly strigose or sparsely pilose above. . . . . . (20)

20a. [19] Fls white or cream, the banner with a brown eyespot at maturity; lfls glabrous to sparsely pilose above, generally conduplicate. **L. argenteus** Pursh ssp **ingratus** (Greene) Harmon [homely]. Grassy slopes, Front Range through the mts into Utah.
20b. Fls normally blue, without the eyespot. . . . . (21)

21a. [20] Fls small and slender, viewed laterally (ca. 8 mm long or less); lfls generally conduplicate, narrow, glabrous or sparsely strigose above. **L. argenteus** ssp **argenteus** var **tenellus** (Douglas) Dunn. Scattered throughout the range of the sp as individuals or local populations.
21b. Fls 8-12 mm long; lfls glabrous or thinly pilose above . . . . . (22)

22a. [21] Fls 8-10 mm long, narrow viewed laterally; lfls narrowly oblanceolate, plane but often drying conduplicate, glabrous above; banner and keel often glabrous. **L. argenteus** ssp **rubri-**

caulis (Greene) Hess & Dunn. Sagebrush parks, usually below 3,000 m.
22b. Fls 10-12 mm long; lfls variable. . . . . (23)

23a. [22] Lfls glabrous above, plane, broadly oblanceolate; fls somewhat pendent; banner and keel often glabrous. **L. argenteus** ssp **spathulatus** (Rydberg) Hess & Dunn. Spruce-fir groves at high altitudes.
23b. Lfls glabrous to sparsely pilose above, at least near the margins; lower valleys and foothills . . . . (24)

24a. [23] Lfls narrowly oblanceolate, generally glabrous above. **L. argenteus** ssp **argenteus**. Arid grassy plains and valleys with sagebrush, N counties.
24b. Lfls linear-lanceolate to elliptical, often strongly conduplicate; plants 5 dm to over 1 m tall, sandy soils, W border. **L. argenteus** ssp **moabensis** Dunn & Harmon.

MEDICAGO L. 1753 [Gr. name for Alfalfa, alluding to the fact that the plant came to Greece from Media]. ALFALFA; MEDIC
1a. Fls yellow, in very tiny clusters; plants decumbent. **M. lupulina** L. [little hops], BLACK MEDIC. ADV, common ruderal weed.
1b. Fls purple to white, sometimes with a greenish-yellow color; heads large; plants erect, branched from the base. **M. sativa** L. [planted], ALFALFA. ADV, escaped from cult.

MELILOTUS Miller 1754 [Gr., *meli*, honey, + *lotos*, some leguminous plant]. SWEET-CLOVER
1a. Fls white. **M. alba** Desrousseaux. ADV, extensively planted for forage, erosion control, and as a honey plant.
1b. Fls yellow. **M. officinalis** (L.) Lamarck. ADV, similar sites.

OXYTROPIS de Candolle 1802 [Gr., *oxys*, sharp, + *tropis*, keel]. LOCO WEED
1a. Pods pendulous, not inflated; stipules only slightly adnate by their bases to the petioles; plants usually with lfy stems. **O. deflexa** (Pallas) de Candolle var **foliolosa** (Hooker) Barneby [reflexed; little lfls]. Dry lodgepole forests, subalpine.
1b. Pods erect or spreading, never pendulous; stipules adnate to the petiole; plants scapose or nearly so. . . . . (2)

2a. Lvs with some lfls in whorls or more than one at a node. **O. splendens** Douglas. Stony subalpine meadows. Woolly-pubescent; fls pink.
2b. Leaves strictly pinnate. . . . . (3)

3a. Scapes short, bearing 1-4 fls; pod papery-inflated; dwarf alpine or subalpine plants. **O. podocarpa** Gray [foot-frt]. Locally abundant on high peaks in the central massifs (absent from the San Juans).
3b. Scapes tall or bearing many fls . . . . (4)

4a. Plants sticky-glandular, at least on the calyx and bracts. **O.**

Fabaceae (Leguminosae) (FAB/LEG)

       viscida Nuttall. Tundra of central massifs.
4b. Plants not sticky-glandular; lower elevations . . . . (5)

5a. Corolla purplish or red except in rare albino forms . . . . (6)
5b. Corolla white or yellowish, keel often purple-tinged, the whole corolla rarely purplish . . . . (7)

6a. Calyx inflated, enclosing the turnip-shaped pod. **O. nana** Nuttall var **obnapiformis** (C. L. Porter) Isely [dwarf; turnip-shaped]. Sandy areas, MF (*O. obnapiformis*).
6b. Calyx not inflated, the pod protruding, elongate. **O. lambertii** Pursh [for A. B. Lambert, British botanist, 1761-1842]. Grasslands. Generally with only a few fl stems, and spreading lvs. Crosses extensively with *O. sericea* at the upper altitudinal limit of its range.

7a. Fls 12-15 mm long. **O. gracilis** (Nelson) Schumann. About 3 dm tall, with rather dense spikes of yellowish-white fls. Montane-subalpine (*A. campestris* var *gracilis*).
7b. Fls 18-25 mm long. **O. sericea** Nuttall [silky]. Sagebrush, upper montane, where it hybridizes with *O. lambertii*, forming spectacular variations of color and habit.

PARRYELLA Torrey & Gray 1868 [for C. C. Parry]
    One sp, **P. filifolia** Torrey & Gray. A low sprawling shrub with pinnate lvs with narrowly elliptic or usually filiform lfls, and slender racemes of yellowish fls. Local, Four Corners.

PEDIOMELUM Rydberg 1919 [Gr., *pedion*, flatland, + *mylon*, apple, alluding to the tubers, from the French vernacular name *Pomme de Prairie*]. INDIAN POTATO (*Psoralea* in part)
1a. Fls 15-20 mm long; lvs forming a basal rosette, gray-pubescent; aerial stems very short. **P. megalanthum** (Wooton & Standley) Rydberg, **54B, PL 13**. Adobe hills, ME-MN.
1b. Fls 10-14 mm long; lvs not forming a basal rosette, green; aerial stems 15-30 cm high, lfy. **P. aromaticum** (Payson) Weber. Infrequent on similar sites, ME-MN.

PSORALIDIUM Rydberg 1919 [dim. of *Psoralea*: Gr., *psoraleos*, scabby, from the gland-dotted foliage] (*Psoralea* in part)
1a. Fls white or cream-colored in dense racemes; lfls linear. **P. lanceolatum** (Pursh) Rydberg. Sandy soils.
1b. Fls blue or purple in loose racemes; lfls elliptic. **P. tenuiflorum** (Pursh) Rydberg. Grasslands.

ROBINIA L. 1753 [for Jean Robin, 1550-1629, herbalist to Henry IV of France, and his son Vespasian, 1579-1662, who first cultivated the tree in Europe]. LOCUST
1a. Fls white, in a hanging raceme; pods smooth; tree. **R. pseudoacacia** L., BLACK LOCUST. ADV, cult as a street tree and persisting around old homesteads.
1b. Fls purple, the raceme not hanging; pods glandular-hirsute;

shrub. **R. neomexicana** Gray. ADV along streamsides, Colorado R Valley.

SPHAEROPHYSA de Candolle 1825 [Gr., *sphaira*, a sphere, + *physa*, a bellows, alluding to the bloated fruit]. BUYAN

One sp, **S. salsula** (Pallas) de Candolle (alluding to the salt flat habitat). ADV, estab near Delta. The plant resembles a gigantic *Astragalus* and is not clearly separated from that genus. However, the strange fl color (red-orange) and the habit and inflated pods mark it sufficiently well. At times the plants may be covered with swarms of blister beetles (Cantharidae); handling them can cause severe skin burns.

THERMOPSIS R. Brown 1811 [Gr., *thermos*, lupine, + *opsis*, like]. GOLDEN BANNER
1a. Pods stiffly erect, straight, pubescent. **T. montana** Nuttall. Widespread in wet mt meadows.
1b. Pods widely spreading, curved, glabrous or nearly so. **T. divaricarpa** Nelson [spreading-frt]. Gravelly meadows and streambottoms. More common on the E slope.

TRIFOLIUM L. 1753 [Lat., *tres*, three, + *folium*, leaf]. CLOVER

1a. Stems scapose, lvs basal (only in *T. gymnocarpum* a few lvs on the fl stalk). . . . . (2)
1b. Stems lfy, not exclusively basal . . . . (9)

2a. Plants from long slender rhizomes, not caespitose; fls pendent, in short racemes and not tight heads. **T. brandegei** Watson. Upper subalpine and alpine, usually on steep rocky slopes; fls purple.
2b. Plants not rhizomatous, commonly caespitose; fls not pendent . . . (3)

3a. Very densely caespitose, with many caudices clothed with dry old lf bases. . . . . (4)
3b. Not or loosely caespitose; caudices few, not strongly clothed with old dry lf bases. . . . . (7)

4a. Fls 1-3 per head. **T. nanum** Torrey [dwarf]. Tundra of the higher peaks. A hard-mat plant, the fls hardly exceeding the lvs.
4b. Fls numerous in each head . . . . (5)

5a. Fls bicolored; banner pale, wings and keel pink- or purple-tipped; usually less than 1 dm tall . . . . (6)
5b. Fls one color, bright rose-purple; usually forming loose mats over 1 dm tall; rocky ledges at timberline. **T. attenuatum** Greene. Rock ledges, San Juans to Mosquito Range. Much larger in every way than the last.

6a. Heads subtended by an invol of stipules. **T. andinum** Nuttall [of the "northern Andes"]. Desert hills, MF.
6b. Heads not subtended by an invol; forming close low mats on dry

tundra. **T. dasyphyllum** Torrey & Gray [shaggy-lvd]. Common in the central massifs, evidently absent from the San Juans.

7a. Spreading, close to the ground; heads less than 1 cm broad, pale purple, no invol; lvs sharply serrate, gray-green, often with a white mark across the blade. **T. gymnocarpum** Nuttall [naked frt]. Sagebrush-oak.
7b. Erect; heads over 2 cm broad, deep rose-purple, with an invol of fused bracts; lvs rarely serrate, grass-green, never marked . . . . (8)

8a. Banner rounded, not much longer than the wings; low, usually less than 1 dm tall. **T. parryi** Gray. Common in subalpine forest openings and moist tundra. Diploid, with 16 chromosomes.
8b. Banner tapered, acute, longer than the wings; tall, larger in every way, usually over 1 dm tall. **T. salictorum** Greene [of willows]. Very wet tundra. A tetraploid with 32 chromosomes. Hybrids are rare and are sterile.

9a. Heads sessile, subtended by a few lvs and a broad papery invol-like bract. **T. pratense** L., RED CLOVER [of meadows]. ADV. Robust perennial often cult for honey and for pasture mixes. The plants have hairy lvs and large pink-purple heads.
9b. Heads pedunculate. . . . . (10)

10a. Invol present, of fused bracts. **T. wormskjoldii** Lehmann [for Morten Wormskjöld, Danish botanist, 1783-1845]. Forests and meadows, S counties (*T. fendleri*).
10b. Invol absent . . . . (11)

11a. Low spreading plants forming dense clumps or rooting at the nodes; introd plants . . . . (12)
11b. Erect plants never forming dense clumps nor rooting at the nodes; fls various; wild plants. . . . . (14)

12a. Fls rose-pink; calyx papery-inflated in fruit; creeping plants introd on lawns and golf-courses, often escaped and estab. **T. fragiferum** L., STRAWBERRY CLOVER. ADV, Colorado R valley.
12b. Fls white or pinkish-white, turning brownish; calyx not inflated; erect or creeping . . . . (13)

13a. Stems erect or ascending; fls pinkish-white; calyx pubescent in the sinuses between the teeth. **T. hybridum** L., ALSIKE CLOVER (pronounced *Ál-si-keh*; this was a hamlet near Linnaeus' summer home). ADV, commonly cult and escaped into meadows.
13b. Stem creeping, rooting at the nodes; calyx glabrous or sparsely pubescent at the base. **T. repens** L., WHITE DUTCH CLOVER [creeping]. ADV, escaped from cult and estab in meadows.

14a. Stem and lvs glabrous; heads large, with purple, reflexed fls. **T. kingii** Watson [for Clarence King]. Infrequent in forests of the plateaus, MN, ME (*T. macilentum*).
14b. Stem and lvs more or less pubescent; heads about 1 cm diam, white or rarely purplish, fls varying in attitude. **T. longipes**

VEXIBIA Rafinesque 1825 [derivation?]. WHITE LOCO

One sp, *V. nuttalliana* (Turner) Weber. Infrequent on dry grasslands, GN-MZ. This small genus previously lumped in *Sophora*, a group of dry-tropics trees, is disjunct between western U.S. and southwest Asia!

VICIA L. 1753 [the classical Lat. name]. VETCH

1a. Lvs densely villous; racemes many-fld. **V. villosa** Roth. ADV, introd for nurse crops for freeways, persisting along roadsides.
1b. Lvs not densely pubescent; racemes few-fld. **V. americana** Mühlenberg. Common in meadows and thickets. The fls are larger than those of the last, hence this sp is commonly mistaken for *Lathyrus*.

FAGACEAE—OAK FAMILY (FAG)

Having grown up in the East, I became well-acquainted with many species of oaks and had little trouble telling most of them apart. In the West, the story is very different. While in Colorado we have only one common and dominant oak, the scrub oak species *Quercus gambelii*, this is so variable that it has been at one time or other divided into *Q. fendleri, gunnisonii, leptophylla, novomexicana, utahensis, venustula* and *vreelandii*, the differences based on leaf shape and pubescence. We can't pass off these differences as imaginary. They are real and striking, but probably they reflect genetic contamination of the *Q. gambelii* genotype by hybridization with species formerly inhabiting the area along with it. Because this oak reproduces by suckering, very large areas can be populated by clones having a single distinctive leaf-form, and this only magnifies the difference. So one should expect our common Gambel Oak to vary in the direction of other southwestern species; absolute identifications are often difficult or impossible.

QUERCUS L. 1753 [the classical Lat. name]. OAK

1a. Lvs usually over 5 cm long, not rigid, the lobes deep, rounded, with broad open sinuses; tall shrubs or small trees above the piñon-juniper. **Q. gambelii** Nuttall, SCRUB OAK, 53E. Abundant and dominating the plateaus.
1b. Lvs usually less than 5 cm long, rigid, the lobes shallow or lvs merely very strongly toothed, the lobes or teeth usually with sharp points.; shrubs less than 2 m tall . . . . (2)

2a. Lvs about 5 cm long, distinctly lobed, usually with basally rounded sinuses narrow at the top. **Q. gambelii** Nuttall x **Q. havardii** Rydberg [for Wm. Gambel, 1821-1849, collector of plants and animals for Phila. Academy; for Lt. V. Havard, U.S. Army, botanist in Texas, 1885], **53H**. Forming large stands of very low shrubs in the piñon-juniper, N edge of Uncompahgre Plateau from Colorado National Monument to the Utah border. **Q. havardii** is a sp of sandy plains of Oklahoma, Texas and New Mexico and there is no evidence that it ever occurred in W Colorado. Nevertheless, the notion of its involvement in this hybrid has been developed seriously by oak specialists.

280   Fagaceae (FAG)

2b. Lvs about 3 cm long, not lobed but with very prominent spine-tipped teeth . . . . (3)

3a. Lvs glabrous and glaucous with attenuate-spinose teeth. **Q. ajoënsis** Muller [from the Ajo Mts., Arizona], **53G**. Known from only from rimrock slopes on the Mesa Verde.
3b. Lvs pubescent, especially along the nerves. **Q. turbinella** Greene [a little top], **53F**. Known from one small stand near Durango, which appears to be intermediate between *Q. gambelii* and *Q. turbinella*.

FRANKENIACEAE—FRANKENIA FAMILY (FNK)

This is a very ancient family now consisting of four genera of very salt-tolerant heath-like plants. *Frankenia*, the largest genus, is found widely scattered on seashores and salt deserts in Australia, the Mediterranean region, southern South America, and southwestern North America. The family must have been once much more diversified and widely distributed, but its evolution and dispersal remains a puzzle.

FRANKENIA L. 1753 [for Johannes Franckenius, 17 Cent. Swedish botanist]

One sp, **F. jamesii** Torrey, **55A**, restricted to gypsum shales, SW MZ. Elsewhere in Colorado this occurs near Canyon City. The sp is evidently an obligate gypsophile. *Frankenia* is very easy to recognize. It has prominently jointed stems with opposite, linear, tightly revolute lvs. The axils are crowded with short shoots bearing lvs so that they appear to be fascicled. The fls are very distinctive. The sepals are united into a narrow tube, the petals are conspicuous, white, but are narrowed to claws within the calyx. There are six stamens in two groups of three long and three short. The style has three terminal branches.

FUMARIACEAE—FUMITORY FAMILY (FUM)

Our only genus of this strange family is a relative of Dutchman's Breeches and Squirrel Corn, well-known spring flowers of the eastern and far-western states, and the ornamental species of rose-colored *Dicentra*, the best-known of which is the Bleeding-heart. All species are noted for their unusual spurred flowers, and the fruit which resembles a bean-pod. *Corydalis* species may be mistaken for legumes. An analysis of the flower might be useful. There are two sepals, very tiny and bractlike. Of the four petals, the two outer ones flare at the top and one of these has a spur at the base. The two inner petals are smaller, narrower and united at the top over the stigmas. There are six stamens, in two sets of three. The fruit is a 2-valved capsule with parietal placentae.

CORYDALIS Ventenat 1804 [ancient Gr. name for the crested lark]

1a. Fls yellow; plants low and sprawling. **C. aurea** Willdenow, GOLDEN SMOKE, **55C**. Common on roadside banks, mostly in the oak woodland. Two forms occur: ssp **aurea**, with the spur about a

Figure 55. **A**, *Frankenia jamesii*, plant, fl; **B**, *Corydalis caseana*, plant, fl left; **C**, *C. aurea*

third the length of the rest of the corolla and the fruits pendent and torulose. This seems to be the plant of the high mountains and intermountain parks; and ssp **occidentalis** (Engelmann) Ownbey has the spur about equalling the body and the frts erect and hardly torulose. This evidently is the low altitude plant.

1b. Fls white; plants up to 2 m tall. **Corydalis caseana** (Gray) ssp **brandegei** (Watson) Ownbey [for its discoverer, Prof. E. L. Case], **55B, PL 20.** Locally abundant in very wet aspen and spruce-fir forests of Grand Mesa and the Elk and San Juan Mountains. This sp also occurs disjunct in the Pacific Northwest, and represents a distinctly eastern-Asiatic section of the genus.

GENTIANACEAE—GENTIAN FAMILY (GEN)

Gentians are characteristic and often among the choicest of alpine wild flowers in the high mountains of the world. In the Rockies we lack the deep blue low gentians of the Swiss Alps, but have some specialties of our own. And we share some of ours with the mountains of the other continents: *Chondrophylla*, most well represented in New Guinea; *Swertia*, *Comastoma*, *Lomatogonium* and *Gentianodes* are found in the mountains of Eurasia. *Gentiana* proper, tall plants with large spotted purple or yellow flowers, occur only in Europe. While the tradition in America has been to lump all gentians into a single genus, the genera recognized here are distinct on morphological grounds, chromosome numbers, electron-microscopic characters of the pollen grains, and life histories.

1a. Corolla lobed to near the base, rotate, never distinctly tubular . . . . (2)
1b. Corolla distinctly tubular. . . . . (4)

2a. Tall and stout, up to 2 m high; lvs fleshy, in whorls; fls greenish-white. **Frasera,** MONUMENT PLANT
2b. Plant slender; lvs opposite or basal; fls blue or white. . . . . . . (3)

3a. Annual; fls white, rarely light blue; several pairs of opposite stem lvs present. **Lomatogonium,** MARSH FELWORT
3b. Perennial; fls deep blue; lvs chiefly basal, elliptic or oblanceolate. **Swertia,** STAR GENTIAN

4a. Corolla salverform (with a narrow tube and wide-spreading lobes), pink and yellow, sometimes white. **Centaurium,** CENTAURY
4b. Corolla not salverform, the tube broad relative to the erect or slightly spreading lobes, usually blue, but occasionally pink or white . . . . (5)

5a. Perennial, without a taproot; corolla never with fringed lobes, usually over 2.5 cm long . . . . (6)
5b. Annual or biennial, or, if a short-lived perennial, then with a taproot; corolla usually small, but if larger than 2.5 cm, then with fringed lobes. . . . . (7)

6a. Fls white with dull purple pleats. **Gentianodes**, ARCTIC GENTIAN
6b. Fls blue or purple. **Pneumonanthe**, BOTTLE GENTIAN

7a. Corolla deep blue, over 2.5 cm long, the principal lobes marginally fringed. **Gentianopsis**, FRINGED GENTIAN
7b. Corolla white, pale, or deep blue, less than 2 cm long, the principal lobes not fringed on the margin . . . . (8)

8a. Sinuses of the corolla plicate, with a smaller tooth-like lobe between the principal ones; lf-pairs connate into a tubular base; lvs less than 1 cm long, rounded-oblanceolate or obovate, white-edged. **Chondrophylla**, SIBERIAN GENTIAN
8b. Sinuses of the corolla not plicate, without subsidiary lobes; lvs larger, not connate-based nor white-edged . . . . (9)

9a. Corolla-lobes with two fringed scales within; fls on long naked peduncles. **Comastoma**, LAPPLAND GENTIAN
9b. Corolla-lobes with a single row of hairs forming a fringe inside (occasionally lacking in very late-blooming plants); fls subtended by bracts, usually in clusters on the stem. **Gentianella**, LITTLE GENTIAN

CENTAURIUM Hill 1756 [Lat., *centaurus*, its medicinal properties said to have been discovered by a Centaur]. CENTAURY

1a. Corolla-lobes 7-8 mm long, at least 3/4 as long as the tube. **C. calycosum** (Buckley) Fernald, **58B**. Infrequent or rare, seasonally moist places in the Montrose area.
1b. Corolla-lobes 3-5 mm long, about 1/2 as long as the tube. **C. exaltatum** (Gray) Tidestrom. Known from a single collection in Colorado Nat. Mon., where it occurs around seasonal pools in cottonwood groves, blooming in late summer. The plants vary incredibly in stature depending on shade and moisture. Large plants may reach 2 dm high.

CHONDROPHYLLA Nelson 1904 [Gr., *chondros*, cartilage, + *phyllon*, leaf]. SIBERIAN GENTIAN
This genus exists widely disjunct in the mountain ranges of the world. I have seen species in the Andes, the mountains of Australia and New Guinea, the Alps, Himalaya and Siberian Altai. All are tiny gentians, often four-merous. Annuals are exceedingly rare in our alpine, but *C. prostrata* seems to be annual or more likely a winter annual (*Ciminalis* of earlier editions).
1a. Capsule broadly obovoid, hardly longer than broad, the two valves gaping widely; base of capsule grading into a rather stout stipe, exserted from the corolla.; corolla pale blue. **C. aquatica** (L.) Weber, **57F**. Common in subalpine wet sedge meadows (*Gentiana fremontii*). Apparently not sensitive to light changes.
1b. Capsule narrow cylindrical, at least 5 times as long as broad, the valves spreading only at the top; stipe slender; corolla deep blue (except for white mutants) . . . . (2)

2a. Flowering stems erect; ripe capsule not fully exserted from the

Figure 56. A, *Gentianella acuta*; B, *Comastoma tenellum*; C, *Swertia perennnis*; D, *Lomatogonium rotatum*

corolla; plants usually not over 5 cm tall. **C. prostrata** (Haenke) J. P. Anderson, **57E**. Corolla light sensitive, closing quickly when shaded by a cloud or hand.

2b. Flowering stems arcuate, fls nodding; ripe capsule fully exserted on a slender stipe up to 3 cm long; plants over 5 cm tall. **C. nutans** (Bunge) Weber. Only recently discovered, a Siberian sp new to the Western Hemisphere, on tundra, PT, ST.

COMASTOMA Toyokuni 1961 [Gr., *coma*, mane, + *stoma*, opening, alluding to the fringe inside the corolla]. LAPLAND GENTIAN

One sp, **C. tenellum** (Rottboell) Toyokuni, **56B**. Infrequent on alpine tundra. Easily recognized by the chiefly basal lvs and long-peduncled fls.

FRASERA Walter 1788 [for John Fraser, colonial American botanist, 1750-1811]. MONUMENT PLANT; GREEN GENTIAN

1a. Tall, unbranched, the floral branches not exceeding the lvs. **F. speciosa** Douglas, **58C**. Common in pine forests and meadows, montane and subalpine, a very conspicuous plant with its whorls of broad lvs and pale greenish fl clusters. Each petal has a midline of stiff glandular hairs and a fringed basal flap covering the nectary. Once considered biennial but better described as monocarpic, since, like the agaves, they take from 20 to 60 years of growth before producing a fl stalk, after which the plant dies.

1b. Low, much-branched from the base, the floral branches much exceeding the narrow white-margined lvs. **F. albomarginata** Watson, **58D**. In Colorado known only from MZ.

GENTIANELLA Moench 1794. LITTLE GENTIAN

1a. Corolla lobes as long as the tube; capsule with 6 or fewer seeds. **G. tortuosa** (Jones) Gillett. Restricted to shale outcrops, Piceance Basin.

1b. Corolla lobes shorter than the tube; capsule with many seeds . . . (2)

2a. Calyx lobes distinctly fused into a basal cup, the lobes relatively narrow and not markedly unequal; cilia of internal corolla fringe free to the base or sometimes lacking; plants most commonly with relatively small flowers and stiffly ascending branches, but exceedingly variable in stature. **G. acuta** (Michaux) Hiitonen, **56A**. A very variable and widespread sp in moist meadows up to subalpine (*G. amarella* is European). The usual form has pale blue fls, but white forms occur. In very late-blooming plants the characteristic internal fringe of the corolla may be absent.

2b. Calyx lobes free to the base, the lobes variable in width and length, at least one of them broad and bractlike; fringe cilia usually united below; plants averaging larger than the last, with usually widely spreading branches. **G. heterosepala** (Engelmann) Holub. Similar sites.

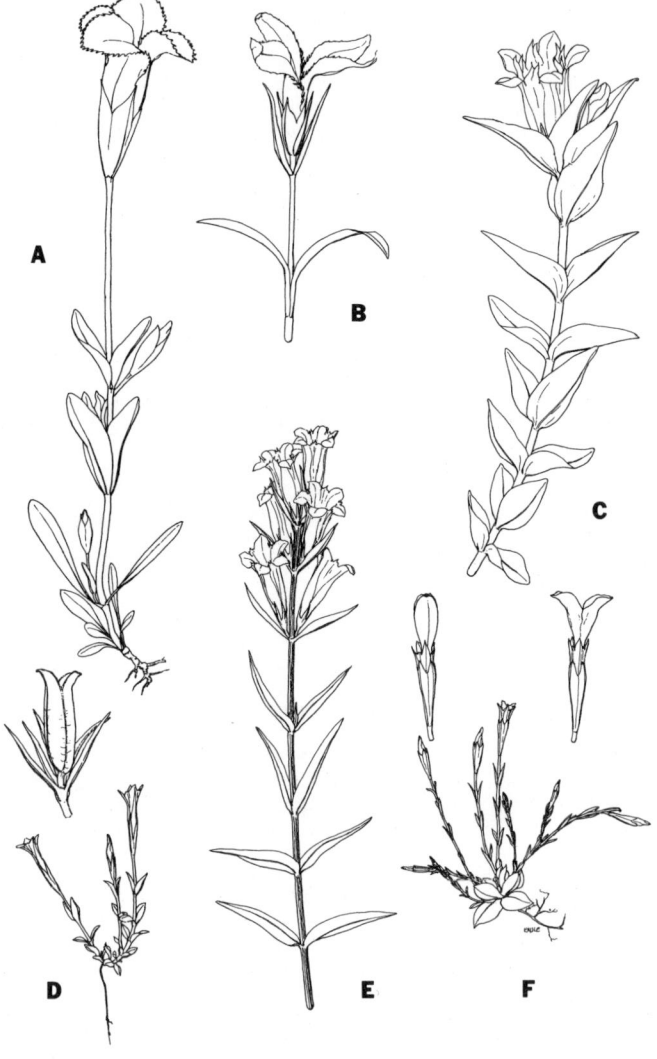

Figure 57. A, *Gentianopsis thermalis*; B, *G. barbellata*; C, *Pneumonanthe parryi*; D, *P. affinis*; E, *Chondrophylla prostrata*; F, *C. aquatica*

GENTIANODES Löve & Löve 1972 [from Gentius, King of Illyria, who, according to Pliny, discovered the medicinal virtues of gentians]. ARCTIC GENTIAN

One sp, **G. algida** (Pallas) Löve & Löve, **58A, PL 9**. A very late summer bloomer in the subalpine and alpine along rills, streambanks and on tundra meadows.

GENTIANOPSIS Ma 1951. FRINGED GENTIAN

1a. Annual; fls on long naked peduncles, not closely bracteate; petals broadened above. **G. thermalis** (Kuntze) Iltis, **57A**. Locally abundant in wet meadows and subalpine snow-melt basins (considered by some a ssp of *G. detonsa*). White or pink flowered mutants are not uncommon.
1b. Short-lived perennial; fls short-peduncled in the axils of two bract-like lvs; petals narrow-strap-shaped. **G. barbellata** (Engelmann) Iltis, **57B, PL 62**. Subalpine grassy slopes.

LOMATOGONIUM A. Braun 1830 [Gr., *loma*, hem, + *gone*, gynoecium, alluding to the decumbent stigmatic lines]. MARSH FELWORT

One sp, **L. rotatum** (L.) Fries ssp *tenuifolium* (Grisebach) Porsild, **56D**. Willow bogs and marshes, subalpine. Our plants have numerous ascending branches and usually white fls, while the typical Arctic plants have few branches and purplish fls.

PNEUMONANTHE Gleditsch 1764 [Gr., *pneumon*, lung, + *anthos*, flower, alluding to the inflated corolla]. BOTTLE GENTIAN

1a. Corolla cylindric, the floral bracts narrow, not scarious; plants ascending from a spreading base. **P. affinis** (Grisebach) Greene, **57D**. A common summer-blooming gentian in the intermountain parks.
1b. Corolla barrel-shaped, the floral bracts broad, scarious. **P. parryi** (Engelmann) Greene, **57C**. The common large gentian of montane and subalpine forests and meadows (incorrectly called *P. calycosa*, a sp of the Pacific Northwest).

SWERTIA L. 1753 [for Emanuel Sweert, Dutch herbalist, born 1552]. STAR GENTIAN

One sp, **S. perennis** L., **56C**. Willow bogs and marshes, subalpine. Mutant individuals may have white fls.

GERANIACEAE—GERANIUM FAMILY (GER)

The geraniums have developed a remarkable method of planting their seeds. The gynoecium splits into five one-seeded units (mericarps), each attached to a split length of style, which coils like a spring. Falling to the ground, the spring coils and uncoils with changes in atmospheric humidity. If the spring lies against a grass stem or other fixed object, it drills the sharp-pointed mericarp containing the seed into the earth. Similar devices have evolved, using different materials, in the grasses (*Stipa*) and in the roses (*Cercocarpus*). Potted 'geraniums' belong to the African genus, *Pelargonium*.

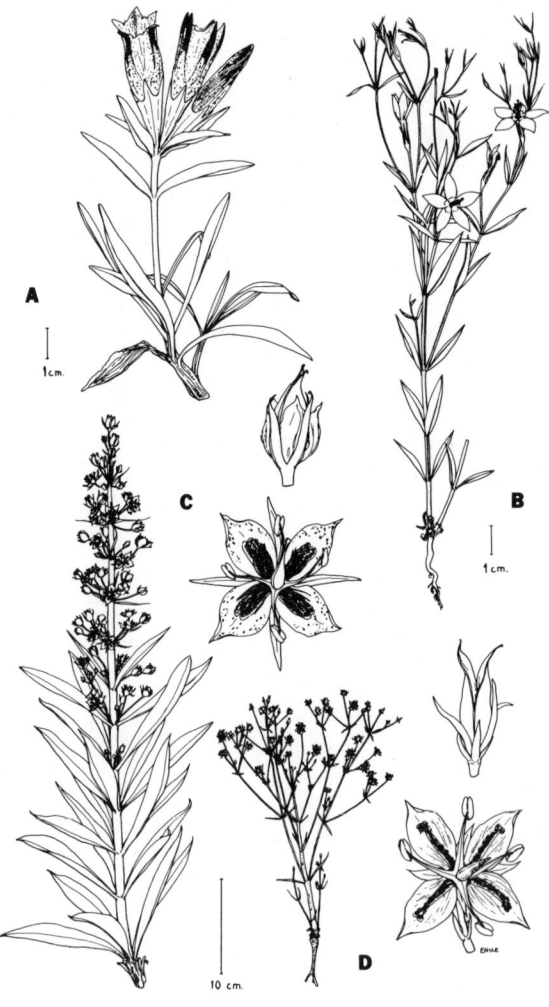

Figure 58. A, *Gentianodes algida*; B, *Centaurium calycosum*; C, *Frasera speciosa*, habit, fl, frt; D, *F. albomarginata*, habit, fl, frt

Geraniaceae (GER) 289

1a. Lvs pinnately compound and dissected. **Erodium**, CRANE'S BILL; FILAREE
1b. Lvs palmately lobed. **Geranium**

ERODIUM L'Heritier 1789 [Gr., *erodios*, a heron, for the long frt beak]. CRANE'S BILL; FILAREE [Sp., *alfiler*, a pin]

One sp, **E. cicutarium** (L.) L'Heritier, **59D**. Fls tiny, pink, the petals falling early. One of the earliest flowering weeds of early spring in ruderal sites. A winter annual, its leafy rosette is already well-developed by October.

GERANIUM L. 1753 [Gr., *geranos*, a crane, for the long fruit beak].

1a. Plants erect, with a single or few stems . . . . (2)
1b. Plants with many stems, these often sprawling . . . . (3)

2a. Petals white with purple veins, pilose on the basal half; plants slender; lvs thin in texture. **G. richardsonii** Fischer & Trautvetter, **59A**. Typically found in aspen groves and spruce-fir forests. In the field this sp is easier to recognize than from pressed specimens.
2b. Petals pink to deep purple, pilose only on the basal quarter; plants stout; lvs thick in texture. **G. viscosissimum** Fischer & Meyer ssp **nervosum** (Rydberg) Weber, **59C**. Wet roadside ditches and meadows.

3a. Plants lacking glandular pubescence; fls ranging from pale pink to deep purple; stems slender, much-branched. **G. caespitosum** James ssp **atropurpureum** (Heller) Weber, **59B**. Common in the S counties and the dominant race in New Mexico. Ponderosa pine zone.
3b. Plants with glandular petioles, stems, or pedicels. **G. caespitosum** ssp **caespitosum**. Relatively infrequent on the W slope, and very variable in the amount and disposition of glandular hairs. The named varieties, while easily separated on technical characters, occur in mixed populations (*G. fremontii, G. parryi*).

GROSSULARIACEAE
CURRANT OR GOOSEBERRY FAMILY (GRS)

The word 'currant' is a corruption of Corinth, from whence Zante Currant, a small variety of grape, comes (raisins of Corinth). Wild currants are so-called because of their resemblance to these. Gooseberries are green, often spiny fruits with an entirely different flavor, and this group is often segregated as the genus *Grossularia*, from which the family gets its name.

RIBES L. 1753 [said to come from Danish colloquial *ribs*, for red currant]. CURRANT; GOOSEBERRY
1a. Spines or prickles absent from the twigs . . . . (2)
1b. Spines or prickles present . . . . (7)

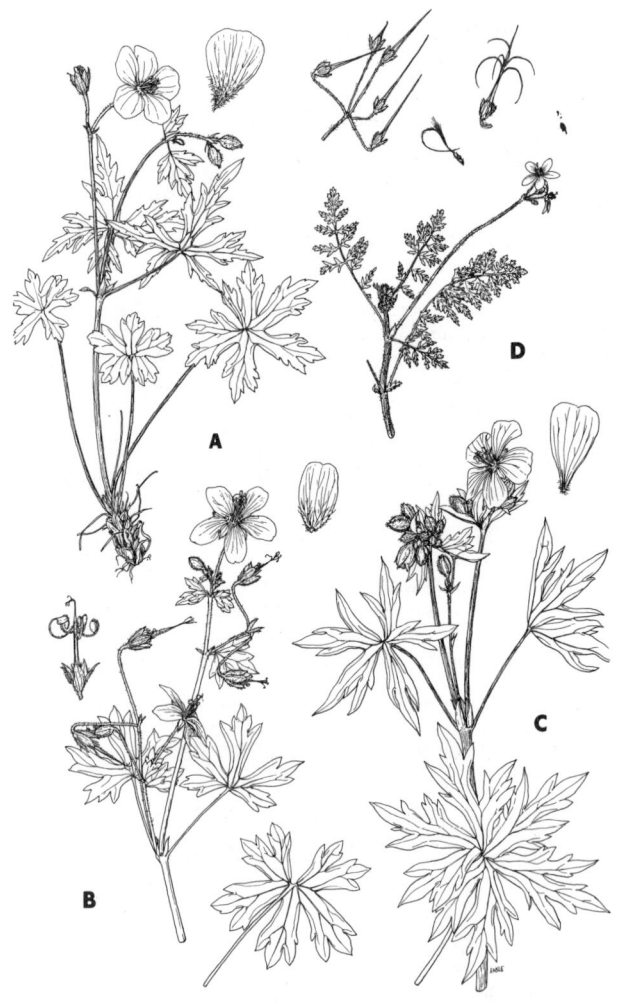

Figure 59. A, *Geranium richardsonii*, habit, petal; B, *G.. caespitosum*, habit, frt, petal; C, *G. viscosissimum*, habit, petal; D, *Erodium cicutarium*, habit, frt

2a. Fls yellow; petals yellow or red; berry black; lvs with three principal lobes. **R. aureum** Pursh, GOLDEN CURRANT, 60C. Streamsides and wet ditches in the lower valleys.
2b. Fls white or pink . . . . (3)

3a. Hypanthium very shallowly developed above the ovary, saucer-shaped. . . . . (4)
3b. Hypanthium short- or long-tubular . . . . (5)

4a. Fls pink, arising from buds on last years' growth, not terminal on the branches; lvs with acute lobes, maple-leaf form. **R. coloradense** Coville, 60B. Common in subalpine forests near the Continental Divide, but mostly replaced on the W slope by the next.
4b. Fls white, in terminal racemes on the current year's growth; lvs with rounded lobes. **R. wolfii** Rothrock, 60A. Common in subalpine forests.

5a. Lvs deeply lobed about half-way to the midrib, not strongly glandular; plant usually with some spines at the nodes. **R. inerme** Rydberg, 60D. Canyons, middle altitudes.
5b. Lvs obscurely lobed, strongly glandular-pubescent. . . . . (6)

6a. Fls pink; hypanthium narrow, 3-4 times as long as wide; lf-blades 1-3 cm diam; frt orange-red. **R. cereum** Douglas [waxy], 60F. Dry gulches, canyonsides, piñon-juniper.
6b. Fls white; hypanthium about as broad as high; lf-blades larger; frt black. **R. viscosissimum** Pursh [sticky]. N counties near the Continental Divide, GA-RT.

7a. Fls 2 to 4 in a sessile cluster; hypanthium tubular . . . . (8)
7b. Fls several in a raceme, each fl on a slender pedicel; hypanthium saucer-or goblet-shaped . . . . (10)

8a. Petals and sepals narrow-oblong; anthers red; style glabrous, white; sepals not reflexed. **R. leptanthum** Gray [slender-fld]. Canyonsides in the lower valleys.
8b. Petals short and broad, much shorter than the usually reflexed sepals; anthers white; styles densely pilose toward their bases .
. . . . (9)

9a. Lvs glabrous; spines straight, slender; petals obovate, ochroleucous; filaments to twice as long as petals. **R. inerme** Rydberg, 60D. Common in canyons, middle altitudes. The specific epithet '*inerme*' is a misnomer.
9b. Lvs pilose to villous; spines stout, often somewhat curved; petals flabelliform, brownish-purple; filaments more than twice as long as petals. **R. divaricatum** Douglas. Only recently detected and distribution not well known, along rushing streams from Middle Park to RT.

10a. Lvs pubescent and glandular; spines 3 at a node but internodes usually unarmed; hypanthium saucer-shaped, red; low spreading bushes of dry spruce forests. **R. montigenum** McClatchie, 60E.

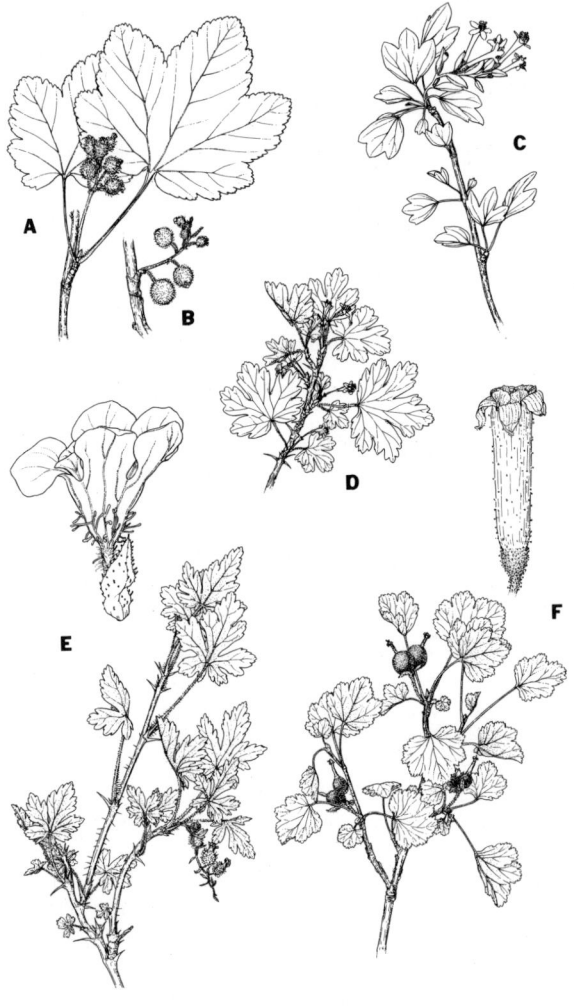

Figure 60. **A**, *Ribes wolfii*; **B**, *R. coloradense*; **C**, *R. aureum*; **D**, *R. inerme*; **E**, *R. montigenum*; **F**, *R. cereum*

Common in spruce-fir forests, along streams, subalpine.
10b. Lvs glabrous; spines single and internodes also spiny or bristly; hypanthium goblet-shaped, green; tall, little-branched shrubs of streamsides. **R. lacustre** (Persoon) Poiret [of lakes]. Wet meadows and willow bogs, montane and subalpine.

HALORAGACEAE
WATER-MILFOIL FAMILY (HAL)

A small family of mostly Australian species, some of which are shrubs. Aquatic species, although very atypical and unrepresentative of the family, are found across the Northern Hemisphere. The plants will be found submerged in lakes and ponds and may be recognized by their whorled filiform-pinnatisect leaves and interrupted terminal spikes of small greenish flowers. The flowering spikes resemble a cord knotted at intervals, similar to spikes of some of the submerged potamogetons, but in that genus the leaves are never divided.

MYRIOPHYLLUM L. 1753 [Gr., *myrios*, innumerable, + *phyllon*, leaf].
WATER MILFOIL
One sp, **M. sibiricum** Komarov, **62B**. Common in lakes and ponds at lower and middle altitudes (*M. exalbescens*).

HELLEBORACEAE—HELLEBORE FAMILY (HEL)

The Hellebore family encompasses all of the former members of the Ranunculaceae that have follicles rather than akenes. It is named for *Helleborus*, a genus of southern Europe and Southwest Asia. The meaning of the word is obscure, and was one used by Theophrastus. The type genus, *Helleborus*, is essentially Mediterranean. Its best known species, *Helleborus niger*, the Christmas Rose, is a common garden plant blooming in midwinter. Larkspurs and aconites include many species poisonous to livestock. Most species of aconite are Asiatic.

1a. Fls bilaterally symmetrical . . . . (2)
1b. Fls radially symmetrical . . . . (3)

2a. Uppermost sepal prolonged into a conspicuous spur. **Delphinium**, LARKSPUR
2b. Uppermost sepal forming a hood that arches over the fl. **Aconitum**, MONKSHOOD

3a. Lvs very large (over 10 dm), compound; carpel solitary, a red (rarely white) several-seeded berry. **Actaea**, BANEBERRY
3b. Lvs smaller, simple lobed or compound; carpels follicular, dry, dehiscent. . . . . (4)

4a. Petals spurred (rarely spurless in occasional mutants); lvs compound. **Aquilegia**, COLUMBINE
4b. Petals spurless; lvs never compound . . . . (5)

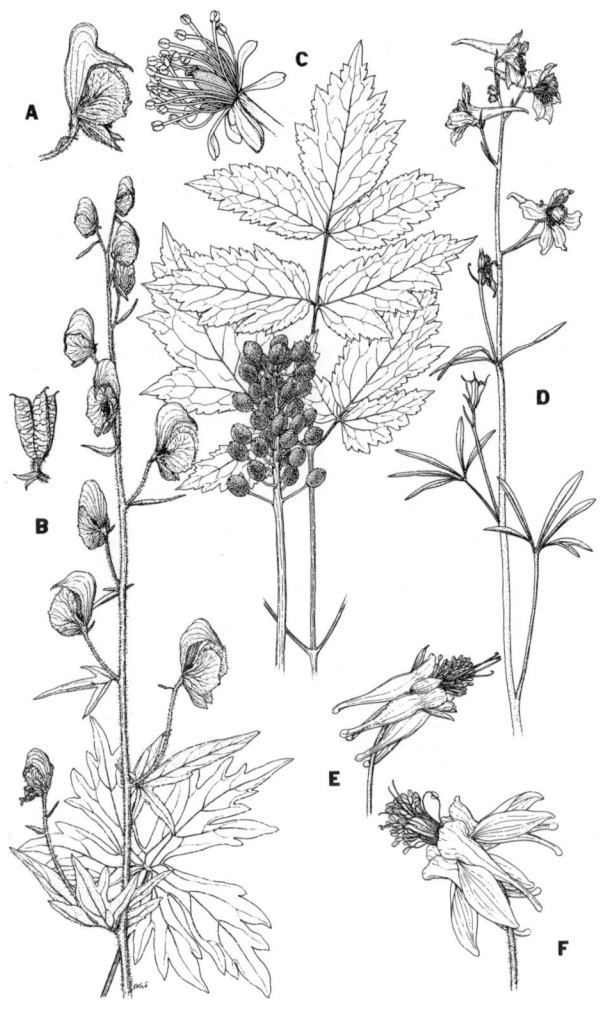

Figure 61. A, *Aconitum "bakeri"*; B, *A. columbianum*; C, *Actaea rubra*; D, *Delphinium nuttallianum*; E, *Aquilegia elegantula*; F, *A. barnebyi*

5a. Lvs chiefly basal, kidney-shaped or rounded cordate, often with a slight lobule-like auricle at the base; tepals white, bluish on the back. **Psychrophila**, MARSH-MARIGOLD
5b. Lvs basal and cauline, palmately-lobed; tepals off-white or cream-colored. **Trollius**, GLOBEFLOWER

ACONITUM L. 1753 [the classical Gr. and Lat. name]. MONKSHOOD
One sp, A. **columbianum** Nuttall, **61B**. Forest openings, montane and subalpine. Fls usually blue-purple. In its typical form the hood has a straight front line with the beak pointed down, but on Grand Mesa there are populations which have the front line curved and concave with the beak abruptly turned out. This has been called *A. bakeri* Greene, **61A**. The greenish-white forma *ochroleucum* St. John, occurs as a sporadic mutant.

ACTAEA L. 1753 [ancient name for the Elderberry]. BANEBERRY
One sp, A. **rubra** (Aiton) Willdenow ssp **arguta** (Nuttall) Hultén, **61C**. Deep moist shade of montane forests. The racemes of red 'berries' are conspicuous in late summer. The occasional white-frted plant is a genetic variation of the same sp and is not, as some assume, the White Baneberry, *A. alba*, of the eastern U. S. In the latter sp the pedicels are much thicker than in *A. rubra*.

AQUILEGIA L. 1753 [Lat., *aqua*, water, + *legere*, to collect, from the evident fluid at the base of the spur]. COLUMBINE
Note: spurless mutant individuals occur in populations of most of the spp. Also, since there are no genetic barriers between spp of *Aquilegia*, hybrids are to be found between any species that come in contact.
1a. Fls blue-and-white, at high altitudes tending to be mostly white . . . . (2)
1b. Fls red-and-yellow, sometimes almost all yellow. . . . . (3)

2a. Dwarf plants with strongly hooked spurs and small fls, the spurs and laminae of the petals together not more than 2 cm long. A. **saximontana** Rydberg, DWARF COLUMBINE. Rare, cliffs and rocky slopes, subalpine and alpine, near the Continental Divide (ST). No spurless form is known in this sp.
2b. Tall plants with essentially straight spurs and much larger fls. A. **coerulea** James, COLORADO COLUMBINE. Very common in open forests, meadows, aspen groves, and talus slopes, foothills to alpine. The Colorado State Flower. A spurless form is forma **daileyae** (Eastwood) Weber.

3a. Lfls and upper stems glandular-pubescent; fls pale, mostly yellow. A. **micrantha** Eastwood. Frequent on rock walls and alcoves of canyons in the W counties. At its eastern limits, this sp hybridizes with *A. elegantula*.
3b. Lfls and stems not glandular-pubescent; fls bicolored, red-and-yellow . . . . (4)

4a. Glaucous; sepals up to twice the length of the laminae. A. **bar-**

nebyi Munz, **61F**. Common on cliff walls, favoring shale outcrops, Glenwood Canyon to the Piceance Basin.
4b. Plants green; sepals not much longer than the laminae. **A. elegantula** Greene, **61E**. Common along mountain streams, spruce-fir forest. This hybridizes with *A. coerulea*, but because the F_1 generation is most like that sp, the backcrosses are with *A. coerulea*, thereby causing some variability in that sp and leaving *A. elegantula* pure.

DELPHINIUM L. 1753 [Lat., *delphinus*, dolphin, in allusion to the shape of the fl bud]. LARKSPUR
1a. Lvs mostly basal or near the base of the stem. . . . . (2)
1b. Lvs basal and cauline, the stem lvs well-developed . . . . (3)

2a. Roots fusiform, clustered; fls deep blue-purple; lvs with many deep narrow lobes. **D. nuttallianum** Pritzel, **61D**. Meadows, sagebrush, open woods (*D. nelsonii*).
2b. Roots elongate, fibrous; fls Wedgewood blue; lvs with few, usually broad rounded lobes. **D. scaposum** Greene. Arid gypsum or clay soils S of the Colorado R Valley.

3a. Fls narrow, the upper sepal and its spur forming nearly a straight line (even in old fls); sepals often widest above the middle, not over 12 mm long; stems usually glandular-pubescent; fls usually pale blue often variegated with white. **D. occidentale** (Watson) Watson. Aspen zone, N counties.
3b. Fls not especially narrow, the upper sepal flaring (at least in older fls); sepals widest at or below the middle; stems either without glandular hairs or if glandular then the sepals 14 mm long or more . . . . (4)

4a. Rachis of raceme and pedicels lustrous, glandular-hirsute; sepals dark purple, often acuminate; stems usually 5-20 from a single root; lf-segs broad. **D. barbeyi** Huth [for William Barbey]. Swampy spruce-fir forests.
4b. Rachis and pedicels non-glandular; sepals dull or bright blue, not acuminate; stems single or few from a root; lf segs narrow. **D. ramosum** Rydberg. Open sites, middle and high altitudes (incl. *D. alpestre*).

PSYCHROPHILA Berchtold & Presl 1823 [Gr., *psychros*, frigid, + *philein*, to love]. MARSH-MARIGOLD
   One sp, **P. leptosepala** (DeCandolle) Weber, **90E**. Wet ground, mt meadows and tundra, flowering right after thaw. This characteristic plant of snowmelt basins belongs to a genus of the mts of S South America and Australia-New Zealand and probably represents an ancient Tertiary element in the flora (*Caltha* of Colorado lit).

TROLLIUS L. 1753 [latinization of *Troll*, a globe, from *Trollblume*, the German common name]. GLOBE-FLOWER
   One sp, **T. albiflorus** (Gray) Rydberg [white-fld], **90D**. Seasonally wet ground around springs, streams and subalpine meadows (*T. laxus* var *albiflorus*). *T. laxus*, of New England, is extremely rare and con-

sidered to be endangered and has yellow-orange fls; phytogeographically, it is likely that our sp is more closely related to Asiatic ones.

HIPPURIDACEAE—MARE'S TAIL FAMILY (HPU)

This family consists of a single genus and species, occurring around the world in the Northern Hemisphere. When emergent, the stems with their whorled leaves stand stiffly out of the water. Submerged forms have very lax leaves that might cause one to mistake the plant for *Elodea*. Fls in *Hippuris* are extremely reduced and simplified. A single flower occurs in the axil of the leaf. The perianth is reduced to an inconspicuous rim around the top of the gynoecium. There is one large stamen. The ovary is inferior, unicarpellate, with a long slender style, and produces a single seed.

HIPPURIS L. 1753 [Gr., *hippo*, horse, + *oura*, tail]. MARE'S TAIL

One sp, **H. vulgaris** L., **62A**, **PL 48**. Common in shallow water of slow streams and ponds, montane and subalpine.

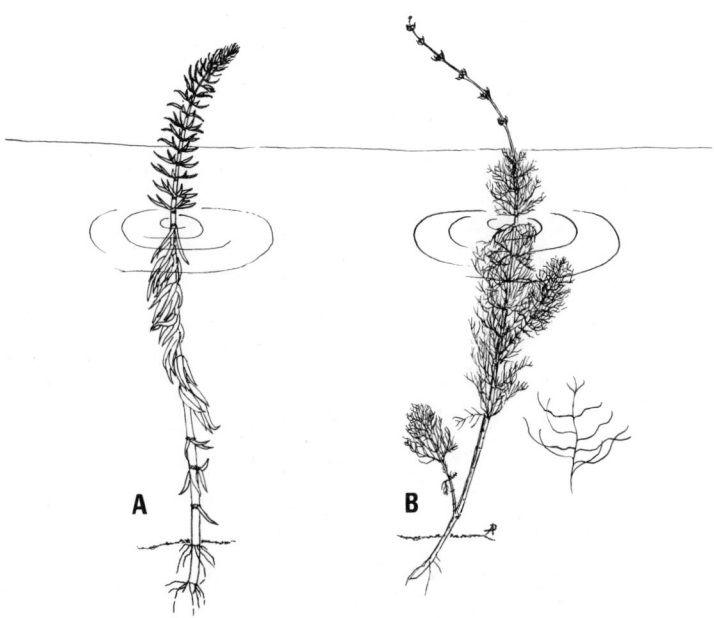

Figure 62. **A**, *Hippuris vulgaris*; **B**, *Myriophyllum sibiricum*

HYDRANGEACEAE—HYDRANGEA FAMILY (HDR)

This family contains shrubs with opposite, elliptic lvs, fragrant flowers with parts in fours, the petals white, ovary half-inferior, the fruits long-persistent. Some treatments still place this distinctive group in the Saxifragaceae. Our *Jamesia* is a 'living fossil' with an interesting distribution including the foothills of the Front Range, a few localities in Utah and Arizona, and the east base of the Sierra Nevada. Belle K. Stewart, working from the University Museum, discovered fossil leaf impressions in the volcanic ash formations in the Creede valley many years ago.

1a. Lvs ovate, regularly crenate, copiously soft hairy beneath. **Jamesia**, WAXFLOWER
1b. Lvs elliptical or lanceolate, glabrous or appressed-hairy. . . . . . (2)

2a. Outer bark reddish-brown, exfoliating to reveal a pale inner bark; lvs elliptic, 1-1.5 cm long; lvs strongly 3-nerved beneath, appressed-hairy, the hairs without swollen bases; petals entire, not clawed. **Philadelphus**, MOCK-ORANGE
2b. Outer bark gray or white, not exfoliating; lvs elliptic, not prominently nerved . . . . (3)

3a. Very low shrub, less than 1 m tall; lvs up to 1 cm long, appressed-hairy, the hairs with swollen bases; fls minute, less than 5 mm long. **Fendlerella**
3b. Tall lanky shrub; lvs up to 3 cm long, clustered at the nodes except on new growth, often curved; fls large, the petals broadly oval, ragged-toothed, narrowed to a long claw. **Fendlera**

FENDLERA Engelmann & Gray 1852 [for August Fendler]
One sp, **F. rupicola** Gray, **63B, PL 39**. Abundant on canyonsides in the Colorado Plateaus region.

FENDLERELLA Heller 1898 [dim. of *Fendlera*]
One sp, **F. utahensis** (Wats.) Heller, **63A**. Infrequent on sandstone outcrops and rimrock, MF, MN.

JAMESIA Torrey & Gray 1840 [for Edwin James, its discoverer]. WAXFLOWER
One sp, **J. americana** Torrey. Common in canyons of the E slope but known in our area only from a single site on the W side of Wolf Creek Pass. A 'living fossil', of which leaf impressions have been found in the Creede Oligocene formation.

PHILADELPHUS L. 1753 [said to be named for Ptolemy Philadelphus, King of Egypt, 283-247 B.C.]. MOCK-ORANGE
One sp, **P. microphyllus** Gray, **63C**. Canyonsides of the Colorado Plateau region. A small-fld relative of the widely cultivated sp.

Figure 63. A, *Fendlerella utahensis*, habit, fl, frt, lf detail; B, *Fendlera rupicola*, habit, frt; C, *Philadelphus microphyllus*, habit, frt

HYDROCHARITACEAE—FROGBIT FAMILY (HDC)

The floral biology of *Elodea*, our only genus, can only be described as bizarre. The plant is submerged. How does pollination take place? The staminate flowers, formed under water, break away and float to the surface, liberating the pollen on the surface film of water. The carpellate flowers are produced on long thread-like stalks that remain attached to the main stem but grow to reach the water surface. There the stigmas encounter the floating pollen grains which move to them by surface attraction.

ELODEA Michaux 1803 [Gr., *elodes*, marshy]. WATERWEED
   We have too few collections of this genus, but evidently the following three spp are present on the W Slope.
1a. Upper and middle lvs opposite. **E. longivaginata** St. John
1b. Upper and middle lvs in whorls of three . . . . (2)

2a. Upper and middle lvs mostly 2-3 mm wide, dark green. **E. canadensis** L.
2b. Upper and middle lvs up to 1.5 mm wide, pale green and limp. **E. nuttallii** (Planchon) St. John.

HYDROPHYLLACEAE—WATERLEAF FAMILY (HYD)

The hydrophylls are probably best recognized by their inflorescences, which are usually tightly coiled into a helix when young, gradually uncoiling as the flowers open. The stamens are usually exserted on long slender filaments. The family name derives from the succulent, watery stems and leaves of the genus *Hydrophyllum*, but many hydrophylls have rough-hairy foliage like the borages, a family that also has helicoid inflorescences but differs in having the fruit divided into four one-seeded nutlets.

1a. Lvs entire or very nearly so . . . . (2)
1b. Lvs coarsely toothed, lobed, or pinnatifid . . . . (6)

2a. Plants stemless, with elliptic succulent lvs from a perennial taproot; fls scapose, solitary on each pedicel. **Hesperochiron**
2b. Plants with distinct stems; fls. purplish. . . . . (3)

3a. Harshly hispid-hairy; lvs narrow, spatulate-linear. **Nama**
3b. Smooth or pubescent, succulent, not harshly hispid . . . . . . (4)

4a. Very delicate plant with an erect stem, lowest lvs largest . . . . . (5)
4b. Stout or coarsely succulent plants, erect and simple or with spreading-branched stems. **Phacelia**

5a. Lvs broadly ovate-elliptic, petiolate, obtuse. **Phacelia**
5b. Lvs linear, not distinctly petiolate, acute. **Nama**

6a. Fls solitary on axillary or terminal pedicels; annual; corolla not longer than the sepals . . . . (7)

6b. Fls in several- to many-flowered terminal or axillary clusters; annual or perennial; corollas usually exceeding the sepals. . . . . (8)

7a. Lvs with only two pairs of lateral lobes; calyx with small reflexed lobules between the sepals. **Nemophila**
7b. Lvs with 4 or more pairs of lateral lobes; calyx without reflexed lobules. **Ellisia**

8a. Fls in ± dichotomous cymes or ball-like clusters, not strongly helicoid sprays; lvs and stems with copious watery juice. **Hydrophyllum**, WATERLEAF
8b. Fls in elongate helicoid cymes with a main axis; lvs and stems often harshly pubescent, not watery. **Phacelia**

ELLISIA L. 1753 [for John Ellis, 1710?-1776, naturalist and correspondent of Linnaeus]

One sp, **E. nyctelea** L. [from *Nyctelius*, an epithet of Bacchus, who celebrated his mysteries at night; Linnaeus did not explain; perhaps he thought the plant was night-blooming?], **64D**. ADV, riparian sites and disturbed soils of gardens and cult ground.

HESPEROCHIRON Watson 1871 [Gr., *hesperos*, west, + *chiros*, hand, or Chiron, the Centaur; the name's meaning not explained]

One sp, **H. pumilus** (Douglas) Porter [dwarfed], **64E**. A very early-flowering plant of clay soils in sagebrush areas, its habit reminiscent of *Lewisia*. Known from only one old record from MN or DL.

HYDROPHYLLUM L. 1753 [Gr., *hydor*, water, + *phyllon*, leaf, alluding to the succulent, watery petioles]. WATERLEAF
1a. Fls blue, in a ball-like cluster, hardly exceeding the few obtusely-lobed lvs. **H. capitatum** Douglas, **64A**. Common in shaded places in open forests and oak woodlands.
1b. Fls ochroleucous, in a more open dichotomous cyme exceeding the lvs; lvs with sharply serrate lobes. **H. fendleri** (Gray) Heller, **64B**. Common in riparian woodlands.

NAMA L. 1753 [Gr., *nama*, a spring, alluding to habitat of some spp]

1a. Harshly hispid-hairy; lvs narrow, spatulate-linear . . . . (2)
1b. Smooth or pubescent, succulent, not harshly hispid-hairy. **N. dichotomum** (Ruiz & Pavon) Choisy. Rare late-summer-blooming annual on sandstone rimrock depressions catching moisture from summer rains, ME.

2a. Branched from the base and the branches spreading out on the ground. **Nama densum** Lemmon, **64F**. Local, in sandy soil, MF.
2b. Simple at the base and branched some distance above, the branches ascending, not wide-spreading. **N. hispidum** Gray. Peripheral, known only from SW MZ.

NEMOPHILA Nuttall 1822 [Gr., *nemos*, a glade, + *philein*, to love]

One sp, **N. breviflora** Gray, **64C**. Common in shaded woodlands, N counties, RT-MF.

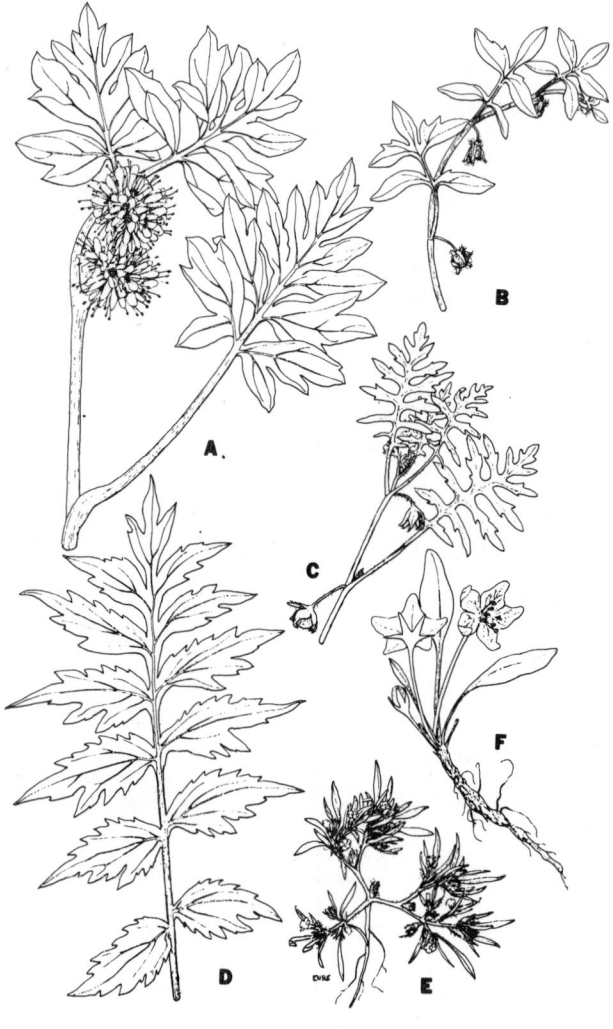

Figure 64. A, *Hydrophyllum capitatum*; B, *H. fendleri*; C, *Nemophila breviflora*; D, *Ellisia nyctelea*; E, *Hesperochiron pumilum*; F, *Nama densum*

Plate 33. ***Ephedra torreyana*** *(male)*   Weber
MORMON TEA

Plate 34. ***Ephedra torreyana*** *(female)*   Weber
MORMON TEA

Plate 35. ***Glycyrrhiza lepidota*** Weber
WILD LICORICE

Plate 36. ***Calochortus nuttallii*** Weber
MARIPOSA

Plate 37. *Oreocarya longiflora* Weber

Plate 38. *Androstephium breviflorum* Weber

Plate 39. *Fendlera rupicola*　　　　　　　　　　　Weber

Plate 40. *Koenigia islandica*　　　　　　　　　　　Weber

Plate 41. *Fraxinus anomala* Weber
Ash

Plate 42. *Acrolasia thompsonii* Weber

Plate 43. *Lygodesmia grandiflora* — Weber

Plate 44. *Lupinus bakeri* — Weber

Plate 45. *Caulanthus crassicaulis* — Weber

Plate 46. *Ptilagrostis* FEATHERGRASS — Weber

Plate 47. Anthills with *Oenothera caespitosa* — Weber
EVENING PRIMROSE

Plate 48. *Hippuris vulgaris* — Weber
MARE'S-TAIL

PHACELIA Jussieu 1789 [Gr., *phakelos*, a fascicle, alluding to the clusters of floral branches]
1a. Lvs entire or very nearly so; ephemeral annuals. . . . . (2)
1b. Lvs coarsely crenate-toothed, lobed, or pinnatifid. . . . . (4)

2a. Delicate plant with an erect stem, the lowest lvs largest. **P. incana** Brand [hoary], **65B**. Local early spring annual of desert hills, RB. Very variable in size depending on moisture.
2b. Coarsely succulent plants with spreading-branched stems; fl clusters short, not exceeding the lvs . . . . (3)

3a. Corolla less than 5 mm long; lvs gray-green, hirsute; seeds transversely corrugated. **P. submutica** Howell [bluntish], **PL 52**. Local on clay over hard-pans, GA, ME.
3b. Corolla up to 8 mm long; lvs bright green, very succulent, minutely pubescent; seeds not corrugated but finely pitted. **P. demissa** Gray [weak]. Local in early spring on Mancos clays.

4a. Stamens shorter than the narrowly tubular corolla; delicate annual. **P. ivesiana** Torrey [for Eli Ives, Yale pharmacy prof.], **65A**. Common in the shade of piñon and juniper, usually with *Cryptantha* spp.
4b. Stamens longer than the campanulate corolla; annual or perennial. . . . . (5)

5a. Lvs large, with entire margins, simple or with a few basal lobes or lfls; coarse harshly-hairy perennials. . . . . (6)
5b. Lvs toothed, regularly lobed or pinnatifid . . . . (7)

6a. Lvs green, not silvery-pubescent; fls white; plants usually with a single stem. **P. heterophylla** Pursh, SCORPION-WEED. Abundant in meadows at low altitudes. Common in open ground of the lower mountain areas.
6b. Lvs appressed silvery-hairy; fls distinctly purplish; stems several from clustered caudices. **P. hastata** Douglas, SCORPION-WEED. Replacing the last at higher altitudes (up to subalpine).

7a. Corolla white, small (4 mm or less), the lobes erose-dentate. **P. alba** Rydberg, **65G**. Sagebrush, Gunnison Basin.
7b. Corolla purplish, over 4 mm; lobes smooth-margined . . . . . . (8)

8a. Perennial; not glandular-hairy but appressed silvery-pubescent; infl condensed to form what appears to be a single spike, not conspicuously helicoid. **P. sericea** (Graham) Gray, PURPLE FRINGE, **65C**. Abundant on gravelly open slopes, subalpine. In the W counties a race with broad lf-segments (ssp **ciliosa** [Rydberg] Gillett) occurs at lower altitudes on the plateaus.
8b. Annual or biennial; usually glandular-hairy; infl of distinctly helicoid units. . . . . (9)

9a. Lvs shallowly lobed or only undulate, or if compound, the segs broad (over 5 mm) . . . . (10)
9b. Lvs pinnately or bipinnately compound, the segs narrow . . . . (12)

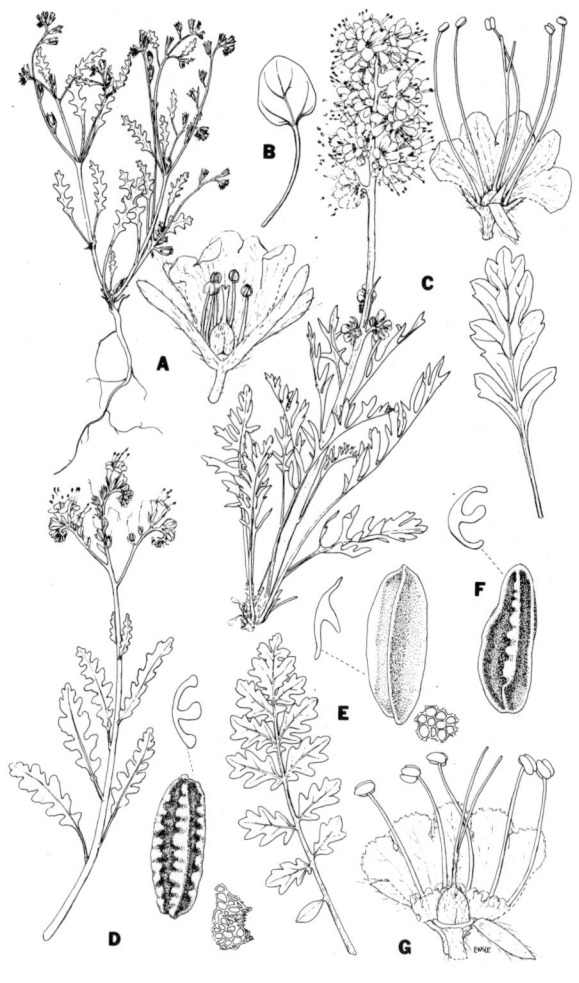

Figure 65. A, *Phacelia ivesiana*, habit, fl; B, *P. incana*, fl; C, *P. sericea*, habit, fl, lf of ssp *ciliosa*; D, *P. crenulata*, habit, seed/x-section, texture; E, *P. bakeri*, lf, seed/x-section; F, *P. integrifolia*, seed/x-section; G, *P. alba*, fl

10a. Plants with an elongate, relatively narrow infl of many short helicoid cymes crowded along the main axis. **P. constancei** Atwood [for Lincoln Constance, HYD specialist]. Peripheral, entering from eastern Utah, local on clay soils, SM.
10b. Plants with several spreading helicoid cymes . . . . (11)

11a. Seeds corrugated ventrally; corolla usually intensely colored. **P. crenulata** Torrey, **65D**. Common in adobe soils from ME southward (*P. corrugata*).
11b. Seeds lacking ventral corrugations; corolla pale. **P. integrifolia** Torrey, **65F**. Similar sites, known from SW MZ.

12a. Corolla distinctly bicolored, purple with yellow tube; lvs green and succulent, not very glandular, the lobes narrowed at the base. **P. splendens** Eastwood, PL. 22. Adobe hills of the Mancos formation, ME-MN.
12b. Corolla not bicolored, purple; lvs strongly glandular, shallowly to deeply pinnatifid, the lobes not narrowed at the base . . . . . (13)

13a. Seeds not excavated ventrally. **P. bakeri** (Brand) Macbride [for C. F. Baker], **65E**. Sagebrush valleys, OR, GN.
13b. Seeds excavated ventrally. **P. glandulosa** Nuttall. Steep shale-clay slopes, GF, RB.

HYPERICACEAE—ST. JOHNSWORT FAMILY (HYP)

Klamath Weed, *Hypericum perforatum*, a European species that is not a nuisance in its homeland, came to us with the westward movement and the livestock industry. Over a span of fifty years it cost Oregon and California millions of dollars in sheep poisoning losses. Two and one-third million acres of California land were infested, and in 1930 this plant was the cause of the worst financial losses on pasture and range lands in California. The plant contains chemicals that sensitize white animals to sunlight, and death usually results from starvation following blindness or refusal to eat.

In Colorado, Klamath Weed first appeared on Rocky Flats in Jefferson County, where it may have been introduced with straw during the building of the Moffat Tunnel route. For many years it dominated about 17,000 acres of the mesa but showed no signs of spreading. In the last decade, however, it has evidently selected a strain that is capable of doing well all over Colorado, and it has spread into the foothills to Estes Park and out onto the Arkansas Divide. Recently a stand was found at Glenwood Springs, so Klamath Weed is on its way to becoming a first-class pest in Colorado. At Rocky Flats the plant has been controlled, as elsewhere, by the introduction of a beetle, *Chrysolina quadrigemina*, for which *H. perforatum* is its sole food. This is a classic example of the value and possibilities of biological control of pests. While the species has not been eliminated, it is kept in check, at least, by this insect.

Hypericum species may be easily recognized by the translucent dots on the oppositely-arranged leaves, seen when held up to the light. In some species the yellow petals have black dots near the margins. The stamens tend to be in five clusters.

HYPERICUM L. 1753 [*Hypericon*, the ancient Gr. name]. ST. JOHNSWORT
1a. Lvs narrowly oblong; plants profusely branched; fls very numerous in a broad, flat-topped cluster. **H. perforatum** L., KLAMATH WEED. ADV, near Glenwood Springs.
1b. Lvs broadly elliptic; plants slender, sparingly branched; fls few, in axillary cymes; infl not flat-topped. **H. formosum** Humboldt, Bonpland & Kunth. Wet meadows and streamsides, upper montane and subalpine.

IRIDACEAE—IRIS FAMILY (IRI)

Irises need no introduction. Our wild iris species is so much like some of the cultivated types as to be instantly recognized. Interpretation of the floral parts is not as easy. The perianth consists of three outer hanging 'falls' and three inner erect or over-arching 'standards'. The three spreading flat structures that cover and hide the three stamens are the style branches. The folded-triangular grooved leaves of the equitant type are common to Iridaceae and some Juncaceae. Other well-known irids in cultivation are the spring-blooming *Crocus* and the late-summer *Gladiolus*.

1a. Fls more than 5 cm wide; falls spreading or reflexed; standards erect; frt a cylindrical capsule. **Iris**
1b. Fls less than 2 cm wide; all perianth segs petaloid and spreading; frt a round berry or capsule. **Sisyrinchium**, BLUE-EYED-GRASS

IRIS L. 1753 [Gr., the rainbow]
One sp, **I. missouriensis** Nuttall, WILD IRIS. Wet meadows in the mt parks and along broad streams.

SISYRINCHIUM L. 1753 [name used by Theophrastus for some Iris-like plant. BLUE-EYED-GRASS
1a. Length ratio of outer to inner bracts generally less than 1.8, the outer tapered evenly to an acute tip; outer tepals with a l:w ratio of 3 or less, broadly oblanceolate or elliptic-lanceolate, the apex rounded or slightly emarginate. **S. idahoense** Bicknell var **occidentale** (Bicknell) Henderson. Wet meadows, parks, GA-GN.
1b. Ratio of outer to inner bracts generally greater than 1.8, the outer often widened above the apex of the inner before tapering to an acuminate tip; outer tepals with a l:w ratio greater than 3, elliptic to elliptic-oblanceolate, apex rounded to retuse. **S. montanum** Greene. Grassy (not necessarily wet) meadows.

JUNCACEAE--RUSH FAMILY (JUN)

The rushes form a neat little group whose diversity of small technical characters should appeal to the biometrically inclined. Vegetatively resembling both grasses and sedges, they can always be recognized by their small brownish or greenish miniature lily flowers with all floral parts present. As in the sedges, some species display inflorescences on what seems to be the side of the stem, while the lowest bract stands erect and appears to continue the stem to the apex. Since this tendency occurs in several unrelated marsh plants (convergent evolution), one might speculate that this life form may present less resistance to wind than a terminal infl and thus prevent 'lodging' of the culms in areas of marshlands swept by strong winds. *Juncus torreyi* and *J. nodosus* often produce galls in which the floral parts are tremendously enlarged, creating a mass of telescoping sheaths. This deformity is caused by a Hemipteran insect, the Sedge Psyllid, *Livia maculipennis* Fitch.

1a. Plants glabrous; lf sheaths with the margins overlapping but not fused; ovary usually more or less 3-loculed; ovules numerous. **Juncus,** RUSH
1b. Plants with a few long weak hairs along the lf-blades or sheaths; lf sheaths with the margins fused; ovary with one locule; ovules three. **Luzula,** WOOD RUSH

JUNCUS L. 1753 [the classical name]. RUSH

1a. Annual; infl making up half the plant or more . . . . (2)
1b. Perennial, or if appearing annual; infl making up less than half the height of the plant. (4)

2a. [1] Plant minute, less than 1.5 cm high, scapose, fl solitary at the apex of the stem; tepals 1.5-2.0 mm long; stamens 3. **J. bryoides** Hermann. Rare or overlooked, flowering very early in spring, on seepy sandstone ledges in ponderosa pine zone, ME, MF. Easily mistaken for a moss.
2b. Plant at least 3 cm high, the fls usually lateral as well as terminal on the stems; tepals 2-7 mm long; stamens 6. . . . . (3)

3a. [2] Capsule oblong, 3.0-4.5 mm long; perianth 4-6 mm long. **J. bufonius** L. [of toads], **66F**. Muddy pond shores and roadside depressions.
3b. Capsule subglobose, 2-3 mm long; perianth 3-4 mm long. **J. bufonius** L. var **occidentalis** Hermann. Similar habitats, but rare.

4a. [1] Lowest lf of the infl erect, terete, and appearing to be a continuation of the stem; infl appearing lateral . . . . (5)
4b. Lowest lf of the infl divergent, not appearing to be a continuation of the stem, or if so, then the lf grooved along the inner side; infl appearing terminal . . . . (9)

5a. [4] Rhizomes present; seed with a short white 'tail' at each end
. . . . (6)
5b. Rhizomes absent; seed with a long tail at each end. . . . . (7)

6a. [5] Fl cluster more than half way up the stem. **J. arcticus** Willdenow ssp **ater** (Rydberg) Hultén, **66H**. Streams, lake shores and alkali flats. From a distance this sp forms a dark green zone, marking the stream course (*J. balticus*).
6b. Fl clusters within a few cm of the ground, the portion of stem above them many times as long as that below. **J. filiformis** L.

Figure 66. A-D, Seeds of *Juncus* spp; E, *J. saximontanus*; F, *J. bufonius*, habit, fls, seed; G, *J. confusus*, habit, seed; H, *J. arcticus*

Similar habitats, local but perhaps overlooked; especially common in Middle Park.

7a. [5] Upper lf sheaths bristle-tipped, the blade lacking; capsule blunt, depressed at the apex. **J. drummondii** Meyer. Very common tuft-forming alpine tundra plant.
7b. Upper lf-sheaths bearing blades. . . . . (8)

8a. [7] Capsule pointed at the apex. **J. parryi** Engelmann. Wet places, subalpine.
8b. Capsule broad and depressed at the apex. **J. hallii** Engelmann. Uncommon in wet places, subalpine.

9a. [4] Lvs septate inside (with papery cross-partitions visible when the lf is slit lengthwise); lvs hollow, terete or folded like the lvs of *Iris* . . . . (10)
9b. Lvs not septate; the blades flat or folded, never hollow or pulpy or folded V-shaped as in *Iris*. . . . . (21)

10a. [9] Infl consisting of a solitary capitate cluster of from 1 to 5 fls; lvs mostly less than 8 cm long. . . . . (11)
10b. Infl consisting of several clusters of more than 5 fls each; lvs over 8 cm long . . . . (13)

11a. [10] Infl with subtending bract longer than the fl cluster and standing erect, pushing the cluster to one side. **J. biglumis** L., **67B**. Infrequent, wet gravels and frost scars on the higher peaks. Bracts and perianth segs always dark.
11b. Infl terminal, without subtending bracts that are longer than the fls, the fl cluster not appearing pushed to one side. . . . . . . (12)

12a. [11] Bracts and perianth uniformly dark reddish brown. **J. triglumis** L., **67C**. Wet gravel and frost scars, upper subalpine and alpine tundra.
12b. Bracts pale, the perianth very pale or white. **J. albescens** (Lange) Fernald. Subalpine peat bogs.

13a. [10] Lf blades like those of *Iris* (thick, pulpy and folded V-shaped) . . . . (14)
13b. Lf blades terete (round in cross-section) or somewhat flattened . . . . (17)

14a. [13] Lf blades involute, mostly basal. **J. castaneus** Smith [chestnut]. Subalpine and alpine bogs and streams.
14b. Lf-blades equitant (like *Iris*) . . . . (15)

15a. [14] Stamens 3. **J. ensifolius** Wikström. Wet meadows and roadsides, RT, PT.
15b. Stamens 6 . . . . (16)

16a. [15] Heads hemispheric, dark purple-black; style exserted; seeds prominently tailed. **J. tracyi** Rydberg. Wet places, especially roadside ditches, subalpine and montane.

16b. Heads more nearly spherical, brown; styles not prominent; seeds not tailed. **J. saximontanus** Nelson, **66E**. Wet places from the lowlands through the montane.

17a. [13] Capsules subulate (very narrow and sharp pointed); fl clusters spherical . . . . (18)
17b. Capsules oblong with pointed tip, or abruptly narrowed to a beak from a rounded apex . . . . (19)

18a. [17] Lf-blade divergent from the stem; inner tepals shorter than the outer; plants usually very robust; fl clusters usually over 1 cm diam. **J. torreyi** Coville. Sloughs and ditches in the lower valleys.
18b. Lf-blade erect; inner tepals longer than the outer; plants usually slender; fl clusters usually less than 1 cm diam. **J. nodosus** L. [knotted, from the rhizomes, which are thickened at intervals]. Similar habitats, often growing with the last.

19a. [17] Head solitary, purplish-black, rarely more than one; fl head usually exceeded by its lowest bract. **J. mertensianus** Bongard [for F. C. Mertens], **67D**. Subalpine and alpine, swampy woodlands, bogs, pond shores and roadsides.
19b. Heads not solitary, nor purplish black, nor exceeded by the lowest bract; at least a few heads pedunculate. . . . . (20)

20a. [19] Fl clusters few (1 to 3), close together, dark, the tepals about as dark as the capsule; capsule abruptly mucronate from a rounded or flattened apex. **J. mertensianus** ssp **gracilis** (Engelmann) Hermann. Infrequent, subalpine (*J. badius*).
20b. Fl clusters numerous, on stiffly divergent peduncles, the light-colored bracts contrasting with the darker tepals and capsules. **J. alpino-articulatus** Chaix. Local, in travertine bogs, GN (*J. alpinus* of manuals).

21a. [9] Each individual fl subtended by a single bract; fls grouped in heads. **Juncus longistylis** Torrey, **67A**. Common in swamps and ponds from the lower valleys to subalpine.
21b. Each fl subtended by two small bracts; fls scattered individually along the branches (if the infl is condensed, the short branchlets are still visible . . . . (22)

22a. [21] Plants with long rhizomes; tepals with incurved tips, clasping the capsule; capsule globose-ovoid, distinctly longer than the tepals. **J. compressus** L., alkaline riverbanks and pond shores, lower valleys.
22b. Plants tufted, without rhizomes; sepals with straight or spreading tips, standing away from the capsule . . . . (23)

23a. [22] Seed with a long tail at each end. **J. vaseyi** Engelmann. Springy slopes and meadows, Grand Mesa.
23b. Seed merely apiculate, not tailed . . . . (24)

Figure 67. A, *Juncus longistylis*; B, *J. biglumis*; C, *J. triglumis*; D, *J. mertensianus*; E, *Luzula spicata*, habit, frt; F, *L. parviflora*

24a. [23] Lf-auricle thin-papery in texture; capsule completely 3-locular. **J. confusus** Coville, **66G**. Moist meadows.
24b. Lf auricle cartilaginous; capsule one-locular, with partial septa separating the carpels. **J. dudleyi** Wiegand [for the discoverer, William R. Dudley]. Wet places, mostly in the lower valleys. Some choose to make this a var of *J. tenuis*, which has papery auricles.

LUZULA De Candolle 1805 [from *Gramen Luzulae* or *Luxulae*, dim. of *lux*, light; a name given to some sp for its lvs shining with dew]. WOODRUSH

1a. Fls on slender pedicels in a loose, drooping, panicle; lvs glabrous except for a few long hairs near the throat of the lf-sheath; perianth about 2 mm long, shorter than or barely equalling the capsule. **L. parviflora** (Ehrhart) Desvaux [small-fld], **67F**. Moist or swampy montane and subalpine forests.
1b. Fls crowded, subsessile, in a few heads or spikes; lvs sparsely villous with long, loose hairs; perianth longer than the capsule
. . . . (2)

2a. Lvs 1-4 mm wide, with subulate (often involute) tips; bracts at bases of fls ciliate-fimbriate; spikes usually nodding; mostly alpine. **L. spicata** (L.) de Candolle, **67E**. Tundra and higher subalpine slopes.
2b. Lvs usually broader, flat, with blunt callous tips; bracts at base of fls entire or merely lacerate . . . . (3)

3a. Spikes short-cylindric, short-peduncled, the bracts and tepals pale brownish or straw-colored, capsules darker brown; lf blades less than 5 mm wide. **L. campestris** (L.) de Candolle. Subalpine streamsides (*L. multiflora*).
3b. Spikes capitate, sessile or a few long-peduncled, the tepals almost as dark as the deep brown capsules; lf blades 5-8 mm wide. **L. subcapitata** (Rydberg) Harrington. END, subalpine and alpine bogs. Extremely similar to *L. pseudosudetica* Kreczetowicz of the Caucasus.

JUNCAGINACEAE—ARROW-GRASS FAMILY (JCG)

This is a very small family with about 16 species worldwide of which all but one belong to *Triglochin*. The genus is marked by its grasslike habit and slender racemes of greenish, inconspicuous flowers. The carpels, although united, separate when mature into three or six mericarps, leaving a terete axis standing between them.

TRIGLOCHIN L. 1753 [Gr., *treis*, three, + *glochis*, point, alluding to the fruit of *T. palustris*. ARROW-GRASS
1a. Fertile carpels and stigmas 3; frts elongate, linear to somewhat clavate. 5-8 mm long; lf ligules bilobed. **T. palustris** L., **68A**. Mt meadows, not necessarily strongly alkaline. A very slender plant compared to the others.
1b. Fertile carpels and stigmas 6; fruits oblong or ovoid-prismatic, 4-6 mm long . . . . (2)

Figure 68. **A**, *Triglochin palustris*; **B**, *T. maritima*; **C**, *T. concinna*

2a. Ligules entire or only slightly bilobate, up to 5 mm long; old lf bases not shredding into many fibers; shoots closely aggregated on the rhizome. **T. maritima** L., **68B**. Alkaline flats and dry washes from the lower valleys to intermountain basins.

2b. Ligules bilobed or emarginate, up to 1 mm long; rhizome clothed with brown fibrous remains of lf bases; shoots well spaced along the rhizome. **T. concinna** Davy, **68C**. Less frequent, but sometimes growing with the last. Whether *T. concinna* or *T. debilis* is the correct name is moot. Both names were published in 1895.

LAMIACEAE/LABIATAE
MINT FAMILY (LAM/LAB)

What would be left of the good life if we did not have this family? For scent, flavor and "that little something extra" in our foods we depend on mints: Rosemary, Lavender, Sage, Spearmint, Peppermint, Basil, Thyme, Horehound, Marjoram, Oregano, Savory! *Citronella* was once the only reliable insect-repellant. *Coleus* plants used to be in every home, before we learned about African Violets. Probably only the Apiaceae come close to supplying as many important culinary needs. The usually aromatic foliage, square stems, and 2-lipped corollas are distinctive features of the family.

1a. Calyx with a prominent transverse ridge across the upper side, this always easily visible because the fls are never tightly clustered. **Scutellaria**, SKULLCAP
1b. Calyx without a transverse ridge, or fls too densely clustered to see this . . . . (2)

2a. [1] Lvs almost round, strongly impressed veiny, very densely white-woolly; fls white. **Marrubium**, HOREHOUND
2b. Not as above . . . . (3)

3a. [2] Fls grouped in heads or in essentially unbroken terminal spikes or racemes . . . . (4)
3b. Fls solitary or in clusters in the axils of lvs, not in unbroken terminal spikes or racemes . . . . (14)

4a. [3] Fls in hemispherical terminal clusters, subtended by an invol of broad lflike bracts . . . . (5)
4b. Fls in dense or often elongated spikes . . . . (7)

5a. [4] Fls large, with arching corolla much longer than the calyx; lvs ovate, toothed, broadest at the base. **Monarda**, HORSE MINT
5b. Fls small, the corolla not obviously arching and not much longer than the calyx . . . . (6)

6a. [5] Lvs elliptic, entire; bushy-branched plants of arid sagebrush sites. **Monardella**
6b. Lvs narrowly ovate, somewhat crenulate; simple-stemmed, somewhat delicate plants of mesic habitats. **Clinopodium**, WILD BASIL

7a. [4] Lvs entire or very shallowly crenate-serrate . . . . (8)

7b. Lvs regularly and distinctly serrate or crenate. . . . . (9)

8a. [7] Spikes or racemes very long and the fls remote; fls pale blue. **Salvia,** SAGE
8b. Spikes dense; fls deep purple. **Prunella,** HEAL-ALL

9a. [7] Fls white; lvs ovate, coarsely crenate; plant with the strong odor of catnip. **Nepeta,** CATNIP
9b. Fls some shade of purple; lvs and odor otherwise . . . . (10)

10a. [9] Spikes containing numerous lf-like, spine-tipped, serrate bracts; lvs with salient spine-tipped teeth. **Dracocephalum,** DRAGONHEAD
10b. Spikes without lflike, serrate bracts; lvs serrate or crenate, not spine-toothed. . . . . (11)

11a. [10] Lvs triangular-ovate, strongly petiolate from a broadly truncate or subcordate base. **Agastache,** GIANT HYSSOP
11b. Lvs narrowly ovate, the petiole short or not sharply delimited from the blade . . . . (12)

12a. [11] Bracts very broadly ovate, partly purplish, abruptly long-acuminate; stamens 2. **Salvia,** SAGE
12b. Bracts lanceolate or narrow-ovate, not purplish nor acuminate; stamens 4 . . . . (13)

13a. [12] Lvs cuneate at the base, with a very narrowly winged petiole; upper lip of the corolla deeply split down the middle, the stamens arching over the open space, the upper lip thus appearing to be part of a five-lobed lower lip; corolla not speckled. **Teucrium,** GERMANDER
13b. Lvs truncate or subcordate at the base; upper lip of corolla not split, covering the stamens. **Stachys,** HEDGE-NETTLE

14a. [3] Plants creeping on the ground, or weak and spreading if semi-erect . . . . (15)
14b. Plants erect. . . . . (16)

15a. [14] Plants creeping; fls few; lvs rounded or reniform. **Glecoma,** GROUND-IVY; GILL-OVER-THE-GROUND
15b. Plants sprawling to semi-erect; fls more numerous, in dense axillary clusters. **Lamium,** DEAD-NETTLE

16a. [14] Lvs linear or elliptic, less than 1 cm long, or usually less than 3 mm wide; plants with a very strong odor. **Hedeoma,** PENNYROYAL
16b. Lvs larger in both dimensions; plants without a very strong odor. . . . . (17)

17a. [16] Fls 1 cm or more long . . . . (18)
17b. Fls less than 0.5 cm long . . . . (19)

18a. [17] Lvs narrowly ovate-lanceolate, shallowly and inconspicuously

toothed; fls in very dense ball-like axillary clusters in the upper lf axils and terminal; pubescence, short, inconspicuous; stamens 2. **Monarda**, HORSE MINT
18b. Lvs broad triangular-ovate, coarsely toothed; fls in looser, few-fld clusters; pubescence of long multicellular vitreous hairs; stamens 4. **Galeopsis**, DEAD-NETTLE

19a. [17] Lvs with long salient teeth, or pinnately cleft; fls white; stamens hidden in the corolla-tube. **Lycopus**, WATER HOREHOUND; BUGLEWEED
19b. Lvs merely shallowly and regularly serrate; fls pink-purple; stamens exserted. **Mentha**, MINT

AGASTACHE Clayton 1762 [Gr., *agan*, many, + *stachys*, spike]. GIANT HYSSOP
1a. Calyx-teeth mostly 1.5-2.5 mm long, triangular, similar in texture to the calyx-tube; upper corolla lip straight to galeate-curved; stamens held under upper corolla lip, exserted only 1-2(3) mm beyond mouth of corolla; lvs less than 3 cm long, crenate with small, rounded teeth. **A. pallidiflora** (Heller) Rydberg. Rocky places in the middle altitudes, southernmost counties.
1b. Calyx teeth mostly 3.5-5.0 mm long, subulate, thinner and more paleaceous than calyx-tube; upper corolla lip spreading or reflexed; stamens spreading, exserted 4-7 mm beyond mouth of corolla; lvs over 3 cm long, with coarse, often sharp serrations. **A. urticifolia** (Bentham) Kuntze. Aspen zone.

CLINOPODIUM L. 1753 [Gr., *klino*, bend, + *pous*, foot]. WILD BASIL
One sp, **C. vulgare** L. ADV, known from one or two old collections from the Steamboat Springs area.

DRACOCEPHALUM L. 1753 [Gr., *draco*, dragon, + *kephalos*, head]. DRAGONHEAD.
One sp, **D. parviflorum** Nuttall, **69B**. Wide-ranging from adobe hills, where it is infrequent, up into mountain meadows and aspen groves and burned forested areas (*Moldavica*).

GALEOPSIS L. 1753 [Gr., *gale*, a weasel, from a fancied resemblance of the corolla to a weasel's head]. DEAD-NETTLE
One sp, **Galeopsis tetrahit** L. [pre-Linnaean name used by Lobel]. ADV weed of shady places in the Aspen and Green Mt Reservoir areas.

GLECOMA L. 1753 [Gr., *glechon*, name of a sp of *Mentha*]. GROUND-IVY; GILL-OVER-THE-GROUND
One sp, **G. hederacea** L. ADV creeping weed in lawns and orchards.

HEDEOMA Persoon 1896 [Gr., *hedys*, sweet, + *osme*, scent]. PENNYROYAL
One sp, **H. drummondii** Bentham. Rimrock, canyons and dry desert ridges, NW counties. A plant with extremely strong odor.

LAMIUM L. 1753 [old Lat. name for a nettle-like plant]. DEAD-NETTLE
1a. Upper stem lvs purple, usually distinctly petioled, not clasping the stem; plant densely pubescent. **L. purpureum** L. ADV. This and the next are not yet reported, but are probably present as weeds in orchards and gardens.
1b. Upper stem lvs green, usually clasping the stem, only the lower lvs with distinct petioles; plant sparingly pubescent. **L. amplexicaule** L., HENBIT. ADV.

LYCOPUS L. 1753 [Gr., *lycos*, wolf, + *pous*, foot]. WATER HOREHOUND; BUGLEWEED
1a. Blades of lower and middle stem lvs tapered to petioles; roots rarely tuberous; nutlets with smooth corky ridge. **L. americanus** Mühlenberg. Swamps and streambanks, lowlands.
1b. Blades of lower and middle lvs sessile; roots tuberous; nutlet without a corky ridge. **L. asper** Greene. Similar habitats.

MARRUBIUM L. 1753 [from Hebrew, *marrob*, a bitter juice]. HOREHOUND
One sp, **M. vulgare** L, **69A**. ADV coarse ruderal weed.

MENTHA L. 1753 [*Minthe*, a nymph fabled to have been changed by Proserpine into Mint]. MINT
One sp, **Mentha arvensis** L., FIELD MINT, **69D**. Along irrigation ditches, sloughs and streambanks in the lowlands.

MONARDA L. 1753 [for Nicolas Monardes, 16th Cent. botanical writer]. HORSE MINT; BEE BALM
1a. Fls large, rose-pink. **M. fistulosa** L., **69C**. Streamsides and meadows in the foothills.
1b. Fls small, pinkish to white. **M. pectinata** Nuttall. Local in the Delta area, and probably introd there. It is native on the eastern plains.

MONARDELLA Bentham 1834 [dim. of *Monarda*]
One sp, **M. odoratissima** Benth. Subalpine, San Juans.

NEPETA L. 1753 [believed to be derived from *Nepete*, an Etruscan city]. CATNIP
One sp, **N. cataria** L. ADV ruderal weed in gardens and shaded pastures on floodplains.

PRUNELLA L. 1753 [of uncertain derivation]. SELF-HEAL; HEAL-ALL
One sp, **P. vulgaris** L. ADV? Common in moist forests and aspen stands.

SALVIA L. 1753 [the old Lat. name]. SAGE

1a. Lvs oblong-cuneate; spikes or racemes long and the fls remote; fls pale blue. **S. reflexa** Hornemann. ADV weedy annual on floodplains, uncommon.

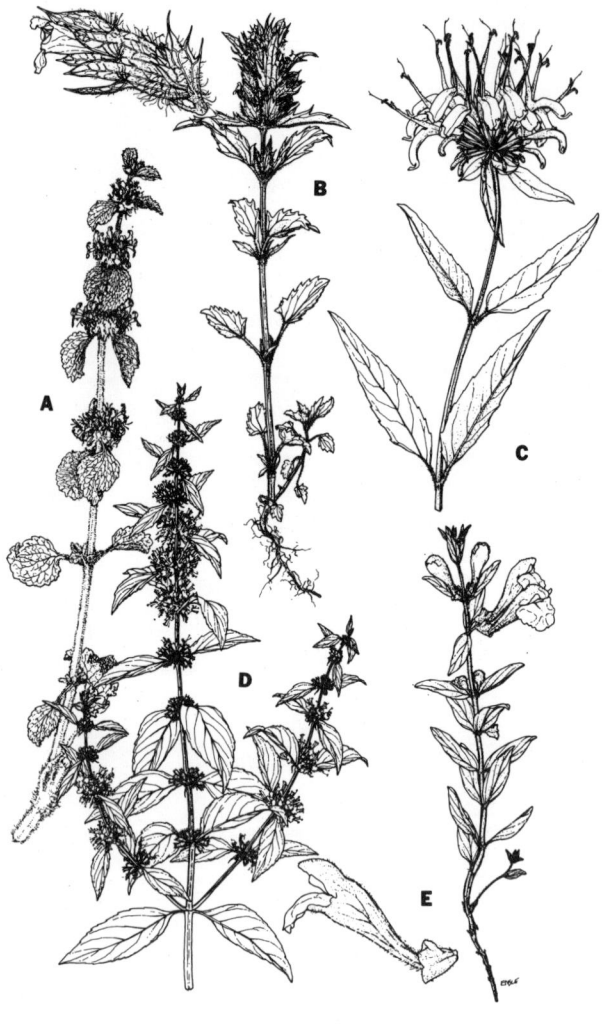

Figure 69, A, *Marrubium vulgare*; B, *Dracocephalum parviflorum*; C, *Monarda fistulosa*;; D, *Mentha arvensis*; E, *Scutellaria brittonii*

1b. Lvs cordate-ovate; spikes dense; fls purple. **S. sylvestris**, Woodland Sage. ADV locally established near Aspen.

SCUTELLARIA L. 1753 [Lat., *scutella*, a dish or little shield, alluding to the hump-backed calyx]. Skullcap
1a. Lvs almost as wide as long, very finely short-pubescent with curved glandular and nonglandular hairs; stems elongate, unbranched except at the base. **S. resinosa** Torrey. A strongly xerophytic species peripheral from its main Utah-Arizona range, piñon-pine zone, W MN.
1b. Lvs at least twice as long as wide; not strongly xerophytic . . . . (2)

2a. Corolla about 2 cm long; middle stem lvs entire, sessile; plants of dry gravelly forest openings. **S. brittonii** Porter (for Nathaniel Lord Britton, American botanist), 69E. Common in pine forests, middle altitudes.
2b. Corolla shorter; middle stem lvs crenate-serrate, petioled; plants of wet meadows. **S. galericulata** L. var **epilobiifolia** (Hamilton) Jordal. Wet places, RT.

STACHYS L. 1753 [Gr., *stachys*, spike]. Hedge-nettle
One sp, **Stachys palustris** L. ssp. **pilosa** (Nuttall) Epling. Frequent in wet meadows and ditches, lower elevations.

TEUCRIUM L. 1753 [for Teucer, king of Troy, acc. to Linnaeus]. Germander
One sp, **T. canadense** L. ssp. **occidentale** (Gray) McClintock & Epling. Frequent in wet meadows and ditches, lower altitudes.

LEMNACEAE—DUCKWEED FAMILY (LMN)

The Lemnaceae represent the ultimate reduction in form and structure in the flowering plants. The entire plant is reduced to a small flat floating or submerged disk, part of which represents a spathe such as one sees in Jack-in-the-Pulpit. The spathe forms a pocket between the upper and lower side of the disk, and new disks, as well as flowers, are produced within this pocket. In our single genus, *Lemna*, there is a single unbranched root. Flowering *Lemna* plants are quite rare collectors' items.

LEMNA L. 1753 [name of a water plant mentioned by Theophrastus]. Duckweed
1a. Fronds submerged, narrowed to a green stalk at the base; margin of fronds distally denticulate; 3 or more fronds cohering together, forming long and branched chains. **L. trisulca** L. [3-furrowed]. Common in slow meanders and ditches.
1b. Fronds floating on the surface, not narrowed at the base; when submerged only a few fronds cohering. . . . . (2)

2a. Fronds with 3-5 veins, broadly rounded . . . . (3)
2b. Fronds with 1 vein, 1-1.7 times as long as wide. **L. minuscula** Herter.

320 *Lemnaceae (LMN)*

3a. Fronds with several papules of ± equal size above the midline on the upper side; very often reddish beneath; forming small obovate to circular, rootless dark green to brown turions under unfavorable conditions, that sink to the bottom. **L. turionifera** Landolt. Common in still water, evidently the most abundant sp.
3b. Papules either lacking or the one above the node and at apex bigger than the ones between; never red beneath; fronds rarely forming turions; if turion-like fronds are formed they have short roots and are slowly reproducing daughter fronds. **L. minor** L.

LENTIBULARIACEAE—BLADDERWORT FAMILY (LNT)

A small family of mostly aquatic, often carnivorous, plants. The bladderworts have flowers resembling the spurred ones of Butter-and-eggs and the submerged, finely divided leaves have some of the leaf-segments inflated to form a sac, open at one end, that acts as a trap for small aquatic animals such as *Paramecium*.

UTRICULARIA L. 1753 [Lat., *utriculus*, little bladder]. BLADDERWORT
Note: The genus is poorly collected in Colorado, and most specimens lack fls, which may be needed for identification. Collectors should note the flower size and shape in the field, and be sure to collect some stems that are not slimy and encrusted with diatoms.
1a. Lf margin and winter buds setose (minute hyaline teeth near the lobe tips, the lobe tips themselves seta-like, hyaline). . . . . . . (2)

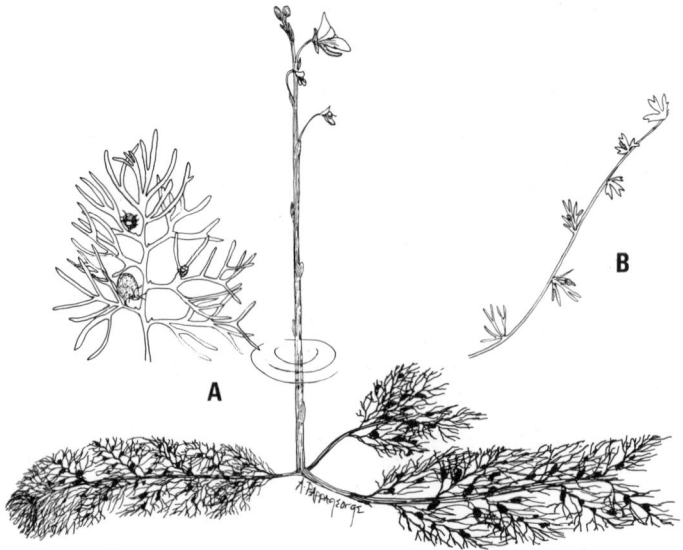

Figure 70. A, *Utricularia vulgaris*; B, *U. minor*

1b. Lf margins and winter buds smooth, not at all setose; plants with very small lvs, the stem and lvs rarely up to 1 cm wide. **U. minor** L., **70B**. Plants are differentiated into aquatic stolons with lvs and subterranean stolons with fewer lvs and more bladders. Until now only known from subalpine ponds on the E slope, but to be expected.

2a. Lvs pinnately divided, with a main rachis and more than 20 terete ultimate segs, the segs usually well over 3 mm long; corolla 10-12 mm broad, the spur conspicuous, 10 mm long, hook-like, slightly shorter than the lower lip. **U. vulgaris** L., GREAT BLADDERWORT, **70A**. Common in ponds in the montane and subalpine.

2b. Lvs dichotomously divided, with fewer than 20 flat ultimate segs, usually without bladders, these usually on lfless stolons; spur pyramidal, 3.0-5.5 mm long, positioned at a right angle to the lower lip. **U. ochroleuca** Hartman. Until now only known from the upper Arkansas drainage and South Park, but to be expected.

LILIACEAE—LILY FAMILY (LIL)

(See also Alliaceae, Asparagaceae, Agavaceae,
Convallariaceae, Calochortaceae, Melanthiaceae,
Trilliaceae, Uvulariaceae)

The lily flower is the model of the monocots, perfect in its symmetry, with the parts all alternating in threes. It probably has received more study from beginning botany students than any other single flower and is a good place to learn the basic structure. Unfortunately, the superficial similarity of the flowers in a number of distantly-related families tended to result in their placement in this family. Detailed study by Dahlgren & Clifford (1982, 1985) shows that the traditional Liliaceae must be divided into two orders and over 20 families, of which our flora contains several.

1a. Lvs appearing basal, the cauline ones, when opposite, much reduced; lvs narrowly linear or grasslike, or, if broader, then definitely basal . . . . (2)
1b. Lvs arising at nodes on the main stem, not reduced . . . . (4)

2a. Lvs elliptic, not grasslike; fls yellow, with recurved tepals. **Erythronium**, AVALANCHE LILY
2b. Lvs linear, grasslike; fls white; tepals erect or at most spreading. . . . . (3)

3a. Tepals united to form a long tube, the base buried among the basal lvs; lowland plants of early spring. **Leucocrinum**, SAND LILY
3b. Tepals separate; stems bearing a few reduced lvs; plants of alpine tundra. **Lloydia**, ALP LILY

4a. Fls 1-2 cm long, nodding, yellow-orange or purple-brown; lvs

322   Liliaceae (LIL)

linear, alternate or somewhat whorled. **Fritillaria**, FRITILLARY
4b. Tepals over 5 cm long, erect or spreading, bright red-orange, spotted; lvs whorled. **Lilium**, LILY

ERYTHRONIUM L. 1753 [Gr., *erythro*, red, alluding to the flower color in some spp]. AVALANCHE LILY

One sp, **E. grandiflorum** Pursh. Abundant in early spring close to melting snowbanks, especially in aspen. Normally the anthers are yellow, but in some populations red-anthered plants are common.

FRITILLARIA L. 1753 [Lat., *fritillus*, dice-box, because of the shape of the capsule]. FRITILLARY
1a. Fls yellow or orange, fading red to purple. **F. pudica** (Pursh) Sprengel, YELLOW-BELLS, **71C**, **PL 3**. A sp of the interior Pacific NW, known in Colorado only from MF.
1b. Fls purplish-brown, speckle. **F. atropurpurea** Nuttall, **71D**. Infrequent, rarely occurring more than a few plants in a stand, in aspen groves and montane sagebrush meadows. The cubical capsules of these spp are very distinctive.

LEUCOCRINUM Nuttall 1837 [Gr., *leucos*, white, + *krinon*, lily]. SAND LILY

One sp, **L. montanum** Nuttall. A very common plant of grasslands on the eastern plains, blooming in very early spring, known on the W slope only from AA. *Leucocrinum* is out of place in the Liliaceae and has been placed by R. M.T. Dahlgren *et al.* in The Funkiaceae or the Amaryllidaceae, with the further suggestion that its relationships may really be with the Hemerocallidaceae.

LILIUM L. 1753 [Lat. form of *leirion*, the classical Gr. name]. LILY

One sp., **L. philadelphicum** L., WOOD LILY. Rare or in small isolated stands, aspen groves, very vulnerable to collecting, AA, LP.

LLOYDIA Reichenbach 1830 [for the discoverer, Edward Lloyd, 1660-1709, curator of the Museum of Oxford University]. ALP LILY

One sp, **L. serotina** Salisbury. Perennial from short underground rhizomes, although the base of plant parts usually collected resembles a slender bulb. Common on the alpine tundra. A remarkable sp, scattered over the high mountains of the Northern Hemisphere, but very rare in the Arctic, where one might expect it.

LIMNANTHACEAE—MEADOW-FOAM FAMILY (LIM)

A very small family of two genera, exclusively western North American. *Limnanthes*, with about a dozen species, mostly Californian, contains wet meadow plants with often large white or yellow flowers. One species, *L. douglasii*, has yellow petals with white tips and has been called the Poached-egg Flower.

FLOERKEA Willdenow [for G. H. Floerke, 18th Cent. German lichenologist]. FALSE MERMAID

One sp, **F. proserpinacoides** Willdenow [for Proserpine, wife of Pluto], a delicate inconspicuous plant of wet montane meadows. The

Figure 71. A, *Disporum trachycarpum*; B, *Streptopus fassettii*; C, *Fritillaria pudica*; D, *F. atropurpurea*

lvs are alternate, pinnately divided into 3-5 oblong or linear lfls. Fl parts are in three's, the sepals about 2-3 mm long and the petals white, only half as long. There are six minute stamens. The gynoecium consists of about 3 carpels, apparently separate but sharing a common style from the gynobase; thus they are schizocarps as in *Geranium*. The ripe segments are one-seeded tuberculate nutlets. A very strange little plant in an equally strange family!

LIMONIACEAE—THRIFT FAMILY (LMO)

This small family contains several genera familiar in cultivation: the Sea Lavender, *Limonium*, and Statice, *Armeria*. Most species occur along seacoasts and on saline desert-steppes. In our genus, *Armeria*, the plants are perennial from tufts of linear basal leaves. The inflorescence is a ball of pale purple flowers subtended by an involucre of papery bracts. Its structure is peculiar and complicated. The outermost bracts of the head are prolonged downward and form a brown sheath around the top of the stem. The conspicuous part of the flower is the calyx; this is tubular and hairy, with 5 lobes and pleats, each lobe with a stout red vein. The petals are short, oblong, united into a tube, and cucullate at the apex, with the stamens attached on and in front of the cucullate apex. The filaments are dilated, and the two-locular anthers curve in over the five styles of the gynoecium; the ovary is superior. Without careful dissection none of this detail is to be made out in a head of what most will see as simply a pink ball of 'paper flowers'.

ARMERIA Willdenow 1809 [name said to be of Celtic origin]. STATICE; THRIFT

One sp, **A. scabra** Pallas ssp **sibirica** (Turczaninow) Hylander, **PL 59**. Very rare, found in America only in the vicinity of Hoosier Pass. Otherwise it occurs in Mongolia. It grows on wet solifluction lobes or even on relatively dry tundra but it is so extremely restricted in range that it should never be collected unless to document a new locality.

LINACEAE—FLAX FAMILY (LIN)

The word 'linen' comes from *Linum*, Flax, cultivated from ancient times as a source of fiber which is obtained by the process of retting (curing the stems in water). *Linum* is also the source of Linseed Oil, a drying oil of a thousand uses. The seeds of flax are used medicinally. Flax blossoms open early in the morning and usually fall by midday. They come in yellow, copper, and one of the truest blues found in nature. Critical differences in the union of the styles, along with different chromosome base numbers, indicate that the genus *Linum* is heterogeneous and that several segregate genera, some proposed over a century ago, are justified.

1a. Fls blue . . . . (2)
1b. Fls yellow or coppery . . . . (3)

2a. Perennial; stigma capitate. **Adenolinum**, WILD BLUE FLAX

2b. Annual; stigma considerably longer than wide. **Linum**, CULTIVATED FLAX

3a. Perennial; fruit separating into ten 1-seeded segments; styles separate. **"Cathartolinum"**
3b. Annual; styles united nearly to the summit; sepals glandular-toothed. **Mesynium**, YELLOW FLAX

ADENOLINUM Reichenbach 1837 [Gr., *aden*, gland, + *Linum*]. WILD BLUE FLAX

One sp, **A. lewisii** (Pursh) Löve & Löve. Plains to upper montane. Petals blue, falling in late morning (*Linum lewisii*).

"CATHARTOLINUM". PERENNIAL YELLOW FLAX

One sp, **C. kingii** (Watson) Small. Infrequent or rare, thus far known from shale slopes in RB. J. K. Small erred in placing this sp in the European genus *Cathartolinum*, but at present there is no other genus name available for the group to which our sp belongs.

LINUM L. 1753 [classical name of flax, hence, linen]. CULTIVATED FLAX

One sp, **L. usitatissimum** L. [most utilized], ADV. Not yet found on the W slope, but to be expected as a volunteer.

MESYNIUM Rafinesque 1837 [Gr., *meso*, middle, + *syn*, united, alluding to the united styles]. YELLOW FLAX

1a. Plants grayish-puberulent throughout. **M. puberulum** (Engelmann) Weber. Adobe soils in the valleys. The fls of this sp are more copper-colored than yellow.
1b. Plants glabrous or essentially so . . . . (2)

2a. Sepals lanceolate to narrowly ovate; lvs quite evident; plant not broom-like, few-branched at the base and in the infl. **M. australe** (Heller) Weber. Dry steppe-desert sites, SW counties. This replaces the E-slope *M. rigidum* on the W slope. It has oblanceolate petals less than 10 mm long, anthers less than 1 mm long (in *M. rigidum* the petals are obovate, 10 mm long or more, anthers more than 1 mm long).
2b. Sepals linear-lanceolate, attenuate; lvs small, the lower tending to be hidden among the branches; plant broom-like, bushy, with long slender, stiffly spreading-ascending few-fld branches. **M. aristatum** (Engelmann) Weber. Known from one collection, MZ.

LOASACEAE—LOASA FAMILY (LOA)

The sandpaper surface of the leaves of Loasaceae is caused by some of the strangest plant hairs known. These multicellular hairs are 'pagodaeform', *i.e.*, broad-based, shaped like a pagoda, each cell capped by a ring of stiff, curved hooks, which, unlike the corners of pagoda roofs, curve down, not up. There is hardly an article of clothing that will not carry away the leaves or fruits. The flowers of the larger species are inconspicuous until they open wide at eventide, like the flowers of the Night-blooming Cereus, which they resemble.

Our plants traditionally have been treated in the genus *Mentzelia*.

1a. Annual; petals 5, only 2-5 mm long; capsule linear-cylindric, widest at the top, less than 5 mm diam; placentae without horizontal lamellae between the seeds; seeds prismatic, irregularly angular. **Acrolasia**
1b. Biennial or perennial; petals more than 5, usually over 1 cm long; capsule broadly cylindric, over 5 mm diam; placentae with horizontal lamellae; seeds flat, often winged. **Nuttallia**

ACROLASIA K. B. Presl 1831 [Gr., *akron*, summit, + *lasios*, hairy, the allusion unclear]
1a. Seeds prismatic, truncate at the ends, grooved along three angles, the surface appearing smooth under low magnification. **A. dispersa** (Watson) Davidson [scattered]. Frequent on dry slopes, but usually not in the hot desert.
1b. Seeds cuboidal, lacking grooves on the angles, the surface generally appearing papillose under low magnification. . . . . (2)

2a. Bracteoles lobed. **A. albicaulis** (Douglas) Rydberg [white-stemmed], **72B**. Common in early spring at low altitudes including desert flats.
2b. Bracteoles entire. . . . . (3)

3a. Basal rosette present; lvs usually narrowly lobed and plant slender. **A. albicaulis** Douglas (see 2a)
3b. Basal rosette absent; lvs all entire, very shiny as if lacquered; plant short and stout. **A. thompsonii** (Glad) Weber [for Henry J. Thompson, monographer], **72A**, **PL 42**. Heavy clay soils, Colorado, Gunnison and San Juan R valleys, abundant but flowering only in very early spring.

NUTTALLIA Rafinesque 1817 [for Thomas Nuttall, British-American botanist and western explorer, 1786-1859]. BLAZING-STAR
1a. Petals 15-30 mm long, or if smaller, white or pale yellow; stems stout, simple, with a rosette of many large basal leaves at flowering time . . . . (2)
1b. Petals up to 10 mm long, or if larger, golden yellow. . . . . . . (3)

2a. Petals less than 20 mm long, white or pale yellow, sometimes with an apricot tint at the apex. **N. rusbyi** (Wooton) Rydberg. Canyons and inermontane basins from the Colorado R southward at middle altitudes.
2b. Petals 30 mm long or more, pale yellow. **N. laevicaulis** (Douglas) Greene. Barely entering Colorado along the N border near Slater, MF.

3a. Lvs entire, oblong-spatulate, rounded at the apex; stems very tortuous, in clumps from deep-seated rhizomes. **N. argillosa** (Darlington) Weber. Local on steep shale slopes, Parachute Creek drainage.
3b. Lvs variously toothed or pinnatisect . . . . (4)

Figure 72. A, *Acrolasia thompsonii*; B, *A. albicaulis*, habit, petal upper right; C, *Nuttallia multiflora*, petal-stamen transitions above

4a. Petals pubescent on outer surface . . . . (5)
4b. Petals glabrous . . . . (6)

5a. Petals 10; stamens with narrow filaments; lvs deeply pinnatifid. **N. cronquistii** (Thompson & Prigge) Weber [for Arthur Cronquist, contemporary floristic botanist].
5b. Petals 5; stamens petaloid (staminodia). **N. marginata** Osterhout [with margined seeds]. Adobe hills, Colorado and Gunnison R valleys.

6a. Lvs broad, shallowly toothed, not pinnatifid; plants stout, sparsely branched. **N. pterosperma** (Eastwood) Greene. Adobe hills, Colorado and Gunnison R valleys.
6b. Lvs narrow, deeply pinnatisect; plants slender, much-branched . . . . (7)

7a. Petals appearing numerous (grading into staminodia), 16-18 mm long. . . . . (8)
7b. Petals 5 (or apparently 10), 9-10 mm long, 6-9 mm wide; next inner whorl consisting of staminodia. . . . . (9)

8a. Lvs shallowly pinnatifid with relatively broad lobes. **L. multiflora** (Nuttall) Greene, **72C**. Scattered in W tier of counties. This and the following are found on clay and shale slopes. The key is tentative because several undescribed spp still are being studied by the monographer and there is no recent treatment.
8b. Lvs deeply pinnatifid with very narrow lobes. **N. laciniata** Wooton & Standley.

9a. Petals and staminodia broad, 6-9 mm wide and 9-10 mm long. **N. multicaulis** Osterhout, **PL 64**.
9b. Petals and staminodia shorter and narrow. **N. humilis** (Gray) Rydberg. Four Corners area.

LYTHRACEAE—LOOSESTRIFE FAMILY (LYT)

A family with an ambiguous common name, because loosestrifes also occur in the Primulaceae. Three genera and only three species occur on the Western Slope, all of them wetland species. Two exotic genera are worth mentioning. *Lagerstroemia indica*, the Crepe-myrtle, is a striking cultivar of the Gulf Coast and Southern California, a small tree with pink, yellow or white fringed and puckered petals with narrow claws; and *Lawsonia indica*, the Henna, was called by Mohammed "chief of the flowers of this world and the next." However, no one has returned to report the existence of this remarkable plant in the next world, and we do not know whether hair dye or nail coloring is useful there. *Lawsonia* was named for a surveyor-general of North Carolina who was burned by the Indians in 1712.

1a. Tall (often over 1 m) plants with racemes of conspicuous pink-purple fls; hypanthium elongated, cylindrical or tubular. **Lythrum**, PURPLE LOOSESTRIFE
1b. Low (less than 0.5 m) plants with inconspicuous axillary fls and

stiffly spreading branches; hypanthium short, hemispheric or
globose. . . . . (2)

2a. Fls two or more in the leaf axils; capsules bursting irregularly.
Ammannia
2b. Fls solitary in the leaf axils; capsule septicidally dehiscent.
Rotala, TOOTHCUP

AMMANNIA L. 1753 [for Paul Ammann, German botanist, 1634-1691]
One sp, **A. robusta** Heer & Regel. ADV in low marshy areas of floodplains in the large river valleys.

LYTHRUM L. 1753 [Gr., *lytron*, a name used by Dioscorides for our sp]. PURPLE LOOSESTRIFE
One sp, **L. salicaria** L. ADV, escaped from old gardens, along irrigation ditches in the valleys.

ROTALA L. 1753 [name an incorrect dim. of Lat., *rota*, a wheel, from the whorled lvs of the original sp]. TOOTHCUP
One sp, **R. ramosior** (L.) Koehne. This occurs with, closely resembles, and has been mistaken for *Ammania* on the E slope. Although it has not yet been collected in our area there is good reason to expect it, since *Rotala* occurs throughout the other far western states.

MALVACEAE—MALLOW FAMILY (MLV)

Everyone knows hollyhocks. Most old folks remember making dolls with long dresses out of the fls, smaller copies of the hollyhock. The main distinguishing feature of mallow flowers is the column of united stamen filaments forming a sheath around the gynoecium and standing in the midst of the flower like a fountain spraying out hundreds of colored droplets—the anthers. Also, the leaves and stems are usually clothed with stellately-branched hairs. Although some species have a capsular fruit, most have a gynoecium resembling a wheel of cheese, with the carpels sloughing away at maturity as one-seeded disks (mericarps). The confection, marshmallow, used to be based on the mucilaginous contents of the root of the Marsh Mallow, *Althaea officinalis*, which grows in marshes of western Europe and New England. Now there are synthetic sources. One of the important crops of man, cotton (*Gossypium*), is a mallow, as are the okra or gumbo, *Hibiscus esculentus*, and an ornamental shrub, Rose-of-Sharon, *H. syriacus*.

1a. Lvs very shallowly lobed, almost circular in outline, crenate; corolla pale pink or white. **Malva**, MALLOW; CHEESEWEED
1b. Lvs not as above . . . . (2)

2a. Low spreading annual; frt a capsule; calyx papery, very strongly veined, enclosing the capsule; corolla bicolored, greenish-yellow with a purple eye; lvs palmately divided. **Hibiscus**
2b. Perennial or tall erect annual; fruit schizocarpous; lvs not palmately divided although sometimes deeply lobed . . . . (3)

3a. Style branches not capitate, the stigmatic surface along the length of the style; lvs with rounded lobes, some divided more than half-way, often the lower merely deeply crenate. **Sidalcea**, CHECKER MALLOW
3b. Style branches broadened above to a capitate or truncate stigmatic surface. . . . . (4)

4a. Lvs cordate, not lobed; fls yellow-orange; carpels with long divergent awns at the apices; tall weedy annual. **Abutilon**, VELVETLEAF
4b. Lvs not cordate, usually somewhat lobed . . . . (5)

5a. Lvs maple-like, with about 5 main lobes, acute and with coarse teeth; fls large, white or pale pink; forest plant. **Iliamna**, WILD HOLLYHOCK
5b. Lvs shallowly or deeply lobed, not maple-like; fls orange; plant of open land. **Sphaeralcea**, GLOBE MALLOW

ABUTILON Miller 1754 [name, *Aubutilum*, given by Avicenna (Ibn Sina), Persian "Prince of Physicians", 980-1037]. VELVETLEAF
One sp, **A. theophrasti** Medikus, INDIAN MALLOW. Infrequent ADV ruderal weed in the Colorado R Valley.

HIBISCUS L. 1753 [ancient name for some large mallow]
One sp, **H. trionum** L., FLOWER-OF-AN-HOUR. frequent ADV weed in tilled land in the valleys.

ILIAMNA Greene 1906 [name not explained, but probably not of Greek origin as usually supposed. In Alaska there are a Mount Iliaminsk and a Lake Iliamna, possibly named by Russian explorers. Perhaps Greene saw this name and found it pretty, like the genus, but kept his readers guessing. Another suggested explanation from Paul Fryxell, MLV specialist, is Gr., *ilyos*, mud, + Lat., *amnis*, river, but Greene would never stoop to mixing two classical languages!]. WILD HOLLYHOCK
1a. Sepals narrowly lanceolate, long-acuminate; pedicels slender, 2-3 cm long; seeds glabrous. **I. crandallii** (Rydberg) Wiggins. END, vicinity of Steamboat Springs.
1b. Sepals broadly triangular-ovate, obtuse or acute; pedicels stout, less than 2 cm long; seeds sparsely puberulent with very short simple or stellate hairs; plants simple or sparingly branched.(2)

2a. Bracts of involucel linear, about half as long as the calyx-lobes; calyx 5-8 mm high at anthesis. **I. rivularis** (Douglas) Greene, 73A. Infrequent along shaded mt streamsides, generally distributed in the mountains.
2b. Bracts of involucel lanceolate, 2/3 as long as the calyx; calyx 8-15 mm high at anthesis. **I. grandiflora** (Rydberg) Wiggins. Mountains southwest of Colorado R drainage. There seems to be doubt about the distinctness of these species, but they are relatively poorly collected. Field observations are needed.

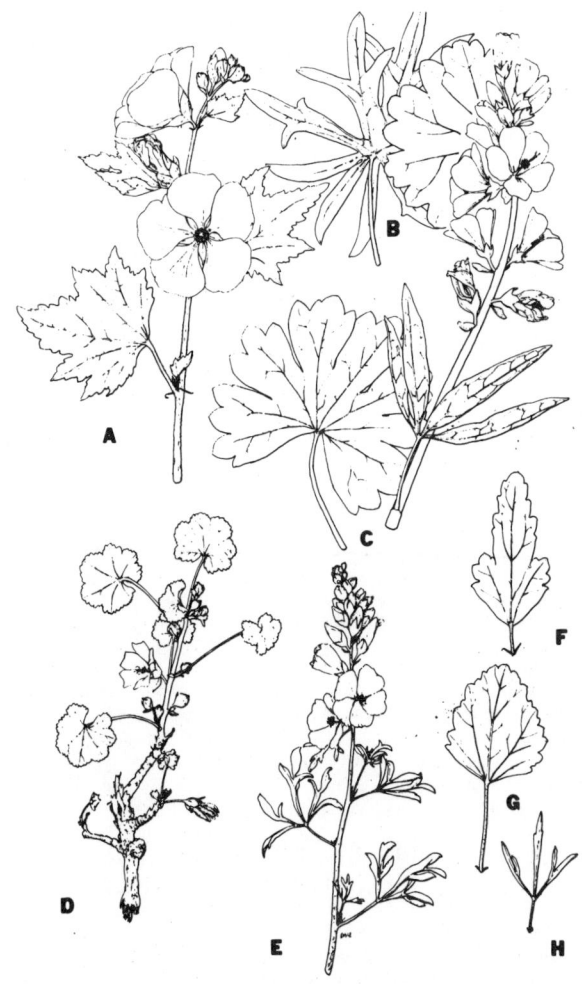

Figure 73. A, *Iliamna rivularis*; B, *Sidalcea neomexicana*, upper and lower lvs; C, *S. candida*; D, *Malva neglecta*; E, *Sphaeralcea coccinea*; F, *S. fendleri*, lf; G, *S. parvifolia*, lf; H, *S. leptophylla*, lf

Malvaceae (MLV)

MALVA L. 1753 [Gr., *malache* or *moloche*, for the emollient leaves]. MALLOW; CHEESEWEED

One sp, **M. neglecta** Wallroth, **73D**. ADV weed in lawns in the valleys. A very tenacious weed with a stout deep taproot and spreading caudices. The frts resemble wheels of cheese.

SIDALCEA Gray 1849 [comb. of two genera, *Sida* and *Alcea*]. CHECKER MALLOW
1a. Fls white. **S. candida** Gray, **73C**. Common in wet meadows in the montane zone.
1b. Fls purple. **S. neomexicana** Gray, **73B**. Common in swampy, often alkaline meadows, middle altitudes. Occasional white mutants are found in normal stands.

SPHAERALCEA St. Hilaire 1825 [Gr., *sphaera*, a sphere, + *alcea*, a mallow]. GLOBE MALLOW
1a. Lower lvs very deeply palmately-divided; lvs silvery from tightly packed stellate hairs . . . . (2)
1b. Lower lvs shallowly lobed; lvs green. . . . . (3)

2a. Lvs with linear lobes, upper lvs simple, lower 3-parted; plants with tall, wand-like form. **S. leptophylla** (Gray) Rydberg, **73H**. Rocky canyonsides and gravelly river benches from Colorado R Valley southward.
2b. Lvs palmately lobed with more than 3 divs; plants with low bushy form. **S. coccinea** (Nuttall) Rydberg ssp **dissecta** (Nuttall) Kearney, Copper Mallow, **73E**. Roadsides and ruderal, often disturbed, sites in the valleys.

3a. Lf blades broadly triangular-ovate, about as long as wide, the three main lobes about equal; pubescence dense, plant grayish. **S. parvifolia** Nelson, **73G**. Common on dry stream benches and in piñon-juniper.
3b. Lf blades narrowly ovate, longer than wide, lower side lobes much exceeded by the terminal one; pubescence thin, plants green. **S. fendleri** Gray, **73F**. Open pine forests, AA-LP. Intermediate forms occur which suggest that there is some hybridization between these.

MELANTHIACEAE
FALSE HELLEBORE FAMILY (MLN)

Recently segregated from the Liliaceae, this family includes the False Hellebore and Death Camas groups. It is interesting to note that, even without any knowledge of the modern evidence for segregation of this and other lilylike families, Rydberg presented essentially the same arrangement in his book on the Rocky Mountain flora, but the taxonomic establishment did not follow him.

1a. Tall, rank herbs up to 2-3 m tall, arising fibrous roots; lvs strongly pleated; infl a pyramidal panicle of greenish-white fls. **Veratrum**, FALSE HELLEBORE, CORN HUSK LILY

1b. Low herbs usually not over 5 dm tall; lvs not pleated; arising from bulbs; infl a raceme sometimes with short branches at its base. . . . . (2)

2a. Tepals 7-11 mm long; stamens not distinctly longer than the perianth; tepal gland notched above. **Anticlea**, DEATH CAMAS
2b. Tepals about 4 mm long; stamens distinctly longer than the tepals; tepal gland obovate or almost orbicular, not notched. **Toxicoscordion**, DEATH CAMAS

ANTICLEA Kunth 1843 [from *Anticlea*, mother of Ulysses]. DEATH CAMAS
One sp, **A. elegans** (Pursh) Rydberg. Subalpine meadows and lower moist tundra. The bulbs are very toxic (*Zygadenus*).

TOXICOSCORDION Rydberg 1903 [Gr., *toxikon*, poison for arrows, + *skorodon*, garlic]. DEATH CAMAS
1a. Infl racemose, rarely with a few lower branches; fls all perfect; outer tepals narrowed to very short claws. **T.venenosum** (Watson) Rydberg. Meadows at lower elevations (*Zygadenus*).
1b. Infl paniculate; fls of the lower panicle branches staminate, those of the main axis perfect; outer tepals lacking claws. **T. paniculatum** (Nuttall) Rydberg. Similar habitats but evidently infrequent.

VERATRUM L. 1753 [Lat., *vere*, true, + *atre*, black, alluding to the black rhizomes of some spp]. CORN HUSK LILY; FALSE HELLEBORE
One sp, **V. tenuipetalum** Heller. Forming very dense stands of tall, rank plants, on open slopes along subalpine streams, often a sign of overgrazing.

MENYANTHACEAE
BUCKBEAN FAMILY (MNY)

A small family of five genera, three in the Northern Hemisphere and two in the Southern, and 40 species. All are aquatic or semiaquatic herbs. Most species are tropical, but our single species is widespread in mountains of the northern Hemisphere. Where abundant, as in northern Eurasia, the leaves are used as a substitute for tea or added to beer, or eaten as an emergency food. Here the plant is uncommon.

MENYANTHES L. 1753 [Gr., *Menyanthos*, name of some other plant in this family]. BUCKBEAN; MARSH TREFOIL
One sp, **M. trifoliata** L., **74**. Upper montane and subalpine ponds (GA, GF, GN). The lvs and flower stalks rise above water level, and the very spongy stalks and rhizomes are rooted in the mud. The fls are unusually attractive, with recurved white petals covered with a dense brush of crinkly white or pinkish hairs. It is a mystery why these plants occur in some ponds and not in others.

Figure 74. *Menyanthes trifoliata*

MONOTROPACEAE—PINESAP FAMILY (MNT)

A small family of somewhat fleshy plants with reduced scale-leaves lacking chlorophyll, parasitic on the roots of conifers. This family has traditionally been placed in the Ericaceae.

1a. Corolla of united petals; stem tall (over 20 cm), stout, red-brown, with numerous reddish fls in a long raceme. **Pterospora**, PINEDROPS
1b. Corolla of separate petals; stem shorter, the entire plant pale yellowish or pinkish, the fls in a nodding terminal cluster, becoming erect in fruit. **Hypopitys**, PINESAP

HYPOPITYS Hill 1756 [Gr., *hypo*, under, + *pitys*, pine]. PINESAP
  One sp, **H. monotropa** Crantz, **88D**. Rare in deep moist forests (*Monotropa hypopitys*).

PTEROSPORA Nuttall 1818 [Gr., *pteros*, a wing, + *spora*, seed]. PINEDROPS
  One sp, **P. andromedea** Nuttall, **88C**. Common in pine-needle duff in forests. The seeds of this plant are unique. They are minute (less than 0.2 mm diam) and are provided with a fragile, lacy, transparent cellular wing many times the size of the seed, attached at one end, providing buoyancy for dispersal.

MORACEAE—MULBERRY FAMILY (MOR)

A family of many economic plants mostly of the tropical and subtropical world. All are trees or shrubs with 4-merous unisexual flowers arranged in heads, catkins, or hollowed out receptacles (as in figs). *Artocarpus*, breadfruit, was the plant that Captain Bligh was assigned to bring back to England, sparking the Mutiny of the H.M.S. "Bounty". *Ficus* is a large genus that includes sources of latex, delicious fruit, and several extremely sacred trees with a vast mythology. *Morus*, the mulberry, provides leafy food for the commercial silkworm.

1a. Lvs entire; branches with stout thorns; frt a baseball-sized mass of individual fruits. **Maclura**, OSAGE-ORANGE
1b. Lvs deeply lobed; branches not thorny; fruit small, blackberry-like. **Morus**, MULBERRY

MACLURA Nuttall 1818 [for Wm. Maclure, 1763-1840, American geologist]. OSAGE-ORANGE
   One sp., **M. pomifera** (Rafinesque) Schneider. Escaped and estab ADV along fencerows in the Colorado R Valley.

MORUS L. 1753 [the classical Latin name] MULBERRY
   One sp, **Morus alba** L., WHITE MULBERRY. Escaped and estab ADV along fencerows, Colorado R Valley.

NAJADACEAE—WATER-NYMPH FAMILY (NAJ)

An obscure little family of submerged aquatics consisting of the single genus, *Najas*. The leaves are linear, opposite but often clustered at the nodes, and tend to be slightly toothed. The flowers are very reduced; male flowers have a single sessile anther, and the female flower consists of a single carpel with 2-4 linear stigmas. Because *Najas* is a common aquarium plant it gets introduced into ponds with the emptying of the fishbowl.

NAJAS L. 1753 [Gr., *Naias*, the water nymph]
   One sp, **N. guadalupensis** (Sprengel) Morong, **36C**. ADV, not yet found on the W slope but probably overlooked, since it occurs in eastern Colorado and Utah. This sp has very narrow, only slightly toothed lvs. A second sp, **N. marina** L., is also to be expected. It has lvs up to 5 mm wide with strongly dentate margins.

NYCTAGINACEAE—FOUR-O'CLOCK FAMILY (NYC)

A small family characterized by the often tubular perianth, which doubles as petals and calyx, the inferior ovary forming a one-seeded, often winged, nutlet, opposite fleshy lvs and umbellate flower clusters subtended by conspicuous, often papery, bracts. The cultivated garden Four-o'clock, *Mirabilis jalapa*, is a native of South America. The flamboyant *Bougainvillea* vines of the tropics are nyctages. The species are most attractive when they are in flower, but the critical characters for identification are in the fruits.

1a. Fls in umbels surrounded by 4-6 separate bracts; stigmas linear or fusiform; anthers not exserted . . . . (2)
1b. Fls in few-flowered clusters surrounded by united bracts or subtended by 3 bracts united at the base; stigmas capitate or hemispheric; anthers exserted. . . . . (3)

2a. Frt over 1 cm long and wide, in a loose cluster, the wings broad, papery, strongly veined, transparent (like a cicada's wing); annual. **Tripterocalyx**, SAND-VERBENA
2b. Frt smaller, in a tight head, the wings not transparent; perennial. **Abronia**, SAND-VERBENA

3a. Lvs 1-2 cm long, elliptic-ovate, densely sticky-glandular; fls small, purplish; branches spreading out on the ground from a cluster of basal lvs. **Allionia**
3b. Lvs larger or of different shapes . . . . (4)

4a. Lvs perfectly cordate, not thick and fleshy; invol less than 1 cm long. **Mirabilis**, FOUR-O'CLOCK
4b. Lvs otherwise; erect or ascending plants with rotate or campanulate invol over 1 cm long or broad . . . . (5)

5a. Invol green, lflike, not enlarging or becoming membranous in frt; frt smooth, not constricted at the base, slightly 5-ribbed. **Mirabilis**, FOUR-O'CLOCK
5b. Invol enlarging and becoming membranous in frt; frt strongly 5-angled, constricted at the base, usually pubescent. **Oxybaphus**, UMBRELLA-WORT

ABRONIA Jussieu 1789 [Gr., *abros*, delicate, referring to the involucre]. SAND-VERBENA
1a. Frts lacking a beak or wings, smooth. **A. argillosa** Welsh & Goodrich. Locally abundant on adobe hills, Colorado and White R valleys. Closely resembling *A. elliptica* except for the frt.
1b. Frts beaked, with 2-5 wings, smooth or loosely villous . . . . . . (2)

2a. Frts thin-walled, delicate, the wings not rigid or stiff, two of them folded together to form a groove; lvs oval-elliptic, glaucous. **A. elliptica** Nelson, **75A, PL 12.** Abundant on adobe hills, flowering in early spring. Abronias are strikingly attractive plants and tend to be collected when they are in flower. One should wait until the fruits are ripe, since fruiting characters are critical for identification.
2b. Frts thick-walled, hard, the wings leathery, not folded together; lvs usually ovate, broadest near the base, usually puberulent. **A. fragrans** Nuttall. Evidently not common on the W slope, SW counties.

ALLIONIA L. 1753 [for Carlo Allioni, 1705-1804, Italian botanist, author of *Flora Piedmontana*]
One sp, **A. incarnata** L., **75B.** Infrequent on steep canyonsides. The small fls are in clusters of three, each invested by a bract forming an invol on a short axillary peduncle.

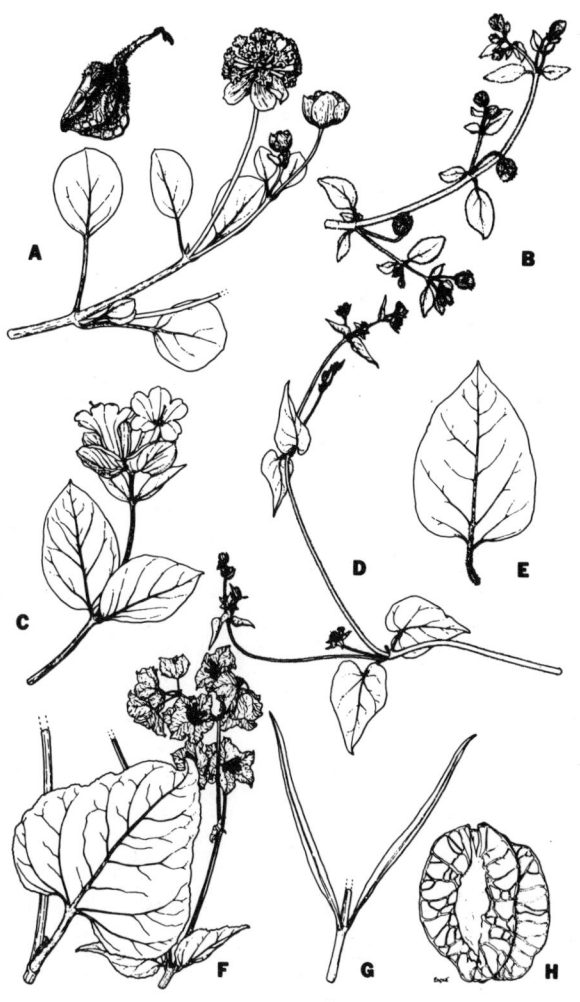

Figure 75. **A**, *Abronia elliptica*; **B**, *Allionia incarnata*; **C**, *Mirabilis alipes*; **D**, *M. oxybaphoides*; **E**, *M. multiflora*, lf; **F**, *Oxybaphus nyctagineus*, lf, frt; **G**, *Tripterocalyx micranthus*, lf, frt

MIRABILIS L. 1753 [Lat., *mirabilis*, wonderful]. FOUR-O'CLOCK

1a. Lvs perfectly cordate, not thick and fleshy; invol less than 1 cm long. **M. oxybaphoides** Gray, 75D. Infrequent, piñon-juniper. The perianth is less than 1 cm long, the invol subrotate, 3-fld; stamens 3, the filaments free.
1b. Lvs otherwise; erect or ascending plants with rotate or campanulate invol over 1 cm broad and or long . . . . (2)

2a. Fls white to pale pink; invol bracts separate to near the base, with the margins turned out, their contiguous sides forming a sort of wing. **M. alipes** (Watson) Pilz, 75C. Peripheral from Utah, on desert shale ridges, RB.
2b. Fls bright pink-purple; invol campanulate, of fused bracts . . . . (3)

3a. Sprawling plant with large, thick, green, rounded-cordate lvs and few branches; infl very glandular-pubescent. **M. glandulosa** (Standley) Weber, PIÑON FOUR-O'CLOCK, **PL 19**. Common by bases of trees in piñon-juniper, Colorado Nat. Mon. Blooming in early spring. The heavily rose-scented fls open in early morning.
3b. Erect plant forming hemispherical bushy growth; lvs triangular-cordate, not very succulent, grayish-pubescent; branches numerous from the base; infl not markedly glandular. **M. multiflora** (Torrey) Gray, 75E. Abundant along roadsides and on open canyonsides, blooming all summer and fall, widely distr.

OXYBAPHUS L'Heritier 1797 [Gr., *oxybaphon*, a saucer, alluding to the broad flat involucre]. UMBRELLA-WORT
1a. Lvs linear or narrowly oblong; stems white. **O. linearis** (Pursh) Robinson. Common in fields and roadsides in the valleys.
1b. Lvs broadly ovate or cordate. **O. nyctagineus** (Michaux) Porter & Coulter, 75F. Ruderal weed, originally native?

TRIPTEROCALYX Hooker 1909 [Gr., *tri*, three, + *pteron*, wing, + *calyx*]. SAND-VERBENA
1a. Perianth 1.5 cm long or less. **T. micranthus** (Torrey) Hooker, 75G. Infrequent, in loose sand, desert-steppe.
1b. Perianth 2 cm long or more. **T. carneus** (Greene) Galloway var. **wootonii** (Standley) Galloway [flesh-colored; for E. O. Wooton, New Mexico botanist]. Canyon bottoms, SW base of Mesa Verde.

NYMPHAEACEAE—WATER-LILY FAMILY (NYM)

The white or pink water-lilies belong to the genus *Nymphaea*. The sacred Lotus of the East is *Nelumbo*, cultivated in India for its edible rhizomes and fruit, and of extreme importance in the Buddhist religion. A South American species, *Victoria amazonica*, has floating leaves up to two meters in diameter, strongly reinforced against buffeting of wave action and having an upturned rim. These leaves are claimed to support the weight of a child. In Scandinavian folklore there is a troll called 'näck' who sits at the bottom of lakes and fishes for people, using the stem and flower of the Water-lily (the 'näck-rose') as a lure.

NUPHAR J. E. Smith 1809 [name said to be of Arabic origin]. YELLOW POND-LILY; SPATTERDOCK

One sp, **N. luteum** Sibthorp & Smith ssp **polysepalum** (Engelmann) Beal. Subalpine ponds, common on Grand Mesa.

OLEACEAE—OLIVE FAMILY (OLE)

The Ash tree has been famous in mythology; the World Ash tree figured prominently in the Nibelungen Lied, from which Wagner built his operatic quadrilogy. Ash, to most of us, signifies a tree with pinnately compound leaves and oar-shaped samaras. But in the American southwest and Mexico several species with simple or trifoliolate leaves occur. They take a bit of getting used to. Privet, *Ligustrum vulgare*, belongs to this family, and our native *Forestiera* bears a close resemblance to it.

1a. Lvs dark green, simple, narrowly elliptic; frt a glaucous blue-black, one-seeded drupe. **Forestiera**, WILD PRIVET
1b. Lvs yellow-green, oval or elliptic-ovate, simple or sometimes 3-foliolate; frt a single-winged pendent samara. **Fraxinus**, ASH

FORESTIERA Poiret 1812 [for Forestier, physician of St. Quentin, ca. 1820, first botany teacher to Poiret]. WILD PRIVET

One sp, **F. pubescens** Nuttall. Common on floodplains of the larger streams, forming dense thickets. The fls appear before the lvs, are unisexual or polygamous and consist of only stamens and/or gynoecium; petals are absent or much reduced (*F. neomexicana*).

FRAXINUS L. 1753 [the classical Lat. name]. ASH

One sp, **F. anomala** Torrey, **PL 41**. Common in gulches, desert canyons, ME-MZ. To accept this strange plant as an ash, one needs only to see the typical samaras.

ONAGRACEAE
EVENING-PRIMROSE FAMILY (ONA)

Evening-primroses are unrelated to true primroses. Many are attractive, morning- and evening-flowering plants pollinated by night-flying long-tongued moths. The floral formula for most of them (four sepals, four petals, eight stamens, four united carpels in an inferior ovary) is unique, but because of their four-merous pattern they sometimes (especially those with small fls) are mistaken for mustards. Hugo de Vries propounded the Mutation Theory in 1901 from studies on an Evening-primrose, *Oenothera*. The mutation theory stands today, despite the fact that the phenomena DeVries thought were mutations in *Oenothera* turned out to be the result of another genetic mechanism. It remained for others to demonstrate true mutations in other plants and animals. Horticulturally, the family is best known for *Fuchsia*, an Andean genus.

1a. Fls with parts in twos; ovary spherical; lvs broadly ovate, long-petioled. **Circaea**, ENCHANTRESS' NIGHTSHADE

1b. Fls with parts in fours; ovary more or less elongate; lvs narrower, short-petioled or sessile . . . . (2)

2a. Seeds with a tuft of hairs (coma) at one end; fls pink or white, never yellow . . . . (3)
2b. Seeds without coma; fls pink, white, or yellow . . . . (4)

3a. Fls large, the petals 1-2 cm long, entire, spreading; hypanthium not prolonged beyond the ovary. **Chamerion**, FIREWEED
3b. Fls smaller, petals usually notched, ascending; hypanthium prolonged beyond the ovary. **Epilobium**, WILLOW-HERB

4a. Frt nut-like, indehiscent; fls always pink. **Gaura**
4b. Frt a dehiscent, usually elongate, capsule; fls white, pink, or yellow. . . . . (5)

5a. Fls minute; plants very delicate, slender, with slender branches; ovary with 2 locules; hypanthium not prolonged beyond the ovary; fls always white or pink. **Gayophytum**, 76A
5b. Fls minute to usually showy; ovary with 4 locules; hypanthium prolonged beyond the ovary as a slender tube. . . . . (6)

6a. Stigma with 4 linear lobes; fls mostly opening in the evening. **Oenothera**, EVENING-PRIMROSE
6b. Stigma capitate, discoid or slightly 4-lobed or -toothed; fls mostly opening in the daytime . . . . (7)

7a. Hypanthium tube 25-50 mm long; stamens almost equal in length. **Calylophus**
7b. Hypanthium 1-15 mm long; stamens of 2 lengths. **Camissonia**

CALYLOPHUS Spach 1835 [Gr., *kalyx*, calyx, + *lophos*, crest, alluding to the dorsal appendages of the sepals]

One sp, **C. lavandulifolia** (Torrey & Gray) Raven [with lvs like lavender]. Rocky ledges on canyonsides in the warm river valleys, W counties.

CAMISSONIA Link 1818 [for Adelbert von Chamisso 1781-1838, poet, explorer and naturalist, creator of Peter Schlemihl].
1a. Ovary with a long slender projection below the hypanthium; plants stemless or nearly so. . . . . (2)
1b. Ovary lacking a sterile projection; plants only occasionally appearing stemless, and then when immature . . . . (3)

2a. Lvs pinnatifid; plants more or less densely pilose or appressed pubescent. **C. breviflora** (Torrey & Gray) Raven. In Colorado known only from North Park, but to be expected on the West slope along the N border, since it occurs in adjacent Wyoming and Utah.
2b. Lvs not pinnatifid; plants almost glabrous. **C. subacaulis** (Pursh) Raven. Meadows, upper Yampa River.

3a. Capsules on well-defined pedicels, not coiled or contorted; seeds

in 2 rows in each locule; lvs ovate or lyrately lobed . . . . (4)
3b. Capsules sessile, often coiled or contorted; seeds in 1 row in each locule; lvs linear or oblanceolate . . . . (6)

4a. Capsules elongate, often linear, usually less than 2 mm thick; pedicels often inconspicuous. **C. walkeri** Nelson) Raven [for Ernest P. Walker, of Paradox Valley]. On loose slides of limestone and sandstone rocks, ME to MZ.
4b. Capsules distinctly clavate, more than 2 mm thick. . . . . (5)

5a. Stigma surrounded by the anthers at maturity, the petals less than 5.5 mm long. **C. scapoidea** (Torrey & Gray) Raven, **76B**. Adobe hills in the lower valleys, blooming in early spring.
5b. Stigma held well above anthers at maturity, the petals usually more than 6 mm long. **C. eastwoodiae** (Munz) Raven. Similar sites.

6a. Petals white; fls opening in the evening; stems slender, little-branched, erect; lvs not in clusters. **C. minor** (Nelson) Raven. Infrequent and very inconspicuous, in adobe, lower Colorado and Yampa drainages.
6b. Petals yellow; fls opening in the morning. . . . . (7)

7a. Plants with naked, capillary stems, each bearing a crowded, lfy infl at its apex; capsule strongly flattened, 0.5-1.0 cm long. **C. andina** (Nuttall) Raven [of the Rocky Mts or Northern Andes]. One record, Blue Mountain Plateau of Dinosaur Nat. Mon.
7b. Plants lfy although not near the base; infl not crowded; capsule not flattened, usually over 1 cm long. **C. parvula** (Nuttall) Raven. Sand blowout areas, MF.

CHAMERION Rafinesque 1833 [Gr. *chamae*, lowly, + *Nerium*, the Oleander, from the lf shape] (formerly incl in *Epilobium*). FIREWEED

1a. Racemes elongate, many-fld, not lfy; styles hairy at the base, exceeding the stamens; lvs 5-20 cm long, veiny. **C. danielsii** D. Löve [for F. P. Daniels, who wrote a Boulder area flora in 1928]. Abundant along roadsides and in burned areas, middle altitudes (an octoploid related to *C. angustifolium*).
1b. Racemes few-fld, lfy; style glabrous, shorter than the stamens; lvs 2-6 cm long, glaucous, not veiny. **C. subdentatum** (Rydberg) Löve & Löve. Talus slopes and along snow-melt streamsides, upper subalpine (a tetraploid related to *C. latifolium*). This group has been called *Epilobium* in America, but belongs to a distinct Eurasiatic genus. The original spelling was *Chamerion*.

CIRCAEA L. 1753 [for Gr. goddess *Circe*]. ENCHANTRESS' NIGHTSHADE

One sp, **C. alpina** L., **76D**. Cool ravines, spruce-fir forests. Delicate, with opposite, ovate, denticulate lvs; fls tiny, in a raceme; frt covered with tiny hooked bristles. Thus far, all collections are from the eastern slope, but it is to be expected since it ranges widely to the far west.

Figure 76. A, *Gayophytum* sp, habit, frt; B, *Camissonia scapoidea*; C, *Gaura coccinea*; D, *Circaea alpina*, habit, fl, frt; E, *Epilobium hornemannii*

EPILOBIUM L. 1753 [Gr. *epi*, upon, + *lobon*, a capsule, alluding to the hypanthium tube]. WILLOW-HERB

1a. Annual; stems with peeling epidermis; lvs usually alternate. **E. brachycarpum** Presl. Common weedy herb, disturbed roadsides in the mts (*E. paniculatum*). Often mistaken for a crucifer or for a very large *Gayophytum*.
1b. Perennial; epidermis not peeling; lvs mostly opposite. . . . . . . (2)

2a. Low and spreading, often in dense clumps, hardly over 20 cm tall, usually shorter; stems often S-shaped; lvs 8-20 mm long . . . . (3)
2b. Erect, solitary or a few together, up to 4 dm or more tall, stems straight; lvs up to 5 cm long. . . . . (4)

3a. Infl nodding in bud; lvs oblong to narrowly ovate, thin, nearly entire; seeds smooth, 1 mm long. **E. anagallidifolium** Lamarck [with lvs like *Anagallis*, the pimpernel]. Snow-melt streamlets, subalpine and alpine.
3b. Infl erect in bud; lvs broadly ovate, thickish, more or less serrulate; seeds papillose, 1.5-2.0 mm long. **E. clavatum** Trelease. Alpine boulderfields, Park Range.

4a. Lvs mostly not more than 3 mm broad, the lateral veins scarcely or not evident. **E. leptophyllum** Rafinesque. Infrequent, wet meadows, Gunnison Basin.
4b. Lvs broader, with distinct lateral veins. . . . . (5)

5a. Seeds with parallel ridges; stems mostly 3-10 dm tall and freely branched especially above, if shorter the upper lvs alternate and more numerous; seeds with longitudinal ridges. **E. ciliatum** Rafinesque. Common weedy species of roadside ditches (incl. *E. adenocaulon*, *E. brevistylum*, and *E. glandulosum*).
5b. Seeds smooth or papillose; stems mostly 1-3 dm tall, simple above, with few pairs of opposite lvs; non-weedy species. . . . . (6)

6a. Turions (globose or ovoid fleshy winter buds) formed on the rhizomes and persisting as scales at the base of the stem of the year. . . . . (7)
6b. Turions not present . . . . (8)

7a. Lvs lance-oblong, not crowded, margins often irregularly dentate; petals white. **E. halleanum** Hausknecht [for Elihu Hall, collector in South Park, 1861-2]. Openings in spruce-fir forests.
7b. Lvs ovate with rounded bases, usually longer than the internodes, margins usually entire. **E. saximontanum** Hausknecht. Moist mt meadows and forest streamsides.

8a. Petals white or with pink tips, 3-4 mm long; seeds smooth; base of stem with several broad withered lvs at flowering time. **E. lactiflorum** Hausknecht [milky-fld]. Common along forest rills, subalpine.
8b. Petals pink-purple, 5-7 mm long; seeds more or less papillose; base of stem with small and inconspicuous or no withered lvs. **E.**

hornemannii Haussknecht [for Jens W. Hornemann, Danish botanist, 1770-1841], **76E**. Similar sites.

GAURA L. 1753 [Gr., *gauros*, superb, not very apt for our species]
1a. Tall plants well over 1 m tall, with spreading branches at the top; anthers oval, 0.5-1.0 mm long; sepals 1.5-3.0 mm long; petals 1.5-2.0 mm long. **G. parviflora** Douglas. Late-summer weedy roadside plant, lower valleys.
1b. Plants under 1 m tall, the branches not noticeably spreading; anthers linear, 2-5 mm long; sepals 5-11 mm long; petals 3-10 mm long. . . . . (2)

2a. Stem erect, 40-70 cm tall; stem lvs 5-10 cm long; hypanthium 7-12 mm, sepals 9-11 mm; petals 8-10 mm long. **G. neomexicana** Wooton. Local and infrequent near Pagosa Springs.
2b. Stem ascending, rarely erect, seldom over 30 cm tall; stem vs up to 3.5 cm long; hypanthium 5-8 mm, sepals 5-8 mm, petals 3-6 mm long. **G. coccinea** Nuttall [scarlet], **76C**. Meadows, roadsides, sagebrush, lower altitudes.

GAYOPHYTUM Jussieu 1832 [for Claude Gay, 1800-1873, French botanist]
1a. Pedicels of mature capsules less than 3 mm long; petals less than 2 mm long. . . . . (2)
1b. Pedicels of mature capsules 3 mm long or longer; petals 0.5-3.0 mm long. . . . . (3)

2a. Branched only in the lower half; secondary branches few or none, the branching not dichotomous. **G. racemosum** Torrey & Gray. Gravelly soils and roadsides, mountains. *G. decipiens* Lewis & Szweykowski is related to this, and reported from Colorado, but it seems to be very difficult to separate from this and the next, not having any distinctive characteristics of its own.
2b. Branched throughout or at least in the upper half; secondary branches evident. **G. diffusum** Torrey & Gray ssp **parviflorum** Lewis & Szweykowski, **76A**. Similar habitats.

3a. Seeds crowded, overlapping, usually 2 rows in each locule; capsules terete. . . . . (4)
3b. Seeds not crowded, in one row in each locule; capsules somewhat flattened or conspicuously torulose (constricted at intervals) (return to 2)

4a. Petals less than 1.5 mm long; pedicels equalling or longer than the capsules. **G. ramosissimum** Torrey & Gray. Similar habitats.
4b. Petals 1.5-3.0 mm long; pedicels equalling or shorter than the capsules. **G. diffusum** Torrey & Gray ssp **parviflorum** L. & S. Similar habitats.

OENOTHERA L. 1753 [name used by Theophrastus for a sp of *Epilobium*]. EVENING-PRIMROSE
1a. Plants stemless or stem very short, hidden among the basal lvs; fls from amid a cluster of basal lvs . . . . (2)

1b. Plants with lfy stems. . . . . (7)

2a. Fls white, turning pink; capsule not strongly winged, but usually warty on the surface. **O. caespitosa** Nuttall, PL 47. Abundant on clay hills and sandy road-cuts in the valleys and canyons. Four ssp occur on the W slope. . . . . (3)
2b. Fls yellow; fruit sharply 4-winged, not warty. . . . . (6)

3a. Plants with short appressed to somewhat spreading hairs and no minute glandular hairs. **O. caespitosa** ssp **caespitosa**. N counties.
3b. Plants hirsute or villous or sometimes only glandular. . . . . . . (4)

4a. Capsule abruptly contracted to a sterile beak, the dehiscing valves incurved; plants shaggy villous. Ssp **navajoensis**. Colorado Plateaus.
4b. Capsule tapering gradually to the beak, the dehiscing valves spreading; plants hirsute . . . . (5)

5a. Capsule straight, with tuberculate ridges or rows of tubercles; lvs typically pinnately lobed. Ssp **marginata**. Widespread.
5b. Capsule curved, the valves with smooth to irregular ridges; lvs oblanceolate to spatulate, the margins dentate. Ssp **macroglottis**. Widespread.

6a. Lvs linear to very narrowly elliptic, irregularly and coarsely dentate to pinnatifid, the lobes triangular; taproot woody, slender, with long lateral branches that sprout new shoots; capsule wings 2-5 mm wide. **O. acutissima** Wagner. END in W MF and adjacent Utah. Seasonally moist areas, sagebrush and ponderosa pine.
6b. Lvs oblanceolate to linear-oblong, irregularly pinnatifid, the lobes variable in shape, rarely the lvs almost entire; taproot fleshy, stout; capsule wings 1-2 mm wide. **O. flava** (Nelson) Munz [yellow]. Moist mt meadows with sagebrush.

7a. Fls yellow, wilting orange . . . . (8)
7b. Fls white, wilting pink. . . . . (10)

8a. Hypanthium tube 8-15 cm long; sepals and petals 4-6 cm long. **O. jamesii** Torrey & Gray. Peripheral from Utah, one record from McElmo Canyon, MZ. The hypanthium tube is extraordinary, resembling a slender red rubber hose. Irrigation ditches and roadsides.
8b. Hypanthium tube much shorter . . . . (9)

9a. Petals and sepals 25-40 mm long. **O. elata** Humboldt, Bonpland & Kunth. [tall]. Common in wet meadows and roadside ditches, middle and lower elevations (*O. hookeri*).
9b. Petals and sepals not over 20 mm long. **O. villosa** Thunberg. Less common than the former on the W slope, and at higher altitudes (*O. strigosa*).

10a. Capsule membranous, somewhat enlarged above the base; seeds in

       2 rows in each locule, with shallow pits in regular rows on the surface. . . . . (11)
10b. Capsule woody, somewhat narrowed toward the apex; seeds in one row in each locule, not pitted. . . . . (12)

11a. Perennial, rhizomatous; hypanthium with a conspicuous tuft of hairs in the throat; petals 7-15 mm long; capsule 8-20 mm long. **O. coronopifolia** Torrey & Gray [with lvs like the crucifer, *Coronopus*]. Gravelly open mt meadows and roadsides.
11b. Annual or winter annual; hypanthium not long-hairy in the throat; petals 20-40 mm long; capsule 20-40 mm long. **O. albicaulis** Pursh [white-stemmed]. Common in early spring on bare sandy or clay flats. A field full of blooming plants looks, from a distance, as if a box of white Kleenex tissues had been blown there by the wind.

12a. Lvs dentate or serrate, to 10 cm long or more; capsule 4-8 cm long; petals over 4 cm long. **O. kleinii** Wagner & Mill, recently described from the W side of Wolf Creek Pass, but the population has already been destroyed by road improvement. Its relationships are with Mohave desert and Californian species, and I suspect that *O. kleinii* was introd here before it was discovered elsewhere and only survived a few seasons. I doubt very much that it was native here.
12b. Leaves entire or nearly so, shorter; capsule and petals shorter. **O. pallida** Lindley. Clay-shale benches in the warm river valleys and piñon-juniper. Plants with prominently pilose sepals belong to ssp **trichocalyx** (Nuttall) Munz & Klein (*O. trichocalyx*).

ORCHIDACEAE—ORCHID FAMILY (ORC)

(see also *Cypripediaceae*)

Paradoxically, the orchid family is the second largest family in numbers of species, and it probably contains more rare and endangered species than any other family. They often have exceedingly delicately tuned pollination mechanisms. The extinction of a unique insect pollinator means the extinction of the orchid species. Their germination depends on the presence of symbiotic fungus species. They have very narrow ecological amplitudes and extremely specialized floral structures. For example, the pollen, instead of being dustlike and easily spread, is aggregated into two sticky bags (pollinia) that must be transmitted whole by an insect from one flower to another, the process often involving elaborate tricks of luring the insect to the proper site, causing a trigger mechanism to force the pollinium onto the insect's head, and holding the insect in place until the pollinium's glue dries. Tropical orchids usually occur in very small numbers. In Colorado, the species that grow in very wet places seem to be in little danger of extinction except through loss of the habitat, but those that grow on dry or only seasonally moist forest floors are often very rare and endangered.

1a. Plants without green lvs, saprophytic or parasitic. **Corallorhiza**, CORAL-ROOT
1b. Plants with green lvs. . . . . (2)

2a. Lip of corolla a pointed slipper-shaped inflated sac. **Calypso**, FAIRY SLIPPER
2b. Lip of corolla not as above. . . . . (3)

3a. Fls with definite spurs (long and narrow or short and sac-like). . . . . (4)
3b. Fls without spurs . . . . (7)

4a. Corolla lip broad, 2-3-lobed at the apex; spur short, scrotiform; bracts usually longer than the fls. **Coeloglossum**, GREEN BOG ORCHID
4b. Corolla lip entire; spur short or elongate; bracts usually not much longer than the fls. . . . . (5)

5a. Lf solitary, basal. **Lysiella**
5b. Lvs several, usually cauline but sometimes most of them basal . . . . (6)

6a. Lvs grouped near the base of the stem; infl very slender, up to 30 cm long; fl bracts ovate, shorter than the ovary; fl small. **Piperia**
6b. Lvs distributed the length of the stem; infl usually stouter, shorter; fl bracts linear or lanceolate, equalling or exceeding the ovary. **Limnorchis**, BOG ORCHID

7a. Lvs two, opposite, near middle of the stem. **Listera**, TWAY-BLADE
7b. Lvs not as above . . . . (8)

8a. Stem lvs absent, or the lvs at least appearing to be basal, usually white along midrib and veins. **Goodyera**, RATTLESNAKE-PLANTAIN
8b. Stem lvs present, green. . . . . (9)

9a. Plants of bogs; fls white, spirally arranged in a tight spike. **Spiranthes**, LADY'S TRESSES
9b. Plants of moist alcoves and ledges of sandstone cliffs; fls few, greenish-brownish-purple, in a few-fld raceme. **Epipactis**, HELLEBORINE

CALYPSO Salisbury 1807 [for the Greek sea-nymph of Homer's Odyssey]. FAIRY SLIPPER
One sp, **C. bulbosa** (L.) Oakes. Deep moist forests; this should never be collected, since its survival is precarious.

COELOGLOSSUM Hartman 1820 [Gr., *koilos*, hollow, + *glossa*, tongue]. GREEN BOG ORCHID
One sp, **C. viride** (L.) Hartman ssp **bracteatum** (Mühlenberg) Hultén. Wet spruce-fir forests near streams.

Orchidaceae (ORC)

CORALLORHIZA Gagnebin 1755 [Gr., *corallion*, coral, + *rhiza*, root]. CORALROOT
1a. Lip striped with purple. **C. striata** Lindley, **77C**. Dry pine forests.
1b. Lip plain or spotted with purple. . . . . (2)

2a. Lip white, not spotted; sepals and petals 1-nerved; plants usually yellowish, but smaller and more slender than albinos of the next. **C. trifida** Chatelain. Subalpine forests.
2b. Lip spotted with purple; sepals and petals 3-nerved. **C. maculata** Rafinesque [spotted], **77D**. Dry pine forests. The plants are usually reddish, but occasional ones are albinos, totally yellow.

EPIPACTIS Zinn 1757 [ancient Gr. name for hellebore]. HELLEBORINE

One sp, **E. gigantea** Douglas, **77E**, **PL 4**. Local, in moist protected alcoves of sandstone canyon walls, W counties.

GOODYERA R. Brown 1813 [for John Goodyer, 1592-1664, British botanist]. RATTLESNAKE-PLANTAIN
1a. Lvs 1-3 cm long, not conspicuously white-veined; lip saccate, with a flaring or recurved margin. **G. repens** (L.) R. Brown ssp **ophioides** (Fernald) Löve & Simon [creeping; snake-like]. Local, in moist spruce forests.
1b. Lvs 5-10 cm long, conspicuously white along the midrib; lip scarcely saccate, the margin involute. **G. oblongifolia** Rafinesque. Infrequent, in duff on fairly dry forest floors.

LIMNORCHIS Rydberg 1900 [Gr., *limnaios*, of a bog]. BOG ORCHID (formerly incl in *Habenaria*)
1a. Fls white; lip rhombic-lanceolate, dilated at the base. **L. dilatata** (Pursh) Rydberg ssp **albiflora** (Chamisso) Löve & Simon. Wet meadows, shores of subalpine ponds.
1b. Fls greenish; lip lanceolate to linear, not dilated at the base . . . . (2)

2a. Infl slender, the fls remote from each other; lip linear-elliptic; spur always long and narrow; plants of relatively dry woods. **L. sparsiflora** Watson. Very infrequent, never forming stands.
2b. Infl dense, the fls often overlapping; lip lanceolate; spur very variable, from elongate to short and sac-like. **L. saccata** (Greene) Löve & Simons. Swampy or boggy forests and meadows (incl *H. hyperborea* of Colorado reports).

LISTERA R. Brown 1813 [for Dr. Martin Lister, 1638-1711, Brit. naturalist]. TWAYBLADE
1a. Corolla lip oblong or linear, 2-cleft for half its length. **L. cordata** (L.) R. Brown ssp **nephrophylla** (Rydberg) Löve & Löve. Cool moist ravines and forests. When ripe, the capsules split lengthwise, remaining attached top and bottom, to form a delicate cage.
1b. Corolla lip broader, not 2-cleft for half its length . . . . (2)

2a. Lip oblong, sagittate and broadest at the base, without lateral

Figure 77. A, *Listera convallarioides*, fl; B, *Spiranthes romanzoffiana*; C, *Corallorhiza striata*; D, *C. maculata*, fl and root; E, *Epipactis gigantea*

teeth and with a fleshy ridge in the center near the base. **L. borealis** Morong. Very local, in deep rich forests, Gunnison Basin.
2b. Lip cuneate to obovate, not auriculate, broadest at the apex, with lateral teeth, without a fleshy ridge. **L. convallarioides** Torrey [with lvs like *Convallaria*, Lily-of-the-valley], **77A**. Cool ravines, subalpine forests.

LYSIELLA Rydberg 1900 [dim. of *Lysias*, another genus]

One sp, **L. obtusata** (Banks) Britton & Rydberg. Mossy streamsides in very rich and deeply-shading forests.

PIPERIA Rydberg 1901 [for Charles V. Piper, 1867-1926, botanist of Washington State]

One sp, **P. unalascensis** (Sprengel) Rydberg. Very local and infrequent, aspen stands. Inconspicuous, easily overlooked.

SPIRANTHES L. Richard 1817 [Gr., *speira*, coil, + *anthos*, flower]. LADY'S TRESSES

One sp, **S. romanzoffiana** Chamisso & Schlechtendal [for Count Romanzoff], **77B**. Common in subalpine meadows and willow bogs.

OROBANCHACEAE—BROOM-RAPE FAMILY (ORO)

By carefully digging around an *Orobanche*, the holdfast connecting this parasite to the host plant can usually be located. Our species of *Orobanche* are commonly parasitic on species of Asteraceae, including *Artemisia* and *Ambrosia*. The flowers remind one of Scrophulariaceae such as *Penstemon*. Orobanches and their relatives are found in the deserts of the temperate parts of all the continents. One species, *O. crenata*, is parasitic on cultivated legumes and is responsible for crop losses when infestations are high.

OROBANCHE L. 1753 [Gr., *orobos*, vetch, + *anchein*, to strangle]. BROOM-RAPE [from the leafless straw-like stems + an allusion to *Brassica*, Rape]
1a. Fls conspicuously long-peduncled, without accessory bractlets
. . . . (2)
1b. Fls sessile or on short peduncles from a stout main stem; a pair of bractlets situated just below the calyx in addition to the normal subtending bract. **O. multiflora** Nuttall, **78B**. Sandy soil of lower canyons, parasitic on sagebrush. In this sp the upper lobes of the corolla are obtuse or rounded. In *O. ludoviciana* Nuttall of the E slope they are acute.

2a. Pedicels 1 to 3, much longer than the short and inconspicuous main stem; calyx lobes slender, longer than the tube. **O. uniflora** L., **78C**. Montane and subalpine meadows.
2b. Pedicels 4 to 10 or more, not longer than the relatively long main stem; calyx lobes broader, shorter than or equalling the tube. **O. fasciculata** Nuttall, **78A**. Usually growing attached to the roots of sagebrush.

Oxalidaceae (OXL) 351

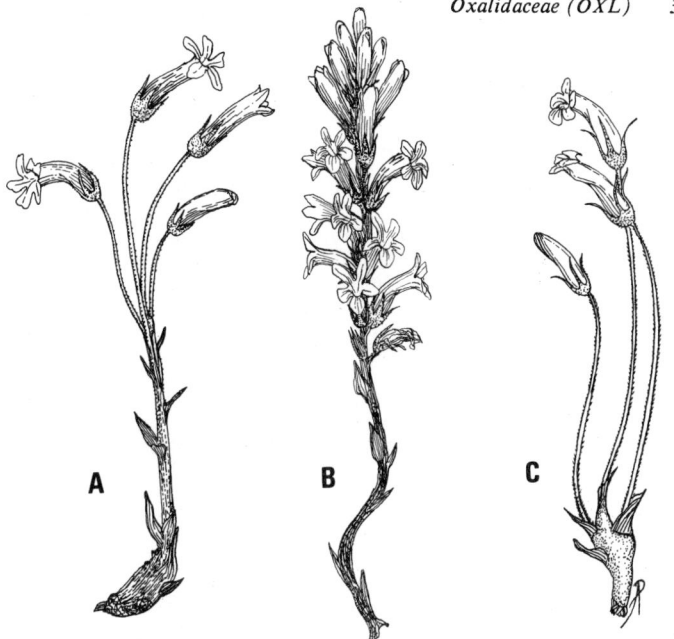

Figure 78. A, *Orobanche fasciculata*; B, *O. multiflora*; C, *O. uniflora*

OXALIDACEAE—WOOD-SORREL FAMILY (OXL)

Oxalis plants, with their three-parted leaves with heart-shaped leaflets, are commonly sold as Irish shamrocks, but whether the original shamrock used by St. Patrick to symbolize the Doctrine of the Trinity was an *Oxalis* or a *Trifolium* is debatable. The leaves of *Oxalis* contain oxalic acid and are pleasantly tart when chewed. Tubers of *Oxalis crenata* (the 'oca' of crossword puzzles) have been an important foodstuff in Peru since ancient Inca times. The capsules of *Oxalis* are elastically dehiscent; the valves split open explosively and describe arcs, shooting the seeds off some distance from the parent plant.

OXALIS L. 1753 [Gr., *oxys*, sour]. WOOD SORREL

1a. Plants with basal lvs from a subterranean tuber; fls purple. **O. violacea** L. Moist forests, S counties.
1b. Plants with aerial stems; fls yellow. . . . . (2)

2a. Stems tall, usually unbranched, from an underground rhizome; stem and petioles with some septate multicellular hairs that become crinkled and show prominent reddish cross-walls; lvs green or sometimes deep red. **O. stricta** L. ADV. Garden weed, not yet found but expected to occur here.

2b. Stems low, branched from the base, without underground horizontal rhizomes; stem and petioles with straight or curved, simple hairs only, usually appressed to the stem; lvs distinctly glaucous. **O. dillenii** Jacquin [for Jacob Dillenius, British botanist, 1684-1747). The native sp, infrequent, AA.

PAPAVERACEAE—POPPY FAMILY (PAP)

In poppy flowers the calyx is united from top to bottom. It does not open, but breaks away by a dehiscence line at its base when forced by the pressure of the expanding corolla, which is crumpled in the bud like a handkerchief. Open flowers, therefore, have no calyx. The unopened flower might be misinterpreted to be a fruit since the calyx may be crowned by style-like horns.

1a. Petals white, large (over 4 cm long); lvs spiny on the margins and veins, pubescent. **Argemone,** PRICKLY POPPY
1b. Petals pale yellow or bright orange, smaller; lvs not as above
    . . . . (2)

2a. Pods short and broad, goblet-shaped; lvs with few short hirsute divisions; alpine tundra plants with pale yellow, often almost white, fls. **Papaver,** POPPY
2b. Pods elongate, linear, curved; lvs with many linear divs; petals orange. **Eschscholzia,** CALIFORNIA POPPY

ARGEMONE L. 1753 [an herb mentioned by Pliny]. PRICKLY POPPY
    One sp, **A. hispida** Gray. An E plains sp, probably introd in the single W slope locality in EA.

ESCHSCHOLZIA Chamisso 1820 [for J. F. Eschscholz, 1793-1831, physician who accompanied Kotzebue's world voyage]. CALIFORNIA POPPY
    One sp, **E. californica** Chamisso. ADV roadside weed probably sown in wild flower packets (GF). Native in the Pacific coast and SW states.

PAPAVER L. 1753 [the ancient name]. POPPY
    One sp, **P. kluanense** D. Löve, ALPINE POPPY, **PL 53**. Infrequent, occurring in very small stands on the high peaks. A commonly cultivated relative, the ADV Iceland Poppy, *P. croceum* Ledebour, with larger, bright orange fls, persists around old mt townsites.

PARNASSIACEAE
GRASS-OF-PARNASSUS FAMILY (PAR)

Usually included in the Saxifragaceae, *Parnassia* shows as little affinity with that family as do the Hydrangeaceae and Grossulariaceae. *Parnassia* is easily recognized. The leaves are basal except for one smaller leaf on the flowering stem (absent in one species). The flowers are white; the row of five normal stamens alternates with five peculiar staminodia which bear a fringe of shining yellow stalked glands. The ovary is quite superior and has four carpels.

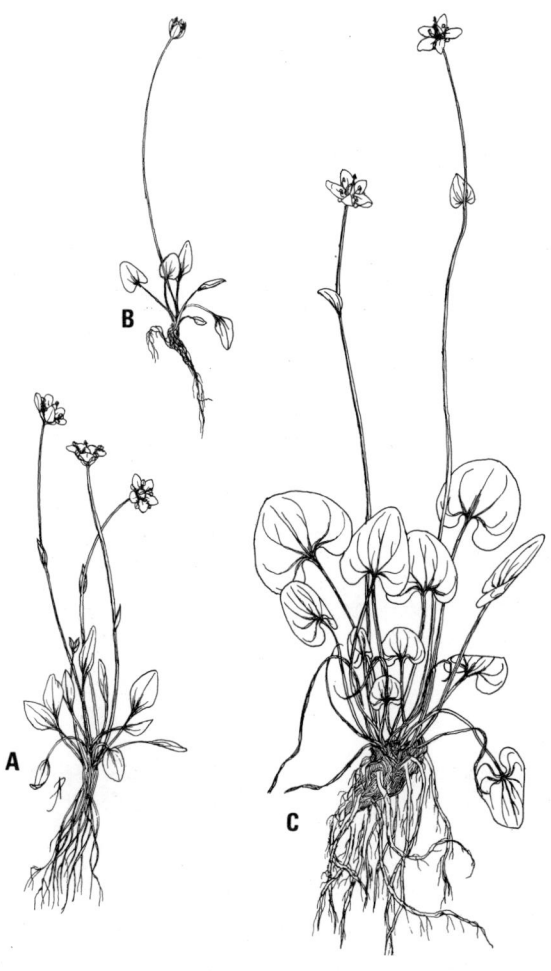

Figure 79. A, *Parnassia parviflora*; B, *P. kotzebuei*; C, *P. fimbriata*

Parnassiaceae (PAR)

PARNASSIA L. 1753 [for Mt. Parnassus, Greece]. GRASS-OF-PARNASSUS

1a. Fl stem with a bractlike lf, usually above the level of the basal lvs; petals large, 5- to 13-veined . . . . (2)
1b. Fl stem bractless; petals small (about equalling the sepals), 1- to 3-veined. **P. kotzebuei** Chamisso [for Otto von Kotzebue, 1787-1846, Russian navigator, commander of northern Pacific exploring expeditions], **79B**. Local, on rocky ledges and rills, subalpine, alpine.

2a. Lvs ovate, lanceolate, or elliptic; petals not marginally fimbriate. **P. parviflora** de Candolle [small-fld], **79A**. Subalpine bogs.
2b. Lvs cordate or reniform; petals marginally fimbriate. **P. fimbriata** Banks [fringed], **79C**. Subalpine bogs and streamsides.

PLANTAGINACEAE
PLANTAIN FAMILY (PTG)

The word *plantain* comes from Latin *planta*, the sole of the foot, and alludes to the usually broad spreading leaf. Plantar warts come from the same stem, and have nothing to do with gardening. The tropical plantains, related to the Banana, bear no relation to our plantains but are monocots in the Musaceae. Some of our plantains are common dooryard weeds, and all are recognized by the cluster of basal leaves, and spikes of flowers with papery corollas, and a peculiar ovary that dehisces by a horizontal rift (circumscissilely).

PLANTAGO L. 1753 [Lat., *planta*, sole of the foot]. PLANTAIN

1a. Lvs linear to filiform, rarely over 1 cm wide; annuals . . . . . . (2)
1b. Lvs lanceolate to ovate, over 1 cm wide; perennials . . . . (3)

2a. Densely woolly-pubescent; lower fl bracts commonly exceeding the fls. **P. patagonica** Jacquin [from Patagonia], WOOLLY PLANTAIN, **80A**. Abundant on barren soils and overgrazed range at low altitudes.
2b. Almost glabrous, none of the bracts exceeding the fls. **P. elongata** Pursh, **80B**. Locally abundant, alkali flats, ME.

3a. Lf blades broadly obovate, abruptly narrowed to the petiole; seeds 6-20 in each capsule. **P. major** L., COMMON PLANTAIN, **80C**. ADV abundant weed in lawns and grazed meadows.
3b. Lf-blades lanceolate, or if broader, then tapering to the petiole; seeds few (2-4) . . . . (4)

4a. Petals broad, 2 mm long, spreading and persistent, hiding the frts; spikes short and broad at fl time, the stamens with long filaments, forming a ring around the spike. **P. lanceolata** L., ENGLISH PLANTAIN, **80D**. ADV lawn weed.
4b. Petals narrow, 1 mm long, never hiding the frts; spikes usually elongate, at least in age, the stamens not as above . . . . (5)

Figure 80. A, *Plantago patagonica*; **B**, *P. elongata*; **C**, *P. major*; **D**, *P. lanceolata*

5a. Lf bases covered with reddish-brown wool; spikes over 5 cm long; lvs thick or succulent. **P. eriopoda** Torrey [woolly-foot], REDWOOL PLANTAIN. Wet places and alkali flats, mt parks.
5b. Lf bases not woolly or only slightly so; spikes usually shorter; lvs not thick nor succulent. **P. tweedyi** Gray [for the collector, Frank Tweedy]. Mountain meadows.

POACEAE/GRAMINEAE
GRASS FAMILY (POA/GRM)

(Parts contributed by Janet L. Wingate)

The grass family is usually considered a difficult group, and the terminology used for its floral parts is unique. Once one understands the fundamental structure of the grass spikelet, which actually is very simple, the grasses become a fascinating and not-too-difficult subject. One must be ready to make measurements of very small things, such as anthers, glumes and lemmas. Every citizen should know the dominant grasses, because these tell a great deal, by their presence, absence, or abundance, about the condition of the range. At the present time, because of new evidence from genetics, comparative anatomy, and scanning electron microscopy, great changes are occurring in the classification of the grasses, resulting in new tribal organization and in the delimitation of genera. The grasses being extremely streamlined plants, their small parts with relatively minute differences have to be more carefully analyzed than those of most other plant families.

Key to the Genera

1a. Plants dioecious (spklts entirely staminate or carpellate, on different plants and usually conspicuously different in appearance). **Key A, (Dioecious Grasses)**
1b. Plants not dioecious (most grasses belong in this category) . . . . (2)

2a. Plants prostrate on the ground and radially spreading, with long naked internodes and dense fascicles of short, stiff lvs with pale thickened margins; spklts hidden in the lf clusters. **Monroa, FALSE BUFFALOGRASS**
2b. Plants not as above . . . . (3)

3a. Spklts consisting of hard burs with sharp, hooked spines. **Cenchrus, SANDBUR**
3b. Spklts not bur-like . . . . (4)

4a. Florets converted to bulblets with shiny purple bases and long green tips. **Poa bulbosa**
4b. Florets not as above . . . . (5)

5a. Spklts sessile, alternating on either side of a flattened rachis . . . . (6)
5b. Spklts not alternating on either side of a flattened rachis . . . . . (7)

6a. Each spklt cluster nested in a group of long white hairs. **Hilaria, Galleta Grass**
6b. Spklt clusters not subtended by hairs. **Key B (Alternating Spklts)**

7a. Foliage and stem harshly retrorse-scabrous (saw-grass); glumes lacking, the spklt with a single lemma and palea. **Leersia, Rice Cutgrass**
7b. Foliage not as above; spklts with glumes . . . . (8)

8a. Spklts sessile, subsessile, or very short-pedicelled on one side of the rachis, forming one-sided spikes or spikelike racemes; spikes often resembling little flags. **Key C (Flagged Grasses)**
8b. Spklts not as above . . . . (9)

9a. Spklts disarticulating below the glumes (falling in one piece); glumes and lemmas flat or curved, never folded (the spklt tends to be terete, without a right and left side) . . . . (10)
9b. Spklts usually disarticulating above the glumes and between the florets (shattering at maturity and leaving the glumes attached to the rachis); glumes and lemmas strongly rounded or folded (spklt tends to lie flat, with a right and left side) . . . . (11)

10a. Spklts in pairs, one sessile and bisexual, the other pediceled and staminate, rudimentary or reduced to a mere pedicel. **Key D (Sorghum Group)**
10b. Spklts not in pairs. **Key E (Panicum Group)**

11a. Spklts with a single floret. **Key F (One-fld Spklts)**
11b. Spklts with at least two florets . . . . (12)

12a. Glumes (at least one) as long as or longer than the lowest floret, usually as long as the whole spklt, the awn, if present, attached on the back of the lemma or appearing so. **Key G, Oats Group)**
12b. Both glumes shorter than the lowermost floret; awn, if present, attached to the tip of the lemma or arising from between the teeth of a bifid lemma apex. **Key H (Poa Group)**

KEY A (Dioecious Grasses)

1a. Florets numerous in the spklt (8 to 15); lemma 5-11-nerved; plants of low alkaline areas in the valleys. **Distichlis, Salt Grass**
1b. Florets relatively few in the spklt (3 to 7); lemma 3-5-nerved; plants of well-drained mountain soils . . . . (2)

2a. Lf-tip boat-shaped; plants forming dense clumps, not over 5 dm tall. **Poa fendleriana**
2b. Lf-tip not boat-shaped; tall rhizomatous plants not forming dense clumps, often a meter tall. **Leucopoa**

Key B (Alternating Spklts)

1a. Spklts arranged so as to form a solid cylinder, the rachis bent to accommodate them; spklts rough and long-awned, the rachis shattering at maturity. **Cylindropyrum**, GOATGRASS
1b. Spklts loose, not forming a solid cylinder. . . . . (2)

2a. Annuals . . . . (3)
2b. Perennials, either rhizomatous or bunch-formers. . . . . (7)

3a. Tall, cultivated for grain and escaping to roadsides or volunteering in fallow fields; stems with large diameter straw . . . . . (4)
3b. Low annual weeds; stems with slender straw . . . . (6)

4a. Glumes subulate, 1-nerved . . . . (5)
4b. Glumes broad, 3-nerved. **Triticum**, WHEAT

5a. Spklts usually 3 at a node (one rare exception). **Hordeum**, BARLEY
5b. Spklts single at each node. **Secale**, RYE

6a. Culms widely spreading; spikes less than 2 cm long; spklts widely spreading. **Eremopyrum**, ANNUAL WHEATGRASS
6b. Culms erect; spikes slender, over 2 cm long, the spklts erect. **Critesion**, FOXTAIL BARLEY

7a. Spklts placed edgewise to the rachis; first glume lacking, its function taken over by the rachis. **Lolium**, DARNEL
7b. Spklts placed with the flat side next to the rachis; both glumes present. . . . . (8)

8a. Glumes and lemmas truncate at the apex, never awned. . . . . . (9)
8b. Glumes and lemmas acute at the apex or awned. . . . . (10)

9a. Glumes squarely truncate, lacking a mucro; bunch grass. **Lophopyrum**, TALL WHEATGRASS
9b. Glumes blunt but with a small slightly off-center mucro; rhizomatous. **Elytrigia intermedia**, INTERMEDIATE WHEATGRASS

10a. Spklts with stiffly and widely spreading florets. **Agropyron**, CRESTED WHEATGRASS
10b. Spklts with erect or strongly ascending florets. . . . . (11)

11a. Spklts 3 or more at a node . . . . (12)
11b. Spklts 1 or 2 at a node. (15)

12a. Three spklts per node, 1 central and fertile, 2 lateral, reduced, sterile and pedicelled. **Critesion**, FOXTAIL BARLEY
12b. Spklts not as above . . . . (13)

13a. Lemma with awns 10 to 30 mm long, divergent at maturity. **Elymus canadensis**
13b. Lemma awnless or short-awned. . . . . (14)

14a. Lemmas soft-pubescent; spklts less than 1 cm long; plants robust but not forming bunches over a meter tall. **Psathyrostachys,** RUSSIAN WILD RYE
14b. Lemmas glabrous; spklts over 1 cm long; plants forming enormous bunches over a meter tall. **Leymus,** GIANT WILD RYE

15a. Rhizomatous . . . . (16)
15b. Not rhizomatous, forming dense bunches (make careful field observations!). . . . . (17)

16a. Glumes tapering from near the base, not widest at the middle. **Pascopyrum,** WESTERN WHEATGRASS
16b. Glumes widest at the middle. **Elytrigia**

17a. Very densely formed bunchgrass of undisturbed grasslands; spklts slender, rather widely separated on the rachis (specimens of *Elytrigia* lacking basal parts may key here). **Pseudoroegneria,** BLUE-BUNCH WHEATGRASS
17b. Medium-dense bunchgrasses of roadsides, disturbed soils or aspen forests; spklts rather densely arranged on the rachis. **Elymus,** WHEATGRASS

Key C (Flagged Grasses)

1a. Infl forming a digitate cluster of spikes or spikelike racemes, like spokes of an umbrella, sometimes with isolated branches below . . . . (2)
1b. Infl not digitate. . . . . (5)

2a. Plants creeping, with above-ground scaly stolons. **Cynodon,** BERMUDA GRASS
2b. Plants lacking stolons, although sometimes tending to root at the decumbent lower nodes. . . . . (3)

3a. Lemmas distinctly awned. **Chloris,** WINDMILL GRASS
3b. Lemmas not awned . . . . (4)

4a. Spklts less than 4 mm long with 1 well-developed floret. **Digitaria,** CRABGRASS
4b. Spklts usually over 4 mm long with 3-8 well-developed florets. **Eleusine,** GOOSEGRASS

5a. Spklts or groups of them pendent. **Bouteloua curtipendula,** SIDE-OATS GRAMA
5b. Spklts or groups of them erect or spreading but not pendent . . . (6)

6a. Infl distinctly brush-like, with the spklts standing out at a wide angle from the rachis . . . . (7)
6b. Infl not brush-like. (8)

7a. Spikes standing out from the culm at nearly right angles; low plants of dry grassland. **Bouteloua,** GRAMA
7b. Spikes more or less appressed to somewhat spreading; coarse tall

grasses of wet ditches or seasonally wet alkali flats. **Spartina**, CORDGRASS

8a. Infl very long and slender, forming recurved arcs, the spklts minute. **Scheddonardus**, TUMBLEGRASS
8b. Infl not as above, the spklts fairly large . . . . (9)

9a. Spklts very broad, almost circular . . . . (10)
9b. Spklts narrow, pointed . . . . (11)

10a. Spklts with the glumes folded, the spklt lying flat, with an open slit where the glumes meet. **Beckmannia**, SLOUGHGRASS
10b. Spklts with the glumes flat, the spklt in face view not bisected. **Paspalum**

11a. Panicle with all spikelets short-pedicelled, or sessile, forming a single close one-sided cluster. **Sclerochloa**
11b. Panicle with several distinct main branches, separating the spikelets into well-defined groups or individuals . . . . (12)

12a. Spklts in 2 or 3 very dense clusters at the ends of a few main panicle branches; pastures and lawns. **Dactylis**, ORCHARDGRASS
12b. Spklts in slender, straight, erect racemes or the infl so condensed as to appear so. **Leptochloa**, SPRANGLETOP

Key D (Sorghum Group)

1a. Infl branches stout, in digitate or densely clustered terminal groups . . . . (2)
1b. Infl branches slender, delicate, not in close groups but spaced along the slender culm. **Schizachyrium**, LITTLE BLUESTEM

2a. Spikes reddish, in a digitate cluster. **Andropogon**, BIG BLUESTEM; TURKEYFOOT
2b. Spikes silvery-white, in a dense plume-like, not distinctly digitate terminal cluster. **Bothriochloa**, SILVER BEARDGRASS

Key E (Panicum Group)

1a. Spklts subtended by slender bristles that represent the pedicels of suppressed spklts, the entire spike resembling a bottlebrush. **Setaria**, FOXTAIL; BRISTLEGRASS
1b. Spklts not subtended by bristles although the lemmas may be slender-tipped . . . . (2)

2a. Spklts long-pedicelled, in open panicles, the glumes and lemmas never awned . . . . (3)
2b. Spklts short-pedicelled or sessile on the panicle branches, the glumes or lemmas usually awned; coarse, weedy grasses with broad lvs and narrowly pyramidal infl. **Echinochloa**, BARNYARD GRASS

3a. Basal lvs on short shoots, distinctly different from those of the fl culm, forming overwintering rosettes. **Dichanthelium**
3b. Basal lvs similar to the culm lvs, not overwintering as rosettes. **Panicum**, PANIC GRASS

Key F (One-fld Spklts)

1a. Panicle very dense and spikelike, forming a cylindric head, the panicle branches suppressed or absent . . . . (2)
1b. Panicle loose or dense, occasionally spikelike but the branches always well-developed although sometimes appressed to the rachis . . . . (3)

2a. Each glume with a short, stout awn, the keel ciliate; lemma awnless or only mucronate. **Phleum**, TIMOTHY
2b. Glumes awnless, the keels densely hairy; lemma with a dorsal awn. **Alopecurus**, FOXTAIL

3a. Lemma with 3 awns. **Aristida**, THREE-AWN
3b. Lemma with a single awn or none. . . . . (4)

4a. Lemma with an awn from the back . . . . (5)
4b. Lemma with a terminal awn or none. . . . . (6)

5a. Lemma with a tuft of hairs at the base; palea about as long as the lemma. **Calamagrostis**, REEDGRASS
5b. Lemma naked at the base; palea up to 2/3 as long as the lemma, or entirely lacking. **Agrostis**, BENTGRASS

6a. Lemma indurate, terete; callus well-developed, often sharp-pointed . . . . (7)
6b. Lemma membranous or firm, not terete; callus not differentiated . . . . (9)

7a. Awn plumose, less than 2 cm long; lemma prolonged beyond the base of the awn into a rounded bifid tip; glumes rounded at apex, often purplish; plants of peat hummocks in subalpine willow bogs. **Ptilagrostis**, FEATHERGRASS
7b. Awn usually naked, but if plumose, then more than 4 cm long; lemma not prolonged beyond the base of the awn; glumes pointed, straw-colored; plants of dry sites and forest floors . . .
. . . . (8)

8a. Awn persistent, bent and twisted; callus sharp-pointed. **Stipa**, NEEDLEGRASS
8b. Awn deciduous, only slightly twisted and bent; callus blunt. **Oryzopsis**, RICEGRASS (Plants with spklts of **O. hymenoides** but with awns up to 2 cm long and ascending panicle branches represent the infrequent intergeneric hybrid, *X Stiporyzopsis*).

9a. Floret with a tuft of long hairs at the base, these at least 1 mm long. **Muhlenbergia andina**, MUHLY
9b. Floret without a tuft of hairs at the base, or the hairs very short . . . . (10)

10a. Articulation below the glumes, the spklts falling as units . . . . (11)
10b. Articulation above the glumes, the florets falling out of the spklts, leaving the glumes attached to the rachis. . . . . (12)

11a. Glumes with awns 4 mm long or more; panicle very dense and compact. **Polypogon**, RABBITFOOT GRASS
11b. Glumes awnless; panicle loose and open. **Cinna**, WOODREED

12a. Lemma awned from the apex, the awn over 1 mm long . . . . (13)
12b. Lemma awned from the back or awnless, or with an awn-tip less than 1 mm long. . . . . (14)

13a. Awn bent and twisted, plumose. **Ptilagrostis**, FEATHERGRASS
13b. Awn straight, never plumose. **Muhlenbergia**, MUHLY

14a. Nerves of the lemma densely silky-hairy. **Blepharoneuron**, PINE DROPSEED
14b. Nerves of the lemma not silky-hairy, and if pubescent, not especially so on the nerves . . . . (15)

15a. Tall reed-grass over 1 m high, in wet ditches in the valleys, with dense spikelike pale infl; lemma smooth and shining, hard, with a minute hairy scale on each side of the lemma base. **Phalaroides**, REED CANARYGRASS
15b. Not as above . . . . (16)

16a. Glumes as long as the lemma. **Agrostis**, BENTGRASS
16b. Glumes one or both shorter than the lemma . . . . (17)

17a. Grain falling free from the lemma and palea at maturity (Sorry, this is a hard one!); seed loose in the seed coat when wetted; ligule mostly of hairs. **Sporobolus**, DROPSEED [see also *Muhlenbergia asperifolia*]
17b. Grain remaining enclosed within the lemma and palea at maturity; seed fused to the seed coat; ligule membranous . . . . . . (18)

18a. Panicle small and inconspicuous, hardly exceeding the enclosing culm lvs; lvs with a boat-shaped tip as in *Poa*; very rare alpine grass of permanently saturated gravels. **Phippsia**
18b. Panicle conspicuous, spikelike or open, exserted; lvs not boat-tipped. **Muhlenbergia**, MUHLY

Key G (Oats Group)

1a. Florets of the spklt unlike, one bisexual and the other staminate . . . . (2)
1b. Florets all essentially alike (the uppermost may be progressively smaller and less developed). . . . . (3)

2a. Spklts with 2 staminate florets alongside the single bisexual one, all 3 falling attached to each other; foliage fragrant especially when dry. **Hierochloë**, SWEETGRASS
2b. Spklts with 2 florets, the upper bisexual, the lower staminate,

with a bent and twisted awn; tall oat-like grass. **Arrhenatherum**, TALL OATGRASS

3a. Annual; spklts very large, the glumes over 2 cm long; awns large and conspicuous except in some cult vars. **Avena**, OATS
3b. Perennial; spklts smaller, the glumes usually less than 2 cm long; awn, when present, less than 1.5 cm long. . . . . (4)

4a. Lemma awnless; plant less than a meter tall. . . . . (5)
4b. Lemma awned (minute or rarely absent in *Trisetum wolfii*, a tall wet-meadow plant usually over a meter tall) . . . . (6)

5a. Articulation above the glumes; glumes unlike, the first narrow, the second wider, broadest above the middle. **Sphenopholis**, WEDGEGRASS
5b. Articulation above the glumes, the glumes essentially similar. **Koeleria**, JUNEGRASS

6a. Lemma with a flattened, twisted awn arising from between the split apex. **Danthonia**, OATGRASS
6b. Lemma with the awn arising from the back, the apex not split . . (7)

7a. Spklts large, the glumes over 8 mm long; awns large and conspicuous . . . . (8)
7b. Spklts smaller, the glumes less than 8 mm long; awn, if present, less than 10 mm long . . . . (9)

8a. Lf-blades flat or folded; spklts with 3-6 florets; terminal florets exserted slightly beyond the glumes; culms usually well over 20 cm tall; infl well-exserted, golden-brown. **Avenula**, MOUNTAIN OAT
8b. Lf-blades involute; spklts usually with 2 florets, these included between the glumes; culm less than 20 cm tall; infl not much overtopping the lvs, pale straw-colored. **Helictotrichon**, ALPINE OAT

9a. Lemma folded, awned from well above the middle. **Trisetum**
9b. Lemma rounded on the back, awned from the middle or below . . . . (10)

10a. Glumes longer than the florets; lf-blades flat; callus hairs over 1 mm long; lemmas awned from near the middle. **Vahlodea**
10b. Glumes not exceeding the upper floret; lf-blades usually folded; callus hairs less than 1 mm long; lemma awned from near the base. **Deschampsia**, TUFTED HAIRGRASS

Key H (Poa Group)

1a. Rachilla with long silky hairs as long as the lemmas; tall reedgrasses with large tassel-like panicles; plants of wetlands. **Phragmites**, GIANT REED
1b. Not as above . . . . (2)

2a. [1] Spklts minute (less than 2 mm long); infl of very fine capillary branches. **Muhlenbergia asperifolia**
2b. Spklts more than 2 mm long; infl not as above . . . . (3)

3a. [2] Lemma 3-nerved; ligule composed of hairs (except in *Catabrosa*) . . . . (4)
3b. Lemma 5- to many-nerved, the nerves usually not conspicuous; ligule membranous (except in **Distichlis**) . . . . (7)

4a. [3] Spklts 2-fld; sheath closed at least half its length; ligule membranous; semiaquatic, usually with lower part of stem in water. **Catabrosa**, BROOKGRASS
4b. Spklts 3- to many-fld; sheath open; ligule composed of hairs; plants of drier sites . . . . (5)

5a. [4] Lemma long-hairy along the nerves, sometimes notched or lobed at apex; perennial . . . . (6)
5b. Lemma glabrous to scaberulous along nerves, awnless; annual. **Eragrostis**, LOVEGRASS

6a. [5] Stoloniferous; spklts in leafy fascicles, not or scarcely surpassing the sharp-tipped lvs; lemma with two lobes separated by a narrow awned central one. **Dasyochloa**, FLUFFGRASS
6b. Bunchgrass; spklts in a terminal cluster from a culm much exceeding the lvs; lemma merely shallowly notched. **Erioneuron**, HAIRY TRIDENS

7a. [3] Sheath completely closed or closed at least half its length . . . . (8)
7b. Sheath entirely open or open more than 1/2 its length . . . . . (17)

8a. [7] Spklts in dense, rather one-sided clusters on a few main branches. **Dactylis**, ORCHARDGRASS
8b. Not as above . . . . (9)

9a. [8] Lemmas of uppermost florets rolled together to form a club-shaped rudiment; spklts 7-15 mm long, awnless . . . . (10)
9b. Lemma of uppermost florets not rolled together . . . . (11)

10a. [9] Culms bulbous at base; articulation above the glumes and between the florets; panicle not particularly one-sided. **Bromelica**, ONIONGRASS
10b. Culms not bulbous-based; articulation below the glumes; panicle one-sided. **Melica**, ONIONGRASS

11a. [9] Lemma with parallel nerves not converging toward the tip (if projected). **Glyceria**, MANNAGRASS
11b. Lemma with nerves converging toward the tip (if projected) . . (12)

12a. [11] Spklts less than 10 mm long, awnless. **Poa**, BLUEGRASS
12b. Spklts over 10 mm long . . . . (13)

13a. [12] Callus with a prominent tuft of straight hairs 1-2 mm long;

rare or infrequent forest grass. **Schizachne**, FALSE MELIC
13b. Callus not as above . . . . (14)

14a. [13] Annual. . . . . (15)
14b. Perennial. . . . . (16)

15a. [14] Lemma long and narrow, tapering to the long awn. **Anisantha**, CHEATGRASS
15b. Lemma broad and rounded at apex, abruptly awned. **Bromus**, BROME

16a. [14] Spklts flattened, the glumes and lemmas sharply folded. **Ceratochloa**, RESCUE GRASS
16b. Spklts more or less terete, the lemmas rounded on the back. **Bromopsis**, PERENNIAL BROME

17a. [7] Spklt with 2 unlike florets, the upper one bisexual with a short straight awn, the lower staminate with a long bent awn. **Arrhenatherum**, TALL OATGRASS
17b. Florets all alike . . . . (18)

18a. [17] Lemma with an awn 1 mm or more long . . . . (19)
18b. Lemma awnless or merely awn-pointed, with the point less than 1 mm long. . . . . (22)

19a. [18] Lemma awned from the back. **Trisetum**
19b. Lemma terminally awned or rarely awned from a minutely bifid apex. . . . . (20)

20a. [19] Annual of very short duration; plants yellow-green, in age reddish-brown, flowering in early spring. **Vulpia**, SIX-WEEKS FESCUE
20b. Perennial; plant green, not turning brown nor flowering early . .
. . . . (21)

21a. [20] Infl of stiff, rigidly spreading, not secund, branches; florets usually 2, with a terminal rudiment; restricted to shales. **Argillochloa**, FALSE RICEGRASS
21b. Infl of secund branches, not stiff or rigidly spreading; florets usually 3 or more. **Festuca**, FESCUE

22a. [18] Lemma tough and leathery; palea serrate; ligule mostly of hairs; dioecious; on alkali flats. **Distichlis**, SALTGRASS
22b. Lemma membranous; palea not serrate; ligules membranous; bisexual, rarely dioecious. . . . . (23)

23a. [22] Articulation below glumes; glumes very unlike, first short and narrow, second longer and broad above middle; spklts usually 2-fld. **Sphenopholis**, WEDGEGRASS
23b. Articulation above glumes; glumes not as above . . . . (24)

24a. [23] Lemma with parallel nerves not converging at the tip (if projected); lemma apex broadly obtuse or truncate. . . . . . . (25)

24b. Lemma with nerves converging toward the tip (if projected); lemma apex usually acute. . . . . (26)

25a. [24] Nerves faint; plants of alkaline flats. **Puccinellia**, ALKALI GRASS
25b. Nerves prominent, raised; plants of freshwater marshes and wet places, generally avoiding alkaline soils. **Torreyochloa**, WEAK MANNAGRASS

26a. [24] Lemmas and glumes folded (keeled) . . . . (27)
26b. Lemmas rounded on the back (glumes may be keeled and lemmas may be slightly keeled at apex . . . . (28)

27a. [26] Rachis and panicle branches minutely pubescent; panicle dense and spike-like (spreading during anthesis); spklts usually 2-fld; lemmas slightly scabrous. **Koeleria**, JUNEGRASS
27b. Rachis and panicle branches glabrous to scabrous; panicle contracted to open; spklts 2- to several-fld; lemmas often with a tuft of cobwebby hairs at base and/or pubescent nerves. **Poa**, BLUEGRASS

28a. [26] Dioecious; stigmas hispidulous all around; tall broad-lvd glaucous plants of dry pine forests. **Leucopoa**, SPIKE FESCUE
28b. Bisexual; stigmas softly plumose; otherwise not as above . . . . (29)

29a. [28] Lf-tip boat-shaped, splitting apart when opened out; lemmas never awned. **Poa**, BLUEGRASS
29b. Lf-tip not boat-shaped; lemmas awnless or awn-pointed. **Festuca**, FESCUE

AGROPYRON Gaertner 1770 [Gr., *agros*, field, + *pyros*, wheat]. CRESTED WHEATGRASS

Note: realignments in the wheatgrasses have moved our spp into several genera, namely *Elymus*, *Elytrigia*, *Eremopyrum*, *Leymus*, *Lophopyrum*, *Pascopyrum*, *Psathyrostachys* and *Trichopyrum*.

1a. Glumes straight, the hyaline margin broad and conspicuous; spklts spreading at a narrow angle. **A. cristatum** (L.) Gaertner ssp **desertorum** (Fischer) Löve. ADV. These are all Asiatic introductions, planted extensively for soil stabilization.
1b. Glumes twisted, margins very narrow; spklts spreading at almost right angles to the rachis. . . . . (2)

2a. Spikes broad, the lemmas prominently awned. **A. cristatum** (L.) Gaertner ssp **cristatum**.
2b. Spikes narrow, the spklts hardly spreading at all, very short-awned. **A. cristatum** ssp **fragile** (Roth) Löve. Because of extensive breeding and selection, these two, being somewhat compatible, are not always clear-cut.

AGROSTIS L. 1753 [Gr., *agros*, field]. BENTGRASS

1a. Anthers 1-1.6 mm long; palea at least half as long as lemma;

	rhizomatous and often stoloniferous; ligules of upper stem lvs 3-6 mm long .... (2)
1b.	Anthers not more than 0.7 mm long; plants otherwise not as above; mostly native spp .... (3)

2a. Rhizomatous; stems erect from the base; panicle narrow before but open after flowering. **A. gigantea** Roth, REDTOP. ADV. Cult in pastures and estab in hay-meadows and ditches (*A. alba*).

2b. Without rhizomes but sometimes stoloniferous; stems decumbent at the base; panicle narrow at maturity. **A. stolonifera** L., REDTOP. ADV. Less common, usually along streams (*A. palustris*).

3a. Palea at least half as long as lemma; glumes mostly 1.3-2.3 mm long, blunt to acute at apex. .... (4)

3b. Palea absent or less than half as long as lemma; glumes 1.5-3.0 mm long, acute or tapered to a fine tip .... (5)

4a. Panicle narrow or open, 3-7 cm long; lf-blades ca. 2 mm wide; rachilla prolonged beyond the palea as a minute prong. **A. thurberiana** Hitchcock. Subalpine bogs and meadows (*Podagrostis*).

4b. Panicle very narrow, spikelike, 1-4 cm long; lf-blades 1 mm wide or less; rachilla not prolonged. **A. humilis** Vasey. Alpine meadows and tundra (*Podagrostis*).

5a. Lvs 2-10 mm wide; ligule 2-6 mm long; panicle narrow, some branches bearing spikelets to the base. **A. exarata** Trinius [plowed out, alluding to the weedy character]. Moist mt meadows and roadsides, apparently introd.

5b. Lvs narrower, 1-3 mm wide and ligule shorter; panicle open or narrow. .... (6)

6a. Lemma with a prominent bent awn exceeding the lemma tip; panicle narrow; dwarf alpine plant. **A. mertensii** Trinius. Common on tundra (*A. borealis* of Colo lit.). Eurasian plants have distinctly open panicles. Possibly the Colorado ones constitute a well-marked subspecies.

6b. Lemma awnless or with a short, very inconspicuous straight awn no longer than the lemma .... (7)

7a. Panicle narrow, at least some of the lower branches spikelet-bearing near the base; lvs short, involute; lemma rarely awned. **A. variabilis** Rydberg. Subalpine and alpine.

7b. Panicle open or or at least with loosely ascending branches, when narrow the lemmas sometimes awned; lvs flat .... (8)

8a. Panicle very delicate, with very slender branches forking beyond the middle; relatively tall and slender. **A. scabra** Willdenow. Roadsides and mt trails; panicles up to 30 cm long.

8b. Panicle with relatively stouter, not capillary branches; usually awnless, but occasionally with a very inconspicuous straight awn no longer than the lemma; subalpine and low alpine. **A. idahoensis** Nash. The awned form has been called *A. bakeri* Rydberg.

Figure 81. A, *Bromus japonicus*; B, *Danthonia parryi*; C, *Anisantha tectorum*; D, *Phleum commutatum*; E, *Bouteloua curtipendula*; F, *B. gracilis*

ALOPECURUS L. 1753 [Gr., *alopex*, fox, + *oura*, tail]. FOXTAIL

1a. Spklts 5-6 mm long; basal lvs curled; introd sp of dry sites. **A. pratensis** L., MEADOW FOXTAIL. ADV. Used for erosion control and reseeding along highways.
1b. Spklts 2-4 mm long; native sp of wet places . . . . (2)

2a. Panicle 1-4 cm long, about 1 cm broad; glumes densely covered with long hairs. **A. alpinus** Smith. Subalpine meadows and gravelly stream-courses.
2b. Panicle 3-7 cm long, 3-5 mm broad; glumes hairy on keel and nerves only. **A. aequalis** Sobol. Widespread in muddy places, ditches and ponds.

ANDROPOGON L. 1753 [Gr., *andr*, man, + *pogon*, beard]. BIG BLUESTEM; TURKEYFOOT
One sp, **A. gerardii** Vitman. Locally abundant along roadsides near Mancos, native on the E slope and probably accidentally introduced here.

ANISANTHA K. Koch [Gr., *anisos*, unequal, + *anthos*, flower, alluding to differential sexuality among the florets]. CHEATGRASS (formerly incl in *Bromus*)
1a. Awns less than 2 cm long; second glume less than 1 cm long. **A. tectorum** (L.) Nevski [of roofs], **81C**. ADV. Abundant in disturbed ground everywhere. The dry plants are fire hazards and the awned spklts are a danger to animals.
1b. Awns over 2 cm long; second glume over 1 cm long . . . . (2)

2a. Awns 3-6 cm long. **A. diandra** (Roth) Tutin [with two stamens], RIPGUT GRASS. ADV. Infrequent weed (*B. rigidus*).
2b. Awns not over 3 cm long. **A. sterilis** (L.) Nevski. ADV. Infrequent weed.

ARGILLOCHLOA Weber 1984 [Gr., *argillos*, clay, + *chloë*, grass]. FALSE RICEGRASS
One sp, **A. dasyclada** (Hackel) Weber [with hairy branches]. Abundant on shale slopes in the Piceance Basin, otherwise known from a small area in Utah (*Festuca*). Superficially similar to Indian Ricegrass, inhabiting similar sites and having stiffly spreading panicle branches.

ARISTIDA L. 1753 [Lat., *arista*, awn]. THREE-AWN
One sp, **A. purpurea** Nuttall. Easily recognized by the unique 3-awned floret; extremely variable, dry grasslands (*A. longiseta, A. fendleriana*).

ARRHENATHERUM P. Beauvois 1812 [Gr., *arrhen*, masculine, + *ather*, awn, alluding to the awned staminate floret]. TALL OATGRASS
One sp, **A. elatius** (L.) Mertens & Koch. ADV, introd as a nurse crop for new highway rights-of-way.

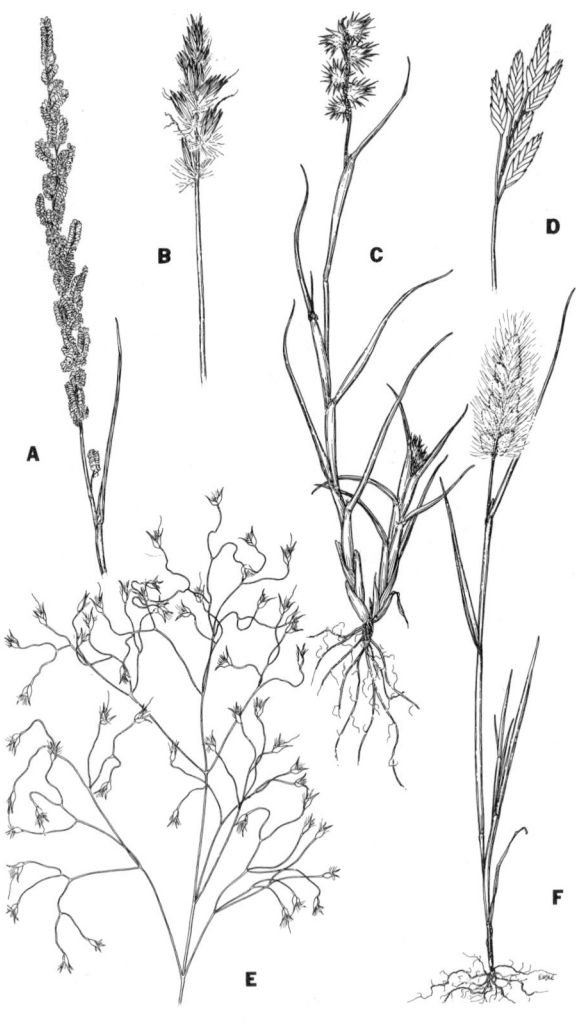

Figure 82. A, *Beckmannia syzigachne*; B, *Hilaria jamesii*; C, *Cenchrus longispinus*; D, *Distichlis spicata*; E, *Polypogon monspeliensis*

AVENA L. 1753 [the classical Lat. name]. OATS

1a. Lemma with stiff, usually reddish-brown hairs; awn bent and twisted. **A. fatua** L. [useless], WILD OATS. ADV weed in grain fields and along roadsides.
1b. Lemma glabrous; awn straight or absent. **A. fatua** var **sativa** (L.) Haussknecht, CULTIVATED OATS. ADV. Widely cult and volunteering on roadsides and horse trails.

AVENULA Dumortier 1868 [dim. of *Avena*]. MOUNTAIN OAT

One sp, **A. hookeri** (Scribner) Holub. Upper subalpine and lower tundra, Continental Divide and South Park. According to Soviet specialists, the Central Asiatic *A. asiatica* is identical to this sp (*Avenochloa, Avena*).

BECKMANNIA Host 1805 [for Johann Beckmann, 1739-1811, German botanist. SLOUGHGRASS

One sp, **B. syzigachne** (Steudel) Fernald [with scissors-like glumes], **82A**. Irrigation ditches and swamps. The unusual spklts are arranged like stacks of poker chips.

BLEPHARONEURON Nash 1898 [Gr., *blepharos*, eyelash, + *neuron*, nerve, alluding to the silky-hairy nerves of the lemma]. PINE DROPSEED

One sp, **B. tricholepis** (Torrey) Nash. Rocky meadows and gravelly open spruce or pine forests.

BOTHRIOCHLOA Kuntze 1891 [Gr., *bothr*, pit, + *chloë*, grass, alluding to a glandular depression on the first glume]. SILVER BEARDGRASS

One sp, **B. barbinodis** (Lagasca) Herter. Infrequent on talus slopes in canyon bottoms, Dolores R (*Andropogon*).

BOUTELOUA Lagasca 1805 [for Claudio and Esteban Boutelou, 18th Century Spanish botanists]. GRAMA [originally spelled *Botelua*]
1a. Spklts arranged in 1-3 brushlike spikes; spikes persisting and curling after the florets fall. . . . . (2)
1b. Spklts arranged in 20-50 small spikes, racemose and pendulous or reflexed on an elongate central axis; spikes falling as a unit. **B. curtipendula** (Michaux) Torrey [short-hanging], SIDE-OATS GRAMA, **81E**. Sagebrush and piñon-juniper.

2a. Annual; spikes one to a culm. **B. simplex** Lagasca. ADV, estab on roadsides, AA, LP.
2b. Perennial; spikes usually 2 or more to a culm. **B. gracilis** (Humboldt, Bonpland & Kunth) Lagasca, BLUE GRAMA, **81F**. Grasslands, lower altitudes.

BROMELICA Farwell 1919 [*Bromus* + *Melica*]. ONIONGRASS

1a. Basal swelling of culm small, globose, 'tailed' at base, i.e., not attached directly to rhizome; first glume 4-5 mm long, less than half as long as the spklt. **B. spectabilis** (Scribner) Weber

[showy]. Aspen woodlands, N and central counties (*Melica*).
1b. Basal swelling of culm stout, attached directly to the rhizome and roots; first glume 6-9 mm long, more than half as long as the spklt. **B. bulbosa** (Geyer) Weber [alluding to the corm]. One record from GF (*Melica*).

BROMOPSIS Fourreau 1869 [*Bromus*, + Gr., *opsis*, like]. PERENNIAL BROME (formerly incl in *Bromus*)
1a. Rhizomes present; floral branches erect or slightly spreading; awn of lemma not over 3 mm long . . . . (2)
1b. Rhizomes absent (bunchgrasses); floral branches nodding; awn of lemma often over 3 mm long . . . . (3)

2a. Lemma scabrous to glabrous; nodes and lvs usually glabrous. **B. inermis** (Leysser) Holub, SMOOTH BROME. ADV. A Eurasian sp widely introduced along roadsides for soil stabilization and pasture forage.
2b. Lemma pubescent; nodes hairy; lvs usually pubescent. **B. pumpelliana** (Scribner) Holub. The native American counterpart of Smooth Brome, montane and subalpine.

3a. First glume (the lower and shorter one; the base of the first glume enfolds that of the second; best examined from inside) 3-nerved. **B. porteri** (Coulter) Holub. Common along roadsides and trails in the mountains.
3b. First glume 1-nerved . . . . (4)

4a. Lower culm sheaths with spreading hairs. **B. lanatipes** (Shear) Holub. Similar habitats.
4b. Lower culm sheaths glabrous. **B. canadensis** (Michaux) Holub. Similar habitats (*B. ciliata, B. richardsonii*).

BROMUS L. 1753 [ancient Gr. name for oats]. BROME

1a. Awns absent or very short; lemmas broad and inflated, papery, the spklts rattling when shaken together. **B. briziformis** Fischer & Meyer [like the genus *Briza*], RATTLESNAKE GRASS. Not yet found on the W slope but to be expected. All spp are ADV introduced weeds of ruderal sites.
1b. Lemmas awned; otherwise not as above . . . . (2)

2a. Lower lf sheaths with slender soft hairs, these more or less reflexed, velvety to ascending shaggy-hairy or loosely hairy to almost glabrous . . . . (3)
2b. Lower lf sheaths with stout, stiff hairs, more or less spreading but never velvety . . . . (5)

3a. Lemma thickish, parchment-like, the veins not very prominent; mature pedicels spreading or pendulous . . . . (4)
3b. Lemma thinner, membranous, with more or less prominent veins; pedicels mostly stiffly erect. **B. hordeaceus** L.

4a. Palea margins narrow (0.5 mm), bluntly infolded above the middle; longest pedicels with 2-4 linear-lanceolate spklts. **B. japonicus** Thunberg, **81A**.
4b. Palea margins 1 mm broad, acutely infolded above the middle; pedicels with 1 or 2 ovate-lanceolate spklts. **B. squarrosus** L.

5a. Sides of the palea hairy or rough with short spikelike cells (compound microscope!); caryopsis of lowest floret usually shorter than the others; panicle large and loose . . . . (6)
5b. Sides of the palea smooth, lacking hairs of any kind; caryopsis of lowest floret almost as long as the others; panicle more or less narrow, not large and loose. **B. racemosus** L.

6a. Margin of palea rounded; caryopsis either ± shriveled or well-developed; ripe spklts with firm axis and thickish florets; lower lf-sheaths glabrous or sparingly hairy. **B. secalinus** L.
6b. Margin of the palea angular-folded; caryopsis always well-developed; ripe spklts with fragile axis and thinner or more slender florets; lower lf-sheaths densely hairy. **B. commutatus** Schrader.

CALAMAGROSTIS Adanson 1763 [Gr., *kalamos*, reed, + *agrostis*, a grass]. REEDGRASS
1a. Awn straight, not over 3 mm long; callus hairs from half to nearly as long as the lemma . . . . (2)
1b. Awn bent, up to 8 mm long; callus hairs less than half the length of the lemma. . . . . (4)

2a. Panicle loose and open; lvs soft-textured, lax. **C. canadensis** (Michaux) P. Beauvois. Very common on borders of montane and subalpine ponds.
2b. Panicle contracted; lvs rather stiff. . . . . (3)

3a. Glumes 2.5-4.0 mm long; lemma 2.2-3.2 mm long. **C. stricta** (Timm) Koeler. Subalpine willow bogs (*C. inexpansa*, *C. neglecta*).
3b. Glumes 4.2-6.0 mm long; lemma 3.5-5.0 mm long. **C. scopulorum** Jones. Seeping ledges of sandstone cliffs in the canyonlands.

4a. Awn 4.5-8.0 mm long, longer than the glumes; glumes 5.5-7.5 mm long; robust, stiff bunch grass (very shortly if at all rhizomatous. **C. purpurascens** R. Brown. Open talus slopes, gravelly low tundra, forested zone to alpine.
4b. Awn 2.2-3.5 mm long, scarcely exceeding the glumes; glumes 3-5 mm long; slender rhizomatous sp. **C. rubescens** Buckley. Lodgepole pine forests, MF.

CATABROSA P. Beauvois 1812 [Gr., *catabrosis*, a devouring, alluding to the chewed appearance of the spklts]. BROOKGRASS
One sp, **C. aquatica** (L.) P. Beauvois. Quiet oxbows of mt streams, usually half-submerged.

CENCHRUS L. 1753 [Gr., *kenchros*, a kind of millet]. SAND BUR
One sp, **C. longispinus** (Hackel) Fernald, **82C**. Sandy soil in the lower valleys.

CERATOCHLOA De Candolle & Beauvois 1812 [Gr., *keratos*, horn, + *chloë*, grass]. RESCUE GRASS

One sp, **C. carinata** (Hooker & Arnott) Tutin. ADV. A sp consisting of a number of interfertile races, introd for range revegetation (*Bromus marginatus*, *B. breviaristatus*).

CHLORIS Swartz 1788 [Gr. goddess of flowers]. WINDMILL GRASS

1a. Panicle branches slender, in several whorls along an axis 20 mm or more long; lemma awned but not hairy. **C. verticillata** Nuttall. ADV weed of gardens and lawns, Grand Junction.
1b. Panicle branches stout, in a single whorl or at least the branches crowded; lemma awned and copiously hairy. **C. virgata** Swartz. ADV. Similar habitats.

CINNA L. 1753 [Gr., *kinni*, a name used by Theophrastus for some grass]. WOOD-REED

One sp, **C. latifolia** (Treviranus) Grisebach. Swampy woodlands, montane and subalpine. A tall, somewhat nondescript grass with broad lvs, a 1-fld spklt, glumes as long as the lemma, lemma tipped with a very short awn point. The large ligules are membranous and lacerate.

CRITESION Rafinesque 1819 [Gr., *krithe*, barley]. FOXTAIL BARLEY (formerly incl in *Hordeum*)
1a. Perennial; awns slender; lvs lacking auricles. . . . . (2)
1b. Annual, branching at the base; awns mostly stouter; lvs sometimes with auricles . . . . (3)

2a. Spike, including awns, as broad as long or nearly so when mature; awns 2-5 cm long. **C. jubatum** (L.) Nevski. Wet ditches and meadows, a very beautiful plant with nodding yellowish or reddish spikes.
2b. Spike, including awns, much longer than broad, the awns not more than 1 cm long. Culms stiffly erect. **C. jubatum** ssp **breviaristatum** (Bowden) Löve. ADV ruderal weed in the valleys (*Hordeum brachyantherum*).

3a. Lf blades with prominent auricles. **C. glaucum** (Steudel) Löve. ADV ruderal weed in the lower valleys.
3b. Lf blades lacking auricles. **C. pusillum** (Nuttall) Löve. Ruderal weed in the lower valleys.

CYLINDROPYRUM Löve 1984 [Gr., cylindric-wheat]. GOATGRASS

One sp, **C. cylindrica** (Host) Löve. ADV weed in the lower Gunnison and Colorado R valleys (*Aegilops*).

CYNODON Richard 1805 [Gr., *kyno*, dog, + *odos*, tooth]. BERMUDA GRASS

One sp, **C. dactylon** (L.) Persoon. ADV. Commonly used for lawns, occasionally escaping and becoming estab, Colorado R Valley. Easily known from the digitate infl and stoloniferous habit.

Poaceae/Gramineae (POA/GRM) 375

DACTYLIS L. 1753 [Gr., *daktylos*, a finger]. ORCHARDGRASS
One sp, **D. glomerata** L. ADV weed in lawns and fields, sometimes grown in pasture mixes. The clumps of succulent, bluish-green folded lvs form unsightly clumps, overspreading bluegrass in lawns and not removed easily by mowing. The pollen is a major cause of hay fever.

DANTHONIA de Candolle 1805 [for Etienne Danthoine, 19th Cent. French botanist]. OATGRASS
1a. Panicle with one, rarely more, spklts; lf sheaths pilose. **D. unispicata** (Thurber) Munro. Sandstone benches, MF.
1b. Panicle with numerous spklts; lf sheaths not pilose. . . . . (2)

2a. Glumes over 15 mm long; lemma over 9 mm long; culms robust, over 1 mm wide. **D. parryi** Scribner, **81B**. Dry gravelly hillsides, upper montane and subalpine. Doubtfully present on the W slope.
2b. Glumes and lemmas shorter; culms slender; old lf sheaths not conspicuous. **D. intermedia** Vasey. Subalpine and alpine grasslands.

DASYOCHLOA Willdenow 1840 [Gr., *dasys*, shaggy, + *chloë*, grass]. FLUFFGRASS
One sp, **D. pulchella** (Humboldt, Bonpland & Kunth) Rydberg [dim. of beautiful]. Piñon-juniper and desert-steppe, ME, MZ (*Erioneuron*).

DESCHAMPSIA P. Beauvois 1812 [for Jean Loiseleur Deslongchamps, 1774-1849, French botanist]. TUFTED HAIRGRASS
One sp, **D. cespitosa** (L.) P. Beauvois. Wet meadows and pond margins, subalpine, one of the most valuable native forage grasses in the mts. It is very tenacious, often being the last survivor when upland wetlands are overgrazed or drained. The lvs are stiff and have sharp points (use palm of the hand), a good identification mark.

DICHANTHELIUM Gould 1974 [Gr., *dicha*, in two, + *anthele*, tuft or plume of a reed, alluding to the branching in the type sp, *D. dichotomum*] (formerly in *Panicum*)
One sp, **D. acuminatum** (Swartz) Frechmann var **fasciculatum** (Torrey) Frechmann [woolly]. Rare on the W slope, known only from a spring in Unaweap Canyon. Var **sericeum** (Schmoll) Frechmann occurs only on steaming travertine at Box Canyon Hot Springs, and is disjunct from Wyoming and Alberta. In the variety the lvs are very short and broad, green and almost glabrous, spreading out on the hot surface (*D. lanuginosum*).

DIGITARIA Heister 1759 [Lat., *digitus*, finger]. CRABGRASS
One sp, **D. sanguinalis** (L.) Scopoli (stanching blood, named for its supposed styptic properties]. ADV, a pest of lawns, fields and roadsides in the lower valleys.

DISTICHLIS Rafinesque 1819 [Gr., *distichos*, 2-ranked]. SALTGRASS
One sp, **D. spicata** (L.) Greene ssp **stricta** (Torrey) Thorne, **82D**. Alkaline swales and borrow-pits, lower valleys. The name *D. stricta*

was thought for a long time to be a different sp but it was found that these were only the carpellate plants, which have more rigid spklts!

ECHINOCHLOA P. Beauvois 1812 [Gr., *echinos*, hedgehog, + *chloë*, grass]. BARNYARD GRASS
  One sp, **E. crus-galli** (L.) P. Beauvois [cockspur]. ADV Coarse weed in gardens, irrigation ditches and farmyards in the lower valleys. Very variable as to awn length.

ELEUSINE Gaertner 1788 [from *Eleusis*, the town where Ceres, goddess of harvests, was worshipped]. GOOSEGRASS
  One sp, **E. indica** (L.) Gaertner [of India]. ADV ruderal weed in the Colorado R valley.

ELYMUS L. 1753 [Gr., *elymos*, name for a kind of millet]. WILD RYE

1a. Spklts solitary at each node of the rachis . . . . (2)
1b. Spklts 2 or more at some or all of the nodes (count the glumes; there are 2 for each spklt) . . . . (4)

2a. Awn of lemma straight or absent. **E. trachycaulus** (Link) Gould [rough-stem]. Meadows and roadsides; an alpine race (ssp **andinus** [Scribner & Smith] Löve & Löve) has very broad glumes and lemmas.
2b. Glumes and lemmas with long, curved awns . . . . (3)

3a. Culms decumbent, spreading. **E. scribneri** (Vasey) Jones [for F. Lamson-Scribner]. Very common on dry alpine tundra.
3b. Culms erect. **E. bakeri** (Nelson) Löve [for C. F. Baker]. Mt meadows, never on tundra. Little known or understood, this resembles *Elytrigia dasystachya* ssp *albicans* but lacks rhizomes.

4a. Glumes subulate, extending into long spreading awns; rachis of infl brittle and shattering at maturity . . . . (5)
4b. Glumes broad or narrow but not subulate or extended into long awns; rachis usually remaining intact, or, if shattering, then the awns less than 2 cm long. (7)

5a. Lowermost floret of one or both spklts at each node sterile and reduced to a subulate or lanceolate awn, giving the appearance of extra glume segs . . . . (6)
5b. Lowermost floret of each spklt fertile, not modified. **E. longifolius** (Smith) Gould. This and the next two are very common weedy grasses (squirreltails) on roadsides and disturbed areas. When ripe the awns spread stiffly and the axis soon breaks apart. Because of minute barbs along the awns, the segments will 'walk' if not glued to herbarium sheets (*Sitanion*).

6a. Glumes entire or bifid. **E. elymoides** (Rafinesque) Swezey (*Sitanion hystrix*). The most abundant sp.
6b. Glumes 3-many-cleft. **E. multisetus** (Smith) Davy (*S. jubatum*). Grasslands, MF.

7a. Lemma with long, divergent awns; spike nodding. **E. canadensis** L., CANADA WILD RYE. Fencerows in the valleys, the spikes persisting long into autumn.
7b. Lemma with short, straight awns; spike strictly erect. **E. glaucus** Buckley, BLUE WILD RYE. Aspen glades in the mts, evidently requiring shade.

ELYTRIGIA Desvaux 1810 [Gr., *elytron*, sheath or husk] (formerly in *Agropyron*)
1a. Glumes blunt, rounded or truncate at the tip and only slightly mucronate. **E. intermedia** (Host) Nevski, INTERMEDIATE WHEATGRASS. ADV, commonly planted to revegetate depleted range. A race with villous lemmas is ssp. **barbulata** (Schur) Löve (*A. trichophorum*). Löve recently proposed the genus *Trichopyrum* for this species. Easily confused with *Lophopyrum elongatum*, which has truncate glumes without a mucro, and lacks rhizomes.
1b. Glumes pointed. . . . . (2)

2a. Lemmas with long outcurved awns. **Elytrigia dasystachya** ssp **albicans** (Scribner & Smith) Dewey [shaggy-spike; whitened]. Usually among rocks on slopes, but commonly in moist borrow pits. In Colorado this behaves more like a legitimate sp than as a race of the next.
2b. Lemmas with straight awns of none . . . . (3)

3a. Lemmas scabrous or villous. **E. dasystachya** (Hooker) Löve & Löve. Common roadside grass.
3b. Lemmas glabrous. **E. repens** (L.) Nevski, QUACK GRASS. ADV weed of cult ground with deep-seated brittle rhizomes.

ERAGROSTIS Wolf 1781 [Gr., *Eros*, god of love, + *agrostis*, a grass]. LOVEGRASS
1a. Tall, erect, 6-10 dm tall, with open panicles. **E. mexicana** (Hornemann) Link ssp **virescens** Presl. Infrequent ADV weed, Colorado R Valley (*E. orcuttiana*).
1b. Low, spreading grass. (2)

2a. Plant with minute glandular depressions on the panicle branches and sometimes on the keels and faces of lemmas . . . . (3)
2b. Plants not glandular on the panicle branches or lemmas. **E. pectinacea** (Michaux) Nees [comb-like]. ADV ruderal weed, late summer.

3a. Largest spklts 2.5 mm wide; glandular depressions prominent on keels of lemmas. **E. cilianensis** (Allioni) Janchen [of Ciliani, an Italian estate]. ADV ruderal weed.
3b. Largest spklts not more than 2 mm wide, mostly less; glandular depressions mostly on the panicle branches and lvs. **E. minor** Host (*E. perplexans*, *E. poaeoides*). ADV ruderal weed, Grand Junction.

EREMOPYRUM Jaubert & Spach 1851 [Gr., *erem*, desert, + *pyros*, wheat]. ANNUAL WHEATGRASS

One sp, **E. triticeum** (Gaertner) Nevski. ADV, introd along the railroad at Grand Junction many years ago and now widespread in the lowlands throughout the Colorado R Valley.

ERIONEURON Nash 1903 [Gr., *erion*, woolly, + *neuron*, nerve) HAIRY TRIDENS

One sp, **E. pilosum** (Buckley) Nash. Piñon-juniper and desert steppe, ME-MN. To be expected also in the southern tier of counties, since it recurs on the E slope in the Arkansas River drainage (see also *Dasyochloa*).

FESTUCA L. 1753 [ancient name for a grass]. FESCUE

1a.	Lf blades flat, averaging over 3 mm wide	(2)
1b.	Lf blades involute or, if flat, less than 3 mm wide.	(5)

2a. Panicle spikelike; plants dioecious; stigmas bearing branches on all sides; lvs without auricles; native in ponderosa pine forests (see *Leucopoa*)
2b. Panicle narrow but not spikelike; plants not dioecious; stigmas with branches on two sides only; auricles sometimes present . . . (3)

3a. Spklts 2-4-fld, 8-11 mm long; auricles lacking. **F. sororia** Piper. Little known, from spruce-fir forest openings, San Juan Mts.
3b. Spklts 5-9-fld, 10-17 mm long; auricles present. . . . . (4)

4a. Lemmas 7-10 mm long; first glume 4-6 mm long, the second 5-7 mm long. **F. arundinacea** Schreber [reed-like], ALTA FESCUE. ADV, introd in pastures and roadsides in the valleys.
4b. Lemmas 4-7 mm long; first glume 2.5-4.0 mm long, the second 3.5-5.0 mm long. **F. pratensis** Hudson, MEADOW FESCUE. ADV, similar habitats.

5a. Ligule 2-4 mm or more long; lemmas awnless or cuspidate. **F. thurberi** Vasey [for George Thurber, botanist for the Mexican Boundary Survey]. A tall and handsome bunchgrass, abundant on forested slopes and forming the dominant grass on high mountain ridges in the San Juans. Distinguished from the habitally similar *F. arizonica* by the broader, not glaucous, lvs.
5b. Ligule shorter; lemma distinctly awned (except in *F. arizonica*)
. . . . (6)

6a. Culm curved at the base, the new shoots breaking out through the old lf-sheath; basal lf sheaths reddish, the vascular strands persisting as fibers; culms in loose tufts. **F. rubra** L. Mt meadows; anthers 2-3 mm long.
6b. Culms erect from the base, the new shoots not breaking out but coming up between a lf sheath and the culm; basal lf sheaths not reddish nor fibrillose. . . . . (7)

7a. Rhizomatous, always growing in *Kobresia* stands in the tundra. **F. hallii** (Vasey) Piper [for Elihu Hall]. Known in recent time only from Cameron Pass, but originally collected somewhere on the PA/ST county boundary, possibly on the W slope.
7b. Plant caespitose, without rhizomes. . . . . (8)

8a. Anthers up to 1.5 mm long; lemmas up to 4 mm long exclusive of the awn. . . . . (9)
8b. Anthers 2.5-4.0 mm long; lemma up to 5-7 mm long excluding the awn, often inrolled, exposing the rachilla . . . . (12)

9a. Anthers 1.0-1.5 mm long; lvs glaucous; culms tall, about 2-3 times the height of the basal lvs; ligule 3 mm long; lemma 6.0-7.5 mm long including the awn. **F. saximontana** Rydberg. Dry mt meadows and forest openings.
9b. Anthers 0.7-0.8 mm long; lvs green; culms usually less than twice the height of the basal lvs; ligule minute or obsolete; lemma 3-4 mm including awn. . . . . (10)

10a. Culm minutely and densely pubescent just below the head; spklts tending to be reddish-brown. **F. baffinensis** Polunin [from Baffin Island]. Infrequent on dry tundra on the Continental Divide, N counties.
10b. Culm not pubescent below the head; spklts dark gray-green. . . (11)

11a. Lvs very slender and lax, the tuft usually less than 10 cm high and tending to spread; culms hardly exceeding the lvs; caryopsis hairy at the apex. **F. minutiflora** Rydberg. Frequent on tundra but not as common as the next.
11b. Lvs stiff, erect, the tuft usually over 10 cm high; culms usually well exceeding the lvs; caryopsis glabrous. **F. brachyphylla** Schultes ssp **coloradensis** Frederiksen. Very abundant and characteristic of dry tundra (often incorrectly called *F. ovina*; that is a European sp with long anthers, only cult in America).

12a. Awn 2-4 mm long; persistent papery basal lf sheaths less than 4 cm long; lvs seldom up to 30 cm high. **F. idahoensis** Elmer. Infrequent, subalpine. The typical plant of the Pacific Northwest has widely spreading panicle branches, not always the case with our plants.
12b. Awn up to 2 mm long; persistent papery lf sheaths 5-10 cm long; lvs filiform, usually over 30 cm long. **F. arizonica** Vasey. Common in dry pine forests, S counties.

GLYCERIA R. Brown 1810 [Gr., *glyceros*, sweet]. MANNAGRASS

1a. Spklts linear, over 7 mm long; panicle narrow. **G. borealis** (Nash) Batchelder. Margins of ponds, upper montane and subalpine, uncommon.
1b. Spklts ovate to oblong, less than 7 mm long; panicle open. . . . . (2)

2a. Lf blades narrow, 2-6 mm wide; first glume 0.5-0.9 mm long; culm mostly less than 1 m tall. **G. striata** (Lamarck) Hitchcock.

Common on swampy streamsides throughout. The ripe florets shatter very easily from the spklts.
2b. Lf blades wider; first glume 1 mm or more long; culm mostly over 1 m tall . . . . (3)
3a. First glume 1.5 mm or more long; spklts 5-7 mm or more long; panicle very compound and open. **G. grandis** Watson. A very tall sp of swamps and irrigation ditches in the lower valleys (*G. maxima* ssp *grandis*).
3b. First glume 1 mm long or less; panicle only moderately compound. **G. elata** (Nash) Hitchcock. Aspen thickets and pond borders, subalpine.

HELICTOTRICHON Besser 1827 [Gr., *helicos*, twisted, + *trichon*, hair]. ALPINE OAT

One sp, **H. mortonianum** (Scribner) Henrard [for J. Sterling Morton, Sec'y of Agriculture]. Dry alpine tundra. Our only representative of a fairly large Asiatic mountain genus.

HIEROCHLOË R. Brown 1810 [Gr., *hieros*, sacred, + *chloë*, grass]. SWEETGRASS

One sp, **H. hirta** (Schrank) Borbas ssp **arctica** (Presl) Weimarck. Frequent in swampy meadows and lower alpine slopes. Spklts rich golden brown. In Poland the plant is favored for flavoring vodka.

HILARIA Humboldt, Bonpland & Kunth 1816 [for Auguste St.-Hilaire, French naturalist]. GALLETA GRASS
1a. Culms and often the lvs woolly-pubescent. **H. rigida** (Thurber) Bentham. Recently discovered in McIntyre Canyon, SM. Desert-steppe and piñon-juniper.
1b. Culms and lvs glabrous to slightly hirsute. **H. jamesii** (Torrey) Bentham, **82B**. Common on river benches and sagebrush stands in the lower valleys. The spklt anatomy in this genus is extremely complex, but it has a unique appearance.

HORDEUM L. 1753 [the classical name for barley]. BARLEY

One sp, **H. vulgare** L. ADV. Widely cult in the valleys and occasionally volunteering along roadsides and in fallow fields. Two forms are commonly cult: 'bearded' barley, with long-awned lemmas, and 'hooded' barley, with awnless lemmas having a blunt, often 3-lobed apical appendage or 'hood'. A third rarely cult type with a single spklt (var. *distichum*) might be confused with wheat, but in barley the florets taper to the awn and in wheat they are truncate.

KOELERIA Persoon 1805 [for Georg L. Koeler, German botanist, 1765-1807]. JUNEGRASS

One sp, **K. macrantha** (Ledebour) Schultes. Very common in meadows. In blossom the panicle is open, glossy, and very different in appearance from its fruiting aspect, a dense, contracted spikelike panicle (*K. gracilis*).

LEERSIA Swartz 1788 [for Johann Leers, German botanist, 1727-1774]. RICE CUTGRASS

One sp, **L. oryzoides** (L.) Swartz. ADV. Frequent in irrigation ditches in the Colorado R Valley. The spklt, of one floret without glumes, and the saw-edged stems, are diagnostic.

LEPTOCHLOA P. Beauvois 1812 [Gr., *leptos*, delicate, + *chloë*, grass]. SPRANGLETOP
One sp, **D. fascicularis** (Lamarck) P. Beauvois. Muddy shores of ponds and oxbows in the lower valleys (*Diplachne*).

LEUCOPOA Grisebach 1852 [Gr., *leucos*, white, + *Poa*]. SPIKE FESCUE
One sp, **L. kingii** (Watson) Weber. A common grass of dry ponderosa pine woods in eastern Colorado, but known on the W slope only from the plateaus of Dinosaur Nat. Mon. (*Hesperochloa*).

LEYMUS Hochstetter 1848 [anagram of *Elymus*]. WILD-RYE (formerly in *Elymus*)
1a. Strongly rhizomatous, definitely not bunchgrasses. **L. triticoides** (Buckley) Pilger. Frequent on benches and clay flats in the lower valleys.
1b. Bunchgrasses with no rhizomes or very short ones . . . . (2)

2a. Plants gigantic, forming dense clumps up to over 2 m high; lvs yellow-green; lf blades up tp 15 mm broad. **L. cinereus** (Scribner & Merrill) Löve, GIANT WILD-RYE. Common on talus slopes in the canyon-bottoms.
2b. Plants smaller; lvs dark- or grayish-green; lf blades narrower . .
. . . . (3)

3a. Lvs involute, dark blue-green; spklts usually solitary at the nodes. **L. salina** (Jones) Löve [from Salina, Utah]. Abundant and dominant grass on desert clay hills.
3b. Lvs flat, yellow-green; spklts commonly 2 at a node. **L. ambiguus** (Vasey & Scribner) Dewey. Frequent on rocky mountainsides in the E Colorado foothills, reported but doubtfully present on the W slope.

LOLIUM L. 1753 [the ancient Lat. name]. RYEGRASS
One sp, **L. perenne** L. ADV. Common admixture in lawns and becoming a troublesome weed because it lodges and resists mowing (*L. multiflorum*).

LOPHOPYRUM Löve 1980 [Gr., *lophos*, crest, mane, + *pyros*, wheat]. SLENDER WHEATGRASS
One sp, **L. elongatum** (Host) Löve. ADV. Extensively planted to retard erosion and stabilize grasslands. Similar to *Elytrigia intermedia* but rhizomes are absent and the glumes are exactly truncate, without a mucro extension of a vein.

MELICA L. 1753 [Lat., *mel*, honey]. ONIONGRASS
One sp, **M. porteri** Scribner [for T.C. Porter]. Rare or only locally abundant on rocky cliffsides in Black Canyon and the San Juans. A beautiful grass growing in massive clumps with many culms, each with pendent racemose spklts (see also *Bromelica*).

MONROA Torrey 1857 [for William Munro, British grass specialist, 1818-1880]. FALSE BUFFALOGRASS
One sp, **M. squarrosa** (Nuttall) Torrey. Sandy depressions on rimrock areas on the plateaus and along roadsides in the lower valleys. Easily recognized by its matted form and very rigid, prickle-

pointed white-edged lvs. In some places a plant louse infests the foliage, resulting in the whole plant being covered by a loose cobwebby material [incorrectly spelled *Munroa*].

MUHLENBERGIA Schreber 1789 [for Gotthilf Mühlenberg, 1753-1815, Pennsylvania botanist]. MUHLY

1a. Annual, mostly weak-rooted and completing a life cycle in six weeks or so. . . . . (2)
1b. Perennial, usually with rhizomes . . . . (4)

2a. Lemma awned. **M. depauperata** Scribner. Known from one collection in Colorado Nat Mon, restricted to small depressions in sandstone rimrock that fill seasonally with shallow water pools.
2b. Lemma awnless. . . . . (3)

3a. Pedicels capillary, elongate; panicle open. **M. minutissima** (Steudel) Swallen. Infrequent and very inconspicuous, on sandy flats, roadsides, borrow pits, without much competing vegetation. A delicate and pretty little sp.
3b. Pedicels short, appressed; panicle narrow, contracted. **M. filiformis** (Thurber) Rydberg. Swampy woodlands, meadows, and boggy streamsides, subalpine.

4a. Rhizomatous . . . . (5)
4b. Bunchgrasses lacking rhizomes . . . . (10)

5a. Panicle narrow; spklts on short pedicels . . . . (6)
5b. Panicles open when fully out of the sheath; spklts on slender, more or less elongated pedicels . . . . (9)

6a. Blades 2 mm broad or less, usually short and involute; anthers 1.0-2.7 mm long . . . . (7)
6b. Blades mostly over 3 mm broad, flat; anthers 0.3-1.0 mm long . . . . (8)

7a. Lemma not at all pilose, 2-3 mm long; lvs several cm long, erect. **M. richardsonis** (Trinius) Rydberg. Common on rocky ledges and gravelly meadows, piñon-juniper to montane.
7b. Lemma pilose at least on lower half, 2.0-3.5 mm long, distinctly awned; lvs about 1 cm long, stiffly spreading. **M. thurberi** Rydberg. Sandstone rimrock, piñon-juniper, ME-MZ.

8a. Callus hairs almost as long as the lemma; awn 2.5-8.0 mm long. **M. andina** (Nuttall) Hitchcock. Around water seeps at the base of rock outcrops in the canyons.
8b. Callus hairs less than half as long as the lemma; awn very short or a mere mucro. **M. racemosa** (Michaux) Britton, Sterns & Poggenberg. Rocky places in sagebrush and aspen zone. Pale scaly rhizomes present.
9a. Glumes awnless; spklts minute (less than 2 mm); lemma hardly longer than the glumes. **M. asperifolia** (Nees & Meyen) Parodi. Infl of very fine branches; plants making extensive stands in alkaline ditches and swales in the lower valleys.

9b. Glumes short-awned (up to 3 mm long including the awn); lemma twice as long as the glumes; blades involute, stiff and sharp-pointed. **M. pungens** Thurber. Sandy blowouts, MF.

10a. Second glume 3-toothed, rarely only ragged. . . . . (11)
10b. Second glume not 3-toothed, usually awned. . . . . (12)

11a. Awn 6-20 mm long; panicles 6-15 cm long; ligules prominent, 4-7 mm long. **M. montana** (Nuttall) Hitchcock. Common on dry montane hillsides.
11b. Awn 2-3 mm long; panicles 2.0-4.5 cm long; ligules up to 4 mm long. **M. filiculmis** Vasey. Common in dry gravels of South Park and to be expected on the W slope, since it recurs in Utah.

12a. Panicles open, loose, naked at the base; culms proliferating from the upper lf-axils. **M. porteri** Scribner. Not yet reported from the W slope, but to be expected in the Four Corners.
12b. Panicles narrow or spikelike, spklt-bearing to the base . . . . . (13)

13a. Lemma 1.5-2.2 mm long; weak perennial with a few short, slender rhizomes. **M. filiformis** (Thurber) Rydberg. Swampy woodlands, meadows and boggy streamsides, subalpine.
13b. Lemma 3-5 mm long; strong perennial . . . . (14)

14a. Lemma tapering to an awn 5-12 mm long; spklts usually purple. **M. pauciflora** Buckl. A southwestern sp peripheral in LP, known from one collection.
14b. Lemma only awn-pointed or with an awn up to 1 mm; spklts green. **M. wrightii** Vasey [for the collector, Charles Wright, 1811-1885]. Ledges of sandstone rimrock, SW counties.

ORYZOPSIS Michaux 1803 [Gr., *oryza*, rice, + *opsis*, like]. RICEGRASS

1a. Lemma densely covered with long hairs . . . . (2)
1b. Lemma glabrous or covered with short appressed hairs . . . . . . (4)

2a. Panicle wide-spreading at maturity. **O. hymenoides** (Roemer & Schultes) Ricker [membranous, referring to the thin glumes], INDIAN RICEGRASS. An attractive bunchgrass of shale or clay soil in the steppe-desert. The seeds were used extensively by Indians for food. Occasionally, first generation hybrids are formed by crossing with any of several *Stipa* spp, resulting in plants with longer awns and narrower infls; these may be referred to as *X Stiporyzopsis bloomeri*.
2b. Panicle narrow, with appressed branches at maturity. . . . . . . (3)

3a. Glumes less than 7.5 mm long, broadest at the middle; short bunchgrass, not over 2 dm high. See *Stipa webberi*.
3b. Glumes up to 10 mm long, tapering from base to apex; tall bunchgrass resembling *O. hymenoides*. **O. contracta** (Johnson) Schechter. One collection from DeBeque.

4a. Spklts 5-8 mm long, not including the awn; callus densely hairy; lf blades flat, 5-9 mm wide. **O. asperifolia** Michaux [rough-lvd]. Shade woods, lower montane.
4b. Spklts 3-4 mm long, not including the awn; callus not densely hairy; lvs narrower . . . . (5)

5a. Panicle branches erect or appressed at maturity . . . . (6)
5b. Panicle branches spreading or reflexed at maturity. **O. micrantha** (Trinius & Ruprecht) Thurber. Usually in deep shade, rocky slopes. A delicate plant with very slender weak culms and minute spklts.

6a. Awn less than 2 mm long or almost lacking. **O. pungens** (Torrey) Hitchcock [sharp]. Infrequent, known on the W slope from pine forests in the Cochetopa Divide.
6b. Awn 5 mm or more long. **O. exigua** Thurber [short]. Frequent on rocky canyon slopes in the northern Park Range.

PANICUM L. 1753 [Lat., *panus*, an ear of millet]. PANIC GRASS

1a. Weedy annual, low and spreading, with filiform, widely-spreading panicle branches; sterile palea lacking. **P. capillare** L. var **occidentale** Rydberg, WITCHGRASS. ADV common late summer weed of fields and roadsides in the valleys.
1b. Perennial, tall bunchgrass; sterile palea present. **P. virgatum** L. [wandlike], SWITCHGRASS. Uncommon on the W slope, frequent in lower Escalante Canyon.

PASCOPYRUM Löve 1980 [Lat., *pascuum*, pasture, + Gr., *pyros*, wheat]. WESTERN WHEATGRASS [formerly *Agropyron*]

One sp, **P. smithii** (Rydberg) Löve [for J. G. Smith, USDA botanist]. Abundant glaucous rhizomatous plant of dry flats and grasslands. Two races occur, var **smithii** with glabrous spklts, and var. **molle** with hairy spklts. Very easily recognized once one masters the subtlety of the glume shape, in this sp tapering from base of apex.

PASPALUM L. 1753 [Gr., *paspale*, meal]

One sp, **P. dilatatum** Poiret, DALLIS GRASS. ADV. Known on the W slope only from a single old record, DT.

PHALAROIDES Wolf 1781 [dim. of ancient Gr. name for some grass]. REED CANARYGRASS

One sp, **P. arundinacea** (L.) Raüschert [reedlike]. ADV, abundant along irrigation ditches and wet meadows, lower valleys. The seed is a common ingredient of bird seed mixes (*Phalaris*).

PHIPPSIA R. Brown 1823 [for Constantine John Phipps, 2nd Baron Mulgrave, 18th Cent. Arctic voyager]

One sp, **P. algida** (Phipps) R. Brown [cold]. Restricted to cold gravels of snow-melt streamlets fed by snowfields of glacial cirques, usually over 12,000 ft. The culms are very low and spreading, 1-3 cm high, and the foliage somewhat succulent. The lf-blades are very short and have a boat-tip as in *Poa*. On the W slope known only from high peaks of the Ten Mile Range, ST. This genus is very close to *Puccinellia*; if it is synonymous, then all spp of *Puccinellia* (there are very many) would have to be transferred to *Phippsia*.

PHLEUM L. 1753 [Gr., *phleos*, name for some marsh reed]. TIMOTHY
1a. Panicle oblong to ovoid, less than 5 times as long as wide; base of culm not bulbous; upper sheaths inflated (loose). **P. commutatum** Gaudin [altered], ALPINE TIMOTHY, **81D**. Common in subalpine meadows (*P. alpinum* is an exclusively European sp).
1b. Panicle cylindrical, over 6 times as long as wide; culm base swollen or bulbous; sheaths tight. **P. pratense** L. [of meadows]. ADV along roadsides and trails, meadows and pastures.

PHRAGMITES Adanson 1763 [ancient Gr. name meaning "growing in hedges"]. COMMON REED
One sp, **P. australis** (Cavanilles) Trinius. Locally abundant and forming great stands along rivers and in irrigation ditches in the lower valleys. The stout culms were used to make arrow-shafts. Occasional populations have spklts that are without floral parts within the glumes and lemmas; in such plants, reproduction must be purely vegetative (*P. communis*).

POA L. 1753 [ancient Gr. name for grass or fodder]. BLUEGRASS
Note: a difficult genus of variable and often hybridizing spp, many forming partly or wholly apomictic populations. The following key will not always work, but should be useful most of the time.
1a. Annual (**Key A, Annuae**)
1b. Perennial. . . . . (2)

2a. Rhizomes present and well-developed; plants not forming tight clumps (**Key B, Pratenses**)
2b. Rhizomes lacking; plants forming tight clumps (although occasionally the culms are decumbent, rooting at the lower nodes . . . . (3)

3a. Lemma with a weft of wavy hairs at the base (sometimes scanty in *P. nemoralis*) (**Key C, Palustres**)
3b. Lemma lacking a weft of wavy hairs at the base (sometimes sparsely so in *P. abbreviata*). . . . . (4)

4a. Spklts flattened; glumes and lemmas keeled (**Key D, Alpinae**)
4b. Spklts rounded, the glumes not keeled, or only obscurely so at the tip (**Key E, Scabrellae**)

KEY A, Annuae

1a. Culms erect, bulbous at the base; fls proliferated into asexual bulblets with short leafy shoots. **P. bulbosa** L., BULBOUS BLUEGRASS. ADV. Commonly cult and spreading in dry land.
1b. Culms low, spreading, succulent, not bulbous; culms not proliferous. **P. annua** L. ADV weedy sp in poorly drained lawns, meadows, along wet trails and clearings.

KEY B, Pratenses

1a. Culm flattened and 2-edged; exposed nodes marked by a prominent black line; sheaths often paler than the culm. **P. compressa** L., CANADA BLUEGRASS. Common on dry hillsides, a native sp, possibly distinct from its Old World counterpart.
1b. Culm not flattened . . . . (2)

2a. Panicle contracted, branches stiffly aacending to erect. **P. arida** Vasey, PLAINS BLUEGRASS. Low, often alkaline flats in the valleys.
2b. Panicle open, branches spreading or reflexed . . . . (3)

3a. Lemmas with long crinkly hairs at the base. . . . . (4)
3b. Lemmas without long crinkly basal hairs . . . . (6)

4a. Ligule on culm lvs 2-4 mm long, obtuse or truncate; lemmas 3.5-5.5 mm long. **P. arctica** R. Brown. Common on tundra but sometimes doing well along subalpine roadsides (*P. grayana*, *P. longipila*).
4b. Ligule on culm lvs 1 mm long, truncate; lemmas 2-3 mm long . .
. . . . (5)

5a. Basal lvs bright green, 2-3 mm broad, flat or channeled, withering and disintegrating after a season; spklts mostly 3-fld; lowest lemma very cobwebby at base. **P. pratensis** L., KENTUCKY BLUEGRASS. ADV. Widely used for lawns and pasture mixes, always in wet sites in natural habitats.
5b. Basal lvs glaucous, 0.8-2.0 mm broad, folded and somewhat revolute, remaining intact through the next season; spklts mostly 2-fld; lemma only slightly cobwebby. **P. agassizensis** Boivin & Löve. The native counterpart of the last, common in dry open forests.

6a. Lower sheaths minutely retrorse-hairy and purplish; spklts commonly purplish. **P. nervosa** (Hooker) Vasey. Common in forests and meadows, montane, subalpine.
6b. Lower sheaths smooth, green. **P. arctica** R. Brown. Upper subalpine and alpine.

KEY C, Palustres

1a. Panicle nodding, open, with flexuous capillary branches; blades short, flat, up to 4 mm wide; anthers 0.4-0.9 mm long . . . . . . (2)
1b. Panicle not nodding nor with flexuous branches. . . . . (3)

2a. Glumes very unequal, the lower ones often ± subulate; lemma 3-4 mm long, acuminate, the nerves pilose to glabrate. **P. leptocoma** Trinius. Springs and boggy subalpine forests.
2b. Glumes subequal, the lower similar to the upper; lemma 2-3 mm long, acute, the nerves pilose. **P. reflexa** Vasey & Scribner. Similar habitats, very common.

3a. Culms 5-12 dm high, loosely tufted; ligule 1.5 mm long or more; panicle pyramidal, 15-30 cm long; moist habitats . . . . (4)
3b. Culms 2-5 dm high, densely tufted, stiff; ligule 0.5-1.5 mm long; panicle 5-15 cm long with short ascending branches; lemma sometimes only scantily cobwebby. **P. nemoralis** L. ssp **interior** (Rydberg) Butters & Abbe. Common on rocky outcrops and mt slopes. The short culm blade stands out stiffly at a wide angle from the stem, a good field character.

4a. Ligule 1.5-3.0 mm long; blades 3-7 mm wide; lemma 3-5 mm long; anthers 1.8-3.0 mm long. **P. tracyi** Vasey. Forest openings, montane, subalpine. The tall stature and wide blades are distinctive.
4b. Ligule 3-5 mm long; blades 1-3 mm wide; lemma 2.4-3.0 mm long, the tip bronzed. **P. palustris** L. SWAMP BLUEGRASS. Common in wet meadows and swampy woods.

KEY D, Alpinae

1a. Lemma pubescent on keel and marginal nerves . . . . (2)
1b. Lemma glabrous or minutely scabrous . . . . (5)

2a. Basal lvs short and broad, 2-4 mm wide; spklts broad, rounded or almost cordate at the base; new shoots extravaginal (breaking through the base of the enclosing sheath), these thus spreading horizontally. **P. alpina** L. Abundant on tundra and gravelly upper subalpine.
2b. Basal lvs narrow, elongate; spklts narrow, not broadly rounded at the base; branching intravaginal, these thus erect . . . . (3)

3a. Culms 25 cm or less tall; spklts 2-3 mm long; panicles narrow and condensed; alpine and subalpine. . . . . (4)
3b. Culms usually over 3 dm tall; spklts 6-8 mm long in a thick, lax panicle; plants dioecious; piñon-juniper to timberline. **P. fendleriana** (Steudel) Vasey, MUTTONGRASS. The basal lf-sheaths are long (4-6 cm), papery, and persistent through the next year.

4a. Lvs stiffly erect, the sheaths not elongate or papery; infl slender, stiff, the branches distinct; forming tight clumps. **P. glauca** Vahl. Dry sites, subalpine and alpine (*P. rupicola*).
4b. Lvs gracefully curved, the sheaths elongate and papery, to 4-5 cm long, persistent; infl dense but soft and lax; forming loose spreading clumps. **P. abbreviata** R. Brown ssp **pattersonii** (Vasey) Löve *et al.* Wet alpine snowbed gravels and frost scars (*P. pattersonii*).

5a. Dwarf alpine 3-10 cm high; spklts 3-4 mm long; lemmas 2-3 mm long; lvs all alike. **P. lettermanii** Vasey [for George Letterman]. Boulderfields and screes on the highest peaks, usually above 3,500 m.
5b. Up to 30 cm tall; spklts 5.0-7.5 mm long; lemmas 4.0-4.5 mm long; culm lvs with broad (2-3 mm) blades, new shoot lvs filiform; plants almost or quite dioecious. **P. cusickii** Vasey ssp

epilis (Scribner) Weber [for W. C. Cusick, Oregon collector; hairless], SKYLINE BLUEGRASS. Gravelly alpine ridges (*P. epilis*).

KEY E, Scabrellae

1a. Tall, loosely clumped to rhizomatous; lf blades usually ± flat; lemma mostly scabrous or glabrous, or puberulent on the nerves; ligule truncate or obtuse. **P. juncifolia** Scribner. Wet meadows and gulches, lower and middle altitudes (*P. ampla*).

1b. Low, densely caespitose; lf-blades narrow, involute; lemma puberulent at the base, sometimes scabrous or glabrous; ligules long, acute. **P. secunda** Presl. Very common and variable on dry grassland and desert-steppe (*P. canbyi, sandbergii, gracillima, nevadensis*).

POLYPOGON Desfontaines 1798 [Gr., *poly*, much, + *pogon*, beard]. RABBITFOOT GRASS

One sp, **P. monspeliensis** (L.) Desfontaines [of Montpelier, France], **82E**. ADV. Common in wet ditches and muddy pond shores in the lower valleys.

PSATHYROSTACHYS Nevski 1934 [Gr., *psathyros*, shattering, + *stachys*, spike]. RUSSIAN WILD RYE (formerly in *Elymus*)

One sp, **P. juncea** (Fischer) Nevski. ADV. Widely cult for range stabilization. The brittleness of the rachis is characteristic.

PSEUDOROEGNERIA Löve 1980 [Gr., *pseudo*, false, + *Roegneria*, a genus]. BLUEBUNCH WHEATGRASS (formerly in *Agropyron*)

One sp, **P. spicata** (Pursh) Löve. The dominant grass of the Palouse grassland in Washington, reaching our area in the NW counties. Most of our collections represent the awnless var. **inermis**. *Elytrigia albicans* is commonly mistaken for this, since rhizomes are not always observed or collected.

PTILAGROSTIS Grisebach 1852 [Gr., *ptilon*, feather, + *agrostis*, grass]. FEATHERGRASS

One sp, **P. porteri** (Rydberg) Weber [for Thomas C. Porter], **83B**. END. Very local on the W slope, known only from Hoosier Pass, usually in peat of willow bogs. A close relative of the Asiatic *P. mongholica*, **83A**, **PL 46**, it is endemic around the north end of South Park.

PUCCINELLIA Parlatore 1848 [for Benedetto Puccinelli, Italian botanist, 1808-1850]. ALKALI GRASS

1a. Lower panicle branches becoming reflexed at maturity; lemma 1.5-2.0 mm long; first glume less than 1.5 mm long; ligule usually less than 1.5 mm long. **P. distans** (L.) Parlatore. Alkali flats and pond margins, lower valleys. ADV. Probably impossible to distinguish from the native sp.

1b. Lower panicle branches spreading or ascending but rarely reflexed; lemma 2-3 mm long; first glume about 1.5 mm long; ligule

Figure 83. A, *Ptilagrostis mongholica* (specimen from USSR); B, *P. porteri*

usually over 1.5 mm long. **P. airoides** (Nuttall) Watson & Coulter [like the genus *Aira*]. Similar habitats (*P. nuttalliana*).

SCHEDONNARDUS Steudel 1854 [Gr., *schedon*, almost, + *Nardus*, a genus]. TUMBLEGRASS

One sp, **S. paniculatus** (Nuttall) Trelease. Mostly a sp of the E plains, but known on the W slope from one old collection (1891) from Grand Junction.

SCHIZACHNE Hackel 1909 [Gr., *schizein*, to split, + *achne*, chaff or lemma], FALSE MELIC

One sp, **S. purpurascens** (Torrey) Swallen. Rare or infrequent on deeply shaded forested slopes.

SCHIZACHYRIUM Nees 1829 [Gr., *schizein*, to split, + *achyron*, chaff]. LITTLE BLUESTEM

One sp, **S. scoparium** (Michaux) Nash [broom-like]. Frequent in the canyon-bottoms, SW counties [*Andropogon*].

SCLEROCHLOA P. Beauvois 1812 [Gr., *sklero*, hard, + *chloë*, grass]

One sp, **S. dura** (L.) P. Beauvois. ADV, known from a single collection in GF. A dryland plant common west of Colorado and to be expected in the western counties. The one-sided spikes have spklts with short rounded glumes and very strongly ribbed, hard-textured glumes and lemmas.

SECALE L. 1753 [classical Lat. name for rye]. RYE

One sp, **S. cereale** L. ADV. Cult in the lower valleys and occasionally volunteering along roadsides and in fallow fields.

SETARIA P. Beauvois 1812 [Lat., *seta*, bristle]. FOXTAIL; BRISTLE-GRASS

1a. Bristles downwardly barbed; panicle branches distinct. **S. verticillata** (L.) P. Beauvois. ADV weed in cult ground and roadsides, lower Colorado R Valley.
1b. Bristles upwardly barbed; panicle branches crowded into a dense spike . . . . (2)

2a. Fertile lemmas strongly transversely wrinkled, 5-16 bristles below each spklt; ripe spklts yellowish. about 3 mm long. **S. glauca** (L.) P. Beauvois. ADV common weed in cult ground.
2b. Fertile lemma only faintly wrinkled, 1-3 bristles below each spklt; second glume about as long as the spklt; ripe spklts green. **S. viridis** (L.) P. Beauvois. ADV common weed in cult ground. While this is usually a relatively small plant, a huge race with heavy nodding spklts occurs in the Colo R Valley, but I cannot assign it to another sp.

SPARTINA Schreber 1789 [Gr., *spartine*, a cord]. CORDGRASS

One sp, **S. gracilis** Trinius. Infrequent on the W slope, known from a single collection from the lower Yampa R.

SPHENOPHOLIS Scribner 1906 [Gr., *sphen*, wedge, + *pholis*, scale]. WEDGESCALE
One sp, **S. obtusata** (Michaux) Scribner. Moist woodlands and gulches, scattered through the montane zone, RT-GN. Somewhat resembling *Poa* except for the very unequal glumes, one much wider than the other.

SPOROBOLUS R. Brown [Gr., *spora*, seed, + *ballein*, to throw]. DROPSEED

1a. Sheaths with only a few spreading hairs at the summit, sometimes nearly glabrous, the old persisting ones at the base of the plant cream-colored, shiny, smooth; branches with spklts borne mostly at the tips; anthers over 1 mm long. **S. airoides** (Torrey) Torrey [for the genus *Aira*], ALKALI SACATON. Abundant on low-lying alkaline flats, forming large stands. The panicles are very open and diffuse.
1b. Sheaths with a conspicuous tuft of hairs at the summit; panicle branches usually spklt-bearing to the base; anthers less than 1 mm long. . . . . (2)

2a. Infl a long slender dense spike, the branches appressed, never any of them spreading. **S. contractus** Hitchcock. Known on the W slope only from Colorado Nat Mon, on canyonsides.
2b. Infl with spreading branches at least after emerging from the sheath . . . . (3)

3a. Spklts usually appressed to the main branches; panicle pyramidal, the lower branches longest, straight. **S. cryptandrus** (Torrey) Gray [hidden fls]. Very common on roadsides and dry grasslands. Commonly the infl only partially emerges from the surrounding lf-sheaths, hence the name.
3b. Spklts spreading away from the branches, the lowest branches no longer than the middle ones, flexuous and often tangled and drooping. **S. flexuosus** (Thurber) Rydberg. Frequent on rimrock and piñon-juniper at Colorado Nat Mon and possibly elsewhere but overlooked.

STIPA L. 1753 [Gr., *stype*, tow, as unraveled fibers]. NEEDLEGRASS

1a. Terminal seg of the awn plumose; glumes 3-6 cm long. **S. neomexicana** (Thurber) Scribner. Common in the lower canyons S of the Colorado R.
1b. Terminal seg of the awn not plumose . . . . (2)

2a. Basal seg of the once-bent (geniculate) awn strongly plumose, the hairs 4-8 mm long. **S. speciosa** Trinius & Ruprecht [showy]. Frequent, canyon country S of the Colorado R.
2b. Basal segment of the awn glabrous, or the hairs less than 2 mm long. . . . . (3)

3a. Lemma densely pilose with white hairs 2-5 mm long. . . . . . . (4)
3b. Lemma smooth or if hairy the hairs less than 2 mm long . . . . . (5)

4a. Awn 5-7 mm long, deciduous, straight, not bent or twisted; low bunchgrass under 2 dm tall. **S. webberi** (Thurber) B. L. Johnson [for H. J. Webber, Calif. botanist, 1865-1946]. Desert-steppe, known here from one collection (*Oryzopsis*).
4b. Awn 11-22 mm loing, persistent, bent and twisted; tall bunchgrass over 2 dm tall. **S. pinetorum** Jones. Pine forests, Gunnison Basin.

5a. Lemma 10-15 mm long; awn 7-16 cm long. **S. comata** Trinius & Ruprecht [maned], NEEDLE-AND-THREAD. Abundant in grasslands; a beautiful grass easily distinguished from a distance because of the very long awns that tend to droop away from the wind.
5b. Lemma 3.5-8.0 mm long or less; awn 0.5-7.0 cm long . . . . . . (6)

6a. Panicle branches few, divaricately spreading, naked for most of their length. **S. richardsonii** Link [for Sir John Richardson, botanist on the Franklin expeditions to find a Northwest Passage]. Locally abundant in lodgepole pine forests.
6b. Panicle branches numerous or at least strongly ascending, not naked for most of their length . . . . (7)

7a. Lf sheath with a tuft of hairs at the throat . . . . (8)
7b. Lf sheath not villous at the throat, margins not ciliate; lemma usually less than 6 mm long . . . . (9)

8a. Hairs at lemma apex over 2 mm long; awn less than 2 cm long; glumes 10-15 mm long. **S. scribneri** Vasey [for C. Lamson-Scribner, American grass specialist]. Common on the E slope and in adjacent Utah, but not yet reported for the W slope although probably here.
8b. Hairs at lemma apex less than 2 mm long; awns over 2 cm long; glumes 7-11 mm long. **S. viridula** Trinius. Frequent tall roadside grass with rather heavy infl.

9a. Awn 4.0-7.5 cm long, faintly bent and loosely twisted for 10-20 mm and flexuous beyond. **S. arida** Jones. Desert canyons S of the Colorado R Valley.
9b. Awn 1.0-3.5 cm long, twice bent and usually tightly twisted below, the terminal seg straight . . . . (10)

10a. Awn 1-5 cm long; lvs not tightly involute, often flat, 2-5 mm wide. **S. nelsonii** Scribner. Common in dry montane forests (*S. columbiana*).
10b. Awn 1-2 cm long; lvs tightly involute and filiform. **S. lettermanii** Vasey [for George Letterman]. Similar but usually drier habitats.

TORREYOCHLOA Church 1949 [for John Torrey, pioneer American botanist, 1796-1873]. WEAK MANNAGRASS

One sp, **T. pauciflora** (Presl) Church [few-fld]. Margins of subalpine ponds (*Glyceria*).

TRISETUM Persoon 1805 [Lat., *tres*, three, + *seta*, bristle, alluding to the awn and two teeth of the lemma]

1a. Awn minute, included within the glumes or sometimes lacking. **T. wolfii** Vasey [for John Wolf]. Infrequent, usually with solitary stems intermixed with other tall marsh grasses, along the borders of swamps and ponds, subalpine. Once learned, this is easily recognized, but being nondescript it is overlooked and commonly misidentified.

1b. Awn large, exserted, divergent . . . . (2)

2a. Panicle dense, thick, often purple; culms densely pilose to nearly tomentose below the panicle. **T. spicatum** (L.) Richter ssp **congdonii** (Scribner & Merrill) Hultén [for Joseph W. Congdon, California collector, 1834-1910]. Upper subalpine and alpine.

2b. Panicle slender, greenish-straw-colored, rarely with purple tinge; culms almost of quite glabrous below the panicle . . . . (3)

3a. Panicle branches short, not lax. **T. spicatum** ssp **majus** Hultén. Frequent in dry forests.

3b. Panicle branches elongate, loose. **T. spicatum** ssp **montanum** (Vasey) Weber. This is a very complicated sp worldwide in distribution, of which the above are three distinguishable races in our area.

TRITICUM L. 1753 [classical name for wheat]. WHEAT

One sp, **T. aestivum** L. [of summer]. ADV. Many varieties are cult, and plants frequent volunteer and survive for a season along roadsides and trails.

VAHLODEA Fries 1842 [for Martin Vahl, Danish botanist, 1749-1804]

One sp, **V. atropurpurea** (Wahlenberg) Fries ssp **latifolia** (Hooker) Porsild. Subalpine meadows and on soil of ledges in rocky gorges. The spklts are usually dark purple, but a pale albino phase occurs (*Deschampsia*).

VULPIA Gmelin 1805 [Lat., *vulpes*, fox]. SIX-WEEKS FESCUE

One sp, **V. octoflora** (Walter) Rydberg. Spklts with 7 or more florets (some early-flowering smaller plants may have fewer); lvs short, some less than 5 cm long. Abundant in early spring in disturbed soil at low altitudes, turning brown when ripe (*Festuca*).

POLEMONIACEAE—PHLOX FAMILY (PLM)

The Phlox family provides many of the characteristic wildflowers of the western slope. They range from extremely dainty and inconspicuous ephemerals (*Linanthus* and *Gymnosteris*) to showy perennials (*Phlox* and *Ipomopsis*), from desert plants to alpine tundra species. The flowers characteristically have a narrow tube suddenly flaring to five wide-spreading lobes, and three styles. Many species are potential rock-garden ornamentals.

1a. Annuals, never with a rosette of basal lvs . . . . (2)

1b. Biennials or perennials, or if winter annual (*Ipomopsis pumila*), then often with rosettes of basal lvs . . . . (10)

2a. Stems lfless except for a few lflike bracts subtending a fl-cluster; plants minute, only 1-2 cm tall, with exceedingly slender stems. **Gymnosteris**
2b. Lvs scattered along the stem . . . . (3)

3a. Stems simple and essentially unbranched, with lanceolate or elliptic simple lvs; fls in a dense terminal cluster. **Collomia**
3b. Stems distinctly branched, or with much narrower lvs, or fls in an open infl . . . . (4)

4a. Lvs linear or divided into linear segs. . . . . (5)
4b. Lvs broader than linear and often toothed or lobed . . . . (9)

5a. Stems and lvs extremely delicate; lvs never sharp-pointed or needlelike . . . . (6)
5b. Relatively robust; lvs either broadly linear or stiff, sharp-pointed and often needlelike . . . . (7)

6a. Branching opposite; not glandular; lvs apparently whorled. **Linanthus**
6b. Branching alternate; glandular; lvs alternate. **Gilia**

7a. Lvs simple, linear, not stiff nor needlelike although the tips may be acicular. **Ipomopsis**
7b. Lvs trifid or pinnatisect, often rigid and needlelike . . . . (8)

8a. Fl clusters in a cobwebby-hairy invol, well-separated from the lvs below; lvs not dense nor very needlelike. **Eriastrum**
8b. Fl clusters glabrous, hidden in masses of needlelike lvs, the whole plant forming a bur-like mass at maturity. **Navarretia**

9a. Lvs simple, entire, oblong, rounded at apex; fls minute; stems simple or branched from the base. **Microsteris**
8b. Lvs toothed, lobed or divided; stems erect or spreading, branched from near the base. **Ipomopsis**

10a. Lvs simple and entire, opposite. **Phlox**
10b. Lvs variously divided or compound, alternate or opposite. . . . (11)

11a. Lvs pinnately compound with distinct lfls; plants never with a basal rosette. **Polemonium**, JACOB'S LADDER; SKY PILOT
11b. Lvs pinnately lobed or dissected, or palmatifid . . . . (12)

12a. Lvs palmatifid, so deeply so as to appear simple. . . . . (13)
12b. Lvs pinnately lobed or dissected. . . . . (14)

13a. Lvs needlelike, sharp-pointed; low cushion-formers or somewhat woody decumbent plants flowering in evening and early morning. **Leptodactylon**, PRICKLY GILIA

13b. Lvs not acerose, appearing whorled; ample herbs forming rounded clumps, flowering during the day. **Linanthastrum**

14a. Fls with a tube but lacking a differentiated wider limb; upper parts of stem clothed with well-developed lvs; seeds large, usually oblong and slightly curved. **Ipomopsis** (but see *Gilia thyrsoidea*)
14b. Fls with a tube and a slightly expanded limb; upper part of stem with reduced lvs, the flowering portion essentially lfless; seeds small, spheroidal. **Gilia**

COLLOMIA Nuttall 1818 [Gr., *colla*, gluten, from the mucilaginous seeds].
1a. Corolla white to salmon-colored, usually over 2 cm long, the limb and lobes 1 cm diam or more; calyx lobes ovate-lanceolate, obtuse. **C. grandiflora** Douglas. Sagebrush, RB, MZ.
1b. Corolla pink or whitish, much less than 2 cm long, the limb and lobes usually less than 6 mm diam; calyx lobes subulate to linear-lanceolate, acute. **C. linearis** Nuttall, **84E**. Common in a variety of habitats, especially in sagebrush meadows and oak brush.

ERIASTRUM Wooton & Standley 1913 [Gr., *erion*, wool, + *aster*, star]
 One sp, **E. diffusum** (Gray) Mason. ADV. Locally abundant in the Colorado R Valley, ME, where it behaves as a weed and probably was introd from farther west. The fls are lavender.

GILIA Ruiz & Pavon 1794 [for Felipe Gil, 18th Cent. Spanish botanist] [Key written with help from Dr. Alva Day]
1a. Delicate annual lacking a basal rosette, branched from near the base; lvs simple; stems covered with dark glandular hairs; corolla pink. **Gilia sinistra** Jones [on the left hand, the allusion unexplained]. Sagebrush stands, RT (*G. capillaris*, incorrectly). Disjunct from southern Idaho.
1b. Annual, biennial or perennial, always with a rosette of basal lvs
. . . . (2)

2a. Anthers distinctly exserted . . . . (3)
2b. Anthers not protruding beyond the corolla tube . . . . (5)

3a. Strong perennial; basal lvs mostly entire or irregularly pinnatisect; restricted to narrow crevices of cliffs, very difficult to extricate with the roots; fls blue. **G. penstemonoides** Jones, **PL 29**. Vertical cliff faces of igneous and metamorphic rock, Blue Mesa and Black Canyon.
3b. Biennial or monocarpic; basal lvs regularly pinnatisect; on level ground, easily collected . . . . (4)

4a. Plant freely branched, never forming a dense spikelike panicle; fls lavender, less than 1 cm long. **G. pinnatifida** Nuttall. Gravelly soils, usually with little other competing vegetation, very common (*G. calcarea*).
4b. Plant essentially unbranched, forming a dense spikelike panicle;

fls white, over 1 cm long. **G. stenothyrsa** Jones. Clay hills, ME-GA, rare or infrequent (*Ipomopsis*, incorrectly).

5a. Corolla over 1 cm long, deep rose-colored . . . . (6)
5b. Corolla shorter, lavender or white. . . . . (7)

6a. Upper surface of basal lvs with white crinkly hairs. **G. haydenii** Gray. Colluvial fans from sandstone parent rock, SW counties.
6b. Upper surface of basal lvs with minute glandular hairs. **G. subnuda** Torrey, **PL 60**. Similar habitat and range. This and the last may blossom the first year and appear to be annual.

7a. Lower stem and basal lvs somewhat cobwebby-pubescent. . . . . (8)
7b. Lower stem and basal lvs glabrous. . . . . (11)

8a. Stem lvs clasping, serrate; calyx glandular-hairy; stem glabrous below the middle. **G. sinuata** Douglas. Infrequent on adobe soils, ME.
8b. Cauline lvs pinnately lobed (lobes longer than the rachis is wide), not clasping; calyx glabrous or glandular-hairy; stems cobwebby-hairy below the middle. . . . . (9)

9a. Corolla barely exserted from the calyx; infl branching strict; calyx glandular-hairy. **G. tweedyi** Rydberg. Infrequent or local, steppe-desert. MF.
9b. Corolla well-exserted; infl widely branching; calyx glabrous (cobwebby only on the earliest fls) . . . . (10)

10a. Calyx lobes acuminate; corolla tube and throat 2-5 times as long as the lobes; capsule ovoid. **G. ophthalmoides** Brand. The most abundant of this group, on adobe hills and flats.
10b. Calyx lobes acute; corolla tube and throat 1.5-2.0 times as long as the lobes; capsule subglobose. **G. clokeyi** Rydberg. Fairly common, Colorado R Valley, ME.

11a. Corolla lobes entire; plants diffusely branched without a dominant leading stem; corolla tube included or barely exserted; capsules globose of nearly so. **G. micromeria** Gray. Infrequent or overlooked, MF-ME.
11b. Corolla lobes trifid; plants usually with a dominant leader; corolla tube well-exserted; capsule ovoid. **G. triodon** Eastwood. Infrequent or overlooked, adobe soils, MF-MZ.

GYMNOSTERIS Greene 1898 [Gr., *gymnos*, naked, + *sterizo*, support, alluding to the naked stems]
One sp, **G. parvula** (Rydberg) Heller, **84C**. A very inconspicuous and ephemeral spring fl in sagebrush meadows at middle altitudes. The slender stem is naked, only a few cm tall; the lvs and tiny fls are clustered at the branch tips.

IPOMOPSIS Michaux 1803 [resembling *Ipomoea*].
(Key adapted from Grant & Wilken, pers. comm.)
1a. Corolla short-tubular. . . . . (2)

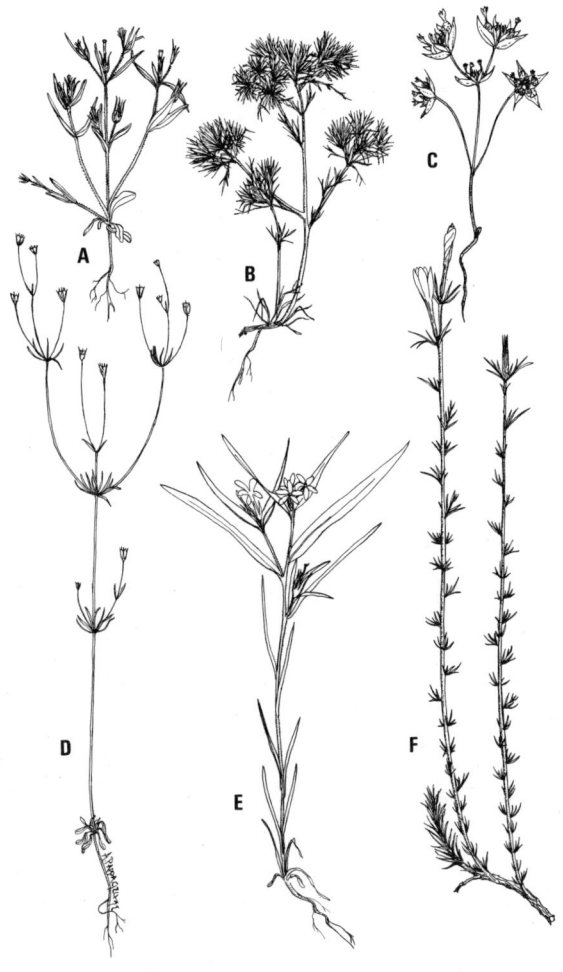

Figure 84. A, *Microsteris gracilis*; B, *Navarretia breweri*; C, *Gymnosteris parvula*; D, *Linanthus harknessii*; E, *Collomia linearis*; F, *Leptodactylon pungens*

1b. Corolla with long tube, well over 1 cm long . . . . (8)

2a. Ephemeral annual. . . . . (3)
2b. Biennial or perennial. . . . . (6)

3a. Lf blades all entire. **I. gunnisonii** (Torrey & Gray) Grant. Sandy ground, Four Corners.
3b. Lf blades, at least the basal ones, pinnatifid or deeply toothed . . . . (4)

4a. Fls in axillary clusters along the stems and branches; stamens strongly exserted; plants over 2 dm tall, biennial. **Ipomopsis polyantha** (Rydberg) Grant. Local, near Pagosa Springs.
4b. Fls in terminal heads; plants usually less than 2 dm tall. . . . . . (5)

5a. Stems widely spreading, prostrate, branches naked except for the conspicuous ring of foliaceous bracts subtending the terminal fl-clusters; anthers included in the corolla tube; corolla 3-5 mm long; styles glabrous at base. **I. polycladon** (Torrey) Grant. Adobe hills, early spring.
5b. Stems ascending, branched from the base, leafy; anthers exserted; corolla 5-9 mm long; styles hairy at the base. **I. pumila** (Nuttall) Grant. Similar habitats. This might be confused with *Eriastrum diffusum*, but the stem of *Eriastrum* is very slender and wiry as in *Navarretia*; the fl clusters are very woolly, and when pressed the individual calyces or fruits are hardly visible. In *I. pumila* the individual fls can be made out because the wool is much more sparse.

6a. Shrubby, with numerous woody stems, forming a hemispherical growth form; corolla 12-14 mm long, the head suffused with pink. **I. roseata** (Rydberg) Grant. END. Common on sandstone ledges, ME, MN.
6b. Herbaceous, caespitose or simple-stemmed, if woody at the base then not having a symmetric form; corolla 6-8 mm long . . . . . (7)

7a. Infl a terminal capitate, woolly-hairy ball over 1 cm diam; fls pale purple; strictly alpine. **I. globularis** (Brand) Weber. Endemic in the Hoosier Pass area. One of the most handsome alpine tundra plants, with a heavy fragrance.
7b. Infl terminal, capitate, less than 1 cm diam, not particularly villous; fls white; lower altitudes. **I. congesta** (Hooker) Grant. Several races occur, the most common being var **congesta** with trifid to pinnatisect arachnoid lvs, and strictly herbaceous stems. Plants with woody lower stems and mostly entire lvs belong to ssp **frutescens** (Rydberg) Day. Ssp **crebrifolia** (Nuttall) Day, is peripheral in LP and MF, is dwarf and has mostly entire, glabrous lvs in dense basal clusters.

8a. Annual; fls white, over 3 cm long. **I. longiflora** (Torrey) Grant. Infrequent in sandy soils, MN-MZ.
8b. Biennial or perennial; fls firecracker red, infrequently white or intermediate in color. . . . . (9)

Plate 49. ***Ranunculus gmelinii*** Weber

Plate 50. ***Arctostaphylos patula*** Weber
MANZANITA

Plate 51. ***Echinocereus triglochidiatus inermis*** Weber
CLARET CUP

Plate 52. ***Phacelia submutica*** Weber

Plate 53. ***Papaver kluanense*** Weber
ALPINE POPPY

Plate 54. ***Chamaechaenactis scaposa*** Weber

Plate 55. ***Braya humilis***   Weber

Plate 56. ***Askellia nana***   Weber

Plate 57. *Physaria alpina*   Weber

Plate 58. *Townsendia rothrockii*   Weber

Plate 60. *Gilia subnuda*   Weber

Plate 59. *Armeria scabra* ssp *sibirica*   Weber
THRIFT

Plate 61. *Cirsium hesperium* — Weber

Plate 62. *Gentianopsis barbellata* — Weber

Plate 64. *Nuttallia multicaulis* Weber

Plate 63. *Rudbeckia occidentalis* Weber

9a. Corolla scarlet to reddish pink, trumpet-shaped, the tube with a flaring throat. . . . . (10)
9b. Corolla white, pink to deep violet (red only in hybridizing populations), salverform, the tube without a conspicuously flaring throat . . . . (12)

10a. Anthers all well-exserted; highest anther 3-5 mm beyond the orifice; calyx lobes 3-4 mm long. **I. aggregata** (Pursh) Grant ssp **formosissima** (Greene) Wherry, TRUMPET GILIA. Peripheral from New Mexico, in southern AA.
10b. All but one anther included; calyx lobes 1-2 mm long . . . . . (11)

11a. Corolla tube filiform, about 1 mm wide at base and flaring gently to a narrow orifice 2-3 mm diam. **I. aggregata** ssp **attenuata** (Gray) Grant & Grant. Park Range, RT.
11b. Corolla tube 1.5 mm or more wide at base and flaring upward to a broader orifice 3-4 mm diam. **I. aggregata** ssp **aggregata**. The most common and widely distributed race.

12a. Corolla tube filiform, 10-22 mm long; highest anther at the orifice. **I. aggregata** ssp **weberi** Grant & Wilken. Rabbit Ears Pass area.
12b. Corolla tube narrow but not filiform, 19-45 mm long; highest anther included in the tube; fls well-spaced in an open infl; calyx lobes 3-4 mm long. **I. tenuituba** (Rydberg) Grant. At higher altitudes than ssp *aggregata*, RT, GN, ME. Superficially it resembles ssp *candida* of the E slope, but that has a more dense infl and shorter calyx lobes.

LEPTODACTYLON Hooker & Arnott 1839 [Gr., *lepto*, slender, + *daktylos*, finger]. PRICKLY GILIA
1a. Fls 5-merous; plants forming elongated loosely asymmetrical stems. **L. pungens** (Torrey) Nuttall, **84F**. Common, piñon-juniper and adobe hills.
1b. Fls 4- or 6-merous, forming dense symmetrical clumps with crowded lvs . . . . (2)

2a. Fls 4-merous; lvs less than 1 cm long (aspect of *Phlox hoodii*), very crowded and ascending; clumps tight. **L. caespitosum** Nuttall. Uncommon on sandstone rimrock, MF.
2b. Fls 6-merous; lvs over 1 cm long, wide spreading, clumps loose. **L. watsonii** (Gray) Rydberg. Restricted to crevices in massive granite cliffs, usually difficult to reach.

LINANTHASTRUM Ewan 1942 [related to *Linanthus*]
One sp, **L. nuttallii** (Gray) Ewan. A stout perennial growing in many-stemmed clumps. The flowers are large, salverform. Open gravelly slopes, upper montane to subalpine.

LINANTHUS Bentham 1833 [Gr., *Linum*, flax, + *anthos*, flower]
One sp, **L. harknessii** (Curran) Greene var **septentrionalis** (Jepson) Bailey, **84D**. Extremely delicate annual with filiform stems and lvs and minute fls, common in sagebrush and oak brush, but usually overlooked.

MICROSTERIS Greene 1898 [Gr., *mikro*, small, + *sterizo*, stem]

One sp, **M. gracilis** (Hooker) Greene, **84A**. Very common but inconspicuous weedy annual of sagebrush and oak zone, flowering in early spring, and almost always to be found together with *Collinsia*.

NAVARRETIA Ruiz & Pavon 1794 [for Francisco Fernando Navarrete, Spanish botanist-physician]

1a. Fls yellow; capsule dehiscent by 3 valves. **N. breweri** (Gray) Greene, **84B**. Common in disturbed sites, sagebrush.
1b. Fls lavender; capsules 2-locular, indehiscent or irregularly dehiscent by disintegration of the lower lateral walls. **N. minima** Nuttall. Similar habitats but evidently not as common.

PHLOX L. 1753 [Gr. word for flame; an ancient name for *Lychnis*]

1a. Cushion-like or densely caespitose; lvs crowded . . . . (2)
1b. Loosely branched or matted; lvs not crowded . . . . (5)

2a. Alpine tundra plants; lvs often ciliate but not cobwebby-woolly . . . . (3)
2b. Desert-steppe plants; lvs not ciliate but usually somewhat cobwebby-woolly . . . . (4)

3a. Tightly cushioned; lvs short (5 mm), erect; fls white, tube 7 mm, lobes 3 mm long. **P. condensata** (Gray) Nelson. Common near the Continental Divide, S counties.
3b. Cushions loose; lvs more spreading, over 1 cm long; fls usually colored, tube 11-12 mm, lobes 5 mm long. **P. pulvinata** Wherry. Near Continental Divide, N counties (*P. sibirica* ssp *pulvinata*).

4a. Lvs densely woolly near their bases, less than 5 mm long, scale-like, closely overlapping. **P. muscoides** (Nuttall) Wherry [moss-like]. Barely entering in the NW corner, MF. Common on the east slope (*P. bryoides*). Depressed forms of *P. hoodii* may be difficult to separate, but in that the lvs are always somewhat spreading and the tips are more strongly apiculate.
4b. Lvs only slightly cobwebby, usually more than 5 mm long, ascending, not closely appressed. **P. hoodii** Richardson ssp **canescens** (Torrey & Gray) Wherry [for a companion of Richardson on the voyage to find the Northwest Passage]. Very common throughout, in sagebrush.

5a. Stems solitary or a few together, never forming mats; lvs usually over 2.5 cm long; fls distinctly pedicelled. . . . . (6)
5b. Stems numerous from a stout taproot, forming mats; lvs less than 2 cm long; fls without obvious pedicels . . . . (7)

6a. Hyaline membranes between calyx-lobes flat, with no hint of a keel. **P. caryophylla** Wherry. END, Pagosa Springs area.
6b. Hyaline membranes between calyx-lobes keeled. **P. longifolia** Nuttall. Abundant throughout on roadsides, adobe hills and sagebrush; fls vary from pale to deep pink.

7a. Membrane between the calyx lobes distinctly convex-keeled in the lower half; lvs steely green, slender, stiffish and sharp-pointed. **P. austromontana** Coville. Sagebrush and piñon-juniper, S counties.
7b. Membrane between the calyx lobes flat; lvs bright green, up to 3 mm wide, not particularly stiff nor sharp. **P. multiflora** Nelson. Common in upper forested zone.

POLEMONIUM L. 1753 [ancient name, possibly commemorating Polemon, Athenian philosopher, or from Gr., *polemos*, war]. JACOB'S LADDER; SKY PILOT

1a. Corolla funnelform; lfls whorled; lvs chiefly basal . . . . (2)
1b. Corolla shallowly bell-shaped; lfls opposite; lvs mostly cauline . . . . (4)

2a. Corolla narrow, 3 times length of calyx, ochroleucous; rockslides in mt canyons and alpine screes, never on stable tundra. **P. brandegei** Greene. Variable fl color (to pale blue) and corolla tube length is the result of introgressive hybridization with the next.
2b. Corolla broadly funnelform, equalling or up to twice as long as calyx, deep blue or purple . . . . (3)

3a. Corolla tubular, little longer than the calyx, deep purple, not strongly flaring at the mouth; anthers yellowish. **P. viscosum** Nuttall. Common on stable alpine tundra. White mutants occur in normal populations.
3b. Corolla tubular-campanulate, twice as long as calyx, light blue, widely flaring at the mouth; anthers orange. **P. grayanum** Rydberg. END, on unstable alpine talus and scree from Mt. Evans southwestward. Like *P. brandegei*, this hybridizes with *P. viscosum* where their habitats make contact.

4a. Stems tall, lfy, stiffly erect, solitary or a few together; plants of open sites . . . . (5)
4b. Stems low (less than 3 dm high), spreading, several to many in tufts; plants of shaded forest floors. **P. pulcherrimum** Hooker ssp **delicatum** (Rydberg) Brand. Dry, open subalpine forests (*P. delicatum*).

5a. Plants from slender rhizomes; lfls narrow, almost glabrous; infl longer than broad. **P. caeruleum** L. ssp **amygdalinum** (Wherry) Munz [blue; with almond odor]. Infrequent in mossy subalpine birch-willow bogs.
5b. Plants with stout woody caudices; lfls broad, pubescent; infl broad, flat-topped. **P. foliosissimum** Gray. Streamsides and mt meadows.

POLYGALACEAE—MILKWORT FAMILY (PGL)

At first glance the *Polygala* flower reminds one of the legumes or the Fumariaceae. The resemblance is only superficial. The flower has five sepals, three of which are minute, the other two large, resembling the 'wing' petals of legumes. Two of the lower petals are united to form a keel, into which the stamens and style are neatly tucked away. The upper two petals of the 'banner' are longer and very narrow. The stamens are united to the petals and by their filaments into two groups. Their eight anthers are tiny, one-locular, and each opens by a terminal pore. The ovary is broadly elliptic, flat, and two-locular. An amazing flower indeed!

POLYGALA L. 1753 [Gr., *polys*, much, + *gala*, milk, a name applied by Dioscorides to a plant reputed to increase lactation]. MILKWORT

One sp, **P. subspinosa** Watson, PL. 6. Rare, on arid clays and shales, western tier of counties S of the Colorado R.

POLYGONACEAE—BUCKWHEAT FAMILY (PLG)

This family contains two important food plants, Buckwheat (*Fagopyrum esculentum*) and Rhubarb (*Rheum rhaponticum*). Rhubarb is known as an escape around old mountain homesteads. The petioles are edible, but the leaves may cause lethal poisoning from oxalic acid. The pleasant flavor of the petioles comes from malic acid. Buckwheat is a photosensitizer like *Hypericum*, and white cattle eating too much of it can develop a lethal sunburn. Like the gentians and the saxifrages, taxonomic treatments have always tended to be very conservative. But as early as 1836 Rafinesque pronounced the genus *Polygonum*, which then included *Bistorta*, *Persicaria*, *Reynoutria* and *Fallopia*, a complete absurdity. He seems to have had more sense than he has been given credit for. A good earmark of the family (except for *Eriogonum*!) is the sheathing stipule (called ochrea). This is what one strips off when preparing rhubarb petioles. Also, the one-locular, 3-sided akene.

1a. Herbaceous vines. **Fallopia**, BLACK BINDWEED
1b. Erect or prostrate, herbaceous or woody, but never vines. . . . . . (2)

2a. Dwarf annuals of wet gravels in tundra, resembling seedlings, red-tinged, with only a few pairs of small oval lvs and minute axillary fls. **Koenigia**
2b. Not as above . . . . (3)

3a. Fl clusters subtended by campanulate, turbinate, or cylindric invols of fused bracts . . . . (4)
3b. Fl clusters not subtended by bracts . . . . (6)

4a. Plant with massive taproot and rosette of oblanceolate basal lvs; flowering stem tall, with panicles of dangling yellow fls; ripe aks 3-angled and winged. **Pterogonum**, WINGED BUCKWHEAT
4b. Annual, perennial or shrubby; basal lvs if present not as above; infl cymose or racemose; aks not winged . . . . (5)

5a. Invol double, of 3 outer and 3 inner bracts; always delicate annuals (only 2 relatively rare spp). **Stenogonum**
5b. Invol of a single circle of fused bracts; habit various, either annuals or perennials or shrubs (many spp). **Eriogonum**, WILD BUCKWHEAT

6a. Tepals 4 or 6, the outer spreading or reflexed, remaining small, the inner usually erect and enlarged in fruit . . . . (7)
6b. Tepals 5, the outer not smaller, usually petal-like, white or bright pink. . . . . (9)

7a. Lf-blades lanceolate to ovate, never basally lobed; stout weedy plants. **Rumex**, DOCK
7b. Lf-blades rounded-reniform or basally lobed; low, relatively delicate plants . . . . (8)

8a. Lvs lanceolate, often with basal hastate lobes; fls mostly unisexual; weed of fallow fields, roadsides or burned areas. **Acetosella**, SHEEP SORREL
8b. Lvs rounded reniform; fls mostly perfect; plants of rocky alpine tundra. **Oxyria**, ALPINE SORREL

9a. Huge weedy herb forming thickets; stem zig-zag; lvs broadly ovate, truncate at the base; fls in axillary panicles; escaped from cult. **Reynoutria**, JAPANESE KNOTWEED
9b. Not as above . . . . (10)

10a. Lvs with a hinge-like joint at point of attachment of blade and sheath; fls in axillary clusters; bracts of the infl with well-developed blades. **Polygonum**, KNOTWEED
10b. Lvs lacking a joint at point of attachment of blade and sheath; fls in terminal or axillary spikelike racemes; bracts of infl reduced to sheaths . . . . (11)

11a. Rhizome thickened and tuber-like; basal lvs well-developed and stem lvs reduced; alpine and subalpine. **Bistorta**, BISTORT
11b. Rhizome, if any, not tuber-like; basal lvs none; plants of various altitudes, mostly wet places at low altitudes. **Persicaria**, SMARTWEED

ACETOSELLA Fourreau 1869 [dim. of the genus *Acetosa*]. SHEEP SORREL
1a. Slenderly rhizomatous; lvs less than 5 cm long, most of them hastate. **A. vulgaris** (Koch) Fourreau, **85A**. Abundant in disturbed areas and sites of recent fires. The plants turn red when mature; the lvs, with their small hastate basal lobes, are unique; the fls are tiny, reddish, in diffuse panicles (*Rumex acetosella*).
1b. Stoutly taprooted; lvs (many basal) over 10 cm long, never hastate. **A. paucifolia** (Nuttall) Löve [few-lvd]. Common in meadows, upper Yampa drainage (*Rumex*).

BISTORTA Adanson 1763 [Lat., *bis*, twice, + *tortus*, a twist, alluding to the knotty rhizomes]. BISTORT
1a. Raceme narrowly cylindric, 4-8 mm wide, bearing reproductive blackish bulblets in place of some of the lower fls. **B. vivipara** (L.) S. Gray. Common, subalpine meadows and tundra. *Bistorta* is a small genus of mt plants common to W North America and Eurasia.

Figure 85. A. *Acetosella vulgaris*; B, *Eriogonum cernuum*; C, *Oxyria digyna*; D, *Polygonum douglasii*

Polygonaceae (PLG) 405

1b. Raceme broadly cylindrical or ovoid, not viviparous, 10-20 mm wide; fls conspicuous, white or pinkish. **B. bistortoides** (Pursh) Small. Subalpine meadows, the spikes of white fls often dominating the landscape.

ERIOGONUM Michaux 1803 [Gr., *erion*, wool, + *gonu*, knee, from the woolly lvs and swollen joints of the type species]. WILD BUCKWHEAT

1a. Annual or winter annual, with slender or stout but easily pulled root system. . . . . (2)
1b. Distinctly perennial, or with heavier root system, not appearing annual. . . . . (9)

2a. [2] Stem lfy, both basal and in pairs at the nodes; branches divaricate; fls minute, in small clusters at the nodes. **E. divaricatum** Hooker. Desert pavements, Four Corners.
2b. Lvs all basal, petiolate, broadly orbicular, the fl stems slender and lfless. . . . . (3)

3a. [2] Invol sessile at the nodes . . . . (4)
3b. Invol distinctly pedicellate . . . . (6)

4a. [3] Tepals white, narrowly fan-shaped; invol ± angular. **E. palmerianum** Reveal [for Edward Palmer, collector of the SW and Mexico]. Piñon-juniper, ME, MZ.
4b. Outer tepals broadly cordate-orbicular; invol not angular. . . . . . (5)

5a. [4] Stem perfectly smooth, somewhat glaucous. **E. hookeri** Watson [for Sir J. D. Hooker, plant geographer of Royal Botanic Gardens, Kew]. Grand and San Juan drainages, on river benches.
5b. Stem floccose-tomentose. **E. scabrellum** Reveal. Local, rimrock benches, ME-MZ.

6a. [3] Fls yellow and densely hairy; stems swollen; lvs green and glabrous except for long spreading hairs on the veins and margins. **E. inflatum** Torrey & Fremont, DESERT TRUMPET. Abundant in early spring on adobe hills. While usually annual, it sometimes behaves as a perennial. Because some plants fail to inflate, the swollen stem has been thought to be caused by an insect that lays eggs in the stem, evoking a growth response. The swollen stems commonly are punctured, but studies suggest that the insect may not cause the inflation. The inflated stem does aid the plant in its function as a tumbleweed.
6b. Fls white or pink, or if yellow, then not densely hairy; fl stem never swollen. . . . . (7)

7a. [6] Lvs green and sparsely hairy to smooth; fls white, the tepals oblong; peduncles ascending or spreading at a wide angle, rarely reflexed. **E. gordonii** Bentham [for Alexander Gordon, collector on the Oregon Trail]. Abundant early spring annual, adobe hills.
7b. Lvs softly tomentose. . . . . (8)

8a. [7] Fls white, large, in large invols on slender reflexed peduncles; branches few; tepals fan-shaped, wavy-margined, suddenly narrowed just above the base. **E. cernuum** Nuttall, NODDING BUCKWHEAT, **85B**. Blossoming in midsummer at middle altitudes, mt parks.

8b. Fls yellow to red, minute, in small invols on filiform peduncles; branches numerous; tepals elliptic, not fan-shaped nor with wavy margins. **E. wetherillii** Eastwood [for Alfred Wetherill, pioneer Mancos rancher]. Infrequent, Four Corners.

9a. [1] Infl (always umbels) subtended by a circle of lflike bracts . . . . (10)
9b. Infl (cymes, racemes or umbels) not subtended by a ring of lflike bracts . . . . (18)

10a. [9] Fls glabrous . . . . (11)
10b. Fls pilose . . . . (16)

11a. [10] Ring of bracts in the middle of the stem, not subtending rays of the infl; fls rose or ochroleucous. **E. heracleoides** Nuttall [from a fancied resemblance to *Heracleum*, presumably because of the umbels]. Sandstone benches, Blue Mt Plateau, MF.
11b. No ring of lflike bracts in the middle of the stem . . . . (12)

12a. [11] Fls ochroleucous or pinkish. **E. subalpinum** Greene. Subalpine meadows and forest openings. Considered by some to be a variety of the next, but in Colorado at least the two are distinct and grow together without mixing.
12b. Fls bright yellow. **E. umbellatum** Torrey. Very abundant throughout the forested region and composed of a number of rather distinct races, as follows . . . . (13)

13a. [12] Lvs pubescent at least below . . . . (14)
13b. Lvs glabrous on both sides . . . . (15)

14a. [13] Infl a simple umbel; plants erect or slightly spreading, not prostrate nor shrubby; abundant in open woods and meadows at lower altitudes. **E. umbellatum** var **umbellatum**.
14b. Infl of compound umbels; erect subshrubs or shrubs. **E. umbellatum** var **subaridum** Stokes. Mesa Verde.

15a. [13] Infl umbellate or merely subcapitate; widespread, middle altitudes. **E. umbellatum** var **aureum** (Gandoger) Reveal.
15b. Infl capitate or nearly so; subalpine and alpine. **E. umbellatum** var **porteri** (Small) Stokes.

16a. [10] Umbels solitary; fl stems lfless except for the bracts at the base of the umbel; dwarf alpines. **E. jamesii** Bentham var **xanthum** (Small) Reveal. Tundra near the Continental Divide.
16b. Umbels several, peduncled, with a ring of bracts at the base of the peduncles; lower altitudes. . . . . (17)

17a. [16] Fls ochroleucous. **E. jamesii** var **jamesii**. Piñon-juniper, San Juan Basin, replacing most yellow varieties.

17b. Fls yellow. **E. jamesii** var **flavescens** Watson. Open woods at low elevations.

18a. [9] Infl of a few lfless elongate stiffly ascending branches with the fl clusters forming spikes; basal lvs oblong-ovate, tomentose; fls pink. **E. racemosum** Nuttall. Sagebrush to pine-oak zone.
18b. Infl capitate or cymosely branched, or if ± racemose, never spicate. . . . . (19)

19a. [18] Caespitose-matted; infl capitate or very nearly so . . . . . (20)
19b. Forming loose clumps, broomy or actually shrubby; infl distinctly cymose or racemose . . . . (26)

20a. [19] Lvs broadly oval or orbicular; infl of a single capitate cluster of sessile invols, on a stem several times longer than the basal lvs. . . . . (21)
20b. Lvs narrower; infl not more than twice as long as the basal lvs . . . . (22)

21a. [20] Fls white or pink. **E. ovalifolium** Nuttall var **ovalifolium**. Sagebrush benches, piñon-juniper and adobe hills.
21b. Fls yellow. **E. ovalifolium** var **nevadensis** Gandoger. Less common than the typical form, MF.

22a. [20] Lvs over 2 cm long; caudices numerous, slender, elongate; fl stem well-differentiated, the umbels not closely invested by the lvs. **E. coloradense** Small. Gravels and clays of high mt parks up to talus slopes of the alpine, South Park and Gunnison Basin.
22b. Lvs less than 2 cm long; caudices short, tightly massed; fl stems hardly longer than the lvs and usually closely invested by them; desert spp . . . . (23)

23a. [22] Lvs linear, 1-3 cm long; fl stems visible, usually more than 1 cm long. **E. bicolor** Jones. Adobe hills in the Colorado R Valley, ME.
23b. Lvs broader or shorter; fl stems very short, the umbels hardly exserted from the surrounding lvs. . . . . (24)

24a. [23] Lvs linear, densely pilose, the hairs all directed forward; umbels not exceeding the lvs. **E. tumulosum** (Barneby) Reveal [mounded]. Gypsum hills, northern MF. Umbels very short, hardly exceeding the lvs.
24b. Lvs oval, thickly white-cottony-tomentose . . . . (25)

25a. [24] Invol solitary at the end of the shoot; fls yellow. **E. acaule** Nuttall. Peripheral, clay hills, northern MF. Invols hidden along the lvs, their peduncles very short.
25b. Invols several; fls ochroleucous or pink. **E. shockleyi** Watson var. **longilobum** (Stokes) Reveal [for Wm. H. Shockley, Nevada collector]. Sandstone ledges, Colorado and San Juan valleys. Invols and fls conspicuous, on evident peduncles.

26a. [19] Infl large and open, the invols racemosely arranged and secund at the ends of the branches. **E. leptocladon** Torrey & Gray var **leptocladon**, with yellow fls, occurs in the lower Colorado R Valley, while var **ramosissimum** (Eastwood) Reveal, with white fls, occurs in the Four Corners.

26b. Without the above combination of characters . . . . (27)

27a. [26] Fls yellow . . . . (28)
27b. Fls white or pink . . . . (30)

28a. [27] Lvs tightly revolute, underside hardly visible; woody stems numerous, several cm tall. **E. contortum** Small. Shales, Colorado R Valley, ME. The lvs are short (2-3 cm long) and fl stems are quite short, not much longer than the above-ground woody stems.
28b. Lvs flat or revolute along the margins, underside visible; woody stems very short, the plant dying back each year almost to the base . . . . (29)

29a. [28] Lvs short, 203 cm long; caudices very short, crowning a stout, knotty root system; fl stems numerous, not over 20 cm high, branching from the base several times, noticeably green from the mass effect. **E. ephedroides** Reveal [like *Ephedra*, alluding to the bunches of green stems]. END, shales, western RB.
29b. Lvs often over 5 cm long; caudices relatively slender, root system not massive; fl stems few, over 30 cm high, branching mostly in the upper half. **E. brevicaule** Nuttall. Common on clay and shale, arid valleys.

30a. [27] Lvs broader than linear (oblong to ovate). . . . . (31)
30b. Lvs oblanceolate to linear. . . . . (33)

31a. [30] Lvs basal; caudices short, from a stout root system; plants without woody stems. **E. batemanii** Jones [for a friend of Jones and Stokes]. Mowry Shale Formation, Dinosaur Nat Mon.
31b. Lvs scattered on an aerial stem; stems woody below, not dying back to the base every year. . . . . (32)

32a. [31] Lvs small, not over 2 cm long, linear to elliptic, revolute on the margins. **E. microthecum** Nuttall [small-fruited]. A puzzlingly variable sp, easily recognized when a definite shrub, but sometimes with very scanty woody stem. Plants with oval lvs belong to var **laxiflorum** Hooker, plants with linear lvs to var **simpsonii** (Bentham) Reveal. Adobe hills and piñon-juniper.
32b. Lvs, including petioles, over 3 cm long, oblong to orbicular or broadly ovate; well-developed shrub. **E. corymbosum** Bentham. Arid lands, western tier of counties. A variable sp consisting of 3 races in Colorado: var **corymbosum**, with lanceolate to oblanceolate or elliptic lvs, MF-MN; var **velutinum** Reveal, with broadly elliptic to oblong lvs with densely matted white tomentum, MN-ME; and var **orbiculatum** (Stokes) Reveal & Brotherson, with floccose to tomentose, orbicular lvs, SM.

33a. [30] Lvs tightly revolute, underside hardly exposed, numerous on

the fl stems up to infl branches . . . . (34)
33b. Lvs only revolute on the margins, underside exposed, widely scattered, mostly near base of fl stem . . . . (36)

34a. [33] Infl of large compound cymes, branched more than 3 times. **E. leptophyllum** (Torrey) Wooton & Standley [slender-lvd]. Local, on black shales, Four Corners.
34b. Infl of simple cymes or umbels, not branched. . . . . (35)

35a. [34] Subshrubs 1-2 dm high; stems glabrous; invols mostly 4.0-4.5 mm long. **E. clavellatum** Eastwood [club-shaped, as to tepals]. Local on shales, Four Corners.
35b. Herbaceous perennials, 0.5-1.0 dm high; stems floccose to glabrous; invols 3.0-3.5 mm long. **E. pelinophilum** Reveal [clay-loving]. END. Local on clay-shale near Delta.

36a. [33] Invols clustered at each node; lvs narrowly oblanceolate or lanceolate; lower peduncles 1-3 cm long. **E. lonchophyllum** Torrey & Gray [lance-leaved]. Canyonsides; extremely variable in stature and leaf length and shape.
36b. Invols solitary at each node; lvs lanceolate; peduncles lacking. **E. saurinum** Reveal [lizard, alluding to the type area]. END, local, Dinosaur Nat Mon.

FALLOPIA Adanson 1763 [not explained but probably honoring Gabriel Fallopius, Italian anatomist, 1523-62]. BLACK BINDWEED

One sp, **F. convolvulus** (L.) Löve [with lvs resembling *Convolvulus*]. ADV herbaceous weedy vine of ruderal sites in and around towns (*Polygonum, Bilderdykia*).

KOENIGIA L. 1753 [for Emmanuel Koenig, Swiss Botanist, 1698-1742]

One sp, **K. islandica** L. [of Iceland], **PL 40**. Infrequent but locally abundant in frost scars and wet gravel on alpine tundra, our only truly alpine annual, with the possible exception of some *Draba* spp. The entire plant is only a few mm high. High mts near the Continental Divide.

OXYRIA Hill 1765 [Gr., *oxys*, sour, as to the lvs]. ALPINE SORREL

One sp, **O. digyna** (L.) Hill [with 2 carpels], **85C**. Rock crevices in tundra, rarely in compensating environments in subalpine. Resembling a dwarf *Rumex*, easily marked by the kidney-shaped lvs.

PERSICARIA Miller 1754 [from *Persica*, the peach, referring to the lf shape]. SMARTWEED (formerly in *Polygonum*)
1a. Aquatic or subaquatic; spikes all terminal or nearly so; fls bright pink or red. . . . . (2)
1b. Terrestrial although sometimes in very wet places, never floating; infl of axillary and terminal racemes or spikes; fls pink or white . . . . (3)

2a. Lf blades obtuse or acute, commonly widest near the middle; fl spikes seldom more than 3 cm long, usually over 10 mm wide. **P. amphibia** (L.) S. Gray, WATER SMARTWEED. Floating on ponds or in mud on pond margins. A single plant may exhibit branches with smooth floating lvs like *Potamogeton* (and often mistaken for that) and erect terrestrial branches with pubescent erect lvs.

2b. Lf blades acuminate, commonly widest near the base; infl 3-10 cm long, seldom more and usually less than 10 mm wide. **P. coccinea** (Mühlenberg) Greene, SCARLET SMARTWEED. Similar sites but not often floating.

3a. Sheaths with marginal bristles. . . . . (4)
3b. Sheaths lacking marginal bristles . . . . (5)

4a. Fls pink, not gland-dotted; racemes dense, thick. **P. maculata** (Rafinesque) S. Gray [spotted], LADY'S THUMB. ADV on pond margins and irrigation ditches. The lvs commonly have a dark spot in the center, "Our Lady's thumbprint".
4b. Fls greenish, gland-dotted; racemes very slender. . . . . (6)

5a. Peduncle with granular yellow glands; tepals usually white or cream-colored; infl commonly elongate, drooping. **P. lapathifolia** (L.) S. Gray [with lvs like dock]. ADV on pond borders and irrigation ditches.
5b. Peduncle with stalked red-purple glands; tepals usually pink; infl usually erect, short and stout. **P. pensylvanicum** (L.) Gomez, PINKWEED. ADV in similar sites.

6a. Sheaths swollen, filled with cleistogamous fls; aks minutely granular-papillose, dull. **P. hydropiper** (L.) Opiz, WATER-PEPPER. ADV, pond shores and irrigation ditches.
6b. Sheaths hugging the stem, not plump from hidden cleistogamous fls; aks smooth and shiny. **P. punctata** (Elliott) Small, DOTTED SMARTWEED. ADV, similar sites.

POLYGONUM L. 1753 [Gr., *polys*, many, + *gonu*, joint, alluding to the nodes]. KNOTWEED

1a. Prostrate-spreading; coarse weedy annual with deep-seated taproot; branches elongate, lfy; lvs relatively uniform on stem and branches; ak dull, brown, minutely roughened. **P. arenastrum** Bourgeau [of sandy places], DEVIL'S SHOESTRINGS (*P. rurivagum*, *P. aviculare* of Colorado lit). ADV in ruderal sites.
1b. Erect or ascending; annuals with stender taproots . . . . (2)

2a. Very delicate plants, creeping or ascending, with elliptic lvs and minute fls (less than 2 mm). **P. minimum** Watson. Mud or wet sand, seeps or streamsides, near Continental Divide, N counties.
2b. Erect annuals with generally narrower, oblong-elliptic to linear lvs . . . . (3)

3a. Tall or at least much-branched from the base; lower lvs usually falling before fruiting time; stem prominently striate, never with regularly reflexed fls and fruits; introd ruderal weeds, low altitudes . . . . (4)

3b. Low plants usually less than 2 dm tall; if taller, then without strongly striate stems and with reflexed fls and fruits . . . . . . (6)

4a. Lvs all narrowly linear; fls and frts less than 2.5 mm long; frt narrow, slightly longer than the tepals; plants with a hemispheric bushy-branched form. **P. graminifolium** Wierzbicki (?). ADV. Evidently recently introd and nowhere common. Identification uncertain.
4b. Lvs broader, or if not, than fls and frts larger; frt enclosed by the tepals; plants not bushy-branched . . . . (5)

5a. Lvs of main stem distinctly larger than the branch lvs; plants virgate, with a main stem and several elongate branches, all strongly ascending, losing the lower lvs early. **P. ramosissimum** Michaux. ADV. Late summer-flowering weed.
5b. Lvs of main stem and branches similar; stiffly spreading horizontal branches at the base, and erect main stem; lvs persistent; fls pink. **P. argyrocoleon** Steudel. ADV ruderal weed. There may be other species of Asiatic origin subsumed under these names, but the taxonomy is not clear.

6a. Less than 5 cm tall, the fls crowded into a dense terminal head with linear bracts longer than the fls. **P. polygaloides** Meisner ssp **kelloggii** (Greene) Hickman [resembling *Polygala*; for Albert Kellogg, Calif. botanist]. Beds of drying ponds.
6b. Usually 1 dm or more tall; fls not as above . . . . (7)

7a. Tepals 1.5-2.5 mm long; lvs narrowly linear. **P. engelmannii** Greene. Dry canyonsides.
7b. Perianth 3-5 mm long; lvs variable, from narrowly linear to elliptic. **P. douglasii** Greene, **85D**. Common in a variety of habitats. Extremely variable in lf form and height. While the fls are usually reflexed in fruit they need not be (*P. sawatchense*, *P. montanum*).

PTEROGONUM Gross 1913 [Gr., *pter-*, wing, + allusion to *Eriogonum*]. WINGED BUCKWHEAT (formerly in *Eriogonum*)

One sp, **P. alatum** (Torrey.) Gross. A striking and unusual herb with a rosette of oblanceolate basal lvs from which arises a tall simple fl stalk crowned with an open paniculate cyme. The pendent frts are yellow-green, trigonous, and conspicuously winged. Our plant is monocarpic, that is, the rosettes grow for several season and the plant, or at least the flowering stem, dies after it finally blossoms.

REYNOUTRIA Houttuyn 1777 [name unexplained]. JAPANESE BUCKWHEAT

One sp, **R. japonica** Houttuyn. ADV. Occasionally cult in gardens but frequently escaping to form dense thickets of rank growth, lower elevations (*Polygonum cuspidatum*). Not yet found on the W slope but very likely present.

RUMEX L. 1753 [the ancient Lat. name]. DOCK

1a. Valves (the inner 3 tepals) in frt 14-20 mm long, no central swellings ('grains') present . . . . (2)
1b. Valves in frt less than 7 mm long; grains present or absent . . . . (3)
2a. Valves in frt over 2 cm wide; plants with elongate caudices and deep roots. **R. venosus** Pursh, WILD BEGONIA. Uncommon on the W slope, sandy soil, lower Yampa drainage.
2b. Valves in frt less than 2 cm wide; plants with clusters of tuberous roots. **R. hymenosepalus** Torrey [with membranous sepals], CANAIGRE. Sandy soil along the lower river valleys. Once commercially grown for its tannin content.

3a. Valves with 1-3 distinct, spine-like teeth on the margins; usually 3 grains present. **R. maritimus** L. ssp **fueginus** (Philippi) Hultén [of shores; from Tierra del Fuego]. Wet ground of drying pools and streamsides, lower valleys. Plant low and sprawling.
3b. Valves entire or merely crenate or denticulate; grains present or absent . . . . (4)

4a. Stems erect, spreading or ascending with well-developed axillary shoots . . . . (5)
4b. Stems erect and lacking axillary shoots . . . . (6)

5a. One or more of the valves with grains. **R. quadrangulivalvis** (Danser) Rechinger. Very common in mountain parks (*R. salicifolius* of manuals]. A diploid species.
5b. No valves with grains. **R. utahensis** Rechinger. More frequent westward. Tetraploid. Both spp sometimes lumped into *R. salicifolius* Weinmann, a Californian sp.

6a. Grains present on at least one of the valves; lf-margins ruffled. **R. crispus** L. CURLY DOCK. ADV weed in wet ditches.
6b. Grains absent . . . . (7)

7a. Plant with a vertical taproot, often solitary. **R. aquaticus** L. ssp **occidentalis** (Watson) Hultén. Wet meadows and roadside ditches in the mts (*R. occidentalis*).
7b. Plant with a stout horizontal rhizome, forming dense patches. **R. densiflorus** Osterhout. Boggy places, mostly subalpine, usually at higher altitudes than the last.

STENOGONUM Nuttall 1848 [Gr., *stenos*, narrow, *gonu*, knee or joint, alluding to the slender axis and branches] (formerly in *Eriogonum*)
1a. Lvs strictly basal; peduncles 1-3 cm long, bent in the middle; plants erect, sparsely glandular; basal lvs orbicular. **S. flexum** (Jones) Reveal & Howell. Adobe soils, lower Colorado and San Juan drainages.
1b. Lvs basal and cauline; peduncles varying from none to 4 cm long, straight; plants widely branched, glabrous; lvs spatulate to linear-oblanceolate. **S. salsuginosum** Nuttall [of salty places]. Adobe hills and flats, Yampa, Colorado and San Juan drainages.

PORTULACACEAE—PURSLANE FAMILY (POR)

This small family makes up for its size in the beauty of its cultivated members. The Moss-rose, *Portulaca grandiflora*, is one of the hardiest ever-blooming plants of hot, sunny gardens in our area, and many kinds of *Lewisia* or *Oreobroma* were at one time nearly exterminated in the Pacific Northwest by root-diggers for the rock garden trade. *Lewisia rediviva*, the bitterroot, is the state flower of Montana.

1a. Prostrate-spreading, much-branched, matted, with fleshy spatulate lvs and inconspicuous yellow or orange-red fls. **Portulaca**, PURSLANE
1b. Erect or stemless, without prostrate spreading branches; fls pink, red, or white . . . . (2)

2a. Stems stolon-bearing at the base, with several pairs of opposite lvs; plants of wet streamsides. **Crunocallis**, WATER SPRING BEAUTY
2b. Stems low or absent; lvs chiefly basal, or fl stalk with a very few lvs; plants of drier habitats . . . . (3)

3a. Plants with a pair or three stem lvs (no basal lf); fl stalk arising from a deep-seated round corm . . . . (4)
3b. Plants with a cluster of linear succulent basal lvs from a stout taproot. . . . . (5)

4a. Fl stem with a single pair of broadly oval-elliptic stem lvs. **Claytonia**, SPRING BEAUTY
4b. Fl stem with three very slender linear lvs. **Erocallis**

5a. Infl an open cyme on a stalk taller than the succulent, linear basal lvs. **Talinum**
5b. Infl not taller than the lvs . . . . (6)

6a. Lvs broadly spatulate, obtuse, in very dense rosettes; fls white with pink veins. **Claytonia**, SPRING BEAUTY
6b. Lvs linear, in small tufts, or lvs absent at flowering time; fls deep solid red or pink, rarely white . . . . (7)

7a. Fls more than 2 cm diam, showy, pink, on jointed pedicels, appearing after the lvs wither. **Lewisia**, BITTERROOT
7b. Fls less than 1 cm diam., red, pink, or rarely white, not on jointed pedicels, appearing with the lvs. **Oreobroma**, PYGMY BITTERROOT

CLAYTONIA L. 1763 [for John Clayton, Virginia botanist, 1686-1739]. SPRING BEAUTY
1a. Plant with a cluster of succulent spatulate basal lvs from a stout taproot. **C. megarhiza** (Gray) Parry, ALPINE SPRING BEAUTY, **86G**. Among rocks on tundra of the higher peaks. Very similar to *C. joanneana* of the Altai.
1b. Plant slender, arising from a deep-seated round corm . . . . . . (2)

414   Portulacaceae (POR)

2a. Basal lvs none; stem with a pair of broadly oval-fusiform lvs. **C. lanceolata** Pursh, **86F**. Common, oak and upper sagebrush zone on the plateaus.
2b. One or more basal lvs present; cauline lvs usually narrowly lance-linear. **C. rosea** Rydberg. Uncommon on the W slope, an extremely early bloomer in pine forests, Mesa Verde.

CRUNOCALLIS Rydberg 1906 [from Gr., *krounos*, spring, + *kalos*, beautiful]. WATER SPRING-BEAUTY

One sp, **C. chamissoi** (Ledebour) Cockerell, **86E**. Petals white, with pink streaks. Common by streams, spruce-fir forests (*Montia*).

EROCALLIS Rydberg 1906 [possibly Gr., *erotema*, question + *kalos*, beautiful, Rydberg questioning its former placement]

One sp, **E. triphylla** (Watson) Rydberg, **86B**. Locally frequent on moist slopes and screes, Park Range (RT) (*Lewisia*).

LEWISIA Pursh 1814 [for Meriwether Lewis, of the Lewis & Clark expedition]. BITTERROOT

One sp, **L. rediviva** Pursh, **86A, PL 7**. Locally abundant in early spring on gravelly flats, Middle Park, and on seasonally wet sagebrush benches, MF.

OREOBROMA Howell 1893 [Gr., *oros*, mountain, + *broma*, food, alluding to the edible fleshy root]. PYGMY BITTERROOT (formerly incl in *Lewisia*).

1a. Sepals glandular-dentate at the ends of the veins, 2-5 mm long; petals less than 7 mm long; lvs linear, less than 8 cm long. **O. pygmaea** (Gray) Howell, **86C**. Common in open, stony subalpine meadows. White-fld mutants are common.
1b. Sepals entire, 5-10 mm long; petals about 1 cm long; lvs usually broader, oblanceolate. **O. nevadensis** (Gray) Howell. Infrequent, at lower altitudes (7-8,000 ft.) on the W plateaus. Sometimes considered a variety of the last, but in our experience they are morphologically and ecologically distinct.

PORTULACA L. 1753 [old Lat. name, mening unknown]. PURSLANE

1a. Lf axils and infl conspicuously villous with long white kinky hairs; lvs linear to narrowly oblanceolate, terete to subterete; fls orange, drying red and orange. **P. parvula** Gray. Local in sandy, seasonally wet places in the piñon-juniper, ME.
1b. Lf axils and infl glabrous or inconspicuously short-pilose; lvs obovate-cuneate to spatulate, thick but flat; annuals; fls yellow
. . . . (2)

2a. Seeds usually iridescent, when viewed at low magn, with minute ridges converged into peg-like projections that are not crowded, very nearly to fully 1 mm in greatest diam; style lobes usually 3-4. **P. retusa** Engelmann. Native, probably present in the SW counties. Ethnobotanical material from Mesa Verde, contains this seed type.

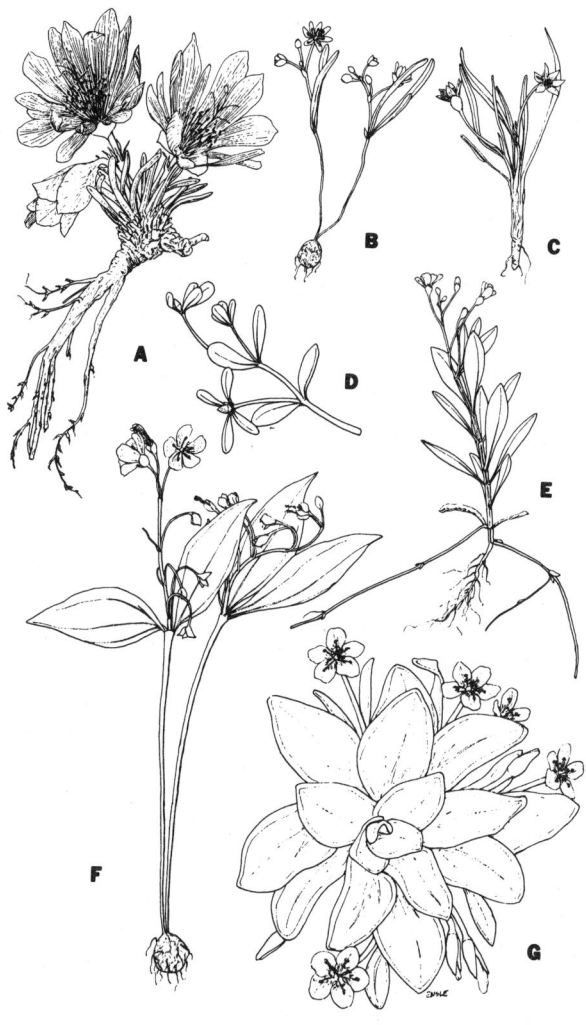

Figure 86. A, *Lewisia rediviva*; B, *Erocallis triphylla*; C, *Oreobroma pygmaea*; D, *Portulaca oleracea*; E, *Crunocallis chamissoi*; F, *Claytonia lanceolata*; G, *C. megarhiza*

416   Portulacaceae (POR)

2b. Seeds dark brown, rounded tuberculate, the tubercles crowded, usually distinctly less than 1 mm diam; style lobes usually 5-6. **P. oleracea** L., **86D**. ADV ruderal weed.

TALINUM Adanson 1763 [from a tribal name for an African sp]
   One sp, **T. parviflorum** Nuttall. Seasonally wet rimrock depressions, piñon-juniper and ponderosa pine woods, MF, ME.

POTAMOGETONACEAE
PONDWEED FAMILY (POT)

The pondweeds are found in midsummer in almost every pond of any size. Their presence is marked by the spikes of dull greenish flowers emerging from the water, and by their floating lily-pad leaves. Some are completely submerged and may be found by dredging with a rake. The floating leaves of *Potamogeton* are very similar to those of *Persicaria*, but the latter has pinnately-veined leaves and spikes of bright pink flowers. Potamogetons are important waterfowl food plants.

POTAMOGETON L. 1753 [Gr., *potamos*, river, + *geiton*, neighbor]. PONDWEED
   Note: our spp are not well-enough collected to justify precise comments on habitat or altitude. We are greatly in need of an energetic collector with a rubber raft and a long rake.
1a. Submerged lvs with stipules adnate to the leaf base and forming a sheath around the stem, the leaf blade or petiole not directly attached to the node. . . . . (2)
1b. Submerged lvs with stipules free from the rest of the lf, the blade or petiole attached directly at the node . . . . (3)

2a. Lvs retuse, blunt or rarely short-apiculate; style lacking; fruiting beak wart-like and central; lvs 2-5 mm wide. **P. filiformis** Persoon. Common in the larger lakes in the mountains.
2b. Lvs sharply pointed; styles short, the stigma on the ventral margin of the ak; lf blade filiform, up to 1 mm wide. **P. pectinatus** L. Very common in ponds (often alkaline) mostly at lower altitudes.

3a. Submerged lvs linear or nearly so, less than 5 mm wide; floating lvs lacking . . . . (4)
3b. Submerged lvs wider, ribbon-like, or plants with floating as well as submerged lvs . . . . (5)

4a. Peduncles stout, to 2 cm long, bearing congested subcapitate spikes; lvs glandless. **P. foliosus** Rafinesque.
4b. Peduncles slender, up to 9 cm long, with more open, elongated spikes; lvs with two small globose basal glands. **P. pusillus** L.

5a. Submerged lvs sessile and clasping the stem, no specialized floating lvs present . . . . (6)
5b. Submerged lvs petiolate or tapering to a sessile base, not

strongly clasping the stem, the floating lvs often well-developed and differentiated from the submerged ones . . . . (7)

6a. Stems usually zig-zag; lvs more than 10 cm long, and over 20 mm wide; stipules rigid, usually persistent; aks 4-5 mm long. **P. praelongus** Wulfen.
6b. Stems not zig-zag; lvs less than 10 cm long and less than 20 mm wide; stipules soon disintegrating into coarse fibres; aks up to 3.5 mm long. **P. richardsonii** (Bennett) Rydberg.

7a. Submerged lvs linear, sessile, 1-2 mm wide; floating lvs lance-ovate to ovate-elliptic, long-petioled; stipules 4-10 cm long, strongly fibrous; aks 3-5 mm long. **P. natans** L.
7b. Submerged lvs broadly linear to ovate, usually over 2 mm wide; floating lvs lacking, or not as above . . . . (8)

8a. Stems flattened; submerged lvs mostly 2-10 mm wide, ribbon-like; aks laterally compressed; stipules 1-4 cm long. **P. epihydrus** Rafinesque.
8b. Stems terete; submerged lvs mostly wider, ovate to elliptic, or if narrower, then not ribbon-like; aks with convex sides . . . . . . (9)

9a. Submerged lvs sessile, the floating lvs (when present) delicate and translucent, short-petiolate, not markedly different from the submerged ones; plants with reddish tinge. **P. alpinus** Balbis.
9b. Submerged lvs sessile or petiolate, different in appearance and texture from the floating lvs, or if not, then the lvs strongly curved. . . . . (10)

10a. Submerged lvs 25-75 mm wide, folded and strongly curved, petiolate, the margins entire; floating lvs 25-50-nerved, ovate to ovate-elliptic. **P. amplifolius** Tuckerman.
10b. Submerged lvs mostly 3-35 mm wide, flat, sessile or petiolate, the margin with minute 1-celled translucent teeth; floating lvs with fewer than 20 nerves . . . . (11)

11a. Submerged lvs on petioles 2-10 cm long; floating lvs elliptic to oblong-elliptic, 5-12 X 2-4 cm, on longer petioles; stipules 4-8 cm long; aks 3.5-4.0 mm long, reddish. **P. nodosus** L.
11b. Submerged lvs sessile or on petioles up to 4 cm long; aks 2.0-3.5 mm long, greenish. . . . . (12)

12a. Stipules 0.5-3.0 cm long; submerged lvs up to 12 mm wide; floating lvs up to 7 cm long; aks under 3 mm long. **P. gramineus** L.
12b. Stipules 3-7 cm long; submerged lvs up to 40 mm wide; floating lvs up to 12 cm long; aks over 3 mm long. **P. illinoensis** Morong.

PRIMULACEAE—PRIMROSE FAMILY (PRM)

Primroses, or cowslips, have been cultivated in gardens since Elizabethan times and still are among the choicest of rock garden plants. The showiest come from the mountains of Asia; our red mountain primroses are close cousins of these. *Cyclamen*, known here as a potted plant, grows wild in Europe, and *Soldanella*, a unique genus with deeply fringed bell-shaped corollas, is a treasure of the Alps. Our own *Dodecatheon*, the Shooting-star, used to be called the American *Cyclamen*. The combination of a united corolla with the stamens inserted opposite to, instead of the usual arrangement of alternate with, the petals, makes this family very easy to recognize (but see *Glaux*!).

1a. Plants lfy-stemmed . . . . (2)
1b. Plants bearing lvs at the base of the stem only . . . . (3)

2a. Fls pink; sepals petaloid, petals absent; lvs oblong; stems low, semiprostrate. **Glaux**, SEA MILKWORT
2b. Fls with yellow petals; lvs ovate; stems tall. **Steironema**, FRINGED LOOSESTRIFE

3a. Corolla lobes reflexed; stamens exserted, the anthers appearing united, forming a beak-like projection. **Dodecatheon**, SHOOTING-STAR
3b. Corolla lobes erect and spreading; stamens included, separate and distinct . . . . (4)

4a. Fls purple-red, only white in rare mutant forms; corolla tube equalling or exceeding the calyx; style filiform, elongate. **Primula**, PRIMROSE
4b. Fls white (or in one sp, faintly pink and yellow); corolla short, with short tube exceeded by calyx; style very short. **Androsace**, ROCK-JASMINE

ANDROSACE L. 1753 [name used by Pliny for some unidentified plant; derivation controversial]. ROCK-JASMINE
1a. Perennial; fls in a dense cluster, almost sessile; capsule few-seeded. **A. chamaejasme** Host ssp **carinata** (Torrey) Hultén, **87D**. Fls white with yellow center, becoming rose-colored in age. Plants only a few cm tall, locally abundant on alpine tundra.
1b. Annual; fls on long pedicels; capsule many-seeded. . . . . (2)

2a. Bracts at base of umbel broad (lance-ovate to obovate). **A. occidentalis** Pursh, **87C**. Open grassy slopes and ledges, canyonsides, flowering in early spring.
2b. Bracts at base of umbel narrow (lanceolate to subulate). . . . . . (3)

3a. Calyx strongly 5-keeled; lvs not distinctly petioled. **A. septentrionalis** L., **87B**. Forested or open sites (except desert), extremely variable in size and length of pedicels and peduncles.
3b. Calyx not keeled; lvs abruptly narrowed to a distinct petiole. **A. filiformis** Retzius, **87A**. Wet places, subalpine.

DODECATHEON L. 1753 [Gr., *dodeca*, twelve, + *theos*, god, name given by Pliny to the primrose, believed to be under the protection of the twelve superior gods]. SHOOTING-STAR

One sp, **D. pulchellum** (Rafinesque) Merrill. Along streams and by springs, from shaded canyons up into spruce-fir forest.

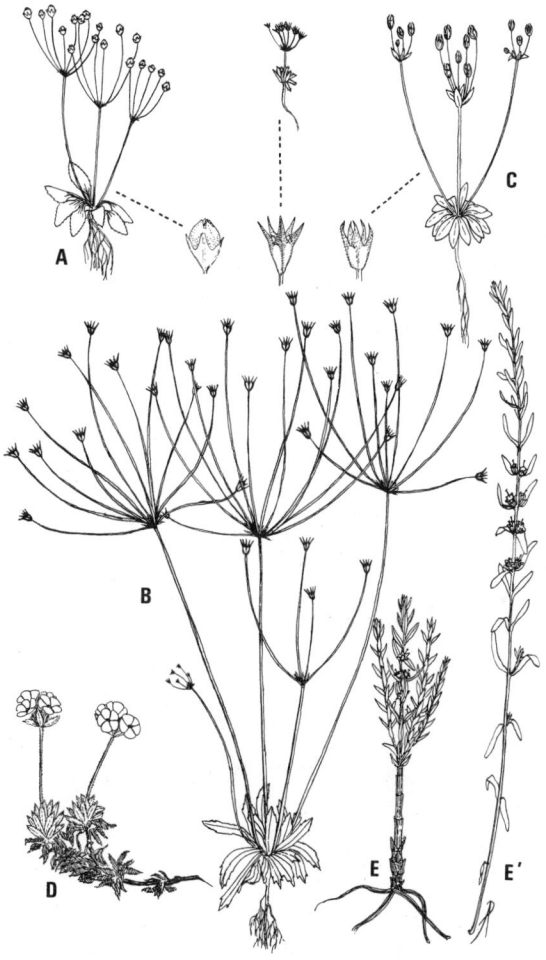

Figure 87. **A**, *Androsace filiformis*; **B**, *A. septentrionalis*; **C**, *A. occidentalis*; **D**, *A. chamaejasme*; **E**, **E'**, *Glaux maritima*, growth forms

GLAUX L. 1753 [Gr., *glaucos*, sea-green]. SEA MILKWORT

One sp, **G. maritima** L., 87E. Alkaline flats along the rivers, and in grazed wet meadows. The stamens are alternate to the petal-like sepals, indicating that a whorl of parts, the petals, are missing, for in the primroses a whorl of stamens is missing to start with, causing the remaining whorl of stamens to be opposite the petals. Confusing?

PRIMULA L. 1753 [dim of Lat. *primus*, early spring]. PRIMROSE

1a. Lvs white-mealy beneath; fls. small, pink . . . . (2)
1b. Lvs green on both sides; fls. small or large, deeply rose-colored. . . . . (3)

2b. Basal lvs less than 5 cm long, entire or very shallowly dentate. **P. incana** Jones, BIRDS-EYE PRIMROSE. Wet meadows, intermountain parks.
2a. Basal lvs usually over 6 cm long, coarsely dentate. **P. specuicola** Jones, CLIFF PRIMROSE. Not yet found in Colorado, but since it occurs as close as Moab and Bluff, Utah, in seeping canyon alcoves at the base of the Wingate Sandstone, it should occur in the Dolores and Colorado R canyons.

3a. Plants large (1.5-4.0 dm high); fls numerous, very showy, with a skunky odor. **P. parryi** Gray, PARRY'S PRIMROSE. Streambanks, subalpine snowmelt seeps.
3b. Plants small (3-10 cm high); fls solitary or few. **P. angustifolia** Torrey, ALPINE PRIMROSE. Dry rocky subalpine meadows and alpine tundra. Occasionally in dry forests where it becomes quite tall, up to 1 dm.

STEIRONEMA Rafinesque 1821 [Gr., *steiros*, sterile, + *nema*, thread, alluding to the staminodia]. FRINGED LOOSESTRIFE

One sp, **S. ciliatum** (L.) Rafinesque. Uncommon in grassy meadows along meandering streams, MF (*Lysimachia*).

PYROLACEAE—WINTERGREEN FAMILY (PYR)

A small family of exquisite forest herbs with waxy, sometimes exceedingly fragrant flowers. They are hallmarks of the most mesic montane and subalpine forests, and are most often found in deep shade. This family, traditionally, has been included in the Ericaceae.

1a. Stems bearing several whorls of sharply serrate, oblanceolate leathery lvs; infl almost umbellate. **Chimaphila**, PIPSISSEWA; PRINCE'S PINE
1b. Stems lfy only at or near the base, not in whorls; lvs ovate or round; infl a raceme, or flower solitary . . . . (2)

2a. Fl solitary, extremely fragrant. **Moneses**, WOOD NYMPH
2b. Fls several on a stem . . . . (3)

3a. Lvs scattered along lower third of stem; infl distinctly one-sided. **Orthilia**, ONE-SIDED WINTERGREEN
3b. Lvs all basal, rarely absent. **Pyrola**, WINTERGREEN

CHIMAPHILA Pursh 1813 [from Gr., *cheima*, winter, + *philein*, to love]. PIPSISSEWA; PRINCE'S PINE

One sp, **C. umbellata** (L.) Barton ssp **occidentalis** (Rydberg) Hultén, **88B**. Frequent in cool ravines, foothills to subalpine.

MONESES Salisbury 1821 [Gr., *monos*, one, and *hesis*, delight]. WOOD NYMPH; ONE-FLOWERED WINTERGREEN

One sp, **M. uniflora** (L.) S. Gray, **88A**. Cold mossy forests, usually near streams. Has fragrance of Lily-of-the-valley.

ORTHILIA Rafinesque 1840 [Gr., *ortho*, straight, alluding to the straight, elongate style]. ONE-SIDED WINTERGREEN

One sp, **O. secunda** (L.) House, **88E**. Mossy forest floors, cool ravines, montane and subalpine (*Pyrola, Ramischia*).

PYROLA L. 1753 [dim. of *Pyrus*, the pear tree, from resemblance in the foliage]. SHINLEAF (corruption of *shingle-leaf*?)

1a. Style straight. **P. minor** L., Lesser Wintergreen, **88F**. Subalpine spruce-fir forests.
1b. Style curved downward and outward. . . . . (2)

2a. Lvs pale along the veins. **P. picta** Smith. Deeply shaded ravines, San Juans. This sp is a hemiparasite, and sometimes most or all of the green leaves may be absent.
2b. Lvs green, not mottled. . . . . (3)

3a. Fls greenish; petals 4-5 mm long; scape usually less than 20 cm long; lvs 2-3 cm diam. **P. chlorantha** Swartz [green-fld]. Upper montane and subalpine forests.
3b. Fls pink; petals 7-8 mm long; scape tall, up to 40 cm long; lvs commonly over 3 cm in diam. **P. rotundifolia** L. ssp **asarifolia** (Michaux) Löve, SWAMP WINTERGREEN. Boggy streambanks, subalpine forests (*P. asarifolia*).

RANUNCULACEAE—BUTTERCUP FAMILY (RAN)

[Note: the genera with follicular or berry-like fruits are now placed in the Helleboraceae]

The petals of buttercups have a high, almost mirror-like gloss. Children test this quality by holding up a flower to another's chin and asking, "Do you like butter?" The basal part of the petal, however, is dull. Lyman Benson explains, in *Plant Taxonomy, Methods and Principles*, that these qualities constitute a device for pollination by rainwater. The stigmas of buttercups are not well situated to be brushed by bees, but bees leave much pollen lying around on the petals. The glossy part of the petal is water repellent, while the dull part is not. If rain or dew falls on the petal, the water will rise only as far as the top of the matte area, draining off between the petals above that point. This water level is usually at about the same level as the stigmas. Pollen thus floats on the water-film and is deposited on the stigmas as the water level recedes.

Figure 88. A, *Moneses uniflora*; B, *Chimaphila umbellata*; C, *Pterospora andromedea*; D, *Hypopitys monotropa*; E, *Orthilia secunda*; F, *Pyrola minor*

1a. Tiny annual plants with linear basal lvs; fruiting receptacle many times longer than wide; petals spurred. **Myosurus**, MOUSETAIL
1b. Plants not as above; receptacle rarely more than 5 times as long as wide; petals, when present, not spurred . . . . (2)

2a. Petals and sepals distinctly different, the petals usually yellow or white . . . . (3)
2b. Petals and sepals similar (tepals), or absent, or only one or the other present, usually white or colored, but rarely yellow. . . . (10)

3a. Submerged aquatics with linear palmatisect lvs and emergent white fls; petals not glossy; aks transversely wrinkled. **Batrachium**, WATER CROWFOOT
3b. Terrestrial plants, or if aquatic, then with yellow glossy petals
. . . . (4)

4a. Ak with a long straight beak and with two pouch-like enlargements at the base; sepals persistent in frt; small desert annuals with linear-dissected lvs. **Ceratocephala**, HORNHEAD
4b. Ak with a short, often curved beak, or beakless, lacking basal pouches; sepals deciduous. . . . . (5)

5a. Strongly stoloniferous, rooting at the nodes, semiaquatic, rooted in mud or floating in water. . . . . (6)
5b. Not stoloniferous, terrestrial . . . . (7)

6a. Lvs linear or narrowly elliptic. **Ranunculus reptans**, SPEARWORT
6b. Lvs not as above . . . . (8)

7a. Lvs round or oval, crenate-toothed, cordate at the base; plants of muddy shores. **Halerpestes**, ALKALI CROWFOOT
7b. Lvs deeply palmately lobed; floating in water or emerging onto muddy banks. **Ranunculus**, BUTTERCUP

8a. Petals narrow, with a claw-like base; fls perfect, but often almost staminate or carpellate (functionally male or female); aks longitudinally ribbed. **Cyrtorhyncha**
8b. Petals broad, clawless; fls with functional stamens and carpels; aks not ribbed . . . . (9)

9a. Style and beak extremely short; aks transversely rugose and minutely alveolate; receptacle cylindric, the aks very numerous. **Hecatonia**, BLISTER BUTTERCUP
9b. Style and beak well-developed; otherwise not as above. **Ranunculus**, BUTTERCUP

10a. Tepals small, less conspicuous than the stamens or carpels . . . (11)
10b. Tepals large and showy, petal-like. . . . . (12)

11a. Lvs simple, mostly basal, palmately lobed, long-petioled; fls perfect. **Trautvetteria**, TASSEL-RUE
11b. Lvs compound, basal and cauline, with many shallowly-lobed lfls. **Thalictrum**, MEADOW-RUE

12a. Tepals commonly 4, not overlapping; lvs not whorled beneath the infl; styles becoming long and feathery at maturity. . . . . . . (13)
12b. Tepals 5 or more, overlapping; upper stem lvs in a whorl below the infl, sometimes forming an invol. . . . . (16)

13a. Tepals thick, purple, forming an urn; plants erect or sprawling, not true vines. **Coriflora**, LEATHER-FLOWER; SUGAR-BOWLS
13b. Tepals white or yellow or blue-purple, spreading; plants sprawling or true vines . . . . (14)

14a. Tepals thin, blue-purple. **Atragene**, BLUE CLEMATIS
14b. Tepals white, cream or yellowish . . . . (15)

15a. Tepals thick, yellow; fls perfect. **Viticella**, ORIENTAL CLEMATIS
15b. Tepals thin, white or cream; flowers imperfect, staminate or carpellate (the carpellate fls with a few sterile stamens). **Clematis**, VIRGIN'S BOWER

16a. Fls appearing before the lvs; tepals over 2 cm long; styles becoming long and feathery at maturity. **Pulsatilla**, PASQUE-FLOWER
16b. Fls appearing after the lvs; tepals about 1 cm long; styles not greatly elongated in fruit. . . . . (17)

17a. Aks glabrous; fls usually several, tepals white or lemon-yellow. **Anemonastrum**, NARCISSUS ANEMONE
17b. Aks pubescent; fls usually few, tepals white to rose, or bluish on the back. **Anemone**, WIND-FLOWER

ANEMONASTRUM Holub 1973 [*Anemone*, + Lat., -*astrum*, resembling]. NARCISSUS ANEMONE

One sp, **A. narcissiflorum** (L.) Holub ssp **zephyrum** (Nelson) Weber, **89A**. The largest-fld and most showy of our anemones, common in the upper subalpine (*Anemone*). The fls are so large that some confuse this with *Trollius*, which has follicles rather than akenes and lacks the conspicuous invol.

ANEMONE L. 1753 [ancient name, corruption of *Na'man*, Semitic name for *Adonis*, from whose blood the crimson-flowered *Anemone* of the Middle East was said to have sprung. Probably has nothing to do with Gr., *anemos*, wind]. WINDFLOWER
1a. Aks densely woolly; receptacle cylindrical; tepals white. **A. cylindrica** Gray, THIMBLEWEED. Meadows and roadside ditches, medium altitudes, GN.
1b. Aks pubescent but not woolly; receptacle not cylindric; tepals various. . . . . (2)

2a. Basal lvs three-parted, with broad, shallowly-lobed glabrous and glossy segs. **A. parviflora** Michaux. Local on cool subalpine rocky slopes.
2b. Basal lvs cleft into 5 or more narrow divs, pubescent . . . . . . (3)

3a. Tepals usually rose-colored; plants of medium altitudes in forests and meadows. **A. multifida** Poiret ssp **globosa** (Nuttall) Torrey & Gray, **89C**. Common in dry open forests.
3b. Tepals white or cream with distinctly bluish dorsal faces; dwarf tundra plants. **A. multifida** Poiret ssp **saxicola** (Boivin) Weber. Infrequent, Mosquito and Elk Mts.

ATRAGENE L. 1753 [derivation unknown]. BLUE CLEMATIS

1a. Lvs with 3 lfls, these large, not cleft. **A. occidentalis** Hornemann, **89D**. Climbing on trees, foothills to subalpine (*Clematis columbiana* of Colorado lit).
1b. Lvs biternately compound, the lfls small, deeply cleft and lobed. **A. columbiana** Nuttall. Scrambling and semi-vine-like, hardly climbing, in open forests (*C. pseudoalpina*). Very similar to the European *C. alpina*.

BATRACHIUM S. Gray 1821 [Gr., *batrachion*, frog, alluding to the habitat]. WATER CROWFOOT
Note: we need more carefully made collections of the water crowfoots, especially in fruiting condition; they, of course, are conspicuous plants when in blossom, but unfortunately the critical characters are in the frts. It is almost certain that the three spp listed below occur in our region in slow streams and ditches.

1a. Style persistent after flowering; ak beak 0.7-1.1 mm long, body coarsely transversely ridged; dissected lvs once- or sometimes twice-trichotomous, then dichotomous. **B. longirostre** (Godron) Schultz.
1b. Style usually deciduous after flowering; ak beak 0.3 or rarely 0.5 mm long, body obovoid, 1-1.5 mm long, finely transversely wrinkled . . . . (2)

2a. Pedicels recurved at fruiting time; submersed dissected lvs usually sessile, the first divisions arising within the usually dilated stipular lf bases (the ends of these are often free), usually not collapsing when withdrawn from the water, circinate, much shorter than the internodes; aks mostly 30 to 45 or 80; dissected lvs usually once- or twice-trichotomous. **B. circinatum** (Sibthorp) Fries ssp **subrigidum** (Drew) Löve & Löve, **92B**.
2b. Pedicels not recurved at fruiting time; submersed dissected lvs usually petioled, the first divisions arising usually but not always well above the non-dilated stipular lf bases (the ends of these not free), usually collapsing when withdrawn from the water, not circinate, usually about equalling or a little shorter than the internodes; aks usually about 10 or 20 or as many as 40; dissected lvs usually repeatedly trichotomous. **B. trichophyllum** (Chaix) Bosch.

CERATOCEPHALA Moench 1794 [Gr., *keratos*, horn, + *kephale*, head]. HORNHEAD

One sp, **C. orthoceras** de Candolle [straight horn], **91B**. ADV weed of Asia Minor, naturalized widely on the W slope, mostly on

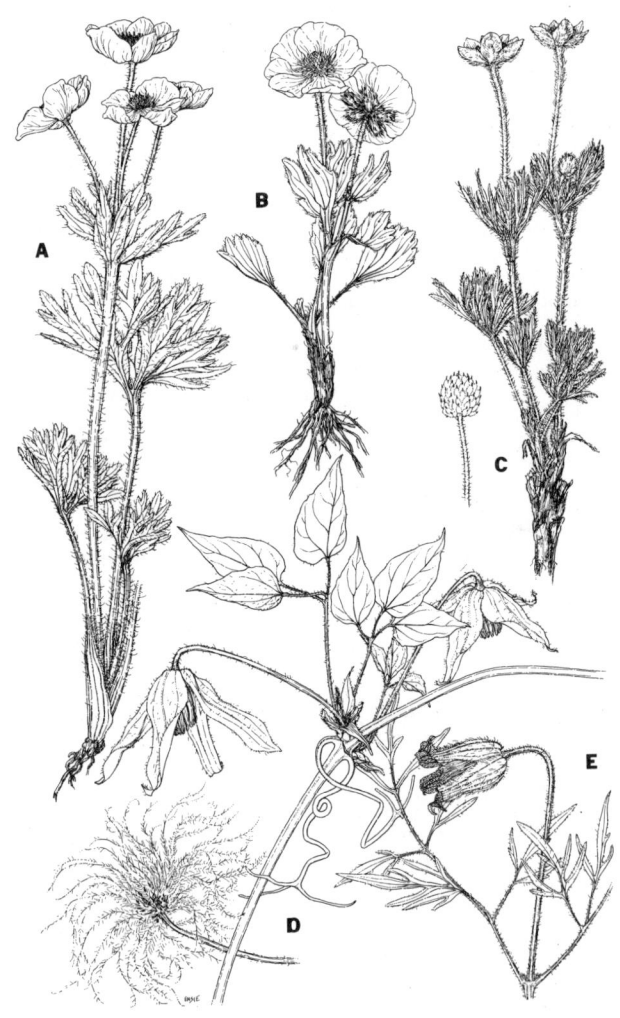

Figure 89. A, *Anemonastrum narcissiflorum*; B, *Ranunculus macauleyi*; C, *Anemone multifida*; D, *Atragene occidentallis*; E, *Coriflora hirsutissima*

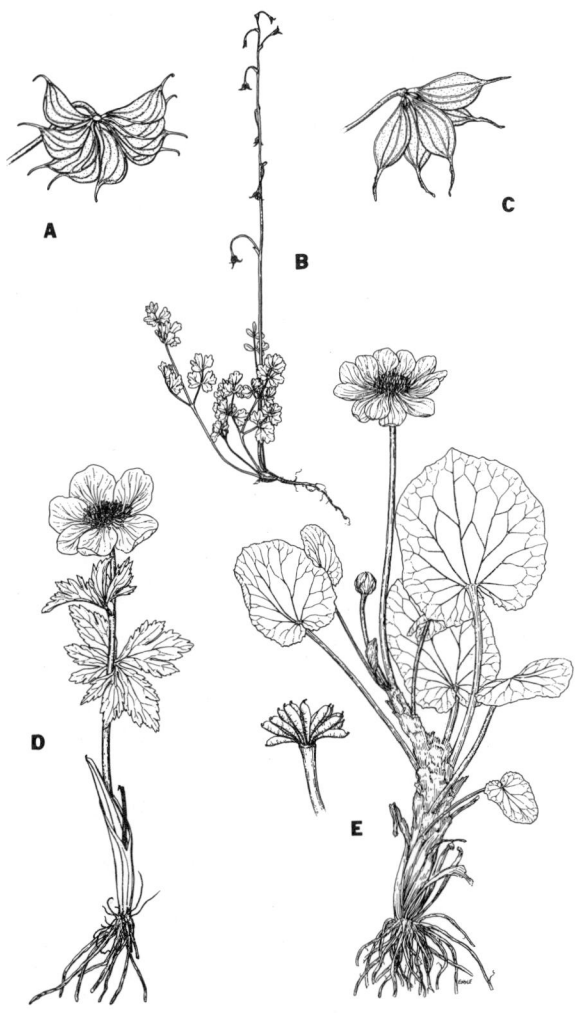

Figure 90. A, *Thalictrum sparsiflorum*; B, *T. alpinum*; C, *T. fendleri*; D, *Trollius albiflorus*; E, *Psychrophila leptosepala*

clay soils of the valleys, very abundant in early springtime (*C. testiculata*).

CLEMATIS L. 1753 [Gr., *clema*, a shoot]. VIRGIN'S BOWER
One sp, **C. ligusticifolia** Nuttall [with lvs like privet]. Common, clambering over fences and trees, valley bottoms. The masses of feathery frts are conspicuous in late summer.

CORIFLORA Weber 1982 [Gr. *coriarius*, of leather, alluding to the texture of the tepals]. LEATHERFLOWER; SUGARBOWLS
One sp, **C. hirsutissima** (Pursh) Weber, **89E**. Grassy slopes, meadows and open pine woods (*Clematis*).

CYRTORHYNCHA Nuttall 1838 [Gr., *kyrtos*, curved, + *rhynchos*, beak]
One sp, **C. ranunculina** Nuttall. Rocky slopes wet in spring from snow runoff, upper Gunnison Basin (*Ranunculus*).

HALERPESTES Greene 1900 [not explained, but possibly from Gr., *halos*, salt, + Lat., *pestis*, plague]. ALKALI CROWFOOT
One sp, **H. cymbalaria** (Pursh) Greene ssp **saximontana** (Fernald) Moldenke, **91D**. Common on muddy shores and flats. Recognized by the combination of stolons, ovate, crenate lvs, and prominently ribbed aks. This is a small genus of 4-6 spp occurring in Central Asia, W North America, and temperate S South America (*Ranunculus*).

HECATONIA Loureiro 1790 [Gr., *hecaton*, hundred, from the large number of aks]. BLISTER BUTTERCUP
One sp, **H. scelerata** (L.) Fourreau, **92C**. ADV weed of muddy places, particularly disturbed sites such as cattle ponds and troughs. Although usually placed in *Ranunculus*, this sp is unique, having very different aks and differing greatly in habit, being a succulent plant with small fls, producing up to a hundred akenes. The lvs are deeply dissected and the stems are stout and hollow.

MYOSURUS L. 1753 [from Gr., *myos*, of a mouse, + *oura*, a tail]. MOUSETAIL
1a. Mature aks roundish, with a flat or concave dorsal shield or border nearly surrounding the base of the beak, the shield often larger than the body of the akene. **M. cupulatus** Watson. Infrequent or overlooked, in muddy (greasewood?) flats, MZ (*M. nitidus*).
1b. Mature aks more or less quadrangular, without shield or border, keeled dorsally from base to apex . . . . (2)

2a. Back of the ak scarcely wider on each side than the very prominent keel, prolonged into a beak at least half as long as the body. **M. apetalus** Gay. Drying ponds, sagebrush (*M. aristatus*, *M. minimus* var *montanus*).
2b. Back of the ak distinctly wider on each side than the relatively low keel, the beak much less than half as long as the body. **M. minimus** L., **91C**. Similar sites.

PULSATILLA Miller 1754 [possibly dim. from Italian, *pulsare*, to throb, alluding to the Passion; first used by Matthioli]. PASQUE-FLOWER

One sp, **P. patens** (L.) Miller ssp **hirsutissima** Zamels. One of the first early spring fls of open forests and sagebrush, but ranging up to timberline. This genus is best developed in the mountain regions of Eurasia (*Anemone*).

RANUNCULUS L. 1753 [dim. of Lat., *rana*, frog, in allusion to the habitat where buttercups abound]. BUTTERCUP

1a. Lvs all entire or at most denticulate or wavy . . . . (2)
1b. Lvs coarsely toothed or lobed or deeply dissected . . . . (3)

2a. Stoloniferous and rooting at the nodes; lvs only a few mm wide, linear or narrowly oblong. **R. reptans** L. [creeping], SPEARWORT, **91A**. Muddy pond shores and drying catchment basins, montane and subalpine.
2b. Not stoloniferous; lvs broadly lanceolate, over 1 cm wide; petals 7-12 mm long. **R. alismifolius** Geyer var **montanus** Watson. Wet mt meadows.

3a. Lvs deeply palmately lobed, floating in water or emerging onto muddy banks. . . . . (4)
3b. Lvs not as above, not floating or emergent . . . . (5)

4a. Lvs broadly 3-lobed, the lobes sometimes shallowly notched; submerged lvs not much different from the floating ones. **R. hyperboreus** B. Brown ssp **intertextus** (Greene) Kapoor & Löve [far-northern; interwoven], FLOATING BUTTERCUP. In small subalpine ponds and peat bogs.
4b. Lvs deeply 3-lobed, the lobes again deeply 3-lobed; submerged lvs usually finely dissected. **R. gmelinii** DeCandolle var **hookeri** (D. Don) Benson [for J. G. Gmelin; for J. D. Hooker], WATER CROWFOOT, **92A, PL 49**. Abundant in meandering streams in the intermountain basins.

5a. Styles and ak beaks lacking or minute, not over 0.2 mm long; basal lvs merely crenate; fls minute. **R. abortivus** L. ssp **acrolasius** (Fernald) Kapoor & Löve [runty; hairy top]. Infrequent, slender plants of shaded streamsides, RT.
5b. Styles and ak beaks longer . . . . (6)

6a. Aks laterally compressed, much wider than thick; sepals not tinged with purple. . . . . (7)
6b. Aks turgid, not more than 2.5 times as broad as thick; sepals tinged with purple. . . . . (9)

7a. Stems harshly spreading-pubescent, commonly rooting at the lower nodes. **R. macounii** Britton [for the Canadian botanist, John Macoun]. Common in riparian woodlands.
7b. Stems smooth or pubescent but not as above, not rooting at the lower nodes . . . . (8)

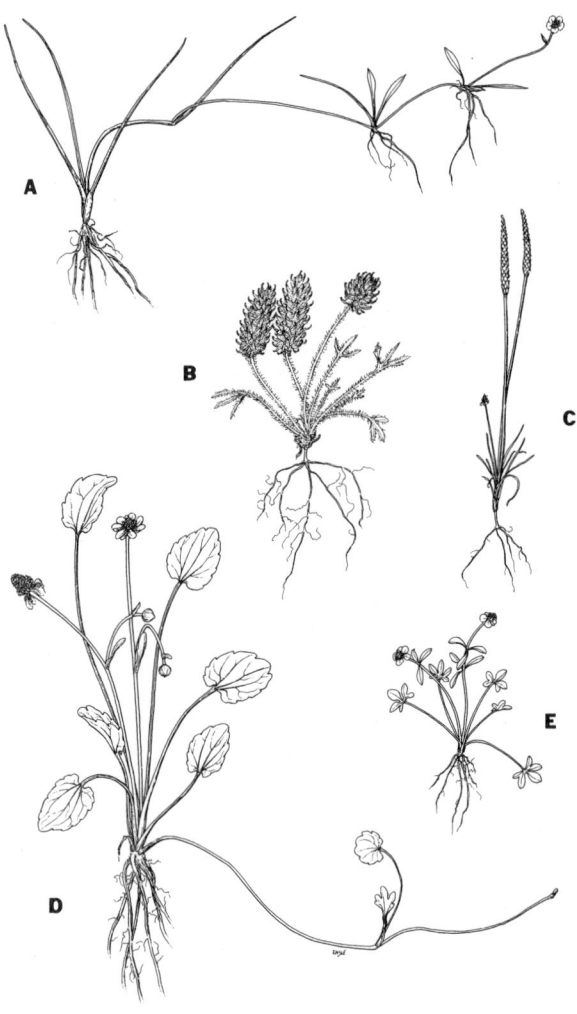

Figure 91. A, *Ranunculus reptans*; B, *Ceratocephala orthoceras*; C, *Myosurus minimus*; D, *Halerpestes cymbalaria*; E, *Ranunculus pygmaeus*

Figure 92. A, *Ranunculus gmelinii*; B, *Batrachium circinatum*; C, *Hecatonia scelerata*; D, *Trautvetteria carolinensis*

8a. Petals not over 3 mm long; aks smooth or hispid. **R. uncinatus** Don [hooked]. Moist woodlands, middle altitudes.
8b. Petals 6-18 mm long; aks glabrous. **R. acriformis** Gray [resembling *R. acris*]. Moist meadows, RT.

9a. Sepals and usually the pedicels covered with blackish or reddish hairs. . . . . (10)
9b. Sepals not covered with dark hairs. . . . . (11)

10a. Basal lvs elliptic to spatulate, toothed at apex. **R. macauleyi** Gray [for the collector, Lt. C. H. McCauley], 89B. Subalpine meadows from the Gore Ranges southwestward.
10b. Basal lvs broader, palmately lobed or parted. **R. nivalis** L. A single specimen, collected by Penland on Capitol Peak, appears to belong to this sp. New collections and field observations are needed.

11a. Tiny alpine plants less than 5 cm tall, with small 3-lobed lvs and minute fls, the petals to 3.5 mm long, only equalling the sepals. **R. pygmaeus** Wahlenberg, 91E. Local in snow-melt areas, extremely inconspicuous.
11b. Taller plants, if alpine with larger fls and different lf form . . .
. . . . (12)

12a. Fruiting receptacle and head of aks globose. . . . . (13)
12b. Fruiting receptacle and head of aks ovoid to cylindrical . . . . (14)

13a. Lvs three-parted; roots tuberous, 3-5 mm diam, in a cluster. **R. jovis** Nelson [for a mountain, The Thunderer, in Yellowstone Park]. Sagebrush areas, MF.
13b. Lvs not three-parted; basal lvs simple, stem lvs lobed; roots not tuberous. **R. glaberrimus** Hooker var **ellipticus** Greene. Early spring, sagebrush to oak-aspen.

14a. Fl stems almost scapose, the plant consisting of a cluster of biternately-dissected basal lvs on slender petioles from a mass of fibrous roots, most of the plant buried in loose scree. **R. gelidus** Karelin & Kirilow [frigid]. Extremely local, growing on the highest peaks. Found also in Alaska and eastern Siberia. There is disagreement as to whether or not *R. grayi*, described from Gray's Peak, is really synonymous.
14b. Fl stems erect, somewhat lfy, otherwise not as above. . . . . . (15)

15a. Lvs very finely dissected into thread-like divs; fls very showy; plants of high tundra. **R. adoneus** Gray [for the god, *Adonis*], SNOW BUTTERCUP. Along snowbanks, often blossoming through the melting snow.
15b. Lvs with broader divs; fls relatively small . . . . (16)

16a. Aks glabrous; most lvs cleft to the middle or below. **R. eschscholtzii** Schlechtendal [for J. F. Eschscholtz, early 19th century collector with Russian expeditions]. Moist subalpine forests.

Some feel that *R. adoneus* is only an alpine race of this, but in Colorado they are distinct.
16b. Aks pubescent . . . . (17)

17a. Most basal lvs cleft to near the base. **R. pedatifidus** Smith [palmately-cleft]. Pond borders, wet meadows, scree slopes, subalpine and alpine.
17b. Blades of the basal lvs, or most of them, merely crenate or shallowly lobed . . . . (18)

18a. Petals large (ca. 1 cm. long). **R. cardiophyllus** Hooker [with heart-shaped lvs]. Margins of ponds, wet meadows, upper montane and subalpine. Both fls and frts should be available for certain identification.
18b. Petals small (ca. 5 mm or less). **R. inamoenus** Greene [unattractive]. Meadows and pond borders, upper montane, subalpine.

THALICTRUM L. 1753 [a name of some plant mentioned by Dioscorides]. MEADOW-RUE. This genus probably belongs in its own family, the Coptaceae.
1a. Stems very low, less than 20 cm high, lvs chiefly basal; fls perfect, in a simple raceme; peat bogs and tundra, alpine and subalpine. **T. alpinum** L., ALPINE MEADOW-RUE, **90B**.
1b. Stem tall and lfy; fls in panicles, perfect or unisexual (fls of each sex, however, may be present on the same stem) . . . . . . (2)

2a. Upper edge of carpel straight or concave, lower edge deeply convex, lateral parallel veins not prominent, but mature carpel with oblique veins. **T. sparsiflorum** Trelease [few-fld], **90A**. Shaded ravines and aspen stands.
2b. Upper and lower edges of carpels convex, lateral parallel veins prominent . . . . (3)

3a. Lvs coriaceous, glaucous; lfls 5-8 x 4-9 mm; carpels 4-5(6). **T. heliophilum** Wilken & DeMott [sun-loving]. END. Open sunny sites on dry shale slopes, GF, RB.
3b. Lvs thin, green; lfls 10-17 X 8-12 mm; carpels 7-14. **T. fendleri** Engelmann, **90C**. Aspen groves and meadows, montane and subalpine, our most common sp.

TRAUTVETTERIA Fischer & Meyer 1835 [for E. R. von Trautvetter, 1809-1889, Russian botanist]. TASSEL-RUE

One sp, **T. carolinensis** Walter) Vail [of the Carolinas], **92D**. Spruce-fir forests and subalpine meadows, AA, LP. The long white staminal filaments are the most conspicuous parts of the fls. The palmately-lobed basal lvs recall *Trollius*.

VITICELLA Moench 1794 [dim. of *Vitis*, the grape-vine]. ORIENTAL CLEMATIS

One sp, **V. orientalis** (L.) Weber. ADV. Originally introd into Colorado into mining towns on the Clear Creek valley, now is estab on W slope roadsides, MF, GF (*Clematis*).

RHAMNACEAE—BUCKTHORN FAMILY (RHM)

This family is characterized by a shrubby habit, leaves with three principal veins, with the remainder closely parallel and pinnate, and flowers in which the stamens are opposite the petals. Few families have this condition (see Primulaceae and Portulacaceae). *Ceanothus* is most diversified in California with over 40 species including some extremely beautiful and decorative shrubs used horticulturally (California Lilac). *Rhamnus purshiana* of the Pacific Coast yielded the bark called *cascara sagrada*, used medicinally as a tonic and laxative. *R. cathartica* is a common cultivated ornamental shrub in Colorado.

1a. Frt fleshy with 2-4 seeds; petals 4, rarely 5, greenish, short-clawed, about 1-1.5 mm long; ovary essentially superior. **Rhamnus**, BUCKTHORN
1b. Frt dry, capsular; petals 5, white, long-clawed, 2 mm long or more; ovary partly inferior. **Ceanothus**, BUCKBRUSH

CEANOTHUS L. 1753 [Gr., *keanothos*, a kind of thistle]. BUCKBRUSH

1a. Lvs 4-8 cm long, strongly toothed, thick, evergreen and with a sticky, strong-scented lacquer coating. **C. velutinus** Douglas [velvety], STICKY-LAUREL, **93A**. Steep canyon slopes. When very abundant it may be a fire hazard because of the volatile oils in the foliage.
1b. Lvs smaller, not evergreen, not sticky, entire or shallowly toothed near the apex . . . . (2)

2a. Lvs oblong-elliptic, entire; low spreading shrub with slender branches and slender spinescent short shoots; lvs silky-pubescent, often grayish beneath. **C. fendleri** Gray, **93B**. Common understory in coniferous forests.
2b. Lvs broadly ovate, often few-toothed at the apex; more erect shrub with stout branches and mostly lacking spinescent short shoots; lvs green and almost glabrous beneath. **C. martinii** Jones [for Rev. George Martin, Utah amateur botanist], **93C**. Oak scrub, Piceance Basin.

RHAMNUS L. 1753 [ancient Gr. name for this genus]. BUCKTHORN

One sp, **R. smithii** Greene [for the collector, Benjamin H. Smith], **93D**. Infrequent shrub 1-2 m tall on usually wooded slopes but occasionally barren shales, White River to San Juan drainage. The lvs are elliptic, rounded at the apex, shallowly crenate from base to apex. Fls appear with the lvs in June. The berry is black.

ROSACEAE—ROSE FAMILY (ROS)

The flowers of most members of the rose family are astonishingly similar, the main differences, besides size and color, being in the number and structure of the carpels. All rosaceous flowers have an hypanthium or fused cup formed by the bases of the calyx, corolla and stamens. There is often a confusing 'extra' set of calyx-like parts alternating with the real sepals. For want of an understanding we

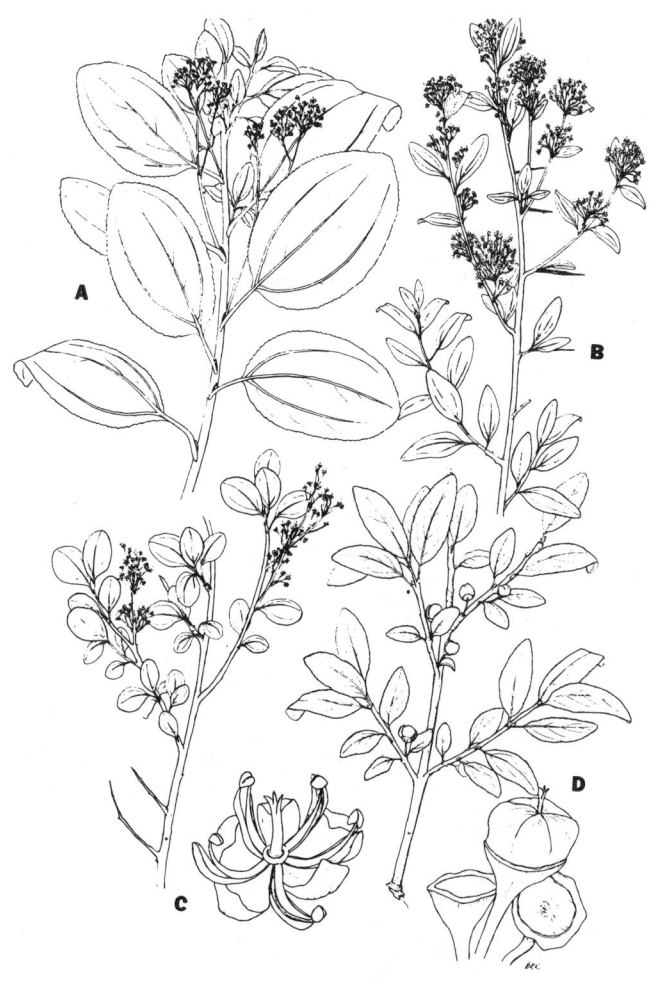

Figure 93. A, *Ceanothus velutinus*; **B**, *C. fendleri*; **C**, *C. martinii*; **D**, *Rhamnus smithii*

give them a name—bracteoles. They also occur in the mallows and mentzelias. In a family that provides so many edible fruits, it is odd to find that the edible parts are formed in many ways from quite different floral parts: hypanthium (Apple, Pear), carpel wall (Cherry, Plum), receptacle (Strawberry), the whole carpel group without the receptacle (Raspberry), and carpels plus receptacle (Blackberry).

1a. Shrubs or small trees. . . . . (2)
1b. Herbs, sometimes woody at the very base. . . . . (17)

2a. [1] Branches and lvs opposite. **Coleogyne**, BLACKBRUSH
2b. Branches and lvs alternate . . . . (3)

3a. [2] Lvs compound. . . . . (4)
3b. Lvs simple or lobed . . . . (7)

4a. [3] Fls yellow; lvs pinnately compound but crowded so as to appear to be palmate. **Pentaphylloides**, SHRUBBY CINQUEFOIL
4b. Fls pink or white; lvs distinctly pinnate . . . . (5)

5a. [4] Lfls 11 to 15; small tree with umbel-like fl clusters and orange berries; thorns or prickles absent. **Sorbus**, ROWAN TREE; MOUNTAIN-ASH
5b. Lfls 5 to 7; shrubs with thorns or prickles . . . . (6)

6a. [5] Lvs strongly glaucous beneath; fls white; frt a 'raspberry'. **Rubus**, RASPBERRY
6b. Lvs green, often pale but not glaucous; fls pink; frt a 'hip'. **Rosa**, WILD ROSE

7a. [3] Plants with thorns formed by modified branches. **Crataegus**, HAWTHORN
7b. Plants not thorny . . . . (8)

8a. [7] Fls and frts in a raceme; lvs and twigs glabrous, lvs finely serrulate, never lobed. **Padus**, CHOKE-CHERRY
8b. Fls and fruits not in a raceme; lvs and twigs either pubescent, or lvs coarsely serrate or lobed . . . . (9)

9a. [8] Lvs simple or shallowly pinnately lobed . . . . (10)
9b. Lvs palmately lobed, often faintly so. . . . . (14)

10a. [9] Lvs narrowly elliptic-oblong, not or very indistinctly toothed; frt a pome. **Peraphyllum**, SQUAW-APPLE
10b. Lvs distinctly toothed or lobed . . . . (11)

11a. [10] Fls, white, in terminal, many-flowered, pyramidal clusters. **Holodiscus**, OCEAN-SPRAY
11b. Fls white or yellowish, axillary or in few-fld clusters . . . . . (12)

12a. [11] Lvs linear, or if ovate or oblong, then tapering to the base; style becoming long and feathery in fruit; frt dry, of a single carpel; lvs permanently and densely pubescent beneath. **Cercocarpus**, MOUNTAIN-MAHOGANY

12b. Lvs broadly ovate, abruptly rounded at the base; petiole distinct; style not feathery; frt several-carpellate; lvs usually losing much of their pubescence at maturity . . . . (13)

13a. [12] Fls small, pink, in a terminal pyramidal infl; stamens conspicuously exserted; low shrub; frt a cluster of dry follicles. **Spiraea**, BRIDAL WREATH
13b. Fls white, large, in axillary clusters; stamens not conspicuously exserted; tall shrub; frt a pome. **Amelanchier**, SERVICEBERRY

14a. [9] Lvs oblanceolate, deeply few-lobed at the apex, white-tomentose beneath. **Purshia**, BITTERBRUSH; CLIFF-ROSE
14b. Lvs not oblanceolate nor otherwise as above . . . . (15)

15a. [14] Fls small, in umbellate cymes; frt a cluster of 2 or more papery carpels. **Physocarpus**, NINEBARK
15b. Fls large, solitary or in few-flowered cymes; frt an aggregate of fleshy aks (raspberry) . . . . (16)

16a. [15] Lvs 3-6 cm wide, the lobes rounded. **Oreobatus**, BOULDER RASPBERRY
16b. Lvs 10-20 cm wide, the lobes acute. **Rubacer**, THIMBLEBERRY

17a. [1] Lvs simple. . . . . (18)
17b. Lvs compound or variously divided . . . . (19)

18a. [17] Lvs simple, crenate, white beneath; loosely matted alpine plants; fls large, white, with usually 8 petals and plumose styles. **Dryas**, MOUNTAIN DRYAD
18b. Lvs narrowly spatulate, in tight rosettes forming extensive hard mats on cliffs; fls small, in delicate spikes. **Petrophyton**, ROCK-SPIRAEA

19a. [17] Lvs palmately compound, with three or more lfls . . . . . (20)
19b. Lvs pinnatifid, ternately subdivided or pinnately compound. . . (23)

20a. [19] Fls yellow . . . . (21)
20b. Fls white or pink . . . . (22)

21a. [20] Petals minute, narrow; lvs few-toothed at the apex; densely matted snowbed plant with only basdal lvs and very short infl. **Sibbaldia**
21b. Not as above. **Potentilla**, CINQUEFOIL; FIVE-FINGER

22a. [20] Lvs not basal; stems very slender, rhizomatous; fls rose-purple; streamsides and willow bogs. **Cylactis**, ARCTIC RASPBERRY
22b. Lvs basal from a stout caudex, stem stoloniferous; fls white; forest floors. **Fragaria**, STRAWBERRY

23a. [19] Lvs several times ternately divided; fls minute, white or pinkish. **Chamaerhodos**
23b. Lvs pinnately compound or cleft . . . . (24)

24a. [23] Lvs pinnately compound, with ± uniform lfls . . . . (25)
24b. Lvs variously pinnatifid, with unequal segs or lfls . . . . (31)

25a. [24] Fls in tight ball-like heads or short spikes . . . . (26)
25b. Fls not as above . . . . (27)

26a. [26] Lfls oval, toothed; fls white. **Sanguisorba**, BURNET
26b. Lfls divided to the base into three lobes; fls yellow. **Ivesia**

27a. [26] Fls yellow . . . . (28)
27b. Fls purple; glaucous-leaved rhizomatous plant of wet pond shores. **Comarum**, PURPLE CINQUEFOIL

28a. [27] Plant with basal lvs only, with 7 to 30 lfls, silvery beneath, spreading by long, usually red, stolons. **Argentina**, SILVERWEED
28b. Plant with lfy stems or at least not stoloniferous . . . . (29)

29a. [28] Fls in a narrow raceme; upper half of mature hypanthium covered with hooked bristles. **Agrimonia**, AGRIMONY
29b. Fls in a branched infl; hypanthium without hooks . . . . (30)

30a. [29] Style attached to near top of ovary; lvs either palmately compound or pinnately compound with narrow lfls. **Potentilla**, CINQUEFOIL; FIVE-FINGER
30b. Style attached near the base of the ovary; lvs pinnately compound with broadly oval lfls. **Drymocallis**

31a. [24] Style jointed, the lower part persistent and with a terminal hook; lvs pinnately compound with few unequal lfls, the uppermost one usually larger; fls erect, yellow, white or rose. **Geum**, AVENS
31b. Style continuous, without a hook; lvs with many narrow segs . .
. . . . (32)

32a. [31] Petals pinkish-white; fls nodding; style plumose at maturity. **Erythrocoma**, PRAIRIE SMOKE
32b. Petals yellow; fls erect. **Acomastylis**, ALPINE AVENS

ACOMASTYLIS Greene 1906 [Gr., *a-*, without, + *coma*, mane, + *stylis*, style]. ALPINE AVENS
One sp, **A. rossii** (R. Brown) Greene ssp **turbinata** (Rydberg) Weber [for Capt. James C. Ross, Arctic explorer; turbinate, as to the hypanthium]. Very abundant on rocky tundra, forming a dense tight turf in areas with relatively little winter snow cover. *Acomastylis* is responsible for the deep red autumn color of the tundra, contrasting with the golden bronze of *Kobresia*. *Acomastylis* is essentially an Asiatic genus.

AGRIMONIA L. 1753 [corruption of *Argemone*, a plant mentioned by Pliny]. AGRIMONY
One sp, **A. striata** Michaux. Brushy areas in the bottoms of gulches, infrequent on the W slope (GN).

AMELANCHIER Medikus 1789 [Provençal name for a European sp]. SERVICEBERRY
1a. Petals broadly oval, not more than 3 times as long as wide; lvs permanently soft-hairy beneath. **A. utahensis** Koehne. Sagebrush and upper piñon-juniper.
1b. Petals narrowly oblong, more than 3 times as long as wide; lvs and young twigs glabrous or glabrate in age. **A. alnifolia** Nuttall [alder-lvd]. Oak-aspen zone (incl *A. pumila*, a glabrous form).

ARGENTINA Hill 1756 [Lat., *argentum*, silver]. SILVERWEED
One sp, **A. anserina** (L.) Rydberg. Mt meadows and poorly drained roadside ditches, montane, subalpine. The bicolored pinnate lvs and long stolons are diagnostic (*Potentilla*).

CERCOCARPUS Humboldt, Bonpland & Kunth 1824 [Gr., *kerkos*, tail, + *karpos*, fruit]. MOUNTAIN-MAHOGANY
1a. Lvs linear, strongly revolute; intricately branched low shrub of rimrock and cliffs. **C. intricatus** Watson [intricately-branched]. Sandstone canyons, W counties.
1b. Lvs broader, if revolute, the undersides still showing; tall open-branching shrubs and trees . . . . (2)

2a. Lvs entire, leathery, strongly revolute; usually a small tree. **C. ledifolius** Nuttall. Piñon-juniper and Douglas-fir, MF-ME.
2b. Lvs crenate-serrate, not leathery nor strongly revolute; tall shrubs. **C. montanus** Rafinesque. Widespread, piñon-juniper. Sporadic intermediates (hybrids) occur between all of the spp where they occur together.

CHAMAERHODOS Bunge 1829 [Gr., *chamae*, dwarf, + *rhodon*, rose]
One sp, **C. erecta** (L.) Bunge ssp **nuttallii** (Pickering) Hultén. Abundant, open gravelly plains of intermountain parks. The typical ssp occurs in Siberia.

COLEOGYNE Torrey 1853 [from Gr., *koleos*, sheath, + *gyne*, fruit]. BLACKBRUSH
One sp, **C. ramosissima** Torrey [much-branched]. Benches of Colorado and Dolores R systems. A low, dark shrub widely branching, known by its opposite lf and branch arrangement, unique among our roses.

COMARUM L. 1753 [Gr., *comaron*, ancient name for some plant, used by the author of *Appuleius' Herbarium*, 4th Cent. A.D.]. PURPLE CINQUEFOIL
One sp, **C. palustre** L. Known in Colorado from only two localities, in the Gunnison Basin and on Grand Mesa. The plant trails and roots at the lower nodes and the purple petals are shorter than the sepals. While the lvs are pinnately-compound, the lfls may be quite close together (*Potentilla*).

440 Rosaceae (ROS)

CRATAEGUS L. 1753 [Gr., *kratos*, strength]. HAWTHORN

1a. Lvs distinctly although shallowly lobed in addition to the normal marginal serrations; frts red. . . . . (2)
1b. Lvs not distinctly lobed although often distinctly serrate; frts red or black . . . . (3)

2a. Lvs and petioles pubescent at maturity; marginal teeth not strongly gland-tipped; spines over 4 cm long; in flat-topped, broad; frts remaining bright red through lf-fall; plants usually quite close to streams. **C. macracantha** Loddiges var. **occidentalis** (Britton) Eggleston [big-thorned; western]. Infrequent, AA.
2b. Lvs and petioles glabrous at maturity; marginal teeth with black glandular tips; thorns shorter or sometimes lacking; infl. racemose; frts soon turning dark purplish red; plants usually on dry hillsides rather than near the streambeds. **C. erythropoda** Ashe [red-based]. Usually growing with the next, in autumn turning color and losing its leaves sooner than the next. Widely distributed in the W tier of counties.

3a. Shrub with long erect stems, hardly branched except for very short lateral shoots; lvs of short shoots elliptic-oblong, smaller and narrower than the others, crenulate; petals less than 5 mm diam; stamens 15-20; frt blue-black, smaller than in the next, 5-8 mm diam. **C. saligna** Greene [willowy, from *Salix*]. END. Most abundant in and near the Gunnison and upper Colorado R basins.
3b. Shrub or tree with wide-spreading branches; lvs of short shoots not different from the rest, very finely and sharply serrate; petals over 5 mm diam; stamens 10; frts red, darkening in age, to 10 mm diam. **C. rivularis** Nuttall [riparian]. The most common hawthorn along streams on the W slope.

CYLACTIS Rafinesque 1819 [Gr, *kylix*, cup, + *actis*, ray, from the fl shape]. ARCTIC RASPBERRY

One sp, **C. arctica** (L.) Rafinesque ssp **acaulis** (Michaux) Weber. Infrequent, mossy willow thickets along mt streams (*Rubus*).

DRYAS L. 1753 [named for the mythological dryads]. MOUNTAIN DRYAD

One sp, **D. octopetala** L. ssp **hookeriana** (Juzepczuk) Hultén. Dry tundra, especially on limestone or where calcium is available as a leachate from the granite.

DRYMOCALLIS Fourreau 1908 [Gr., *drymos*, woodland, + *callis*, trail] (formerly in *Potentilla*)
1a. Fls cream-colored, scarcely longer than the sepals. **D.arguta** (Pursh) Rydberg, STICKY CINQUEFOIL. Montane meadows and open rocky flats in sagebrush.
1b. Fls bright yellow, usually longer than the sepals. . . . . (2)

2a. Infl an open cyme; stems slender. **D. glandulosa** (Lindley) Rydberg. A peripheral N Rocky Mt sp, RT.

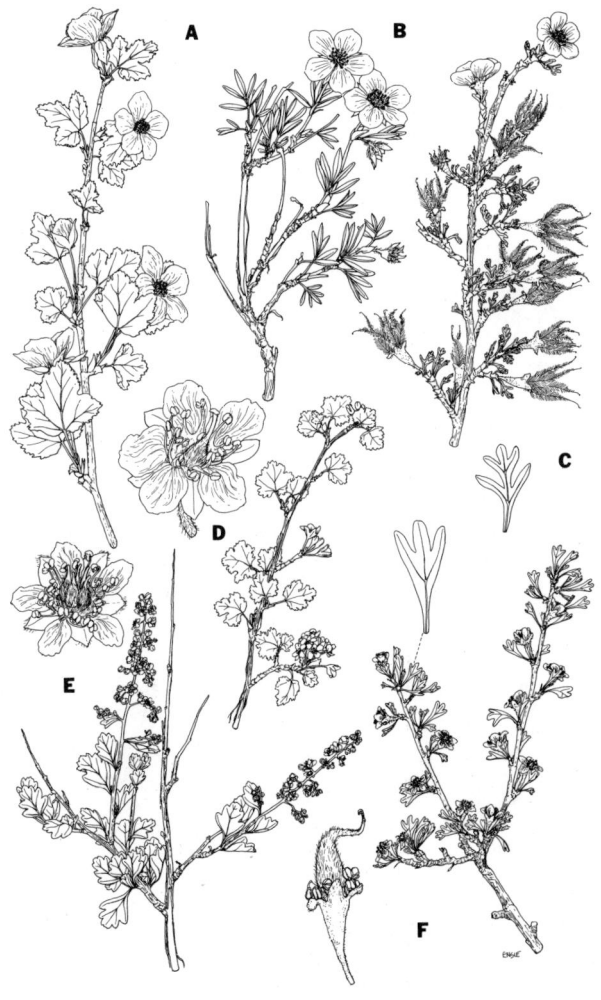

Figure 94. A, *Oreobatus deliciosus*; B, *Pentaphylloides floribunda*; C, *Purshia stansburiana*; D, *Physocarpus alternans*; E, *Holodiscus dumosus*; F, *Purshia tridentata*

2b. Infl a dense, congested cyme; stems stout. **D. fissa** (Nuttall) Rydberg. Abundant on E slope, but reaching the W slope only in GA.

ERYTHROCOMA Greene 1906 [Gr., *erythro*, red, + *coma*, mane]. PRAIRIE SMOKE

One sp, **E. triflora** (Pursh) Greene. Mt meadows and forest openings. The pink nodding fls, beautifully plumose styles, and pinnatifid basal lvs are diagnostic (*Geum*).

FRAGARIA L. 1753 [Lat., *fraga*, strawberry, implying its fragrance]. STRAWBERRY

1a. Lvs pure green, not glaucous on the upper surface, relatively thin and with raised veins, upper surface silky-pilose, veins impressed; terminal tooth of the lfls ± well-developed, usually projecting beyond the uppermost lateral teeth; infl commonly equalling or surpassing the lvs. **F. vesca** L. ssp **bracteata** (Heller) Staudt. In more mesic sites than the next.
1b. Lfls glaucous and somewhat bluish-green above, rather thick and not prominently veiny, the veins on the upper surface not impressed and usually glabrous; terminal tooth of the lfls small, usually surpassed by the adjacent lateral teeth; infl commonly shorter than the lvs. **F. virginiana** Miller ssp **glauca** (Watson) Staudt. In dry forests.

GEUM L. 1753 [a name used by Pliny]. AVENS

1a. Petals yellow; sepals purplish, reflexed after blossoming . . . . . (2)
1b. Petals pale violet; sepals green, not reflexed after blossoming. **G. rivale** L. [of brooksides], PURPLE AVENS. Swamps and wet meadows, subalpine.

2a. Lower section of style glabrous or sparsely pubescent at the base, not glandular; terminal lf-seg not greatly enlarged. **G. aleppicum** Jacquin [of Aleppo, Syria], YELLOW AVENS. Ravines and canyonsides, montane.
2b. Lower section of style glandular-puberulent; terminal lf-seg usually greatly enlarged. **G. macrophyllum** Willdenow, LARGE-LEAVED AVENS. Moist meadows and streamsides, montane to subalpine. The terminal lfl is fan-shaped in the typical form, but narrower and incised in ssp **perincisum** (Rydberg) Hultén.

HOLODISCUS Maximovicz 1879 [Gr., *holo*, entire, + *diskos*, circular plate, describing the fl]. OCEAN SPRAY

One sp, **H. dumosus** (Hooker) Heller, **94E**. Cliff faces and rocky escarpments, middle altitudes (incl *H. microphyllus*).

IVESIA Torrey & Gray 1858 [for Eli Ives, Professor of pharmacy, Yale University]

One sp, **I. gordonii** (Hooker) Torrey & Gray. Rocky pavements in sagebrush zone up to dry alpine meadows, scattered over the area but rather local.

Rosaceae (ROS) 443

OREOBATUS Rydberg 1903 [Gr., *oreos*, mountain, + *batos*, bramble].
BOULDER RASPBERRY
One sp, **O. deliciosus** James, **94A**. Local, on Pre-Cambrian granite outcrops, Unaweap Canyon, a smaller-fld and -lvd race than the E slope plant, but not *O. exrubicundus* Bailey as once supposed (*Rubus*).

PADUS Miller 1854 [the ancient Gr. name]. CHOKE-CHERRY
One sp, **P. virginiana** (L.) Miller ssp **melanocarpa** (Nelson) Weber. Along streams in the lower valleys (*Prunus*).

PENTAPHYLLOIDES Duhamel 1755 [Gr., *pente*, five, + *phyllon*, leaf].
SHRUBBY CINQUEFOIL
One sp, **P. floribunda** (Pursh) Löve, **94B**. Locally abundant along drainage lines, sagebrush-aspen (*Potentilla*). This is as clear-cut a genus as we have in the Rosaceae, differing from *Potentilla* in morphology and chemistry, and it seems to have been kept there purely as a matter of tradition.

PERAPHYLLUM Nuttall [Gr., *per*, very, + *phyllon*, leaf, alluding to the crowded lf-clusters]. SQUAW-APPLE
One sp, **P. ramosissimum** Nuttall [much-branched]. Frequent in the oak-serviceberry zone, W counties.

PETROPHYTON Nuttall 1900 [Gr., *petra*, rock, + *phyton*, plant].
ROCK-SPIRAEA
One sp, **P. caespitosum** (Nuttall) Rydberg. On precipitous and often inaccessible limestone canyon walls or sometimes stone pavements on summits. The mats are extremely hard, difficult to separate without a heavy knife.

PHYSOCARPUS Maximovicz 1879 [Gr., *physa*, bellows, + *karpos*, fruit, from the inflated carpels]. NINEBARK

1a. Carpel solitary; lf blades less than 2 cm long; filaments of 2 alternating and distinctly unequal lengths. **P. alternans** (Jones) Howell, **94D**. Canyonsides, W counties.
1b. Carpels 2 or more; lf blades larger; filaments more or less equal in length. **P. monogynus** (Torrey) Coulter [with one carpel]. Rocky canyonsides and talus slopes, generally distributed. This genus is sometimes confused vegetatively with *Ribes*, but *Physocarpus* has stellate hairs on the lvs and calyx. The bark also flakes off in long thin strips.

POTENTILLA L. 1753 [dim. of Lat., *potens*, powerful, originally applied to *Anserina*, for its curative powers]. CINQUEFOIL; FIVE-FINGER
(Key contributed by Barry Johnston)

1a. Annuals or short-lived perennials, mostly weedy spp; basal lvs dry and not functional at anthesis . . . . (2)
1b. Perennials; native plants; basal lvs functional at anthesis . . . . . (4)

2a. [1] Stems stiffly hirsute below with more or less pustular-based, spreading hairs; aks usually strongly undulate-corrugate longitudinally; stamens about 20; petals mostly at least 3/4 the length of the sepals. **P. norvegica** L., NORWAY CINQUEFOIL. ADV weed of pastures and grazed meadows.

2b. Stems soft-pubescent below, often with glandular or multicellular pubescence; aks smooth or very slightly striate; stamens mostly 10-15; petals usually less than 3/4 the length of the sepals . . . . (3)

3a. [2] Basal portion of stems soft-pubescent, often ± lanate; plants without glandular hairs; lower cauline lvs commonly 5-foliolate. **P. rivalis** Nuttall [of brooks]. Floodplains and wet depressions.

3b. Basal portion of stems with multicellular, often glandular hairs; lower cauline lvs trifoliolate; infl glandular. **P. biennis** Greene. Ruderal sites and meadows.

4a. [1] Style 1.0 mm long or shorter, often conical and thickened at the base and tapered to the stigma, relatively thick just below the stigma . . . . (5)

4b. Style 1.2 mm long or often much longer, usually thin just below the stigma . . . . (9)

5a. [4] Lvs always digitate, ternate, or subdigitate, with 3-5 lfl, often with flat margins; style often uniformly thickened; lower lf pubescence usually snow-white and formed of long entangled hairs; stems short, decumbent-ascending; infl openly branched; strictly alpine. . . . . (6)

5b. Lvs 7-15-pinnate to (less commonly) (5)7-subdigitate, with revolute margins; infl tight-branched, the fls clustered; plants sometimes alpine but then lvs either clearly pinnate, stems erect-ascending, or with greenish or yellowish pubescence; stems often tall and erect, especially at lower elevations. **P. pensylvanica** L. Moist bottomland with clay soil to rocky montane and alpine ridges. The alpine, subdigitate form is var **paucijuga** (Rydberg) Welsh & Johnston.

6a. [5] Lvs 5-foliolate, digitate to subdigitate; petioles conspicuously spreading-pilose, rarely also obscurely tomentose. **P. rubricaulis** Lehmann [red-stemmed]. Rocky exposed alpine ridges. Resembles *P. subjuga*, but *P. rubricaulis* has short styles that often are papillose at the base.

6b. Lvs 3-foliolate; petioles conspicuously tomentose, sometimes also with spreading straight pubescence . . . . (7)

7a. [6] Fls (1)2-3 per stem; plants densely matted; petioles usually not visible, hidden in the base of the plant, densely pilose, with or without additional dense tomentum. **P. uniflora** Ledebour. Fls seem large in comparison to the rest of the plant. Alpine talus slopes and fell-fields (*P. ledebouriana*).

7b. Fls 5-40 per stem, or else petioles plainly visible and plants not matted on talus slopes; petioles sparsely pilose or else densely tomentose . . . . (8)

8a. [7] Petioles densely tomentose, often with a few straight hairs as well; plants often low, matted. **P. nivea** L. [of snow]. Wind-scarred ridges and edges of exposed alpine ledges; lfls sometimes broadly and shallowly toothed.

8b. Petioles spreading-pilose, sometimes tomentose as well; plants taller. **P. hookeriana** Lehmann [for W. J. Hooker]. Grassy tundra and protected scree slopes; lfls usually more deeply and narrowly toothed than in the last.

9a. [4] Blossoming in early spring, before lf maturity; pedicels arched downward in frt. **P. concinna** Richardson [neat]. Pine woods, rocky ridges, sagebrush to lower alpine. Lvs digitate, white-tomentose below, strigose-pustulose above; calyx broader than long when pressed. Var **bicrenata** (Rydberg) Welsh & Johnston has only 3 teeth on each lfl.
9b. Blossoming in summer, after lf maturity; fruiting pedicels erect to ascending . . . . (10)

10a. [9] Lvs pinnate, with (5)7-more lfls . . . . (11)
10b. Lvs digitate or subdigitate, with 5 lfls . . . . (17)

11a. [10] Lvs subdigitate with 7 lfls . . . . (12)
11b. Lvs plainly pinnate, with 9 or more lfls . . . . (13)

12a. [11] Alpine or high subalpine, above 3000 m, ridges or upper slopes. **P. subjuga** Rydberg [somewhat paired]. Lfls narrowly toothed, tomentose below, always with some visible rachis between the terminal 3 lfls and the lower pairs. A high-alpine form occurs with more finely dissected lfls.
12b. Montane to submontane meadows and lower slopes, usually below 3000 m. **P. pulcherrima** x **P. hippiana**.

13a. [11] Lvs uniformly and sparsely silky or pilose, not tomentose, often green. . . . . (14)
13b. Lvs uniformly and densely hirsute, or else densely tomentose, appearing silvery or grayish-green on lower lf surfaces. . . . . (15)

14a. [13] Dry rocky ridges and slopes, submontane to alpine. **P. ovina** Macoun [of sheep].
14b. Moist to wet bottoms, streamsides, and mt meadows. **P. plattensis** Nuttall [of the Platte River]. Uncommon on W slope, so far known only from upper Gunnison Basin, sometimes nearly invisible (except for the fls) in tall sedge-grass.

15a. [13] Lfls narrow, folded, 3-toothed only in upper third, densely silvery-gray hirsute throughout. **P. crinita** Gray [with tufts of long hairs]. Dry submontane shale outcrops, San Juan Basin.
15b. Lfls broader, several-toothed throughout their length, densely tomentose below. . . . . (16)

16a. [15] Bracteoles darker than the calyx, bicolored; calyx small, densely white-tomentose; fls small; lvs usually not bicolored, more or less equally tomentose above and below, often toothed only in the upper third. **P. effusa** Douglas [straggling]. Dry hillsides, uncommon on the W slope.
16b. Bracteoles the same color as the calyx, which is often green or sparsely tomentose and larger; lvs often bicolored, toothed

throughout. **P. hippiana** Lehmann [for Carl Frederick Hippio, a revered colleague of Lehmann]. Dry hillsides, abundant.

17a. [10] All lvs strictly digitate, with no rachis evident between the lfls even with magnification; lfls either not tomentose or else not strongly bicolored, more or less equally pubescent above and below . . . . (20)
17b. Lvs subdigitate, at least a short rachis visible between lfls on some lvs; lvs bicolored, tomentose below, less pubescent above . . . . (18)

18a. [17] Lvs slightly subdigitate; plants large, with fine-toothed bicolored lfls. **P. pulcherrima** Lehmann [very beautiful]. Meadows and rocky slopes, submontane to lower alpine. Often forms hybrid swarms with *P. hippiana*.
18b. Lvs clearly subdigitate, the rachis visible without magnification . . . . (19)

19a. [18] Alpine and upper subalpine above 3,000 m, ridges or slopes; lvs always with a definite rachis between lfls; upper lfls usually 3, the lower 1 or 2 pairs. **P. subjuga** Rydberg. Large for an alpine plant, but smaller in all parts than *P. pulcherrima*.
19b. Montane to submontane, slopes and meadows; lvs highly variable, some pinnate, some subdigitate; upper lfls usually 5. **P. pulcherrima x hippiana**. A common cross producing many distinctive apomictic clones.

20a. [17] Lfls finely short-toothed (teeth go less than half way to the midrib) the length of the lfl, bicolored, densely tomentose below. **P. pulcherrima** Lehmann.
20b. Lfls either toothed only in upper third, or else more deeply toothed; lfls not densely tomentose, otherwise pubescent or not bicolored (if strongly bicolored then narrowly and deeply toothed) . . . . (21)

21a. [20] Plants small, often less than 20 cm tall; lvs green, glaucous, or sparsely silky, never tomentose; lfls toothed only in upper third. **P. diversifolia** Lehmann. Abundant in alpine and subalpine; closely related to *P. ovina*, which is obviously pinnate.
21b. Lvs grayish green or sparsely tomentose at least below; lfls deeply toothed throughout into long narrow teeth. Uncommon, montane and lower subalpine . . . . (22)

22a. [21] Lfls strongly bicolored, densely tomentose below. **P. flabelliformis** Lehmann. Local, upper Gunnison Basin.
22b. Lfls not strongly bicolored, subglabrous to more or less equally pubescent above and below. **P. gracilis** Douglas [slender]. Uncommon. The var **brunnescens** (Rydberg) Hitchcock has strigose lower lf surfaces, and var **glabrata** (Lehmann) Hitchcock has sparser, finer pubescence on lower lf surfaces.

PURSHIA de Candolle [for Frederick Pursh (1774-1820), describer of the Lewis & Clark collections]. BITTERBRUSH; CLIFF-ROSE

1a. Carpel solitary; style not plumose, **P. tridentata** (Pursh) de Candolle, BITTERBRUSH, **94F**. Abundant in rocky sagebrush and pinyon-juniper.
1b. Carpels several; style long, plumose. **P. stansburiana** (Torrey) Henrickson, CLIFF-ROSE, **94C**. Sandstone rimrock, SW counties (*Cowania mexicana* of Colorado lit). Hybrids sometimes occur between this and **P. tridentata**.

ROSA L. 1753 [the ancient Latin name]. WILD ROSE

1a. Fl stems densely bristly to the apex; infl usually single-fld. **R. sayi** Schweinitz [for Thomas Say, zoologist with the Long Expedition]. Evidently not as common as the next, throughout the wooded areas (*R. acicularis* of manuals). Plants with very large ellipsoid frts are considered to be the result of introgression with the more northwestern *R. nutkana* Presl, which does not occur in Colorado.
1b. Fl stems with infrequent recurved thorns, never densely bristly, drying black; infl commonly with more than one fl in a cluster. **R. woodsii** Lindley [for Joseph Woods, English botanist]. Generally distributed from lowlands to subalpine.

RUBACER Rydberg 1903 [from *Rubus* + *Acer*]. THIMBLEBERRY
One sp, **R. parviflorum** (Nuttall) Rydberg [small-flowered, a misnomer]. Frequent in moist, shaded forests.

RUBUS L. 1753 [the ancient Latin name, related to *ruber*, red]. RASPBERRY (see also *Cylactis, Oreobatus, Rubacer*]
One sp, **R. idaeus** L. ssp **melanolasius** Focke, RED RASPBERRY [from Mount Ida; black-haired]. Moist forests. The frts are delicious but in this region they rarely are produced in any quantity.

SANGUISORBA L. 1753 [Lat., *sanguis*, blood, + *sorbere*, to absorb, for reputed styptic properties]. BURNET
One sp, **S. minor** Scopoli. ADV, infrequent in disturbed mountain meadows.

SIBBALDIA L. 1753 [for Sir Robert Sibbald, 1641-1722, Scottish botanist]
One sp, **S. procumbens** L. [prostrate]. Common on tundra, usually near snow-accumulation areas.

SORBUS L. 1753 [Lat., *sorbum*, ancient name of the fruit of *Sorbus domestica*]. ROWAN TREE; MOUNTAIN-ASH
One sp, **S. scopulina** Greene [of rocks]. Shaded moist gulches, montane zone, mostly near the Continental Divide.

SPIRAEA L. 1753 [the ancient name, mentioned by Theophrastus]. BRIDAL WREATH
One sp, **S. douglasii** Hooker var **menziesii** (Hooker) Presl. Infrequent, forests at medium altitudes, RT.

RUBIACEAE—MADDER FAMILY (RUB)

The madder family gets its name from Madder (*Rubia tinctorum*), cultivated since ancient times for a red dye obtained from its roots. It is a large, mostly tropical family. Our little genus *Galium* is a pale shadow of the many useful and handsome ornamental trees and shrubs belonging to the group. Familiar members of the family are Coffee (*Coffea arabica*), Quinine (*Cinchona* spp) and Ipecac (*Cephaëlis* spp.). The name 'Bedstraw' derives from the fact that masses of the lightweight stems of *Galium* form a springy 'ticking' because the hooked hairs on the corners of the stems and leaves catch on each other and prevent the stack from matting down. *Galium*, our only genus, is unmistakeable with its combination of square stems, retrorse prickles on the stems and leaves of many species, tiny 4-merous flowers and 'double', usually hairy or spiny fruits that separate at maturity into one-seeded ball-like nutlets (mericarps). For long-haired animals these are as nasty as burdock fruits.

GALIUM L. 1753 [Gr., *gala*, milk, which is curdled by some spp].
BEDSTRAW

1a. Fls yellow; lvs narrowly linear; lvs 4 to 6 at a node; plants tall with very many fls. **G. verum** L. [true], YELLOW BEDSTRAW, 95G. ADV along irrigation ditches, especially in the Gunnison Valley.
1b. Fls white or greenish; lvs usually broader. . . . . (2)

2a. Plants definitely woody at the base, growing in dense erect clumps, dioecious. **G. coloradoense** Wight, 95A. Bases of cliffs and rock outcrops in desert canyons.
2b. Plants not woody at the base; fls usually perfect. . . . . (3)

3a. Lvs two or four at a node . . . . (4)
3b. Lvs at least 6 at a node . . . . (6)

4a. Stems tall, erect; lvs 4 at a node, lanceolate, blunt-tipped, broadest at the base; fls white, in a ± pyramidal infl. **G. septentrionale** Roemer & Schultes, NORTHERN BEDSTRAW, 95C. This has been lumped with the Eurasian *G. boreale*, which differs in having cream-colored fls and other measurable differences. *G. boreale* is tetraploid and *G. septentrionale* hexaploid. Common in moist meadows and woodlands, montane, subalpine.
4b. Stems slender and weak, either erect and less than a foot tall, or decumbent-creeping. (5)

5a. Lvs usually two at a node (or if four, one pair smaller than the other); frts bristly-hairy; plant weak but erect, the stem hardly prickly; fls solitary at the nodes. **G. bifolium** Watson [two-leaved], 95B. Common in shaded woodlands, N and C counties.
5b. Lvs 4 at a node; frts smooth; plant weak and trailing; fls often more than 1 at a node. **G. trifidum** L. ssp **brevipes** (Fernald & Wiegand) Löve & Löve [3-cleft; short-stemmed], 95F. Wet ground of willow-bogs and meadows (*G. brandegei*).

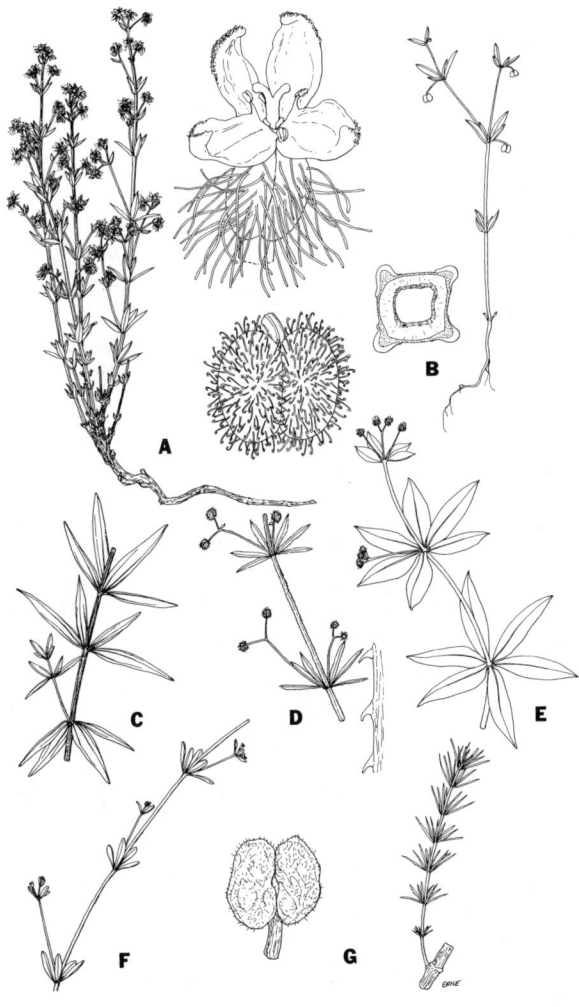

Figure 95. A, *Galium coloradoënse*, habit, fl; B, *G. bifolium*, habit, stem sect, frt; C, *G. septentrionale*; D, *G. spurium*; E, *G. triflorum*; F, *G. trifidum*; G, *G. verum*, habit, frt

6a. Lvs broadly elliptic about 1 cm wide, abruptly mucronate . . . . (7)
6b. Lvs narrowly oblanceolate, not over 5 mm wide, narrowed to a hyaline point . . . . (8)

7a. Ovary with white spreading hairs (about as long as the width of the frt), hooked at the tips; fls white or greenish, mostly in few-fld axillary cymes. **G. triflorum** Michaux [three-fld], FRAGRANT BEDSTRAW, 95E. Deeply shaded woodlands, montane to subalpine.
7b. Ovary with very short hairs curving over the frt, hooked from near the base; fls purplish, mostly in terminal compound cymes. **G. mexicanum** Humboldt, Bonpland & Kunth ssp **asperrimum** (Gray) Dempster [Mexican; very harsh]. Evidently preferring more open sites than the last. The lvs of this sp are usually not over 2 cm long, but at times they may be as long as in the last sp, up to 3 cm.

8a. Fls greenish-yellow, up to 1.5 mm diam; frts 1.5-2.8 mm long (top to bottom); nodes glabrous or slightly hairy; lvs about 3 mm broad. **G. spurium** L. [false], CLEAVERS, GOOSE-GRASS, 95D. ADV, brushy places and talus.
8b. Fls white, 2 mm diam; frts 2.8-4.0 mm long; nodes usually tomentose; lvs about 5 mm broad. **G. aparine** L. [old generic name, meaning to scratch or cling]. ADV, less common than the last, in more mesic sites.

RUPPIACEAE—DITCH-GRASS FAMILY (RUP)

A very small family consisting of a single genus, *Ruppia*, and containing either one extremely polymorphic species or about seven or poorly-delimited ones. The plant resembles a finely-linear-leaved pondweed, but the fruiting peduncles are very distinctive, being loosely coiled like springs, at the end of which are a cluster of small black akenes.

RUPPIA L. 1753 [for H. B. Ruppius, German botanist, 1688-1719].
DITCH-GRASS

One sp, **R. cirrhosa** (Petagna) Graham ssp **occidentalis** (Watson) Löve & Löve, 36D. Not yet collected on the W slope, but surely overlooked, since it is extremely inconspicuous, growing in shallow water of alkali ditches and ponds in E Colorado and E Utah (*R. maritima*). The drying plants form masses of blackish wiry stems and lvs in late summer.

SALICACEAE—WILLOW FAMILY (SAL)

Willows are difficult to identify because the important characters are ephemeral. One needs to know young leaves, mature leaves, flowering and fruiting catkins, and stipules. These parts appear, mature and fall at different times of the year and in order to see them all one must tag a bush or tree and return to it through a season. Twig color and plant height are also important. Most of us do not have enough patience, hence the difficulty of telling which willow is which. Much of the variability of willows is developmental. At least in our region we have hardly any real evidence of interspecific hybridization although this is common in higher latitudes. Anyone living near willow stands and in search of a productive hobby would do well to study them. They actually are easy to know if the species are seen in all seasons.

1a. Buds with several overlapping scales, resinous; bracts lacerate (jagged-edged); stamens numerous in each fl; fls on broad cup-shaped disks; aments (catkins) pendulous. **Populus**, POPLAR; ASPEN; COTTONWOOD

1b. Buds enclosed by a single scale, not resinous; bracts entire or denticulate; stamens few, 2 to 5; fls not borne on disks; catkins usually erect. **Salix**, WILLOW

POPULUS L. 1753 [classical Lat. name]. POPLAR; ASPEN; COTTONWOOD

1a. Petiole flattened perpendicular to the plane of the lf; lvs little or no longer than broad . . . . (2)
1b. Petiole not flattened as above; lvs mostly one-third longer than broad . . . . (3)

2a. Lf broadly ovate to suborbicular, 3-8 cm diam, finely serrate; bark smooth, white or greenish; buds conical; stigmas 2, filiform. **P. tremuloides** Michaux [resembling the Eurasian species, *P. tremula*], QUAKING ASPEN, **96B**. There are no genetic barriers whatsoever between the American and Eurasian species, hence our plants recently have been proposed as a ssp of *P. tremula*. The much whiter bark of W slope trees is sometimes the result of a powdery thallus of a lichen.

2b. Lf deltoid, 5-10 cm long, coarsely serrate; bark furrowed; buds ovoid; stigmas 3 to 4, broad. **P. deltoides** Marsh ssp **wislizenii** (Watson) Eckenwalder [triangular; for the collector, Adolphus Wislizenus, 1810-1889], **96C**. Lower river valleys, reaching to the lower limit of *P. angustifolia*.

3a. Lf ovate to ovate-lanceolate, paler below; terminal bud 2.0-2.5 cm long, very sticky-resinous. **P. balsamifera** L., BALSAM POPLAR, **96A**. Montane, subalpine, uncommon.

3b. Lf lanceolate to ovate-lanceolate, green on both sides; terminal bud less than 2 cm long, slender (may or may not be sticky) . . . (4)

4a. Lf with an abruptly acuminate apex; blade ovate-lanceolate to rhombic-lanceolate, never narrowly lanceolate; petiole at least half the length of the blade; buds 6-7-scaled, non-aromatic, not sticky. **P. x acuminata** Rydberg, **96E**. A first generation hybrid between *P. deltoides* and *P. angustifolia* in the lower canyons where they overlap, and reproducing by suckers and branch rooting.

4b. Lf with merely an acute apex; blade usually lanceolate, but sometimes quite broad; petiole a third the length of the blade or shorter; bud 5-scaled, aromatic, rather sticky. **P. angustifolia** James, NARROWLEAF COTTONWOOD, **96D**. Floodplains and

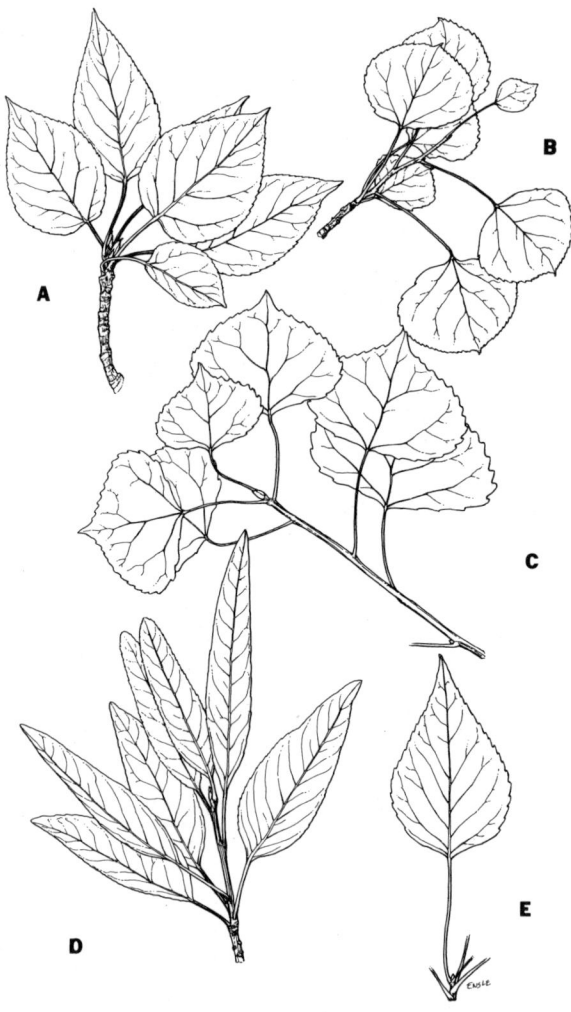

Figure 96. A, *Populus balsamifera*; B, *P. tremuloides*; C, *P. deltoides wislizenii*; D, *P. angustifolia*; E, *P. X acuminata*

streamsides in the middle altitudes. Our most abundant wild cottonwood, except for aspen.

SALIX L. 1753 [the classical Lat. name]. WILLOW

1a. Lvs linear, many times longer than wide; plants exclusively of wet, sandy places in the lower river valleys. **S. exigua** Nuttall [small], SAND-BAR WILLOW. Very variable in lf pubescence (*S. interior*).
1b. Lvs broader . . . . (2)

2a. [1] Depressed, prostrate-creeping, strictly alpine plants less than 10 cm high. . . . . (3)
2b. Taller plants, sometimes dwarfed by grazing or alpine conditions, but rarely creeping or less than 10 cm high. . . . . (4)

3a. [2] Aments terminating the terminal shoots of the season; apex of most lvs obtuse, the blades glaucous and reticulate beneath. **S. reticulata** L. ssp **nivalis** (Hooker) Löve *et al.* A tiny alpine plant, easily overlooked. Typical *S. reticulata* of the Arctic has lvs about 5 cm long; most of our plants have very tiny lvs, but on Trail Ridge very large lvs occur (*S. nivalis* ssp *saximontana*).
3b. Aments on short lateral shoots, not on the terminal shoots of the season; apex of most lvs acute, the blades not reticulate beneath. **S. arctica** Pallas. Common tundra sp.

4a. [2] Capsules hairy (the key treats only carpellate plants, since it is often extremely difficult to distinguish spp from staminate catkins alone, which often appear before the lvs. Unknown staminate specimens usually can be matched up with the corresponding carpellate plants in the field by vegetative comparison) . . . . (5)
4b. Capsules glabrous . . . . (14)

5a. [4] New twigs tomentose with matted hairs; lvs white-tomentose beneath, narrowly oblong. **S. candida** Fluegge [white]. Known from localities in the Rawah Range and South Park on the E slope, but there is no reason why it should not occur in the Park Range. It is an inconspicuous willow growing in *Betula glandulosa* bogs. The stems are unbranched except at the very apex, where they produce a few short lfy branchlets.
5b. New twigs not tomentose with matted hairs; lvs not white-tomentose beneath. . . . . (6)

6a. [5] Twigs pruinose (with a blue-white waxy coat; this is destroyed if plants are dried by heating) . . . . (7)
6b. Twigs not pruinose . . . . (8)

7a. [6] Aments subglobose, numerous, 10 (rarely up to 20) mm long, on pubescent lfy peduncles 5-10 mm long; lvs silky-pubescent on both sides or glabrate, more or less glaucous beneath. **S. geyeriana** Andersson [for Carl A. Geyer, collector on the Oregon Trail]. Montane and subalpine, along streams.

7b. Aments longer, 10-50 mm long, usually sessile or nearly so, bracteate at the base; lvs sparingly pubescent above, glaucescent and silky-hairy below. **S. drummondiana** Barratt [for Thomas Drummond, botanist with the 2nd Franklin Expedition, 1825-27], Blue Willow. Upper montane and subalpine, along streams.

8a. [6] Capsules on long pedicels 2-3(-5) mm long. **S. bebbiana** Sargent [for M. S. Bebb, Oklahoma botanist]. Streambanks and lake shores, foothills to subalpine. The lvs tend to be thin-textured, oblanceolate and rounded at the apex, difficult to describe but easily recognized with experience.
8b. Capsules short-pedicellate or sessile . . . . (9)

9a. [8] Aments sessile or nearly so . . . . (10)
9b. Aments on lfy peduncles or terminating lfy branches, sometimes sessile when immature. . . . . (12)

10a. [9] Lvs glabrous or sparsely pubescent above, variously pubescent beneath . . . . (11)
10b. Lvs glabrous above, glabrous and glaucous beneath (except young lvs, which can be sparsely hairy on both sides); twigs smooth, purplish-black. **S. planifolia** Pursh. Subalpine bogs, streamsides and lower tundra slopes (*S. phylicifolia* ssp *planifolia*).

11a. [10] Lvs dark green and sparsely pubescent above, glaucous and silky-hairy beneath. **S. drummondiana** Barratt.
11b. Lvs dark green and glabrous above, thinly pubescent beneath, the pubescence consisting in part of reddish hairs. **S. scouleriana** Barratt [for Dr. John Scouler, companion of David Douglas in 1825]. The only willow in our area growing in forests away from streamsides.

12a. [9] Low shrubs 0.5-2.0 m high; lvs entire. **S. brachycarpa** Nuttall. Subalpine willow thickets along streams, and forming dense stands of low shrubs on the lower tundra. Extremely variable in lf and ament size (incl *S. glauca* of Colorado lit).
12b. Shrubs 3-5 m high; lvs entire to sub-entire or serrulate . . . . (13)

13a. [12] Lvs obovate or oblanceolate, dark green and glabrate above, glaucous, strongly reticulate and often thinly pubescent beneath, the pubescence consisting in part of reddish hairs; capsules tomentose; pedicels 1-2 mm long. **S. scouleriana** Barratt.
13b. Lvs elliptic-oblong or oblong-lanceolate, dull green and minutely downy above, pale and sparsely hairy beneath; capsules puberulent. **S. planifolia** Pursh.

14a. [4] Trees. . . . . (15)
14b. Shrubs. . . . . (19)

15a. [14] Branches pendulous or crown neatly spherical. . . . . . . (16)
15b. Branches not pendulous nor crown neatly spherical . . . . . . (17)

16a. [15] Branches pendulous. **S. babylonica** L., WEEPING WILLOW

[Psalm 137: "by the waters of Babylon, we sat down and wept"]. ADV, commonly cult, and persisting after abandonment.
16b. Crown neatly spherical. **S. matsudana** Koidzumi [for a Japanese botanist, Sadahisa Matsuda, 1857-1921], GLOBE WILLOW. ADV, widely cult in the Colorado R Valley, not naturalized yet, but included here because it is such a striking feature of the landscape.

17a. [15] Lvs with a few raised glands at the base of the blade; branchlets very brittle, easily broken by pressing the base toward the main stem. **S. fragilis** L., CRACK WILLOW. ADV, cult and becoming estab in the lower valleys. Hybridizes with *S. alba vitellina.*
17b. Lvs without raised glands; branchlets not excessively brittle at the base . . . . (18)

18a. [17] Branchlets greenish; lvs not very different beneath, abruptly slender-acuminate. **S. amygdaloides** Andersson [like *Amygdalus*, the peach], PEACH-LEAVED WILLOW. Common native sp along streams in the lower valleys.
18b. Branchlets yellow; lvs pale beneath, acute or abruptly acuminate. **S. alba** L. var *vitellina* (L.) Koch [white; egg-yolk color], GOLDEN OSIER. ADV, commonly cult on ranches in the valleys, the branches strikingly yellow in winter.

19a. [14] Lvs glaucous or glaucescent below. . . . . (20)
19b. Lvs not glaucous beneath. . . . . (22)

20a. [19] Styles averaging over 0.7 mm long. . . . . (21)
20b. Styles averaging 0.7 mm or less long. . . . . (23)

21a. [20] Erect shrub of streamsides; lvs relatively narrow, acute, not strongly glaucous; aments less than 5 cm long, not stiffly erect. **S. monticola** Bebb. Very common along mt valley streams.
21b. Depressed shrub of alpine tundra; lvs broadly oval, obtuse, glaucous; aments 5 cm or more long, stiffly erect. **S. lanata** L. ssp **calcicola** (Fernald & Wiegand) Hultén. A disjunct sp of the Canadian Eastern Arctic, recently discovered on calcareous ground in the Mosquito Range just E of the Continental Divide, but to be expected wherever there are extensive alpine outcrops of the Leadville Limestone.

22a. [19] Capsule stalks 1-2 mm long; lvs often entire. **S. ligulifolia** Ball. Streamsides at low and medium altitudes.
22b. Capsule stalks 2-4.5 mm long; lvs usually toothed. **S. lutea** Nuttall [yellow]. Similar habitats.

23a. [20] Lf blades lanceolate and long-acuminate at tip; petioles with glands near base of blade on upper side. **S. lucida** Mühlenberg ssp **caudata** (Nuttall) Argus [shiny; acuminate]. Streamsides at low and middle altitudes. The staminate plants are extremely handsome, with large fat aments with many yellow stamens subtended by large oblong yellowish bracts. Lvs not glaucous beneath. Plants with lvs glaucous beneath belong to ssp *lasiandra* (Bentham) Argus.

23b. Lf blades never long acuminate; petioles usually lacking glands
. . . . (24)

24a. [23] Plants less than 2 m high; catkins mostly 0.8-2.0 cm long; capsule stalks 0-0.8 mm long. **S. wolfii** Bebb [for John Wolf]. Snow-melt basins, often forming large continuous stands.

24b. Plants often over 2 m high; catkins 2-6 cm long; capsule stalks up to 4 mm long. **S. boothii** Dorn [for the author's teacher, W. E. Booth]. Montane streamsides.

SANTALACEAE—SANDALWOOD FAMILY (SAN)

Comandra is what we call a hemiparasite. It has pale green leaves but at the same time it is parasitic, attached to the roots of other plants and deriving some nutrition from them. Our little herbaceous species is unlike the majority of the Santalaceae, which are usually shrubs or trees, some parasitic on other trees, others on the roots of grasses! Most of them are, or were, found in Australia and southeast Asia. One of the earliest conservation tragedies was the wholesale extermination, in the 18th and 19th centuries, of the fragrant wild sandalwoods of Australia and New Caledonia by exploiters for the perfumery, incense, and fine woodcarving trades. Sandalwoods are now cultivated for these purposes in India.

COMANDRA Nuttall 1818 [Gr., *kome*, hair + *andros*, male, alluding to the hairs of the calyx lobes which are attached to the anthers].
BASTARD-TOADFLAX

One sp, **C. umbellata** (L.) Nuttall. Steppe-desert and sage-brush benches. The roots are blue in cross-section, a very unusual color in such organs. Hemiparasite on many different plants. Presumably the lvs were thought to resemble the Toadflax, *Linaria*, hence the common name.

SAXIFRAGACEAE—SAXIFRAGE FAMILY (SAX)

Because so many saxifrages are rock garden plants and grow, in nature, in rocky crevices, many assume that the name alludes to the ability of these plants to break up rocks. Gerard, on the contrary, wrote in *The Herbal* (1633): "This name, *Saxifraga* or Saxifrage, hath of late been imposed on sundry plants farre different in the shapes, places of growing, and temperature, but all agreeing in this one facultie of expelling or driving the stone out of the Kidneies, though not all by one meane or manner of operation." Saxifrages are much more important horticulturally than they ever might have been in medicine. The fleshy-leaved *Bergenia* of the Himalaya and Siberia, and the deep red Coral Bells, *Heuchera sanguinea*, native in our SW, are favorite rock garden plants. Note that *Parnassia*, usually included in this family, has been moved to its own family; also, that I take a narrower view of the genus *Saxifraga* than is currently popular, and adopt a number of additional genera, a move suggested by Rafinesque as early as 1834!

Saxifragaceae (SAX) 457

1a. Lvs deeply palmately lobed or even divided into narrow lfls . . . (2)
1b. Lvs entire, toothed or shallowly lobed, never compound . . . . . (4)

2a. Stamens 5; lvs deeply lobed like a circular saw; wiry plants with open panicles of small white fls, on limestone cliffs. **Sullivantia**
2b. Stamens 10; lvs otherwise; plants of level ground . . . . (3)

3a. Petals entire or merely notched; lvs deeply 3- or 5-lobed. **Muscaria**, MOSS SAXIFRAGE
3b. Petals deeply and irregularly cleft into slender, pointed divisions; lvs very deeply lobed, some of them compound. **Lithophragma**, STAR SAXIFRAGE

4a. Plants creeping, imbedded in moss, the lvs round-kidney-shaped, shallowly-lobed; fls in an involucrate cluster, petals lacking. **Chrysosplenium**, GOLDEN CARPET
4b. Plants not as above . . . . (5)

5a. Lvs broadly ovate, cordate at the base, ± pentagonal, serrate or serrulate, never coarsely dentate. . . . . (6)
5b. Lvs variously shaped, otherwise not as above . . . . (8)

6a. Petals trifid or pectinately lobed. **Mitella**, BISHOP'S CAP; MITREWORT
6b. Petals entire . . . . (7)

7a. Fls paniculate, at least in the lower part of the almost spicate infl. **Heuchera**, ALUMROOT
7b. Fls racemose. **Conimitella**

8a. Fls yellow. **Hirculus**, GOLDEN SAXIFRAGE
8b. Fls white or pink . . . . (9)

9a. Lvs evergreen, broadly linear, ciliate, branches forming mats; fls white with purple or orange spots, in few-fld bracteate racemes. **Ciliaria**, SPOTTED SAXIFRAGE
9b. Lvs neither evergreen, linear nor ciliate . . . . (10)

10a. Stems with basal lvs only; fls in loose or compact spikes or panicles. **Micranthes**, SAXIFRAGE
10b. Stems lfy (the stem lvs, however, sometimes considerably reduced). . . . . (11)

11a. Fls in open panicles (at least 2 fls on the lowermost branches); lvs basically 5-lobed, with several deep teeth on each lobe. **Sullivantia**
11b. Fls in few-(1-10)-fld racemes or spikes . . . . (12)

12a. Lvs oblanceolate, merely toothed at the apex; stems with reduced lvs. **Muscaria adscendens**
12b. Lvs reniform, deeply 3-7-lobed. **Saxifraga**, SAXIFRAGE

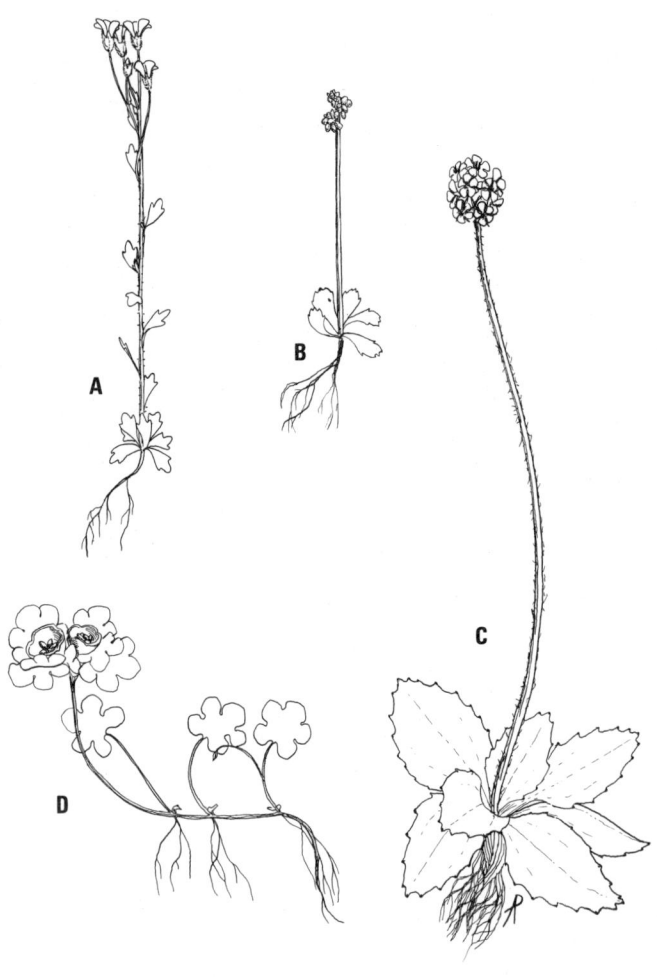

Figure 97. **A**, *Muscaria adscendens*; **B**, *Spatularia foliolosa* (E slope only); **C**, *Micranthes rhomboidea*; **D**, *Chrysosplenium tetrandrum*

CHRYSOSPLENIUM L. 1753 [Gr., *chrysos*, gold, + *splen*, the spleen, probably from reputed medicinal value]. GOLDEN CARPET

One sp, **C. tetrandrum** Fries [4-stamens], **97D**. Rare or at least overlooked plant of cold mossy banks along subalpine and alpine snow-melt streams along the Continental Divide.

CILIARIA Haworth 1821 [Lat., *cilium*, eyelash, alluding to the lf margins]. SPOTTED SAXIFRAGE

One sp, **C. austromontana** (Wiegand) Weber [of southern mountains], **99D**. Dry rocky forested canyons from the foothills to subalpine. Plants forming dense mats, the lvs awl-shaped (like a tiny *Juniperus communis*); fls white with purple or orange spots, in loose, few-fld open panicles (*Saxifraga bronchialis* ssp *austromontana*).

CONIMITELLA Rydberg 1905 [Gr., *konos*, cone, alluding to the turbinate hypanthium differing from the shallow one of *Mitella*]

One sp, **C. williamsii** (Eaton) Rydberg [for R. S. Williams, Montana botanist; Mr. Williams also was my first tutor in bird watching in New York City]. In Colorado, known only from margins of *Pseudotsuga* 'islands' on the slopes between the Blue River Valley and Ute Pass (ST). A very distinctive plant, resembling in lf form either a *Heuchera* or a *Mitella*. The lvs are rounded-reniform, not at all pentagonal, and the margins are strongly ciliate with rather stout, curved hairs that follow the lf margin. The fls are in a slender raceme of up to 10-15 blossoms. The pinkish petals are clawed, the hypanthium narrowly campanulate and minutely glandular-pubescent, with small pink sepals. The nearest other populations are in northern Wyoming.

HEUCHERA L. 1753 [for J. H. Heucher, 1677-1747, German botanist]. ALUM-ROOT

1a. Stamens equalling or exceeding the sepals; lvs with sharp, coarse dentations . . . . (2)
1b. Stamens shorter than the sepals; lvs with blunt or rounded teeth. **H. parvifolia** Nuttall [small-lvd], **99C**. Common on cliffs and rock outcrops from the piñon-juniper to the alpine tundra, where the normal tall form is replaced by a dwarf var **nivalis** (Rosendahl) Löve *et al.*

2a. Infl an open panicle; sepals and upper part of hypanthium pink. **H. rubescens** Torrey [reddish]. A plant of inaccessible granitic cliffs, ME-MT.
2b. Infl a dense spike; sepals and upper part of hypanthium yellowish. **H. bracteata** (Torrey) Seringe. Rocky canyon walls, mostly E slope, reaching W to Grand Lake.

HIRCULUS Haworth 1821 [Lat., *hirculus*, a little goat, perhaps alluding to the spreading short styles or 'horns']. GOLDEN SAXIFRAGE

1a. Lower lvs not arranged in a basal rosette; plants neither in dense mats nor with flagella-like stolons. **H. prorepens** (Fischer) Löve & Löve [creeping], **98F**. Frequent in alpine bogs (*S. hirculus* of Colorado lit).

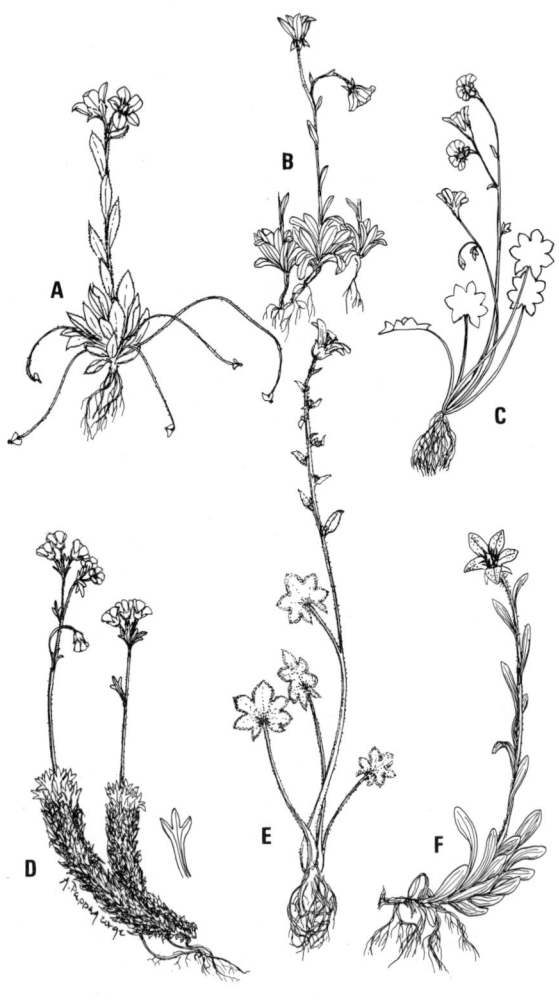

Figure 98. A, *Hirculus platysepalus*; B, *H. serpyllifolius*; C, *Saxifraga hyperborea*; D, *Muscaria delicatula*; E, *Saxifraga cernua*; F, *Hirculus prorepens*

1b. Lower lvs arranged in a basal rosette; plant in dense mats or with flagella-like stolons. . . . . (2)

2a. Slender flagellar stolons present; plant very glandular-pubescent; lvs ciliate-margined. **H. platysepalus** (Trautvetter) Weber ssp **crandallii** (Gandoger) Weber, (*S. flagellaris* of Colorado lit) [broad sepals; for C. S. Crandall], **98A**. Rocky tundra.
2b. Stolons absent; plants almost glabrous; lf margins not ciliate. **H. serpyllifolius** (Pursh) Weber ssp **chrysanthus** Gray) Weber [thyme-lvd, + yellow fls], **98B**. Rocky tundra (*S. chrysantha*).

LITHOPHRAGMA Torrey & Gray 1840 [Gr. equivalent of Lat., *Saxifraga*]. STAR SAXIFRAGE
1a. Basal lvs glabrous or very sparsely pubescent; cauline lvs usually bearing red bulblets; petals usually 5-cleft; seeds muricate. **L. glabrum** Nuttall. Montane sagebrush.
1b. Basal lvs moderately to copiously pubescent at least on the lower surface; bulblets not produced; petals often only 3-cleft; seeds smooth or warty or reticulate, but never muricate . . . . . (2)

2a. Calyx narrowly campanulate (3)4-6 mm long at anthesis, mostly 6-10 mm long in fruit; ovary at least 2/3 inferior; petals commonly 3-cleft. **L. parviflorum** (Hooker) Nuttall [small-fld]. Similar habitats.
2b. Calyx broadly campanulate, 2-3 (3.5) mm long at anthesis and 3.5-5.0 mm long in fruit; ovary about 1/2 inferior; petals mostly 5 (7)-lobed. **L. tenellum** Nuttall [delicate]. Similar habitats.

MICRANTHES Haworth 1812 [Gr., *micro*, small, + *anthos*, flower]. SAXIFRAGE
1a. Lvs circular in outline, cordate at base, coarsely dentate; petioles long and slender; panicle loose and open. **M. odontoloma** (Piper) Weber [toothed margin], **99A**. Along mountain cascades in the spruce-fir zone.
1b. Lvs lanceolate or broader, toothed or entire, tapering to a short, broad petiole; infl a dense head or spike . . . . (2)

2a. Lvs short, rhomboid; spikes usually simple, headlike in anthesis; open ground, not wet meadows or streamsides. **M. rhomboidea** (Greene) Small, **97C**. Rocky meadows from the foothills to the lower tundra.
2b. Lvs elongate, narrowly oblanceolate; spikes often compound; wet meadows and streamsides. **M. oregana** (Howell) Small.

MITELLA L. 1753 [Lat., *mitella*, turban]. BISHOP'S CAP; MITREWORT

1a. Stamens opposite the greenish, pinnatifid petals; lvs rather distinctly lobed, the lobes coarsely toothed. **M. pentandra** Hooker [5 stamens]. Deep shade in spruce-fir forests.
1b. Stamens alternating with the 3-parted or entire petals; lvs scarcely lobed, the teeth very shallow and blunt. **M. stauropetala** Piper var **stenopetala** (Piper) Rosendahl [cruciform; slender petals]. Less frequent than the last, in similar habitats.

Figure 99. A, *Micranthes odontoloma*; B, *Telesonix jamesii* (E slope only); C, *Heuchera parvifolia*; D, *Ciliaria austromontana*

MUSCARIA Haworth 1821 [from *Saxifraga muscoides*, ultimately from Lat., *muscus*, moss]. MOSS SAXIFRAGE

1a. Basal lvs with slightly 3-toothed blades; stems solitary. **M. adscendens** (L.) Small, **97A**. Infrequent and very inconspicuous, on moist tundra (*Saxifraga*).
1b. Basal lvs with prominently 3-cleft blades; caespitose plants . . . . (2)

2a. Hypanthium and sepals ca. 5 mm high; petals ca. 4 mm long; fl stems stout, usually tall (commonly up to 6 cm). **M. monticola** Small. Stony tundra. All of the following were lumped together under the name *Saxifraga* (=*Muscaria*) *cespitosa*, a European and Arctic sp.
2b. Hypanthium and sepals 3-4 mm high; petals 3 mm or less long; fl stems slender, rarely more than 4 cm high, usually less. . . . . . (3)

3a. Petals equalling or slightly exceeding the sepals. **M. delicatula** Small, **98D**. Probably the most abundant sp of this group on the tundra.
3b. Petals minute, much shorter than the sepals. **M. micropetala** Small. Infrequent and overlooked on tundra.

SAXIFRAGA L. 1753 [see introd for derivation]. TRUE SAXIFRAGE

1a. All but the relatively large terminal fl replaced by reddish bulblets. **S. cernua** L., **98E**. Frequent along snow-runoff rivulets.
1b. Bulblets absent; all fls normal. . . . . (2)

2a. Infl strict, the pedicels erect; hypanthium narrowly campanulate; calyx lobes usually shorter than the hypanthium; glandular hairs on the pedicel short, straight. **S. hyperborea** R. Brown ssp **debilis** (Engelmann) Löve *et al.*, **98C**. Subalpine and alpine, usually in dry shaded hollows under boulders.
2b. Infl with spreading pedicels; hypanthium broadly campanulate; calyx-lobes equalling or exceeding the hypanthium; glandular hairs on pedicels long and crinkly. **S. rivularis** L. Edges of alpine rivulets.

SULLIVANTIA Torrey & Gray 1842 [for William Starling Sullivant, American bryologist]

One sp, **S. hapemanii** (Coulter & Fisher) Coulter [for Dr. H. Hapeman, private Nebraska collector]. Vertical, often dripping cliffs, Gunnison and White R basins (ours is ssp *purpusii*, unpublished).

SCROPHULARIACEAE—FIGWORT FAMILY (SCR)

The showy tubular bilabiate flowers of many scrophs show diverse adaptations to insect pollination. In *Penstemon* one of the stamens lacks anthers and instead has a tuft of golden hairs possibly attractive to insects, or at least offering a claw-hold. Scarlet penstemons are hummingbird-pollinated. The corolla of *Castilleja* is so dingy that the floral bracts and calyx substitute as attractants, and the corolla is so narrow that the stamens can hardly fit unless staggered, a challenge neatly met by attaching them at different points and elongating the anther-sacs. Some scrophs, such as *Pedicularis*, have developed such complicated flowers that potential pollinators either cannot reach the nectar or become so impatient that they bite a hole through the base of the corolla, bypassing the stamens and style completely and cancelling the whole adaptation.

1a. Anther-bearing stamens 5: corolla nearly radially symmetrical, rotate, yellow; tall, coarse, very velvety-pubescent herb. **Verbascum,** MULLEIN
1b. Anther-bearing stamens 4 or 2; corolla usually somewhat or quite zygomorphic; fls variously colored . . . . (2)

2a. [1] Fleshy-lvd plants rooted in mud and either stoloniferous or prostrate and rooting at the nodes; fls white, not strongly zygomorphic . . . . (3)
2b. Plants not as above in all details. . . . . (4)

3a. [2] Lvs orbicular; plants prostrate, rooting at the nodes; fls solitary in the lf-axils. **Bacopa,** WATER-HYSSOP
3b. Lvs narrowly spatulate or linear; plants erect but spreading by short stolons; fls in a basal cluster, the pedicels about 1 cm long. **Limosella,** MUDWORT

4a. [2] Corolla distinctly spurred. **Linaria,** TOADFLAX
4b. Corolla not spurred but sometimes somewhat swollen or sac-like at the base . . . . (5)

5a. [4] Upper lip of the strongly two-lipped corolla helmet-shaped, keeled or deeply concave; stamens always either 4 or 2. . . . . . (6)
5b. Upper lip of the corolla not helmet-shaped, keeled, nor deeply concave; stamens 5, 4, or 2; staminodia often present . . . . . (10)

6a. [5] Anther cells equal, parallel; stamens 4. . . . . (7)
6b. Anther cells unequal, separated; bracts often colored. . . . . . . (8)

7a. [6] Lvs opposite, merely toothed; calyx 4-toothed, becoming bladderlike and veiny, completely enclosing the frt and not filled by it. **Rhinanthus,** YELLOW RATTLE
7b. Lvs alternate or basal, pinnatifid in all but two spp; calyx cleft on one or both sides, becoming distended but neither bladderlike nor completely enclosing the frt. **Pedicularis,** LOUSEWORT

8a. [6] Bracts highly colored or white; upper corolla lip (galea) very much longer than the small, 3-toothed or 3-keeled lower lip; plants perennial with few exceptions. **Castilleja,** PAINTBRUSH
8b. Bracts green or purplish; galea not or little surpassing the inflated, saccate lower lip; always annual. . . . . (9)

9a. [8] Calyx with 4 equal or nearly equal lobes; lvs entire or three-cleft; plants generally unbranched. **Orthocarpus,** OWL-CLOVER
9b. Calyx split down the side, lacking lobes, resembling the opposing bract; lvs linear, 3-5-parted. **Cordylanthus,** CLUBFLOWER

10a. [5] Corolla distinctly hump-backed; dainty annuals with minute blue-and-white fls; lvs generally purplish at least on the underside; anther-bearing stamens 4. **Collinsia**, BLUE-EYED MARY
10b. Corolla not hump-backed; otherwise not as above . . . . (11)

11a. [10] Stamens 5, four of these anther-bearing, the fifth a staminode . . . . (12)
11b. Stamens 4 or fewer, without a staminode. . . . . (14)

12a. [11] Sterile stamen represented by a scale on the upper inside of the corolla throat; corolla greenish, somewhat urn-shaped, broad and open, with little distinction of tube and throat. **Scrophularia**, FIGWORT
12b. Sterile stamen an elongate, often bearded filament not much shorter than the anther-bearing stamens; corolla colored or white . . . . (13)

13a. [12] Calyx deeply 5-parted or divided; corolla not strongly flattened; plants of various habitats, not restricted to tundra. **Penstemon**, BEARD-TONGUE
13b. Calyx obtusely 5-lobed; corolla strongly dorsiventrally flattened; low plants of tundra; fls yellowish-white. **Chionophila**, SNOW-LOVER

14a. [11] Anther-bearing stamens 4 . . . . (15)
14b. Anther-bearing stamens 2 . . . . (16)

15a. [14] Corolla green with maroon or purplish tint, urn-shaped with little differentiation of tube and limb; lvs triangular-ovate, dentate; staminode present (may be overlooked). **Scrophularia**, FIGWORT
15b. Corolla colored, usually showy, yellow or reddish; stems not four-angled; lvs various. **Mimulus**, MONKEY-FLOWER

16a. [14] Lvs chiefly basal, cauline lvs reduced in size and alternate; corolla very irregular, cleft nearly to the base, or absent; fls in a dense spike, with strongly exserted stamens. **Besseya**, KITTENTAIL
16b. Lvs chiefly cauline, opposite; corolla zygomorphic but not as above; fls axillary or terminal. . . . . (17)

17a. [16] Corolla 2-lipped, zygomorphic and deeply tubular, yellow. **Gratiola**, HEDGE-HYSSOP
17b. Corolla 4-lobed, only slightly zygomorphic, rotate, never deeply tubular, usually blue. . . . . (18)

18a. [17] Weedy annuals . . . . (19)
18b. Perennials, rooting at the lower nodes or with rhizomes . . . . (20)

19a. [18] Fls solitary in axils of normal foliage lvs. **Pocilla**
19b. Fls in a single slender terminal raceme. **"Veronica"** peregrina

20a. [18] Fls in axillary racemes. **Veronica**, SPEEDWELL

20b. Fls in terminal spikes . . . . (21)

21a. [20] Decumbent and with creeping rhizomes; lower lvs petiolate; capsule orbicular to obcordate. **Veronicastrum**, THYME-LEAVED SPEEDWELL
21b. Erect, rhizomes not obvious; lvs all sessile, blackening in drying; capsule elliptic, emarginate. **Veronica**, SPEEDWELL

BACOPA Aublet 1775 [an aboriginal South American name]. WATER-HYSSOP

One sp, **B. rotundifolia** (Michaux) Wettstein. Low sprawling succulent herb of muddy shores of small ponds, Durango.

BESSEYA Rydberg 1903 [for Rydberg's teacher, Dr. Charles E. Bessey]. KITTENTAIL
1a. Corolla deep violet-purple; less than 15 cm tall, the fl stem compact; lfy bracts 6 or fewer; usually alpine. **B. alpina** (Gray) Rydberg. Common throughout the high mts; on north slopes of cliffs in the Grand Mesa this and other alpine plants sometimes occur below timberline in compensating environments.
1b. Corolla white or yellow, sometimes purple-tinged; usually much over 15 cm tall; lfy bracts more than 6; never strictly alpine
. . . . (2)

2a. Corolla lemon-yellow; lower lip of corolla with lobes not over 1.5 the length of the lip. **B. ritteriana** (Eastwood) Rydberg [for B. W. Ritter of Durango], **PL 15**. END. Restricted to high altitudes, usually cliff-sides near timberline, San Juans.
2b. Corolla white or pinkish-purple; lower lip of corolla with lobes over half the length of the lip. **B. plantaginea** (Bentham) Rydberg [with lvs and floral spike like *Plantago*]. Sagebrush, infrequent in the W counties.

CASTILLEJA Mutis 1782 [for Domingo Castillejo, 18th Century Spanish botanist]. PAINTBRUSH
Note: The keys will be easier to follow if one examines the fls when they are fresh, to see the relative lengths of the upper and lower lips, and to determine the relative incisions of the calyx.
1a. Plant clearly annual, with slender taproot stem simple, unbranched. **C. minor** Gray. Infrequent in sagebrush, ME, MF; fls yellowish or pinkish.
1b. Plant perennial, often more or less woody-based; stems of previous year often persisting . . . . (2)

2a. Lower corolla lip prominent, 1/3 to 2/3 as long as the upper lip or galea; galea short, half as long as the corolla tube or shorter; bracts yellowish, never red. **C. puberula** Rydberg. Rocky tundra, high peaks of the Continental Divide, PA to LR.
2b. Lower corolla lip relatively small, usually less than 1/3 the length of the galea, never over 1/2 as long; galea over 1/2 length of tube; bracts variously colored. . . . . (3)

3a. Calyx incised much more deeply below than above; bracts divided into linear lobes, often less conspicuous than the calyx. . . . . . . (4)
3b. Calyx about equally incised above and below; bracts divided or entire, broad and conspicuous. . . . . (5)

4a. Corolla 1.5-2.5 cm long; bracts yellow, rarely reddish-tipped; calyx yellowish. **C. flava** Watson [yellow]. In sagebrush, GA-MF.
4b. Corolla 3-5 cm long; bracts red or scarlet; calyx red or scarlet. **C. linariifolia** Bentham [with lvs like *Linaria*]. Tall branched plant with very narrow lvs, upper sagebrush and aspen.

5a. Lvs and stems ± densely tomentose; seed coats dark and often pubescent . . . . (6)
5b. Glabrous to variously pubescent but never tomentose; seed coats light-colored, never pubescent . . . . (7)

6a. Bracts orange-crimson, entire or shallowly cleft; corolla over 2.5 cm long; infl short and broad. **C. integra** Gray. Sagebrush in the southern counties, AA-LP.
6b. Bracts dull yellowish, deeply lobed; corolla under 2.5 cm long; infl narrow. **C. lineata** Greene. END, AA.

7a. Plants with yellow bracts and fls . . . . (8)
7b. Plants with red bracts and fls (note: normally red-fld populations of *C. chromosa* occasionally sport a yellow-fld plant; *C. sulphurea* and *C. rhexifolia* form hybrid swarms that display a wide variety of colors). . . . . (9)

8a. Plants low, usually under 2 dm high. **C. occidentalis** Torrey [western]. Common in the tundra, generally at lower altitudes than *C. puberula*, which has much narrower lvs and bracts. Difficult to distinguish from *C. sulphurea* except by size and habitat. However, *C. occidentalis* is tetraploid and *C. sulphurea* diploid. They do not intergrade.
8b. Plants tall, usually more than 2 dm high. **C. sulphurea** Rydberg. Subalpine aspen-spruce zone.

9a. Alpine; bracts with linear lobes. **C. haydenii** (Gray) Cockerell [for F. V. Hayden, U. S. Geological surveyor of the western mts]. Tundra, San Juans.
9b. Plants of forests and lowlands. . . . . (10)

10a. Lvs deeply cleft into linear, spreading lobes; desert, sagebrush and piñon-juniper. . . . . (11)
10b. Lvs entire or upper shallowly lobed near apex; forests . . . . . (12)

11a. Stems erect, lfy to the slender root crown; bracts and lvs little incised, softly pilose; lower lip and most of the galea usually included in the calyx tube; fresh roots yellow. **C. chromosa** Nelson [colorful]. In deep sandy loam, sagebrush.
11b. Stems decumbent, naked near the massive root crown; bracts and lvs narrow, much incised, with short reflexed hairs; lower lip and galea usually exserted from the calyx; roots not yellow. C.

scabrida Eastwood [rough], **Pl 10**. Rimrock ledges, shallow soils, Colorado Nat. Mon.

12a. Bracts entire or very shallowly lobed, typically rose-colored. **C. rhexifolia** Rydberg [the strongly 3-veined lvs resembling *Rhexia*]. Meadows in subalpine spruce-fir, commonly hybridizing with *C. sulphurea* and forming stands of variable bract colors.
12b. Bracts usually deeply cleft, typically bright red. **C. miniata** Douglas [painted with red lead]. Montane forests to lower subalpine.

CHIONOPHILA Bentham 1846 [Gr., *chion*, snow, + *philein*, to love]. SNOW-LOVER

One sp, **C. jamesii** Bentham [for Edwin James]. Alpine tundra. The yellowish fls are dorsiventrally flattened, unlike any other scroph. The lvs turn brown or black on drying. This sp is thought to be free of any fungal rust parasite. Since rusts evolve along with their hosts, it would be of great interest to discover a rust on *Chionophila* since its relationships with other scrophs are unknown.

COLLINSIA Nuttall [for Zaccheus Collins, Philadelphia botanist, 1764-1831]. BLUE-EYED MARY

One sp, **C. parviflora** Lindley [small-fld]. Very common but inconspicuous and delicate annual, blossoming very early at low altitudes and following the season upslope to the oak and aspen zone. Lvs usually strongly purplish-tinged. The hump-backed corolla is distinctive.

CORDYLANTHUS Nuttall 1846 [Gr. *kordyle*, club + *anthos*, flower]. CLUBFLOWER

Note: in *Cordylanthus*, what appears to be a calyx is a bract, opposite which the calyx proper also looks to be a bract, split down the inner side, lacking any lobes.

1a. Corolla over 2 cm long, purple; bract and calyx slender-pointed, glabrous; stems and lvs glabrous or nearly so. **C. wrightii** Gray [for Charles Wright, plant collector of the SW]. Sandy soils, lower valleys, W counties.
1b. Corolla less than 2 cm long, yellow with purple streaks; bract and calyx rounded, very minutely short-glandular-pubescent; lvs puberulent. **C. ramosus** Nutt. [branched]. Sandy soil, MF.

GRATIOLA L. 1753 [dim. of Lat., *gratia*, grace, favor, for supposed medicinal properties]. HEDGE-HYSSOP

One sp, **G. neglecta** Torrey [overlooked]. ADV, infrequent in mud of lake shores and drying springs at fairly low altitudes, widely scattered, MN, RT. The plant has the aspect of a small yellow *Mimulus* but with a more tubular corolla.

LIMOSELLA L. 1753 [dim. of Lat., *limus*, mud]. MUDWORT

One sp, **L. aquatica** L. Drying borders of ponds and springs, middle altitudes. Plant with a rosette of linear lvs and very small inconspicuous white fls.

LINARIA Miller 1754 [from *Linum*, flax, because of similar foliage]. TOADFLAX; BUTTER-AND-EGGS

1a. Lvs linear; much less than 1 m tall. **L. vulgaris** Miller [common]. ADV, locally abundant around the sites of former homesteads, not a very aggressive colonizer.
1b. Lvs ovate; often 1 m tall. **L. genistifolia** (L.) Miller ssp **dalmatica** (L.) Maire *et al* [like the genus *Genista*; from Dalmatia]. ADV, a recently established aggressive weed now rampant in many parts of our semi-arid areas (*L. dalmatica*). Hybrid individuals intermediate between the two spp have been found recently.

MIMULUS L. 1753 [dim. of Lat., *mimus*, buffoon, from the 'grinning' corolla]. MONKEY-FLOWER

1a. Fls large, red or purple . . . . (2)
1b. Fls yellow, or if reddish, then less than 5 mm long . . . . (3)

2a. Fls red; glandular-pubescent, sprawling or hanging. **M. eastwoodiae** Rydberg, **PL 32**. Local and very beautiful sp inhabiting 'hanging gardens' of massive sandstone cliffs of the Wingate formation, SW counties.
2b. Fls pink-purple; plants glabrous, erect. **M. lewisii** Pursh [for Meriwether Lewis]. Peripheral sp of the Pacific Northwest, along rushing mt streams, RT.

3a. Low viscid-pubescent creeping perennial forming mats; lvs broadly ovate, with very short petioles; anthers hairy; corolla yellow with red stripes. **M. moschatus** Douglas [musky]. Streamsides, Park Range, RT.
3b. Not conspicuously viscid pubescent, or if somewhat so, then annual. . . . . (4)

4a. Petiole-base modified to form a pocket that when mature falls away from the lf and stem as a disk-shaped functional propagulum containing a dormant embryonic shoot; fls usually abortive or absent, but if present the pollen sterile. **M. gemmiparus** Weber [forming gemmae]. END. Restricted to massive smooth sloping granite outcrops in Rocky Mt Nat Park, provided with surface seepage water; growing with other *Mimulus* spp.
4b. Petiole-bases not modified; fls always present. . . . . (5)

5a. Calyx-teeth decidedly unequal, the uppermost longer than the rest . . . . (6)
5b. Calyx-teeth equal or nearly so . . . . (8)

6a. Throat of corolla open, the whole corolla less than 2 cm long; some of the calyx teeth reduced or absent; plants usually decumbent. **M. glabratus** Humboldt, Bonpland & Kunth. Muddy ditches and pond borders at low altitudes.
6b. Throat of corolla partly or nearly closed by a prominent palate, the whole corolla usually over 2 cm long; calyx teeth all present and distinct; plants usually erect unless dwarfed and alpine . . . . (7)

7a. Plants with definite creeping, sod-forming rhizomes, often stoloniferous as well; fls few (mostly 1-5), large, the corolla mostly 2-4 cm long. **M. tilingii** Regel [for S. H. Tiling, Russian botanist]. Low plants, 2 dm tall or less, upper subalpine and alpine rills.
7b. Plants with stolons but only rarely with distinct creeping rhizomes; fls often more than 5, usually less than 2 cm long. **M. guttatus** de Candolle [speckled, referring to the corolla]. Usually over 2 dm tall; springs and streams.

8a. Lvs triangular-ovate, coarsely-toothed, with distinct petioles, these often longer than the blades; calyx inflating at maturity. **M. floribundus** Douglas [many-fld]. Seepy ledges; extremely variable in size of plant and fls, depending on availability of water.
8b. Lvs oblong or elliptic, entire, sessile or narrowed to a very short petiole; calyx not inflated at maturity. . . . . (9)

9a. Usually over 5 cm tall, on clay flats in the lower river valleys; blooming in early spring. **M. rubellus** Gray [reddish]. In my experience the fls are yellow although they are said to vary to reddish and white. The distinctions between this and the next are still unclear.
9b. Less than 5 cm tall, on mossy streamsides in the mts; blooming in midsummer. **M. suksdorfii** Gray [for Wilhelm N. Suksdorf, 1850-1932, pioneer botanist of Washington State]. Infrequent. This sp often has reddish fls.

ORTHOCARPUS Nuttall 1818 [Gr., *orthos*, straight, + *carpos*, fruit]. OWL-CLOVER
1a. Fls yellow. **O. luteus** Nuttall. Common in mt meadows.
1b. Fls purple-and-white. **O. purpureoalbus** Gray. Piñon-juniper and sagebrush.

PEDICULARIS L. 1753 [Lat., *pediculus*, louse, because of a belief that cattle, feeding where *P. palustris* abounded, became covered with lice]. LOUSEWORT
1a. Plants with basal lvs forming loose mats from stout branched caudices; fls over 2 cm long, in loose clusters at ground level, exceeded by the lvs. **P. centranthera** Gray [*centrum*, a prickle or sharp point, referring to the unique long-spurred anthers], **PL 18**. Piñon-juniper woodlands, ME-MZ, blossoming so early that the fls and lvs are often withered and gone by June.
1b. Plants with erect stems and terminal spikes of smaller fls, blooming in summer. . . . . (2)

2a. Lvs crenulate, not pinnatifid . . . . (3)
2b. Lvs deeply pinnatifid or incised. . . . . (4)

3a. Corolla white; lvs glabrous. **P. racemosa** Douglas ssp **alba** Pennell. Dominant in subalpine spruce forests.
3b. Corolla pink or rose-colored; lvs or stems pubescent. **P. crenulata** Bentham. Wet meadows, particularly along broad stream valleys, montane and subalpine.

4a. Corolla yellowish or white . . . . (5)
4b. Corolla pink or purplish . . . . (7)

5a. Lvs simple, but shallowly or deeply pinnatifid; lfls joined together by a common winged rachis; upper lip of corolla terminating in a prominent sickle-shaped beak. **P. parryi** Gray. Dry subalpine and alpine slopes.
5b. Lvs divided into separate lfls; plants always over 2 dm tall . . . . (6)

6a. Up to 1 m tall; fls streaked with reddish; corolla 3.0-3.5 cm long; lower lip almost reaching the tip of the galea. **P. procera** Gray [tall]. Tall rank herb of deeply shaded spruce-fir forests; the lvs are commonly mistaken for fern fronds (*P. grayi*).
6b. Much less than 1 m tall; fls not streaked with reddish; corolla less than 3 cm long; lower lip not reaching the tip of the galea. **P. bracteosa** Bentham ssp **paysoniana** (Pennell) Weber. Dry spruce-fir forests.

7a. Beak of galea short and straight; infl woolly-pubescent, fls crowded in a short spike. **P. scopulorum** Gray [of the Rockies]. Swampy meadows and lake shores, subalpine and alpine. Formerly considered to be a race of *P. sudetica*.
7b. Beak of galea long and curved, the flower resembling an elephant's head; infl glabrous or nearly so, fls in an elongated spike. **P. groenlandica** Retzius [erroneously thought to come from Greenland], ELEPHANTELLA. Wet mountain meadows.

PENSTEMON Schmidel 1763 [Gr., *pente*, five, + *stemon*, stamen].
BEARD-TONGUE
1a. Corolla scarlet . . . . (2)
1b. Corolla blue or purple, rarely pink or white . . . . (5)

2a. [1] Calyx and pedicel glandular-pubescent; corolla strongly bilabiate. **P. bridgesii** Gray [for its collector, Thomas Bridges]. Piñon-juniper, DT-MZ, blooming in late summer; lvs evergreen.
2b. Calyx and pedicel glabrous or puberulent, not glandular . . . . . (3)

3a. [2] Corolla strongly bilabiate, the prominent lower lip reflexed, upper lip projecting. **P. barbatus** (Cavanilles) Roth, [bearded, alluding to the inside of the corolla in the species proper], 100C. Rocky canyonsides and piñon-juniper. Two races occur: var **torreyi** (Bentham) Keck, with glabrous anthers, is widely distributed; var **trichander** (Gray) Keck [hairy anthers] is limited to the Four Corners.
3b. Corolla hardly bilabiate, lips erect or spreading . . . . (4)

4a. [3] Corolla lobes small, directed forward; lvs green. **P. eatonii** Gray [for its discoverer, D. C. Eaton]. Piñon-juniper and canyonlands, SW counties. Var **eatonii** (MZ only) has glabrous stems; var **undosus** (Jones) Keck [wavy leaf margins], more widely distributed, has puberulent stems.
4b. Corolla lobes large, rounded, flaring; lvs glaucous. **P. utahensis** Eastwood. Rocky slopes, canyonlands, ME-MZ.

5a. [1] Dwarf, only 2 cm high, completely lacking aerial stems, the narrowly oblanceolate lvs and fls sessile on a stout subterranean caudex. **P. yampaensis** Penland [from the Yampa valley]. END. Gravelly river benches in the sagebrush zone, MF.
5b. Aerial stems present, creeping or erect. . . . . (6)

6a. [5] Anther-sacs pubescent along their sides (away from the line of dehiscence), sometimes sparsely so . . . . (7)
6b. Anther-sacs glabrous along the sides (or only microscopically puberulent). . . . . (17)

7a. [6] Anthers sparsely long-villous to lanate, the hairs usually much longer than the anther sacs and sometimes nearly hiding the anthers. . . . . (8)
7b. Anthers with short, straight or sometimes flexuous hairs shorter than the length of the anther sacs, often sparse . . . . (10)

8a. [7] Corolla pale blue, the much narrower tube nearly as long as the throat; at least the lower peduncles elongate and somewhat divergent; basal lvs usually oval to oblong-spatulate. **P. comarrhenus** Gray [Gr., *kome*, mane, referring to the hairy anthers]. Rocky canyonsides, piñon-juniper, SW counties.
8b. Corolla usually deep blue, the tube much shorter than the throat; lower peduncles short and more or less appressed; basal lvs linear-lanceolate to spatulate. . . . . (9)

9a. [8] Corolla 24-30 mm long; anther hairs longer than anther width; plants of sagebrush, piñon-juniper, and relatively mesic mt meadows; basal lvs usually broadly lanceolate. **P. strictus** Bentham [straight]. Throughout the middle altitudes, variable, the races not well-marked (incl. *P. strictiformis* Rydberg).
9b. Corolla 20-22 mm long; anther hairs variable, often relatively short; basal lvs narrowly lanceolate, withering early. **P. scariosus** Pennell var **albifluvis** (England) N. Holmgren [papery; for the White R]. Barren shale slopes, RB. This sp is still poorly known and is uncomfortably similar to the last.

10a. [7] Stems and often the lvs short-pubescent; corolla limb not strongly bilabiate, the tube not or only slightly bloated. . . . . (11)
10b. Stems and lvs usually glabrous and green; corolla usually strongly bilabiate and bloated. . . . . (13)

11a. [10] Lvs linear, 1-2 mm wide, involute or folded. **P. penlandii** Weber [for C. W. T. Penland]. END on seleniferous clay hills, Middle Park.
11b. Lvs broader, usually flat. . . . . (12)

12a. [11] Infl not glandular; stems and lvs densely short-pubescent, usually cinereous, the basal broadly oval, over 1 cm wide. **P. fremontii** Torrey & Gray [for J. C. Frémont, the "pathfinder"]. Dry slopes, piñon-juniper, NW counties.
12b. Infl glandular; stems short-pubescent but lvs glabrous, the basal less than 1 cm wide. **P. gibbensii** Dorn [for its discoverer, Robert Gibbens]. Arid open land, MF.

Figure 100. A, *Penstemon secundiflorus*; **B**, *P. whippleanus*; **C**, *P. barbatus*

13a. [10] Corolla 22-40 mm long, usually hairy in the throat; sepal tips acuminate, as long as or longer than the body. . . . . . . (14)
13b. Corolla 15-20 mm long, glabrous inside the throat. . . . . . . (15)

14a. [13] Staminode scarcely or shallowly-notched, usually bearded at the apex with yellow hairs; corolla 24-32 mm long; stem glabrous. **P. alpinus** Torrey. Gravelly slopes, middle altitudes, near the Continental Divide in Middle Park.
14b. Staminode deeply notched, glabrous or with a few hairs; corolla 30-38 mm; stem puberulent below. **P. brandegei** Porter [for T. S. Brandegee, botanist on the Hayden Surveys]. Mt. slopes, S counties. Usually treated as a ssp of the last.

15a. [13] Calyx strongly glandular-puberulent; corolla sparsely glandular externally. **P. mensarum** Pennell [of the mesa]. END, mt slopes, Grand Mesa.
15b. Calyx and corolla glabrous externally, or very obscurely glandular-puberulent . . . . (16)

16a. [15] Lvs narrowly oblong, plane-margined; anther-sacs opening completely; upper bracts, pedicels and calyces sparsely glandular. **P. saxosorum** Pennell [of the Rockies]. Rocky slopes, EA, MF.
16b. Lvs broadly oblong, wavy-margined; anther sacs opening partially; bracts, pedicels and calyces essentially glabrous. **P. cyanocaulis** Payson [blue-stemmed, from the very showy infl]. END, Uncompahgre Plateau.

17a. [6] Lvs all narrowly linear or narrowly oblanceolate, not over 5 mm wide and very rarely over 20 mm long; plants decumbent, often mat-forming. . . . . (18)
17b. Lvs various, the lower ones at least wider and usually over 20 mm long. . . . . (22)

18a. [17] Corolla rounded, not 2-ridged, on the lower inside (best examined fresh; dried plants must be boiled to determine this), the throat abruptly widened above the tube. **P. linarioides** Gray ssp **coloradoensis** (Nelson) Keck [with lvs like *Linaria*]. Piñon-juniper, SW counties.
18b. Corolla flattened beneath, 2-ridged on the lower inside, throat not abruptly widened above the tube. . . . . (19)

19a. [18] Calyx lobes usually with prominent scarious margins; lvs glabrous at least toward the tips. **P. crandallii** Nelson [for C. S. Crandall). Piñon-juniper, SW counties, variable in habit from decumbent to erect. The extreme with narrowly linear lvs is var **glabrescens** (Pennell) Keck.
19b. Calyx lobes without prominent scarious margins; lvs from cinereous-pubescent to puberulent or glabrate. . . . . (20)

20a. [19] Lvs essentially linear, usually not over 1.5 mm wide. **P. teucrioides** Greene [resembling the mint, *Teucrium*]. Sagebrush, Gunnison Basin; very close to *P. caespitosus* and may be comparable to the linear-leaved extremes found in *P. crandallii*.

Figure 101. A, *Veronica nutans*; B, *Pocilla biloba*; C, *Veronica peregrina*; D, *V. catenata*; E, *V. americana*

20b. Lvs narrowly oblanceolate or spatulate, more than 1.5 mm wide. . . . . (21)

21a. [20] Creeping and forming very low mats, the fls not greatly exceeding the normal lvs. **P. caespitosus** Nuttall. Abundant in Middle Park, where the lvs tend to be glabrate, extending W and N where the lvs are more pubescent.
21b. Flowering stems erect, greatly exceeding the basal lvs. **P. retrorsus** Payson. END, adobe hills, MN.

22a. [17] Plant with long flexible branched caudices, growing in loose alpine scree slopes; low, with a few fls from the axils of unmodified lvs at the stem apex. **P. harbourii** Gray. The fls are a peculiar powder-blue.
22b. Stems erect, with well-differentiated infl. . . . . (23)

23a. [22] Some or all of the stamens strongly exserted from the corolla, not merely visible in the open throat; anthers sagittate with parallel sacs . . . . (24)
23b. Stamens included in the corolla, or if somewhat exserted, then anthers with divaricate sacs. . . . . (25)

24a. [23] Fls 9-15 mm long, in a dense spike; all stamens exserted; anthers 2 mm long; bracts mostly as broad as long. **P. cyathophorus** Rydberg [cupped-base, referring to the subtending bracts]. Sagebrush meadows of Middle Park.
24b. Fls 18-24 mm long, in a loose spike; only 2 stamens exserted; anthers 2.5-3.0 mm long; bracts longer than broad. **P. harringtonii** Penland [for H. D. Harrington]. Road-cuts and sagebrush, Middle Park (GA) to EA, RT.

25a. [23] Lvs sessile, broadest at the base and tapering gradually to the apex (narrowly triangular), widely spreading; fls in loose interrupted spikes. **P. watsonii** Gray (for the collector, Sereno Watson). Sagebrush and piñon-juniper, N counties.
25b. Lvs petiolate or broadest above the base or ascending; fls various. . . . . (26)

26a. [25] Pubescent in some degree (either throughout or at least in the infl or lower stem, sometimes visible only under strong magnification) . . . . (27)
26b. Glabrous throughout. . . . . (40)

27a. [26] Corolla glabrous on outside; rest of infl glabrous or pubescent; fls in densely congested spikes . . . . (28)
27b. Corolla and infl distinctly glandular-pubescent; fls not in densely congested spikes. . . . . (29)

28a. [27] Corolla 6-10 mm long; fls usually declined; sepals not conspicuously scarious-margined. **P. confertus** Douglas ssp **procerus** (Douglas) Clark [crowded; tall]. Wet mt meadows, not as common as the next.

28b. Corolla 10-16 mm long; fls usually horizontal; sepals scarious-margined. **P. rydbergii** Nelson. Common in wet mt meadows.

29a. [27] Lvs of lower stem completely glabrous, bright or dark green . . . . (30)
29b. Lvs of lower stem either pubescent throughout or at least on veins and margins near the base, usually dull or grayish green . . . . (31)

30a. [29] Low plants generally forming large colonies; corolla bright blue, 10-17 mm long. **P. virens** Pennell [green]. Rocky slopes, Front Range, GA. Lvs finely serrulate.
30b. Tall plants with only a few stems; corolla dull wine-red, milky-white, or rarely pale blue, 17-28 mm long. **P. whippleanus** Gray [for Capt. A. W. Whipple, Pacific RR Surveys], **100B**. Dry subalpine forests, both dark and pale color variants often found in the same population.

31a. [29] Corolla somewhat flattened beneath, with 2 strong longitudinal grooves (ridges) within; basal rosette lvs absent. **P. radicosus** Nelson [with many roots]. Brushy hillsides with Douglas-fir and chokecherry, MF.
31b. Corolla more or less rounded, without strong grooves or ridges . . . . (32)

32a. [31] Plants with glandular-viscid pubescence, at least in the infl; staminode prominently bearded . . . . (33)
32b. Plants without this combination of features. . . . . (38)

33a. [32] Stem lvs tending to be in whorls of three; anther sacs dehiscent quite to the proximal ends, not explanate (not opening up flat); corolla 12 mm long, 5 mm wide at the throat. **P. parviflorus** Pennell. END [small-fld]. Local near Mancos, flowering in June; not collected since 1890.
33b. Stem lvs opposite; anther sacs dehiscent throughout and through the partition, explanate (opening up flat). . . . . (34)

34a. [33] Staminode exserted . . . . (35)
34b. Staminode included . . . . (36)

35a. [34] Corolla 14-20(22) mm long, throat 7-10 mm broad when pressed, internally glandular-pubescent; calyx 6-10 mm long; fls deep lavender-purple; basal lvs lanceolate, puberulent. **P. ophianthus** Pennell [snake-flower]. Adobe clays, MN-MZ.
35b. Corolla 30-35 mm long, very strongly expanded above the narrow tube; fls light lavender with red stripes; basal lvs broadly oval, strongly villous-glandular, picking up soil fragments. **P. grahamii** Keck [for Edward H. Graham, specialist on the Uintah Basin Flora]. Barren shale slopes, W RB.

36a. [34] Corolla with narrow tube and limb; basal lvs 2-8 cm long, elliptic, acute; plants low, with few whorls of fls. **P. humilis** Nuttall [humble, small]. Rocky slopes, Dinosaur Nat. Mon.

36b. Corolla with expanded limb; basal lvs longer, lanceolate; plants tall, with several whorls of fls . . . . (37)

37a. [36] Anther sacs widely divaricate but not explanate (not opening up flat); basal leaves broadly elliptic. **P. moffatii** Eastwood [for David Moffat, of the D. & R. G. Railroad]. Adobe hills, Colorado R Valley.
37b. Anther sacs explanate (opening up flat, forming a single disk with the central suture plainly exposed); basal lvs lanceolate. **P. breviculus** (Keck) Nesbit & Jackson. Adobe hills, MN-MZ.

38a. [32] Fls with distinct pedicels, in loose infls; corolla 17-30 mm long, purple; alpine tundra. **P. hallii** Gray [for the collector, Elihu Hall]. Common on high rocky tundra near the Continental Divide.
38b. Fls with very short pedicels, in densely congested whorls; corolla up to 16 mm long. . . . . (39)

39a. [38] Corolla 6-10 mm long; fls usually declined; sepals not conspicuously scarious-margined. **P. confertus** Douglas ssp **procerus** (Douglas) Clark [crowded; tall]. Wet mt meadows, less common than the next.
39b. Corolla 10-16 mm long; fls usually horizontal; sepals scarious-margined. **P. rydbergii** Nelson. Wet mt meadows.

40a. [26] Lflike bracts of the infl very broad-orbicular, abruptly pointed; infl a congested interrupted spike; fls bright blue . . . (41)
40b. Bracts of the infl not as above; infl loosely-fld; fls magenta . .
. . . . (42)

41a. [40] Internodes numerous and short, not much longer than the lvs; flowers in dense congested whorls, their pedicels hardly evident. **P. mucronatus** N. Holmgren. Common, desert-steppe, MF.
41b. Internodes few and longer than the lvs; flowers fewer, in looser whorls, several with evident erect pedicels. **P. pachyphyllus** Gray. Western RB.

42a. [40] Basal lvs broadly oblanceolate to obovate-spatulate or orbicular, usually broader than those of upper stem. **P. osterhoutii** Pennell [for George Osterhout]. Clay hills and slopes, Colorado R drainage southwestward (incl *P. lentus* Pennell).
42b. Basal lvs linear to narrowly or somewhat broadly oblanceolate, usually narrower than those of upper stem . . . . (43)

43a. [42] Infl secund; corolla magenta; stem lvs usually lance-ovate, cordate-clasping, broadest at the base. **P. secundiflorus** Bentham [one-sided infl], **100A**. Abundant on E slope, reaching our area only on Cochetopa Pass, where the plants tend to be dwarfed, quite unlike the normal type.
43b. Infl not secund; corolla typically blue but sometimes magenta; stem lvs usually longer and narrower. . . . . (44)

44a. [43] Fls 10-14 mm long; lobes of upper lip about equal to or

larger than those of the lower. **P. arenicola** Nelson [of sand]. Extreme NW corner of MF.
44b. Fls 15-20 mm long; lobes of upper lip smaller than those of the lower. **P. angustifolius** Nuttall var **vernalensis** Holmgren [the var named for Vernal, Utah]. Essentially a sp of the E plains, but fairly common in W MF.

POCILLA Fourreau 1869 [Lat., *pocillum*, little goblet, alluding to the capsule] (formerly incl in *Veronica*)
1a. Erect; corolla 2-4 mm wide. **Pocilla biloba** (L.) Weber, **101B**. ADV, a newly estab weed rapidly spreading along roads, middle altitudes.
1b. Plant decumbent and trailing; corolla 5-11 mm wide. **P. persica** (Poiret) Fourreau. ADV weed in gardens.

RHINANTHUS L. 1753 [Gr., *rhinon*, snout, + *anthos*, flower, the name applying to plants now excluded from the present genus and thus meaningless in our context]. YELLOW RATTLE

One sp, **R. minor** L. ssp **borealis** (Sterneck) Löve. Mt meadows and clearings. The calyx is very conspicuous in fruit, being almost circular and flat, with a small aperture.

SCROPHULARIA L. 1753 [from the fleshy knobs on the rhizomes of some spp, which, by the doctrine of signatures was supposed to cure scrofula and to remove 'fig warts']. FIGWORT

One sp, **S. lanceolata** Pursh. Fence-rows, ravines and roadside ditches, middle altitudes. The lvs are triangular-ovate and coarsely dentate.

VERBASCUM L. 1753 [the ancient Lat. name used by Pliny]. MULLEIN

One sp, **V. thapsus** L. [classical name, from ancient Thapsus, in North Africa near Tunis, where Julius Caesar defeated the Pompeiians and ended the war in Africa]. ADV, introd from Europe and now an abundant roadside weed. It is said that in colonial times young ladies reddened their cheeks by rubbing them with the tomentose lvs.

VERONICA L. 1753 [from St. Veronica]. BROOKLIME; SPEEDWELL [so named for its alleged curative powers] . . . .
(See also *Pocilla*, *Veronicastrum*)

1a. Fls in racemes arising from the lf-axils . . . . (2)
1b. Fls in terminal spikes or racemes . . . . (4)

2a. Lvs narrowly linear, to narrowly lanceolate; pedicels filiform, reflexing in frt; capsule much wider than long, deeply 2-lobed. **V. scutellata** L. [with a shield, probably referring to the capsule]. Marshes, RT and GA, infrequent or inconspicuous.
2b. Lvs ovate-oblong . . . . (3)

3a. Lvs all short-petioled, serrate. **V. americana** (Rafinesque) Schweinitz, American Brooklime, **101E**. Muddy places, valleys.
3b. Lvs sessile and clasping the stem, or only the lowermost short-

petioled, serrulate or entire. **V. catenata** Pennell [in chains, possibly referring to the fruiting racemes], **101D**. Common in similar habitats (*V. salina*). In this sp the pedicels are widely-spreading; in *V. anagallis-aquatica* L. at least the uppermost ones are said to be ascending; this is a very difficult matter to decide; furthermore, the two spp hybridize forming a very robust sterile hybrid.

4a. Fls. pale pink to white; lvs narrowly elliptic. **V. peregrina** L. ssp **xalapensis** (Humboldt, Bonpland & Kunth) Pennell [wandering; from Xalapa, Mexico], PURSLANE SPEEDWELL, **101C**. Ruderal weed of disturbed and wet places. Probably merits status as a distinct genus, differing from other spp not only in morphology, but with a unique basic chromosome number.

4b. Fls deep blue; lvs ovate, blackening in drying. **V. nutans** Bongard [nodding], Alpine Speedwell, **101A**. Subalpine meadows and tundra; fls dark blue (*V. wormskjöldii* of northeast America is tetraploid; our western plant is diploid, 2n=18).

VERONICASTRUM Heister 1759 [Gr., *-astrum*, dim. suffix]. THYME-LEAVED SPEEDWELL

One sp, **V. serpyllifolium** (L.) Fourreau ssp **humifusum** (Dickson) Weber [thyme-lvd]. Muddy ground, montane and subalpine. Lower lvs petioled, drying green; plant decumbent, rooting at the nodes (*Veronica*).

SIMAROUBACEAE—QUASSIA FAMILY (SMR)

A small tropical family with plants having medicinal and other economic uses. *Kirkia*, the White Syringa from South Africa, has swollen roots which store liquid that can be tapped in times of drought. Our representative is a Chinese tree cultivated for its attractive lvs, rapid growth, ornamental fruit, and as a host for the domesticated silkworm. In America it has become a symbol of ultimate urbanization. This is the tree alluded to in the title of the novel, *A Tree Grows in Brooklyn*. Its exceptional hardiness under most extreme urban conditions symbolized the stamina of the novel's protagonists.

AILANTHUS Desfontaines 1788 [said to be derived from a Moluccan common name, alluding to the great height it achieves in the wild]. TREE OF HEAVEN

One sp, **A. altissima** (Miller) Swingle. ADV. I know of no records of its occurrence on the W slope, but I should be very much surprised if it does not already occur in the valley of the Gunnison and Colorado from Montrose to Grand Junction as a weed tree in back yards and vacant lots. The leaves have a strong odor (in New York City we called it "stinkweed"), the branches are weak and contain a disproportionate amount of pith, but in autumn the great masses of oblong, twisted samaras are very attractive with tints of red and brown. The tree is becoming a pest in the E slope cities.

SOLANACEAE—NIGHTSHADE FAMILY (SOL)

More than most families, the Solanaceae has affected, for good or ill, the course of history. Many species are gifts to Western civilization from the American Indian. The white potato, *Solanum tuberosum*, went from Incan Peru to Europe where it became the major crop of Ireland. A catastrophic fungal blight destroyed potato farming there, and thousands of Irish migrated to Boston and New York. Sir Walter Raleigh introduced tobacco, *Nicotiana*, into British society with well-known results. The tomato, *Lycopersicon esculentum*, was a native American, thought poisonous not too long ago. Eggplant, *Solanum melongena*, native in southern Asia, is as important in Greek cooking as in Indian. Mexican foods would not be the same without the multitude of races of chile and bell peppers, *Capsicum frutescens*. The drug, atropine, used for dilating eyes, comes from *Atropa belladonna*, and in Delibes' grand opera, *Lakme*, the heroine commits suicide by eating the flower of *Brugmansia*. In our gardens, *Petunia violacea* continues to brighten the patio long into autumn. Read Charles Heiser's fascinating account of the family in his book, *Nightshades, the Paradoxical Plants*.

1a. Shrubs. **Lycium**, MATRIMONY-VINE
1b. Herbs or woody vines . . . . (2)

2a. Fls white, over 10 cm long. **Datura**, JIMSONWEED
2b. Fls various, but not enormous. . . . . (3)

3a. Fls pale violet, with a network of purple veins, in a one-sided spike; frts in two rows; capsule circumscissile, the calyx much enlarged at maturity. **Hyoscyamus**, HENBANE
3b. Fls and frts not as above. . . . . (4)

4a. Fls narrowly long-tubular, yellowish-white; very glandular; lvs with pungent taste. **Nicotiana**, TOBACCO
4b. Fls short-tubular or rotate . . . . (5)

5a. Calyx not enlarging nor inflated and not at all enclosing the frt (except in one spiny sp); anthers opening by terminal pores or slits, not dehiscent throughout. **Solanum**, NIGHTSHADE
5b. Calyx inflated and concealing the fruit, or enlarging and enclosing the fruit except at the top; plants never spiny; anthers longitudinally dehiscent throughout their length . . . . (6)

6a. Calyx closely fitted to the fruit, thin and obscurely veined, the lobes not closing at apex (hence the top of the fruit exposed). **Chamaesaracha**
6b. Calyx bladdery-inflated and conspicuously veiny, the lobes closing or connivent over the top of the berry. **Physalis**, GROUND-CHERRY

CHAMAESARACHA Bentham 1876 [Gr., *chamae*: on the ground, + *Saracha*, a tropical American genus named for Isadore Saracha, an 18th century Spanish Benedictine]

One sp, **C. coronopus** (Dunal) Gray [for the mustard genus *Coronopus*, because of the similarity of the lvs]. A low, widely branching weedy herb with small yellow fls and stellate or branched hairs on lvs and stems; the lvs are oblong-lanceolate to linear and sinuate-dentate.

DATURA L. 1753 [altered from the Arabic name, *Tatorah*, or the Hindustani *Dhatura*? Linnaeus disagreed, derived it from Lat., *dare*, to give, because "given to those whose sexual powers are weak or enfeebled"]. JIMSONWEED; THORN-APPLE

One sp, **D. wrightii** Regel [for Charles Wright, botanist of the SW], **102A**. ADV now, probably encouraged and used by the early Americans as a drug and medicinal plant. A coarse weedy herb with ovate, dentate lvs and fls up to 20 cm long, with a broad flaring tube and attenuate lobes. The fruit is spiny, nodding, and dehisces irregularly. Four Corners area.

HYOSCYAMUS L. 1753 [Gr., *hyos*, of a hog, + *kyamos*, bean, because poisonous to swine]. HENBANE

One sp, **H. niger** L. [black], **102C**. ADV. A huge weed of disturbed sites, with large deeply dentate-lobed lvs and bracteate spikes, not widely distributed but locally abundant where it occurs. Contains a very poisonous alkaloid, hyoscyamine.

LYCIUM L. 1753 [ancient Gr. *lycion*, a prickly shrub growing in Lycia]. MATRIMONY-VINE
1a. Corolla purple, the tube 3-7 mm long; lvs narrowly oblong; stems arching and curving down; berry salmon-red, not glaucous. **L. barbarum** L. [foreign; originally brought to Linnaeus from China]. ADV, escaped from old gardens and occasionally estab on roadsides [*L. halimifolium*].
1b. Corolla greenish or purple-tinged, the tube 15-20 mm long; lvs oblong to elliptic; berry red to reddish-blue, glaucous. **L. pallidum** Miers. Native sp, Four Corners.

NICOTIANA L. 1753 [for Jean Nicot, who sent seeds of tobacco to France in 1650]. TOBACCO

One sp, **N. attenuata** Torrey, **102B**. Glandular annual with ovate to lanceolate lvs; fls greenish-white, 2-4 cm long,
narrowly tubular.

PHYSALIS L. 1753 [Gr., *physa*, a bellows, referring to the inflated calyx]. GROUND-CHERRY
1a. Peduncles usually 3-8 mm long; lvs rhomboidal, strongly glandular-pubescent; corolla limb often reflexed when fully opened. **P. hederifolia** Gray [ivy-leaved]. San Juan River drainage, often under scrub oak. Native perennial with deep-seated rhizomes.
1b. Peduncles usually 10-15 mm long; lvs usually lanceolate, glabrous or pubescent; corolla limb usually not reflexed when fully open. **P. virginiana** Miller. Ruderal, possibly ADV, W counties. The genus is very poorly collected in W Colorado; better material, with root systems, is needed for a proper understanding of what we have.

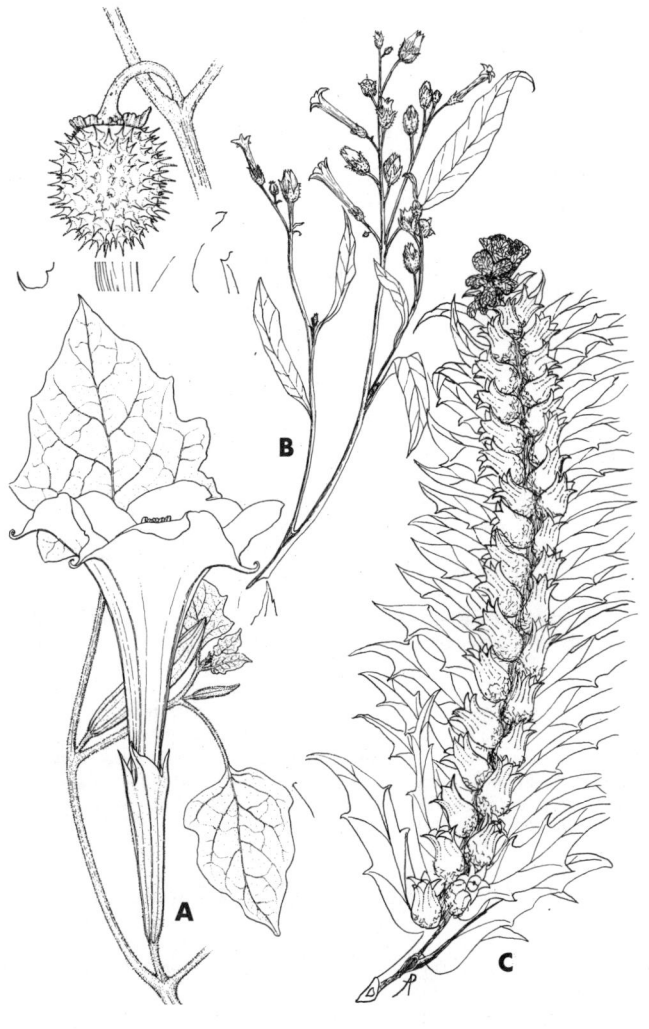

Figure 102. A, *Datura wrightii*; B, *Nicotiana attenuata*; C, *Hyoscyamus niger*

SOLANUM L. 1753 [the classical Latin name]. NIGHTSHADE

1a. Stems and lvs with prickles. . . . . (2)
1b. Stems and lvs lacking prickles. . . . . (3)

2a. Fls yellow; lvs green, deeply lobed, with flat prickles; calyx prickly, enclosing the frt. **S. rostratum** Dunal [beaked, referring to the odd anther], BUFFALO-BUR. ADV weed of cult ground in the valleys. The anthers are dissimilar, the lowest one much larger and longer, with an incurved beak.
2b. Fls purple; lvs and stems white with a dense scurfy stellate pubescence. **S. elaeagnifolium** Cavanilles [with lvs resembling those of *Elaeagnus*]. ADV, estab in the lower Gunnison Valley.

3a. Lf-blades deeply lobed or pinnatifid. . . . . (4)
3b. Lf-blades entire. . . . . (6)

4a. Lf-blades deeply pinnatifid with acute, triangular segs. **S. triflorum** Nuttall. ADV weed of cult ground, lower river valleys; fls white, with yellow anthers.
4b. Lf-blades with broad, rounded lobes. . . . . (5)

5a. Fls purple; plant a somewhat woody vine, climbing over other plants and fences. **S. dulcamara** L. [sweet; bitter], BITTERSWEET NIGHTSHADE. ADV fencerow weed, Gunnison-Colorado R valley.
5b. Fls white; low herb with small round tubers. **S. jamesii** Torrey, WILD POTATO. Piñon-juniper, Four Corners. Probably gathered for food by the Indians.

6a. Lvs thin, translucent; glabrous or nearly so; calyx remaining small, not covering part of the berry at maturity. **S. americanum** Miller, BLACK NIGHTSHADE. Weed of cult ground, lower valleys. In *Solanum* the peduncles, instead of arising from the lf-axils as one would expect, arise from the middle of the internode!
6b. Lvs thick; plants hirsute or glandular-villous; calyx enlarged at maturity, covering the lower half of the berry. **S. physalifolium** Rusby var **nitidibaccatum** (Bitter) Edmonds [with lvs like *Physalis* ± shiny berry]. ADV ruderal weed, sandy soil, lower valleys (*S. sarachoides*, incorrectly, of Colorado lit).

SPARGANIACEAE—BUR-REED FAMILY (SPG)

The bur-reeds inhabit the margins of ponds. With their balls of fls, the lower clusters carpellate and the upper staminate, sessile on a zig-zag rachis, they are unmistakeable. When they get out in deep water, however, they do not flower, their lvs become extremely long and the ribbon-like blades float on the water. Identification of *Sparganium* species requires specimens with mature fruits.

SPARGANIUM L. 1753 [Gr., *sparganion*, a swaddling-band, alluding to the lvs]. BUR-REED
1a. Carpellate heads about 1 cm diam; staminate heads solitary;

plants small, with lvs 1 cm or less wide. **S. minimum** Fries. Infrequent in subalpine bogs.

1b. Carpellate heads over 1 cm diam; staminate heads 2 or more; plants usually robust, with broader lvs. **S. angustifolium** Michaux. Common in ponds in the mts and intermountain parks.

TAMARICACEAE—TAMARISK FAMILY (TAM)

Tamarix and certain other plants that grow in low alkaline areas are able, by means of salt-excreting glands, to get rid of surplus salts, sometimes in such quantity that the salt may be gathered by humans. *Tamarix* is a phreatophyte, that is, a plant capable of reaching the water table. Phreatophytes are so successful in using water that they can actually lower the water table and therefore they are a real problem in areas of water impoundment such as the Colorado River Basin. It is claimed that *Tamarix* was introduced from the Middle East within recent times, but in 1776 the Spanish explorer, Padre Escalante, mentions in his journals that he saw it in the American Southwest, indicating that it had been introduced by the Spanish in the 16th Century or earlier!

TAMARIX L. 1753 [the classical name]. TAMARISK; SALT CEDAR

1a. Fls four-merous, appearing before the lvs; mostly cult and never as abundant as the next. **T. parviflora** de Candolle. ADV, Colorado R Valley.

1b. Fls five-merous, appearing with and after the lvs. **T. ramosissima** Ledebour, **103A**. ADV. Widely naturalized in canyon-bottoms and floodplains. The fls can be pink or white. Some claim that the correct name for this is *T. chinensis* Loureiro.

TRILLIACEAE—TRILLIUM FAMILY (TRL)

Trilliums are among the most beautiful of American monocots. Anyone raised in the East, Midwest or Far West needs no introduction to these striking plants: a stem with three lvs in a whorl, supporting a handsome white, pink or red flower with parts in threes, the outer ones clearly sepals and the inner ones clearly petals. One curious species appears to be stemless, with the lvs at ground level; but the stem extends vertically deep below the surface, so it really is like all the rest. Actually, one of the species native to the Pacific Northwest extends barely into the Park Range of Northern Colorado, giving us a small taste of the Northern Rocky Mountain flora.

TRILLIUM L. 1753 [Lat., *trilix*, triple, alluding to the parts in three's]. WAKE-ROBIN

One sp, **T. ovatum** Pursh. In Colorado restricted to subalpine forests of the Park Range, RT, **PL 2**. Unfortunately, once the general public learned of the presence of this desirable garden plant in Colorado, the accessible stands of it were all but wiped out, and it is to be regarded as an endangered sp here.

Figure 103. **A**, *Tamarix ramosissima*; **B**, *Celtis reticulata*

TYPHACEAE—CAT-TAIL FAMILY (TYP)

The flat leaves of cat-tails seem to be too weak to stand up to high winds, but note that the cat-tail leaves are spirally twisted so that the whole leaf surface is never presented to the wind. Cat-tail marshes are important nesting grounds for sora rails, blackbirds and marsh wrens and should be preserved and encouraged as miniature wildlife sanctuaries.

TYPHA L. 1753 [*typhe*, the ancient Gr. name]. CAT-TAIL

1a. Staminate and carpellate parts of the spike not separated by a bare portion of the axis; pollen remaining in tetrads; carpellate spikes 1.5-3.0 cm, thick; lvs broad, up to 20 mm wide. **T. latifolia** L., BROAD-LEAVED CAT-TAIL. Very common along ditches and ponds in the lower valleys.
1b. Staminate and carpellate parts of the spike separated by a bare portion of the axis; pollen usually separating to single grains; carpellate spikes slender; lvs narrower . . . . (2)

2a. Mature carpellate spike dark brown to reddish-brown; uppermost lf-sheaths lacking auricles, open at the throat, the margins free, tapering to the blade. **T. domingensis** Persoon. Similar habitats.
2b. Mature carpellate spikes buff-colored; uppermost lf-sheaths with auricles, usually closed at the throat, margins free but parallel, not tapering at the throat. **T. angustifolia** L. NARROW-LEAVED CAT-TAIL. A difficult group because the spp hybridize. Pertinent observations must be made in the field because it is difficult to preserve the important features in pressed plants, partly because of their great size.

ULMACEAE—ELM FAMILY (ULM)

Most members of this family characteristically have lvs with unequal (oblique) bases, and the fruit is a samara with a circular wing. Our species flower early in the spring, before the period of leafing-out.

1a. Lvs sharply serrate, smooth above, cuneate at the base. **Ulmus**, ELM
1b. Lvs sparingly serrate or entire, the contours rounded, often somewhat cordate at the base. **Celtis**, HACKBERRY

CELTIS L. 1753 [Pliny's name for the "Lotus with sweet berries" described by Herodotus]. HACKBERRY

One sp, **C. reticulata** Torrey, **103B**. Canyons and arroyos, W counties. The trees are often stunted and misshapen, with the lvs and twigs infested by insect galls of many kinds. A common one on the lvs, caused by *Pachypsylla pubescens*, is a nipple-shaped gall with long hairs and a crater-like depression at the top; the opposite side of the lf has a smooth depression. Another insect produces characteristic 'witches brooms', clusters of affected twigs.

488   Ulmaceae (ULM)

ULMUS L. 1753 [the classical Lat. name]. ELM
 One sp, **U. pumila** L. CHINESE ELM. ADV. This Central Asian import was brought here because of its drought-hardiness. It has been extensively planted around homesteads for shade and shelter from wind. As the land was abandoned the elms have survived and now colonize floodplains in the vicinity.

URTICACEAE—NETTLE FAMILY (URT)

Nettles sting by means of epidermal hairs that are filled with an irritant substance, including acetylcholine and histamine. The hairs are silicified at the tip, thus are brittle and break when brushed against. The irritation is brief but severe in humans. Hunting dogs are prone to more serious systemic disorders. This family contains a major fibre plant, Ramie (*Boehmeria nivea*), a native of Asia.

1a. Lvs alternate, entire; plants without stinging hairs; fls axillary, few. **Parietaria**, PELLITORY
1b. Lvs opposite, sharply serrate; plants with stinging hairs; fls in axillary spikes, numerous. **Urtica**, NETTLE

PARIETARIA L. 1753 [Lat., *paries*, wall, from the habitat of the original sp]. PELLITORY
 One sp, **P. pensylvanica** Mühlenberg, **104A**. Small, weak herb found in shade of trees and rocks in the canyons. The generic name is very apt, since in Europe it commonly grows on walls.

URTICA L. 1753 [Lat., *uro*, to burn]. NETTLE

1a. Lvs green, hirsute or hispid. **U. gracilis** Aiton, **104B**. Along irrigation ditches and streams.
1b. Lvs softly gray-pubescent. **U. gracilis** ssp **holosericea** (Nuttall) Weber. Entering Colorado only in MF.

UVULARIACEAE—BELLWORT FAMILY (UVU)

A segregate family formerly in Liliaceae, characterized by having leafy stems with elliptic-lanceolate lvs and axillary or terminal fls with narrow recurved tepals, and a round or angular berry.

1a. Fls axillary, dangling at the ends of slender pedicels; tepals recurved; berry smooth, round, red. **Streptopus**, TWISTED-STALK
1b. Fls terminal at the ends of the branches, on stout pedicels; tepals erect; berry angular, orange. **Disporum**, BELLWORT

DISPORUM Salisbury 1825 [Gr., *dis*, double, + *spora*, seed, alluding to the two-seeded berries of some spp]. BELLWORT
 One sp, **D. trachycarpum** (Watson) Bentham & Hooker [rough-fruited, from the strongly papillose frt], **71A**. Deep shade in conifer forests.

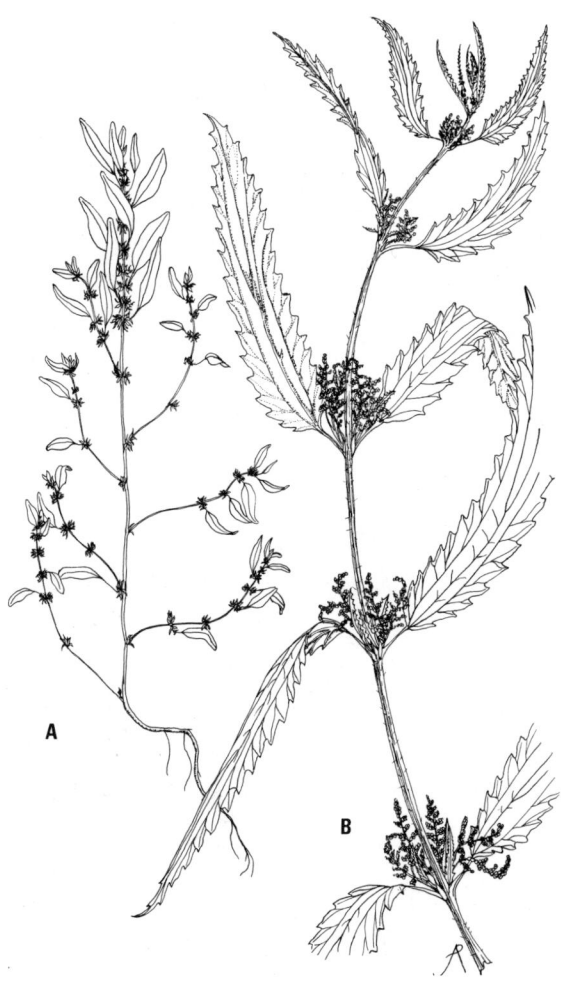

Figure 104. A, *Parietaria pensylvanica*; B, *Urtica gracilis*

STREPTOPUS Michaux 1803 [Gr., *streptos*, twisted, + *pous*, foot, alluding to the bent or twisted peduncles]. TWISTED-STALK

One sp, **S. fassettii** Löve & Löve, **71B**. Moist, deeply shaded forest floors near streams (*S. amplexifolius* var *chalazatus*). Our plant is diploid and distinct from the tetraploid *S. amplexifolius* on morphological grounds.

VALERIANACEAE—VALERIAN FAMILY (VAL)

Although the valerians are a small family, they are very conspicuous in moist forests and meadows in late summer. Because of their compound leaves and umbel-like flower clusters they are often mistaken for Apiaceae but actually they are more closely related to Asteraceae. Two features clearly mark our species: the corolla with a small swelling at the base on one side, and the plumose parachute at the top of the fruit; this unrolls when the fruits are mature and functions just as a dandelion pappus.

VALERIANA L. 1753 [in honor of Publius Aurelius Valerianus, Roman emperor, 253-260]. VALERIAN

1a. Plants with thick, fleshy vertical taproots; lvs and lfls thick, narrow; venation almost parallel; infl very open even at fl time; fls unisexual. **V. edulis** Nuttall, **105A**. Gravelly hillsides and meadows, montane and subalpine.
1b. Rhizomatous; lvs and lfls thin, broad; veins distinctly pinnate; infl a dense compound cyme, becoming more open in frt; fls perfect or evidently so. . . . . (2)

2a. Corolla narrowly cup-shaped, without a definite cylindric tube and not noticeably swollen at the base. **V. occidentalis** Heller. Wet meadows and streamsides, montane and subalpine. The fls in this sp tend to be more greenish than in the next.
2b. Corolla funnel-shaped or trumpet-shaped, with a definite cylindric tube and usually swollen at the base on one side. **V. capitata** Pallas ssp **acutiloba** (Rydberg) Meyer, **105B**. Similar sites but not so much a forest plant and going higher into the subalpine and lower alpine.

VERBENACEAE—VERVAIN FAMILY (VRB)

Our verbenas might be mistaken for mints, but the foliage lacks any minty odor. The stems are often square, however, and the fls mint-like. Verbenas are cultivated for their handsome flower clusters. This family includes teak (*Tectona grandis*), one of the finest of timbers for furniture, and, in the days of wooden ships, shipbuilding. Teak was especially sought for armored vessels because, unlike oak, the wood did not corrode iron. Oddly enough, the wood sinks in water unless dried for two years. Trees were girdled and left standing that long before harvesting.

1a. Fls showy, lavender; corolla tube much exceeding the calyx; lvs very deeply pinnatifid. **Glandularia**, SHOWY VERVAIN

Figure 105. A, *Valeriana edulis*; B, *V. capitata*, habit, fls, frt

1b. Fls small, blue or purple; corolla tube scarcely longer than the calyx; lvs merely toothed or very shallowly pinnatifid. **Verbena**, VERVAIN

GLANDULARIA Gmelin 1792 [Lat., *glandula*, acorn, alluding to the shape of the frt]. SHOWY VERVAIN

One sp, **G. bipinnatifida** (Nuttall) Nuttall. A low, spreading roadside plant, S counties (*Verbena ambrosifolia*).

VERBENA L. 1753 [lat. name for any sacred herb]. VERVAIN

1a. Floral bracts lflike, equalling or exceeding the fls; lvs not especially thick, not rugose-reticulate; plant prostrate or strongly spreading. **V. bracteata** Lagasca & Rodriguez. ADV ruderal weed.
1b. Floral bracts shorter than the fls, not lflike; lvs thick and rugose-reticulate; tall, erect plants. **V. macdougalii** Heller. Fields and roadsides, AA, LP.

VIOLACEAE—VIOLET FAMILY (VIO)

Many violets produce attractive and fragrant flowers, but these often do not produce seeds. The effective seed-producing flowers are cleistogamous, that is, they never open, lack attractive floral parts, and are subterranean or emerge only after fruit is matured. They are obviously self-pollinated in such instances. Many violets are adapted for dispersal of the seeds by ants, and, aiding the ant in grasping the seed there may be a small irregularly-shaped growth on the side of the seed (a caruncle). This relationship between ants and plants is called myrmecophily.

VIOLA L. [the classical name]. VIOLET

1a. Petals yellow, often brown on the back and with brown pencilling . . . . (2)
1b. Petals white or some shade of blue-violet. . . . . (8)

2a. Lvs deeply dissected into narrow segments. **V. sheltonii** Torrey, 106G,M. Oak brush on the plateaus.
2b. Lvs simple . . . . (3)

3a. Lvs deeply cordate-reniform, regularly crenate, hardly showing a terminal point. **V. biflora** L., 106B. Alpine plants in shelter of boulders, also lower altitudes in moss along streams in deep forests.
3b. Lvs lanceolate or elliptic or triangular-ovate, always distinctly pointed, entire, crenate or dentate. . . . . (4)

4a. Lvs triangular-ovate, coarsely few-toothed or -lobed. . . . . . . (5)
4b. Lvs lanceolate-ovate, or elliptic-lanceolate, entire or shallowly crenate. . . . . (6)

5a. Plants weak, spreading, with well-developed stems; lvs and petals usually purple on the back. **V. purpurea** Kellogg ssp **venosa**

(Watson) Baker & Clausen, **106H**. Unstable rocky screes in the higher mountains, Park Range, RT.

5b. Plants sturdy, erect, the stems short and not easily seen; lvs and petals not strongly purple-tinged. **V. utahensis** Baker & Clausen, **106I**. Deep soils in sagebrush, MF.

6a. Lf-blades narrowly lanceolate or lance-elliptic, at least 3 times as long as wide, gradually narrowed to the petiole; plants small (usually less than 5 cm). **V. nuttallii** Pursh, **106K**. Blossoming in early spring at lower altitudes, often in protection of rocks.

6b. Lf-blades broader and often much larger, abruptly narrowed to the petiole; plants small or large. . . . . (7)

7a. Plants small, lvs less than 5 cm long, ± truncate at the base (otherwise like *V. nuttallii*). **V. vallicola** Nelson, **106L**. Same habitats as *V. nuttallii* but evidently not as common or widespread, RB.

7b. Plants large, lvs usually more than 5 cm long, more gradually tapering to the base. **V. praemorsa** Douglas ssp **major** (Hooker) Baker, **106J**. Common in relatively mesic sites at higher altitudes and blooming longer into the summer than the two last. These three taxa comprise a polyploid series, with *V. vallicola* diploid, n=6, *V. nuttallii* tetraploid, n=12, and *V. praemorsa* octoploid, n=24. *V. utahensis* is thought to be an amphiploid, combining the genotypes of *V. praemorsa* and *V. purpurea*.

8a. Plants with erect lfy stems bearing fls in the lf axils. . . . . . . (9)
8b. Plants stemless, sometimes with creeping stolons from which lvs may appear. . . . . (11)

9a. Petals white, usually violet on the back; stem well-developed; lvs cordate. **V. canadensis** L., **106C**. Aspen groves, streamsides. Two distinct types of plant occur, one with small and one with large lvs. The large lvd plant may best be called **V. rugulosa** Greene, for the two seem to be distinct spp.

9b. Petals blue-violet; stem short, often obscure; lvs seldom distinctly cordate . . . . (10)

10a. Lvs pubescent; plants of middle altitudes, usually more than 5 cm tall. **V. adunca** Smith [hooked, alluding to the spur], **106A (left)**. The most abundant summer-blooming violet. Tetraploid. Löve claimed that this plant should be called *V. aduncoides* and that the next is the real *V. adunca*, but the question is not settled.

10b. Lvs glabrous; alpine plants, usually less than 5 cm tall. **V. labradorica** Schrank, **106A (right)**. A diploid species usually treated as a variety of *V. adunca*, but in Colorado at least they are distinct. This small violet occurs from Greenland to Alaska essentially identical to the Rocky Mountain plant and is genetically distinct from the lowland sp. They also differ in the structure of the style (*V. bellidifolia, V. adunca var. minor*).

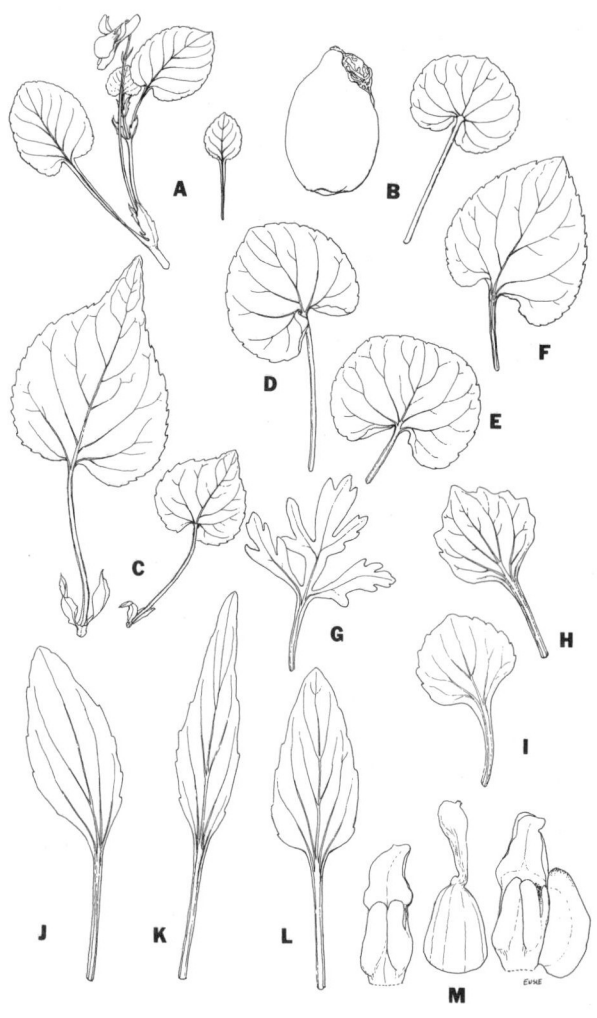

Figure 106. A, *Viola adunca*, habit, lf of *V. labradorica*; B, *V. biflora*, lf, seed; C, *V. canadensis*, large and small lvs; D, *V. epipsiloides*; E, *V. renifolia*;; F, *V. sororia*; G, *V. sheltonii*; H, *V. purpurea*; I, *V. utahensis*; J, *V. praemorsa*; K, *V. nuttallii*; L, *V. vallicola*; M, *V. sheltonii*, stamen left, gynoecium center, appendage stamen right

Figure 107. **A**, *Tribulus terrestris*; **B**, *Parthenocissus inserta*, habit, tendril; **C**, *P. quinquefolia*, tendril

ZANNICHELLIA L. 1753 [for Gian G. Zannichelli, 1662-1729, Venetian botanist]. HORNED PONDWEED

One sp, **Z. palustris** L., 36A. In slow streams and ditches, lower elevations.

ZYGOPHYLLACEAE-CALTROP FAMILY (ZYG)

The single genus and species in our flora gives no clue to the extent of this family, which is distributed mostly in the tropics and Southern Hemisphere. *Lignum vitae*, a durable tropical hardwood, comes from *Guaiacum*, and seeds of a Mediterranean genus, *Peganum*, produce the dye, turkey red. Australia has many species of *Zygophyllum*, adapted to desert or saline sites. The schizocarpous fruit, a capsule that breaks into indehiscent one-seeded units, is characteristic of many genera.

TRIBULUS L. 1753 [Gr., *tribulosus*, thorny]. PUNCTURE-VINE

One sp, **T. terrestris** L., 107A. ADV. Prostrate-spreading weed with small pinnately-compound lvs and yellow fls, common in sandy soil along roadsides and back yards in the valleys. The frts break up into spiny segments that can puncture bicycle tires.

GLOSSARY OF TERMS

Achene—see *akene*.
Acicular—needle-like.
Actinomorphic—having a radial symmetry (same as *regular*).
Acuminate—drawn out at the apex into a gradually tapering point.
Acute—terminating in a sharp or well-defined point.
Adaxial—facing the axis (ventral, in the botanical sense).
Adnate—attached or fused to.
ADV—adventive.
Adventive—not native in the area; introduced by accident or spreading after being deliberately planted for another purpose.
Akene [achene]—a small, dry indehiscent, one-loculed, one-seeded fruit consisting usually of a single carpel (in Asteraceae it is derived from two carpels).
Alternate—[leaves] having one leaf arising at each node;[floral parts] having the members of one whorl attached between the members of the next outer or inner whorl.
Alveolate—honeycombed.
Ament—same as *catkin*.
Amphi[di]ploid—a fertile population arising from the doubling of chromosome sets from two incompatible parental stocks.
Androecium—collective name for the stamens. The total set of stamens is called the *androecium*.
Androgynous—[in *Carex*] having the staminate flowers above the carpellate ones, and in the same spike.
Angiosperms—seed plants in which the ovules are enclosed in carpels; flowering plants.
Annual—living through one season only.
Anterior—[in flowers] the side of the flower facing away from the axis of the inflorescence.
Anthelmintic—used to treat worm infestations.
Anther—the pollen-bearing organ of the flower. See *stamen*.
Anthesis—flowering time.
Aphyllopodic—[in *Carex*], having only bladeless sheaths (originally bud scales) at the base of the flowering culm; this culm matures in one season.
Apiculate—suddenly prolonged to a small point (*apiculus*).
Apomictic—producing seeds from unfertilized ovules, by parthenogenesis. The result is progeny genetically identical to the parent. A common phenomenon in several genera (ex. *Agoseris*, *Taraxacum*).
Appressed—lying close to, or flat against.
Arachnoid—cobwebby.
Areole—in cacti, the point at which a cluster of spines arises, equivalent to a node.
Aril—a fleshy, usually colored appendage or covering on a seed.

Articulate—jointed.

Articulation—[in grasses] the point at which organs (glumes or lemmas) break away from the stem. In a grass spikelet, if, at maturity, the florets fall away from the plant and leave the glumes attached, we say the spikelet disarticulates above the glumes and between the florets. If the spikelet falls completely without leaving the glumes attached to the plant, we say the spikelet disarticulates below the glumes. Manipulating the spikelet with one's fingers or with a tweezers helps to determine the type of disarticulation.

Ascending—growing obliquely upward or curving upward during growth.

Attenuate—drawn out into a long, slender tip (extremely acuminate).

Auricle—[in milkweeds] an ear or flap-like appendage at the base of the hood; (in grasses) a similar appendage at the summit of the leaf-sheath.

Auriculate—with auricles.

Awn—a stiff, bristle-like appendage.

Axil—the angle formed by a leaf with the stem to which it is attached. Buds, for example, are found in the axils of leaves, that is, at the place where the leaf joins the stem.

Axile—a type of placentation in which the ovules are attached to the adaxial (ventral) suture of the carpel. Peas and beans, for example, show axile placentation involving only one carpel. Tomato or apple shows axile placentation involving several united carpels.

Axillary—situated in, or arising from, the axil of a leaf. Usually opposed to terminal.

Axis—an imaginary line running lengthwise through the center of an organ such as a flower or stem.

Banner—the broad, erect, upper petal of the flower of legumes, as in sweet-peas.

Barbellate—having minute prongs. Commonly refers to the pappus of Asteraceae, in which each bristle has very short barbs, as seen with a lens.

Basal—[leaves] produced at ground level; [placentation] having the ovules attached at the base of the ovary only (as in green peppers). In many instances the ovary contains only one seed, which is attached at the base of the ovary and fills the locule.

Basifixed—attached at the base, as anthers to the filament.

Beak—a prominent, firm, slender tip. In *Oxytropis* the keel petals are abruptly narrowed to form a beak; in mustards the tip of the fruit is sometimes abruptly narrowed with the non-ovule-bearing portion forming a beak.

Bearded—having a tuft of long hairs.

Bidentate—two-toothed. In *Carex*, this is an important characteristic in some species in which the tip of the perigynium is bidentate.

Biennial—of two years duration. A biennial plant produces a rosette of basal leaves the first year, sends up a flower stalk the second year, produces seed, and dies. See also *monocarpic*.

Bifid—cleft in two.

Bilabiate—two-lipped, referring especially to the corolla in such groups as mints and scrophs.

Bipinnate—twice pinnately compound.

Bipinnatifid—twice pinnatifid.

Biseriate—in two rows.
Bisexual—(in flowers) having both stamens and carpels in the same flower; same as *perfect*.
Blade—the flat, expanded portion of a leaf or petal.
Bloom—a whitish waxy or powdery (glaucous) covering on leaves or twigs, easily rubbed off; pruinosity.
Bract—a much-reduced leaf, usually subtending a flower.
Bracteole—small bracts on the cup of a calyx, as in mallows.
Bulb—a spherical underground bud or stem with fleshy scales or roots, as in onions. In a bulb the spherical structure consists mostly of scales, whereas in a corm the scales are minute and the round mass consists of the fleshy stem.
Bulblets—asexually reproductive structures derived from flowers or branch primordia, or divisions of a bulb.

Caducous—dropping off early, as the sepals in Papaveraceae.
Caespitose—growing in clumps.
Calcareous—having to do with limestone.
Calciphile—growing on limestone.
Callous (callose)—hard and thick in texture.
Callus—hardened base of the lemma in some grasses, especially *Stipa*.
Calyx—the outer set of perianth segments, usually green; collective name for the sepals (see *tepals*).
Campanulate—bell-shaped.
Canescent—having a hoary, grayish pubescence of short hairs.
Capillary—thread-like.
Capitate—head-like; collected into a dense, short cluster.
Capsule—a dry, dehiscent fruit composed of more than one carpel (ex. *Yucca*).
Carpel—the basic unit of a gynoecium, a single 'inrolled spore-bearing leaf' (stigma, style and ovary). A good example of a typical carpel is the pod of a pea, or a peanut. See also *gynoecium, pistil*.
Caryopsis—the grain (fruit) of grasses, a 2-carpellate akene containing one seed.
Catkin—a spike of inconspicuous and usually unisexual flowers, as in willows and birches. Same as *ament*.
Caudate—tailed.
Caudex (plural, caudices)—the persistent woody, underground base of an otherwise herbaceous stem; an erect or ascending underground stem (*rootstock* is a less precise term).
Cauline—borne on the stem, above ground. Refers to leaves; opposed to basal.
Centimeter—ten millimeters (2.54 cm = 1 inch).
Chartaceous—papery.
Ciliate—marginally fringed with hairs (cilia).
Cinereous—ashy-gray.
Circinate—coiled.
Circumscissile—dehiscent by a transverse circular line, as the capsules of plantains.
Circumpolar—distributed around the world in the Northern Hemisphere.
Cladode (cladophyll; phylloclad)—a branch consisting of a single internode flattened and expanded to function as a leaf.
Clavate—club-shaped.

Claw—the narrow stalk of some petals, esp. mustards.
Cleft—deeply cut.
Cleistogamous—with fertilization occurring within unopened flowers.
cm—centimeter.
Collar—a horizontal line crossing the outside of a grass leaf where the blade joins the sheath. The collar is often thickened or covered with hairs.
Colluvial—(sediments) accumulated through torrential rains.
Coma—a tuft of hairs, as on the seeds of *Epilobium*.
Compound—composed of from two to many similar united parts, as carpels in a compound ovary (a tomato fruit is a compound ovary, consisting of four or five united carpels), or, divided into a number of similar parts, as the leaflets of compound leaves.
Concavo-convex—with one side concave and the other convex.
Compressed—flattened. For example, in a laterally-compressed grass spikelet the flattening involves the side of the spikelet, so that the individual lemmas are folded in half. In a dorsally-compressed spikelet the florets on opposite sides of the axis are pressed towards each other, and the lemmas are flattened out rather than folded.
Concolorous—without differentiation by color.
Conduplicate—folded, with the halves together.
Confluent—running together.
Connate—united, usually by fusion or pressure in the bud.
Connivent—coming into contact or converging.
Cordate—heart-shaped, referring to the outline or the base of a leaf.
Coriaceous—leathery in texture.
Corm—enlarged fleshy base of a stem, bulb-like but solid. Example: gladiolus, spring beauty. See *bulb*.
Corolla—collective name for the petals, the inner whorl of perianth segments.
Corona—a crown or collar attached to the inside of the corolla, as in daffodils and milkweeds.
Corymb—a flat-topped inflorescence.
Cotyledons—the first, or seed-leaves of a plant; the two halves of a peanut kernel are its cotyledons. The two great groups of flowering plants, Monocots and Dicots, are so called because of the difference in the number of cotyledons in the seeds.
Crenate—with rounded marginal teeth (diminutive, *crenulate*).
Crescentic—of a crescent-shape.
Cruciform—cross-shaped.
Cucullate—hooded.
Culm—the 'stem' of grasses and sedges, consisting principally of overlapping leaf-sheaths.
Cuneate—wedge-shaped, usually referring to the base of a leaf.
Cuspidate—tipped with a firm, sharp point.
Cyme—a flower cluster, usually opposite-branched, in its simplest form consisting of three flowers, the central or terminal one blooming first. Same as *dichasium*.

Deciduous—falling off at the end of a growing season; not persistent or evergreen (see also *caducous*).
Decimeter—ten centimeters.

Declined—directed down toward the base (not as sharply as reflexed).
Decumbent—prostrate except for the ascending tips of the branches.
Decurrent—referring to the bases of leaves, which sometimes continue down the stem beyond the point of attachment.
Decussate—in pairs alternately at right angles.
Dehiscent—splitting open at maturity.
Deltoid—triangular, shaped like the Greek letter *delta*.
Dentate—toothed, with the teeth directed outward rather than forward (dim., *denticulate*).
Denticle—an extremely small tooth.
Depauperate—impoverished as if starved, reduced in size or function.
Diadelphous—[stamens] united into two sets. In some legumes, nine of the ten stamens in a flower are united by the filaments, the tenth is separate.
Dichasium—a simple inflorescence consisting of a terminal flower, plus a pair of flowers produced by the nearest pair of subtending leaves or bracts (a *simple cyme*).
Dichotomous—equal forked branches, most commonly occurring in ferns.
Digitate—compounded or veined in a way as to suggest fingers of a hand.
Dimorphic—having two different sized parts or positions of parts. See discussion under borages and pinks.
Dioecious—bearing the staminate flowers on one individual and the carpellate on another of the same species (note: *plants* may be dioecious; their *flowers* are then imperfect or unisexual; flowers are never themselves dioecious.
Diploid—having two sets of homologous chromosomes.
Disarticulating—breaking off from the main axis, as spikelets of grasses. See *articulation*.
Disjunct—occurring in two widely separated geographic areas.
Disk-flowers—the central actinomorphic tubular flowers of Asteraceae. In sunflowers and daisies the central part of the 'flower' (head) is composed of a great number of disk-flowers, while the 'petals' are really each whole flowers (rays). See introduction to Asteraceae.
Dissected—cut into numerous narrow segments.
Distal—remote from the place of attachment; opposite of *proximal*.
Distinct—separate, not united (this has nothing to do with visibility!).
Divaricate—extremely divergent, at right angles.
Divergent—spreading apart, curving away from the main axis.
Divided—cut to the base into lobes or segments.
dm—decimeter.
Dolabriform—of trichomes, attached at the middle, with two arms in a straight line.
Dorsal—pertaining to the part of an organ facing away from the axis, as the underside of a leaf (preferably called *abaxial*). This is a usage quite different from that of zoölogy.
Dorsiventral—with an upper and lower side (-ly compressed: flattened from the back rather than the sides).
Drupe—the fruit of cherry or plum, a fleshy one-seeded fruit in which the seed is enclosed in a hard 'stone'.

Elliptical—having the shape of an ellipse.
Emarginate—having a shallow notch at the tip.
END—endemic.
Endemic—confined to a given region; narrowly endemic, confined to a very small area.
Endosperm—nutritive tissue in the seed, other than the embryo.
Entire—without marginal teeth or lobes.
Epigynous—borne on top of the ovary (flowers are epigynous if they have an inferior ovary).
Equitant—folded over, as if astride, as the leaves of *Iris*.
Erose—ragged-edged.
-escent (-ascent)—becoming.
Even-pinnate—pinnately compound, with the terminal leaflet missing.
Exfoliating—coming off in thin sheets.
Explanate—spread out flat, as opened anthers of some *Penstemon*.
Exserted—projecting beyond the enveloping organs.
Extravaginal—of buds or branches that push through the side of a leaf-sheath, thus arise "outside of the sheath", in grasses and sedges.

Facultative—optional.
Falcate—sickle-shaped.
Farinose—with a mealy or powdery covering of wax or inflated hairs.
Fascicle—bundle, cluster.
Fertile—having a functional gynoecium; producing seed; in ferns, bearing sporangia.
Fibrillose—shredding into fine fibers, usually the vascular bundles, as in some grass and sedge leaf-sheaths.
Filament—the stalk supporting an anther.
Filiform—thread-like.
Fimbriate—fringed.
Fistulose—hollow, as the stems of onions.
Flabellate (-iform)—fan-shaped.
Flagelliform—slender, whip-like.
Flexuous—curved, wavy.
Floccose—having loose tufts of soft, cottony hairs.
Floret—a small flower, specifically applied to those of grasses, sedges, and compositoes.
Foliaceous—leaf-like, either in texture or shape, or both.
Foliolate—referring to leaflets in a compound leaf (a clover leaf, unless you are lucky, is trifoliolate).
Follicle—a single carpel that dehisces along one edge only (*Delphinium, Aquilegia*).
Forma—the lowest taxonomic category; a sporadic mutant in a population.
Fornix—a scale or gland-like protuberance in the flower tube, as in many borages.
Free—not united; separate.
Free-central—a type of placentation in which the ovules are attached to a central stalk within the ovary that is not connected to the carpel margins by partitions.
Fruit—the part of a plant that bears the seeds; usually an ovary, its contents, and any floral parts which may be associated with it at

maturity. The term is also loosely used to refer to cones of gymnosperms and to spore-bearing structures of ferns, mosses, and other lower plants.
Fruticose—shrubby.
Fusiform—thick but tapering toward each end.

Galea—a hood- or helmet-shaped sepal or petal or the upper lip of some zygomorphic corollas.
Geniculate—bent abruptly, like a knee. Most commonly refers to the bent awns of some grasses.
Gibbous—swollen on one side.
Glabrate—becoming glabrous, almost glabrous.
Glabrescent—becoming glabrous.
Glabrous—completely smooth, without trichomes.
Gladiate—sword-shaped, like the leaves of *Iris*.
Gland—an organ of secretion; also commonly used to refer to any minute structure in flowers whose function is unknown.
Glandular—having glands; sticky. Glandular hairs are usually ball-tipped, and stems having these hairs may collect dirt and trash, are sticky to the touch, or stain the pressing-papers.
Glaucous—having a bloom or whitish covering, usually waxy, on the stem or leaf. This may disappear if the plants are dried with heat.
Globose—spherical.
Glochid—a barb.
Glochidiate—pubescent with barbed bristles.
Glomerate—crowded into a compact, spherical mass.
Glume—one of the two basal empty bracts forming the enclosing base of the grass spikelet (used to be called *sterile lemmas*).
Glutinous—sticky.
Graduate—(in Asteraceae) having the inner phyllaries longer than the outer.
Granulate—composed of small grains.
Gynaecandrous—(in *Carex*) having the carpellate flowers above the staminate ones in the same spike.
Gynobase—the often swollen or otherwise differentiated base of the style.
Gynoecium—a carpel or an aggregation of carpels, either separate or united; collective name for all the carpels in a single flower.
Gypsophile—a plant adapted to soils containing gypsum.

Habitat—the kind of locality in which a plant usually grows. If very specific, it is called a *microhabitat*.
Habitus—the growth form of a plant.
Hastate—like an arrowhead but with the basal lobes pointing outward.
Head—a compact, usually hemispherical flower-cluster.
Helicoid—curled in the form of a spring or snail shell.
Herbaceous—not woody.
Herbage—the vegetative portion of the plant.
Hirsute—clothed with coarse straight spreading hairs.
Hispid—clothed with stiff, bristle-like hairs.
Hispidulous—dim. of hispid.
Hyaline—transparent or translucent.

Hypanthium—a cup or tube bearing formed by the fused bases of the stamens, petals, and sepals.
Hypogynous—refers to flowers in which the stamens, petals and sepals are attached below the ovary; flowers with superior ovaries are hypogynous.

Imbricate—overlapping like shingles.
Imperfect—having only stamens or carpels, not both.
Incised—cut sharply, deeply and irregularly into lobes or segments.
Included—not protruding beyond the enveloping organs (opposite of *exserted*).
Indehiscent—not splitting open at maturity.
Indurate—hardened.
Indusium—a membranous flap or 'umbrella' covering the sorus of ferns; usually withers and disappears as the sporangia ripen.
Inferior—refers to ovaries which are either imbedded in the receptacle or fused with the surrounding floral parts. The ovary of an apple is inferior, *i.e.*, it is imbedded in the fused floral parts, which form a fleshy covering.
Inflorescence—flower cluster.
Internerves—in grasses, the portion of a lemma, palea, or glume situated between the nerves or veins.
Internode—the portion of a stem between two nodes.
Interrupted—having parts of the inflorescence not continuous but separated by spaces of stem.
Intravaginal—of buds or branches that arise between the sheath and culm of a grass or sedge.
Introgressant—transferring genes from one population into another through backcrossing following hybridization.
Involucel—a bract of the smallest umbel, in Apiaceae.
Involucre—a circle or cluster of bracts at the base of a flower cluster, sometimes fused into a cup. In the Asteraceae these bracts are called *phyllaries*.
Involute—having the edges rolled inward (revolute lvs are rolled outward).
Irregular—showing inequality in size, shape or arrangement of the parts, often loosely used as a synonym for *zygomorphic*.
Isodiametric—of equal dimensions.

Keel—a prominent dorsal rib, ridge, or crease (or, in the legumes, the name given to the two fused petals enclosing the stamens).

Labiate—with a differentiated, usually larger, lower lobe, as the corollas of orchids, mints and scrophs.
Lacerate—ragged, as if torn.
Lamella—a thin plate.
Lamina (pl. -ae)—blade.
Lanate—woolly.
Lanceolate—long and narrow, but broadest at the base.
Lateral—referring to the side, as opposed to *dorsal* or *ventral*, sometimes used in contrast to *terminal*.
Leaflet—a segment of a compound leaf.

Legume—the fruit (pod) (a single carpel with two sutures), of plants belonging to the Fabaceae; also, any member of the family.
Lemma—the outer bract of the grass floret.
Lenticels—wart-like, usually light-colored, spots on the bark of twigs.
Lenticular—disk-shaped, with two convex sides (lens-shaped).
Ligule—in grasses, the flap of tissue on the ventral (*adaxial*) side of a leaf at the place where the blade joins the sheath, *i.e.*, the ligule is between the blade and the culm; in Asteraceae, a ray-flower or strap-shaped corolla is called a ligule or ligulate corolla.
Limb—the expanded part of a tubular corolla, between the tube and the throat.
Linear—long and narrow, with parallel margins.
Lobe—a partial division or segment of an organ.
Lobule—dim. of lobe.
Locule—one of the cavities or chambers in an ovary or anther (commonly called a '*cell*').
Loculicidal—dehiscing by the rupture of the outer wall of the locule (see *septicidal*).
Loment—a legume which is constricted and jointed between the seeds, breaking up into several indehiscent, one-seeded segments.
Lyrate—pinnatifid with the terminal lobe large and rounded, the lower ones small.

m—meter.
Marcescent—persisting beyond a single season as dried parts.
Marginal—along the edge.
Massif—a more or less discrete group of peaks in a mt range.
Megaspore—the large spore, which in *Selaginella*, produces the female gametophyte (see *microspore*).
Mericarp—a segment of an ovary that separates intact, as in Apiaceae, Malvaceae and Zygophyllaceae.
-merous—refers to the number of segments in a whorl of floral parts (a flower with 3 petals, stamens, and carpels is 3-merous).
Mesic—having medium conditions as to moisture and light.
Mesophyte—a plant adapted to medium conditions as to moisture and light.
Meter—10 decimeters; 39.36 inches.
Microhabitat—a very special or narrowly restricted environment.
Microspore—the minute spore that in *Selaginella*, produces the male gametophyte.
Millimeter—one-tenth of a centimeter.
mm—millimeter.
Monad—of pollen grains, dispersed singly (as opposed to *dyad* or *tetrad*).
Monadelphous—united into a single group, as the filaments of a group of stamens.
Moniliform—like a string of beads.
Monocarpic—flowering and fruiting but once in its lifetime (as in *Agave* and *Frasera*).
Monoecious—having the stamens and carpels in different flowers on the same plant. A *plant* may be monoecious; its *flowers* are unisexual or imperfect.

Monotypic—having only one species in the genus (or one genus in a family), etc.
Mucro—a minute and abrupt point at the apex.
Mucronate—with a mucro (does not have the connotation of stiffness implied in *cuspidate*).
Muricate—having minute sharp-pointed outgrowths (usually on fruits or seeds).

Nectary—a gland or locus of nectar production.
Nerve—vein.
Nodal spines—thorns situated at the nodes.
Node—the point on a stem where leaves, buds, or branches usually arise. Occasionally flowers arise on internodes (*Solanum*) and buds appear above nodes (*superposed buds*).

Ob—a prefix implying 'the reverse'. For example, an obovate leaf is ovate with the widest part near the apex rather than the base.
Obligate—without exception (opposite of *facultative*).
Oblong—rectangular in general outline but with the corners rounded.
Obsolete—describing a part or organ usually present but in this instance much reduced.
Obtuse—blunt or rounded at the tip.
Ochroleucous—off-white, buff.
Odd-pinnate—pinnately compound, with the terminal leaflet present (having an odd number of leaflets).
Opposite—(leaves) originating in pairs at the nodes; (stamens) attached directly in front of a petal, rather than between petals.
Orbicular—round, circular.
Ovary—the basal part of the gynoecium or carpel which contains the seeds.
Ovate—egg-shaped and broadest near the base (a two-dimensional concept).
Ovoid—egg-shaped (three-dimensional).
Ovule—the seed before fertilization.

Palate—an upward-arching part of the lower lip of a zygomorphic corolla, tending to close the throat (as in snapdragon).
Palea—the adaxial (inner) of the two bracts of a grass floret; the bract opposite and enfolded by the lemma.
Paleae (receptacular)—bracts subtending the individual fls in a composite head (often referred to as *chaff*).
Palmate—having veins, lobes or segments which radiate from a single point, as maple lvs. See also *digitate*.
Palmatifid—partially divided in a palmate way (compare *pinnatifid*).
Panicle—a repeatedly branched inflorescence with pedicelled flowers.
Paniculate—arranged in panicles.
Pannose—with the appearance of felt or woolen cloth.
Pap—abbr. of pappus
Papilla(e)—minute epidermal wart(s).
Papillose (-ate)—minutely warty or pimply.
Pappus—appendages at the apex of the ovary, in Asteraceae.
Papule—in *Lemna*, a minute pimple on the surface of the frond, seen best when fresh and with a strong lens.

Parasitic—depending on living tissue of other organisms as a source of food.
Parietal—a type of placentation in which the ovules are attached to the side of the ovary. This term only applies to ovaries which consist of more than one carpel.
Parthenogenesis—production of fruit without benefit of fertilization.
Pectinate—comb-like.
Pedatifid—palmately cleft, with the divisions again cleft (as opposed to *pinnatifid*).
Pedicel—the stalk of a single flower.
Pedicellate—having a pedicel.
Peduncle—the common stalk of a flower cluster (adj: *pedunculate*).
Peltate—shield-shaped, attached in the center as by a stem of an umbrella.
Perennial—living year after year.
Perfect—having all the essential organs (stamens and carpels); bisexual.
Perianth—collective name for the sepals and petals. See also *tepals*.
Pericarp—the ovary wall.
Perigynium—the inflated sac enclosing the ovary of *Carex*, represented in *Kobresia* by an open sheath.
Peripheral—marginal, as concerning species that barely enter Colorado from neighboring states.
Persistent—lasting, not deciduous, remaining attached to the stem.
Petal—one of the white or colored inner perianth segments (adj: *petaloid*).
Petiole—leaf stalk (adj: *petiolate*).
Phyllary—a bract of the involucre in Asteraceae.
Phyllopodic—in *Carex*, having leaves with blades at the base of the flowering culm (the culm is in its second year of growth).
Pilose—having long soft hairs (more sparsely so than *villous*).
Pinna—a primary division of a fern frond (the whole fern 'leaf' is called a frond). Fronds are divided into main branches, or pinnae; pinnae may be divided further into pinnules).
Pinnate—having veins, lobes, or divisions in the form of a feather, *i.e.*, with one main axis having lateral offshoots.
Pinnatifid—pinnately cleft into segments, but the segments not stalked.
Pinnatisect—pinnately dissected.
Pinnule—a secondary division of a fern frond (a division of a pinna).
Pistil—a vague term applying variously to a carpel or an entire gynoecium (not used in this book).
Placenta—the part of the ovary to which the ovules are attached. Not referring to the stalk of an ovule, but merely to the point of attachment.
Placentation—the mode of attachment of the ovules to the ovary wall (axile, parietal, basal, or free-central).
Plane—level, flat.
Plano-convex—flat on one surface, convex on the other.
Plicate—pleated.
-ploid—suffix referring to numbers of sets of chromosomes; -ploid has no intrinsic meaning, having been cut away from the word diploid [*diplo-oid*], then grafted, part from one stem and part from an-

other, to form *tetraploid*, *hexaploid*, etc.

Plumose—feathery (usually applied to a style, bristle, or awn having delicate side-branches).

Polygamo—bisexual, used with *dioecious* or *monoecious*, implying the presence of perfect as well as unisexual flowers on the same plant.

Pome—the fruit of apples and their close relatives, a fleshy inferior ovary with several carpels.

Posterior—the side of the flower facing the axis of the inflorescence (in *Castilleja*, the upper side).

Processes—a term referring to projecting appendages, otherwise difficult to name, that stand out from a plant organ (e.g., knobs on the fruits of *Atriplex*).

Proliferous—producing new plants as offshoots.

Prostrate—lying flat on the ground.

Proteolytic—capable of destroying proteins.

Propagulum (pl., -a)—means of propagation.

Proximal—nearest the point of attachment.

Pruinose—with a white wax or dusty coating; glaucous.

Pseudoscape—in Apiaceae, a slender, erect, usually partly subterranean, stem connecting the root and the first leaves.

Puberulent—very minutely pubescent.

Pubescent—hairy, a deliberately vague term often used to refer generally to hairiness.

Pustulose—hirsute, with basally swollen trichomes.

Raceme—an elongated inflorescence with a single main axis along which single, stalked flowers are arranged. Compare with *panicle*, *spike*, and *cyme*.

Rachilla—in grasses, the axis within the spikelet; the stalk of the individual floret.

Rachis—the axis of the inflorescence or of a compound leaf.

Ray-flowers—the strap-shaped marginal flowers of Asteraceae. Although they resemble petals, each ray-flower is complete with corolla and, usually, essential organs.

Receptacle—the tip of the floral axis, to which the sepals, petals, stamens and gynoecium are attached.

Reflexed—bent abruptly downward.

Regular—radially symmetrical.

Regularly—evenly, uniformly.

Relict—rare survivor of past times.

Remote—widely separated, as flowers on a raceme.

Reniform—kidney-shaped, broader than long, usually curved.

Repand—of teeth, tending to be directed backward; with slightly uneven margin.

Replum—(in mustards) the partition between the two valves of the fruit.

Reticulate—forming a network.

Retrorse—directed backwards or downwards, like hairs on the nape of the neck.

Retuse—with a shallow notch at a rounded apex.

Revolute—having the margins rolled back or under; opposite of *involute*.

Rhizome—a prostrate underground stem or branch, rooting at the nodes; differs from a root in possessing nodes and internodes, and usually scale leaves. See also *caudex*.

Rhombic—equilateral, with obtuse lateral angles.

Rib—a prominent vein or ridge, particularly on carpel walls.

Riparian—of riversides.

Rootstock—a loose or vague term for the underground parts.

Rosette—a cluster of closely crowded radiating leaves at ground level.

Rosulate—forming a small rosette.

Rotate—wheel-shaped, flat and circular in outline; term applied to very open united corollas.

Ruderal—growing in waste places or among rubbish.

Rugose—wrinkled (dim., *rugulose*).

Runcinate—saw-toothed or sharply incised, the teeth retrorse.

Saccate—bag-shaped.

Sagittate—arrow-shaped, with the basal lobes directed downward.

Salient—projecting, protruding.

Salverform—referring to a narrow tubular corolla that opens out to form a very open dish-like apex, as in primroses.

Samara—an indehiscent winged fruit, such as that of maple.

Saprophytic—depending on dead organic materials for a source of food.

Scabrous—rough to the touch.

Scape—a leafless flower stalk arising from the ground or from a cluster of basal leaves (adj: *scapose*).

Scarious—dry, thin, scale-like, not green.

Schizocarps—carpels of a united gynoecium which separate as indehiscent units, as in *Geranium*.

Scrotiform—pouch-shaped.

Scurfy—minutely scaly in appearance.

Secund—one-sided.

Seed—a ripened ovule.

Seleniferous—containing selenium salts; soils with selenium, and the plants growing on them, usually have a distinctive unpleasant odor. *Selenium*-loving plants are usually toxic.

Sepal—one of the outer perianth segments; a segment of the calyx.

Septate—having obvious cross-partitions, usually referring to hollow lvs.

Septate-nodulose—(in sedges) having minute knob-like partitions crossing between the veins. These can usually be seen without splitting the leaf.

Septicidal—dehiscing by the breaking or separation of the septa dividing the carpels (see *loculicidal*).

Sericeous—silky, clothed with closely pressed soft straight trichomes.

Serrate—having sharp teeth pointing forward, like teeth of a rip-saw (dim: *serrulate*).

Sessile—lacking a stalk.

Setaceous—bristle-like.

Setose—covered with bristles.

Sheath—the basal portion of a lf of a grass-like plant, the part which surrounds the stem.

Sigmoid—'S'-shaped.

Silicle—a short silique.

Silique—the fruit of mustards. A silique consists of two carpel walls, called *valves*, separated by a partition, the *replum*. The seeds are attached to the rim of the replum. At maturity, the valves fall away from the fruit, the replum remaining as a very thin, papery plate. If the silique is flattened parallel to the replum, the valves are flattened against the face of the replum, and the replum is roughly the same shape as the valve. If the silique is flattened perpendicular to the replum, the valves are folded and the replum bisects the face of the silique.

Simple—not branched [stems]; not compound [leaves].

Sinuate—wavy-margined.

Sinus—the cleft or indentation between lobes.

Solifluction—downslope creep of alpine soils aided by subsoil water, commonly resulting in terraces.

Sorus (plural, sori)—a cluster of sporangia. The sori are the dark dots on the underside of fruiting fern fronds.

Spatulate—oblong, but narrowed at the base.

Spicate—arranged in or resembling a spike.

Spike—an elongated inflorescence bearing sessile flowers.

Spikelet—(in grasses and sedges) the smallest unbranched flower cluster in an inflorescence, usually forming a distinct and compact unit.

Spinescent—ending in a spine or sharp point.

Spinulose—having minute spines.

Sporangium—structure containing spores.

Spore—the asexual reproductive cell in ferns (other meanings, not applicable here, also apply).

Sporocarp—[in *Marsilea*] a hard nutlike organ containing sporangia.

Sporophyll—a structure, often lflike, bearing sporangia.

spp—species (plural).

Spur—a hollow projection of a petal or sepal, as in columbine and violet.

Squamellate—having small scales.

Squamiform—scale-like.

Squarrose—spreading or recurved at the tip.

ssp (also subsp)—subspecies.

Stamen—the pollen-producing organ of the flower, situated between the petals and the carpels.

Staminate—having stamens but not carpels.

Staminodia—non-functional stamens, usually lacking well-developed anthers, or with the filament broadened and petal-like; many petals of double flowers (roses) arise from stamens as staminodia.

Stella(ae)—the cluster of rays of a stellate trichome.

Stellate—star-shaped.

Sterile—not producing seed; lacking a gynoecium, or (in stamens) lacking anthers.

Stigma—the part of the style that is receptive to pollen, usually recognized by its sticky, pollen-covered surface.

Stipe—a stalk, as of a gynoecium (adj: *stipitate*).

Stipule—an appendage, sometimes leaflike, sometimes papery, at the base of the petiole of a leaf. Stipules usually occur in pairs.

Stolon—a slender modified stem running along the ground above the soil surface, as in strawberry.

Strap-shaped—oblong, as the ray-flowers of Asteraceae.
Striate—marked with fine longitudinal stripes (striae) or furrows.
Strict—close or narrow and upright, very straight.
Strigose—beset with sharp-pointed straight appressed hairs.
Style—the slender upper part of the carpel or gynoecium. A style is not necessarily present on a gynoecium.
Stylopodium—the enlarged base of the style, as in *Eleocharis* and Apiaceae.
Sub-—prefix meaning *almost*, as in *subequal*.
Submersed—growing under water (same as *submerged*).
Subspecies—a subdivision of a species, usually having a distinct geographic range as well as morphological differences. See *variety*, a term sometimes used for the same thing although the category is lower than that of subspecies.
Subtend—to occur below, as a bract subtends a flower.
Subulate—awl-shaped.
Superior—referring to the gynoecium, when it is attached only at its base and is not fused to the surrounding parts. The ovary is superior even if surrounded by a floral tube or hypanthium (as in rose hips), so long as its wall is not fused to the surrounding parts. See *hypogynous*.
Suture—a junction or seam or union; also, the line of dehiscence. In the pea, the pod splits along the dorsal and ventral sutures. The ovules are attached along the ventral suture.
Syncarpous—having united carpels.

Taproot—a primary, often fleshy, vertical root.
Tawny—tan or brownish.
Taxon—any named taxonomic category (plural, *taxa*), such as a genus, family, or species.
Tendril—a slender clasping or twining threadlike outgrowth of stems or leaves, often a modified leaflet or stipule.
Tepal—one of the segments of a perianth when these are not differentiated into sepals and petals.
Terete—cylindrical; circular in cross-section.
Ternate—compounded into divisions or groups of three.
Tessellate—like a mosaic pavement.
Tetrad—a group of four, as pollen grains.
Tetraploid—having four sets of homologous chromosomes.
Thallus—a relatively undifferentiated plant body, without stems or leaves, as in liverworts.
Thyrse—a compact cylindrical or conical panicle.
Tomentose—densely clothed with woolly or cottony hairs without definite orientation (noun: *tomentum*).
Tor—a prominent isolated rocky outcrop.
Tortuous—bent or twisted in various directions.
Torulose—constricted at intervals.
Travertine—rock formed by the action of hot springs.
Trichome—the specific term for any type of plant hair.
Trifid—split into three parts.
Trifoliolate—having three leaflets.
Trigonous—3-angled, 3-sided (generally applied to akenes).
Triquetrous—three-cornered.

Truncate—abruptly cut off at the end.
Tuber—a fleshy, underground stem, as in potato, or root, as in *Dahlia*.
Tubercle—a small expanded structure, such as the base of the style in some sedges, or very large papillae on fruits.
Tuberculate—having tubercles.
Turbinate—top-shaped; inversely conical.
Turion—a fleshy, scaly winter bud at the base of the stem.
Type—in taxonomy, the original specimen to which the name of a taxon is forever attached.
Type locality—the place from which the original specimen, from which a species was named, came.

Umbel—an inflorescence in which the pedicels radiate from a single point, like the spokes of an umbrella.
Undulate—wavy.
Unisexual—having only stamens or carpels, never both.
Utricle—an inflated akene-like fruit in which the carpel wall loosely invests the single seed (in amaranths).

Valve—one of the pieces into which a capsule splits.
Var—variety.
Variety—a subdivision of a species occupying an area within the range of the species; a minor category lower than subspecies.
Ventral—on the side facing the axis (the upper side of the leaf is its ventral side); adaxial.
Vesicle—a little bladder.
Vesicular—with little bladders.
Vesture—clothing, covering.
Villous—clothed with long, soft hairs, often without special orientation (less matted than *tomentose*).
Vitreous—transparent, hyaline.
Viscid—sticky.

Whorl—a circle or ring of organs. When three or more leaves occur at a node, they are said to be whorled.
Winter annual—a plant that begins growth in the autumn, but flowers, sets seed and dies the following season, as *winter wheat*.

Xerophytes—plants adapted to very dry conditions.

Zygomorphic—bilaterally symmetrical. A zygomorphic flower can be divided only one way to produce mirror images (example: snapdragon).

INDEX TO COMMON NAMES

Agrimony: *Agrimonia*	ROS	Bilberry: *Vaccinium*	ERI
Alder: *Alnus*	BET	Bindweed: *Convolvulus*	CNV
Alfalfa: *Medicago*	FAB	Bindweed, Black: *Fallopia*	PLG
Alkaligrass: *Puccinellia*	POA	Bindweed, Hedge:	
Alum-root: *Heuchera*	SAX	*Calystegia*	CNV
Alyssum, Hoary: *Berteroa*	BRA	Birch: *Betula*	BET
Amaranth: *Amaranthus*	AMA	Bishop's Cap: *Mitella*	SAX
Anemone, Narcissus:		Bistort: *Bistorta*	PLG
Anemonastrum	RAN	Bitterbrush: *Purshia*	ROS
Arabis, False: *Boechera*	BRA	Bitterroot, Pygmy:	
Arrow-grass: *Triglochin*	JCG	*Oreobroma*	POR
Arrowhead: *Sagittaria*	ALI	Bitterroot: *Lewisia*	POR
Ash, Mountain-: *Sorbus*	ROS	Bitterweed: *Tetraneuris*	AST
Ash: *Fraxinus*	OLE	Black-eyed Susan:	
Aspen: *Populus*	SAL	*Rudbeckia*	AST
Aster, Golden: *Heterotheca*	AST	Blackbrush: *Coleogyne*	ROS
Aster, Poison: *Xylorhiza*	AST	Bladder-pod, Double:	
Aster, Sand: *Leucelene*	AST	*Physaria*	BRA
Aster, Tansy:		Bladder-pod: *Lesquerella*	BRA
Machaeranthera	AST	Bladderwort: *Utricularia*	LNT
Aster: *Aster*, *Virgulus*	AST	Blanket-flower: *Gaillardia*	AST
Avens, Alpine: *Acomastylis*	ROS	Blazing Star: *Nuttallia*	LOA
Avens: *Geum*	ROS	Blazing-star: *Liatris*	AST
		Blue-eyed Mary: *Collinsia*	SCR
Baby's-breath: *Gypsophila*	CRY	Blue-eyed-grass:	
Bahia, Desert:		*Sisyrinchium*	IRI
Platyschkuhria	AST	Bluebells: *Campanula*	CAM
Balsam-apple: *Echinocystis*	CUC	Bluebells: *Mertensia*	BOR
Balsam-root: *Balsamorhiza*	AST	Blueberry: *Vaccinium*	ERI
Baneberry: *Actaea*	HEL	Bluegrass: *Poa*	POA
Banner, Golden: *Thermopsis*	FAB	Bluestem, Big: *Andropogon*	POA
Barberry: *Berberis*	BER	Bluestem, Little:	
Barley, Foxtail: *Critesion*	POA	*Schizachyrium*	POA
Barley: *Hordeum*	POA	Bouncing Bet: *Saponaria*	CRY
Barnyard Grass:		Box-elder: *Negundo*	ACE
Echinochloa	POA	Bracken: *Pteridium*	HPL
Basil, Wild: *Clinopodium*	LAM	Bridal Wreath: *Spiraea*	ROS
Bear-claw: *Sclerocactus*	CAC	Bristlegrass: *Setaria*	POA
Bearberry: *Arctostaphylos*	ERI	Brittle Fern: *Cystopteris*	ATY
Beard-tongue: *Penstemon*	SCR	Brome, Keeled: *Ceratochloa*	POA
Beardgrass, Silver:		Brome, Perennial:	
Bothriochloa	POA	*Bromopsis*	POA
Bedstraw: *Galium*	RUB	Brome: *Bromus*	POA
Bee Balm: *Monarda*	LAM	Brookgrass: *Catabrosa*	POA
Bee-plant: *Cleome*	CPP	Brooklime: *Veronica*	SCR
Beggar's Tick: *Bidens*	AST	Broom-rape: *Orobanche*	ORO
Beggar's Tick: *Lappula*	BOR	Buckbean: *Menyanthes*	MNY
Begonia, Wild:		Buckbrush: *Ceanothus*	RHM
Rumex venosus	PLG	Buckthorn: *Rhamnus*	RHM
Bellwort: *Disporum*	UVU	Buckwheat, Japanese:	
Bentgrass: *Agrostis*	POA	*Reynoutria*	PLG
Bermuda Grass: *Cynodon*	POA	Buckwheat, Wild: *Eriogonum*	PLG

Buckwheat, Winged:
  Pterogonum — PLG
Buffalo-berry: *Shepherdia* — ELE
Buffalograss, False:
  Monroa — POA
Bugleweed: *Lycopus* — LAM
Bugseed: *Corispermum* — CHN
Bulrush: *Scirpus* — CYP
Bunchberry:
  Chamaepericlymenum — COR
Bur-cucumber: *Echinocystis* — CUC
Bur-reed: *Sparganium* — SPG
Burdock: *Arctium* — AST
Burnet: *Sanguisorba* — ROS
Bush Honeysuckle: *Distegia* — CPR
Butter-and-eggs: *Linaria* — SCR
Buttercup, Blister:
  Hecatonia — RAN
Buttercup: *Ranunculus* — RAN
Butterfly-weed: *Asclepias* — ASC
Butterweed: *Senecio* — AST
Buyan: *Sphaerophysa* — FAB

Cactus, Ball: *Pediocactus* — CAC
Cactus, Hedge-hog:
  Echinocereus — CAC
Cactus, Nipple:
  Coryphantha — CAC
Cactus, Potato: *Opuntia* — CAC
Cactus, Sitting:
  Echinocereus — CAC
Cactus, Strawberry:
  Echinocereus — CAC
Camas, Death: *Anticlea* — MLN
Camas, Death:
  Toxicoscordion — MLN
Campion: *Gastrolychnis*,
  Melandrium, Silene — CRY
Canaigre:
  Rumex hymenosepalus — PLG
Canarygrass, Reed:
  Phalaroides — POA
Candytuft, Wild: *Noccaea* — BRA
Caraway: *Carum* — API
Carnation: *Dianthus* — CRY
Cat-tail: *Typha* — TYP
Catchfly: *Silene* — CRY
Catnip: *Nepeta* — LAM
Cedar: *Sabina* — CUP
Centaury: *Centaurium* — GEN
Chainpod: *Hedysarum* — FAB
Chamomile: *Anthemis* — AST
Chamomile: *Matricaria* — AST
Cheatgrass: *Anisantha* — POA

Chickweed: *Alsine* — ASN
Chickweed: *Stellaria* — ASN
Chicory: *Cichorium* — AST
Chiming Bells: *Mertensia* — BOR
Chives: *Allium* — ALL
Choke-cherry: *Padus* — ROS
Cholla: *Cylindropuntia* — CAC
Christmas Fern:
  Polystichum — ASD
Cinquefoil: *Potentilla* — ROS
Cinquefoil, Purple:
  Comarum — ROS
Cinquefoil, Shrubby:
  Pentaphylloides — ROS
Clammyweed: *Polanisia* — CPP
Clematis, Blue: *Atragene* — RAN
Clematis, Oriental:
  Viticella — RAN
Cliff Brake: *Cryptogramma* — CRG
Cliff Brake: *Pellaea* — SIN
Cliff-rose: *Cowania* — ROS
Clover, Owl-: *Orthocarpus* — SCR
Clover, Sweet-: *Melilotus* — FAB
Clover: *Trifolium* — FAB
Club-moss, Fir: *Huperzia* — LYC
Club-moss: *Lycopodium* — LYC
Clubflower: *Cordylanthus* — SCR
Cocklebur: *Xanthium* — AST
Cuckoldbur: *Xanthium* — AST
Coltsfoot, Sweet:
  Petasites — AST
Columbine: *Aquilegia* — HEL
Comfrey: *Symphytum* — BOR
Coneflower, Prairie:
  Ratibida — AST
Coral-root: *Corallorhiza* — ORC
Cordgrass: *Spartina* — POA
Cornflower: *Jacea* — AST
Cotton-sedge: *Eriophorum* — CYP
Cottonwood: *Populus* — SAL
Cow Cockle: *Vaccaria* — CRY
Cowbane: *Oxypolis* — API
Crabgrass: *Digitaria* — POA
Cranberry, Bush-: *Viburnum* — CPR
Crane's Bill: *Erodium* — GER
Cress, Bitter: *Cardamine* — BRA
Cress, Penny-: *Thlaspi* — BRA
Cress, Rock: *Arabis* — BRA
Cress, Water-: *Nasturtium* — BRA
Cress, Winter: *Barbarea* — BRA
Cress, Yellow-: *Rorippa* — BRA
Crowfoot, Alkali:
  Halerpestes — RAN
Crowfoot, Water: *Batrachium* — RAN

Crown, King's: *Rhodiola*	CRS	Fir: *Abies*	PIN
Crown, Rose: *Clementsia*	CRS	Fireweed: *Chamerion*	ONA
Crownbeard: *Ximenesia*	AST	Five-finger: *Potentilla*	ROS
Cudweed: *Filaginella*	AST	Flax, Cultivated: *Linum*	LIN
Cudweed: *Gnaphalium*	AST	Flax, False: *Camelina*	BRA
Currant: *Ribes*	GRS	Flax, Wild Blue:	
Cutgrass, Rice: *Leersia*	POA	*Adenolinum*	LIN
		Flax, Yellow: *Mesynium*	LIN
Daisy, Cow-pen: *Ximenesia*	AST	Fleabane: *Erigeron*	AST
Daisy, Easter: *Townsendia*	AST	Flower-of-an-hour:	
Daisy, Ox-eye:		*Hibiscus*	MLV
Leucanthemum	AST	Fluffgrass: *Dasyochloa*	POA
Daisy: *Erigeron*	AST	Forget-me-not, Alpine:	
Dallis Grass: *Paspalum*	POA	*Eritrichum*	BOR
Dandelion, Desert:		Forget-me-not: *Myosotis*	BOR
Malacothrix	AST	Four-o'clock: *Mirabilis*	NYC
Dandelion, False: *Agoseris*	AST	Foxtail Barley: *Critesion*	POA
Dandelion: *Taraxacum*	AST	Foxtail: *Alopecurus*	POA
Dayflower: *Commelina*	CMM	Fritillary: *Fritillaria*	LIL
Dead-nettle: *Galeopsis*	LAM		
Dead-nettle: *Lamium*	LAM	Galleta Grass: *Hilaria*	POA
Ditch-grass: *Ruppia*	RUP	Gentian, Arctic:	
Dock: *Rumex*	PLG	*Gentianodes*	GEN
Dodder: *Grammica*	CUS	Gentian, Bottle:	
Dogbane: *Apocynum*	APO	*Pneumonanthe*	GEN
Douglas-fir: *Pseudotsuga*	PIN	Gentian, Fringed:	
Dragonhead: *Dracocephalum*	LAM	*Gentianopsis*	GEN
Dropseed: *Sporobolus*	POA	Gentian, Green: *Frasera*	GEN
Dropseed, Pine:		Gentian, Lappland:	
Blepharoneuron,	POA	*Comastoma*	GEN
Dryad, Mountain: *Dryas*	ROS	Gentian, Little:	
Duckweed: *Lemna*	LMN	*Gentianella*	GEN
Dwarf Mistletoe:		Gentian, Siberian:	
Arceuthobium	VIS	*Chondrophylla*	GEN
		Gentian, Star: *Swertia*	GEN
Elderberry: *Sambucus*	CPR	Germander: *Teucrium*	LAM
Elm: *Ulmus*	ULM	Gilia, Prickly:	
Espanta Vaquero:		*Leptodactylon*	PLM
Cladothrix	AMA	Gilia, Trumpet: *Ipomopsis*	PLM
Evening-primrose: *Oenothera*,		Gill-over-the-ground:	
Camissonia, Calylophus	ONA	*Glecoma*	LAM
Everlasting, Pearly:		Glasswort: *Salicornia*	CHN
Anaphalis	AST	Globe-flower: *Trollius*	HEL
		Goatgrass: *Cylindropyrum*	POA
Fairy Slipper: *Calypso*	ORC	Golden Carpet:	
Fanweed: *Thlaspi*	BRA	*Chrysosplenium*	SAX
Feathergrass: *Ptilagrostis*	POA	Goldenrod, Rock:	
Felwort, Marsh:		*Petradoria*	AST
Lomatogonium	GEN	Goldenrod: *Solidago*	AST
Fescue: *Festuca*	POA	Gooseberry: *Ribes*	GRS
Fescue, Six-weeks: *Vulpia*	POA	Goosefoot: *Chenopodium*	CHN
Fescue, Spike: *Leucopoa*	POA	Goosegrass: *Eleusine*	POA
Figwort: *Scrophularia*	SCR	Gourd: *Cucurbita*	CUC
Filaree: *Erodium*	GER	Grama: *Bouteloua*	POA

Grape Fern: *Botrychium*	OPH	Ironweed: *Bassia*	CHN
Grape, Holly-, or Oregon-: *Mahonia*	BER	Jacob's Ladder: *Polemonium*	PLM
		Jasmine, Rock-: *Androsace*	PRM
Grass-of-Parnassus: *Parnassia*	PAR	Jimsonweed: *Datura*	SOL
		Junegrass: *Koeleria*	POA
Greasewood: *Sarcobatus*	CHN	Juniper: *Juniperus, Sabina*	CUP
Ground-cherry: *Physalis*	SOL		
Ground-ivy: *Glecoma*	LAM	Kinnikinnik: *Arctostaphylos*	ERI
Groundsel-tree: *Baccharis*	AST	Kittentail: *Besseya*	SCR
Groundsel: *Senecio*	AST	Knapweed, Russian: *Acroptilon*	AST
Gumweed: *Grindelia*	AST		
		Knotweed: *Polygonum*	PLG
Hackberry: *Celtis*	ULM		
Hairgrass, Tufted: *Deschampsia*	POA	Lady Fern: *Athyrium*	ATY
		Lady's Slipper: *Cypripedium*	CPD
Harebell: *Campanula*	CAM		
Hare's Ear: *Conringia*	BRA	Lady's Tresses: *Spiranthes*	ORC
Hawksbeard, Alpine: *Askellia*	AST	Lamb's Quarters: *Chenopodium*	CHN
Hawksbeard, American: *Psilochenia*	AST	Larkspur: *Delphinium*	HEL
		Laurel, Pale or Swamp: *Kalmia*	ERI
Hawkweed: *Chlorocrepis*	AST		
Hawthorn: *Crataegus*	ROS	Leatherflower: *Coriflora*	RAN
Heal-all: *Prunella*	LAM	Lettuce, White-: *Prenanthes*	AST
Heliotrope, Bindweed: *Euploca*	BOR	Lettuce: *Lactuca*	AST
		Lily, Alp: *Lloydia*	LIL
Heliotrope: *Heliotropium*	BOR	Lily, Avalanche: *Erythronium*	LIL
Hellebore, False: *Veratrum*	MLN		
Helleborine: *Epipactis*	ORC	Lily, Corn Husk: *Veratrum*	MLN
Hemlock, Poison: *Conium*	API	Lily, Sand: *Leucocrinum*	LIL
Hemlock, Water: *Cicuta*	API	Lily, Sego: *Calochortus*	CCT
Hemlock-parsley: *Conioselinum*	API	Lily, Yellow Pond-: *Nuphar*	NYM
		Lily: *Lilium*	LIL
Hemp, Indian: *Apocynum*	APO	Lip Fern: *Cheilanthes*	SIN
Henbane: *Hyoscyamus*	SOL	Liquorice, Wild: *Glycyrrhiza*	FAB
Hollyhock, Wild: *Iliamna*	MLV		
Honeysuckle: *Lonicera*	CPR	Little Club-moss: *Selaginella*	SEL
Hop-sage: *Atriplex*	CHN		
Hops: *Humulus*	CAN	Loco: *Oxytropis*	FAB
Horehound, Water: *Lycopus*	LAM	Loco, White: *Vexibia*	FAB
Horehound: *Marrubium*	LAM	Locust: *Robinia*	FAB
Hornhead: *Ceratocephala*	RAN	Loosestrife, Fringed: *Steironema*	PRM
Hornwort: *Ceratophyllum*	CRT		
Horsebrush: *Tetradymia*	AST	Loosestrife, Purple: *Lythrum*	LYT
Horsetail: *Equisetum*	EQU		
Horseweed: *Conyza*	AST	Lousewort: *Pedicularis*	SCR
Hound's Tongue: *Cynoglossum*	BOR	Lovage: *Ligusticum*	API
		Lovegrass: *Eragrostis*	POA
Huckleberry: *Vaccinium*	ERI	Lupine: *Lupinus*	FAB
Hyacinth, Wild: *Androstephium*	ALL		
		Madwort: *Asperugo*	BOR
Hyssop, Giant: *Agastache*	LAM	Mahogany, Mountain-: *Cercocarpus*	ROS
Hyssop, Hedge-: *Gratiola*	SCR		
Hyssop, Water-: *Bacopa*	SCR		

Maidenhair Fern: *Adiantum*	ADI	Nailwort: *Paronychia*	ASN
Mallow, Checker: *Sidalcea*	MLV	Needlegrass: *Stipa*	POA
Mallow, Globe: *Sphaeralcea*	MLV	Nettle, Hedge-: *Stachys*	LAM
Mannagrass: *Glyceria*	POA	Nettle: *Urtica*	URT
Manzanita: *Arctostaphylos*	ERI	Nightshade, Enchantress':	
Maple: *Acer*	ACE	*Circaea*	ONA
Mare's Tail: *Hippuris*	HPU	Nightshade: *Solanum*	SOL
Marigold, Fetid: *Dyssodia*	AST	Ninebark: *Physocarpus*	ROS
Marigold, Marsh-: *Psychrophila*	HEL	Oak Fern: *Gymnocarpium*	ATY
Marijuana: *Cannabis*	CAN	Oak: *Quercus*	FAG
Mariposa: *Calochortus*	CCT	Oat: *Avena*	POA
Marsh-elder: *Cyclachaena*	AST	Oat, Alpine:	
Matrimony-vine: *Lycium*	SOL	*Helictotrichon*	POA
Meadow-rue: *Thalictrum*	RAN	Oat, Mountain: *Avenula*	POA
Medic: *Medicago*	FAB	Oatgrass: *Danthonia*	POA
Mermaid, False: *Floerkea*	LIL	Oatgrass, Tall:	
Milfoil, Water: *Myriophyllum*	HAL	*Arrhenatherum*	POA
		Ocean Spray: *Holodiscus*	ROS
Milkweed: *Asclepias*	ASC	Old-man-of-the-mountain:	
Milkwort, Sea: *Glaux*	PRM	*Rydbergia*	AST
Milkwort: *Polygala*	PGL	Onion: *Allium*	ALL
Mint, Horse: *Monarda*	LAM	Oniongrass: *Bromelica*	POA
Mint: *Mentha*	LAM	Oniongrass: *Melica*	POA
Mistletoe, Dwarf: *Arceuthobium*	VIS	Orache: *Atriplex*	CHN
		Orchard Grass: *Dactylis*	POA
Mistletoe, Juniper: *Phoradendron*	VIS	Orchid, Bog: *Limnorchis*	ORC
		Osage-orange: *Maclura*	MOR
Mock-orange: *Philadelphus*	HDR	Oshá: *Ligusticum*	API
Monkey-flower: *Mimulus*	SCR	Oysterplant: *Tragopogon*	AST
Monkshood: *Aconitum*	HEL		
Monument Plant: *Frasera*	GEN	Paintbrush: *Castilleja*	SCR
Moonwort: *Botrychium*	OPH	Panic Grass: *Panicum*	POA
Mormon Tea: *Ephedra*	EPH	Paper-flower: *Psilostrophe*	AST
Moschatel: *Adoxa*	ADX	Parsley Family: *Apiaceae*	API
Mountain-lover: *Paxistima*	CEL	Parsley, Alpine: *Oreoxis*	API
Mouse-ear: *Cerastium*	ASN	Parsnip, Cow: *Heracleum*	API
Mousetail: *Myosurus*	RAN	Parsnip, Water: *Berula*	API
Mudwort: *Limosella*	SCR	Parsnip, Water: *Sium*	API
Muhly: *Muhlenbergia*	POA	Parsnip: *Pastinaca*	API
Mulberry: *Morus*	MOR	Pasqueflower: *Pulsatilla*	RAN
Mule's Ears: *Wyethia*	AST	Pearlwort: *Sagina*	ASN
Mullein: *Verbascum*	SCR	Peavine: *Lathyrus*	FAB
Mustard, Jim Hill: *Sisymbrium*	BRA	Pellitory: *Parietaria*	URT
		Pennyroyal: *Hedeoma*	LAM
Mustard, Purple: *Chorispora*	BRA	Peppergrass: *Lepidium*	BRA
		Pepperwort: *Marsilea*	NSL
Mustard, Skeleton: *Schoenocrambe*	BRA	Pigweed, Winged: *Cycloloma*	CHN
		Pincushion: *Chaenactis*	AST
Mustard, Syrian: *Euclidium*	BRA	Pine: *Pinus*	PIN
Mustard, Tansy: *Descurainia*	BRA	Pineapple Weed: *Lepidotheca*	AST
		Pinedrops: *Pterospora*	MNT
Mustard, Tower: *Turritis*	BRA	Pinesap: *Hypopitys*	MNT
Mustard: *Brassica*	BRA		

Pink: *Dianthus*	CRY	Rowan Tree: *Sorbus*	ROS
Pipsissewa: *Chimaphila*	PYR	Rush, Wood-: *Luzula*	JUN
Plantain, Rattlesnake-: *Goodyera*	ORC	Rush: *Juncus*	JUN
		Russian-olive: *Elaeagnus*	ELE
Plantain: *Plantago*	PTG	Rye: *Secale*	POA
Plume, Prince's: *Stanleya*	BRA	Rye, Giant Wild: *Leymus*	POA
Poison Ivy, Oak: *Toxicodendron*	ANA	Rye, Russian Wild: *Psathyrostachys*	POA
Polypody: *Polypodium*	PLP	Rye, Wild: *Elymus*, *Leymus*	POA
Pondweed, Horned: *Zannichellia*	ZAN	Ryegrass: *Lolium*	POA
Pondweed: *Potamogeton*	POT	Sage: *Salvia*	LAM
Poppy, California: *Eschscholzia*	PAP	Sagebrush: *Seriphidium*	AST
		Sagebrush, Spiny: *Picrothamnus*	AST
Poppy, Prickly: *Argemone*	PAP		
Poppy: *Papaver*	PAP	Sagewort: *Artemisia, Oligosporus*	AST
Poverty Weed: *Iva*	AST		
Poverty Weed: *Monolepis*	CHN	Salsify: *Tragopogon*	AST
Prairie Smoke: *Erythrocoma*	ROS	Saltbush: *Atriplex*	CHN
Prickly-pear: *Opuntia*	CAC	Saltgrass: *Distichlis*	POA
Primrose: *Primula*	PRM	Sand Spurry: *Spergularia*	ASN
Prince's Pine: *Chimaphila*	PYR	Sand-aster: *Leucelene*	AST
Privet, Wild: *Forestiera*	OLE	Sand-bur: *Ambrosia*	AST
Puccoon: *Lithospermum*	BOR	Sand-bur: *Cenchrus*	POA
Puncture-vine: *Tribulus*	ZYG	Sand-verbena: *Abronia, Tripterocalyx*	NYC
Purslane: *Portulaca*	POR		
Pussy-toes: *Antennaria*	AST	Sandwort, Alpine: *Lidia*	ASN
		Sandwort, Desert: *Eremogone*	ASN
Quack Grass: *Elytrigia*	POA		
Queen Anne's Lace: *Daucus*	API	Sarsaparilla: *Aralia*	ARL
Quillwort: *Isoëtes*	ISO	Saxifrage: *Micranthes, Saxifraga*	SAX
Rabbitbrush: *Chrysothamnus*	AST	Saxifrage, Moss: *Muscaria*	SAX
Rabbitfoot Grass: *Polypogon*	POA	Saxifrage, Spotted: *Ciliaria*	SAX
Ragweed: *Ambrosia*	AST	Saxifraga, Star: *Lithophragma*	SAX
Raspberry: *Rubus*	ROS		
Raspberry, Arctic: *Cylactis*	ROS	Saxifrage, Golden: *Hirculus*	SAX
Raspberry, Boulder: *Oreobatus*	ROS	Scouring-rush: *Hippochaete*	EQU
		Sea-blite: *Suaeda*	CHN
Rattlesnake Fern: *Botrypus*	OPH	Sedum: *Amerosedum, Clementsia, Rhodiola, Sedum*	CRS
Rattlesnake Grass: *Bromus*	POA		
Red-osier: *Swida*	COR		
Reed, Common: *Phragmites*	POA	Sego Lily: *Calochortus*	CCT
Rhododendron, White: *Azaleastrum*	ERI	Self-heal: *Prunella*	LAM
		Serviceberry: *Amelanchier*	ROS
Ricegrass: *Oryzopsis*	POA	Shad-scale: *Atriplex*	CHN
Ricegrass, False: *Argillochloa*	POA	Shepherd's Purse: *Capsella*	BRA
		Shield Fern: *Dryopteris*	ASD
Ripgut Grass: *Anisantha*	POA	Shinleaf: *Pyrola*	PYR
Rock Brake: *Cryptogramma*	CRG	Shooting-star: *Dodecatheon*	POR
Rose: *Rosa*	ROS	Silverberry: *Shepherdia*	ELE
Rose, Cliff-: *Purshia*	ROS	Silverweed: *Argentina*	ROS

Skeleton-weed: *Lygodesmia*	AST	Sunflower, Little:	
Skullcap: *Scutellaria*	LAM	*Helianthella*	AST
Sky Pilot: *Polemonium*	PLM	Sweet Cicely: *Osmorhiza*	API
Sloughgrass: *Beckmannia*	POA		
Smartweed: *Persicaria*	PLG	Tamarisk: *Tamarix*	TAM
Smoke, Golden: *Corydalis*	FUM	Tansy: *Tanacetum*	AST
Snakeroot: *Sanicula*	API	Tarragon: *Oligosporus*	AST
Snakeweed: *Gutierrezia*	AST	Tarweed: *Madia*	AST
Sneezeweed, Orange:		Tassel-rue: *Trautvetteria*	RAN
Dugaldia	AST	Teasel: *Dipsacus*	DPS
Sneezeweed: *Helenium*	AST	Thimbleberry: *Rubacer*	ROS
Snow-lover: *Chionophila*	SCR	Thistle: *Carduus, Cirsium*	AST
Snow-on-the-mountain:		Thistle, Musk: *Carduus*	AST
Agaloma	EUP	Thistle, Russian-: *Salsola*	CHN
Snowberry: *Symphoricarpos*	CPR	Thistle, Scotch: *Onopordum*	AST
Soapwort: *Saponaria*	CRY	Three-awn: *Aristida*	POA
Solomon's Seal, False:		Thrift: *Armeria*	LMO
Maianthemum	CVL	Tickseed: *Corispermum*	CHN
Sorrel, Alpine: *Oxyria*	PLG	Timothy: *Phleum*	POA
Sorrel, Sheep: *Acetosella*	PLG	Toadflax, Bastard-:	
Sorrel, Wood-: *Oxalis*	OXL	*Comandra*	SAN
Sow-thistle: *Sonchus*	AST	Toadflax: *Linaria*	SCR
Spanish Bayonet: *Yucca*	AGA	Tobacco: *Nicotiana*	SOL
Spectacle-pod:		Tree of Heaven: *Ailanthus*	SMR
Dimorphocarpa	BRA	Trefoil, Marsh: *Menyanthes*	MNY
Speedwell: *Veronica*	SCR	Tridens, Hairy: *Erioneuron*	POA
Speedwell, Thyme-leaved:		Trumpet Creeper: *Campsis*	BIG
Veronicastrum	SCR	Tuber Starwort:	
Spiderwort: *Tradescantia*	CMM	*Pseudostellaria*	ASN
Spike-rush: *Eleocharis*	CYP	Tule: *Schoenoplectus*	CYP
Spikenard: *Aralia*	ARL	Tumblegrass: *Scheddonardus*	POA
Spiraea, Rock-:		Turkeyfoot: *Andropogon*	POA
Petrophyton	ROS	Twayblade: *Listera*	ORC
Spleenwort: *Asplenium*	ASL	Twinflower: *Linnaea*	CPR
Spring Beauty: *Claytonia*	POR	Twisted-stalk: *Streptopus*	UVU
Spring Beauty, Water:		Twistflower: *Streptanthus*	BRA
Crunocallis	POR		
Spruce: *Picea*	PIN	Umbrellawort: *Oxybaphus*	NYC
Squaw-apple: *Peraphyllum*	ROS		
Squirreltail: *Elymus*	POA	Valerian: *Valeriana*	VAL
St. Johnswort: *Hypericum*	HYP	Velvetleaf: *Abutilon*	MLV
Starwort, Water:		Venus' Hair Fern: *Adiantum*	ADI
Callitriche	CLL	Vervain: *Verbena*	VRB
Stickseed: *Hackelia,*		Vervain, Showy:	
Lappula	BOR	*Glandularia*	VRB
Stinkweed: *Cleomella*	CPP	Vetch: *Vicia*	FAB
Stitchwort: *Stellaria*	ASN	Vetch, Crown: *Coronilla*	FAB
Stonecrop, Yellow:		Vetch, Milk: *Astragalus*	FAB
Amerosedum	CRS	Violet: *Viola*	VIO
Strawberry: *Fragaria*	ROS	Virgin's Bower: *Clematis*	RAN
Sugarbowls: *Coriflora*	RAN	Virginia Creeper:	
Sumac: *Rhus*	ANA	*Parthenocissus*	VIT
Sundew: *Drosera*	DRS		
Sunflower: *Helianthus*	AST	Wake-robin: *Trillium*	TRI

Wallflower: *Erysimum*	BRA	Wheatgrass, Blue-bunch:	POA
Water-nymph: *Najas*	NAJ	*Pseudoroegneria*	
Water-plantain: *Alisma*	ALI	Wheatgrass, Crested:	POA
Waterleaf: *Hydrophyllum*	HYD	*Agropyron*	
Waterweed: *Elodea*	HDC	Wheatgrass, Intermediate:	POA
Waterwort: *Elatine*	ELT	*Elytrigia*	
Wheat: *Triticum*	POA	Wheatgrass, Tall:	POA
Wheatgrass: *Elymus*	POA	*Lophopyrum*	
Wheatgrass, Annual:	POA	Wheatgrass, Western:	POA
Eremopyrum		*Pascopyrum*	
		White-top: *Cardaria*	BRA

INDEX TO GENERA

Names of genera are on the left. If I do not accept a genus, the name is followed by (see . . .). If I have divided a genus, the name is followed by (also . . .). Instead of page references, the right-hand column gives the family acronym. Since families are alphabetically organized, the acronym is a convenient finding device even though the acronyms do not strictly parallel the spelling of families. Acronyms for Fern and Gymnosperm families are preceded by F or G.

Abies	G-PIN	*Alopecurus*	POA
Abronia	NYC	*Alsinanthe*	ASN
Abutilon	MLV	*Alsine*	ASN
Acer (also *Negundo*)	ACE	*Alyssum*	BRA
Acetosella	PLG	*Amaranthus*	AMA
Achillea	AST	*Ambrosia*	AST
Acomastylis	ROS	*Amelanchier*	ROS
Aconitum	HEL	*Amerosedum*	CRS
Acosta	AST	*Ammannia*	LYT
Acrolasia	LOA	*Amphiscirpus*	CYP
Acroptilon	AST	*Amsonia*	APO
Actaea	HEL	*Anaphalis*	AST
Adenolinum	LIN	*Andropogon* (also *Bothriochloa*	
Adiantum	ADI	*Schizachyrium*)	POA
Adoxa	ADX	*Androsace*	PRM
Agaloma	EUP	*Androstephium*	ALL
Agastache	LAM	*Anemonastrum*	RAN
Ageratina	AST	*Anemone*	RAN
Agoseris	AST	*Angelica*	API
Agrimonia	ROS	*Anisantha*	POA
Agropyron (also *Pascopyrum*,		*Anotites*	CRY
Pseudoroegneria)	POA	*Antennaria*	AST
Agrostis	POA	*Anthemis*	AST
Ailanthus	SMR	*Anticlea*	MLN
Aletes (*Lomatium*,		*Apocynum*	APO
Cymopterus in part)	API	*Aquilegia*	HEL
Alisma	ALI	*Arabis* (also *Boechera*,	
Allionia	NYC	*Turritis*)	BRA
Allium	ALL	*Aralia*	ARL
Alnus	BET	*Arceuthobium*	VIS

Index to Genera

Arctium	AST
Arctostaphylos	ERI
Arenaria (also *Alsinanthe*, *Eremogone*, *Lidia*, *Minuartia*, *Pseudostellaria*, *Spergulastrum*, *Tryphane*)	ASN
Argemone	PAP
Argentina	ROS
Argillochloa	POA
Aristida	POA
Armeria	LMO
Arnica	AST
Arrhenatherum	POA
Artemisia (also *Oligosporus*, *Picrothamnus*, *Seriphidium*)	AST
Asclepias	ASC
Askellia	AST
Asparagus	ASG
Asperugo	BOR
Asplenium	F-ASL
Aster (also *Brachyactis*, *Eucephalus*, *Machaeranthera*, *Virgulus*)	AST
Astragalus	FAB
Athyrium	F-ATY
Atragene	RAN
Atriplex	CHN
Avena	POA
Avenula	POA
Avenochloa (see *Avenula*)	POA
Axyris	CHN
Azaleastrum	ERI
Baccharis	AST
Bacopa	SCR
Baeothryon	CYP
Bahia (also *Platyschkuhria*)	AST
Balsamorhiza	AST
Barbarea	BRA
Bassia	CHN
Batrachium	RAN
Beckmannia	POA
Berberis (also *Mahonia*)	BER
Berteroa	BRA
Berula	API
Besseya	SCR
Betula	BET
Bidens	AST
Bistorta	PLG
Blepharoneuron	POA
Boechera	BRA
Bolboschoenus	CYP
Bolophyta	AST
Bothriochloa	POA
Botrychium (also *Botrypus*)	F-OPH
Botrypus	F-OPH
Bouteloua	POA
Brachyactis	AST
Brassica	BRA
Braya	BRA
Brickellia	AST
Bromelica	POA
Bromopsis	POA
Bromus (also *Anisantha*, *Bromopsis*, *Ceratochloa*)	POA
Bupleurum	API
Calamagrostis	POA
Callitriche	CLL
Calochortus	CCO
Caltha (see *Psychrophila*)	HEL
Calylophus	ONA
Calypso	ORC
Calystegia	CNV
Camelina	BRA
Camissonia	ONA
Campanula	CAM
Campsis	BIG
Cannabis	CAN
Capsella	BRA
Cardamine	BRA
Cardaria	BRA
Carduus	AST
Carex	CYP
Carum	API
Castilleja	SCR
Catabrosa	POA
Cathartolinum	LIN
Caulanthus	BRA
Ceanothus	RHM
Celtis	ULM
Cenchrus	POA
Centaurea (see *Acosta*, *Acroptilon*, *Jacea*, *Leucacantha*)	AST
Centaurium	GEN
Cerastium	ASN
Ceratocephala	RAN
Ceratochloa	POA
Ceratophyllum	CRT
Cercocarpus	ROS
Chaenactis	AST
Chamaechaenactis	AST
Chamaepericlymenum	COR
Chamaerhodos	ROS
Chamaesaracha	SOL
Chamaesyce	EUP

Index to Genera

Chamerion	ONA	Crepis (see *Askellia*,	
Cheilanthes	F-SIN	*Psilochenia*)	AST
Chenopodium (also *Teloxys*)	CHN	Critesion	POA
Chimaphila	PYR	Croton	EUP
Chionophila	SCR	Crunocallis	POR
Chloris	POA	Cryptantha (also *Oreocarya*)	BOR
Chlorocrepis	AST	Cryptogramma	F-CRG
Chondrophylla	GEN	Cucurbita	CUC
Chorispora	BRA	Cuscuta (see *Grammica*)	CUS
Chrysosplenium	SAX	Cyclachaena	AST
Chrysothamnus	AST	Cycloloma	CHN
Cichorium	AST	Cylactis	ROS
Cicuta	API	Cylindropuntia	CAC
Ciliaria	SAX	Cylindropyrum	POA
Ciminalis		Cymopterus	API
(see *Chondrophylla*)	GEN	Cynodon	POA
Cinna	POA	Cynoglossum	BOR
Circaea	ONA	Cyperus	CYP
Cirsium	AST	Cypripedium	CPD
Cladothrix	AMA	Cyrtorhyncha	RAN
Claytonia	POR	Cystopteris	F-ATY
Clematis (also *Atragene*,			
Coriflora, *Viticella*)	RAN	Dactylis	POA
Clementsia	CRS	Danthonia	POA
Cleome	CPP	Dasyochloa	POA
Cleomella	CPP	Datura	SOL
Clinopodium	LAM	Daucus	API
Coeloglossum	ORC	Delphinium	HEL
Coleogyne	ROS	Deschampsia	POA
Collinsia	SCR	Descurainia	BRA
Collomia	PLM	Dichanthelium	POA
Comandra	SAN	Dicoria	AST
Comarum	ROS	Digitaria	POA
Comastoma	GEN	Dimorphocarpa	BRA
Commelina	CMM	Diplachne (see *Leptochloa*)	POA
Conimitella	SAX	Dipsacus	DPS
Conioselinum	API	Disporum	UVU
Conium	API	Distegia	CPR
Conringia	BRA	Distichlis	POA
Convolvulus	CNV	Dithyrea	
Conyza	AST	(see *Dimorphocarpa*)	BRA
Corallorhiza	ORC	Dodecatheon	PRM
Cordylanthus	SCR	Draba	BRA
Coreopsis	AST	Dracocephalum	LAM
Coriflora	RAN	Drosera	DRS
Corispermum	CHN	Dryas	ROS
Cornus (see *Chamaeperi-*		Drymocallis	ROS
clymenum, *Swida*)	COR	Dryopteris	F-ASD
Coronilla	FAB	Dugaldia	AST
Corydalis	FUM	Dyssodia	AST
Coryphantha	CAC		
Cosmos	AST	Echinocereus	CAC
Cowania (see *Purshia*)	ROS	Echinochloa	POA
Crataegus	ROS	Echinocystis	CUC

Elaeagnus	ELE	*Fragaria*	ROS
Elatine	ELT	*Frankenia*	FRK
Eleocharis	CYP	*Franseria* (see *Ambrosia*)	AST
Eleusine	POA	*Frasera*	GEN
Ellisia	HYD	*Fraxinus*	OLE
Elodea	HDC	*Fritillaria*	LIL
Elymus (also *Elytrigia*, *Eremopyrum*, *Leymus*, *Lophopyrum*, *Psathyrostachys*)	POA	*Gaillardia*	AST
		Galeopsis	LAM
Elytrigia	POA	*Galium*	RUB
Enceliopsis	AST	*Gastrolychnis*	CRY
Ephedra	G-EPH	*Gaultheria*	ERI
Epilobium (also *Chamerion*)	ONA	*Gaura*	ONA
Epipactis	ORC	*Gayophytum*	ONA
Equisetum (also *Hippochaete*)	F-EQU	*Gentiana* (see *Comastoma*, *Chondrophylla*, *Gentianella*, *Gentianodes*, *Gentianopsis*, *Pneumonanthe*)	GEN
Eragrostis	POA		
Eremogone	ASN	*Gentianella*	GEN
Eremopyrum	POA	*Gentianodes*	GEN
Eriastrum	PLM	*Gentianopsis*	GEN
Erigeron	AST	*Geranium*	GER
Eriogonum (also *Pterogonum*, *Stenogonum*)	PLG	*Geum* (also *Acomastylis*, *Erythrocoma*)	ROS
Erioneuron	POA	*Gilia* (also *Ipomopsis*)	PLM
Eriophorum	CYP	*Glandularia*	VRB
Eritrichum	BOR	*Glaux*	PRM
Erocallis	POR	*Glecoma*	LAM
Erodium	GER	*Glyceria*	POA
Erysimum	BRA	*Glycyrrhiza*	FAB
Erythrocoma	ROS	*Gnaphalium* (also *Filaginella*)	AST
Erythronium	LIL		
Eschscholzia	PAP	*Goodyera*	ORC
Eucephalus	AST	*Grammica*	CUS
Euclidium	BRA	*Gratiola*	SCR
Eupatorium (also *Ageratina*)	AST	*Grayia* (see Atriplex)	CHN
Euphorbia (see *Agaloma*, *Chamaesyce*, *Tithymalus*, *Poinsettia*)	EUP	*Grindelia*	AST
		Gutierrezia	AST
Euploca	BOR	*Gymnocarpium*	F-ATY
Euthamia	AST	*Gymnosteris*	PLM
Eutrema	BRA	*Gypsophila*	CRY
Evolvulus	CNV		
		Habenaria (see *Coeloglossum*, *Limnorchis*, *Lysiella*, *Piperia*)	ORC
Fallopia	PLG		
Fendlera	HDR	*Hackelia*	BOR
Fendlerella	HDR	*Halerpestes*	RAN
Festuca (also *Argillochloa*, *Leucopoa*)	POA	*Halimolobos*	BRA
		Halogeton	CHN
Filaginella	AST	*Haplopappus* (see *Macronema*, *Machaeranthera*, *Oreochrysum*, *Pyrrocoma*, *Stenotopsis*, *Stenotus*, *Tonestus*)	AST
Flaveria	AST		
Floerkea	LIM		
Forestiera	OLE		
Forsellesia	CRO	*Hecatonia*	RAN

Index to Genera

Hedeoma	LAM	Koenigia	PLG
Hedysarum	FAB	Krascheninnikovia	CHN
Helenium (also *Dugaldia*)	AST	Kuhnia (see *Brickellia*)	AST
Helianthella	AST		
Helianthus	AST	Lactuca	AST
Helictotrichon	POA	Lamium	LAM
Heliomeris	AST	Lappula	BOR
Heliotropium (see *Euploca*)	BOR	Lathyrus	FAB
Heracleum	API	Leersia	POA
Hesperochiron	HYD	Lemna	LMN
Heterocodon	CAM	Lepidium	BRA
Heterotheca	AST	Lepidotheca	AST
Heuchera	SAX	Leptochloa	POA
Hibiscus	MLV	Leptodactylon	PLM
Hieracium		Lesquerella	BRA
(see *Chlorocrepis*)	AST	Leucanthemum	AST
Hierochloë	POA	Leucelene	AST
Hilaria	POA	Leucocrinum	LIL
Hippochaete	F-EQU	Leucopoa	POA
Hippuris	HPU	Lewisia (also *Erocallis*,	
Hirculus	SAX	*Oreobroma*)	POR
Holodiscus	ROS	Leymus	POA
Holosteum	ASN	Liatris	AST
Hordeum (also *Critesion*)	POA	Lidia	ASN
Humulus	CAN	Ligularia	AST
Huperzia	F-LYC	Ligusticum	API
Hydrophyllum	HYD	Lilium	LIL
Hymenolobus	BRA	Limnorchis	ORC
Hymenopappus	AST	Limosella	SCR
Hymenoxys (see *Picradenia*,		Linanthastrum	PLM
Rydbergia, *Tetraneuris*)	AST	Linanthus	PLM
Hyoscyamus	SOL	Linaria	SCR
Hypericum	HYP	Linnaea	CPR
Hypopitys	MNT	Linum (also *Adenolinum*,	
		Cathartolinum, *Mesynium*)	LIN
Iliamna	MLV	Listera	ORC
Ipomopsis	PLM	Lithophragma	SAX
Iris	IRI	Lithospermum	BOR
Isatis	BRA	Lloydia	LIL
Isocoma	AST	Lolium	POA
Isoëtes	F-ISO	Lomatium	API
Iva (also *Cyclachaena*)	AST	Lomatogonium	GEN
Ivesia	ROS	Lonicera (also *Distegia*)	CPR
		Lophopyrum	POA
Jacea	AST	Lotus	FAB
Jamesia	HDR	Lupinus	FAB
Juncus	JUN	Luzula	JUN
Juniperus (also *Sabina*)	G-CUP	Lycium	SOL
		Lycopodium	
Kalmia	ERI	(also *Huperzia*)	F-LYC
Knautia	DPS	Lycopus	LAM
Kobresia	CYP	Lygodesmia	AST
Kochia	CHN	Lysiella	ORC
Koeleria	POA	Lysimachia (see *Steironema*)	PRM

Lythrum	LYT	*Nama*	HYD
		Nasturtium	BRA
Machaeranthera	AST	*Navarretia*	PLM
Maclura	MOR	*Negundo*	ACE
Macronema	AST	*Nemophila*	HYD
Madia	AST	*Nepeta*	LAM
Mahonia	BER	*Nicotiana*	SOL
Maianthemum	CVL	*Noccaea*	BRA
Malacothrix	AST	*Notholaena*	
Malcolmia	BRA	(see *Cheilanthes*)	SIN
Malva	MLV	*Nuphar*	NYM
Mariscus	CYP	*Nuttallia*	LOA
Marrubium	LAM		
Marsilea	MSL		
Matricaria		*Oenothera* (also *Calylophus*,	
(also *Lepidotheca*)	AST	*Camissonia*)	ONA
Medicago	FAB	*Oligosporus*	AST
Melandrium		*Onopordum*	AST
(also *Gastrolychnis*)	CRY	*Opuntia*	
Melica (also *Bromelica*)	POA	(also *Cylindropuntia*)	CAC
Melilotus	FAB	*Oreobatus*	ROS
Mentha	LAM	*Oreobroma*	POR
Mentzelia (see *Acrolasia*,		*Oreocarya*	BOR
Nuttallia)	LOA	*Oreochrysum*	AST
Menyanthes	MNY	*Oreoxis*	API
Mertensia	BOR	*Orobanche*	ORO
Mesynium	LIN	*Orogenia*	API
Micranthes	SAX	*Orthilia*	PYR
Microseris	AST	*Orthocarpus*	SCR
Microsteris	PLM	*Oryzopsis*	POA
Mimulus	SCR	*Osmorhiza*	API
Minuartia (see *Lidia*)	ASN	*Oxalis*	OXL
Minuopsis	ASN	*Oxybaphus*	NYC
Mirabilis (also *Oxybaphus*)	NYC	*Oxypolis*	API
Mitella	SAX	*Oxyria*	PLG
Moehringia	ASN	*Oxytenia*	AST
Moldavica		*Oxytropis*	FAB
(see *Dracocephalum*)	LAM		
Monarda	LAM	*Packera*	AST
Monardella	LAM	*Padus*	ROS
Moneses	PYR	*Panicum*	
Monolepis	CHN	(also *Dichanthelium*)	POA
Monotropa (see *Hypopitys*)	MNT	*Papaver*	PAP
Monroa	POA	*Parietaria*	URT
Montia (see *Crunocallis*)	POR	*Parnassia*	PAR
Morus	MOR	*Paronychia*	ASN
Muhlenbergia	POA	*Parryella*	FAB
Munroa (see *Monroa*)	POA	*Parthenium* (see *Bolophyta*)	AST
Muscaria	SAX	*Parthenocissus*	VIT
Myosotis	BOR	*Pascopyrum*	POA
Myosurus	RAN	*Paspalum*	POA
Myriophyllum	HAL	*Pastinaca*	API
		Paxistima	CEL
		Pedicularis	SCR
Najas	NAJ	*Pediocactus*	CAC

Index to Genera

Pediomelum	FAB	Prunella	LAM
Pellaea	F-SIN	Prunus (also *Padus*)	ROS
Pennellia	BRA	Psathyrostachys	POA
Penstemon	SCR	Pseudocymopterus	API
Pentaphylloides	ROS	Pseudoroegneria	POA
Peraphyllum	ROS	Pseudostellaria	ASN
Perideridia	API	Pseudotsuga	G-PIN
Persicaria	PLG	Psilochenia	AST
Petasites	AST	Psilostrophe	AST
Petradoria	AST	Psoralidium	FAB
Petrophyton	ROS	Psychrophila	HEL
Phacelia	HYD	Pteridium	F-HPL
Phalaris (see *Phalaroides*)	POA	Pterogonum	PLG
Phalaroides	POA	Pterospora	MNT
Philadelphus	HDR	Ptilagrostis	POA
Phippsia	POA	Puccinellia	POA
Phleum	POA	Pulsatilla	RAN
Phlox	PLM	Purshia	ROS
Phoradendron	VIS	Pyrola	
Phragmites	POA	(also *Moneses, Orthilia*)	PYR
Physalis	SOL	Pyrrocoma	AST
Physaria	BRA		
Physocarpus	ROS	Quercus	FAG
Picea	G-PIN		
Picradenia	AST	Ranunculus (also *Cyrtorrhyncha,*	
Picrothamnus	AST	*Halerpestes, Hecatonia*)	RAN
Pinus	G-PIN	Ratibida	AST
Piperia	ORC	Reynoutria	PLG
Plagiobothrys	BOR	Rhamnus	RHM
Plantago	PTG	Rhinanthus	SCR
Platyschkuhria	AST	Rhodiola	CRS
Pneumonanthe	GEN	Rhus (also *Toxicodendron*)	ANA
Poa	POA	Ribes	GRS
Pocilla	SCR	Robinia	FAB
Podistera	API	Rorippa (also *Nasturtium*)	BRA
Poinsettia	EUP	Rosa	ROS
Polanisia	CPP	Rotala	LYT
Polemonium	PLM	Rubacer	ROS
Polygala	PGL	Rubus (also *Cylactis,*	
Polygonum		*Oreobatus, Rubacer*)	ROS
(also *Bistorta, Fallopia,*		Rudbeckia	AST
Persicaria, Reynoutria)	PLG	Rumex (also *Acetosella*)	PLG
Polypodium	F-PLP	Ruppia	RUP
Polypogon	POA	Rydbergia	AST
Polystichum	F-ASD		
Populus	SAL	Sabina	G-CUP
Portulaca	POR	Sagina	ASN
Potamogeton	POT	Sagittaria	ALI
Potentilla (also *Argentina,*		Salicornia	CHN
Comarum, Drymocallis,		Salix	SAL
Pentaphylloides)	ROS	Salsola	CHN
Prenanthella	AST	Salvia	LAM
Prenanthes	AST	Sambucus	CPR
Primula	PRM	Sanguisorba	ROS

Sanicula	API	Sporobolus	POA
Saponaria	CRY	Stachys	LAM
Sarcobatus	CHN	Stanleya	BRA
Saussurea	AST	Steironema	PRM
Saxifraga		Stellaria (also *Alsine*)	ASN
(also *Ciliaria, Hirculus,*		Stenogonum	PLG
Micranthes, Muscaria)	SAX	Stenotopsis	AST
Schedonnardus	POA	Stenotus	AST
Schizachne	POA	Stephanomeria	AST
Schizachyrium	POA	Stipa	POA
Schoenocrambe	BRA	Streptanthella	BRA
Schoenoplectus	CYP	Streptanthus	BRA
Scirpus (also *Amphiscirpus,*		Streptopus	UVU
Baeothryon, Bolbostylis,		Suaeda	CHN
Schoenoplectus)	CYP	Sullivantia	SAX
Sclerocactus	CAC	Swertia	GEN
Scrophularia	SCR	Swida	COR
Scutellaria	LAM	Symphoricarpos	CPR
Secale	POA	Symphytum	BOR
Sedum (also *Amerosedum,*			
Clementsia, Rhodiola)	CRS	Talinum	POR
Selaginella	SEL	Tamarix	TAM
Senecio		Tanacetum	AST
(also *Ligularia, Packera*)	AST	Taraxacum	AST
Seriphidium	AST	Tecoma (see *Campsis*)	BIG
Setaria	POA	Teloxys	CHN
Shepherdia	ELE	Tetradymia	AST
Sibbaldia	ROS	Tetraneuris	AST
Sidalcea	MLV	Teucrium	LAM
Silene (also *Anotites*)	CRY	Thalictrum	RAN
Sinapis	BRA	Thelesperma	AST
Sisymbrium		Thelypodiopsis	BRA
(also *Schoenocrambe*)	BRA	Thelypodium	BRA
Sisyrinchium	IRI	Thermopsis	FAB
Sium	API	Thlaspi (also *Noccaea*)	BRA
Smelowskia	BRA	Tidestromia	
Smilacina	CVL	(see *Cladothrix*)	AMA
(see *Maianthemum*)		Tiquilia	EHR
Solanum	SOL	Tithymalus	EUP
Solidago (also *Euthamia,*		Tonestus	AST
Petradoria)	AST	Torreyochloa	POA
Sonchus	AST	Townsendia	AST
Sophora (see *Vexibia*)		Toxicodendron	ANA
Sorbus	ROS	Toxicoscordion	MLN
Sparganium	SPG	Tradescantia	CMM
Spartina	POA	Tragia	EUP
Spergularia	ASN	Tragopogon	AST
Spergulastrum	ASN	Trautvetteria	RAN
Sphaeralcea	MLV	Tribulus	ZYG
Sphaeromeria	AST	Trifolium	FAB
Sphaerophysa	FAB	Triglochin	JCG
Sphenopholis	POA	Trillium	TRL
Spiraea	ROS	Tripterocalyx	NYC
Spiranthes	ORC	Trisetum	POA

Index to Genera

Triticum	POA	*Veronicastrum*	SCR
Trollius	HEL	*Vexibia*	FAB
Tryphane	ASN	*Viburnum*	CPR
Turritis	BRA	*Vicia*	FAB
Typha	TYP	*Viguiera* (see *Heliomeris*)	AST
		Viola	VIO
Ulmus	ULM	*Virgulus*	AST
Urtica	URT	*Viticella*	RAN
Utricularia	LNT	*Vulpia*	POA
Vaccaria	CRY	*Woodsia*	F-WDS
Vaccinium	ERI	*Wyethia*	AST
Vahlodea	POA		
Valeriana	VAL	*Xanthium*	AST
Veratrum	MLN	*Ximenesia*	AST
Verbascum	SCR	*Xylorhiza*	AST
Verbena (also *Glandularia*)	VRB		
Veronica (also *Pocilla*, *Veronicastrum*)	SCR	*Yucca*	AGA
		Zannichellia	ZAN

DATE DUE

DEMCO 38-297